STATUE OF THE IMMACULATE CONCEPTION, PIAZZA DI SPAGNA, ROME.

Rejoice, O Virgin Mary, thou alone hast destroyed all heresies.
Who didst believe the words of the archangel Gabriel.
Whilst a virgin thou didst bring forth God and man:
and after childbirth thou didst remain a virgin.
O Mother of God, intercede for us.

TRACT, FROM THE VOTIVE MASS OF THE BLESSED VIRGIN MARY

Words of Appreciation

Illustrious Sir,

Please receive my sincere thanks for your kindness in sending me your book on liberation theology. At first glance, it seems very interesting. I wish it wide distribution.

Greetings and blessings,
✠ Walter, Card. Brandmüller

Cardinal Brandmüller is the former president of the Pontifical Committee for Historical Sciences

Dear Mr. Loredo,

I am deeply grateful that you sent me your work on liberation theology in which, competently and thoroughly, you tackle one of the most problematic and disputed chapters of theology's contemporary history. I take advantage of this letter to wish you every good in Our Lord Jesus Christ.

✠ Giampaolo Crepaldi, archbishop-bishop of Trieste
[in Italy]

Very illustrious Mr. Loredo,

I received the book *Liberation Theology: A Lead-Filled Life Jacket for the Poor*, and thank you for the gift of this interesting and profound work.

Indeed, the topic you analyze continues triggering discussion and fascination in many who sometimes conflate ideas with authentic Christian doctrine. I pray wholeheartedly that your book may guide its readers to a wholesome discernment between what is true and evangelical and that which is not so, in addition to a loyal reading of history.

Thank you for this gift, which I greatly appreciated.

May the Lord bless you.
✠ Francesco Cavina, bishop of Carpi
[in Italy]

Prof. Julio Loredo,

I received your study *Liberation Theology*, and thank you for it.
Your work will permit me to know better this movement whose value was checkered, surpassed, and rehabilitated (*ab in albis sedente?*).

Thank you and good toil.

Patti, September 17, 2015
✠ Ignazio Zambito
[bishop of Patti, in Italy]

Dear Mr Loredo,

I have received a copy of your book, *Liberation Theology, a Lead-Filled Life Vest for the Poor*. I will read it with great interest. Dr. Plinio's teaching, of which you are a faithful interpreter, is evermore important at this crucial moment of history as the clash between the revolution and the counter-revolution has become dramatic.

Your book will certainly help to understand many events that are disturbing the Church. . . .

Sincerely,
In Jesu et Maria,
Fr. Roberto Spataro, S.D.B.

Review by Ettore Gotti Tedeschi
Liberation Theology by Julio Loredo
(Cantagalli, 2014)

As a Catholic and a non-academic economist, I have always thought and recognized that moral misery should be eradicated in order to eliminate material misery. Recalling the doctrinal teachings of my (Jesuit) teachers, the origin of evil and misery is found in the sin that generates greed, selfishness, indifference, etc.

When reading Loredo's well-documented book, I learn that the so-called liberation theology practically affirms the opposite: one overcomes moral misery by eradicating material misery. That is not all. I also learned that inequality in the distribution of resources is the origin of all evils; I would even say of sin itself. Alas, this book must be read and discussed, and precisely at this historical moment. Toward the end of the reading, I wondered if it was "only" an analysis of liberation theology or also an analytical study of the process of dechristianization that has developed and transformed in history over time.

I even wonder whether it is appropriate to evaluate the book from an "economic" point of view. I would conclude by saying no. The subject of this book is, above all, "theological and apologetic." It ponders that capitalism (as an economic system) is a sign of contradiction since it produces material well-being for many but confuses those lacking a mature ability to discern the meaning of [human] life and actions, and do not consider the economy simply as a means to achieve altogether different ends. On the other hand, Marxist-progressive socialism (always as an economic system), is not a sign of contradiction but produces material and moral malaise. It does not confuse but deceives. It hurts to see it defended by theologians.

The author offers extremely didactic reflections on these "illusions." Let me quote one of them referring to the great revolutions in Western history: "Progressives...saw modern history as a succession of constructive 'liberations': Humanism freed the human mind from scholastic thought; Protestantism freed humanity from papal 'absolutism'; the Enlightenment liberated reason from the tyranny of faith; the French Revolution freed the citizenry from the tyranny of kings; and now Socialism was about to liberate the worker class from the oppression of its masters."

However, instead of immediately going to Confession and doing spiritual exercises, progressive theologians see this "social movement" as "the reconciliation between the Church and the modern world, of *democracy and the papacy*" (Fr. Felix Klein in *L'Eglise et la démocratie*, 1893). On the other hand, when evaluating such "theories," the popes sought to ascertain whether they were consistent with and corresponded to the natural order. Thus, the popes condemned Socialism and Modernism and approved some premises of the market economy while rejecting its abuses. Progressive theologians did

not. That may be the reason why so many "Christian Democrat theologians" (such as Romolo Murri) strove to "liberate the Catholic religion from its old superstructure" while naturally praising Modernism as tomorrow's new Catholicism. Modernist liberal Catholicism (which affirms the sovereignty of individual conscience by emancipating the person from the supernatural and moral order) generated the so-called "Nouvelle Théologie," which Pius XII defined and condemned. It gave rise to the present liberation theology.

In this regard, the author draws a very interesting parallel with the philosophical current of the moment: Existentialism. This philosophical fashion states that it is not the essence that gives meaning to existence but the opposite. As if to say (as perhaps would Cardinal Kasper) that it is not the doctrine that gives meaning to practice, but practice gives meaning to doctrine. The power of ideas that draw their meaning from behavior rather than determining it.

But let us return to the author's considerations on liberation theology. He destroys it with great elegance and obvious competence from the beginning by defining it as not being properly theology since theology is the study of God. Instead, said theology deals with studying "socio-political movements for liberation from societies considered oppressive," thus managing to transform revelation into the evolution of truth. Perhaps even worse, as Leonardo Boff, its most famous theologian, characterizes it: "What we propose is not to put theology into Marxism, but to put Marxism—historical materialism—into theology."

Reading on, I discovered that liberation theologians have also revolutionized the sacred Scriptures by writing the Newest Testament. I was greatly intrigued by reading that, for them, the Bible is the story of the struggle of subversion by the poor: "The Old Testament was written by an oppressed people. The New Testament was written with the very life of Jesus, a poor man of Nazareth...We, today's poor, are writing the Newest Testament with our lives." As my curiosity waned, I became worried upon discovering that, for this theology, virtue consists in carrying out revolutionary activities (rather than following the Commandments), and being a saint is not to fight against sin but actually to combat capitalism, while converting means committing oneself to free the poor and exploited. All this would have sufficed. Yet, I also learned that environmentalism, a universal religion, also finds its foundations in liberation theology (ecological revelation). Therefore, I would not write off this theological current as something out of a faraway Latin America but warmly invite you to seriously deepen your knowledge by reading this work by Julio Loredo.

[Ettore Gotti Tedeschi is an Italian economist and banker and was president of the Vatican Bank for a few years.]

Contents

Liberation Theology

How Marxism Infiltrated the Catholic Church

BY JULIO LOREDO DE IZCUE

Translated by José Aloisio Schelini

The American Society for the Defense of Tradition, Family, and Property—TFP

Spring Grove, Pennsylvania

Italian original *Teologia della liberazione: Un salvagente di piombo per i poveri*
© Copyright 2014 Julio Loredo de Izcue
Edizioni Cantagalli
Massetana Romana, 12
53100 Siena SI
Italy

Published in Spanish as *Teología de la liberación: Un salvavidas de plomo para los pobres*
© Copyright 2015 Tradición y Acción por un Perú Mayor
Maria Parado de Bellido 296, Magdalena del Mar
Lima, Peru
(511) 462-0314 * TFPLima@gmail.com

Published in Portuguese as *Teologia da libertação: Um salva-vidas de chumbo para os pobres*
© Copyright 2016 Associação Instituto Plinio Corrêa de Oliveira
Rua Visconde de Taunay, 364—Bom Retiro
01132-000 São Paulo, S.P.
Brazil

Printed in the United States of America

ISBN: 978-1-877905-67-4
      978-1-877905-68-1 (ebook version)

Library of Congress Control Number: 2022931845

B111

Foreword

Many look at liberation theology as a Latin American phenomenon that need not concern Americans. In 1971, Fr. Gustavo Gutiérrez, a Peruvian theologian, released the movement's seminal book, *A Theology of Liberation: History, Politics, and Salvation*, which claimed to represent "the cry of the people." These ideas spread rapidly and then reached their peak in the seventies and eighties when they inspired the popular movements and basic Christian communities in left-agitated Latin America.

In 1984 and later in 1986, the Vatican's Congregation for the Doctrine of the Faith (C.D.F.) condemned certain aspects of liberation theory, especially its use of Marxist analysis. Afterward, the movement slowly faded, and the more progressive elements in the Church moved on to environmentalism, homosexuality, race, and other leftist causes.

However, liberation theology never disappeared. It is not over. Many are now surprised to see that it is having a worldwide resurgence. It shows up in places like President Joe Biden's Oval Office in the form of a bust of Cesar Chavez, the California farmworker agitator. It shows up in President Biden's inaugural address. The president's words, "A cry for survival comes from the planet itself," is an echo of the more famous "the cry of the poor, the cry of the earth" from Leonardo Boff, a leading liberation theologian, and a friend of Pope Francis. It is said that he was consulted during the writing of the encyclical *Laudato Si'*.

Indeed, liberation theology is off the back burner and into the headlines where it enjoys the favor of the media and liberal establishment. Its message has come charging back with more radicalized doctrines and applications. Thus, *Liberation Theology: How Marxism Infiltrated the Catholic Church* could not be timelier.

Like Father Gutiérrez, author Julio Loredo de Izcue is a Peruvian. He has studied Latin America's problems first hand and has lectured on the Catholic left and liberation theology for over forty years. Currently living in Italy, where he is the president of the Italian Association Tradition, Family, and Property (T.F.P.), Mr. Loredo is a well-known writer, speaker, and commentator on Church affairs.

Mr. Loredo understands that liberation theology is built on powerful myths that, once debunked, render it much less dangerous. He also knows its points of vulnerability that allowed him to deliver a stunning broadside against this theological current that threatens the Church.

Readers of this book will learn four important lessons that will help them understand better this theology that may soon be coming to a parish nearby.

The first one is that liberation theology is not theology. The body of work related to liberation theology would place it more in the fields of political philosophy and sociology. Its Marxist analysis, and especially its class struggle dialectics, has caused immense damage throughout the world. Its use of the 'theology' label and vocabulary makes it more dangerous since it relies upon people's goodwill toward religion.

Resorting to such sociological sources is tragic considering the Church's vast treasury of social teaching based on the writings of saints, doctors, and theologians. Unlike the Church—which promotes love of neighbor and social harmony for the love of God—liberation theology excludes all supernatural means of dealing with misfortune and poverty. Moreover, liberation theology is rooted in egalitarianism and fueled by hatred, not love. Liberation theology also lacks originality as it recycles old philosophical errors, changing only the exterior packaging.

The second lesson is that liberation theology is part of a process. The author is well trained in the school of historical analysis of Prof. Plinio Corrêa de Oliveira. The noted Catholic thinker taught that historical currents follow processes that are not always clear to ordinary laymen. However, a careful look at a current will reveal the origin of the error. At times, an evil may seem to disappear, then suddenly reappear, fortified and worse than ever. Once seen as a process, however, such currents are easier to refute.

Thus, Mr. Loredo shows that liberation theology did not suddenly appear on the horizon. Readers of this book will find the process meticulously traced in its development from theological and sociological currents after the French Revolution and the advance of liberalism. He cuts to the root of where liberation theology originated.

Yet another lesson comes through the author dispelling the myth of liberation theology being a purely Latin American phenomenon that sprang from the cry of the people. The real story is more complex and less dramatic. The origins of this 'theology' are much more based on European theological currents than the reflections of villagers in the Andes. Highly educated priests and laymen formulated its doctrines, not the poor subjected to its process of "conscientization."

The final lesson is that liberation theology threatens us here in America. This theology has found its way into the American context. It has long infiltrated through Hispanic Catholic communities and parishes in the United States. Catholic leftists like Dorothy Day and others saw liberation theology as inspiration for their activism. In addition, many liberation theology theories that applied only to the poor are now used for identity politics and the present "woke" revolution.

American readers will appreciate the exhaustive research that will allow them to see liberation theology in this new light. As with all cancerous movements inside the Church, the whole Church is affected. The movement has metastasized and can be found everywhere in the Church now, especially under the reign of Pope Francis.

Readers need to be aware that the final goal of liberation theology is not to introduce another manner of looking at problems inside the Church. Its worldview excludes all others. The goal is to transform the Church, her structures and doctrines, into a new church and religion. That is why it is so dangerous.

Like all things leftist, the author shows that liberation theology will harm the people it claims to help. The poor are the victims of this strange theology. Mr. Loredo recalls the metaphor that liberation theology is a lead-filled life jacket for the poor. Indeed, it drags them to destruction. Its proposed political structures impoverish nations and consign the poor to abject misery.

This book comes at the right time for Catholic American readers. It will prove useful for those seeking to understand the crisis in the Church. By pointing out liberation theology's origins, core beliefs, and ruinous goals, Mr. Loredo arms readers to oppose it better. However, the author's supernatural spirit also points to the need to resort to God and the Blessed Mother. They are the key to crushing this terrible heresy.

John W. Horvat II, vice president
The American Society for the Defense of
Tradition, Family, and Property (TFP)

Abbreviations

C.E.   *Catholic Encyclopedia*, 16 vols. (New York: Robert Appleton Company, 1907–1914).

D.A.F.C.   *Dictionnaire apologétique de la foi catholique*, edited by Adhémar d'Alès, 5 vols. (Paris: Gabriel Beauchesne, 1922).

D.C.   *Documentation Catholique* (Paris: Maison de la Bonne Presse).

D.T.C.   *Dictionnaire de théologie catholique*, edited by Jean Michel Alfred Vacant, Eugène Mangenot, and Émile Amann, 30 vols, (Paris: Letouzey et Ané, 1902–1950).

E.C.   *Enciclopedia cattolica*, 12 vols. (Vatican: Ente per l'Enciclopedia Cattolica e per i Libro Cattolico, Soc. p. a., 1948–1954).

LT   liberation theology.

Preface:
Old Ghosts...From the Dead of Winter to a New Springtime?
Perplexities and Apprehensions

No es que crea en las brujas, pero de haberlas las hay ... (Not that I believe in witches, but they exist all right). This old Spanish proverb came to mind as I leafed through Italian newspapers in recent months. My disbelief gradually turned into amazement as I watched an old ghost emerge from the mists of the past, a ghost I thought had been buried forever. Instead, it was now making the headlines of national newspapers and even appearing in *L'Osservatore Romano*, the Vatican's daily.

I refer to liberation theology (LT), which has resurfaced thanks to a series of lectures given in Italy by LT's father, Peruvian priest Gustavo Gutiérrez Merino, along with Gerhard Ludwig Cardinal Müller, then-prefect of the Congregation for the Doctrine of the Faith and a Father Gutiérrez disciple. Both presented their book, *On the Side of the Poor: The Theology of Liberation*, co-written in 2004, and brought to light today in its Italian translation in a bid to provide LT with "doctrinal health certificates," in the expression of the Uruguayan Jesuit theologian Horacio Bojorge.[1] Cardinal Müller writes, "In my judgment ... 'liberation theology' ... is one of the most significant currents of Catholic theology in the twentieth century."[2]

In fact, in Rome LT had already resurfaced since January 2011, when Brazilian Bishop João Braz de Avis, now a cardinal, was appointed prefect of the Congregation for the Institutes of Consecrated Life and Societies of Apostolic Life. Indeed, His Eminence is an enthusiastic champion of LT.[3]

Observers are beginning to proclaim that the Vatican has ended its hostility toward liberation theology. Some would like to resurrect LT, presenting it as a valid Christian response to alleged situations of misery and oppression in Latin America and elsewhere. More recently, a version of LT—the so-called indigenous theology—inspired the Pan-Amazon Synod that took place in Rome in October 2019. Yet other versions, dubbed ecological theology, are inspiring radical environmentalism.

My mind flew back to August 6, 1974, when, not yet nineteen, I had to flee to exile in a friend's old pickup truck. I would not see Peru, my native country, for more than three decades. What prompted me to take that step? As a founding member of the association Tradición y Acción por un Perú Mayor, in 1973 I had participated in a campaign against liberation theology (it was the first such campaign in the world), which had just been launched in Peru with the publication of the book *Una Teología de la liberación: Perspectivas*, by Father Gutiérrez.[4]

Peru was then going through the darkest phase of the Marxist and pro-Castro dictatorship of General Juan Velasco Alvarado (1910–1977). Unwilling or unable to respond to our criticism, LT advocates kept an eloquent silence. The counterattack came directly from the government. A month after we launched our campaign, the government's official periodical published two full pages against Tradición y Acción.[5] In April 1974, the dictator himself railed against "those gentlemen in suit and tie who, wearing symbols, distribute their magazine in churches of elegant neighborhoods." Prudently, we decided to suspend the campaign. However, General Velasco Alvarado did not stop there. In a televised speech in late July, after threatening, "I will not tolerate any counter-revolution!" he vowed to "bring down the full weight of revolutionary justice on these gentlemen." That was the straw that broke the camel's back. Within a few days, all members of the association were abroad, from where it seemed more effective to continue the campaign against the Marxist regime. Our oldest member was twenty-two.

Five months later, Soviet-made T-55 tanks choked in blood a popular reaction against the dictatorship, leaving on the streets of Lima nearly a hundred people dead and more than a thousand wounded. That was revolutionary justice.

After spending three years between Colombia and Ecuador, where I was able to study LT in action, I moved to Brazil. In 1982, I participated in a campaign to distribute the book written by Prof. Plinio Corrêa de Oliveira with the brothers Gustavo and Luiz Solimeo, *The BCCs, Much Talked About but Little Known: The TFP Describes Them as They Are*.[6] It is a comprehensive critical study of LT and the so-called Basic Christian Communities (B.C.C.s) inspired by it. With seven editions totaling 72,000 copies, the book became one of the great bestsellers in the history of Brazil. A comic book version sold 240,000 copies. The blow turned out to be fatal and marked the beginning of LT's decline in Brazil, and consequently in other Latin American countries.

Soon afterward, American friends called my attention to LT's infiltration in the southern United States and especially among Texas Chicanos (Mexican-Americans), in symbiosis with Alinsky-inspired People's Organizations. They asked me to write a book denouncing that danger. That was the starting point of this study. Various circumstances, including the decline of the LT current

---

1. Horacio Bojorge, *Teologías deicidas: El pensamiento de Juan Luis Segundo en su contexto*, 2nd ed. (Montevideo: Centro Cultural Católico, 2011), 329. See Gianni Valente, "The War Between the Liberation Theology Movement and Rome Is Over," *Vatican Insider-La Stampa*, June 21, 2013. [Publisher's Note: When provided, access dates and hyperlinks to online sources are shown only in the bibliography.]

2. Gerhard Ludwig Müller, "Liberating Experience: A Stimulus for European Theology" in *On the Side of the Poor: The Theology of Liberation*, by Gustavo Gutiérrez and Gerhard Ludwig Müeller, trans. Robert A. Krieg and James B. Nickoloff (Maryknoll, N.Y.: Orbis Books, 2015), 11.

3. See Alessandro Speciale, "João Bráz de Aviz, The Liberation Theologian Receives the Red Biretta," *Vatican Insider-La Stampa*, Feb. 16, 2012. See also Nicola Gori, "Come parole del Vangelo lungo la storia: A colloquio con l'arcivescovo João Braz de Aviz," *L'Osservatore Romano*, Feb. 2, 2011.

4. See Gustavo Gutiérrez, *Una teología de la liberación: Perspectivas* (Lima: Centro de Estudios y Publicaciones, 1971). Tradición y Acción por un Perú Mayor was the first to denounce, see "Teología de la liberación, ¿o marxismo para cristianos?" *Tradición y Acción* (Lima), nos. 6–7 (Dec. 1973).

5. See "La ultraderecha y sus activistas," *La Nueva Crónica* (Lima), Jan. 5, 1974, 14–15.

6. See Plinio Corrêa de Oliveira, Gustavo Antonio Solimeo, and Luiz Sergio Solimeo, *As CEBs, das quais muito se fala, pouco se conhece: A TFP as descreve como são* (São Paulo: Editora Vera Cruz, 1982). Later published in English as *Grassroots Church Communities (GRCCs): Perestroika in Latin America?* (Carmel, N.Y.: Western Hemisphere Cultural Society, 1991).

and the consequent attenuation of its threat, caused the study in the English language, although finished, to remain in the drawer.

After the 1984 Instruction *Libertatis Nuntius* of the Congregation for the Doctrine of the Faith and the downfall of the historical praxis that served as its instrument, namely Communism, LT entered a long twilight. While some of its leaders such as Father Gutiérrez and the Brazilian Fr. Clodovis Boff, O.S.M. made a half-hearted *mea culpa*, others joined more up-to-date theological currents. The roaring dynamism of the sixties and eighties was followed by a long hibernation.

After years of Socialism and revolution, Latin America itself entered a new historical stage with the introduction, in several countries, of economic systems in stark contrast with those advocated by LT. These systems brought about a strong economic development and an equally sharp decline in poverty, allowing those countries, including Peru, to become emerging markets.

However, the global economic crisis begun in 2007 seems to change the situation.

1. From Winter to a New Springtime?

The crisis, interpreted as the demise of the free market, revived long fossilized socialist currents. The left again began to rule major Latin American countries and to implement outdated statist policies. From the mists of the past the LT specter was resurrected. In a few months, that revolutionary current emerged from the twilight of time to the pages of *Avvenire* (the Italian bishops' daily) and *L'Osservatore Romano*, even creeping into the Roman Curia.

It is not the old Marxist LT, friendly to guerrilla violence and leftist dictators. This time it is presented simply as a friend of the poor. LT advocates state that, purified from specific aspects of Marxism, it could now provide adequate responses to difficult situations. They also hope it will inspire a new social conscience after years of rampant capitalism. Others hope that, in up-to-date versions, it can help boost the environmentalist movement. "It is a spring for the Church," proclaims the Brazilian Leonardo Boff, an exponential figure of that current.[7]

The appointment, in July 2012, of Gerhard Cardinal Müller as Prefect of the Congregation for the Doctrine of the Faith surely contributed to this spring. As mentioned, he is a personal friend of Father Gutiérrez, who convinced him to acquire a long pastoral experience in Peru, thus bringing him close to LT. On September 4, 2013, as the above-mentioned book was being presented in Italy, *L'Osservatore Romano*, for the first time and in a positive tone, devoted two full pages to LT.[8] The magic expression seemed to be *sdoganamento* (customs clearance).

"The Church has given liberation theology a customs clearance," commented vaticanist Andrea Tornielli, later named chief of the Vatican's communications. "The Vatican and the Liberation Theology movement have made peace. After all the condemnations of the '80s, the exaggerations and misunderstandings, the Church has finally granted the Theology of Liberation movement full citizenship. This peaceful handshake is being witnessed within the context of the new climate set by the Catholic Church's first Latin American pope and the resumption of the bishop and martyr

Oscar Romero's beatification process."[9] Vaticanist Sandro Magister also commented, "Peace made between Müller and Gutiérrez. ... Müller's positive judgment on liberation theology—read through the lens of Gutiérrez—can be grasped from the very first lines."[10] Not to be outdone, left-wing magazine *L'Espresso* trumpeted, "Condemned by Ratzinger, the theology of liberation is now rehabilitated by a pope who comes from afar."[11]

Some want to give the impression that the 1984 condemnation is outdated. Others point to Pope Francis's role in the liberationist renaissance.[12] Many commented, for example, on the private audience the pope granted Cardinal Müller, accompanied by Father Gutiérrez, on September 11, 2013, followed by the celebration of a Mass with the Peruvian theologian. They interpreted that meeting as a papal endorsement of LT.[13] "The liberation Mass," Gian Guido Vecchi headlined in *Corriere della Sera*, observing: "A book and an interview mark a change."[14]

A few months later, on January 18, 2014, the pope received at Casa Santa Marta another well-known liberation theologian, Arturo Paoli. The media also interpreted that gesture as a sign of his closeness to that current. Ultra-progressive theologian Vito Mancuso commented on Facebook, "I have just learned that tonight Pope Francis received Arturo Paoli, 101 years old and spiritual father of liberation theology. The meeting lasted about 40 minutes and was characterized by a most friendly empathy. Perhaps a liberation Magisterium is being born! Forge ahead, Francis!"[15]

Sensing the new climate, after years of relative hibernation, over seven hundred liberation theologians and activists gathered in São Leopoldo, Brazil, at the Continental Conference of

7. Pierluigi Mele, "La teologia della liberazione sta vivendo una nuova primavera, grazie anche a Papa Francesco: La forza storica dei poveri. Intervista a Leonardo Boff," *RaiNews*, Sept. 20, 2013.

8. See Gustavo Gutiérrez, "I preferiti di Dio"; Gerhard Ludwig Mueller, "Fare la verità e non solo dirla"; Ugo Sartorio, "Una Chiesa che ha bisogno di tutti," *L'Osservatore Romano*, Sept. 4, 2013, 4–5. On Cardinal Müller's relations with LT, see his lecture at the then Pontifical Catholic University of Lima on November 28, 2008 (Gerhard Müller, "Mis experiencias sobre la teología de la liberación," in *Religión*, Lima, July 3, 2012).

9. Andrea Tornielli, "The Vatican and the Liberation Theology Movement Make Peace," *Vatican Insider-La Stampa*, Sept. 5, 2013.

10. Sandro Magister, "Peace Made Between Müller and Gutiérrez. But Bergoglio Isn't Falling For It," *L'Espresso online*, Sept. 5, 2013.

11. Wlodek Goldkorn, "Ho ispirato Bergoglio," *L'Espresso*, Mar. 27, 2014, 88.

12. A typical example of the desire to enlist Pope Francis in the liberationist camp is the comment by João Pedro Stedile, the leader of Brazil's Landless Workers Movement (Movimento dos Sem Terra, M.S.T.), of Marxist and subversive orientation. "The fact of having a Latin American pope is a victory for the poor of this continent," Stedile said at a conference organized by the Pontifical Council of Sciences in Rome. "We are finally leaving behind two conservative and backward pontificates, those of John Paul II and Benedict XVI. Instead, Pope Francis has broken with European tradition and shows signs every day of wanting to change relations between the Church and society." "Líder do MST diz que papa Francisco é uma vitória para os pobres," *Agencia EFE*, Feb. 6, 2014. On LT's role within Brazil's Landless Workers Movement, see Antonio Julio de Menezes Neto, *A ética da teologia da libertação e o espírito do socialismo no MST* (Belo Horizonte: F.M.G., 2012).

On Pope Francis's position on poverty and misery, see two documents, his preface to Cardinal Müller's *Povera per i poveri: La missione della Chiesa* (Vatican City: Libreria Editrice Vaticana, 2014), 5–12, and the pope's interview with Ferruccio de Bortoli, director of *Corriere della Sera* ("Vi racconto il mio primo anno da papa," *Corriere della Sera*, Mar. 5, 2014).

On LT's "Argentine" variety, see Enrico Ciro Bianchi, *Pobres en este mundo, ricos en la fe: La fe vivida en el cristianismo popular latinoamericano en la obra 'El cristianismo popular según las virtudes teologales' de Rafael Tello* (master's thesis, Universidad Católica Argentina, 2011); M. Gonzalez, *La reflexión teológica en la Argentina, 1962–2004: Apuntes para un mapa de sus relaciones y desafíos hacia el futuro* (Córdoba: Universidad Católica de Córdoba, 2005); S. Politi, *Teología del pueblo: Una propuesta argentina a la teología latinoamericana, 1967–1975* (Buenos Aires: Ed. Castañeda—Ed. Guadalupe, 1992).

13. See Sandro Magister, "Il Papa ha ricevuto Gutiérrez, ma non ha dimenticato un suo sgarbo," *L'Espresso online*, Sept. 13, 2013. The Roman pontiff distanced himself from that interpretation. When asked if that audience was an endorsement of LT, the pope answered, "That is what [Cardinal] Müller thinks, that is what he thinks." Sandro Magister, "Due battute del papa contro Müller e Bertone," *L'Espresso online*, Sept. 16, 2013.

14. Gian Guido Vecchi, "La messa della liberazione: Il pontefice concelebra con il teologo degli ultimi," *Corriere della Sera*, Sept. 22, 2013.

15. See "Il papa riceve Paoli, tra i padri teologia della liberazione," *La Stampa*, Jan. 19, 2014. Pope Francis's position on LT is much more complex than some media present it. See, for example, Filippo Santoro, "La liberazione che viene dal Vangelo," *Avvenire*, Sept. 28, 2013; Gian Guido Vecchi, "Mons. Becciu: Parla anche a chi investe in modo intelligente," *Corriere della Sera*, Sept. 28, 2013.

Theology held at UNISINOS University, of the Jesuit Fathers.[16] There was talk of a "new beginning." Even the Basic Christian Communities seem to be experiencing a new springtime. The 13th Interchurch Encounter of the Basic Christian Communities was held in Juazeiro do Norte, Brazil, in January 2014. Pope Francis sent the conference a message of encouragement and support. That is the first time it happened. "With Pope Francis, the moment becomes propitious for BCCs once again," said Alver Metalli in *Vatican Insider*.[17]

LT seems to have awakened in Europe as well. In September, the John XXIII Association of Theologians, spearhead of LT in the Old Continent, held its 33rd conference in Madrid with over one thousand participants. Its theme: "Liberation theology today." The meeting opened with a message from Most Rev. Pedro Casaldáliga, bishop emeritus of São Felix do Araguaia, Brazil, a Spaniard who describes himself as "Monsignor hammer and sickle." The prelate asked, "Who's afraid of Liberation Theology? With the arrival of Francis the topic becomes relevant again."[18]

LT's "customs clearance" appears to have come to fruition with the presentation in Rome on February 25, 2014 of the book, *Poor for the Poor*, by Gerhard Cardinal Müller, published by Libreria Editrice Vaticana with a foreword by Pope Francis. "Liberation theology has been definitely and solemnly 'cleared,'" headlined Vatican correspondent Giuseppe Rusconi in *Corriere del Ticino*, quoting the Vatican spokesman, Father Federico Lombardi: "Liberation theology has now definitively entered the normal life of the Church."[19] During the conference, attended by Cardinals Rodríguez Maradiaga and Müller, Father Gutiérrez received a standing ovation as a sign of definitive consecration right at the heart of Christianity.

More recently, the resurrection of LT has been powerfully aided by the Pan-Amazon Synod of bishops, convened in Rome in October 2019. Here, a newer version of LT—the so-called indigenous theology—was presented in the heart of the Church, with the support of cardinals, bishops, and the pope himself.

2. Misgivings and Apprehensions

For my part, spurred by this and other news, I thought I could make a contribution to the current debate by pulling my unpublished study out of the drawer duly translated and updated. This is a modest and unassuming contribution. I am a journalist specialized in the study of history and have closely followed for many years the situation in Latin America, where the LT phenomenon takes place, and would thus like to share my own experiences and reflections with others, all the more so since the topic is not very well known in Italy. Perhaps the time has come to help bridge this gap, especially in view of the momentous changes that the election of Pope Francis seems to have set in motion.

In a historical era in which clarity is more needed than ever, the panorama is becoming ever more ambiguous. For faithful observers trying to discern some clear pastoral approach in terms of liberation theology, recent ecclesiastical pronouncements have brought a feeling of confusion: While some reiterate objections to LT, others solemnly clear it and take steps to endorse it. In practice, which elements of LT are censored, and which are cleared or endorsed? That is not clear, and especially since there is not always a perfect harmony between some statements by cardinals and others by Pope Francis. Antonio Socci goes so far as to talk of "waffling language."[20]

A typical example is the use of Marxist analysis by liberation theologians. Whereas the then-prefect of the Congregation for the Doctrine of the Faith, Joseph Cardinal Ratzinger, condemned it in no uncertain terms asserting that it is impossible to employ Marxist analysis without *ipso facto* assuming the ideology,[21] the next prefect, Gerhard Cardinal Müller, praised it, saying, "There are no alternative theories that can clarify more accurately the phenomena and the factors of exploitation, poverty, and oppression."[22] Sometimes people try to obfuscate this issue by talking about a partial use of Marxist analysis. However, the confusion remains: Which of its elements should be used, and which should instead be rejected?[23]

For those who have studied and experienced it firsthand, its revival, albeit in updated versions, raises many concerns and even apprehension. The concerns revolve on two axes:

1) It is said that LT's problem would be the use of Marxist analysis. If you remove Marxism, or at least part of it, we would have a *correct* rather than an *erroneous* LT. Nothing could be more simplistic. In fact, as we shall see in the following pages, the use of Marxist analysis is almost a peccadillo compared with more serious theological and philosophical deviations. Moreover, the same liberation theologians have been recycling old Marxism since the eighties by supplementing it with doctrines more suited to the new revolutionary season.

2) It is also claimed that, in the context of the severe economic crisis we are experiencing after years of neoliberalism, a renewed LT would be able to inspire a new social consciousness that places the poor at the center of attention. Such awareness would be legitimate, indeed desirable. The problem is whether LT is able to do it. In this case, a careful analysis shows that, much more than the poor, LT favors poverty as such by advocating socioeconomic systems historically found to cause bankruptcy and severe harm to the lower classes—precisely those it claims to help. Ironically, Jesuit theologian Fr. Horacio Bojorge defines LT as a "lead-filled life jacket" for the poor.[24]

As the former Pope Benedict XVI recalled in a recent interview, we must oppose LT "precisely for the sake of the poor and the

---

16. See Fundación Amerindia, ed., *Teología de la liberación en perspectiva* (Montevideo: Amerindia-Doble Clic Editoras, 2012). See also Andrés Beltramo Álvarez, "Brasile, tornano in campo i teologi della liberazione," *Vatican Insider-La Stampa*, Oct. 9, 2012.

17. Alver Metalli, "Vuelven las comunidades eclesiales de base," *Vatican Insider-La Stampa*, Dec. 30, 2013. Metalli comments: "They had not disappeared but entered a dark period in the years of John Paul II and Benedict XVI. Today they are talked about once again and reflect about their mission and role in the Church of the Latin American pope."

18. Juan Bedoya, "Mil teólogos piden al papa que rehabilite a los castigados por Ratzinger," *El País*, Sept. 8, 2013. The conference's Final Message reads, "We have confirmed that liberation theology remains alive and active in the face of attempts by conservative thought and traditional theology to condemn it and declare it dead." Bedoya, "Mil teólogos." To read the Message's full text, see: Asociación de Teólogos as Juan XXIII, "Mensaje del 33 Congreso de Teología," *Atrio*, Sept. 8, 2013.

19. Giuseppe Rusconi, "Maradiaga, Müller e Gutiérrez: Chiesa povera per i poveri," *Rossoporpora.org*, Feb. 26, 2014.

20. Antonio Socci, "Francesco chiama Benedetto accanto a sé: Le tempeste si avvicinano," *Libero*, Mar. 6, 2014.

21. "The thought of Marx is such a global vision of reality that all data received form observation and analysis are brought together in a philosophical and ideological structure, which predetermines the significance and importance to be attached to them. The ideological principles come prior to the study of the social reality and are presupposed in it. Thus no separation of the parts of this epistemologically unique complex is possible. If one tries to take only one part, say, the analysis, one ends up having to accept the entire ideology." Sacred Congregation for the Doctrine of the Faith, *Instruction on Certain Aspects of the Theology of Liberation* (Aug. 6, 1984), VII, no. 6.

22. Gerhard Ludwig Müller, "Liberation Theology in Context," in *On the Side of the Poor*, 77. "The chief point of concern is always liberation theology's social-analytical reflection and its partial use of Marxist concepts." Müller, "Liberation Theology in Context."

23. When asked by journalists whether his participation in the launching of Cardinal Müller's book in Rome with the presence of Fr. Gustavo Gutiérrez implied support of LT, Cardinal Rodríguez Maradiaga allegedly answered with a musical metaphor: *Allegro ma non troppo.* Which of LT's aspects merit "allegro"? Which deserve "non troppo"?

24. Bojorge, *Teologías deicidas*, 9. As we will see in chapter 6, an exponential increase in poverty and social hardship has occurred wherever LT postulates have been applied.

service that should be rendered to them."[25] Add to these concerns apprehensions over the possible effects of LT's "customs clearance" on the Latin American reality and around the world. Again, those effects would result more from propaganda manipulation than from reality. LT has always been anchored in the extreme left. Any ecclesiastical endorsement of this current would run a serious risk of being interpreted as political support for the left. Is that the impression they want to convey? There are many who hope that it is not, starting with Juan Luis Cardinal Cipriani, then-archbishop of Lima, Peru, who attributes the recent ecclesiastical faux pas to naiveté. "[Cardinal Müller] knows theology and is preparing Ratzinger's complete works. He is an academic coming from the academic world. No one doubts his intellectual capacity," Cardinal Cipriani stated regarding the book launching in Italy. "Cardinal Müller is in charge of defending the sound doctrine of the faith in the Church and therefore must give up this naiveté and be more cautious. I tell him this in all humility."[26]

Naiveté can lead, for example, to disregarding the existence of a powerful propaganda machine which escapes churchmen's control and will certainly appropriate (as it already has) the liberation theology label. Employing the well-known revolutionary stratagem of "unperceived ideological transshipment" denounced by Plinio Corrêa de Oliveira, it will then be loaded with ambiguous and elusive content always favorable to the far left.[27] For example, the propaganda machine has glossed the recent participation by João Pedro Stedile, leader of the Landless Workers Movement (M.S.T.), of Marxist and subversive orientation at a conference organized by the Pontifical Council of Sciences in Rome, as a Vatican endorsement of the far left in Brazil; no clarification on it was issued by the competent authorities.[28]

Is that the impression they want to convey? Clarity and definition are needed to avoid manipulation, a clarity which I hope this study will help to bring about.

◆ ❖ ◆

"In large measure, Christians today feel lost, confused, perplexed and even disappointed. Ideas opposed to the revealed and perennially taught Truth have been scattered abundantly. Real heresies in the full and proper sense of the word have been spread in the area of dogma and morals, creating doubts, confusions and rebellion. The liturgy has been altered ..."[29]

This is the dramatic image of the Church as described by Pope John Paul II in 1981. Since then, the situation has only worsened.

Which barriers have been torn down that allowed the free movement of such heresies? How have religious practices changed to the point of becoming in many cases almost unrecognizable to those accustomed to the Church of all time? What factors have led large Church sectors to participate in Marxist-inspired social revolutions? Is this a transient trial that will readily fade away like a fleeting nightmare, or is it a lasting situation with strong and deep roots that may last for decades and perhaps even centuries? In that case, does it have a potential to evolve into even more harmful forms?

In this book, the result of many years of research, I offer a panoramic vision of today's religious crisis, its roots and history, its present and possible future developments. The analysis focuses on the so-called 'liberation' theology, condemned by two popes and yet hailed today even in the Vatican as a Christian response to situations of misery and oppression allegedly created by economic crisis. Is liberation theology really a friend of the poor?

This book would not have been possible without the participation of many friends and colleagues who have graciously contributed to its publication by researching documentation and revising the text. I believe I interpret their feelings by addressing my heartfelt thanks to our common mentor, Prof. Plinio Corrêa de Oliveira, of whom we are proud to be disciples. From him we received an example of the love for God, the Virgin Mary, Holy Church, and Christian Civilization which has guided the preparation of this work.

Julio Loredo de Izcue
Palm Sunday, 2020

25. Benedict XVI, "Il ricordo del pontefice emerito," in *Accanto a Giovanni Paolo II: Gli amici & i collaboratori raccontano,* ed. Wlodzimierz Redzioch (Rome: Ares, 2014), 18.

26. Andrea Tornielli, "Teologia della liberazione, Cipriani contro Müller: Sia più prudente," *Vatican Insider-La Stampa,* Oct. 17, 2013. To Cardinal Cipriani's praise of the prefect of the Congregation for the Doctrine of the Faith's intellectual depth, it is only right for us to add an applause for the strong stands Cardinal Müller has taken on moral matters to the point of polemicizing with other prelates. However, that praise does not dispel apprehensions in other fields. During the Rome presentation of Cardinal Müller's latest book, Cardinal Rodríguez Maradiaga also chided Cardinal Müller in an interview with a German newspaper: "The world isn't like that, my brother." "Cardinal Oscar Rodríguez Maradiaga Tells Doctrinal Watchdog Archbishop Gerhard Mueller to Loosen Up," *Reuters,* Jan. 21, 2014.

27. Plinio Corrêa de Oliveira, *Unperceived Ideological Transshipment and Dialogue.*

28. See Bertrand of Orleans-Braganza, "Quo Vadis, Domine? Reverent and Filial Message to His Holiness Pope Francis," TFP.org, Feb. 13, 2014.

29. John Paul II, "Speech to the First National Conference on Popular Missions During the 1980s (Feb. 6, 1981)," no. 2.

Chapter 1:
A Long and Troubled History

In Latin America, communist expansionism hopelessly ran into an obstacle that had already caused it many difficulties in Europe: the strong cohesion of the Catholic Church in opposition to the doctrines coming from Moscow. When that spiritual force entered the fray, the result was foreseeable. Striking confirmations of this fact were the defeat of Communism in Spain in 1939 and in Italy in 1948. Outspoken and pragmatic, Americans say, "If you can't beat them, join them." Unable to destroy the Church, the communists tried to co-opt her. They started the *politique de la main tendue*, the policy of the outstretched hand, inaugurated in 1937 by Maurice Thorez and Leon Blum, respectively secretaries-general of the French Communist Party and of the S.F.I.O. (Section Française de l'Internationale Ouvrière), i.e., the Socialist Party.

That politique de la main tendue found many open doors in the Catholic camp. A leftist current of social activism had long been propagating in the Church. It began in the nineteenth century as *social Catholicism*, became *Christian Democracy*, and finally *Christian Socialism*. Intimately linked to this activism and sharing its doctrinal foundations was a philosophical, theological, and pastoral movement that began in the nineteenth century as *liberal Catholicism*, became *Modernism*, and finally *Nouvelle Théologie*.

Liberation theology comes directly from the confluence of those two currents. One cannot talk about one without the other. Let us begin with the social activism current.

A. From Social Catholicism to Christian Socialism: The Story of a Drift

1. A New Presence: The Proletariat

While generating increased economic output and many useful technological advances that improved living conditions, the Industrial Revolution also shattered the old order, which in its framework and human relationships still bore the imprint of organic society. American sociologist Robert Nisbet (1913–1996) is right when he accuses the Industrial Revolution of having caused "the most traumatic social change ... since the beginnings of settled culture in the Neolithic age."[30] Despite shortcomings, traditional organic society had the advantage of stability. Its structures formed a complex and organic network, admirably balanced, in which each individual had a place and, therefore, a sense of purpose and belonging.

The structures of traditional organic society, primarily the family and guilds, had an innate ability to absorb human problems which, thus, rarely turned into a burden for society as a whole. There were social problems, but not a social question.[31] Industrialization introduced in the economy and society what some analysts now call frenetic intemperance, demolishing centuries-old institutions and dissolving traditions and long-standing customs.[32] From the social standpoint, the Industrial Revolution was the most destructive revolution of modern times and, in its turn, opened the way for yet other no-less-ruinous revolutions.[33]

Eclipsed by machinery and new technologies, craftsmanship (until then the mainstay of the economy) went into decline. Corporations disappeared, and with them the mechanisms that protected the working class. Increasingly large and anonymous companies swallowed up small family businesses. Rural life, which until then had set the tone for society, fell into a rapidly deteriorating situation, thus breaking the balance between town and country. Forced by the collapse of their supporting structures, and attracted by the mirage of progress and the prospect of wage-earning in factories, a growing number of peasants and artisans poured into the slums of new industrial centers. Deprived of family, guild, and parish—the very structures which had given them a social role and a reason for being until then—they lost any reference point and found themselves obliged to live in an

---

30. Nisbet comments:

> During the past two centuries mankind has undergone the most traumatic social change it has experienced since the beginnings of settled culture in the Neolithic age. I refer to the decline—even disappearance in spreading sections—of the local community, the dislocation of kinship, and the erosion of the sacred in human affairs. ...
>
> It is a striking fact that through approximately ten thousand years, the period since the appearance of agricultural arts made settled community possible, the basic strength of these social ties remained intact, this despite the innumerable wars, migrations, famines, plagues, and other kinds of catastrophes to which mankind was subjected.
>
> Very different, however, has been the case since the onset of the two great revolutions of modern times: the democratic and the industrial at the end of the eighteenth century. Unlike all preceding major changes in human history, these revolutions went below the superstructure of society, went right to man's most ancient and cherished sources of identity. With the rise of the

factory system and the mass electorate, there was inevitably a wrenching of the individual from his accustomed family, local, and religious contexts. (Robert Nisbet, *Twilight of Authority* [New York: Oxford University Press, 1975], 78–79)

31. On traditional organic society, see Numa Denis Fustel de Coulanges, *The Ancient City: A Study on the Religion, Laws, and Institutions of Greece and* Rome, trans. Willard Small (Boston: Lee and Shepard, 1877); Henri Delassus, *L'esprit familiale dans la maison, dans la cité et dans l'État* (Lille: Desclée de Brouwer, 1910); Frantz Funck-Brentano, *The Old Regime in France: The Social Institutions and Traditions of the Eighteenth Century and Their Influence on the Government of the Monarchy*, trans. Herbert Wilson (London: E. Arnold & Co., 1929).

32. For a penetrating analysis of frenetic intemperance in the economy and in society, see John Horvat II, *Return to Order: From a Frenzied Economy to an Organic Christian Society* (York, Penn.: York Press, 2013).

33. Throughout, the term *revolution* is used mostly in the sense given to it by Prof. Plinio Corrêa de Oliveira in his book *Revolution and Counter-Revolution*, 3rd ed. (York, Penn.: The American Society for the Defense of Tradition, Family, and Property, 1993). In *Civilization and Capitalism 15th–18th Century*, French historian Fernand Braudel comments:

> Since its original appearance in England the industrial revolution has engendered a series of other revolutions and is evolving before our eyes, still moving on toward new horizons. ...
>
> The industrial revolution in Britain opened the door to a series of revolutions which are in its direct line of descent. (Fernand Braudel, *The Perspective of the World*, vol. 3, *Civilization and Capitalism 15th–18th Century*, trans. Sian Reynolds [New York: Harper & Row Publishers, 1984], 536, 539.)

environment that severely hindered religious practice and the maintenance of their own identity.[34]

Thus, a new class was born, the proletariat, immersed in a previously unknown poverty. It was a "reality, of chimneys and soot on the outside, and misery and degradation inside."[35]

2. The Social Question Is Born as a Controversial Issue

Rootless and defenseless, and surrounded by factors that seemed tailored to ruin the last vestiges of its Christian tradition, this nascent class posed a whole array of new religious and social problems.[36] Foremost among these was its need for spiritual and material support. The proletarians' plight created a new social sensibility that took hold of large sectors of public opinion toward the middle of the century. The so-called social question was born.

By leading many to ascribe an inordinate weight to sentiment at the expense of reason, the prevailing Romanticism greatly bolstered this new social sensibility. The noble compassion that men should feel toward the poor was thus infected in many cases by a morbid sentimentalism easily exacerbated by social inequalities, and consequently open to utopias and panaceas.

Being Mother and Teacher, the Church had always exerted a salutary influence that permeated all society. Showing special concern for the neediest classes, she attenuated the effects of poverty through charities and long-established social works. The almost self-healing nature of traditional society—where the extended family naturally absorbed most human problems—greatly diminished the need for any other specifically social initiative. With the Industrial Revolution, all this changed. The collapse of the old order, the dissolution of the family, and the rise of a new class with new problems challenged the Church to find new ways to meet the needs of the rising proletariat.

However, ecclesiastical authorities did not react immediately to the new social environment. Faced with the dangers of an increasingly materialistic society, deteriorating public and private morality, new heresies, and the rise of militantly anti-Catholic governments in several countries, the ecclesiastical authorities perhaps judged it more prudent to first carefully observe the new phenomenon and to act upon it later. One should also bear in mind that Pope Pius IX (1792, 1846–1878) was grappling with extremely serious problems, both internally and on the international scene, culminating with the breach of Porta Pia.[37] This initial cautiousness offered grounds for an impression of hesitancy that allowed some Catholic sectors to consider the problem in equivocal terms. In the absence of a clear word from Rome, theories about the social question and the practical ways of coping with it soon became controversial issues where disparate voices were heard.

On the other hand, the subversive action of socialist sects complicated things further. The crumbling of the old order offered a propitious culture for revolutionary proselytism through the exploitation of the suffering of the working class. Far from condemning early industrial capitalism, socialists greeted it as a positive development, as it was useful to destroy the traditional order and therefore conducive to their historical perspective.[38]

3. The Spirit and Doctrines of the French Revolution Further Poison the Air

The Industrial Revolution, however, was not the only factor at play. As devastating as the upheavals it produced may have been, traditional organic society could have largely—and in some cases easily—assimilated them and continued its course were it not for another powerful force: the influence of the liberal ideas born of the French Revolution of 1789.

The destructive impulse of the spirit and doctrines of the French Revolution in the religious, philosophical, moral, and even economic realms was equal to or greater than that of the Industrial Revolution in the social sphere. The Industrial Revolution was a concrete phenomenon that unhinged the old order and created a new situation that gave rise to the social question. However, it was the doctrines of the French Revolution that provided the distorted criteria by which to evaluate the social question, resulting in solutions obviously polluted by those doctrines.

The doctrines of the French Revolution are expressed in the famous trilogy: Liberty, Equality, Fraternity. While admitting a Christian sense,[39] this motto was construed by revolutionary factions through successively more radical interpretations until it came to openly designate a thoroughly liberal and egalitarian,

---

34. Braudel writes:

> The industrial revolution represented a new and completely disorienting division of labour, preserving and refining the mechanisms at work, but bringing disastrous consequences in social and human terms. ...
> ... Rural workers began to abandon their small-holdings and joined the ranks of the full-time weavers. ...
> ... The new division of labour, as it urbanized working-class society, was tearing apart the world of the poor, as they chased after work which vanished in front of them; it eventually took them to unfamiliar places, far from the countryside they knew and in the end diminished their way of life. Living in towns, deprived of the traditional resources of kitchen garden, cow, and farm-yard fowls, working in great factories under the stern gaze of the overseers, being forced to obey, losing all freedom of movement, accepting fixed working-hours—all these were immediate effects hard to bear. It meant changing a whole way of life and view of the world. (Braudel, *The Perspective of the World*, 592–93, 595)

From another point of view, renowned conservative scholar Russell Kirk comments:

> With the coming of democracy and industrialism, the physical and intellectual props of conservative order were knocked away. ...
> Modern industrialism, in Britain and America and most of western Europe, had smashed the economic defenses of conservative society. ...
> ... The poor man ceased to feel that he had a decent place in the community; he became a social atom, starved for most emotions except envy and ennui, severed from true family-life, and reduced to mere household-life, his old landmarks buried, his old faiths dissipated. Industrialism was a harder knock to conservatism than the books of the French equalitarians. (Russell Kirk, *The Conservative Mind: From Burke to Eliot*, 6th rev. ed. [Chicago: Regnery Gateway, 1978], 197, 199)

35. Fiorenza Tarozzi, *Dizionario di storiografia*, ed. A. De Bernardi and S. Guarracino (Milan: Mondadori Bruno, 1998), s.v. "Questione sociale." A University of Bologna professor, Tarozzi is a scholar specializing in labor, trade union, and cooperative movements.

36. On the hardships experienced by the early industrial proletariat, see E. Royton Pike, *Human Documents of the Industrial Revolution in Britain* (London: George Allen & Unwin, 1970). For an analysis on the uprooting of the proletariat and the emergence of Socialism, see Yvan Blot, "Socialisme, les raisons d'un déclin morale," *Figaro Magazine* (Paris), Mar. 15, 1986, 19–26.

37. Rome's invasion by the Piedmontese army on September 20, 1870, resulted in the popes' being held prisoner in the Vatican. The situation was only resolved with the 1929 Lateran Treaty.

38. Engels wrote, "So just fight bravely on, most gracious masters of capital! We need you for the present. ...You have to clear the vestiges of the Middle Ages and of absolute monarchy out of our path; you have to annihilate patriarchalism; you have to carry out centralisation [of the economy]; you have to convert the more or less propertyless classes into genuine proletarians, into recruits for us; by your factories and your commercial relationships you must create for us the basis of the material means which the proletariat needs for the attainment of freedom." Frederick Engels, "The Movements of 1847," in *Marx and Engels 1845–48*, vol. 6, *Collected Works*, by Karl Marx and Frederick Engels (n.p.: Lawrence & Wishart Electric Book, 2010), 529.

39. In his homily at the Mass celebrated at the Le Bourget airport, in Paris, on June 1, 1980, Pope John Paul II said, "How much the sons and daughters of your nation have done for the knowledge of mankind, to express humanity through the formulation of their inalienable rights! The role that the idea of liberty, equality, and fraternity plays in your culture is well known. Deep down, they are Christian ideas. I say this conscious of the fact that those who first formulated this ideal were not referring to man's alliance with eternal wisdom, but wanted to act for the attainment of freedom." John Paul II, "Homily at Le Bourget Airport" (June 1, 1980), no. 5. For a discussion on the trilogy in Church Magisterium, see Plinio Corrêa de Oliveira, *Nobility and Analogous Traditional Elites in the Allocutions of Pius XII: A Theme Illuminating American Social History* (York, Penn.: The American Society for the Defense of Tradition, Family, and Property, 1993), 381–89.

that is, communist, utopia.[40] The fascination of this utopia has played a central role in most of the revolutions that have rocked the world since then, in both the temporal and religious spheres.

The spirit and doctrines of 1789 inspired the revolutions of 1830 and 1848, which gave rise to liberal Catholicism (extensively covered in the next chapter). They also inspired so-called social Catholicism, the topic of this chapter. "The 1848 Revolution gave the signal for the upsurge of social Catholicism all over Europe," explains French Catholic historian Georges Hourdin (1899–1999).[41]

B. Social Catholicism

Numerous Catholic sectors sensed a need to carry out a social action that would improve worker conditions and at the same time serve as a response to the new social sensibility. Thus, a current known as social Catholicism arose. "The expression 'social Catholicism,'" explains Alec Vidler (1899–1991) professor at Cambridge, "designates those individuals and groups in Catholicism that became aware of these social changes, that were shocked by their inhumanity, that refused to sit down under the doctrine of *laissez-faire,* and that determined to do something more to ameliorate the consequences of industrialization than could be done by traditional charity."[42]

Moved by this commendable aspiration, a large number of Catholics devoted themselves to social action with such an enthusiasm that it suggested a revival of the Church. As a whole, the current observed the Magisterium of the Church and followed the example of its best elements, exercising a salutary, Gospel-inspired influence on society. However, some sectors gradually allowed themselves to be infected with the revolutionary spirit and doctrines, giving rise to a progressive current. Hence the distinction between the conservative social Catholicism, and the liberal or progressive one.

Progressive sectors downplayed the importance of moral and religious factors in the social question, but no social regeneration would be possible without the actual practice of religion and a consequent rejection of a pragmatic and sensual lifestyle. Nor did they keep in mind that the social question was the result of a broader and deeper phenomenon: the revolutionary process unleashed in 1789. They tended to exclude, therefore, the deleterious presence of revolutionary influences from their analyses.

1. Conservative Social Catholicism

This book is not about conservative social Catholicism, faithful to the Magisterium. For the sake of completeness, though, we will devote a few lines to it. Representatives of this tendency

maintained that the problem was one of morals, not institutions. The solution, in their view, had to start with a profound strengthening of the Catholic faith and moral principles, not social engineering.

Still, realizing that the root cause of the proletarian problem was the breakdown of organic society, they proposed solutions based on the recovery of organic institutions such as the family, the guilds, and corporations. Since the downfall (or at least weakening) of those institutions had eliminated the intermediate bodies between the individual and the State, there was a twofold revolutionary trend: either the State tended to swallow everything (State Socialism), or rampant individualism tended to dissolve the social fabric (social anarchism). Only the restoration of intermediate bodies could protect people from that double danger and restore balance to society. This is the principle of subsidiarity, cornerstone of Catholic social doctrine. In this matter, it is worth noting the works of Italian Jesuit Fr. Luigi Taparelli (1793–1862), co-founder of the magazine *Civiltà Cattolica* in Rome.[43]

Opposed to both Socialism and Liberalism, conservative social Catholics were often associated with sectors then called intransigent, counter-revolutionary, or ultramontane, that is, with the political right. Among its best-known representatives in France were Frédéric LePlay (1806–1882), Charles Périn (1815–1905), and Emile Keller (1828–1909). There was also a school led by Most Rev. Charles Emile Freppel, bishop of Angers (1827–1891). This school upheld the rights of private property and vindicated a greater role for free enterprise, limiting the role of the State to the protection of individual rights and the correction of abuses. Suspicious of labor unions, often infiltrated by socialists, it proposed instead a constant cooperation between management and labor to solve the social question. In sum, it steered closer to capitalism than other segments of social Catholicism, though it rejected its liberal inspiration and laissez-faire excesses.

In Italy, social Catholicism arose in a peculiar historical context. In 1868, the anticlericalism of the Savoy monarchy had driven Pius IX to enact the policy known as *non expedit* (it is not convenient), which declared it unacceptable for Italian Catholics to participate in political elections and, by extension, in political life. Pope Leo XIII reiterated that provision in 1886. Excluded from politics, many Catholics devoted themselves to charitable initiatives and educational and social works. That was the era of great social saints like St. Joseph Benedict Cottolengo (1786–1842), St. John Bosco (1815–1888), St. Leonard Murialdo (1828–1900), St. John Piamarta (1841–1913), St. Louis Guanella (1842–1915), Blessed Bartolo Longo (1841–1926), St. Hannibal of France (1851–1927), Blessed Contardo Ferrini (1859–1902), and many others. Social initiatives often came from the aristocracy, as was the case with the Servant of God Giulia Falletti Colbert de Maulévrier, Marchioness of Barolo (1785–1864).

They lived their social commitment not only with dutiful works of charity toward the poor, but also as defiance in the face of the liberal persecution against the Church, an affirmation of Catholic spirit in opposition to the new political class, and a tool to organize the Catholic masses and especially the young.

As the growing Catholic social movement coalesced, the Italian Catholic Youth Society was founded on June 29, 1867. Attorney

---

40. One of the trilogy's more radical interpretations can be enunciated as follows: Justice demands that there be absolute equality among men. Equality alone, by suppressing all authority, completely attains liberty and fraternity. Liberty can only have one limit, namely, whatever is indispensable for preventing more gifted men from setting up, for their own benefit, any superiority of command, prestige, or possessions. True fraternity characterizes the relations among entirely free and equal men. See Plinio Corrêa de Oliveira, *Autogestion socialiste: Les têtes tombent à l'entreprise, à la maison, à l'école* (Paris: Tradition Famille Proprieté, 1983), 79.

41. Georges Hourdin, in *La Documentation Catholique*, no. 997 (Aug. 17, 1947), 1059.

42. A.R. Vidler, *A Century of Social Catholicism: 1820–1920* (London: S.P.C.K., 1964), xi–xii. An Anglican clergyman, Dr. Vidler was one of the greatest historians of religion in the twentieth century. See: A.R. Vidler, *The Church in an Age of Revolution: 1789 to the Present Day,* vol. 5, *The Penguin History of the Church* (London: Penguin Books, 1962); A.R. Vidler, *Prophecy and Papacy: A Study of Lamennais, the Church and the Revolution* (London: S.C.M. Press, 1954). See also J.B. Duroselle, *Les débuts du catholicisme social en France, 1822–1970.* (Paris: Presses Universitaires de France, 1951). Francesco Nitti comments: "And when Socialism discarded a great part of its primitive revolutionary tendencies, the more intelligent and cultured and intrepid among the French Catholics felt the necessity of interesting themselves in the social question." Francesco S. Nitti, *Catholic Socialism,* trans. Mary MacKintosh (London: Swan Sonnenschein & Co., 1895), 262.

43. See Luigi Taparelli D'Azeglio, *Esame critico degli ordini rappresentativi nella società moderna,* 2 vols. (Rome: 1854). Fr. Taparelli developed his thought in over two hundred articles in *Civiltà Cattolica,* all of them with such a tenor that he was called the "hammer of liberal concepts" (Antonio Messineo). He opposed the unification of Italy. While defending the primacy of society over the State he criticized the centralizing tendency of the Savoy government. For him, living organisms as the family, the community, and the village were foreign to the liberal, nationalist ideology.

Giovanni Acquaderni (1839–1922) assumed its presidency. His police record classified him as a "clerical reactionary." Later, Count Mario Fani Ciotti (1845–1869) joined him. Pope Pius IX approved the new association in 1868, with the brief *Dum filii belial*. The Society defended Pius IX and his anti-liberal policy. The sovereign pontiff reciprocated with a phrase that became a motto:

> "Together we will fight error. ..."
> "... You are with me, I am with you."[44]

The Society's program, published on January 4, 1868, began with an attack on Freemasonry ("those men without faith and without God that have invaded and corrupted everything"), and stressed the urgency of religious education for the youth. In the social sphere, it proposed a society based on family, morality, and faith.

The first national Catholic Conference was held in Venice in June 1874. Presided over by Giovanni Acquaderni, the five hundred delegates agreed to safeguard Italian religious traditions against liberal society. In their speeches, they strongly attacked the Revolution, "this snake that poisons, this tiger that dismembers, this she-wolf that devours, this dirty witch."[45] At a second conference, held in Florence in 1875, they created the Opera dei Congressi, entrusting the presidency to Acquaderni. The climate was one of great enthusiasm. Giovanni Spadolini spoke of "King's heralds of militant Catholicism."[46]

2. Ideological Transshipment in Social Catholicism

In order to trace the history of liberation theology (LT), however, we need to look at the progressive currents: those sectors of social Catholicism that, opening up to revolutionary influences, began to slide to the left all the way to Socialism. In its sociopolitical connotations, LT is a result of this process.

An indicative case was that of Count Albert de Mun (1841–1914), the principal figure of a vast Catholic movement—the Oeuvre des Cercles Catholiques d'Ouvriers (Catholic Workers' Circles)—that had a profound influence throughout France in the second half of the nineteenth century. The span of the Oeuvre's doctrinal migration makes it an almost paradigmatic example of the kind of ideological transshipment at work within social Catholicism. Counter-revolutionary in its beginnings, the Oeuvre attracted ultramontane and legitimist Catholics into its ranks. Two decades after its founding, however, several of its sectors were already walking hand in hand with the socialists.

De Mun was a monarchist and a cavalry officer. His motto was simple and direct: "War on the Revolution!" His program was equally clear: "Opposition to the Declaration of the Rights of Man, foundation of the Revolution, and proclamation of the rights of God, foundation of the Counter-Revolution."[47] When asked to define his position, he wrote, "The Syllabus will be our flag."[48] De Mun called his movement the "Counter-Revolution on the move."

However, such ultramontane declarations of faith did a poor job hiding the lack of doctrinal foundations. The French nobleman's social commitment, as was the case with many social Catholics, was inspired by a generous, albeit vague and romantic, desire to help the poor rather than by sound principles derived from a profound knowledge of Catholic doctrine and a methodical observation of reality. Historian Fr. Emmanuel Barbier observed: "Initially, the Oeuvre des Cercles had no structured social doctrine; only later will it develop."[49]

This lack of firm doctrinal foundations and a deep optimism regarding the times caused de Mun and many conservative social Catholics to fall prey to a devious process of ideological transshipment that gradually moved them to the left. Carried away by this process, de Mun began to champion collectivist solutions also propounded by the left and to depart from the positions of the right. At first, the coincidences were more in the concrete measures than in doctrine, but, as he rationalized his attitude, he began to slide toward Socialism. Though de Mun himself never wholly embraced Socialism, other segments of social Catholicism did. The importance of this process, which affects many Catholic circles to this day, deserves a brief discussion.

a. The Interplay of Sympathies and Phobias

At first glance, that drift from the right to Socialism may appear puzzling. Instead, it is the result of a deceitful revolutionary propaganda ploy Brazilian Catholic thinker Plinio Corrêa de Oliveira called "unperceived ideological transshipment."[50] The trick is based on the manipulation of two sets of conflicting impressions—some of sympathy, others of phobia—and from their coincidence or discrepancy with seemingly similar dispositions on the part of the socialists. Let us look at this process in slow motion.

b. Sympathy: Predilection for Medieval Guilds

A fact to take into account in order to understand this baffling ideological transshipment is the great predilection that Catholics (and particularly traditionalists) showed for medieval corporations. This predilection was part of an ideal of restoration of Christian civilization. In the wake of the French Revolution, the secularization of European society was greatly accentuated. In a natural reaction of defense against this dechristianization, ample sectors of public opinion began to wistfully look back to the "time when States were governed by the philosophy of the Gospel"[51] and yearn for its restoration as the only remedy for the revolutionary quagmire. Throughout the nineteenth century, the Middle Ages were highly revalued. Consider, for example, the flourishing neo-Gothic style and the rediscovery of Gregorian chant. Catholics were, almost by definition, defenders of the restoration of Christian civilization. The restoration of corporations and other intermediate bodies of organic society was particularly sought.

44. Giacomo De Antonellis, *Storia dell'Azione Cattolica dal 1867 a oggi* (Milan: Rizzoli, 1987), 56–57. On Acquaderni and Fani, see Paola Dal Toso and Ernesto Diaco, *Mario Fani e Giovanni Acquaderni: Profilo e scritti dei fondatori dell'Azione Cattolica* (Rome: AVE, 2008); Mario Agnes, ed., *Giovanni Acquaderni: Ricordi ai suoi amici* (Rome: AVE, 1977).

45. Gabriele De Rosa, *Il movimento cattolico in Italia: Dalla restaurazione all'età giolittiana* (Bari: Editori Laterza, 1988), 59. During the Spanish civil wars of the 1800s between traditionalists and liberals, the Catholic Youth Society unwaveringly sided with Catholics. See Lorenzo Bedeschi, *Le origini della gioventù cattolica dalla caduta del governo pontificio al primo congresso cattolico di Venezia su documenti inediti d'archivio* (Bologna: Cappelli, 1959), 102.

46. Giovanni Spadolini, *L'opposizione cattolica da Porta Pia al '98* (Florence: Vallecchi, 1964), quoted in De Antonellis, *Storia dell'Azione Cattolica*, 17. The Camelots du Roi (King's Heralds) were a monarchical and anti-liberal militant youth sector linked to Action Française.

47. Albert De Mun, *Discorso inaugurale alla camera dei deputati*, 1876, quoted in Emmanuel Barbier, *Histoire du catholicisme libéral et du catholicisme social en France:*

Du concile du Vatican à l'avénement de S.S. Benoît XV (1870–1914) (Bordeaux: Imprimerie Y. Cadoret, 1924), 1:349.

48. Albert De Mun, *Questions sociales*, vol. 1, *Discours du Comte Albert de Mun* (Paris: Librairie Poussielgue Frères, 1888), 99. He was obviously referring to the *Syllabus errorum*, an 1864 document issued by Pius IX containing a detailed list of liberal errors in the theological, philosophical, moral, and sociopolitical fields.

49. Barbier, *Histoire du catholicisme libéral*, 1:358.

50. See Corrêa de Oliveira, *Unperceived Ideological Transshipment*.

51. Leo XIII, encyclical *Immortale Dei* (Nov. 1, 1885), no. 21. "Medieval Christendom was not just any order, or merely one of many possible orders. It was the realization, in the circumstances inherent to the times and places, of the only authentic order among men, namely, Christian civilization." Corrêa de Oliveira, *Revolution and Counter-Revolution*, 41.

c. Phobia: An Ingrained Rejection of Liberal Capitalism

At the other extreme, we find in many nineteenth-century Catholics an ingrained rejection of liberal capitalism, defined by the American thinker Michael Novak as "democratic capitalism."[52] A child of the Enlightenment, linked to the Protestant spirit to the point of being considered one of its emanations,[53] liberal capitalism caused not only a doctrinal rejection in many Catholics but also an emotional one. That reaction was aggravated by the anti-Catholicism sported by many representatives of the liberal capitalist current, beginning with Adam Smith (1723–1790), who wrote, "The constitution of the Church of Rome may be considered as the most formidable combination that was ever formed against the ... liberty, reason, and happiness of mankind."[54] It is not surprising, then, that many Catholics saw liberal capitalism as a subversive phenomenon, destructive of the traditional order. This perception was not exclusive to Catholics. It was also dominant, for example, among the English Tories and Old Whigs, usually akin to High Anglicanism.

This aversion was aggravated by the rise of a new middle class of Voltairean spirit, which replaced the old aristocracy in the conduct of public affairs, imposing coarse, pragmatic, and calculating ways where refinement, generosity, and heroism had prevailed before, and replacing the primacy of education and good manners with that of money.[55]

d. Incipient Sympathy for the Left's Positions

Both the predilection for corporations and the rejection of liberal capitalism overlapped (at least in appearance) with similar positions of the socialists, provoking in some areas of social Catholicism a nascent sympathy for the positions of the left. Once the left's often secular and anti-Catholic side had been removed, did it not show a commendable desire to improve the condition of the proletariat? Did the leftists not also want to organize intermediate bodies—trade unions—which at least formally resembled guilds? Did Catholics and socialists not coincide in their refusal of democratic capitalism? Revolutionary propaganda cleverly exploited these formal coincidences to trigger in many sectors of social Catholicism a process of ideological transshipment to the left.

e. Strategy of Ideological Transshipment

Ideological transshipment evolved around two axes: First, the workers' sufferings were greatly magnified, exacerbating sentimental compassion for their plight, an attitude supposedly shared by the left. Secondly, a growing apathy was created regarding the advance of the socialist movement, supposedly imbued with the *spirit of the times.* The actual process of ideological transshipment can be outlined as follows:

1) Overvaluation, both doctrinal and temperamental, of social Catholics' dislike for democratic capitalism and, conversely, of their sympathy for the guild system.
2) Attenuation of points of discord with the left: Any issue that might bring social Catholics into conflict with the left was attenuated or hidden as much as possible.
3) Manipulation of impressions: Sympathies and antipathies were then gradually emptied of their significance and loaded with new meanings. The rejection of democratic capitalism was magnified until it included even its legitimate aspects. The defense of corporations was transformed into a defense of labor unions.
4) Search of affinities with the left: It was then suggested that these dispositions were shared by the left.
5) Sympathy for the left: The left was idealized as the kind-hearted party of the poor, and its leaders portrayed as generous, idealistic, and open-minded.
6) Aversion toward the right: Gradually, the same propaganda depicted the right as the party of the greedy rich, and their leaders were loathed as callous and insensitive.
7) Collaboration with the left: The nascent sympathy for the left led to some punctual cooperation, for example, to call a strike. Such occasions tended to multiply, leading ever larger sectors of social Catholics to join the left in popular initiatives.
8) Acceptance of Socialism: The last step was to convince the social Catholics ensnared in this process that the overvalued issues were better defended by the ideology of their new comrades, that is, the socialists.

f. An Example: The Slide Toward Statism

A typical example of ideological transshipment was Albert de Mun's slide toward statism. Initially Count de Mun simply wished to ameliorate the workers' lot by introducing in labor relations not only justice but also charity. He proposed the traditional ideal of having charity exercised through patronage, that is, an employer's commitment to the welfare of his employees. This approach, however, offended the romantic and egalitarian atmosphere of the time, which beheld any social hierarchy (particularly when it generated dependence) as causing the inferior to suffer. Workers, it was argued, were now grown-ups and did not ask for alms but for rights. Yielding to the dominant environment, de Mun did not hold on to his original position for long. He gradually abandoned the idea of patronage and adopted instead that of free association

52. Michael Novak, *The Spirit of Democratic Capitalism* (New York: American Enterprise Institute/Simon and Schuster, 1982), 14. Novak uses the expression in the sense of a triple system encompassing bourgeois democratism in the sociopolitical sphere; liberal capitalism in the economic sphere; and pluralism in the religious, moral, and cultural spheres.

53. German sociologist Max Weber (1864–1920) wrote the well-known thesis that capitalism and, therefore, the modern economic and technological development are largely derived from Protestant ethics. Rejecting the medieval Catholic vision of an earthly life aimed at the hereafter and thus fully inspired by symbolic and spiritual values, Protestantism, he says, generated a worldly asceticism, which involved the rationalization of economic and social life on the basis of efficiency and technical knowledge, the bases of modern progress. That would explain the remarkable material development of Protestant powers and, conversely, the backwardness of Catholic countries. See Max Weber, *The Protestant Ethic and the Spirit of Capitalism*, trans. Talcott Parsons (New York: Charles Scribner's Sons, 1930). Modern analysis has dispelled the myth that progress comes only from Protestant ethics. See for example, Rodney Stark, *The Victory of Reason: How Christianity Led to Freedom, Capitalism, and Western Success* (New York: Random House, 2006).

54. Adam Smith, *An Inquiry Into the Nature and Causes of the Wealth of Nations*, ed. Edwin Cannan, vol. 2 (London: Methuen & Co. 1904).

55. We can apply to this new class Edmund Burke's (1729–1797) rebuke of the French Revolution:

It is now sixteen or seventeen years since I saw the queen of France, then the dauphiness, at Versailles, and surely never lighted on this orb, which she hardly seemed to touch, a more delightful vision. I saw her just above the horizon, decorating and cheering the elevated sphere she just began to move in—glittering like the morning star, full of life and splendor and joy. Oh! what a revolution! and what a heart must I have to contemplate without emotion that elevation and that fall! Little did I dream when she added titles of veneration to those of enthusiastic, distant, respectful love, that she should ever be obliged to carry the sharp antidote against disgrace concealed in that bosom; little did I dream that I should have lived to see such disasters fallen upon her in a nation of gallant men, in a nation of men of honor and of cavaliers. I thought ten thousand swords must have leaped from their scabbards to avenge even a look that threatened her with insult. But the age of chivalry is gone. That of sophisters, economists; and calculators has succeeded; and the glory of Europe is extinguished forever. (Edmund Burke, *Reflections on the Revolution in France* [1790], 63)

of patrons and workers or mixed trade unions. "The substitution of the regime of patronage by that of association," de Mun later recalled, "was a profound idea that had enormous consequences. It was destined to transform Catholic social action to its roots."[56] Even though de Mun conceived these associations in the mold of guilds and corporations, following the restorationist belief, the leftist propaganda applauded this step.

At first de Mun carefully distinguished Christian associations from the labor unions advocated by the socialists, which were accused of being tools for class struggle. However, few employers were open to the idea and preferred to hire non-associated workers.[57] Given the failure of the project, the Oeuvre's more progressive wing, led by the Marquis René de la Tour du Pin Chambly (1834–1924), began to propose a compulsory application of government options. According to an Oeuvre executive, Paul Tailliez, la Tour du Pin argued that "the guild system will fully bear fruit only if neither employer nor worker is able to escape it."[58]

Since only the State was able to apply forced corporatism, those sectors began to consider it the natural protector of the working classes against the greed of capitalists. Hence, they called for increasing the State's powers to intervene in labor relations and ultimately in the entire economy. "The State ... does it have the right to intervene in these matters?" asked de Mun in an 1888 speech in the Chamber of Deputies. "For me, it obviously does. I have no doubt, and I'll make my thought clearer by saying that it actually has the duty."[59] At first, de Mun and his school tried to steer a middle-course between Liberalism and Socialism in a forerunner version of the twentieth century's third way. "We equally reject anti-Christian Liberalism and State Socialism," explained de Mun in his speech closing the *Oeuvre* Conference in 1884.[60]

Once the Pandora box of State interventionism was opened, however, it was difficult to draw a line, particularly when the predominant trends of the time (clearly of socialist inspiration) called for increasing State interventionism, usually on the pretext of taming laissez-faire capitalism. While some trends of social Catholicism moved toward leftist statism and eventually merged with Marxist Socialism, others went toward a right-wing statism that produced the so-called social right.[61] In both cases, the victim would still be the traditional organic society.

Francesco Nitti, an Italian economist and contemporary of de Mun, summarizes the Oeuvre's slide: "The form of Catholic Socialism taught by Count de Mun has passed through three distinctly different periods. In the first the *Oeuvre* maintained the absolute necessity of a return to the guild system; in the second ... it sought to bring about the development of mixed syndicates [unions]; finally, in the third ... it has supported the necessity

for profound economic reforms on the part of the State, thus accentuating its tendency toward State Socialism."[62]

g. Doctrinal Ambiguities

This slide within the Oeuvre—a sample of what was going on in ample sectors of social Catholicism—called for a rationalization. Seeking to justify their slide, many social Catholics began to sustain ideas increasingly closer to socialist doctrine.

Reacting against the excessive individualism of liberal capitalism, social Catholics tended to belittle the legitimate rights of the person, placing emphasis on social or community elements instead. Had they been inspired by a wholesome intention of restoring organicity to society, it would have helped to restore the social balance. However, those Catholics seemed to ignore the presence of powerful revolutionary forces moving in a similar direction and with which they were objectively in sync. By making *social* the dominant criterion, they ended up forgetting the person and advocated an interventionist statism that is the exact opposite of traditional organic society, which is always built up from below and never imposed from above. This is the hotbed that later engendered Fascism and other movements incorrectly defined as right-wing.

On the other hand, the Christian injunction to help the poor began to be unilaterally emphasized until it became a sort of super commandment. The greatest iniquity of the time, it was simplistically said, was the plight of proletarians and their consequent desertion of the Church. Christians' primary duty began to be depicted as a sort of "preferential option for the poor" (to use modern language). Some Catholic theologians and writers began to exalt proletarians as the privileged people of the Gospel, as the foundation on which the future world would be built. It is no exaggeration to say that legitimate concerns about the lower classes were misrepresented as a kind of mystique of the poor, which led to a climax in the twentieth century by LT and certain populist currents.

Aided by widespread romanticism, this mystique was easily infected by the egalitarian spirit so that concern for the poor was readily coupled with a bias against those who supposedly oppressed them: employers. Even as leftist propaganda burnished the poor with an affectionate touch, it lampooned employers as heartless and greedy. The lamentable apathy or even disdain displayed by some employers in relation to their employees only reinforced that perception. As a result, an incipient savor of class struggle began to creep into sectors of social Catholicism, replacing the mood of Christian cooperation and partnership. The sectors opened to this outlook were sometimes referred to as the populist wing of social Catholicism.

h. Hand in Hand With the Socialists

As a result of this ideological transshipment, many social Catholics found themselves increasingly siding with the socialist left. Far from concealing this situation, they actually flaunted it. "I don't balk from this convergence with the socialists," Albert de Mun conceded in 1889. "We will certainly concur in many other points yet. Far from fearing this, I congratulate myself for it."[63] For their part, the socialists reciprocated. Speaking on behalf of socialist deputies, A. Ferroul stated, "I have read M. de Mun's declarations, and, together with my friends, cannot but commend

---

56. Albert de Mun, *Ma vocation sociale: Souvenirs de la fondation de l'Oeuvre des Cercles Catholiques d'Ouvriers* (Paris: P. Lethielleux, Libraire-Éditeur, 1950), 217.

57. In Italy, St. Leonard Murialdo suffered a similar failure. Highly successful in organizing Catholic trade unions, with which he formed the Sub-Alpine Worker Federation, he was much less so organizing similar unions for employers. See Armando Castellani, *Il beato Leonardo Murialdo*, 2 vols. (Rome: Tipografia S. Pio X, 1966–1967).

58. Paul Tailliez, letter to Fr. Emmanuel Barbier, quoted in Barbier, *Histoire du catholicisme libéral*, 1:357.

59. Albert de Mun, speech to the Chamber of Deputies (May 28, 1888), in *1888–1891*, vol. 4, *Discours et écrits divers du Comte Albert de Mun* (Paris: Librairie Ch. Poussielgue, 1895), 49.

60. Albert de Mun, speech closing the twelfth conference of the Oeuvre des Cercles Catholiques d'Ouvriers (June 7, 1884), in *Discours du Comte Albert de Mun*, 1:424.

61. The drift of the Marquis de La Tour du Pin, for example, led him toward "right wing" corporatism. In 1899, he joined the Action Française, becoming a prominent figure. See René de la Tour du Pin, *Vers un ordre social chrétien* (Paris: Éditions du Trident, 1987).

62. Nitti, *Catholic Socialism*, 300.

63. Albert de Mun, *Discours à l'Assemblée de Romans* (Nov. 10, 1889), quoted in Barbier, *Histoire du catholicisme libéral*, 2:224.

them; his demands are, in reality, identical with those formulated by the socialist conferences."[64]

By the end of the century, convergence with the socialists had become almost complete. "With the exception of a few points touching on religious matters," Francesco Nitti observed at the time, "the programme of de Mun ... is identical with that of the most advanced socialists."[65]

The Marquis de la Tour du Pin, who would later become a leading figure of the French nationalist right, was the greatest enthusiast of convergence with the socialists. Explaining his position, in 1889 he wrote, "In the light of the principles with which we have conducted our studies, it is easy to say the dose of materialism advocated by revolutionary Socialism is no more preponderant than in liberal economy. Nevertheless, we find humanity in Socialism. ... Virtually all that is just in the claims of revolutionary Socialism, in substance if not in form, is perfectly reflected in our vision of the corporate system."[66] Not surprisingly, he proclaimed, "We are marching along with the socialists. ... I repeat once again: we don't care about having the conservatives and their moribund wails on our side."[67] He often called his position Christian Socialism.

Socialist trends were particularly strong in the Association Catholique de la Jeunesse Française, a kind of youth section of the Oeuvre, which played a leading role in the birth of progressivism in the twentieth century.

i. The Italian Front

Although with particular nuances, the process of ideological transshipment to the left also took place in Italy's social Catholicism. The Opera dei Congressi had spread everywhere, participating in local elections and organizing cultural and social activities, pilgrimages, and so on. In a few years, the Opera peaked at twelve regional, one hundred and nine diocesan, and over eight hundred parish committees.

Unfortunately, just as in France, Italian social Catholics displayed a doctrinal vacuum, especially regarding the evaluation of the socialist danger. During the conference of the Italian Catholic Youth Society held in Venice in 1874, historian Gabriele De Rosa recounts, "They discussed Socialism. There was some disagreement on assessing the danger posed by the spread of socialist doctrines. ... On the whole, the intransigents showed no knowledge or ability to properly evaluate socialistic doctrines, which then permeated the working press and caused concern among the ruling class: from Proudhon's texts to those of Benoît Malon, Mazzini, to the speeches of Bakunin."[68] This doctrinal vacuum caused many social Catholics to fall into the trap of ideological transshipment.

There was no lack of contrast between the two souls of the movement: the Italian Catholic Youth Society founded and

directed by Giovanni Acquaderni, and the Opera dei Congressi, nominally entrusted to Acquaderni, but in practice managed by the Venetian Committee, presided by Giovanni Battista Paganuzzi (1841–1923), who espoused a different orientation.

A process occurred which was repeated fifty years later with Catholic Action: As efforts grew to group all components of social Catholicism into one association, i.e., the Opera, its more conservative sectors were targeted by a negative propaganda that tried to annihilate them. "The Catholic Youth is going through some pretty sad times," wrote Giacomo de Antonellis. "Acquaderni is a morally elevated figure but does not seem to be able to react to the whirlwind unleashed by multiple quarters."[69] A Jesuit, Fr. Carlo Maria Curci (1809–1891), stood out in the war against Catholic Youth. He wrote a pamphlet accusing the movement of closing itself in a greenhouse Christianity that is, one not open to the modern world.[70]

On May 17, 1878, Acquaderni was forced to resign while some Vatican circles, after the death of Pius IX, seemed to prefer progressive sectors of social Catholicism at the expense of traditional ones. "The first years of the pontificate of Leo XIII were especially difficult for hardliners," De Rosa comments.[71] In a letter dated April 24, 1880, Leo XIII stated his desire to see all Catholics unite in Opera dei Congressi. One by one, the various components of social Catholicism broke up and regrouped in Opera, which thus could present itself as the sole and exclusive representative of militant Catholicism.

At the same time, a leftist-oriented pro-worker current gained ground inside Opera. While traditionalist and moderate Catholics still considered that the social question could be solved by joint unions, the new pro-worker groups, according to De Rosa, "upheld the principle that workers should stand alone and adopt the criterion of resistance in conflicts with employers."[72] In other words, they should join the socialists by participating in class struggle.

3. The American Scene

While far from having the extension and importance it had in Europe, social Catholicism also penetrated the United States. Many American Catholics were dedicated to a social activism that followed lines similar to those in Europe. For example, the Central Verein, an association of German-Americans, introduced the views of the German school of Catholic economics known as Solidarism. Under the stormy leadership of Fr. Peter Dietz, the Verein played a decisive role in the dissemination of leftist social Catholic ideas, particularly through the pages of its periodical, the *Central-Blatt and Social Justice*. To further the Verein programs, Father Dietz organized the Militia of Christ for Social Service,

64. H. de Moly, "La règlementation du travail en France et les catholiques," *La réforme sociale* 10 (May 16, 1890), in *La Réforme Sociale* 2e. serie, vol. 9, year 10 (Jan.–Jun. 1890) (Paris: Secrétariat de la Société d'Économie Sociale, 1890), 601. Commenting on these frequent coincidences, Nitti writes, "Although this second school combats the claims of Democratic Socialism on theoretic grounds, it nevertheless accepts, in practice, a good part of its economic programme. And the socialists themselves, though far from sharing the religious tendencies of the party, do not attempt to conceal their sympathy toward the Oeuvre and its principal inspirer, Count de Mun." Nitti, *Catholic Socialism,* 268)

65. Nitti, 290.

66. Barbier, *Histoire du catholicisme libéral,* 2:224–25.

67. Jean de Fabrègues, *Le Sillon de Marc Sangnier: Un tournant majeur du mouvement social catholique* (Paris: Librairie Académique Perrin, 1964), 70.

68. De Rosa, *Il movimento,* 61. De Rosa noted particularly "the typical intransigence trend which fitted the critique of Socialism into the broader context of a global criticism of the entire 'liberal revolution' starting with the Protestant Reformation" (De Rosa, 61). In our view, it is a most just and necessary criticism, which should, however, be completed with a specific critique of Socialism to avoid failing to grasp

the proper characteristics of the socialist revolution. In chronological and doctrinal order, it is a third Revolution, different from the first (Protestantism) and from the second (Liberalism). The lack of a specific criticism of Socialism implied the absence of a specifically anti-socialist action, being limited to an anti-liberal action. This doctrinal vacuum showed all its harmfulness when, in order to fight Liberalism, many social Catholics joined the socialists, embracing in practice a much more radical form of the Revolution. A typical example was the support of many Catholics for the May 1898 Milan riots. In order to oppose the liberal regime, they did not hesitate to go to the barricades with the socialists. For a historical view of the revolutionary process, see Corrêa de Oliveira, *Revolution and Counter-Revolution,* 13–18.

69. De Antonellis, *Storia dell'Azione Cattolica,* 89.

70. At odds with Church authorities, Father Curci left the Society of Jesus and dedicated himself to writing liberal books. He published numerous works in which he advocated a broad reconciliation between the Church, liberal thought, and the modern world. In 1885, he was suspended *a divinis* and his works were placed on the Index. Shortly before his death, Curci submitted to the Vatican decisions and publicly recanted his previous statements. Readmitted into the Society, he wrote another book, *Di un socialismo cristiano (On Christian Socialism).*

71. De Rosa, *Il movimento,* 115.

72. De Rosa, 95–96.

composed of workers involved in labor causes, and the American Academy for Christian Democracy for young women.[73]

a. The Knights of Labor Controversy

The most conspicuous manifestation of social Catholicism in the U.S. was the widespread involvement of Catholics with the semi-secret brotherhood called the Noble and Holy Order of the Knights of Labor, which at its height (1886) counted some 700,000 members. This strange mixture of trade union and Masonic order was founded in Philadelphia in 1869 by a tailor named Uriah Stephens, a Mason and member of two other secret societies condemned by the Holy See, the Knights of Pythias and the Odd Fellows. The founding members were for the most part Masons.[74]

The Knights of Labor were structured like a Masonic order with initiation rituals, clandestine lodges, secrecy oaths, passwords, and sign grips. Of socialist inspiration, the Order sought to organize the workers in a mass movement that would deliver ownership of company property into their hands. Accordingly, its members engaged in vicious labor strikes and proletarian warfare, even resorting to violence, for which they were repeatedly accused of having close relationships with the Molly Maguires terrorist group.

Since a considerable segment of the working class was composed of Catholic immigrants, it is understandable that they comprised upward of two thirds of the Knights' ranks. In some places, the Knights were almost exclusively Catholic. Catholics frequently joined the Order with the overt, or at least the tacit, approval of their parish priest, since provision was made in its bylaws that membership could be disclosed to the confessor. The existence and doings of the Order were, indeed, well known to Church authorities. Opposed by most pastors, the Knights unfortunately countered with the support of many left-leaning priests and even of some bishops. Catholic involvement with the Knights was heightened in 1880 when Terence V. Powderly (1849–1924), an outspoken Catholic well connected with Church authorities, was elected president. He remained in office until 1893.

While decrying some of the riotous excesses of the anarchist factions within the Knights, Powderly was nonetheless overt about his socialist penchant. A member of the Socialist Labour Party, he "agree[d] with 'some of the aims of the advanced socialists.'"[75] "There are certain socialistic principles upon which we can all agree," he further explained.[76] "I and the majority of the Knights are socialists, in the proper sense of the term."[77] Sidestepping the fact that the terms had a very definite revolutionary meaning, he proclaimed, "If Socialism or Communism means the restoration of man's natural rights, I am a socialist and a communist!"[78] Powderly joined the Knights with the explicit approval of his bishop, Most Rev. William O'Hara of Scranton, Pennsylvania. Under his leadership, the Order became so strongly

identified with left-wing Catholicism that it ended up by drawing Rome's intervention.

At the request of Canadian bishops, the Holy See had formally condemned the Canadian branch of the Knights of Labor in 1884. In the aftermath of the condemnation, several American prelates petitioned Rome for its extension to the United States. In order to forestall such a move, Powderly multiplied contacts with friendly bishops, and eventually obtained the rare privilege of being invited to appear before the Third Plenary Council of Baltimore in 1884.

Archbishop Gibbons—fearful to restrain this labor movement since he was "unreservedly, almost belligerently friendly to organized labor," in the words of well-known historian Aaron Abell[79]—met personally with Powderly and then introduced him to the august assembly, seconded by Archbishop Patrick Feehan of Chicago, also a Knights' partisan. The socialist labor organizer had reassured the cardinal beforehand "that he [was] a devoted Catholic; that he practice[d] his religion faithfully, and receive[d] the sacraments regularly."[80]

Soothed by his guarantee that the Knights of Labor did not exact an oath of secrecy, but merely a pledge, nine of the eleven prelates voted in favor of supporting the trade union and of interceding in Rome against its condemnation.[81]

In 1887, while in Rome to receive the cardinal's hat, Archbishop Gibbons presented a memorial on behalf of the Knights of Labor. Originally written by Bishop John Ireland of Saint Paul (1838–1918), the document, it was said, was backed by 70 of America's bishops. Cleverly sidestepping the central and thorny issue of whether or not the Knights were socialists, the memorial revolved around the argument that the association should not be included in the Vatican's condemnation of secret societies. This strong-handed intervention bore its fruits, and the American branch of the Knights of Labor was spared the condemnation, provided that some minor adjustments be made in the preamble of its constitution.[82]

To appease Church authorities during the process, Powderly had toned down his socialist utterances. However, as soon as the favorable verdict was obtained from Rome, he reverted to a revolutionary position, officially adopting the extreme brand of Socialism advocated by Henry George (see below) and putting the Knights at the service of the latter's political campaigns. This leftward shift eventually led him out of the Church. He apostatized in 1901 and became a Mason, dying as one in 1924.

b. Georgism

Symptomatic of the more radical side of social Catholicism was the widespread acceptance that Henry George's (1839–1897) ideas enjoyed among left-leaning Catholics, including some clerics. George promoted an extreme brand of agrarian Socialism that denied the private ownership of land. Dubbed Georgism, his ideology was rightly qualified at the time by the liberal magazine *Catholic World*, a publication of the New York Paulist Fathers, as

73. For insights into the history and nature of the Verein, see Mary Harrita Fox and Peter E. Dietz, *Labor Priest* (Notre Dame: University of Notre Dame Press, 1953); Mary Liguori Brophy, *The Social Thought of the German Roman Catholic Central Verein* (Washington, D.C.: The Catholic University of America Press, 1941). For an overview of social Catholicism in the U.S., see Aaron I. Abell, *American Catholicism and Social Action: A Search for Social Justice, 1865–1950* (Notre Dame: University of Notre Dame Press, 1963); James Edmund Roohan, *American Catholicism and the Social Question, 1865–1900* (New York: Arno Press, 1976).

74. See Henry J. Browne, *The Catholic Church and the Knights of Labor* (New York: Arno Press, 1976), 36.

75. Browne, *The Catholic Church*, 139–40.

76. Browne, 90.

77. Browne, 298.

78. Browne, 90.

79. Aaron I. Abell, headnote to "The Stake of the Catholic Church in the Labor Movement" by James Gibbons, in Aaron I. Abell, ed., *American Catholic Thought on Social Questions* (Indianapolis: The Bobbs-Merrill Company, 1968), 143.

80. Taken from the Feb. 20, 1887 Memorial on the Knights of Labor presented in Rome by James Cardinal Gibbons to Cardinal Simeoni. James Cardinal Gibbons, *A Retrospect of Fifty Years* (Baltimore: John Murphy Company, 1916), 1:193.

81. See Robert D. Cross, *The Emergence of Liberal Catholicism in America* (Chicago: Quadrangle Paperbacks, 1968), 115–16.

82. Evidencing the brotherhood of Christian democrats worldwide, the French *abbés démocrates* publicly praised the American liberals' campaign to save the Knights of Labor. As Robert Cross comments, the *abbés démocrates* and their followers "regarded Ireland and Gibbons as true prophets of social Catholicism." Cross, *The Emergence*, 190.

"philosophical Communism."[83] In 1887, conservative American prelates attempted to include George's seminal work *Progress and Poverty* in the Index of Forbidden Books.

The move did not succeed, chiefly because of Cardinal Gibbons's personal intervention with the Sacred Congregation of the Index on behalf of the socialist leader. In 1889, however, the Holy Office of the Inquisition did issue a document defining George's doctrines as "deserving condemnation," and enjoined Catholics to "beware of the false theories of Henry George." The condemnation, however, was kept secret.

The most notable cleric to embrace Georgism was Fr. Edward McGlynn, pastor of St. Stephen's in New York. "Private ownership of land is against natural justice," expounded Father McGlynn, echoing George. "I ... would confiscate private property in land without one penny of compensation to the mis-called owners."[84] Along with Terence Powderly, Father McGlynn campaigned for Henry George in his unsuccessful run for mayor of New York in 1886. This campaign, officially endorsed by the socialist parties, acted as a rallying banner for leftist Catholics, with the Knights of Labor at their forefront. Father McGlynn's outspoken socialist militancy was all the more dangerous since he commanded the sympathy of a good number of young priests. Particularly, Fr. Sylvester Malone, pastor of Sts. Peter and Paul Church in Brooklyn, was a well-known Father McGlynn supporter.

During his early Georgist militancy, Father McGlynn enjoyed the disconcerting support of John Cardinal McCloskey, archbishop of New York, who even shielded him against an impending Vatican censure. As early as 1882, Cardinal Simeoni, prefect of the Sacred Congregation of Propaganda Fide (American dioceses were under its jurisdiction) had written Cardinal McCloskey a letter noting that "certain speeches ... attributed to the Rev. Dr. Edward McGlynn contain propositions openly opposed to the teachings of the Catholic Church."[85] Later that year, Cardinal Simeoni wrote a new missive wherein, after condemning again Father McGlynn's doctrines, he transmitted an order from the pope: "The Holy Father has just now commanded me to write to Your Eminence to suspend the above-mentioned priest McGlynn from his sacred ministry, unless you should judge such measure excessive."[86] The archbishop of New York chose not to suspend the socialist priest.

Cardinal McCloskey's successor, Archbishop Michael Corrigan, was more heedful of the Vatican's admonitions. Several attempts at reconciliation having failed, he suspended *a divinis* the radical priest in 1886 and removed him from his parish. After further acts of disobedience, including an insolent remonstrance against a personal order from Leo XIII summoning him to Rome, Father McGlynn was finally excommunicated in 1887. Although obstinate in his stand concerning social matters,[87] the feisty priest eventually worked out a carefully worded statement that was accepted by the Vatican, after the insistent intervention of Cardinal Gibbons,

Archbishop Ireland, and Bishop John Keane of Richmond. His excommunication was lifted in 1892 and he died in 1900.

The whole episode so emboldened left-leaning social Catholics that in 1894 Leo XIII was forced to warn Bishop Keane against aligning sectors of the Church with the growing socialist movement in America. Bishop Keane replied by begging the pope to "avoid whenever possible the condemnation of well-intentioned reform movements."[88]

4. Tendential Factors

We must now introduce a concept that will be a recurring theme in this study: the role played by tendential factors in the revolutionary process.

Much has been written about the doctrines and events of the great revolutions that have marked contemporary history. Little or nothing, however, is said about a prior and more profound aspect: the tendential element manifested through ambiences, music, clothes, art styles, and human types, creating not so much a doctrine as a *humus* that gives rise to doctrines. Just as plants only thrive in a previously prepared soil, so also revolutions develop only in societies already tendentially prepared for them.

Here is a relevant contribution by Prof. Plinio Corrêa de Oliveira to modern Catholic thought. In the centuries-old revolutionary process we can distinguish three depths: in tendencies, ideas, and facts:

> We can also distinguish in the Revolution three depths, which, chronologically speaking, overlap to a certain extent.
>
> The first and deepest level consists of a crisis in the tendencies. These disorderly tendencies by their very nature struggle for realization. No longer conforming to a whole order of things contrary to them, they begin by modifying mentalities, ways of being, artistic expressions and customs, without immediately touching directly—at least habitually—ideas. ...
>
> The crisis passes from these deep strata to the ideological terrain. ... Inspired by the disorder of these deep tendencies, new doctrines burst forth. In the beginning, they at times seek a modus vivendi with the old doctrines, expressing themselves in such a way as to maintain a semblance of harmony with them. Generally, however, this soon breaks out into open warfare. ...
>
> This transformation of the ideas extends, in turn, to the terrain of facts. Here, by bloody or unbloody means, the institutions, laws, and customs are transformed both in the religious realm and in temporal society. It is a third crisis, now fully within the field of facts.[89]

Every revolution has these three depths. Consider the French Revolution, which is clearly the result of Enlightenment doctrines. These doctrines were not spawned out of thin air by the *philosophes*. The latter produced an ideological justification for the profound changes already underway in the tendential field. For example, the excessive passion of Queen Marie-Antoinette of France (1755–1793) for her farm, the Hameau, where she took

---

83. Cross, 120.

84. Frederick J. Zwierlein, *The Life and Letters of Bishop McQuaid* (Rochester, N.Y.: The Art Print Shop, 1927), 3:14.

85. Zwierlein, *Life and Letters*, 3:3.

86. Zwierlein, 3:3.

87. In an 1887 speech, Fr. McGlynn roared:

> I shall not so stultify myself as to permit anyone to say that, because of this suspension ... I have changed one tittle or jot in my belief in those truths [i.e., Georgism]. ...
>
> And if I shall not be permitted to preach those truths from those familiar pulpits, I shall preach them as best I may wherever I may be permitted. (Edward McGlynn, "An Insurgent Priest's Defense of Common Property

in Land," from *The Standard*, Apr. 2, 1887," in *American Catholic Thought on Social Questions*, edited by Abell, 163)

See also Sylvester L. Malone, *Dr. Edward McGlynn* (New York: Dr. McGlynn Monumental Association, 1918); and Stephen Bell, *Rebel, Priest, and Prophet: A Biography of Dr. Edward McGlynn* (New York: Devin Adair, 1937).

88. Cross, *The Emergence*, 124.

89. Corrêa de Oliveira, *Revolution and Counter-Revolution*, 26–27.

shelter to escape court protocol, already displayed a profound satiation of younger generations for the glories of the Ancien Régime. As we know, boredom is the antechamber of rejection. "One must live as one thinks, under pain of sooner or later ending up thinking as one has lived," Paul Bourget wrote.[90]

In turn, the French Revolution produced a series of tendential manifestations that contributed powerfully to its spread. Suffice it to mention its symbolic song, the *Marseillaise*, which has probably attracted more people to the revolutionary cause than the books of Rousseau or Montesquieu.[91]

Without denying the importance of doctrines, Plinio Corrêa de Oliveira goes on to focus on the role of passions as the foundation and driving force of the revolutionary process. According to the illustrious Brazilian thinker, the most profound cause of the revolutionary process is an explosion of pride and sensuality that inspired a whole chain of ideological systems and actions:

> The most powerful driving force of the Revolution is in the disordered tendencies. ...
>
> Two notions conceived as metaphysical values express well the spirit of the Revolution: absolute equality, complete liberty. And there are two passions that most serve it: pride and sensuality. ...
>
> Pride leads to hatred of all superiority and, thus, to the affirmation that inequality is an evil in itself at all levels, principally at the metaphysical and religious ones. This is the egalitarian aspect of the Revolution.
>
> Sensuality, per se, tends to sweep aside all barriers. It does not accept restraints and leads to revolt against all authority and law, divine or human, ecclesiastical or civil. This is the liberal aspect of the Revolution.[92]

What tendential factors were at play in the case of social Catholicism?

a. Optimism About the Modern World

First, we should note an element that will be constantly present in all currents we will deal with all the way to LT: a fundamental optimism about the new times.

Other than doctrinal differences, traditionalists and progressives were divided by something much more profound and fundamental: their attitude vis-à-vis the historical process underway. Consistent with a correct theology of history reflected in various pontifical documents, including the encyclical *Immortale Dei* of Leo XIII, from the perspective of faith and Christian civilization the traditionalists saw modern history as a process of decay which had increasingly distanced humanity from the ways of God since the end of the Middle Ages. That process, generically called the Revolution, developed in stages through the three great revolutions of Western history: Protestantism, the French Revolution, and, more recently, Socialism and Communism.

With a diametrically opposed view, progressives instead saw modern history as a succession of constructive "liberations": Humanism freed the human mind from scholastic thought; Protestantism freed humanity from papal 'absolutism'; the

Enlightenment liberated reason from the tyranny of faith; the French Revolution freed the citizenry from the tyranny of kings; and now Socialism was about to liberate the worker class from the oppression of its masters.

The nineteenth century saw the emergence of the rationalist and scientific spirit as an expression of that modernity. It was the era of so-called strong minds. There was rampant enthusiasm for progress, as shown for example in grandiose Universal Exhibitions symbolized by the Eiffel Tower, built for the Paris Exhibition of 1889. Progress was seen as liberation from Christian civilization. "I believe science is simply the best counterweight to the papacy," thundered Quintino Sella in the Italian Chamber of Deputies on May 21, 1876.[93] One could never exaggerate the role played by that overwhelming enthusiasm for modernity—more tendential than doctrinal—in the spread of liberal and socialist ideas and in the revolutions that resulted.

Poisoned by an egalitarian and permissive spirit, progressive-oriented social Catholics felt growing discomfort with traditional society, its hierarchies, traditions, and customs. To them, it all seemed rigid, inflexible, and contrary to Christian charity as understood in the light of the prevailing romanticism. For similar reasons, they felt a growing unease toward a hierarchically structured Church whose teaching in their view was too strict. They perceived all this as a straitjacket incompatible with the increasingly dynamic and fluid spirit of the times. As a result, they showed a profound temperamental affinity with nineteenth-century modernity.

Modernity catered to these deep emancipatory aspirations. The innovators greeted with relief the destruction of the old order, applauding the dawn of a new, less stifling society, like a waft of fresh air in a stuffy room. Inclined to turn these aspirations into life habits, people allowed themselves to be absorbed by the new world. Social activism offered them a favorable vehicle to achieve their aspirations. Moved by the spirit of innovation, they conceived that activism as a form of lay apostolate in tune with the times, and their social ideas as a modern form of Magisterium. "That broad social movement ... seems to announce to the century that is aborning the reconciliation between the Church and the modern world, of *democracy and the papacy*," 'democratic' priest Félix Klein exclaimed in 1893.[94]

In Italy, according to their respective views on modernity, social Catholics split between intransigents and conciliators. While the former continued the counter-revolutionary line of Pius IX, the latter advocated not only a political agreement between the Vatican and the Kingdom of Italy, but, in a broader and more profound way, a reconciliation of the Church with the society resulting from the liberal nineteenth-century revolution. That understanding could not occur without making profound changes to the Church herself. Initially a minority, the conciliators became an important current as the twentieth century began.

b. Destruction of the Barriers of Horror Between Catholicism and Socialism

A strategic problem with grave moral implications confronted social Catholics. Since socialists were also active in the social field, could Catholics collaborate with them in specific tasks? If yes, how far could that collaboration go?

Until then the dominant relationship between Catholics and socialists was one of overt and irreconcilable discrepancy.

---

90. Paul Bourget, *Le demon du midi*, 2 vols. (Paris: Librairie Plon, 1914), 2:375.

91. In her *Mémoires*, the Marchioness de la Tour du Pin Gouvernet (1770–1853), a legitimist and lady-in-waiting to the queen, recounts how, against her personal convictions, she became so enraptured hearing the "Marseillaise" that her husband had to slap her to break the trance. More than once, dragged by that frenetic song, she found herself crying out loud, *"à la lanterne les aristocrates!"* [hang the aristocrats on the lampposts!]. See Lucie de la Tour du Pin Gouvernet, *Mémoires de la marquise de la Tour du Pin* (Paris: Mercure de France, 1979).

92. Corrêa de Oliveira, *Revolution and Counter-Revolution*, 29, 46, 3.

93. Quintino Sella, *Discorsi parlamentari*, prepared by the Chamber of Deputies (Rome: 1887–1888), 1:229, quoted in De Rosa, *Il movimento*, 102.

94. Félix Klein, *L'église et la démocratie*, quoted in Barbier, *Histoire du catholicisme libéral*, 3:55.

Moreover, the wall of horror that separated both was reinforced by the popes' continuous condemnations of Socialism, particularly Leo XIII's 1878 encyclical *Quod apostolici muneris* against "the pest of Socialism." However, because of doctrinal ambiguities and the influence of the revolutionary spirit in many social Catholics, that wall of horror tended to crack, if not altogether crumble. Formerly an exception, collaboration with the socialists became the norm.

Some were driven by a reaction (in itself healthy, though perhaps unbalanced) against reprehensible aspects of liberal capitalism. Others were led by the naive hope that a more egalitarian and community-oriented order could alleviate the suffering of the poor by distributing wealth more equitably. A third group was composed of those who, motivated by a deep sympathy for Socialism, tried to bring about a strategic convergence with it.

Sometimes they tried to justify the collaboration alleging that it was restricted to the field of action and had no doctrinal implications. It did not matter to them that socialists were atheists and wanted to destroy Christian civilization; nor that they employed social activism as a tool of class struggle; nor yet that they had a revolutionary ideology. The only thing that mattered was that both sides had common ground to proceed hand in hand. The wall of horror between the two camps was thus demolished.

In the twofold process of a growing rejection of capitalism and, conversely, an expanding sympathy for Socialism, increasingly important areas of social Catholicism slid toward what began to be called, at the end of the nineteenth century, Christian Socialism.

5. The Rise of Christian Socialism

The first manifestations of Christian Socialism came directly from the French Revolution and thus predate social Catholicism. During the Revolution there were factions which, taking the motto of "liberty, equality, fraternity" to its ultimate consequences, adopted communist positions. The most prominent representative of this trend was François-Noël Babeuf, called Gracchus (1760–1797). "The French Revolution is nothing but the precursor of another revolution, one that will [be] greater, more solemn, and which will be the last."[95] "His idea," says historian Pierre Gaxotte, "is that the Revolution had failed because it had not been carried out to the end. All the measures it had taken were good. ... But this was just a first step toward the 'radical reform of property,' that is, toward 'the community of goods and works.' Obviously, full collectivism would have been dictatorial."[96]

For those radical factions, one had to eliminate not only the king in the State, but also the "king" in society—the employer— and the king in the family, that is, paternal authority. The clearly utopian dream of a perfectly egalitarian and free society without classes, property, or the monogamous family loomed then on the horizon. Fascination with this dream brought about the so-called utopian Socialism, represented in France by Claude Henri de Saint-Simon (1760–1825), Charles Fourier (1772–1837), Louis Blanc (1811–1882), Philippe Buchez (1796–1865), and Pierre Proudhon (1809–1865). Buchez exerted a particularly significant influence on the left wing of social Catholicism.

Founder of the French Carbonari,[97] Buchez converted to Catholicism in 1830 but did not abandon the socialist ideology. Alec Vidler explains: "He found in Christianity a faith that promised to realize the equality and brotherhood of men, and deliver them from the egoism that sets one against another."[98] Buchez then became an apostle of revolutionary Christianity. With words that seem to come from the pen of a present-day liberation theologian, he proclaimed, "Christianity and revolution are the same thing. The Church's only mistake is not to be revolutionary."[99]

Buchez's influence went beyond social Catholicism, penetrating even the liberal Catholic current. Some of his disciples joined the Dominican Order, which had been restored in France by a close friend of his, Fr. Henri Lacordaire (1802–1861).[100] This was the origin of the progressive wing in France's Dominican community, which, as we shall see in the next chapter, played a central role in the development of neo-modernist theology, and eventually of LT itself.

In the wake of the 1848 revolution there arose in France a Christian socialist current and many priests joined it. On April 29, 1849, a banquet of socialist priests was held in Paris with more than six hundred guests, including clergy and workers. There were many toasts to "Jesus of Nazareth, the father of Socialism." In the closing speech, a priest proclaimed, "Yes, citizens, I say this at the top of my voice, I am a republican socialist priest, one of those who are called red republicans; but also a Catholic priest. ... [Then turning to the working-men, he added:] We want your emancipation, we will no longer allow the exploitation of man by man."[101] Interestingly, only three of the more than thirty priests present were wearing the cassock, while the remaining were in civilian clothes. Evidently, they wanted to emancipate themselves not only from employers but also from ecclesiastical rules, flaunting a revolutionary spirit even in the field of tendencies.

If utopian Christian Socialism had no great following, at least in its public events, and remained a mere ideal on a distant horizon, that was not the fate of the Socialism born from the left of social Catholicism in the late nineteenth century. In France, they usually indicate as a watershed the Workers' Conference held in Lyon in 1896; in Italy, it was the appearance in 1891 of the Fasci Democratici (Democratic Squads) inspired by Fr. Romolo Murri (1870–1944). Initially a minority, the socialists grew in importance to the point of controlling large sectors of social Catholicism.

However, the current never became a majority. The popes' condemnations of Socialism were clear and found an echo among the faithful. On the other hand, the Christian socialists could not count yet on a theology that would give them a doctrinal basis. Forced to choose between fidelity to the Church and socialist commitment, many opted for the latter. Such was the case with Father Murri.

C. The Voice of Rome

Although Pius IX had already addressed some aspects of the social question, we owe the first great synthesis of Catholic social

---

95. Sylvain Marechal, et al., *Manifesto of the Equals*, trans. Mitchell Abidor (1796). See M. Victor Advielle, *Histoire de Gracchus Babeuf et du babouvisme d'après de nombreux documents inédits*, 2 vols. (Paris: self-published, 1884); Filippo Buonarroti, *Gracchus Babeuf et la conspiration des égaux* (Paris: Armand le Chevalier, 1830). On Buonarroti, Babeuf's comrade, see Alessandro Galante Garrone, *Filippo Buonarroti i rivoluzionari dell'ottocento (1828–1837)* (Turin: Einaudi, 1972). On Babeuf's passage from the French Revolution to utopian Socialism, see Julius Braunthal, *Geschichte der Internationale* (Berlin-Bonn: Dietz Nachf Verlag, 1978), 1:45–51.

96. Pierre Gaxotte, *La révolution française* (Paris: Arthème Fayard, 1962), 466.

97. The Carbonari were members of a secret liberal revolutionary movement that incited or participated in most of the nineteenth-century revolutions in Italy and other countries.

98. Vidler, *A Century of Social Catholicism*, 14.

99. Philippe Buchez, "L'atelier," quoted in Henri Verbist, *Les grandes controverses de l'église contemporaine: De 1789 à nos jours* (Veviers, Belgium: Éditions Marabout, 1971), 207.

100. See André Duval, *Lacordaire et Buchez,* "Idéalisme révolutionnaire et réveil religieux en 1849," *Revue des Sciences Philosophiques et Théologiques* 45 (1961): 422–55. See also Andrea Lanza, *All'abolizione del proletariato: Il discorso socialista fraternitario—Parigi 1839–1847* (Milan: Franco Angeli, 2010), 47–52.

101. Vidler, *A Century of Social Catholicism*, 48.

doctrine to Leo XIII (1810, 1878–1903). The 1891 encyclical *Rerum novarum* is rightly considered the cornerstone of the Church's social teaching; it was the first to deal comprehensively with problems related to the social question.[102]

It is interesting to note that Leo XIII started by denouncing the tendential aspects of the social question even before dealing with doctrinal ones. In fact, he blamed the ardent desire for novelty that for a long time began to agitate people and would naturally move from the political order to the socioeconomic one. He goes on to condemn Socialism, calling it a false remedy and unacceptable solution.

While rejecting the abuses of unbridled capitalism, the pope clarifies that the Church approves some foundations of the market economy as derived from the natural order. On private property, he teaches:

> There is no need to bring in the State. Man precedes the State, and possesses, prior to the formation of any State, the right of providing for the substance of his body. ...
> ... Private ownership is in accordance with the law of nature. ...
> The authority of the divine law adds its sanction, forbidding us in severest terms even to covet that which is another's. ...
> ... Private ownership ... is the natural right of man.[103]

The freedom to make employment contracts and to own and manage business enterprises stem from this natural right. Leo XIII goes on to list, along with the rights arising from private property, those deriving from work as something inherent in the person that cannot be limited either by the employer or by the State, including the right to free association, all of it within a hierarchical design, that includes the need for social inequalities. In addition to the precepts of justice, social relations must be inspired by charity; and since this field is outside the scope of the law, it follows that only with the practice of Christian virtue can one attain social balance.

In the encyclical *Graves de communi*, Leo XIII reiterates, "For, it is the opinion of some, and the error is already very common, that the social question is merely an economic one, whereas in point of fact it is, above all, a moral and religious matter, and for that reason must be settled by the principles of morality and according to the dictates of religion."[104]

Unfortunately, sectors of social Catholicism read Pope Leo XIII's encyclicals in a different light, starting a period of hermeneutic abuse that was clarified only in 1903 by Pope St. Pius X with the motu proprio *Fin dalla prima*. Some people even claimed that *Rerum novarum* was opposed to the "dark *Syllabus Errorum*" of Pius IX.[105] Gabriele De Rosa writes:

> *Rerum novarum* destroyed many misgivings and resistance among intransigent Catholics, giving confidence to the most reckless generation of social Christians, to the Christian democratic current, which eventually outgrew the old guard. ...
> All European Christian democratic currents received a boost from *Rerum novarum* [and] felt comforted in

their action tending to prove that a priest, a militant Catholic, was not on the side of the employer.[106]

Fr. Luigi Sturzo recalls how the publication of the encyclical *Rerum novarum* aroused "great wonder ... it seemed almost socialistic, and even the more liberal governments were in fear in their bourgeois soul; many churchmen also feared that new force united to the people."[107]

D. The Christian Democratic Current

1. A Daughter of Social Catholicism

By the end of the nineteenth century, the Catholic social movement had become a power. In Italy, the Opera dei Congressi had 188 diocesan and 3,982 parish committees, 708 youth sections, 17 university circles, 24 newspapers, and 155 periodicals. It was a force that augured well for the future of the Church and of Christian civilization, raising the hope of a new dawn after the revolutionary dusk.[108] Unfortunately, that dawn never came. Indestructible from the outside, the Church would be ever more undermined from within.

A bit everywhere, progressive currents, which took the generic name Christian democracy in a context where democracy was a synonym for the left, gradually gained ground and replaced the old guard. "The new name, Christian Democracy, already circulated among young people," De Rosa recounts. "Extremely active nuclei of priests and laity, followers of Romolo Murri, existed in all regions of Italy."[109]

Christian Democracy is the daughter of social Catholicism. "The social Catholicism of the Oeuvre des Cercles already contained the seeds of the social doctrines of Christian democrats," says historian Father Barbier.[110] Likewise, in 1898, Pierre Monicat observed that "Christian democratic organizations present themselves as heirs of the Cercles, from which they took almost all of their social program."[111]

In Italy, replacing the old guard, Christian democrat sectors became predominant. De Rosa reports.

> As concerns for Socialism spread in Opera ranks ... the organization also became imbued with a party mindset.
> Under a seeming unanimity ... new and contrasting political and social currents actually fermented. ... The times ... of old intransigence were about to end; new ferments stirred the Catholic world and especially young people, who felt called by *Rerum novarum* to become proactive to reconquer the masses running after socialist preaching. ... Intransigent people like [Giuseppe]

---

102. See Daniele Menozzi, "Cristianità e questione sociale: Da Pio IX a Leone XIII," in Daniele Menozzi, *La chiesa cattolica e la secolarizzazione* (Turin: Einaudi, 1993).

103. Leo XIII, encyclical *Rerum novarum* (May 15, 1891), nos. 7, 9, 11, 22.

104. Leo XIII, encyclical *Graves de communi* (Jan. 18, 1901), no. 11.

105. De Antonellis, *Storia dell'Azione Cattolica*, 103.

106. De Rosa, *Il movimento*, 75, 121.

107. Luigi Sturzo, "Leone XIII e la civiltà moderna," speech given at Caltagirone on August 2, 1903, quoted in De Rosa, *Il movimento*, 120.

108. This is, for example, Antonio Gramsci's opinion. Quoting Fr. Ernesto Vercesi—*Il papato nel secolo XIX* (Turin: Società Editrice Internazionale)—the Marxist thinker states, "The nineteenth century attacked Christianity in its different aspects, on political, religious, social, cultural, historical, philosophical grounds, etc. The end result was that, at the nineteenth century's sunset, Christianity in general, and Roman Catholicism in particular, were stronger and more robust than at the dawn of that same century. This fact cannot be challenged by unbiased historians." Antonio Gramsci, *Il Vaticano e l'Italia*, ed. Elsa Fubini (Rome: Editori Riuniti, 1974), 62.

109. De Rosa, *Il movimento*, 141.

110. Barbier, *Histoire du catholicisme libéral*, 3:124. See also Robert Havard de la Montagne, *Histoire de la démocratie chrétienne de Lamennais à Georges Bidault* (Paris: Amiot-Dumont, 1948); Hans Maier, *Revolution and Church: The Early History of Christian Democracy* (Notre Dame, Ind.: University of Notre Dame Press, 1969).

111. Pierre Monicat, *Contribution à l'étude du mouvement social chrétien en France au XIXème siècle* (Paris: Rondelet, 1898), 114, quoted in Barbier, *Histoire du catholicisme libéral*, 2:184–85.

Sacchetti immediately sensed the changing times and realized that the Christian Democrats were displacing them from their leading positions. Hostilities began.[112]

The Christian democratic current's main characteristic was to renounce the ideal of a specifically Catholic social order, namely, a Christian civilization inspired by the Church and her Magisterium. Instead, it accepted a society molded by modern revolutions, in which the Church would be merely a presence, a leaven, and not its founding and leading institution. They no longer spoke of restoring Christian civilization but of Christianizing the modern world, while accepting its premises, beginning with democratic freedoms, all of it topped by the egalitarian and liberal spirit of the Revolution. De Rosa comments: "What changes from Paganuzzi to Murri ... is the perspective of the relationship between the Church and modern society." The former saw "a model, devoted and obedient civil society. ... [a] worldview of which the Church had been the bearer in previous centuries." Father Murri would rather bury the past and with it a "fossilized religion," opening up to new democratic trends in a spirit of independence from ecclesiastical authority. "There was no possibility of understanding ... between the two trends," De Rosa concludes.[113]

The Christian democratic current was actively devoted to rejuvenating (this was the buzzword) the conservative mentality in Catholic associations, and asking for a clearer commitment in defense of democratic freedoms alongside republicans and socialists.

In their infatuation with the modern world, Christian democrats attained almost childish excesses, hoping for a profound reform of the Church to bring it into line with the new times. Fr. Pierre Dabry (1864–1916), a leading member of the Christian democratic current in France, writes:

> The altar, built in the style of the seventeenth century, is destined to join the throne. We must rebuild the entire building to put our tastes and needs in harmony with future generations.
> There is one whose words shall not pass who said: "One cannot pour new wine into old wineskins." *Democracy*, with all its ardent and deep aspirations, has awoken in the light of science and universal suffrage. A new society will be born tomorrow from which we will be excluded if we continue to look at it as the incarnation of the Antichrist. It is the new wine fermented in the bosom of the twentieth century, and we cannot put it into old wineskins. These are only good for the currant syrup of nostalgic Catholics.[114]

The opinion of Fr. Luigi Sturzo was no different. In his famous 1905 speech at Caltagirone, he railed against "Legitimists, Bourbon supporters, believers in the monarchical government of divine right. All museum stuff!"[115] Indeed, the idea was to bury the past, and with it a model of the Church.

Going beyond social Catholicism, which minimized the moral and religious aspects of the social question, Christian democrats now proclaimed the primacy of social and political activism. Here too they prefigured LT. "Earthly society is for the earthly life.

We will think about paradise later," argued 'democratic priest' Jules Lemire (1853–1928).[116] His colleague Fr. Paul Naudet (1859–1929) added, "Until we have improved the situation of workers it is useless to speak to them about supernatural life and religious duties."[117] According to the historian of religions Daniele Menozzi, "What characterizes the 'abbés démocrates' is their attempt to bring social commitment into the political sphere. They want to participate in the political life of the French Republic by building a party capable of adapting Christian doctrine to the government's designs."[118]

Christian democrats showed less concern for the religious and moral crisis of modern society than for economic and social problems, seen from a leftist perspective, naturally. "Today's society is rotten with injustice and oppression, particularly regarding the distribution of wealth," the editors of the monthly *La Démocratie Chrétienne* wrote.[119] In unison with socialists, Christian democrats proclaimed the need for profound changes to correct so-called injustices caused by the unequal distribution of wealth. "Christian Democrats. ... believe that the old order is definitely broken," said Father Naudet.[120]

The Christian democratic current was thus born from the populist wing of social Catholicism. While the more moderate factions preached concord between bourgeoisie and proletariat, the populist wing exhorted them to class struggle. "Like it or not, democratic propaganda excites the populace against the aristocracy, the poor against the rich, with grave damage to the Church and to the social order," warned Most Rev. Emiliano Manacorda, bishop of Fossano, Italy.[121]

In its most radical versions, the Christian democratic current argued that the bourgeoisie was irredeemable and should thus be overthrown to make room for the emancipation of the proletariat. "Our bourgeois society tends to turn workers into a race of serfs, inferior, as in times past, to the caste of free men," thundered the Christian democratic paper *Terre de France*, a leading mouthpiece of revolution. "This imminent revolution, more visible by the day, can only be averted with the proletariat's rise to power."[122] Far from preaching Christian resignation, the Christian democrats instilled a revolutionary spirit in the people. "If I preached patience and resignation to a worker who complains of his situation, I would feel like a misfit in my role as a priest," Father Naudet explained.[123]

As in France, the Italian Christian democratic current eschewed moderate social positions. These were represented, for example, by Giuseppe Toniolo (1845–1918) and the Opera directors. Instead, they emphasized support for class struggle, often in close collaboration with the far left. "My democracy," said Father Murri,

112. De Rosa, *Il movimento*, 129–30.

113. De Rosa, 145–47.

114. Pierre Dabry, *Peuple français*, 436–37, quoted in Barbier, *Histoire du catholicisme libéral*, 3:107. See also Pierre Dabry, *Les catholiques républicains* (Paris: Chevalier et Rivière, 1905).

115. Luigi Sturzo, "La croce di Costantino," 243, quoted in De Rosa, *Il movimento*, 136.

116. Jules Lemire, speech at Orleans (1899), quoted in Barbier, *Histoire du catholicisme libéral*, 3:111. Fr. Lemire is another example of ideological transshipment in social Catholicism. Initially an ultramontane and legitimist partisan of the Count of Chambord, he ended his days as a G.D.R. congressman (*Gauche Démocrate Républicaine*). See Jean-Marie Mayeur, *L'abbé Lemire, 1853–1928, un prêtre démocrate* (Paris: Casterman, 1968).

117. Paul Naudet, *La Justice Sociale*, Mar. 17, 1894, quoted in Barbier, *Histoire du catholicisme libéral*, 3:111.

118. L. Prezzi and P. Stefani, "Dehon e gli ebrei: liberalismo, cattolicesimo e antisemitismo" (interview with Daniele Menozzi), *Il Regno*, no. 16 (2005), 515.

119. Paul Six, *La Démocratie Chrétienne*, Nov. 8, 1894, quoted in Barbier, *Histoire du catholicisme libéral*, 3:77.

120. Paul Naudet, *La démocratie et les démocrates chrétiens* (Paris: Librairie Delhomme & Briguet, 1900), 124.

121. De Rosa, *Il movimento*, 152.

122. *Terre de France*, Apr. 1, 1894, quoted in Barbier, *Histoire du catholicisme libéral*, 3:108.

123. Naudet, *La justice sociale*, Mar. 24, 1896, quoted in Barbier, 3:111.

"implied criticizing capitalism, organizing labor, class struggle, and political struggle."[124]

This conception was based on the clearly Marxist doctrine that private property necessarily generates two antagonistic classes: owners, who control the means of production, and workers, who must sell their labor and thus become enslaved. "We have a concept of a different society from the one that inevitably generates antagonism between two classes. That is, between that which, unable to survive without working, must sell itself to another simply because it owns the means of production," Father Naudet explained.[125]

For their part, more moderate Christian democratic currents, while affirming private property in principle, began to emphasize its social function and clamor for State intervention to regulate it and thus carry out a radical reform of the free market system.[126]

However, extremist factions went so far as to deny the right to private property, thus subscribing to the essence of Marxism, which is precisely to eliminate property and impose equality. Fr. Antoine Pottier (1849–1923), leader of the Christian democratic current in Belgium, summarized their position in the *Bien du Peuple* on December 31, 1893:

> When the economic system is such that it allows owners to monopolize the means of production ... public authority ... must take measures to stop that situation. ...
> ... That situation is against nature. A social system that produces such results is essentially corrupted ... and should be changed at its roots. ... The so-called right to private property is only a right of usufruct. The false theory on the right to private property proposed by economic liberalism is a perpetual crime against nature.[127]

On the horizon of Christian democracy, the lure of the communist utopia of a classless society emerged. "Christian democrats don't believe that [the role of the higher classes] is a necessary principle for a good social order," affirmed Father Naudet.[128] In a more explicit tone, Georges Fonsegrive, another prominent figure in the Christian democratic movement, avowed, "Deep down, the idea of social classes tends to disappear more and more. Some people decry this. I don't see why we should feel sorry. If we are true democrats, ... we should, on the contrary, rejoice."[129] In sum, as Father Barbier comments, "The Christian democrats aim at suppressing the very distinction of classes ... hearing them, one feels that they are tormented by the passion of egalitarian democracy and social leveling."[130]

Summarizing the tenets of Christian democracy, Spanish writer and sociologist Fr. José María Llovera, a partisan of this school, wrote: "1) in *politics* it evinces a bias toward the republican form of government; 2) in *political economy* it proposes the abolition of the wage system and its replacement by worker participation in the profits ... and the management of companies by the workers themselves; in *social economy* it strives to suppress the distinction of classes ... as *means of action* it proposes the organization of labor unions, popular education concerning social matters, peoples' action in every realm and sense."[131]

2. The Catholic Social Guild

The Christian democratic current in England is closely linked to the Catholic Social Guild, founded in 1909 in Manchester by Fr. Charles Plater, S.J. (1875–1921), considered the father of the movement and its most prominent figure. Most of its better-known figures were Jesuits. Like other Christian democratic movements, the Guild enfolded a variety of tendencies. While some of its sectors remained in line with Catholic social Magisterium and even adopted some anticommunist stances during the fifties at the height of the Cold War, others openly supported the socialist-inspired Labour Party and even showed sympathy for Fabian Socialism.

The Guild maintained the Catholic Workers College, known as Plater Hall, in Oxford, and sponsored hundreds of study circles made up of Catholic workers throughout the country. Starting in 1921, it published the monthly magazine *The Christian Democrat*. Its publishing house was one of the main sources of Christian democratic ideas in Great Britain. Although there are still remnants of the Catholic Social Guild in some English dioceses, the movement as such disintegrated in the mid-1960s.[132]

The bishop of Nottingham, Most Rev. Edward Gilpin Bagshawe (1829–1915), was notorious among the representatives of left-wing Christian democracy in England. Finding the Christian democratic label too moderate, he advanced one step further. An ardent partisan of Christian Socialism, he was a regular contributor to *The Christian Socialist*, a magazine founded in 1846 by Kingsley, Maurice, Hughes, and other representatives of Evangelical Socialism.[133] The French *Révue Socialiste* of December 1885 called Bishop Bagshawe's views "a true manifestation of religious Socialism."[134] Fortunately, his extreme views had scant relevance in Victorian England.

3. Fr. Romolo Murri and the Christian Democrats

The drift to the left by Italian social Catholicism is inextricably linked to the figure of Father Murri. From Marxist scholar Antonio Labriola (1843–1904), his college professor, Father Murri drew, as he recalls, "the sense of history, that is, progress, and with it the idea of the proletariat. I also absorbed intimately an interest and sympathy for the modern world and its culture."[135] According to the leader of the Christian democratic current, Labriola's Marxism was "an excellent tool to become aware of the things of one's time and to correct the serious shortcomings in the mentality prevailing in Catholic circles."[136]

Thus, not unlike liberation theologians half a century later, Father Murri used Marxism (supposedly stripped of its atheism)

124. *Aspettiamo un'altra generazione di italiani* (da Romolo Murri), written by Il Centro Studi "Romolo Murri," dir. Gabriela Eleonori, Gualdo, Italy town square, Sept. 26, 2010, 11.

125. Naudet, *La démocratie et les démocrates chrétiens*, 193. This is the essence of the Marxist concept of 'alienation,' which we will discuss later on.

126. Fr. Luigi Sturzo later stated: "[Popularism] is social in the sense of a radical reform of the present capitalist system, but it parts company with Socialism because it admits of private property while insisting on the social function of such property." Luigi Sturzo, *Church and State*, trans. Barbara Barclay Carter (New York: Longmans, Green and Co., 1939), 479.

127. Antoine Pottier, *Le Bien du Peuple*, Nov. 27, 1892, Mar. 3, 1893, and Mar. 5, 1893, quoted in Barbier, *Histoire du catholicisme libéral*, 3:129.

128. Naudet, *La démocratie et les démocrates chrétiens*, 180.

129. Barbier, *Histoire du catholicisme libéral*, 3:128. Fonsegrive identifies democracy with an egalitarian conception of society, which is the very opposite of true democracy according to the Church's social doctrine.

130. Barbier, 3:127.

131. Llovera, *Tratado elemental*, 346.

132. See J.M. Cleary, *Catholic Social Action in Britain 1909–1959: A History of the Catholic Social Guild* (Oxford: Catholic Social Guild, 1961); Georgiana Putnam McEntee, *The Social Catholic Movement in Great Britain* (New York: Macmillan, 1927).

133. On Protestant Socialism in England, see Lujo Brentano, *Die christlich soziale bewegung in England* (Leipzig: Dunke & Humboldt, 1883).

134. Cleary, *Catholic Social Action*, 21.

135. L. Dal Pane, "Antonio Labriola e Romolo Murri," in *Scritti di sociologia e politica in onore di Luigi Sturzo*, ed. Istituto Luigi Sturzo, 3 vols. (Bologna: Nicola Zanichelli Editore, 1953), 1:526. See also Lorenzo Bedeschi, *Murri, Sturzo, De Gasperi: Ricostruzione storica ed epistolario (1898–1906)* (Cinisello Balsamo, Italy: San Paolo, 1994), 24.

136. Dal Pane, "Antonio Labriola e Romolo Murri," 1:529–30.

as a tool to analyze the social and political reality. With some nuances, the criticism Cardinal Ratzinger addressed to liberation theologians (quoting Paul VI) can be applied to him: It is impossible, "illusory and dangerous to ignore the intimate bond which radically unites them, and to accept elements of the Marxist analysis without recognizing its connections with the ideology, or to enter into the practice of class-struggle and of its Marxist interpretation while failing to see the kind of totalitarian society to which this process slowly leads."[137]

In 1891, Father Murri inspired the formation of youth groups called the Fasci Democratici. In 1894, he founded in Rome the Catholic University Circle. The following year he launched the newspaper *La Vita Nuova*, which became the mouthpiece of the university circles that, in 1896, gathered around F.U.C.I., the Italian Catholic University Students Federation. In 1898, the first issue of *Social Culture*, the main periodical of the Christian democratic current, came out. It is estimated that at their high-water mark, Father Murri's Fasci had about one hundred thousand followers.[138]

Claiming to be the wave of the future, the Fasci began to oppose the leadership of Giovanni B. Paganuzzi and of the Opera's old guard, disdained by Father Murri as "asleep to the sound of brass bands."[139] They were supported by some prelates who adhered to the new trends. For example, Most Rev. Igino Bandi, bishop of Tortona, wrote Paganuzzi warning him "not to despise *a priori* the young Christian Democrats' work."[140]

It is interesting to note that, in addition to Marxism, Father Murri drew much inspiration from Americanism (a phenomenon we will consider extensively further on). The Christian democratic leader took advantage of that current "to show our Italian peers and the new generation, the new intellectual and moral acquisitions necessary for Catholics to be operational in modern life."[141]

The controversy became increasingly bitter. Some traditionalist circles even challenged the use of the expression Christian democracy because socialists spoke of social democracy as a synonym for the proletarian revolution. To clarify the situation, in 1901, Pope Leo XIII issued the encyclical *Graves de communi* in which he comprehensively dealt with the problems raised by the Christian democratic movement.

"The consciousness of duty warns Us to put a check on this controversy and to define what Catholics are to think on this matter," the Roman pontiff begins.[142] After making the necessary distinctions between the socialists' social democracy (which he condemned) and Christian Democracy, an expression of itself acceptable, the pope goes on to define its contents. Warning that "it would be a crime to distort this name of Christian Democracy to politics," he says that it means "nothing else than this beneficent Christian action in behalf of the people" under the Church's authority.[143] The pope goes on to show that Christian Democracy cannot be egalitarian, that is, founded on class struggle: "Let there be no question of fostering under this name of Christian

Democracy any intention of diminishing the spirit of obedience, or of withdrawing people from their lawful rulers."[144]

However, ignoring the obvious condemnation of socialist doctrines, Christian democrats interpreted Pope Leo's document to their advantage. Father Murri wrote, "That encyclical ended up by signaling the beginning of a vigorous expansion of the [Christian Democratic] movement."[145] Moreover, some of the pope's expressions seemed to suit them, such as calling Christian democrats in the brief he addressed to the Opera's national congress held in Rome in 1901, a "squad of fresh and strong-willed young forces."[146]

Other than the "liberation" of the proletariat, the Christian democratic movement began to speak of other "liberations," for example that of women, thus anticipating some LT currents. In 1901, the Christian Democratic Women's Fascio, a starting point of the feminist movement, was founded in Milan.[147]

Insensitive to the Church's admonitions, Christian democrats continued their revolutionary contestation undeterred. At the Opera National Congress in Bologna in November 1903, already under Pope St. Pius X (1835, 1903–1914), the clash between the two camps of Italian social Catholicism degenerated into open warfare. "The split between the two mentalities [regarding] the hierarchy-laity relationship, political action, and religious action, the ways of obeying and being faithful to the papacy became irreconcilable," Giacomo de Antonellis writes.[148] Pressed by unrelenting opposition from Christian democrats, Opera leaders left the premises.

St. Pius X, who had been closely following the development of the debates, was not pleased with the outcome of the conference and sent the archbishop of Bologna, His Eminence Domenico Cardinal Svampa, a letter in which he pointed out, "I will not hide my concerns over: 1) the conflict that arose in the assembly; 2) the lack of foresight shown by the presidency; 3) the sensational and repeated demonstrations in favor of Father Murri."[149] A telltale sign is that the Bologna Congress closed without the traditional St. Peter's Pence collection for the pope.

Concerned about the rise of the Christian democratic movement, and seeking to stamp out any hermeneutic manipulation of the documents of his predecessor, in December 1903, St. Pius X published the motu proprio *Fin dalla prima*. It is a very concise document containing a "fundamental plan of Catholic popular action" in nineteen points. In conclusion, the pope teaches, "The necessary characteristic which should shine forth in all the members of every Catholic association is that of openly manifesting their faith by the holiness of their lives, the spotlessness of their morals, and the scrupulous observance of the laws of God and of the Church."[150]

The Holy See disavowed a circular letter by Opera's new president, Giovanni Grosoli (1859–1937), clearly contrasting with the papal directives. The strong penetration of Christian democratic tendencies in social Catholicism left Pope Saint Pius X no other choice but to dissolve the Opera dei Congressi, which he did, on July 28, 1904. The Study Group for popular and social

137. Congregation for the Doctrine of the Faith, *Instruction on Certain Aspects*, VII, no. 7.

138. See Luigi Civardi, *Compendio di storia dell'Azione Cattolica italiana* (Rome: Coletti, 1956), 92–94.

139. Romolo Murri, "Lettera a Giovanni Semeria," *Cultura Sociale*, Sept. 16, 1898, quoted in De Rosa, *Il movimento*, 194.

140. Igino Bandi, "Lettera a Giambattista Paganuzzi" (June 15, 1899), in F.P.O.C., Cartella *Corrispondenza del comitato permanente*, quoted in De Rosa, *Il movimento*, 161.

141. Romolo Murri, "Una lettera da Roma," *L'Osservatore cattolico*, Apr. 17, 1899, quoted in De Rosa, *Il movimento*, 156.

142. Leo XIII, encyclical *Graves de communi*, no. 4.

143. Leo XIII, no. 7.

144. Leo XIII, no. 9.

145. De Rosa, *Il movimento*, 166.

146. De Rosa, 167.

147. See Paola Gaiotti de Biase, *Le origini del movimento cattolico femminile* (Brescia: Morcelliana, 1963); Lucetta Scaraffia and Anna Maria Isastia, *Donne ottimiste: L'associazionismo femminile borghese fra otto e novecento* (Bologna: Il Mulino, 2002); Fiorenza Taricone and Isabella Grassi, *Associazionismo femminile e modernismo* (Milan: Marietti, 2000).

148. De Antonellis, *Storia dell'Azione Cattolica*, 121.

149. De Antonellis, 122.

150. St. Pius X, motu proprio *Fin dalla prima* (Dec. 18, 1903), no. 19.

action headed by Count Stanislao Medolago-Albani of Bergamo (1851–1921) was the only group that remained open.

On June 11, 1905, St. Pius X published the encyclical *Il fermo proposito* to define the lines for a new Catholic Action able to "to restore Jesus Christ to the family, the school, and society by re-establishing the principle that human authority represents the authority of God. They take to heart the interests of the people, especially those of the working and agricultural classes."[151]

With unprecedented insolence, Christian democrats defied the pope by founding in Bologna the openly socialist-inspired National Democratic League.[152] In the general election, for example, the League joined socialist slates. In the encyclical *Pieni l'animo*, of July 28, 1906, St. Pius X wrote, "Under penalty of exclusion from Sacred Orders for clerics and suspension *ipso facto a divinis* for priests, We forbid them to become members of the National Democratic League."[153] Unrelenting, Father Murri was suspended *a divinis* in 1907 and excommunicated two years later. In 1912, he married and had a son. An early follower of Fascism, he soon left it, criticizing the 1929 Lateran Treaty. Pius XII (1876, 1939–1958) revoked his excommunication in 1943, a year before his death.[154]

We cannot close this topic without mentioning the sympathies of a large number of Christian democrats for the modernist heresy, beginning with Father Murri, who in a speech in San Marino invited the audience to "liberate the Catholic religion from its old superstructure."[155] By promoting and leading revolutions in different fields, although similar in inspiration, the two movements could only look at each other with empathy, exchanging "functions" to hold "men and ideas together," as de Antonellis observes.[156] Father Murri believed modernism was "the new Catholicism of tomorrow, the universal religious practice."[157]

In addition to the tendential factors mentioned above, the ease with which Christian democratic ideas spread in the Church is also explained by the existence of a semi-secret society composed mainly of priests and seminarians. With branches in different countries, this cabal published mimeographed bulletins circulated by hand in seminaries, intoxicating future priests with the new ideas. A newsletter boasted of "the irresistible pull of the current dragging the younger clerical generations."[158] It is not surprising, therefore, that the reports by many apostolic visitors at the time mention complaints such as those by the Dominican Tommaso Pio Boggiani (1843–1942) who, after visiting the diocese of Cesena in 1904, wrote, "Most of the new priests leave the seminary with proclivities for Murrism."[159]

4. Early Catholic Socialism in the United States

In the United States, the more radical figures within Christian democracy were quite overt about their socialist sympathies. There was even a short-lived Catholic Socialist Society in 1909. Fr. Thomas McGrady of Kentucky declared that "American Socialism is entirely compatible with religion."[160] In 1905, another priest,

Fr. Thomas Haggerty of Dallas, was among the founders of the extreme-left organization Industrial Workers of the World (I.W.W., whose members were sometimes called Wobblies).[161] As so many of their fellow social activists, both priests eventually left the Church.

There were also some Catholic enthusiasts of utopian Socialism. For example, a Louisiana lawyer and judge, T. Wharton Collens (1812–1879), advocated a Christian Socialism and managed to mobilize a following of sorts. Collens—who styled himself a "Catholic communist and labor reformer"—considered trade unionism and labor legislation mere palliatives that would not solve the social question at its roots. Influenced by European utopian socialists, he proposed instead the formation of evangelical communities of married couples who, supposedly imitating the primitive Church, would embrace voluntary poverty and obedience, within an apostolic community of goods. His views are expressed in his 1876 book, *The Eden of Labor, or the Christian Utopia*.

As the Knights of Labor declined toward the end of the century, Catholic social militants became increasingly involved in the liberal American Federation of Labor (A.F.L.), heir to the labor movement previously epitomized by the Knights. Indeed, the number of Catholics in the organization was such that, by 1918, they were a majority. A number of Catholic-dominated A.F.L. chapters worked with the socialists in what were known as mixed or dual unions.[162]

5. The Ralliement Favors the Spread of Christian Democracy

Temporarily halted in Italy by St. Pius X's firm intervention, the Christian democratic current experienced strong growth in France, favored by a particular combination of circumstances. To fully understand it, we need to step back to 1789.

The French Revolution was not only anti-monarchist but also deeply anti-Catholic. Hostile to hierarchy in the temporal sphere, could the revolutionaries tolerate it in the spiritual one? For example, Georges Clemenceau (1841–1929), president of the French Republic, stated, "Ever since the Revolution we have been in revolt against Divine and human authority, with whom, with just one blow, we settled a terrible score on January 21, 1793 [date of the beheading of Louis XVI]."[163]

The persecution of the French Revolution against the Church was no less ruthless than against the nobility: Dozens of bishops and twelve thousand priests were slaughtered, while more than thirty thousand went into exile. Public worship was forbidden, religious congregations abolished, and many churches and monasteries destroyed. At the height of the Terror, King Louis XVI and Queen Marie Antoinette, both clearly innocent, were guillotined in the name of equality. In the consistory of June 17, 1793, Pope Pius VI called the king's death a martyrdom inflicted *in hatred of the Faith*.[164]

151. St. Pius X, encyclical *Il fermo proposito* (June 11, 1905), no. 7.

152. See Francesco Leoni, *Storia dei partiti politici italiani* (Naples: Guida Editori, 1971), 218.

153. St. Pius X, encyclical *Pieni l'animo* (July 28, 1906), no. 14.

154. For an account on Opera dei Congressi, see Ernesto Vercesi, *Il movimento cattolico in Italia (1870–1922)* (Florence: Società Editrice La Voce, 1923).

155. De Rosa, *Il movimento*, 233.

156. De Antonellis, *Storia dell'Azione Cattolica*, 127.

157. De Rosa, *Il movimento*, 238.

158. Barbier, *Histoire du catholicisme libéral*, 3:115.

159. De Rosa, *Il movimento*, 243. Fr. Boggiani was consecrated bishop in 1908 and created cardinal in 1929, becoming chancellor of the Holy Roman Church.

160. Mel Piehl, *Breaking Bread: The Catholic Worker and the Origins of Catholic Radicalism in America* (Philadelphia: Temple University Press, 1982), 40.

161. See Robert E. Doherty, "Thomas Haggerty, the Church, and Socialism," *Labor History* (Winter 1965): 43–46. See also Robert T. Handy, "Christianity and Socialism in America 1900–1920," *Church History* 21 (Mar. 1982): 39–54; John Spargo, "Christian Socialism in America," *The American Journal of Sociology* 15 (July 1, 1909): 16–20; James Dombrowski, *The Early Days of Christian Socialism in America* (New York: Octagon Books, 1966); John C. Cort, *Christian Socialism: An Informal History* (Maryknoll, N.Y.: Orbis Books, 1988).

162. See Philip Sheldon Foner, *The AFL in the Progressive Era, 1910–1915*, vol. 5 of *History of the Labor Movement in the United States* (New York: International Publishers, 1980).

163. Louis Billot, *Les principes de '89 et leurs conséquences* (Paris: Téqui, 1989), 33.

164. See Pius VI, *Acta* (Rome: Typis Sacra Congregatione de Propaganda Fide, 1871), 17–33. In chapter 2, we examine the French Revolution and its consequences in detail.

The bloodbath woke up a society benumbed by the delights of the "sweetness of life" celebrated by Talleyrand,[165] triggering a reaction which, once consolidated, later became the counter-revolution. Having to face a common enemy, both altar and throne united in the defense of order. That union was first manifested during the Vendée war in 1793, when the famous Catholic and Royal Army was formed.[166]

In the subsequent decades, followers of the French Revolution, including liberal Catholics, supported the various republics resulting from 1789. Conversely, counter-revolutionaries, faithful to the Church and Tradition, proclaimed themselves "Catholic monarchists" and refused to recognize those republics. Their position was known as "intransigent," that is, opposed to the revolutionary innovations.

That choice was not only political but had religious implications as well. For intransigent Catholics, defending the Faith against Liberalism naturally entailed rejecting the form of civil government it had engendered. Then there was the question of egalitarianism, the foundation of liberal republicanism, whose acceptance or rejection in the political sphere had serious metaphysical, moral, and even religious implications that no Catholic could ignore. While Catholics tended to be monarchists, liberals were usually republican.

Popes Gregory XVI (1765, 1831–1846) and Pius IX were uncompromising. They thought it their duty to defend not only the Catholic heritage but civilization itself against the onslaught of an enemy increasingly opposed to both. The camps were sharply demarcated and clashed head-on. While the Roman pontiffs stood up to the onslaught of Liberalism (and, soon after, of Socialism), revolutionary persecution against the Church became more and more brutal.

After the resignation of President Patrice de MacMahon (1808–1893) in 1879, the French Republic became increasingly anti-Catholic, launching an anticlerical policy summarized by the cry of Léon Gambetta (1838–1882): "Behold the enemy: Clericalism!"[167] French Catholics faced a crucial question: Is it licit to agree with such a regime? Is this not making a deal with Satan?[168] Up until then, most Catholics had responded with a firm rejection of the Revolution and its offshoots.

However, toward the end of the nineteenth century, new winds began to blow in Europe. The dream of building a modern, technological civilization spread. The triumph of progress seemed to usher in an era of well-being and happiness. Social life became more joyful and refined. The Belle Époque introduced a new, smiling, and optimistic spirit of the times expressed in the delicate harmonies of the Viennese waltz and the blazing lights of Parisian boulevards.

Elevated to the papal throne in 1878, Pope Leo XIII had to deal with the sensitive issue of relations with the French Republic. In doctrinal matters he continued the line of his predecessor, condemning Liberalism in several documents, especially in the 1888 encyclical *Libertas praestantissimum*. His pontificate, however, was not always immune to the new spirit of the times strongly blowing from society into Church ambiences. French theologian Fr. Jean Rivière talks about the "climate of optimism that characterized Leo XIII's pontificate."[169]

Consequently, in some respects Leo XIII's pastoral line began to deviate from that of Pius IX. While the latter had always favored the intransigent sectors, Leo XIII began to attenuate manifestations of antagonism against the Revolution in the hope that his enemies, seeing the outstretched hand of the Church, would mollify and stop the persecution. The intransigent Catholics were the most fervent and enthusiastic partisans of the papacy, the defenders of dogma. Alongside them, however, were also fearful Catholics who felt the need for a good neighbor policy with the Republic, even regarding some demands of state secularism as long as its advocates diminished their hostility to the Church.

In a move he would bitterly deplore later, Leo XIII decided to abandon the intransigent diplomatic approach and adopt a policy of dialogue. That policy, Plinio Corrêa de Oliveira wrote, "meant precisely to discourage and undercut the support of these courageous people who had suffered from the Revolution every sort of persecution and harm with a joyful heart, knowing well that they were sacrificing themselves for altar and throne, for God and for their King. In compensation, Leo XIII won the applause of the many Catholics who were heedless of the close interaction between temporal and spiritual problems, and of those willing to compromise."[170] Was it worth the price? To the sovereign pontiff, it seemed so.

Leo XIII's policy of dialogue, known as *Ralliement*, was launched on November 12, 1890, with the toast that Charles Martial Cardinal Lavigerie (1825–1892), archbishop of Carthage and Algiers, offered to officers of the French Mediterranean fleet in his palace. It is known to history as the Algiers toast. The officers, all monarchists, were greeted with the Marseillaise, played by students of the White Fathers at a time when the anthem was still rejected by most Catholics precisely because of its revolutionary nature. At dessert, the cardinal stood up and, after stating that the republican form of government needed "unreserved loyalty," invited his guests to rally, that is, to reconcile with the French Republic. The cardinal gave to understand that the order came from above: "In speaking thus, I am convinced I shall not be repudiated by the voice of anyone in authority." The shock was such that everyone remained silent, without applauding. The cardinal then turned to the fleet commander, Admiral Duperré, and said, "'Admiral … will you not reply to the toast proposed by the cardinal?'" The admiral said only, "'I drink to his Eminence the cardinal and to the clergy of Algeria.'"[171]

On February 16, 1892, Leo XIII gave his policy a doctrinal basis in the encyclical *Au milieu des sollicitudes* in which he taught that, in theory, there are three legitimate forms of government: monarchy, aristocracy, and democracy. The Church cannot choose one form over another, just as long as it fulfills the end of the State, i.e., the common good. Therefore, a Catholic can lawfully choose the republican form of government. While unobjectionable from a theoretical standpoint, Leo XIII failed to distinguish clearly between the republican form of government as such and the French

---

165. "Whoever has not lived before 1789 does not know the sweetness of life," said Charles Maurice de Talleyrand-Périgord (1754–1838). François Guizot, *Mémoires pour servir à l'histoire de mon temps*, 8 vols., 2nd ed. (Paris: Michel Lévy Frères, 1859–1872), 1:6.

166. On the *Catholic and Royal Army*, see Jacques Cretineau-Joly, *Histoire de la Vendée militaire*, 5 vols. (Paris: Pays & Terroirs, 1895); Pierre Victor Jean Berthre de Bourniseaux, *Histoire des guerres de la Vendée et des chouans, depuis l'année 1792 jusqu'en 1815* (Paris: Brunot-Labbe, 1819).

167. Phrase used on May 4, 1877, in a speech before the National Assembly answering the bishop of Nevers, Most Rev. Thomas de Ladoue. It seems that the republican Alphonse Peyrat used it in 1863.

168. See Corrêa de Oliveira, *Nobility*, "Forms of Government in the Light of the Church's Social Doctrine: In Theory and in Practice," Appendix IV, 391–418.

169. J. Rivière, s.v. "Modernisme," in Jean Michel Alfred Vacant, Eugène Mangenot, and Émile Amann, eds. *Dictionnaire de théologie catholique* [*D.T.C.*], 30 vols. (Paris: Letouzey et Ané, 1902–1950), 10–2e.:2016.

170. See Corrêa de Oliveira, *Nobility*, ("Forms of Government").

171. Adrien Dansette, *Under the Third Republic*, vol. 2, *Religious History of Modern France*, trans. John Dingle (New York: Herder and Herder, 1961), 2:79. See also Adrien Dansette, *Histoire religieuse de la France contemporaine sous la troisième république* (Paris: Flammarion, 1951), 129–31.

Republic established by the Revolution of 1789. That gave rise to much confusion around the subject. It seemed, to more than a few, that by ordering Catholics to rally around the French Republic the pope not only thwarted a century-old, uncompromising struggle, but also asked them to accept, or at least not oppose, the legacy of 1789.

It is difficult to exaggerate the importance of this diplomatic turnaround. Just as the French Revolution was a watershed in human history, we can perhaps say that the Ralliement was a watershed in the history of contemporary Catholicism, with consequences felt to this day. While until then the line of fidelity to the Church had been very clear—opposition to Liberalism and its consequences, including those in the temporal sphere—the Ralliement split the Catholic camp and discouraged its best members.

Catholics who already showed sympathies for 1789—that is, Christian democrats, liberals, and modernists—applauded Leo XIII's policy and even said it vindicated their position. Others, disoriented, accepted it without asking too many questions in a spirit of blind fidelity to the supreme pontiff. However, that posed a serious problem of conscience for Catholics faithful to tradition. Should they accept the pope's political line, abandoning their counter-revolutionary militancy, or should they protest?

Some pointed out that the pope is infallible when speaking *ex cathedra in rebus fidei et morum*, that is, when teaching from the chair on faith and morals; this privilege, however, does not extend to his diplomatic acts. Catholics were therefore free to reject the Ralliement without compromising their fidelity to the Holy See.[172] While perfectly well grounded from the theological point of view, that distinction left Catholics faithful to tradition vulnerable to accusations of being disobedient to the tack chosen by the Roman pontiff.

Concretely prevented from being "Catholic monarchists," those faithful to tradition faced a crucial choice: Some chose to pursue a Catholic route and were thus drawn by currents polluted with Christian democratic ideas; others preferred a monarchist one and were attracted to currents polluted with positivist and nationalist ideas. In any case, the possibility of forming or perpetuating a current that was both Catholic and counter-revolutionary seemed to have received a mortal blow.[173]

At that point, presenting themselves as a right-wing alternative, new counter-revolutionary movements arose that were no longer founded on the Catholic ideal of restoring Christian civilization, but on nationalist ones.

Such is the case of Action Française, founded in France in 1899 by Henri Vaugeois (1864–1916) and Maurice Pujo (1872–1955),[174] and later led by Charles Maurras (1868–1952). With a positivist and nationalist inspiration, Action Française defended Catholicism not as supernatural truth but as the historical religion of the French people, and the Catholic Church not as the Mystical Body of Christ but as a political component that had historically formed some essential characteristics of the French nation.[175] Likewise, his defense of the monarchy was not based on meta-physical or religious reasons, but pragmatic ones. By accusing the republican system of damaging the national fiber, Action Française supported monarchy as a venerable French institution that had proven suitable to maintain order and tradition.[176] *"Politique d'abord!"* (Politics first!) was the motto of Maurras.[177]

6. Marc Sangnier and the Sillon

The anticlerical policy of the French Republic included many measures that were seriously harmful to the rights of the Church, such as the educational laws of 1882 and 1886, which consigned public education to the State. Anticlericalism reached its climax with the Waldeck-Rousseau government (1899–1902), which, in 1901, passed the "Loi des congrégations," whereby religious congregations had to be authorized by the State, and with the Combes government (1902–1905), which, in 1905, approved the "Loi de séparation," whereby France officially became a secular State. Pope St. Pius X condemned this policy, particularly in the encyclicals *Vehementer* (1905) and *Gravissimo officii* (1906).

---

172. The sovereign pontiff has direct power over matters that relate to his spiritual mission. He also has indirect power over temporal matters *ratione peccati*, that is, in situations involving sin. This is the symbolism of the gold and silver keys on the papal coat of arms. In the case of the *Ralliement*, a political and diplomatic issue, none of the two powers was involved but only what Jesuit theologian Fr. Yves de la Brière called the "directive power." The French scholar writes:

> In addition to the indirect power there is reasonably room for a governing power. For example, that happens when the pope intervenes to suggest to Catholics a specific political tactic rather than another. He does not consider the question in its temporal or political connotations but only inasmuch as it touches on religion and the good of souls. ... In this case the pope's intervention has at least the authority of fatherly advice to be taken very seriously and with great respect, lest one run the risk of committing a moral fault against the virtue of prudence. (Yves de la Brière, s.v. "Pouvoir pontifical dans l'ordre temporel," *Dictionnaire apologétique de la foi catholique [D.A.F.C.]*, ed. Adhémar d'Alès, 5 vols. [Paris: Gabriel Beauchesne, 1922], 4:114)

However, when there are serious reasons it is possible to disagree with the pope's political approach without sinning.

173. Explaining the Ralliement, Leo XIII expressed his conviction that the French Republic did not persecute the Church out of revolutionary hatred but only in retaliation for the attacks of numerous Catholics who adhered to the monarchical cause. From this standpoint he thought that if Catholics were to cease such attacks, the Republic would stop its persecution. Unfortunately, events failed to justify the Roman pontiff's hopes. In a letter to French President Emile Loubet in June 1900, Leo XIII had to admit the failure of his policy: "Having reached the sunset of life,

---

it would be for Us a bitter sorrow and pain to see vanish without bearing fruits, all Our benevolent intentions regarding the French nation and its government, to which We have repeatedly shown not only Our most delicate attentions but also Our effective and special affection." Barbier, *Histoire du catholicisme libéral*, 2:531. Shortly afterward, the pope expressed similar sentiments to the archbishop of Paris, François Cardinal Richard:

> Since the beginning of Our pontificate We have spared no effort to realize in France this work of pacification, which would have resulted in innumerable advantages for her, not only in the religious sphere, but also in the civil and political ones. We have not retreated in the face of difficulty. We have never ceased to give France special proofs of deference, solicitude, and love, hoping at all times that she would respond in a manner befitting a great and generous nation. We would experience extreme sadness if, having arrived at the evening of Our life, We should find ourselves disappointed in these hopes, frustrated by the cost of Our paternal solicitudes and condemned to see, in the country We love, passions and factions struggling ever more desperately without being able either to measure the extent of their excesses or ward off misfortunes which We have done everything possible to prevent. (Leo XIII, "Lettre à son Éminence le Cardinal Richard, archevéque de Paris" [Dec. 23, 1900])

174. Significantly, both founders of Action Française came from the republican left. Vaugeois descended from a regicide and belonged to *Union pour l'action sociale*, the circle of leftist intellectuals to which Pujo (much appreciated by the socialist leader Jean Jaurès) also belonged.

175. See Stéphane Giocanti, *Maurras: Le chaos et l'ordre* (Paris: Flammarion, 2006), 216–17.

176. "Action Française ... resolved to implement its nationalist solutions in the political constitution of the French State, calling itself integral because the monarchical solution meets all of the country's needs just as an integral in mathematics represents the sum of all values of an algebraic function." Bernard de Vesins, "XIIIe congrès d'Action française—Déclarations de Bernard de Vesins, Président de la Ligue d'Action française," *L'Action Française*, Nov. 24, 1926, 1. See also Domenico Fisichella, *La democrazia contro la realtà: Il pensiero politico di Charles Maurras* (Rome: Carocci Editore, 2006).

177. In his later years, Maurras, an agnostic and positivist, drew closer to the Faith. At the Carmel of Lisieux they prayed for his conversion. A nun offered her life for him, a fact communicated in a letter from the Mother Superior, Mother Agnès, a sister of St. Thérèse of the Child Jesus. In 1937, Pius XI wrote exhorting him to convert. Three days before his death, in November 1952, he asked for the last rites and for rosary beads to pray on, a fact usually interpreted as a sign of conversion. We must also remember that, at the request of the Lisieux Carmelites, Pius XII lifted the condemnation of Action Française in 1939.

That anticlericalism was aggressive and rampant. Priests were ridiculed in the streets, religious services interrupted, processions opposed, churches vandalized, religious symbols defaced.[178] Action Française and Sillon stood out among the movements that militantly opposed this anticlericalism, the former in the name of national tradition, the latter on behalf of the Catholic faith.

Founded in 1894 by Marc Sangnier (1873–1950) in the wake of social Catholicism, Sillon (furrow) was born with the blessing of Albert de Mun. Among its early members were some *abbés démocrates*. Sillon sported a messianic rhetoric centered on the cult of its founder's personality. Sangnier was hailed as "a new Messiah"[179] with the "providential mission"[180] of spreading liberal democracy by proclaiming "a democratic and social Christianity. ... [at] the service of democracy."[181] In a February 1904 speech, the French leader exclaimed, "Slowly, this democracy rises up, imposing itself little by little ... it will topple the present, selfish, and pagan social structure and build the future city upon its ruins."[182]

Announcing Sangnier's arrival at Chambéry in December 1905, the daily paper *La Savoie Libérale* exulted:

> Christmas! On the eve of the great Christian feast, a new Messiah has come to announce to democracy the reign of human fraternity. ... From all corners of the horizon, led by an invisible star, shepherds and magi have come to hear the good news.
>
> This young apostle exerts on those surrounding him a powerful attraction. The most varied audiences receive his words with almost religious attention and the triumphant acclamations that greet his passage recall, to some extent, those of the people of Israel hailing Jesus during his entrance into Jerusalem.[183]

Sangnier inaugurated a style of charismatic oratory that was copied by others in the twentieth century. He often fell into an ecstasy of sorts accompanied with tremors and jerky movements. He confessed that he was frequently overtaken "by a sort of violent passion that carried me away almost against my will, and dictated everything to me, without my exercising, so to speak, any voluntary role."[184]

Sillon's militant approach fascinated the young. In order to protect religious ceremonies from attacks by secularists, in 1901 Sillon formed a paramilitary force called Jeune Garde, presented as a chivalry for modern times. Wearing paramilitary uniforms, its members were trained in *savate* (French boxing) and fencing. The Jeune Garde took part in numerous scuffles with secularists in the streets that came to bloodshed, thus earning an aura of crusade that attracted scores of young idealists eager to fight for the Church.[185]

Maurras himself was perhaps inspired by the Jeune Garde when, in 1908, he established a militant section within Action Française: the Camelots du Roi (King's Heralds). The Camelots' task was to distribute street propaganda, confronting republicans, with physical force if necessary.

In the absence of a counter-revolutionary Catholic movement that would meet both the needs of the Faith and those of monarchical militancy, many young Catholics eager to fight the anticlericalism of the Third Republic had to face a substantially flawed dilemma: either defending the Faith by joining Sillon and thus assimilating democratic doctrines, or defending monarchy by joining Action Française and thus absorbing positivist nationalism. This particular set of circumstances enabled Sillon's tremendous growth in the first decade of the twentieth century, a situation not entirely different from the one Italian Catholics faced twenty years later. They were forced to choose between the Italian Popular Party of Father Sturzo and the National Fascist Party of Benito Mussolini.[186]

Over time, however, Sillon's militant Catholic character withered even as its Christian democratic side stood out, which, translated into political action, amounted to a left turn. Trying to justify the change, Sangnier stated, "Sillon's goal is to establish the democratic Republic in France. Therefore, properly speaking, it is not a Catholic association. ... The Sillon is a secular movement."[187]

In 1906, Sillon joined the political left. Many of its members enrolled in the C.G.T. (Confédération Générale du Travail, the socialist trade union), and their collaboration with the Republican left became ever closer.[188] The Jeune Garde turned into storm troopers of the left, taking part in street demonstrations along with the socialists, and even clashing with the Camelots du Roi.[189]

Marc Sangnier had participated in numerous meetings of Christian democrats in Italy, with whom he maintained close relations. It is no surprise, therefore, that Father Murri was one of the staunchest supporters of Sillon's turn to the left.

Sillon now presented itself as "heir to the great republican revolutionaries."[190] In the movement's meetings they praised "Sillon's revolutionaries, definitely successors of those of 1792."[191] "Sillon having asked rhetorically, 'Was the 1793 revolution anti-religious?' answered categorically, 'NO! Robespierre, Danton and Camille Desmoulins were religious minds. ... Their religious philosophy was

---

178. A typical example of aggressive anticlericalism was the daily *Action*, directed by the apostate priest Charbonnel. Calling itself "anticlerical, republican, and socialist," *Action* stood "in favor of all liberties and against all clericalism. ... We will denounce, overthrow, and destroy the enemy of truth, justice, and life: the Church." Fabrègues, *Le Sillon*, 97.

179. *Le Sillon*, Jan. 10, 1906, quoted in Barbier, *Histoire du catholicisme libéral*, 4:390.

180. "Le Petit Démocrate de Limoges," Oct. 24, 1907, quoted in Barbier, 4:387.

181. Marc Sangnier, *Discours*, 1:139, quoted in Barbier, 4:391.

182. Marc Sangnier, *Discours*, 1:262, quoted in Barbier, 4:400. Obvious allusions to the "new city" of Prophet Isaiah (Is. 65:17) and the "new Jerusalem" of the Apocalypse (Apoc. 3:12).

183. *Le Sillon*, Jan. 10, 1906. Quoted in Barbier, 4:390.

184. Fabrègues, *Le Sillon*, 13.

185. That early Sillon movement was encouraged by St. Pius X, who often praised the young men's idealism. In September 1904, he received Marc Sangnier accompanied by a large group of Jeune Garde members. See Jean-Jacques Greteau, *Marc Sangnier:*

Le semeur d'espérances (Paris: L'Harmattan, 2009), 74–75. Constrained to condemn Sangnier in 1910, St. Pius X still made a friendly reference to "Sillon's good times."

186. The Popular Party initially collaborated with Fascism and even allowed two of its members, Vincenzo Tangorra and Stefano Cavazzoni, to join the first Mussolini government. After the 1923 Turin conference, however, the Popular Party had an internal split because the right adopted pro-fascist positions, while the left, led by Fr. Sturzo, advocated collaboration with the socialists, opposing the fascists. It was again a fundamentally flawed choice. What was missing was a political organization that was both Catholic and anticommunist.

187. Marc Sangnier, *La Croix*, Aug. 19, 1906, quoted in Barbier, *Histoire du catholicisme libéral*, 4:437.

188. See Jean-Marie Leuwers, "Étapes de l'action des laïcs et conceptions successives de l'apostolat du laïcat," in *Évangélisation collective: Dossier masses ouvrières*, ed. P. Barrau (Paris: Les Éditions Ouvrières, 1964), 23.

189. Recalling those years, in 1950 the socialist leader Jean Texier wrote,

> I remember the clashes in the Latin Quarter. ... The Camelots du Roi had come looking for trouble. The youth of the Jeune Garde fought alongside us, splitting the heads of those with Action Française.
>
> For us ... the Sillon boys were a revelation. It was incredible! Catholics could be republicans like us? They could clash with monarchists who went to Mass like them, at our side? (Jean Texier, *La Documentation Catholique*, no. 1078 [Sept. 24, 1950], 1268–69)

190. *L'Éveil Démocratique*, July 19, 1908, quoted in Fabrègues, *Le Sillon*, 208.

191. Fabrègues, 208. In 1792, the Jacobins seized power. They were the most radical faction in the French Revolution. In that same year, they initiated the period known as *The Terror*, which historian Pierre Gaxotte called "communist terror." Gaxotte, *La Révolution Française*, 350.

the very substance of Christianity.'"[192] Sangnier himself extolled "the truly Christian character in the temperament of the revolutionaries (those of 1789 and even those of 1792)."[193]

So what were the key doctrinal points Sillon shared with other Christian democratic tenets?

a. Religious Democracy

We find in Sillon a feature later replicated in many versions of Catholic progressivism: an exacerbated sentimentality. Sillon, explains a follower of Sangnier, the historian Jean de Fabrègues, "was more an impulse than a thought, more a feeling than an idea, more a movement than a doctrine."[194] Such sentimentality can easily trigger antipathy for hierarchy, inspired by the false idea that differences necessarily cause suffering in the inferior and consequently violate human dignity. When not restrained by sound reason, exacerbated sentimentality can lead to an egalitarian position. This is the foundation of Sillon's egalitarian democratism. "We are egalitarians!" Sangnier proclaimed.[195] Sillon activists called one another *comrade*. There was absolute parity within the movement. In their print shop, comrade janitor was equal to comrade editor.

This egalitarianism affected even the most fundamental plane, in which dependence should be radically evident, namely, man's relations with God. Avoiding the conception of God as a transcendent Being over and above His created universe, and to Whom man owes obedience and adoration, Sillon preferred to see God as a life democratically participated in by all men. "If man cannot democratize the divinity, God can," affirmed Sangnier in one of his theological reveries. "Christianity is nothing else than the democracy of divine life. ... Through it, God's sovereignty is really opened up to participation. ... God, who could have treated us as a king, preferred instead to propose to us the republican ideal in our relations with him. He sent his son and invited us to unite ourselves intimately with him, to become like him. Thus, God enjoins us to be united with his second person and so become an adjunct member of the Trinity. Through their assimilation to the second person of the Trinity, men have access to the society of the three persons and participate in their majestic equality."[196]

One consequence of this egalitarianism was a creeping ecumenism toward other religions. Nothing could be more logical. To claim that the Catholic religion is the one true religion not only would establish a hierarchy, but would also offend the human dignity of non-Catholics. Thus, to include Protestants, in 1906 Sangnier launched the Plus Grand Sillon (The Greater Furrow).

b. Social Democracy

The Sillon's democratic egalitarianism also applied to the secular sphere by seeking the attenuation, if not suppression, of inequalities between the governing and the governed. Monarchy and aristocracy were proscribed by Sillon as intrinsically evil regimes, for they are hierarchical. Not even representative democracy was sufficiently 'democratic' for Sillon. It thus promoted the dissemination of direct or participatory democracy, that is, the distribution of State power to the greater possible number of hands at the most basic possible level.

In a first phase, this would imply a society in which the division in classes is greatly attenuated or altogether suppressed. "This division of men in classes or professions is an ancient conception," stated the Sillon leader Paul Gemahling. "We must explode from the inside this system of closed social classes."[197] According to the Sillon, as the democratic conscience progressed among the people, the State would lose its reason for being. "Within our democratic conception," wrote Georges Hoog, a close associate of Sangnier, "the State would be nothing and the free associations of citizens everything."[198]

Thus, on the horizon, Sillon contemplated the dissolution of the State in its modern form as a radical exigency of participatory democracy. Marc Sangnier himself explained this: "The modern State, in our view, is not perennial. To the extent that the value of the individual citizen develops, the coercive action of the State seems to us less and less necessary. ... By increasing the conscience and the sense of civic responsibility of a growing number of citizens, democracy also tends to turn the means of government—the laws—less and less necessary. In a perfect society ... laws will become totally useless."[199]

c. Economic Democracy

From political democracy and social equality, Sillon naturally moved to economic democracy, that is, to Socialism. Could it be otherwise? Having decried social inequalities as intrinsically oppressive and offensive to human fraternity, how could Sillon accept economic inequalities? Sillon appeared to find in employer-employee relations a residual image of the relations between a king and his people. "The passage from the patronal regime to the cooperative regime," said Sangnier, "demands a development of conscience and responsibility similar to that in the passage from the monarchy to the Republic."[200]

Just as kings had been dethroned in society, Sillon now intended to dethrone the kings of the economy by eliminating their sovereignty in the business enterprise. Léonard Constant, Sangnier's right arm, affirmed that the central goal was "to transfer from the employer to the body of workers most of the functions that the business enterprise property now permits the owner to exercise."[201] "Comrades," Marc Sangnier proclaimed in his turn, "we wish to develop among the workers enough conscience and vital energy *so they can have the influence and power* heretofore restricted to a caste or closed class. ... This patronage and the wage system ... will tend to disappear."[202]

According to Sillon, the road to economic democracy must pass through a reform of private property and the way it is managed. Sillon rejected statist Socialism but drew close to the so-called self-managing Socialism.[203] With the gradual disappearance of private property, replaced by types of communal property, owners would also pass on company management to workers' assemblies. Sillon presented this system as a consequence of the people's socioeconomic sovereignty in the political sphere: "When common property spreads and large companies are managed by worker collectives..."[204] He proposed, therefore, "a harmonious State, that is, a collectivist one."[205]

---

192. *Le Sillon*, Apr. 25, 1907, quoted in Fabrègues, *Le Sillon*, 208.

193. André Latreille, J.R. Palanque, E. Delaruelle, and R. Remond, *Histoire du catholicisme en France* (Paris: Spes, 1962), 3:524.

194. Fabrègues, *Le Sillon*, 227.

195. Barbier, *Histoire du catholicisme libéral*, 4:421.

196. Marc Sangnier, *Le Sillon*, Aug. 10, 1903, quoted in Fabrègues, *Le Sillon*, 155.

197. *Le Sillon*, Feb. 18, 1907, quoted in Barbier, *Histoire du catholicisme libéral*, 4:399.

198. Georges Hoog, *Le Sillon*, Sept. 10, 1905, quoted in Barbier, 4:398.

199. Marc Sangnier, *Discours* I, 3, *Le Sillon,* July 10, 1905, quoted in Barbier, 4:398.

200. Marc Sangnier, *Le Sillon*, Feb. 10, 1905, quoted in Barbier, 4:405.

201. Léonard Constant, *Le Sillon*, Feb. 10, 1906, quoted in Barbier, 4:402.

202. *Discours* I, 300, quoted in Barbier, 4:402.

203. For a discussion on self-managing socialism, see Plinio Corrêa de Oliveira, "What Does Self-Managing Socialism Mean for Communism: A Barrier? Or a Bridgehead?" TFP.org.

204. Marc Sangnier, *Discours*, 1:359, quoted in Barbier, *Histoire du catholicisme libéral*, 4:403.

205. *Le Sillon*, July 25, 1904, quoted in Barbier, 4:405.

d. International Democracy

As Prof. Plinio Corrêa de Oliveira explains, "The State is constituted by an independent people exercising full dominion over a territory. Sovereignty is, therefore, in public law, the image of property. Once we admit the idea of a people, whose characteristics distinguish it from other peoples, and the idea of sovereignty, we are perforce in the presence of inequalities: of capacity, virtue, number, and others. Once the idea of territory is admitted, we have quantitative and qualitative inequality among the various territorial spaces."[206]

One can thus understand how Sillon's fundamental egalitarianism led it to reject the idea of the sovereign State. "The very conception we have today of the State and of territorial country will necessarily evolve," we read in their program.[207] "The territorial country seems to us a mere phase in the evolution of this sentiment of the human soul," asserted Sangnier in his turn, in his utopian dreams of a universal republic.[208]

e. The Sillon and Modernism

Being a transposition to the social and political plane of the liberal and modernist errors, Sillon displayed an understandable sympathy for Modernism, condemned by St. Pius X as a heresy in 1907. Fr. Lucien Laberthonnière, a leading modernist, was considered by the *sillonistes* the *maître à penser de la maison* (house mentor).[209] Another modernist, Paul Sabatier, was much more explicit: "Although the Sillon sees itself as being far from Loisy and Fogazzaro, it is the manifestation of the same fundamental sap run on a different terrain."[210]

f. Condemnation and Twilight of the Sillon

In 1906, as we said, the Sillon veered to the left in the political arena, and a growing number of bishops began to issue formal censures against it.[211] The Holy See itself began to multiply the admonitions. Alas, to no avail. Finally, on August 25, 1910, St. Pius X issued the apostolic letter *Notre charge apostolique*, formally condemning the Sillon, and with it the whole Christian democratic current.

After manifesting his paternal grief for having to take such a step, "for We love the courageous youth enrolled under the flag of the Sillon," and praising the early Sillon's "noble enthusiasm," the Holy Father lamented that "Our hopes have in great measure been deceived. A day came when the Sillon revealed to the eyes of those who could see clearly, disquieting tendencies. The Sillon went astray."[212]

After condemning Sillon's craving for social leveling, the pope entered into the analysis of the movement's doctrinal core:

> The Sillon is nobly solicitous for human dignity, but it understands that dignity in the manner of certain philosophers of whom the Church does not at all feel proud. The first element of that dignity is liberty, understood in the sense that, except in the matter of religion, each man is autonomous. From this fundamental

principle, it draws the following conclusions: Today the people are in tutelage under an authority distinct from themselves; they ought to free themselves from it: *political emancipation*. They are dependent upon employers who hold their instruments of labor, exploit them, oppress them and degrade them; they ought to shake off the yoke: *economic emancipation*. Finally, they are ruled by a caste, called the directing caste, to whom their intellectual development gives an undue preponderance in the direction of affairs; they must break away from their domination: *intellectual emancipation*. The leveling down of conditions from this triple point of view will establish equality amongst men, and this equality is true human justice. A political and social organization founded upon this double basis, liberty and [equality] (to which will soon be added fraternity)—this is what they call democracy. ...

> [The Roman pontiff concluded,] The breath of the Revolution has passed this way, and We may conclude that if the social doctrines of the Sillon are erroneous, its spirit is dangerous and its education disastrous.[213]

With his career as a Catholic leader effectively ended, Marc Sangnier dedicated himself to political action in a typically Christian democratic style aimed at transshipping Catholics to the left. In 1912, Sangnier founded the Ligue de la Jeune République. Socialist leader Amédée Dunois wrote him, "You have assumed an idea that, once accepted, could lead very far and all the way to integral Socialism, toward which you are steering some social groups that our propaganda would barely be able to reach."[214] Dunois turned out to be a good prophet: Fifty years later the Ligue de la Jeune République joined the Socialist Party, taking with it a good part of the Christian democratic Catholic left in France.[215]

In 1921, Sangnier created a Comité International d'Action Démocratique pour la Paix with the participation of Italians Rufo Ruffo, Domenico Russo, and Giuseppe Aiello of the Popular Party of Father Sturzo, who sent Sangnier a letter of adhesion.[216] The bylaws of the Comité were published by *Ère Nouvelle*, a mouthpiece of the Radical Socialist Party, showing how their content would appeal to that particular segment of the political spectrum.

Marc Sangnier died in Paris on May 28, 1950, while the 42nd Conference of the French Socialist Party was in session. On receiving the news its Secretary-General, Guy Mollet, stopped the proceedings and asked for a minute of silence. "He was a bit one of us," he said.[217] The assembly decided to send a delegation to his funeral.

7. U.S.A.: Catholics and the New Deal

In the United States, Christian democratic ideas continued to progress during the early decades of the twentieth century, generating the involvement of Catholics, first in the doctrinal justification and elaboration of legislation that would later be incorporated into the New Deal, and then in the implementation

206. Corrêa de Oliveira, *Revolution and Counter-Revolution*, 49–50.

207. *Le Sillon*, Jan. 10, 1905, quoted in Fabrègues, *Le Sillon*, 164.

208. *Le Sillon*, Feb. 25, 1905, quoted in Barbier, *Histoire du catholicisme libéral*, 4:414.

209. See Fabrègues, *Le Sillon*, 181.

210. Fabrègues, 211–12.

211. Bishop Dubillard, of Quimper, for example, warned, "For me, he (Marc Sangnier) is still a collectivist from the social viewpoint, a revolutionary democrat from the political one, and a liberal Protestant from the religious perspective." Barbier, *Histoire du catholicisme libéral*, 4:430.

212. St. Pius X, apostolic letter *Notre charge apostolique*, *The American Catholic Quarterly Review* 35, no. 140 (Oct. 1910), 693–94.

213. St. Pius X, *Notre charge apostolique*, 697, 703. The ACQR mistranslated the original French's *l'égalité* as *legality*. See also Henri Delassus, *La condamnation du modernisme social dans la censure du Sillon* (Cambrai: Desclée de Brouwer, 1910).

214. Jean-François Kesler, *De la gauche dissidente au nouveau Parti Socialiste: Les minorités qui ont rénové le P.S.* (Toulouse: Editions Privat, 1990), 30.

215. See Albert Samuel, *Le socialisme: Courantes, histoire, pratiques* (Lyon: Chronique Sociale, 1981), 330.

216. See "Luigi Sturzo nella storia d'Italia," in *Atti del convegno internazionale di studi promosso dall'Assemblea Regionale Siciliana*, ed. Francesco Malteri (Rome: Edizioni di Storia e Letteratura, 1973), 2:533.

217. *La Documentation Catholique*, no. 1078 (Sept. 24, 1950), 1261.

of New Deal programs. Indeed, in the early years of Roosevelt's first administration, before the New Deal coalition had matured, one of the main pillars on which his reformist projects rested was this wing of the Catholic Church. This was heightened by the overwhelming identification of Catholics with the Democratic Party.[218]

The most notorious representative of this period of social Catholicism in the U.S. was Fr. John A. Ryan (1869–1945), dubbed the "Right Reverend New Dealer" for his brassy identification with Franklin D. Roosevelt (he twice delivered the inaugural invocation for him), the New Deal, and the Democratic Party. Much influenced by Georgism, British Fabian Socialism, and Protestant Social Gospel, Father Ryan saw "valuable truth" in Marxism, and was a fervent partisan of some strains of Socialism, which he sought to identify with aspects of the Catholic doctrine of distributive justice. He was an early member of the American Civil Liberties Union (A.C.L.U.), founded by communist sympathizer Roger Baldwin, and sat on its board of directors.

Father Ryan was the ghostwriter of the pastoral letter published in 1919 by the National Catholic War Council (N.C.W.C., later National Catholic Welfare Conference, the embryo of the present United States Catholic Conference). Titled *Program of Social Reconstruction*, this pastoral letter defended a thesis easily manipulated by the growing socialist propaganda: "The majority [of the workers] must somehow become owners, or at least in part, of the instruments of production. They can be enabled to reach this stage gradually through cooperative productive societies and copartnership arrangements."[219] The *Program*, indeed, was praised by the left throughout the country as a watershed document whereby the bishops joined the progressive fold. A copy of it was promptly sent to Lenin "for his guidance and salvation," as Msgr. Michael Splaine of the N.C.W.C. beamed.[220]

Several American bishops openly opposed the *Program* due to its socialist penchants. Bishop William Turner of Buffalo labelled some of its proposals "a plank in the socialist platform"; and William Cardinal O'Connell of Boston called it "Soviet legislation."[221]

Summing up Father Ryan's role in American social Catholicism, his biographer Francis Broderick writes, "On social and economic questions, Ryan more than any other single person brought Catholics abreast of American progressive thought."[222]

E. Catholic Action

The 1917 Bolshevik Revolution produced a shock wave—psychological as well as political—that hit hard a world already shaken by the horrors of the First World War. The gruesome details of the massacre of the Russian imperial family in Ekaterinburg were commented on with dread in newspapers and salons, raising disturbing images of communist barbarism.[223] As the Spartacist revolution

in Germany and the proclamation of the Soviet Republic of Béla Kun in Hungary demonstrated, Europe was not at all immune to that barbarism. Were it not for the "miracle on the Vistula," the Red Army would have penetrated the heart of Europe, joining local revolutionary forces and placing part of the Old Continent under the Soviet yoke.[224]

Instead of producing a climate of optimism and confidence, the victory Italy achieved in the War saw the country fall into a downward spiral. It went through the so-called red biennium characterized by worker and peasant struggles that culminated in the occupation of factories by Red Guards, a first step to general revolution. The 1919 elections gave a majority to the Italian Socialist Party, which had sided with the Russian revolution. Its paper proclaimed, "The red flag hoisted by the proletariat of Petrograd ... has much more meaning than an adhesion by Russia's working masses to the present situation created by imperialists from all countries."[225] The country was in chaos. A communist revolution seemed imminent.

Apprehension over a possible communist revolution in Europe strengthened the vigorous spiritual rebirth already visible in many countries, and not only in the Old Continent. Pope Pius XI (1857, 1922–1939) was fully able to grasp that rebirth and proclaimed the Holy Year 1925 as the year of the social Kingship of Christ. "We were led in the meantime to indulge the hope of a brighter future at the sight of a more widespread and keener interest evinced in Christ and His Church," the Roman pontiff stated.[226] Animated by new fervor, Catholic mass movements flourished everywhere with such strength and freshness as to warrant great hopes.[227]

1. "A Crucial Turning Point for the Church"

In order to give the Catholic revival substance and direction, Pius XI sought to reorganize the laity by dividing it into specialized sectors devoted to specific fields of apostolate. In 1922 Italy, adult associations were grouped into the Union of Catholic Men. In 1923, Pius XI approved the bylaws of the Italian Catholic Action, dividing it into four sections: Italian Federation of Catholic Men, Female Italian Catholic Union, Italian Catholic University Federation, and Italian Catholic Youth Society. The organization

218. See David O'Brien, *American Catholics and Social Reform: The New Deal Years* (New York: Oxford University Press, 1968).

219. National Catholic War Council, "Program of Social Reconstruction" in *Pastoral Letters of the American Hierarchy, 1792–1970*, ed. Hugh J. Nolan (Huntington, Ind.: Our Sunday Visitor, 1971), no. 36, 210.

220. Joseph M. McShane, S.J., *"Sufficiently Radical": Catholicism, Progressivism, and the Bishops' Program of 1919* (Washington, D.C.: The Catholic University of America Press, 1986), 193.

221. McShane, *"Sufficiently Radical,"* 185.

222. Francis L. Broderick, "John A. Ryan," *New Catholic Encyclopedia*, 2nd ed., 12:446. See also Francis L. Broderick, *Right Reverend New Dealer: John A. Ryan* (New York: The Macmillan Company, 1963); Patrick W. Gearty, *The Economic Thought of Monsignor John A. Ryan* (Washington, D.C.: The Catholic University of America Press, 1953), especially pp. 67–92 for a description of Christian democracy.

223. Those images actually corresponded to reality. See Stéphane Courtois, et al., ed., *The Black Book of Communism: Crimes, Terror, Repression*, trans. Jonathan Murphy and Mark Kramer (Cambridge, Mass.: Harvard University Press, 1999).

224. The Battle of Warsaw, also known as the Miracle on the Vistula, was the decisive battle in the Polish-Soviet War that began shortly after the end of the First World War and ended in 1921 with the Peace of Riga. It was fought on August 16, 1920, between the Red Army of Gen. Michajl Tukhachevsky and the Polish army commanded by Marshal Jozef Pilsudski. Against all expectations, the Poles overran the communists, forcing them to a disorderly retreat which, in practice, prevented the invasion of Central Europe, as planned by Lenin and Trotsky. The outcome, generally attributed to the supernatural intervention of Our Lady of Czestochowa, is remembered in a large fresco at the Polish Chapel of the Basilica of Loreto in the Italian province of Ancona. In fact, Pope Benedict XV had called for a crusade of prayer to implore Our Lady to grant victory over the Soviets. See Adam Zamoyski, *16 agosto 1920: La battaglia di Varsavia* (Milan: Corbaccio, 2009).

225. Roberto Vivarelli, *Storia delle origini del fascismo*, 3 vols. (Bologna: Il Mulino, 2012), 1:106.

226. Pius XI, encyclical *Quas primas* (Dec. 11, 1925), no. 1. In his history of Italian Catholic Action, de Antonellis detects "a return to broad popular devotion. This is demonstrated by the success of the Eucharistic Congress of Genoa, the resumption of patron saint processions, the ever larger pilgrimages to shrines, customs, and initiatives long overlooked by the masses." De Antonellis, *Storia dell'Azione Cattolica*, 156.

227. As a backlash to the trauma caused by the Bolshevik Revolution, nationalist movements arose. They established themselves as an alternative to revolutionary chaos despite their frequently secular and neo-pagan orientation. Often lacking an anticommunist political movement to support, many Catholics were seduced by these movements, which replaced the ideal of a Christian restoration with worship of the State or race. Even great figures of Catholic traditionalism, such as Rafael Cardinal Merry del Val, former secretary of state of Pope St. Pius X, were enthralled by some of the rising nationalist figures. "With a clear vision of the reality of things, Mussolini wanted and wants religion to be respected, honored, and practiced. Visibly protected by God, he has wisely elevated the fate of the nation," the cardinal wrote. Gian Carlo Zuccaro, *Lui, Mussolini, nel giudizio di mille personaggi internazionali* (Genoa: E.R.G.A., 1983), 39. See Pio Cenci, *Il Cardinale Raffaelle Merry del Val* (Rome-Turin: Roberto Berruti Editore, 1933).

was directed by a national council chaired by the Milanese Luigi Colombo (1886–1973).

Beginning in 1924, in Belgium and France there arose the Jeunesse Ouvrière Chrétienne (J.O.C.), the Jeunesse Agricole Catholique (J.A.C.), the Jeunesse Étudiante Chrétienne (J.E.C.), the Jeunesse Maritime Catholique (J.M.C.), the Jeunesse Indépendante Chrétienne (J.I.C.), and the Jeunesse Indépendante Chrétienne Féminine (J.I.C.F.). This model was then exported all over the world through missionary teams composed mostly of Belgians and Frenchmen.

Pius XI's original intent was very clear: "The *holy battle* waged on so many fronts."[228] The battle was against Communism, Socialism, and also Protestantism.[229] Its purpose: "The restoration of the Kingdom of Christ and the re-establishment of that true peace which can be found only in His Kingdom."[230] Pius XI wanted to engage the laity in this battle, entrusting them with the task of re-Christianizing society. Hence, he defined Catholic Action as a "participation of the laity in the apostolate of the Church hierarchy."

Unfortunately, from its inception, the project of Pius XI suffered in many sectors the influence of the Christian democratic and neo-modernist currents. Under the guidance of thinkers such as Jacques Maritain (1882–1972) and Emmanuel Mounier (1904–1950), and theologians such as Fathers Marie-Dominique Chenu (1895–1989) and Henri de Lubac (1896–1991) the progressives literally took over many areas of Catholic Action, turning them into instruments to disseminate their errors, and into the breeding ground from which LT would arise shortly thereafter.

The years of expansion of Catholic Action "marked ... a crucial turning point for the Church," writes historian Adrien Dansette.[231] Catholic Action marked a turning point in two ways:

—It absorbed, relegated to a marginal role, or, in some cases, suppressed older Catholic lay associations that represented the traditional Catholic spirit, particularly that of St. Pius X's pontificate, thus clearing the way for the dominance of new ideas. Describing the rise of American Catholic Action, liberal priest Andrew Greeley, for example, reveals, "New national organizations were founded, and old national organizations were infiltrated and reorganized."[232]

—It fostered a process of ideological transshipment among the Catholic laity that dismantled in many their traditional Catholic upbringing, replacing it with a new one, and inducing more proactive individuals to assume a liberal or even leftist position.

The first development in that turnaround was greatly aided by the fact that Catholic Action was given top priority everywhere, even to the serious detriment of more traditional lay associations such as confraternities, Marian Sodalities, and the Apostleship of Prayer. This priority was grounded by members of Catholic Action on a debatable interpretation—to say the least—of some expressions used by Pius XI in documents relating to the organization. Some of its leaders (the most liberal ones) even claimed a *special mandate* from the hierarchy for Catholic Action militants, and vindicated the exclusiveness of Catholic lay apostolate.[233] In their view, Catholic Action should absorb and supersede all other lay associations in order to bring the Church abreast with the times.

Alleging such a mandate, those sectors presented themselves as standard-bearers of a new spirit that should replace the one which had hitherto been predominant in the Church. This new mentality was inspired not only by Moscow's Socialism, but, above all, by an Americanism that arose with the Roaring Twenties, which was even more insidious because harder to attack. This spread mostly through Hollywood movies, musical rhythms, fashions, and human models. We can define it as an electrifying feeling of discontinuity and rupture with tradition in the name of modernity. According to this view, the First World War had buried Old Europe and its traditions forever. A new world was arising to which Catholic Action should ferry the laity. This was the reason for the bubbly optimism that characterized vast sectors of Catholic Action.

Such a spirit produced manifestations of egalitarianism and Liberalism that allowed the easy spread of neo-modernist and Christian democratic errors, accentuating the drift to the left started by social Catholicism, a drift that was not uniform across all sectors and countries. It is undeniable, for example, that the leadership of Luigi Gedda (1902–2000) slowed this process in Italian Catholic Action.[234]

2. The Condemnation of Action Française

Among the factors that contributed to the expansion of Catholic Action and the simultaneous disappearance of many traditional Catholic groups, especially in Europe, one should mention the dismay caused among traditionalist Catholics by the 1926 condemnation of Action Française, the monarchist movement led by Charles Maurras. The historian André Latreille recounts, "It is difficult to imagine the effect of Pius XI's condemnation of the school and doctrines of Action Française. ... Catholics linked to Action Française were deeply shaken."[235] As he came to their rescue, Louis Cardinal Billot (1846–1931), a leader in the struggle against Modernism, was forced to resign the cardinalate.[236]

The condemnation, issued in a decree by the Holy Office, dated back to the time of St. Pius X. However, worried that it would be misinterpreted as a rejection of traditional Catholicism, the holy pope limited it to a personal reprimand of Maurras. With the decree's publication in 1926, Pope St. Pius X's apprehensions came true. Gabriele De Rosa comments, "With the new pope, the fundamentalists received a mortal blow and Cardinal Billot lost his influence. Even the power of Maurras, cultivated by fundamentalist cardinals and bishops, began to decline."[237]

As explained above, a series of circumstances had allowed Action Française, despite its positivist inspiration, to attract the sympathy of many Catholics, forming a Catholic wing, in fact larger than the positivist one. As the standoff between the two currents of the movement remained unresolved, Pius XI's condemnation objectively ended by striking also its Catholic wing. Traditional Catholicism, already weakened by the Ralliement, thus appeared

228. Pius XI, encyclical *Ubi arcano* (Dec. 23, 1922), no. 54.

229. See Pius XI, Allocution to the Sacred College (July 22, 1934), quoted in Alfredo Maria Cavagna, ed., *La parola del papa su l'Azione Cattolica*, 3rd ed. (Milan: Società Editrice Vita e Pensiero, 1936), 69.

230. Pius XI, encyclical *Ubi arcano*, no. 55.

231. Adrien Dansette, *Destin du catholicisme français 1926–1956* (Paris: Flammarion, 1957), 5.

232. Andrew M. Greeley, *The Catholic Experience: An Interpretation of the History of American Catholicism* (Garden City: N.Y.: Doubleday & Company, 1967), 257.

233. For a penetrating analysis of the legal nature of Catholic Action and a refutation of the progressive interpretation of its *mandate*, see Plinio Corrêa de Oliveira, *In Defense of Catholic Action* (Spring Grove, Penn.: The American Society for the Defense of Tradition, Family, and Property, 2006).

234. See Carlo Falconi, *Gedda e l'Azione Cattolica* (Florence: Parenti, 1958); Marco Invernizzi, *Luigi Gedda e il movimento cattolico in Italia* (Milan: Sugarco, 2012).

235. Latreille et al., *Histoire du catholicisme*, 3:585–86.

236. See Sergio Pagano, "Dalla porpora al chiostro: L'inflessibilità di Pio XI verso il cardinale Louis Billot," in *Il papato contemporaneo (secoli xix–xx)* (Vatican: Archivio Segreto Vaticano, 2009), 395–410.

237. De Rosa, *Il movimento*, 303. "The fundamentalists wanted to honor the Syllabus of Pius IX. The proposal of Action Française to have a churchman teach the Syllabus in its schools contained an able provocation, but Pius XI not only did not want to make the Syllabus relevant again but sought to mitigate and sweeten the encyclical *Pascendi*." Gramsci, *Il Vaticano e l'Italia*, 116.

to receive a new setback. "Concerned with distancing itself from right-wing parties, the Church broke with monarchist publications close to Action Française," says Latreille.[238] As a result, during its expansion Catholic Action found no competitors on its right.

Progressives, on the contrary, saw Pius XI's move as a green light. According to historian Joseph Dusserre, the condemnation of Action Française expressed "disengagement from a policy [integralism] that still weighed heavily on the Church."[239]

3. Jacques Maritain and Emmanuel Mounier

Two French thinkers were the main promoters of Catholic Action's leftward drift: Jacques Maritain and Emmanuel Mounier.

An anarchist and atheist in his youth, Maritain converted to Catholicism in 1906 and contributed to the revival of Thomism as a philosopher, along with brilliant theologians like Fr. Réginald Garrigou-Lagrange. Under the influence of the Dominican Fr. Humbert Clerissac, he drew closer to the Catholic circles of Action Française. In the thirties, however, Maritain gradually moved away from these positions and started to defend democratic Socialism. As the philosophical mentor of Catholic Action worldwide, Maritain led generations of lay people to make the same ideological about face, of which he denounced some excesses at the end of his life in the book, *The Peasant of the Garonne* (1966). His influence was such that rumor had it that Pope Paul VI named him cardinal *in pectore*.[240] To fully understand his thought we need to briefly consider the context in which it arose and developed.

As already stated, as a natural reaction to the growing secularization of society, large sectors of public opinion had begun to look sympathetically at medieval Christian civilization, longing for its restoration. Faced with these opposite processes—the growing secularization of society and the revival of the ideal of Christendom—two currents had arisen in the Church: one faithful to tradition that wanted the restoration of Christian civilization, i.e., the conformity of society with the Church's ideal, and a liberal one that would rather conform the Church to the modern world, whose process of secularization it considered irreversible.

The dilemma became particularly acute with the foundation of Catholic Action, whose purpose was precisely to do lay apostolate in order to shape society according to the Gospel of Our Lord Jesus Christ. The historical juncture seemed particularly favorable for the project. The Crash of 1929 had shattered the optimism of the Roaring Twenties, opening the hearts of many to alternative solutions. Describing the environment in which Catholic Action was born, Plinio Corrêa de Oliveira, then president of its Archdiocesan Board in São Paulo, wrote:

> Like shipwreck victims, men try to grasp even at straws floating on the waves, attributing saving qualities to them. ...
> ... Pius XI beckoned to the world with the great remedy of Catholic Action and thus showed it [as] the only means of salvation.[241]

With which current would Catholic Action side? While Pius XI pointed the way of restoration, powerful forces pointed in the opposite direction. Jacques Maritain, especially in his book *Integral Humanism*, offered them a doctrinal justification.[242] A skilled polemicist, Maritain took as his motto a word that characterized the conservative position, *Christendom*, loading it however with a new content. When speaking of Christendom he was not referring to the Middle Ages, but to a "new Christendom."[243]

Maritain commenced from a seemingly undeniable fact: Medieval Christendom had ended for good and any attempt to restore it was utopian. Likewise, to uphold its moribund remnants was a bottomless pit of futile efforts that could otherwise be used constructively. Maritain grounded this cornerstone of his system in two *a priori* arguments one is amazed to find in a self-proclaimed Thomist philosopher. For him, "humanity, [was] borne on by this irresistible [forward] movement." How so? Because of "the radical irreversibility of historical movement." Perhaps feeling the shallowness of his reasoning, Maritain introduces yet a third *a priori* argument: "A fully lived experience [in this case, medieval Christendom] cannot be begun again."[244]

The anthropocentrism of modern times, Maritain acknowledges, was harmful. It even had some "catastrophic" consequences for Christianity[245]—but, he slyly adds, "Every great experience, even one accomplished in error, is orientated by the attraction of a certain good." He continues, "It is impossible to conceive that the sufferings and experiences of the modern world have been useless."[246] We must learn from these experiences. According to Maritain, "this world, I have said, has sought the rehabilitation of the creatures; and if it has sought it by wrong roads, still we ought to recognize and to save the truth which was there hidden."[247]

What truth is hidden in revolutionary modernity that a Catholic must recognize and save?

Maritain condemns the free market system without reservation: "Capitalism needs no longer to be brought to trial; its

---

238. Latreille et al., *Histoire du catholicisme*, 3:603.

239. Joseph Dusserre, "L'histoire de la 'main tendue' des origines à 1952," 368, quoted in Francis J. Murphy, *Communists and Catholics in France 1936–1939: The Politics of the Outstretched Hand* (Gainsville: University of Florida Press, 1989), 6.

240. See Stanislas Fumet, "Jacques Maritain," *I.C.I.*, no. 432 (May 15, 1973), 21. One of the most disquieting points about Jacques Maritain is his intimate friendship with Saul David Alinsky (1909–1972), the father of the populist left in the United States. They met in 1941 when Maritain taught at the University of Chicago. The French philosopher's influence over Alinsky was such that he called Maritain "my teacher." In a letter to the editor of *Harper's Magazine*, Maritain wrote, "I have known and loved him [Alinsky] for more than twenty years. I consider him to be one of the few really great men of our century." Jacques Maritain, "The Professional Radical: Conversations with Saul Alinsky," *Harper's Magazine* (Aug. 1965), 6. In his last book, Maritain praises Alinsky as a true revolutionary: "Among those of my contemporaries still living as I write these lines, I see in the Western world no more than three revolutionaries worthy of the name—Eduardo Frei in Chile, Saul Alinsky in America, ... and myself in France." Jacques Maritain, *The Peasant of the Garonne: An Old Layman Questions Himself About the Present Time*, trans. Michael Cuddihy and Elizabeth Hughes (New York: Holt, Rinehart and Winston, 1968), 23. The Catholic Action mentor's friendship with the American revolutionary leader is all the more disturbing if we recall that Alinsky had a penchant for the devil. For example, he dedicated his main book "To the very first radical . . . who rebelled against the establishment and did it so effectively that he at least won his own kingdom—Lucifer." Saul D. Alinsky, *Rules for Radicals: A Practical Primer for Realistic Radicals* (New York: Vintage Books, 1989), ix. In an interview with *Playboy* magazine, shortly before his death, Alinsky stated, "If there *is* an afterlife, and I have anything to say about it I *will* unreservedly *choose to go to hell*. ... Hell *would* be heaven for me." "*Playboy* Interview: Saul Alinsky—A Candid Conversation with the Feisty Radical Organizer" *Playboy* (Mar. 1972), 178. See St. Matthews Research Committee, ed. *Report on El Paso Inter-Religious Sponsoring Organization (EPISO)* (El Paso, Texas: unpublished, 1982), Addendum no. 14 (interview full transcript); Hamish Frazer, "Jacques Maritain and Saul Alinsky: Fathers of Christian Revolution," *Approaches* (Scotland), 1981, 2. See also P. David Finks, *The Radical Vision of Saul Alinsky* (New York: Paulist Press, 1984).

241. Corrêa de Oliveira, *In Defense of Catholic Action*, 21.

242. See Jacques Maritain, *Humanisme intégrale* (Paris: Aubier, 1936); *Integral Humanism: Temporal and Spiritual Problems of a New Christendom*, trans. Joseph W. Evans (New York: Charles Scribner's Sons, 1968). The title was meant as a response to Charles Maurras's "integral nationalism," which Maritain had abandoned.

243. In *A Theology of Liberation*, Fr. Gutiérrez explains that this "New Christendom" approach served as an important stepping-stone for the development of liberation theology. See Gustavo Gutiérrez, *A Theology of Liberation* (Maryknoll, N.Y.: Orbis Books, 1973), 56. Reprinted by permission of Orbis Books.

244. Maritain, *Integral Humanism*, 139–40.

245. Maritain, 242.

246. Maritain, 140.

247. Maritain, 140.

condemnation has even become a commonplace to which minds who dread platitude fear to return." Not wishing to contradict the encyclical *Quadragesimo anno*, that affirms the legitimacy of free market economics, Maritain cautiously adds that "the ideal mechanism of the capitalist economy is not essentially evil and unjust." Right afterward, he flings his poisoned dagger: "Yet, when we consider the spirit which makes concrete use of that mechanism and which determines its concrete forms and its particular realizations, it must be said that a radical disorder is hidden there."

Maritain compares this disorder to a capital sin: "The energy which stimulates and maintains this economy has been progressively spoiled by a 'capital' sin: not, certainly, by a sin which inflicts death on the souls of the individuals ... but by a sin which little by little inflicts temporal death on the social body." Capitalism, the Catholic Action mentor continues, acts like a social murderer driven by a "spirit of hatred of poverty and scorn for the poor man."[248] The logical consequence of Maritain's visceral anti-capitalism is his hatred of the bourgeoisie: "From the point of view of integral humanism, it appears that this bourgeois type of humanity is seriously endangered and that its condemnation is deserved." He therefore proposes "to change bourgeois man."[249]

Maritain's reasoning concerning Socialism is exactly the opposite. Since he could not fail to condemn Socialism without countering the popes' magisterium, he acknowledged its "errors in 'first philosophy' and in social philosophy." However, for Maritain its basic impulse is good. "Socialism in the nineteenth century was a protest of the human conscience and of its most generous instincts against evils which cried to heaven. It was a noble work to institute the trial of capitalist civilization. ... It has fought a hard and difficult battle, in which have been expended innumerable devotions, and the most moving human quality, devotion to the poor. It loved the poor."[250]

Maritain's pro-socialist lyricism extended to Soviet Communism: "'For the first time in history,' wrote Maxime Gorky recently [about Soviet Communism], 'the true love of man has been organized as a creative force and takes as its task the emancipation of millions of workers.' I believe in the profound sincerity of these words."[251]

In an environment saturated with socialist propaganda, such thinking consolidated the leftward drift in large sectors of Catholic Action. Thus, Maritain played a major role in turning Catholics into militant anti-capitalists while opening their hearts to the lure of the socialist utopia.

Maritain weaves similar considerations to justify the transshipment to an increasingly egalitarian and permissive society. He embraces the modern world born from all revolutions since the end of the Middle Ages—Humanism, Protestantism, French Revolution, Communism: "I am content to owe something to Voltaire in what concerns civil tolerance, and to Luther in what concerns non-conformism, and to honor them in this."[252] However, the Revolution errs in that it fails to offer a transcendental horizon. Maritain therefore proposed to inject into the revolutionary process a particular "spirit" to make it "vitally Christian."[253] He proposes an "integral humanism" that, far from seeking a restoration of medieval Christendom, accepts some consequences of the revolutionary process and strives to build with them a "new Christendom," no longer sacral and fundamentally Catholic but

pluralistic and democratic. In short, Maritain proposed a canny formula that permitted left-leaning Catholics to collaborate with contemporary revolutionary movements, under the pretext of "revitalizing" their Christian sense.

Emmanuel Mounier lacked Maritain's doctrinal stature. His thought—called "personalism"—is muddled and unsystematic. It is based on the idea of the person as a free and creative subject; the opposite is individualism and totalitarianism. Mounier disdained philosophical discussion and was more an activist. From 1932 to 1947 Mounier edited the magazine *Esprit*, perhaps the main mouthpiece of the Catholic left in France. It defined itself as "a magazine of the new generation, for the deepening of spiritual values and the pursuit of the secular revolutions they impose."[254]

Mounier coined the terms "committed Catholic" and "committed Christian" to indicate a Catholic engaged in temporal revolutions. For him, the solutions proposed by liberal and social Catholicism, even those offered by Christian democracy, were utterly passé. Instead of wasting time trying to find the right doctrinal formula to reconcile the Church with Liberalism or Socialism, or trying to justify social apostolate from within Catholic doctrine, Mounier maintained that a Catholic militant should take all that for granted, open his soul to the modern world, and "commit" himself unreservedly to the struggle for establishing the "civilization of the future" which, of course, meant the socialist world. "The critique of the historical organism in which we live," explained Mounier, "prompted us to adopt revolutionary positions against capitalism, formal democracy, and their related institutions."[255]

The movement created around *Esprit* magazine played a pivotal role in fostering the march of considerable segments of Catholics toward Socialism. "While Sangnier sought to reconcile Catholicism with the Republic, Emmanuel Mounier sought reconciliation between Catholicism and Socialism," comments socialist militant Jean-François Kesler.[256] Mounier himself was candid as regards his political feelings: "It [socialism] is a new political force ... that today requires the construction of an authentic socialist regime. ... We place our hopes and desires in it [socialism]."[257] *Esprit*'s positions were so close to those of the socialists that during one of its conventions in 1947 a speaker asked, "In short, what separates us from the Socialist Party?"[258]

Kesler recounts, "[*Esprit*] was an important element within the current that gave birth to the PSU [Parti Socialiste Unifié]. It exerted a determinant influence on the left-wing Catholics who participated in the foundation of the PSU."[259] Speaking about the leftward drift of French Catholic Action, Georges Suffert writes,

> The change of mentality occurred throughout this bubbling process. ...
> ... Without the obstinacy of a man like Mounier, the movement would never have found its guiding ideas, justifications, and hope.[260]

4. Social Apostolate

The new spirit that animated large sectors of Catholic Action gave rise to the so-called social apostolate inspired by the slogan,

---

248. Maritain, 114–15.
249. Maritain, 92–93.
250. Maritain, 88–89.
251. Maritain, 89.
252. Maritain, 92.
253. Maritain, 139.

254. Kesler, *De la gauche dissidente*, 47.
255. Emmanuel Mounier, *Qu'est-ce que le personalisme?* (Paris: Éditions du Seuil, 1946), 16.
256. Kesler, *De la gauche dissidente*, 48.
257. Emmanuel Mounier, "Devant Nous," *Esprit* 16, no. 140 (Dec. 1947): 941–42.
258. Kesler, 51.
259. Kesler, 46–47.
260. Georges Suffert, *Les catholiques et la gauche* (Paris: F. Maspero, 1960), 121. See also John H. Hellman, *Emmanuel Mounier and the New Catholic Left, 1930–1950* (Toronto: University of Toronto Press, 1981).

"Take Christ to the world." It started from the premise that, despite some drawbacks, the modern world was basically good and advancing toward better times, and that, instead of opposing it, the Church would do well to embrace it. "An economic regime, an entire civilization is collapsing before our eyes," exclaimed Most Rev. Henri Alexandre Chappoulie, bishop of Angers, during a French Catholic Action conference. "As children of the Church we have a duty to stand firm in the face of these transformations that are changing the face of the world. We must not succumb to fear or anger but try to understand and love these changes."[261]

The buzzword was for Catholic Action activists to become *incarnate* in the modern world as Our Lord had become incarnate in our human nature. They should seek to incarnate particularly into environments where the modern spirit blew more strongly: avant-garde artistic schools, fashionable youth hangouts, progressive political parties, and the trade union and proletarian worlds. Having abandoned the prudential norms regulating the conduct of lay association members, Catholic Action activists began to frequent ambiences which until then were considered off-limits for practicing Catholics. In order to blend in with those environments, they also began to change their attitude by adapting to fashions in clothing, language, tastes, and habits.

Plinio Corrêa de Oliveira writes, "A spirit of unlimited concessions in face of the outbreak of new fashions and customs began to take shape. This attitude further disguised itself in the cloak of a serious obligation to do apostolate in ambiences proscribed by moral theology for any Catholic unwilling to fall from the supernatural dignity granted him at Baptism."[262]

This huge revolution in the field of tendencies caused another in that of ideas. Feverish exposure to the modern world by large sectors of Catholic Action made them fertile ground for all sorts of dangerously innovative theories and practices. Rashly immersed in the world of the left, many militants of Catholic Action gradually abandoned their beliefs and adopted a Marxist mindset focused on class struggle.

This dynamic stood out particularly in workers' movements. Seeking to incarnate into the proletarian world, many Catholic Action militants began to participate in union activism along with the communist and socialist left. The left welcomed its new allies and began its policy of the outstretched hand toward Catholics.

This policy was also applied in Italy. "The Communist Party paid particular attention to Catholics," Massimiliano Tenconi wrote.[263] In April 1931, at the fourth conference of the Communist Party, a speaker stated the need to not disregard a maneuver to infiltrate the Catholic Church in order to take advantage of the only non-fascist organization left in Italy. Since the Communist Party had been forced to go underground, militants were recommended to contact and even to join Catholic Action to remain active. Historian De Antonellis writes, "This happened especially in academia through F.U.C.I."[264] The Communist Party reiterated this policy of infiltration in August 1944 in its "Declaration on Relations between communists and Catholics."

Unsurprisingly, F.U.C.I. thus became one of the major forces of opposition to Fascism from a leftist perspective, even establishing direct contacts with the Soviet Union. German historian Reinhard Raffalt claims that a senior F.U.C.I. executive confided to Palmiro Togliatti (1893–1964), Secretary General of the Communist

Party, that "the anti-communism of the Church should not be considered eternal, and it would be appropriate to inform the Soviet government about the existence within the Church of a current ready for dialogue."[265]

Leftist infiltration in Italian Catholic Action showed its malice in 1952 on the occasion of the so-called Sturzo operation. With the blessing of Pius XII, Luigi Gedda, then president of the Central Council of Catholic Action, sought to present Father Sturzo (who had adopted more moderate positions) as a candidate to local elections in Rome with the support of the National Monarchist Party, the Italian Social Movement, and the Christian-Democratic center-right. This was intended not only to defeat the candidate of the People's Block but also to isolate the left wing of the Christian Democrats, which had become a thorn in the side of Pius XII, with whom, according to Giulio Andreotti, it was "in sharp contrast."[266]

From the beginning, however, Gedda met the opposition of large sectors of Catholic Action: "To my surprise I found that some did not adhere to the directives I had received [from Pius XII], nor did they share the goals; Carretto (GIAC—Gioventù Italiana di Azione Cattolica), Badaloni (Italian Association of Catholic teachers), Miceli (Gioventù Femminile—Feminine Youth) and Carmela Rossi (Catholic Women), neither did FUCI and Catholic Graduates. This was because the Sturzo operation involved the right-wing electorate."

The operation did not go ahead. Gedda says, "While [Carlo] Carretto had refused to adhere, prompted by people of the Christian Democratic left, [Mario] Rossi (GIAC) was inspired by the so-called liberation theology."

Gedda concludes, citing Armando Zerbinato: "The presidency of GIAC had become a den of rebels, a reason for scandal for young Catholics, and more or less consciously, a tool of the communists." It is no wonder, therefore, that Pius XII lamented to Gedda, "Catholic Action, for which so many sacrifices have been made, is no longer ours!"[267]

5. A New Conception of Religion and the Church

In the wake of this social apostolate, a new conception of religious practice began to make its way in many Catholic Action circles. Traditional pious practices such as devotion to Our Lady and the saints, spiritual exercises, the Rosary, the Stations of the Cross, and so forth were despised as individualistic and, therefore, obsolete. Those more committed to sociopolitical activities replaced traditional religious practices with forms of social apostolate, presented as the new frontier of Christian existence. Thus began a slippery confusion between the spiritual and temporal spheres, between religious practice and sociopolitical activism, between the life of grace and revolutionary commitment. LT took that confusion to a paroxysm.

A new vision of the Church also began to make its way. The same egalitarian hatred that fueled class struggle in the temporal sphere to create a proletarian society inspired a class struggle

---

261. Homily at Reims (Oct. 5, 1952), *La Documentation Catholique*, no. 1173 (May 16, 1954), 623.

262. Corrêa de Oliveira, *In Defense of Catholic Action*, 23.

263. Massimiliano Tenconi, "I cattolici nella resistenza contro l'anticristo nazifascista."

264. De Antonellis, *Storia dell'Azione Cattolica*, 162. See also Francesco Luigi Ferrari, *L'Azione Cattolica e il "regime"* (Florence: Parenti, 1952).

265. Luigi Brazzoli, *Papa Paolo VI: Tormento e grandezza di un'anima* (Milan: C.O.G.E.D., 1978), 55. See also Gabriella Fanello, *Storia della FUCI* (Rome: Editrice Studium, 1971); F.U.C.I., *Coscienza universitaria, fatica del pensare, intelligenza della fede* (Milan: San Paolo, 1996).

266. Giulio Andreotti, *Intervista su De Gasperi*, ed. Antonio Gambino (Bari: Laterza, 1977), 103.

267. Luigi Gedda, *18 aprile 1948: Memorie dell'artefice della sconfitta del Fronte Popolare* (Milan: Mondadori, 1998), 155, 153–54. See Paolo Trionfini, *Carlo Carretto: Il cammino di un innamorato di Dio* (Rome: AVE, 2010). On the Italian Catholic Action, see Ernesto Preziosi, *Obbedienti in piedi: La vicenda dell'Azione Cattolica in Italia* (Turin: S.E.I., 1997); Giovanbattista Guzzetti, *Il movimento cattolico italiano dall'unità ad oggi* (Naples: Edizioni Dehoniane, 1980); Liliana Ferrari, *L'Azione Cattolica in Italia dalle origini al pontificato di Paolo VI* (Brescia: Editrice Queriniana, 1982); Tommaso Turi, *L'Azione Cattolica nella chiesa postconciliare* (Bari: La Scala, 1982).

inside the Church to build a new people's church opposed to the hierarchical one, which was seen as an ally of the bourgeois world. This was another point that LT took to a paroxysm.

6. Liturgism

Among those with a prevailing interest in spiritual things, traditional pious practices were replaced with the participation of the laity in the Church's liturgy. They spoke of an "irruption of laity in the active participation of the life of the Church."[268] They even claimed that the graces of Catholic Action came exclusively through participation in the liturgy. "The liturgy … is the soul of their social movement, as it must be the soul of all Catholic Action," claimed Fr. John Fitzsimmons and Paul McGuire in the *Guide to Catholic Action*, a manual intended to present the movement to the public at large.[269]

Thus was born *liturgism* or the liturgical movement, not to be confused with the liturgical restoration that the Benedictine abbot Dom Prosper Guéranger started in France in the mid-nineteenth century.[270] In order to avoid any confusion with the authentic liturgical movement, we call liturgism the one that emerged within Catholic Action and became known as such in various countries.

With liturgism, neo-modernist errors updated by more radical currents of the Nouvelle Théologie also crept into Catholic Action. We will cover them in depth in the next chapter. Dominican theologian Father Chenu, a leading figure of the Nouvelle Théologie and mentor of Catholic Action, discloses, "The new Catholic Action born in the 1920s and 1930s overhauled the [traditional theological] method, and we were intimately linked with that revolution."[271]

Liturgists advocated a new ecclesiology of an egalitarian and democratic nature. They manipulated the concept of priesthood (the whole Church is a "priestly people") tending almost to erase the substantial distinction between the sacramental priesthood of the clergy and the common priesthood of the laity. By exploiting the notion of *participation* contained in Catholic Action's definition, the liturgists favored the increasing participation of laymen in liturgical acts and their assumption of functions reserved until then to the ordained clergy. According to American Catholic Action chaplain Msgr. Joseph Merrison, "The Liturgical Revival effects a deeper and more active participation by the laity in the Liturgy or public worship of the Spouse of Christ: in the Sacrifice of the Mass, in the Sacraments of Redemption, in the Divine Office, and in the sacramentals."[272]

In its proper sense and within limits, such participation is possible and even necessary, as Pius XII teaches in his encyclical *Mediator Dei* (1947). However, the liturgists presented it as substantially equal to that of the clergy, thus confusing the two priesthoods. The substantial distinction between laity and clergy was thus slowly obliterated in people's minds. Perhaps nowhere was this outcome clearer than in the liturgists' encroaching participation in the Mass. Insinuating the sense of this participation, Theodore Maynard wrote in 1941, "We, like the priest on the altar, have a true priesthood by virtue of our membership in the Mystical Body obtained at baptism, and … we can and should offer Mass with the priest."[273] A document issued by the French Catholic Action in 1932 reads, "As a result of very profound [theological] works, we have re-centered the Mass … on the community of officiants (priest and people together)."[274]

Celebrations of the Catholic Mass *versus populum* or with the faithful around the altar began in the 1930s in Catholic Action circles. "The celebration of the Mass facing the people was an essential component of contemporary liturgical revival," one reads in the above-quoted French document.[275] It is also in Catholic Action circles that they began to introduce the guitar, tambourines, and other profane instruments in the liturgy, and that priests began to shed liturgical vestments. This was happening thirty years before the Council. According to Henri Fesquet, these and other practices in Catholic Action "questioned the very nature of the priesthood. … [It] posed the problem of the role of the laity in the Church. … This is a new stage in the internal evolution of the Church."[276]

The so-called irruption of laity in the Church was facilitated by the decrease in the number of priests, already seen in the first post-war period. Catholic Action mentors saw it as a providential sign, as if God was pushing the laity to occupy the spaces left empty. The twentieth century, they said, would be that of the laity, and Catholic Action was the instrument of Providence. As such, it would be commendable and even a duty for a layman to try and help the overburdened clergy while fully respecting the hierarchical constitution of the Church. That was not, however, the spirit that animated large sectors of Catholic Action. Their eagerness to assume roles until then reserved to the clergy was fueled by a desire to subvert the organic constitution of the Church. Thus began to take shape an entirely new theology of the laity, with an egalitarian and democratic flavor. If lay people could participate in the apostolate of the Church, why could they not participate also in her liturgy? Why not in her government? So they began to tread a path toward what André Latreille defines as a "communitarian religion."[277]

7. The Catholic Action Cells

The ecclesiology underlying liturgism assumed a new model of Church. More radical Catholic Action activists shunned the parish, considered an anachronism proper to a juridical and hierarchical concept of the Church. Instead, they organized in small cells in which they spent most of their religious life. Inspired by this ecclesiology, many parishes were divided into cells. The idea was to transfer to them a considerable part of parish life. On the pretext of "bringing the Church to the people," many priests began to celebrate Mass, administer the sacraments, and hold pastoral

268. Erwin Iserloh, *Il movimento liturgico* in HKG (Milan, 1980), It. Tra. 10 no. 1, 237, quoted in Roberto de Mattei, *The Crusader of the 20th Century: Plinio Corrêa de Oliveira* (Leominster, Herefordshire, U.K.: Gracewing Publishers, 1998), 74.

269. John Fitzsimons and Paul McGuire, ed., *Restoring all Things: A Guide to Catholic Action* (New York: Sheed & Ward, 1938), 75.

270. In the mid-nineteenth century, the Benedictine abbey of Solesmes, France, refounded by Dom Prosper Guéranger (1805–1875) began a restoration of the monastic movement and the traditional Roman liturgy after the devastation caused by the French Revolution, Protestantism, Jansenism, and Gallicanism. This liturgical movement led, among other things, to the restoration of the Roman liturgy and Gregorian chant. Dom Guéranger's cause of beatification was initiated in 2005. See Dom Paul Delatte, *Dom Guéranger: Abbé de Solesmes* (Paris: Plon-Nourrit, 1909).

271. Jacques Duquesne, *Un théologien en liberté: Jacques Duquesne interroge le père Chenu* (Paris: Le Centurion, 1975), 58–59. See pages 88–89 for an explanation on the relationship between Catholic Action and *Nouvelle Théologie*. Fr. Chenu himself wrote the preface to the above-mentioned *Guide to Catholic Action*.

272. Joseph P. Morrison, "The Liturgical Revival and the Family," in Family Life Bureau, ed., *Family Catholic Action* (Washington, D.C: National Catholic Welfare Conference, n.d.), 14.

273. Theodore Maynard, *The Story of American Catholicism* (New York: The Macmillan Company, 1941), 604. In chapter 4 we shall return to this idea of baptismal priesthood.

274. Dansette, *Destin du catholicisme français*, 328.

275. Dansette, 328. In Brazil, the first dialogued and *versus populum* Mass was celebrated on July 11, 1933 by Dom Martin Michler for youths of Catholic University Action. See José Arivaldo da Silva, *O movimento liturgico no Brasil* (Petrópolis: Editora Vozes, 1983), 41–42.

276. Henri Fesquet, "La crise de l'A.C.J.F. repose le problème du rôle des laïcs dans l'église," *Le Monde*, Nov. 27, 1956, in *La Documentation Catholique*, no. 1237 (Oct. 28, 1956), 1398–99.

277. Latreille et al., *Histoire du catholicisme*, 3:600.

meetings in private homes. This situation naturally tended to dilute and disintegrate parish structures.

Inside these groups, partly shielded from the vigilance of the ecclesiastical authorities, Catholic Action priests and militants felt free to create their own spirituality and liturgy adapted to their peculiar conception of Church and religion. Supposedly recovering long-lost elements of the primitive, early Church, Masses were said in living rooms over bare tables, the celebrant clad in a turtle neck and drill slacks, the participants sprawled on the floor. Driven by the desire to make people participate in the Mass, canonical formulas were cast aside and the very texts of the Mass freely improvised according to the participants' whims. These Masses would frequently be followed by a "fraternal meal" conceived as a sort of prolongation of the Mass. The faithful were thus accustomed to a free-wheeling community life often filled with antipathy for the hierarchical Church. In the words of André Latreille, they "molded a new type of Christian, for whom communitarian life is like a second nature."[278]

Catholic Action cells are the direct ancestor of the Basic Christian Communities (B.C.C.s) advocated by liberation theologians. American liberation theologian Phillip Berryman writes, "Catholic antecedents included ... the 'cell' approach to Catholic Action which formed small groups of 'apostles' in milieux of workers, students and families."[279] Analyzing LT's ecclesiology during the world conference of liberation theologians held in Brazil in 2012, Sérgio Coutinho explains, "The B.C.C.s also result from other important ecclesial experiences. We cannot ignore all the work done on our continent by Specialized Catholic Action—ACE. ... With its pastoral method—to see, judge, act—and with great participation by the laity, Catholic Action brought the fundamental elements for the future systematization of liberation theology."[280]

As the direct ancestors of the B.C.C.s, Catholic Action cells also broke ground in another way: They were the first to systematically apply the so-called awareness-raising or conscientization method LT later applied. This method consists of employing techniques derived from group psychology designed to subtly change people's temperament and mentality, triggering a process of ideological transshipment to the left in order to turn them into militant revolutionaries. Some have compared it to a real brainwashing.[281]

The method, initially promoted by Canon Joseph Cardijn and applied in the cells of the Belgian J.O.C., followed the lines of the classic scheme, "see, judge, act." Activists had to observe a situation, analyze it according to particular criteria, and then develop a policy to address it. Since many of those cells were led by people with a neo-modernist and Christian democratic tendency, it is not surprising for them to see through the distorting lens of such ideologies. As a result, their judgment and action also followed on the same tracks.[282]

8. American Catholic Action: A Rather Secretive Plot

a. The Chicago Experience

The way in which Catholic Action penetrated the United States offers some elucidating insights into the movement. Chicago served as a test site for the ideas and methods of Catholic Action in the United States; it then remained the virtual powerhouse of the movement during the ensuing decades. This development was particularly favored by the succession of three liberal archbishops: Cardinals George Mundelein, Albert Meyer, and Samuel Stritch, aided by no less liberal auxiliary bishops such as Bishop Bernard Sheil, a brassy partisan of left-wing organized labor and founder of the Catholic Youth Organization (C.Y.O.).

Well-known liberal priest and novelist Fr. Andrew Greeley offers an interesting insider account of the experiments made by the Chicago Catholic Action, which he sees as foreshadowing the Second Vatican Council. "In the late 1930s," he comments, "there began in the archdiocese of Chicago a series of experiments that would anticipate in many respects the spirit and teachings of the Vatican Council. These experiments in lay action, social action, catechetics, liturgy, and marriage education would be imitated all over the United States, and the men who began them would become national figures and the heroes of many of the progressive Catholics of the country."[283]

So as not to shock the generally conservative Catholic laity, these experiments—which actually introduced into the United States the social and liturgical errors that infected many sectors of Catholic Action worldwide—had to be done in a circuitous and partially covert way. Nurtured by clergy who were influenced by either social apostolate or liturgism, and at times both, small clusters of Catholic militants began to form. The process itself was crafty. In order not to give the impression of being an articulated movement, these small groups seldom adopted a name, they rarely met each other, and each one restricted its proselytism to a specific constituency: high school students, college undergraduates, businessmen, married couples, workers, and so on. They initially adopted what Father

278. Latreille, 3:601.

279. Phillip Berryman, "Latin America: 'Iglesia que nace del pueblo,'" *Christianity and Crisis* 41, no. 14 (Sept. 21, 1981), 238.

280. Graziela Wolfart, Luis Carlos Dalla Rosa, and Márcia Junges, "O crescimento de correntes teológicas e eclesiológicas" (interview with Sérgio Coutinho), *IHU online* 12, no. 404 (Oct. 2012), 27.

281. In the sense used by liberation theologians, the term *conscientization* was coined by Marxist thinkers linked to the Instituto Superior de Estudos Brasileiros and spread by Most Rev. Helder Câmara, Brazil's "red archbishop." See Instituto Ecumenico al Servicio del Desarrollo de los Pueblos, *El mensaje de Paulo Freire: Teoría y práctica de liberación* (Madrid: Editorial Marsiego, 1973), 15. The method, then called "pedagogy of the oppressed," was developed in the fifties by the Marxist educator Paulo Freire (1921–1997), a mentor of the Brazilian Catholic Action and an intellectual who borrowed from Maritain and Mounier. See Paulo Freire, *Pedagogy of the Oppressed*, trans. Myra Bergman Ramos (New York: Continuum, 1982; Paulo Freire, *L'educazione come pratica della libertà* (Milan: Mondadori, 1974); Paulo Freire, *Pedagogia dell'autonomia: saperi necessari per la pratica educativa* (Turin: E.G.A., 2004); Paulo Freire, *Teoria e pratica della liberazione: Testi scelti* (Rome: AVE, 1974). See also Giulio Girardi, *Educare: per quale società?* (Udine: Forum, 2008). Understood as a literacy method to educate the most disadvantaged classes, the pedagogy of the oppressed was intended not only to educate but also to "liberate" the poor from alleged "cultural oppression," inculcating in them a rejection of the established order. "Conscientization" thus appeared as a "pedagogy for revolution" aimed at transforming peaceful citizens into revolutionary activists. As such, it was assumed by LT and employed as a leading pastoral method within the Basic Christian Communities. See Carlos Rodrigues Brandão, *O que é o método Paulo Freire* (São Paulo: Editora Braziliense, 1981); Armando Bandera, *Paulo*

Freire: Un pedagogo (Caracas: Universidad Católica Andrés Bello, 1981). LT's founder, Fr. Gutiérrez, recognizes Freire's contribution to the development of LT: "One of the most creative and fruitful efforts which has been implemented in Latin America is the experimental work of Paulo Freire, who has sought to establish a 'pedagogy of the oppressed.'" Gutiérrez, *A Theology of Liberation*, 91.

282. Discussing the process of conscientization, liberation theologians Joe Holland and Fr. Peter Henriot, S.J., comment, "Our discussion of [conscientization] will be recognized by many who are familiar with the 'see/judge/act' trilogy of Canon Joseph Cardijn, the Belgian priest who, prior to World War II, inspired Catholic social action groups such as the Young Christian Workers, Young Christian Students, and, indirectly, the Christian Family Movement. When Cardijn urged social activists to 'see,' he called upon them to do more than simply *look* at the facts and figures of a particular situation. Beyond these facts and figures lies a framework that provides meaning, a perspective that makes sense of disparate elements." Joe Holland and Peter Henriot, S.J., *Social Analysis: Linking Faith and Justice* (Washington, D.C. and Maryknoll, N.Y.: Center of Concern/Orbis Books, 1983), 10.

283. Greeley, *The Catholic Experience*, 247. Even though he is better known as a novelist of dubious taste, Fr. Greeley's testimony is noteworthy. As a Chicago Catholic Action insider, he narrates facts that directly involved himself or close personal friends. Introducing the chapter on "The Chicago Experience," he writes, "It is difficult to write contemporary history. It is even more difficult to do so when one is writing about one's friends." Greeley, 247. For an account on Cardinal Mundelein's tenure see Edward R. Kantowicz, *Corporation Sole: Cardinal Mundelein and Chicago Catholicism* (Notre Dame: University of Notre Dame Press, 1983), particularly the chapter on "Varieties of Catholic Action," at pages 189–202.

Greeley calls a "somewhat secretive" approach: "Catholic action groups, at first somewhat secretive in their approach, began to appear in Catholic high schools and colleges as well as among Catholic businessmen, the businessmen's wives, and also young working people. The young clergy ... became deeply involved as moderators for these groups."[284]

This young clergy, of course, was usually that infected with the new liberal ideas streaming from Europe. In these groups, under the cloak of deepening their Catholic faith and commitment, the participants went through a gradual process of consciousness raising that mollified their traditional Catholic upbringing and opened them to the new winds blowing from the progressive quarters.

As the membership of these somewhat secretive groups swelled and their level of conscientization deepened, they began to adopt a variety of names, some inspired by Catholic Action denominations, others referring to a vague renewal or other similar buzzwords. Presenting themselves as the dynamic wave of the future, these groups tended to supersede the more traditional lay movements—which they qualified as anachronistic and without a future—thus facilitating the introduction of the germs of neo-modernism and Christian democracy into the capillaries of American Catholic laity. Traditional organizations that initially resisted were later infiltrated and changed from within.

In the early stages, few participants in those small groups were aware that they were actually part of a worldwide movement, a fact that was, of course, clear to the mentors from the beginning. When a particular commitment level was reached by members, the group began to come out of the closet and was steered by its moderators into the folds of the international Catholic Action movement. Old makeshift names were dropped, and the official Catholic Action denominations in use throughout the world were adopted. In his insider account, Father Greeley describes this development:

> Eventually, as they [the members of these groups] began to attend national meetings, they became aware of influences beyond the United States. The international meeting of the Young Christian Workers at Montreal in 1947 was a turning point in many ways for the younger Catholic Action organizations who now began to drop their own names and assume translations of the European names such as Young Christian Workers (YCW) and Young Christian Students (YCS). The English Catholic action leaders ... spent lengthy periods of time in Chicago and provided the links in the communication network by which the Chicago movements were plugged in to what was going on in the rest of the world.[285]

b. The Alinsky-Progressive Symbiosis

Within this milieu of early Chicago Catholic Action and against this historical-doctrinal background, a development began that has had momentous consequences in the history of the Catholic left in the United States. We are referring to the symbiosis between the radical movement fathered by late socialist organizer Saul Alinsky and the progressive Catholic current that eventually resulted in liberation theology.

A former Communist Party supporter and C.I.O. (Congress of Industrial Organizations) labor agitator, Saul David Alinsky (1909–1972) began to dedicate himself in the late 1930s to community organizing in his native Chicago. His blueprint was ambitious, entailing the creation of thousands of "people's organizations" across the country. Under the motto of "power to the people," these grassroots outfits, composed of duly educated (i.e., politically aware) neighborhood residents, would gradually take the political power away from the prevailing structures of democratic representation. After effecting profound changes at neighborhood and city levels, the people's organizations—according to the blueprint—would then unite in statewide coalitions and eventually coalesce into a broad national revolutionary movement. The final goal was to establish what Alinsky defined as a people's democracy, whose inspiration would be self-managing socialism.[286]

To carry out his plans for revolution in the U.S., Alinsky founded the Industrial Areas Foundation (I.A.F.) in 1940, and the I.A.F. Training Institute (today the I.A.F. Alinsky Institute) in 1969. The latter was to serve, in his own words, as a "school for professional radicals." Originally based in Chicago, they both operate now in New York. The I.A.F. oversees a web of people's organizations that spans several states. It also coordinates a small battalion of organizers, many of whom are priests and nuns. The web is known as the I.A.F. Network.

The influence of the principles and strategies developed by Saul Alinsky extends far beyond the I.A.F. Network. They have been, in one way or another, adopted by most of the so-called populist left in the U.S. Populist militant Heather Booth, director of the Chicago-based Midwest Academy, called Alinsky "the Sigmund Freud of modern community organizing."[287] Alinsky's mark on the populist left can be seen well in the designation that *Time* magazine lavishly bestowed on him in 1970: "Prophet of Power to the People." The magazine further commented that "American democracy is being altered by Alinsky's ideas."[288]

Alinsky's influence is also strong inside the Democratic Party's left. Suffice it to recall that former President Barack Obama is an I.A.F.–trained community organizer, and former presidential candidate Hillary Clinton made her doctoral thesis on the Chicago agitator, whom she met twice. Many also point out the coincidences between Bernie Sanders's socialism and that of Saul Alinsky.[289]

Since his earliest forays in social agitation, Alinsky perceived that without the support of the Catholic left his plans would not get much beyond paper. "I recognized," he says, "that if I could win the support of the Church, we'd be off and running. Conversely, without the Church, or at least some elements of it, it was unlikely that we'd be able to make much of a dent."[290] Unfortunately, such disconcerting support never failed him, and it came mostly from Catholic Action milieus. Alinsky initially enlisted the sponsorship of Bishop Bernard Sheil and Cardinal Mundelein, both Catholic Action enthusiasts. This was the beginning of the intimate collaboration between the Chicago archdiocese and the self-styled

284. Greeley, *The Catholic Experience*, 251.

285. Greeley, 252–53.

286. Saul D. Alinsky's ideas are contained in his two books *Reveille for Radicals* (New York: Random House, 1969) and *Rules for Radicals*. Further insights are given in Marion K. Sanders, *The Professional Radical: Conversations with Saul Alinsky* (New York: Harper & Row, 1970). A short yet penetrating study of Alinsky's doctrines is William Lester, S.J., *Basic Principles of Saul Alinsky* (San Jose, Calif.: St. Dismas Publishers, 1970). A comprehensive but flatteringly rosy biography of Alinsky is Finks, *The Radical Vision*.

287. Robert Fisher, *Let the People Decide: Neighborhood Organizing in America* (Boston: Twayne Publishers, 1984), 129. This book also contains interesting insights into Alinsky's doctrines and strategies, as well as on the so-called populist left as a whole. See also Harry C. Boyte, *The Backyard Revolution: Understanding the New Citizen Movement* (Philadelphia: Temple University Press, 1981).

288. "Radical Saul Alinsky: Prophet of Power to the People," *Time*, Mar. 2, 1970, 56–57.

289. See, for example, Theo Anderson, "What Is Actually Radical About Bernie Sanders' Democratic Socialism Isn't the Socialism," *In These Times* 39, no. 12 (Dec. 2015).

290. Alinsky, "Playboy Interview with Saul Alinsky," 72.

professional radical, a type of collaboration that gradually spilled over to liberal Catholic sectors in the rest of the country. Later, Alinsky was hired by Cardinal Stritch to train the archdiocesan clergy in the principles and tactics of community organizing. Alinsky found an eager audience in priests and seminarians dedicated to social apostolate.

Over the years, this collaboration grew into a full-fledged symbiosis and became so encompassing that the Catholic left eventually turned into the very backbone of Alinskyism, as liberal priest and I.A.F. organizer Fr. David Finks acknowledges.[291] One of many examples is the long association between Alinsky and Fr. John O'Grady, a pivotal figure of social Catholicism in the United States. He was executive secretary of the National Conference of Catholic Charities, a Church body set up in 1910 and co-opted since its inception by the social Catholics. He was also secretary of the Committee on Special War Activities, a Church body created in 1918 to draft and implement programs for social reconstruction in the aftermath of World War I. It was Father O'Grady who called upon Father Ryan to write the bishops' *Program for Social Reconstruction* mentioned earlier. Msgr. O'Grady became a domestic prelate in 1935 and secured Church sponsorship and financial support for many I.A.F. projects in the forties and fifties. His goal was, in the words of Father Finks, to "reorganize Catholic Charities and make it part of the network of people's organizations across the country."[292]

Today, the I.A.F. Network is intertwined with the liberation theology–inspired Basic Christian Communities movement, particularly in the Southwest, where, in many cases, they are virtually indistinguishable. Moreover, Alinsky's organizational tactics have become commonplace today among leftist Catholics dedicated to social activism, many of whom, indeed, have been trained by the Alinsky Institute.[293]

c. The Catholic Worker Movement

For its importance and its manifestation of the more radical tendencies of social apostolate, the Catholic Worker Movement of the United States bears discussion. Founded in 1933 by Dorothy Day (1897–1980), it remains active even today, although it maintains a considerably lower profile.[294] The movement arose from the same ideological background as Catholic Action, and worked in close association with a number of its organizations, although it placed itself farther to the left.

Miss Day began her revolutionary career during World War I as a communist activist, feminist militant, and labor organizer. After a series of tumultuous liaisons with communist militants (one of which resulted in an abortion in 1919), a stint as a prostitute in New Orleans, and the birth of a daughter fathered out of wedlock by an anarchist, Miss Day proclaimed herself a convert to Catholicism in 1927. She publicly abandoned her atheism

and agnosticism, although not her radical social commitment, which, if anything, grew stronger. Indeed, she never recanted the profound influence of her communist-anarchist past. "The bottle always smells of the liquor it once held," she used to say.[295] The only significant change was that from then on she would pursue her revolutionary commitment on different grounds, namely, an extreme-left social Catholicism. The move also permitted her to address a larger constituency, thus giving her an appeal she would never have had as an overt communist.

In 1932, she met Frenchman Peter Maurin, a former member of the Sillon, who introduced her to the European strain of Christian democracy, a doctrinal influence that would remain with her for the rest of her life. Maurin coaxed Day into founding the Catholic Worker movement, which quickly became a fixture in the scene of American religious radicalism. The first issue of *The Catholic Worker*, the movement's newspaper, was sold May 1, 1933, at a Communist Party rally.

The socially troubled ambiance of the 1930s provided a field day for socialist initiatives. Adopting a radical interpretation of Catholic social doctrine, Catholic Worker militants became involved in leftist labor movements, not disdaining the partnership of communist front organizations, nor even that of the Communist Party itself. They were conspicuously associated with the C.I.O., then a communist-riddled union.[296]

In 1962, Dorothy Day travelled to Cuba and devoted several of her monthly columns in *The Catholic Worker* to singing paeans to Fidel Castro and his bloody revolution. In 1968, she became enthusiastic about the revolutionary example of Fr. Camilo Torres, a Colombian priest-guerrilla who died in 1966 while ambushing an Army patrol. Day wrote a lavishly panegyrical preface for the English edition of Father Torres's works.[297] In it we read:

> Camilo Torres joined the guerrillas, their life in mountain and jungle, joined their pilgrimage to the people, the campesinos. He broke bread with them, and so truly became the *companero* [comrade], the one who breaks bread, the companion. ...
>
> Suppose a priest like Father Torres looked at his companions sitting around a fire by night, hunted men, but men bringing a gospel of hope to the poor, men who were workers themselves, unlearned men like the twelve apostles. ...
>
> ... Father Camilo Torres, pray for us, that we may have your courage in offering our lives for our brothers.[298]

The esteem in which Dorothy Day is held by the American Catholic left can hardly be overstated. We only need to remember that in 1972 this guerrilla sympathizer was named recipient of the Laetare Medal, the University of Notre Dame's highest award. A cardinal and several bishops were present at the reception ceremony to pay homage to Miss Day. On the other hand, some of the most notorious leftist Catholics in the United States consider

291. P. David Finks was Vicar of Urban Ministry in the diocese of Rochester, N.Y. under Bishop Fulton Sheen but abandoned the priesthood in 1973. He writes:

> [In the fifties] Saul ... saw the churches ... as the backbone of his community organizations. ...
> ... [In the early sixties] the neighborhood parish priests continued to be the backbone of IAF's organizing efforts. ...
> ... In the 1970s, the IAF organizers depended upon local churches as the backbone of the local [people's] organizations. (Finks, *The Radical Vision*, 76, 166, 273)

292. Finks, 76.

293. See for example Gregory F. Pierce, *Activism That Makes Sense: Congregations and Community Organizing* (New York: Paulist Press, 1984).

294. See Rick Hampson, "Day's Followers Seen Losing Vision," *The Washington Times*, May 13, 1988. For a history of the Catholic Worker movement, see Piehl, *Breaking Bread*; Nancy L. Roberts, *Dorothy Day and the Catholic Worker* (Albany, N.Y.: State University of New York Press, 1987).

295. Stephen J. Krupa, "An Introduction to Dorothy Day," *America Magazine*, Aug. 27, 2001.

296. In the thirties, the C.I.O. served as a political playpen not only of the Communist Party but also of the "Catholic left," for which the A.F.L. was too moderate. The C.I.O. could even boast the support of bishops. The most conspicuous was Bishop Bernard Sheil, who more than once sat beside C.I.O. boss John Lewis at labor rallies, and encouraged Catholic participation in the union.

297. See Marc H. Ellis, "Liberation Theology and the Crisis of the Western Society," in *Liberation Theology: The Challenge to U.S. Public Policy,* ed. Richard L. Rubenstein and John K. Roth (Washington, D.C.: The Washington Institute Press, 1988), 58ff.

298. Dorothy Day, preface to *Camilo Torres: Priest and Revolutionary; Political Programme and Messages to the Colombian People,* ed. John Alvarez Garcia and Christian Restrepo Calle, trans. Virginia M. O'Grady (London: Sheed and Ward, 1968), 21, 36.

themselves Day's spiritual children. When she died in 1980, the half-page obituary published by *The New York Times* evidenced the significance liberals attribute to her work. Written by former Communist Party member Alden Whitman, it stated, among other things, "Dorothy Day played a seminal role in developing the social and economic thinking of a generation of American priests and laymen."[299]

d. The Civil Rights Movement and the Delano Grape Strike

This overview of the religious-inspired, left-wing social activism that led to liberation theology would not be complete—from a U.S. perspective—without at least a cursory reference to the civil rights movement of the 1950s and 1960s, and also to the 1965–1970 Delano, California grape strike, sparked by labor organizer Cesar Chavez and the United Farm Workers of America (U.F.W.A., later U.F.W. A.F.L.-C.I.O.). We shall not attempt here to give a historical analysis of both developments, nor shall we discuss their eventual merits or faults. Rather, we are interested in the role they played in the history of liberation theology in the United States.

Both movements afforded the religious left—Catholic as well as Protestant—with an opportunity to make common cause with the political left. Along with the overt involvement of radicals and even communists, both movements counted on the brazen participation of priests, nuns, and ministers in the frontlines, and upon the clear and sometimes enthusiastic support of Church bodies. Both movements drew the best part of their mystique from a religious inspiration and used religious rhetoric and imagery to plead their causes. Both, each in its own way, were taken by left-wing clergy and religious activists to be American equivalents of liberating struggles, which afforded the opportunity to flex their muscles against the so-called oppressors and spawn particular theologies of liberation.[300]

The civil rights movement, and its radical offspring the Black Power movement, served as an inspirational source for the so-called Black Theology of Liberation. "The origin of Black Theology," explains James Cone, perhaps the best-known American Black theologian, "has three contexts: (1) the civil rights movement of the 1950s and 1960s, largely associated with Martin Luther King, Jr.; (2) the publication of Joseph Washington's book, *Black Religion* (1964); and (3) the rise of the black power movement, strongly influenced by Malcolm X's philosophy of black nationalism."[301]

In its turn, the California grape strike greatly enlivened the Hispanic liberation movement, which was then called the Chicano or Brown Power movement. From within it came the so-called Chicano or Mestizaje Theology of Liberation, which—in varying degrees of explicitness—plays an important role in the Catholic pastoral work with millions of Hispanics in the United States. "The Chicano movements gave inspiration to the Chicano clergy and later to all the Hispanic clergy in this country. We began to organize and to work for change," affirms Fr. Virgilio

Elizondo, then-rector of the San Fernando Cathedral in San Antonio, Texas.[302]

Many of those involved in the American LT movement today were drawn into radical activism by the civil rights movement, and, so to speak, were reared on the marches, rallies, and picket lines it sparked. Others were already active in Catholic Action or Catholic Worker causes, or in their Protestant equivalents, and saw their participation in those struggles as a logical corollary of their religious commitment. During the nostalgic reminiscences of the revolutionary pasts of today's LT figures in the United States, it is quite common to hear them speak of being veterans of famous marches, their participation in bus boycotts, or other such engagements in civil rights causes.

A booklet published by the self-described Christian socialist Interreligious Task Force for Social Analysis explains that "much of the churches' present concern for justice derives from the leadership of Martin Luther King, Jr., and the black churches in the civil rights movement."[303]

The religious element was even more conspicuous in the California grape strike, the much-publicized *Huelga*. Cesar Chavez, the strike's media star, was a typical product of left-wing social Catholicism.[304] In 1952, he was hired by Fred Ross, Saul Alinsky's man in California, and worked for ten years with the C.S.O. (Community Service Organization), the Industrial Areas Foundation outfit in California at the time. Chavez received thorough training as a professional agitator, and became an Alinsky disciple.

In 1962, his boss instructed him to organize farm workers in the San Joaquín Valley. In 1965, his National Farm Workers Association joined Larry Itliong's Agricultural Workers Organizing Committee (A.W.O.C.) for the Huelga, and the two organizations merged into the U.F.W. the following year. The strike, in itself a local labor dispute, was adroitly turned into a national *Causa*, a radical cause that galvanized the Christian left, both Catholic and Protestant. Saul Alinsky was, so to speak, an *éminence grise* behind the strike, which basically amounted to a textbook case of the socialist-progressive symbiosis we are discussing.[305]

The vote to declare the strike was cast in a Catholic church after an invocation by the pastor at a meeting presided over by the portrait of Mexican socialist leader and guerrillero Emiliano Zapata. Despite the flagrant participation of communist agitators—including some who had just arrived from Cuba—a continuous stream of priests, nuns, ministers, and rabbis made their "pilgrimage" to the San Joaquín Valley to join the picket lines. Several were arrested. Religious symbols, like the banner of Our

299. Alden Whitman, "Dorothy Day, Catholic Activist, 83, Dies," *New York Times*, Dec. 1, 1980, p. D12.

300. Martin Luther King, Jr., himself beheld the civil rights struggles as "part of [an] overall movement in the world in which oppressed people are revolting against ... imperialism and colonialism." Martin Luther King, "The Legitimacy of the Struggle in Montgomery," Statement, May 4, 1956, quoted in James H. Cone, "Martin Luther King, Jr., and the Third World," in *The Future of Liberation Theology: Essays in Honor of Gustavo Gutiérrez*, edited by Marc H. Ellis and Otto Maduro (Maryknoll, N.Y.: Orbis Books, 1989), 347.

301. James Cone, "Black Theology: Its Origin, Method and Relation to Third World Theologies," in *Churches in Struggle: Liberation Theology and Social Change in North America*, ed. William K. Tabb (New York: Monthly Review Press, 1986), 32. Republished with permission of Monthly Review Press, from *Churches in Struggle: Liberation Theologies and Social Change in North America*, ed. William K. Tabb, 1986; permission conveyed through Copyright Clearance Center, Inc.

302. Virgilio Elizondo, "Mestizaje as a Locus of Theological Reflection," in *The Future of Liberation Theology: Essays in Honor of Gustavo Gutiérrez*, edited by Marc H. Ellis and Otto Maduro (Maryknoll, N.Y.: Orbis Books, 1989), 359.

303. The Inter-Religious Task Force for Social Analysis, ed., *Must We Choose Sides? Christian Commitment for the 1980s* (Oakland, Calif.: The Inter-Religious Task Force for Social Analysis, 1979), 97.

304. Chavez was introduced into the world of social Catholicism by Fr. Donald McDonnell, an agitator-priest who roamed California's fields in the 1950s. "Young Chavez met Father Donald McDonnell ... who had a passion for labor history," recalls Stan Steiner in his book about the Mexican-Americans, "Night after night they discussed the doctrines of social justice and the encyclicals of the popes." Stan Steiner, *La Raza: The Mexican Americans* (New York: Harper & Row, 1970), 313.

The literature on the Delano strike is abundant. Among other sources are: Jacques Levy, *Cesar Chavez: Autobiography of La Causa* (New York: W.W. Norton & Company, 1975); Ronald B. Taylor, *Chavez and the Farm Workers* (Boston: Beacon Press, 1975); Peter Mathiesen, *Sal Si Puedes: Cesar Chavez and the New American Revolution* (New York: Random House, 1969). Like so many liberal *causes célèbres*, the Delano strike was to a great extent a media propaganda stunt that was artificially inflated by the Christian left and some in the liberal chic. See, for example, Ralph de Toledano, *Little Cesar* (New York: Anthem Books, 1971).

305. See "Saul Alinsky: The Guiding Spirit Behind Delano," *California Farmer*, Mar. 19, 1966, 31.

Lady of Guadalupe, were ubiquitous. "GOD IS BESIDE YOU ON THE PICKET LINES!" became one of the picketers' rallying cries. Daily Masses were offered for the strikers and picketers by activist priests clad in red chasubles bearing the U.F.W.'s black eagle. In their sermons, fiery revolutionary rhetoric compensated for the lack of traditional religious themes. With the consent of Bishop Hugh Donohoe of Fresno, several priests served as chaplains to the strikers. Among them were: Fr. Mark Day; Fr. Eugene Boyle, chairman of the Social Justice Committee of the San Francisco diocese; and Fr. Keith Kenny of Sacramento.[306]

Msgr. William Quinn, former director of Chicago Catholic Action, traveled to Delano to lend support, along with Fr. James Vizzard, S.J., the Washington, D.C. office director for the National Catholic Rural Life Conference. The National Council of Churches officially endorsed the strike, and its California Migrant Ministry played an important role in it. Among the main Protestant spokesmen for the strike was Robert McAfee Brown, who was on his way to becoming one of the most conspicuous American liberation theologians. The Huelga eventually ended after complex negotiations between growers and workers, where Bishop Roger Mahony of Stockton (later a cardinal and archbishop of Los Angeles) was the principal mediator.

Emboldened by their participation in the strike, several left-leaning Chicano priests decided to start an association of Hispanic clergy akin to the current that would shortly afterward yield liberation theology. The result was PADRES (Padres Asociados para Derechos Religiosos Educativos y Sociales; Priests Associated for Religious, Educational, and Social Rights), which came into being in early 1970 under the leadership of Fr. Ralph Ruiz.

Following the example of PADRES, a group of Hispanic nuns resolved to found Las Hermanas (The Sisters), an association of LT-aligned Hispanic activist religious women. Both organizations would eventually become central players in the so-called new Hispanic Church, perhaps the most conspicuous feature of the LT movement of Latin American inspiration in the United States.[307]

A 1966 lead editorial of *Political Affairs*, the theoretical journal of the Communist Party U.S.A., commented:

> Profound changes are unfolding within the Church. …
>
> In our country the great rise of democratic struggles during the past several years has brought into the frontlines of battle representatives of all religious faiths. Catholic priests, Jewish rabbis and Protestant ministers. … And in the sphere of economic struggles, we may note as an outstanding case in point the militant support being given by Catholic priests to the grape strikers in Delano, California.[308]

In sum, both the civil rights movement and the California grape strike unquestionably served to energize the religious left, to favor its merger with the political left, and to trigger developments that would help shape the LT movement.

9. The First Cry of Alarm: *In Defense of Catholic Action*

In his book on the Second Vatican Council, Prof. Roberto de Mattei writes:

> With regard to the new heterodox tendencies that were beginning to spread in the Church, the first cry of alarm came unexpectedly from Latin America, where progressivism had arrived during the thirties via the central European liturgical movement. …
>
> … In June 1943 his [Plinio Corrêa de Oliveira] book entitled *In Defense of Catholic Action* was published with a preface by the nuncio Benedetto Aloisi Masella. … The work … was the first thoroughgoing refutation of the deviations that were lurking within Catholic Action in Brazil and, upon reflection, in the world.[309]

At the time, Plinio Corrêa de Oliveira was president of the Archdiocesan Board of Catholic Action of São Paulo and already a prominent Catholic figure in Brazil. A sharp observer, he saw the deleterious action of the revolutionary process that, while diluting the influence of the Church by driving people ever further away from religious practice, undermined in their mentality the very foundations of the Faith. That process, later called secularization, was welcomed by the Catholic sectors influenced by the humanist, anti-capitalist, and anti-bourgeois new Christendom approach proposed by Jacques Maritain. On the other hand, there was the challenge posed by the equally secularized totalitarian movements, in that the solutions they offered were false and founded on nationalistic or racist ideals rather than on the restoration of Christian principles.

Faced with this double challenge, Plinio Corrêa de Oliveira defended the autonomy of the Church: "Catholics must be anti-communist, antinazi, antiliberal, antisocialist … precisely because they are Catholic."[310] He advocated a strong and resolute apostolate that would challenge secular movements on their own ground, for example, through marches of young Catholics with lots of flags and marching bands. He thus correctly interpreted their appetite for symbols that evoked order and hierarchy, certain that they would attract scores of young idealists to the Church. However, his proposals were not taken up by the leadership, already more prone to dialogue and compromise than to teach and lead. History has recorded the archbishop of São Paulo's prohibition for 15,000 young men to parade through the city streets during the Regional Conference of Marian Sodalities in 1935.

While it is difficult to make historical conjectures, it is legitimate to wonder (and some scholars have),[311] what the outcome would have been had the hierarchy adopted the pastoral policy proposed by Plinio Corrêa de Oliveira. In other words, a strong, defined, and militant Catholicism that tended to a sacralization of civil society, i.e., the restoration of Christian civilization. The Catholic leader was convinced that such an approach could reverse the impending crisis. Massimo Introvigne comments that from Plinio Corrêa de Oliveira's action "emerges the idea that the 'less religion' instead of a 'more religion' solution to the Church's problems … does not date from 1950 and the influence of Brazilian and foreign priests enraptured with Marxism but was already very much present in the 1940s."[312]

---

306. See Mark Day, *Forty Acres: Cesar Chavez and the Farm Workers* (New York: Praeger Publishers, 1971), particularly the chapter "The Churches and the Struggle," at pages 53–60. See also Frank Bergon and Murray Norris, *Delano: Another Crisis for the Catholic Church* (Fresno, Calif.: Rudell Publishing Company, 1968); Cletus Healey, S.J., *Battle for the Vineyards* (New York: Twin Circle, 1969), especially the chapter "Involvement of the Catholic Church," at pages 41–46; "The Clergy and the Grapes," *News & Views* 32, no. 5 (May 1969).

307. See Antonio M. Stevens Arroyo, *Prophets Denied Honor: An Anthology on the Hispanic Church in the United States* (Maryknoll, N.Y.: Orbis Books, 1980), 136–37.

308. "Communism and the Church," *Political Affairs* 45 (July 1966), no. 7, 1.

309. Roberto de Mattei, *The Second Vatican Council: An Unwritten Story* (Fitzwilliam, N.H.: Loreto Publications, 2012), 55, 56.

310. Plinio Corrêa de Oliveira, "Pela grandeza e liberdade da Ação Católica," *O Legionário* (São Paulo), no. 331 (Jan. 15, 1939).

311. See Massimo Introvigne, *Una battaglia nella notte: Plinio Corrêa de Oliveira e la crisi del secolo XX nella chiesa* (Milan: Sugarco Edizioni, 2008).

312. Introvigne, *Una battaglia nella notte*, 44.

As many Catholic circles tended to engage in dialogue and succumb to modern errors ("less religion"), the infiltration of such errors grew, finding justification in new theological schools. As president of the archdiocesan Catholic Action, Plinio Corrêa de Oliveira realized the vast scope of that infiltration. Initially, he tried to counter it by intervening in the movement to bring it back to the intent of Pius XI. However, his action was severely hampered. At that point, he made a decision he himself explains:

> It was precisely then that tragedy struck, provoked by the progressive germs. …
> … Evil was being spread with great art, skill, and capacity to recruit. So, amid general incautiousness, we needed to sound a cry of alert to call everyone's attention. Thus it was that … we published the bombshell book, *In Defense of Catholic Action*. It was a kamikaze gesture. Either progressivism would be blown up, or we would.[313]

Without underestimating a theological and canonical analysis, to which he devotes several chapters, Prof. Plinio Corrêa de Oliveira was especially intent on denouncing the crisis as it was actually lived in the ranks of the Catholic movement, with special attention to the new mentality that undergird it. Of particular interest is the third part ("Internal Problems of Catholic Action"), in which the Brazilian leader denounces the growing laxity in the admission of new members and in the expulsion of those who had shown themselves unworthy. Those who subscribed to the new mentality refused to condemn erroneous doctrines or punish improper attitudes, justifying their liberalism as an obligation of charity. They explicitly rejected the Church's militant character and adopted instead a do-good attitude tending to relativism. The author then devotes several pages to the question of fashions, ambiences, dances, manners and customs, and other similar issues, showing how much his attention was turned to tendential aspects of the revolutionary phenomenon.

In the introduction, he calls for action: "Catholic Action … would already risk being turned against its own ends if the action of (fortunately) small groups where error did find enthusiastic adepts were not courageously checked."[314] Unfortunately, as Massimo Introvigne observes, "The analysis of the evils of Catholic Action proposed by *In Defense of Catholic Action* remained unheeded. … by the majority of bishops and priests."[315] In this regard, we cannot fail to recall Bernardino Cardinal Echeverría's lament at the Catholic leader's 1995 passing, "Ah, if only that voice had been heeded!"[316]

10. The Leftward Drift

The infiltration of neo-modernist and Christian democratic tendencies and ideas in Catholic Action triggered a shift that led large numbers of its members increasingly to the left until they adhered to Socialism and even Communism. LT is the daughter of that drift, which was not uniform in all areas nor did it manifest itself in an equally virulent way in all countries. The aim of this study is not to make a detailed history of it, but to analyze some developments that directly contributed to the rise of LT.

a. French Catholic Action

France was undoubtedly the main hotbed of innovating ideas on Catholic Action. From liberal Catholicism to social Catholicism, from Modernism to the Nouvelle Théologie, the phenomena we are addressing in analyzing the origins of liberation theology had paradigmatic connotations in France. From here, well-trained missionary teams took those ideas to the Americas and throughout the world.

The French Catholic Action arose from the Association Catholique de la Jeunesse Française (A.C.J.F.). "The ACJF," explains historian Adrien Dansette, "gave the best of itself to social Catholicism, following its evolution. Counter-revolutionary in its origins, the A.C.J.F. drew closer and closer to Christian democracy."[317] As early as 1892, the more politically aware sections of A.C.J.F. had constituted the Ligue Catholique et Sociale, to the left of the movement's mainstream, and more oriented toward social activism. In 1926, France saw the foundation of J.O.C., followed by J.E.C., J.I.C., and other specialized groups. In 1931, the Assembly of Cardinals and Bishops of France approved the bylaws of Catholic Action.

The rise of Catholic Action led to the disappearance of many traditional lay associations. The most striking example was perhaps that of the Fédération Nationale Catholique (F.N.C.), founded in 1924 by General Edouard de Castelnau (1841–1944).[318] A fervent Catholic and traditionalist, Castelnau rejected A.C.J.F., calling it "a political movement, a nursery of activists at the service of dangerous utopias and revolutionary doctrines."[319] In 1931, the French bishops forced F.N.C. to become a general movement of Catholic Action, only to dissolve it in 1945. The same fate befell the Ligue Patriotique des Françaises, a women's movement close to F.N.C., which was forced to integrate into Catholic Action in 1933, after having withstood several assaults from J.O.C.

The drift to the left was particularly evident in J.O.C., which switched from an apostolate to improve the condition of workers to social activism and leftist politics. Dansette explains: "Influenced by the prevailing atmosphere, J.O.C. militants were dragged toward extremism. … They strove to blend apostolate works with social action aiming at liberating workers from the prevailing economic regime."[320] A 1952 survey revealed that almost half of J.O.C.'s activists sympathized with the Communist Party.[321]

An identical story is that of the Mouvement Populaire des Familles (M.P.F.), part of the Catholic Action family outreach. Invaded by progressive tendencies, in 1950 M.P.F. adopted an openly socialist program and changed its name to Mouvement de Libération du Peuple (M.L.P.). "The notion of family disappears, replaced with the idea of liberation, revealing an awakening of revolutionary consciousness," said Dansette.[322] At its 1953 conference, M.L.P. defined itself as a "revolutionary" party.[323] Many of its activists migrated to the Communist Party.

Speaking about Action Catholique Ouvrière, Georges Suffert reveals that "nine out of ten activists of this organization vote

313. Plinio Corrêa de Oliveira, "Kamikaze," *Folha de S. Paulo*, Feb. 15, 1969.
314. Corrêa de Oliveira, *In Defense of Catholic Action*, 23–24. The book's preface was by Most Rev. Benedetto Aloisi Masella, then apostolic nuncio to Brazil and later made a cardinal. In 1949, the book received a letter of praise from the Holy See, signed on behalf of Pope Pius XII by Msgr. Giovanni Battista Montini, then substitute secretary of state.
315. Introvigne, *Una battaglia nella notte*, 48.
316. Bernardino Cardinal Echeverria Ruiz, "Plinio Corrêa de Oliveira: Distinguished Apostle, Ardent and Intrepid Polemist," TFP.org, Nov. 12, 1995.
317. Dansette, *Destin du catholicisme français*, 88.
318. See Yves Gras, *Castelnau ou l'art de commander* (Paris: Delanoël, 1990). It was F.N.C.'s example that inspired Prof. Plinio Corrêa de Oliveira to found the Catholic Electoral League in Brazil in 1933. See de Mattei, *Crusader of the 20th Century*, 59–60.
319. Dansette, *Destin du catholicisme français*, 110.
320. Dansette, 399.
321. See Dansette, 400.
322. Dansette, 376.
323. Kesler, *De la gauche dissidente*, 131.

for the left, while five out of ten are active members in left-wing parties."[324] As could be expected, Jeunesse Étudiante Chrétienne also increasingly turned to the left. "The prospects of JEC were innovative," Adrien Dansette explains. "Its different religious perspective was simply a radical change of mentality." While traditional student associations "were well established within the existing order and did not conceive the idea of challenging it, JEC militants willingly accepted the idea of its end. ... They did not balk at great economic and social transformations."[325] In 1931, J.E.C.'s *Message* magazine proclaimed, "The time to set the foundations of the proletarian civilization, toward which we are quickly marching, has yet to come. But we already proclaim that we do not belong to the number of those who are frightened by this perspective."[326]

J.E.C.'s left wing eventually joined Vie Nouvelle (New Life), a movement founded in 1940 by former priest André Cruziat under the influence of Emmanuel Mounier's personalist philosophy. Vie Nouvelle members organized in small cells where, according to socialist historian Albert Samuel, "faithful to a rather communitarian utopia, they created structures of participation and co-responsibility" that foreshadowed what later would be called "self-managing Socialism."[327] In 1971, Vie Nouvelle merged into the Socialist Party.

While not officially part of Catholic Action, we should also mention Jeune République, a movement founded by Marc Sangnier in 1912 to take up the Sillon mantle. Animated by the idea of a "permanent revolution," Jeune République called for "the promotion of workers and peasants within a new republic whose economic structures would finally break away from the snares of capitalist feudalism."[328] In 1935, Jeune République participated in the Front Populaire, advocating "the socialization of the means of production."[329] Finding that nothing separated it anymore from the socialists, in 1957 Jeune République became Union de la Gauche Socialiste, later merging with the Parti Socialiste Unifié. Jean-François Kesler writes, "Starting from a democratic tradition, Jeune République ended up subscribing to the socialist one."[330]

b. The Catholic Left Emerges

This leftward drift led to the so-called Catholic left from which the LT movement arose. André Latreille explains. "Beginning in 1950, a small but consistent current took shape that increasingly dragged to the left ... working-class militants, Christian unionized workers, readers of *Témoignage Chrétien*, members of Vie Nouvelle, and veterans of Catholic Action. Leaving aside the purely political aspects and consequences of this leftward slide ... we must point out the rise of a Catholic left, more advanced than Christian democracy."[331]

Even radicalism, however, has its fringes. Part of that Catholic left slid so far to the left as to become indistinguishable from Marxism, forming what we know as *progressivism*. "Christian progressivism," explains Fr. Pierre Bigo, S.J., quoted by Adrien

Dansette, "was born out of the unsettling discovery by Christians ... of an ongoing proletarian revolution ... of a proletarian world pervaded by painful struggles ... of which Communism was one of the intellectual and organizational poles. ... Christian progressivism was born from the encounter of Catholics with Communism. It represents the positive reaction of some Christians vis-à-vis Marxism."

Developing the point, Dansette writes:

> Progressives encountered these social and religious realities ... and this marked their innermost being. Communism offered them an appealing interpretation they had never known [in their Catholic education]. They thus became revolutionaries and began to realize that the evils of capitalism were inherent to its nature, and that therefore it had to be done away with altogether. That was precisely what the communists were striving to accomplish ... and they supported themselves on the masses. ... Communism was the political truth, the future. ...
>
> If these young people were revolutionaries marching hand-in-hand with the communists, they remained Christians.[332]

In 1946, Henri Moiroud, leader of the Union des Chrétiens Progressistes (Union of Christian Progressives) wrote, "Formed by Catholic Action and introduced to political activism through the Resistance ... I [found] a valid explanation of history in Marxism. ... Determined to fight alongside workers, I believed that only the Communist Party was faithful to them."[333]

Unlike Marxists, however, progressives sought to offer a religious and not just a political justification for revolution. Sounding a theme that seems to come right from the pen of a liberation theologian, *Terre Nouvelle* editor Maurice Laudrain wrote, "To cooperate in the revolution is to make possible through Socialism the full flowering of the supernatural and Christian life."[334]

Thus, the end result was reached—at least for now—of the long process begun by nineteenth-century social Catholicism, accentuated by Christian democracy, and then assumed by the left wing of Catholic Action. Summarizing the meaning of this leftward slide, socialist leader Jean Poperen affirmed in 1986, "Undoubtedly, the most important phenomenon in the history of leftist ideas—and not only of ideas—during this latter half of the century was the surge within the left of the political thought of Christian inspiration."[335]

c. Italy: From the Historic Compromise to the Red Brigades

The bibliography on the Italian Catholic left is vast and authoritative.[336] It is not our intention to add anything new about it, let alone make a detailed account of it.

After the 1922 fascist March on Rome, some sectors of Catholic Action maintained a reserved, wait-and-see attitude vis-à-vis the

---

324. Suffert, *Les catholiques et la gauche*, 40.

325. Dansette, *Destin du catholicisme français*, 102–3.

326. Dansette, 103.

327. Samuel, *Le socialisme*, 95.

328. "André Denis adhère à la Jeune République," *La Jeune République* (Jan. 1954), 2, quoted in Kesler, *De la gauche dissidente*, 176.

329. Kesler, 187.

330. Kesler, 189.

331. Latreille et al., *Histoire du catholicisme*, 3:635. Having begun as a clandestine bulletin, *Témoignage Chrétien* was directed by the Jesuit Fr. Pierre Chaillet. Most of its editors were from Catholic Action. From 1950 onward, the magazine was directed by Georges Suffert, former director of *Les Mal Pensants,* a leftist magazine staffed mainly by Catholic Action members. See Kesler, *De la gauche dissidente*, 137.

332. Dansette, *Destin du catholicisme français*, 226.

333. Kesler, *De la gauche dissidente*, 136. See also Jean Verlhac and Maurice Caveing, "Monde chrétien et monde moderne," *Esprit* (Aug.–Sept. 1946), 245–49.

334. Maurice Laudrain in *Terre Nouvelle*, Oct. 1935, quoted in Murphy, *Communists and Catholics in France*, 46.

335. Jean Poperen, "Y a-t-il encore des idées de gauche?" *Le Débat* 42, 1986/5:105.

336. See Carlo Felice Casula, *Cattolici comunisti e sinistra cristiana 1938–1945* (Bologna: Il Mulino, 1976); Francesco Malgeri, *La sinistra cristiana 1937–1945* (Brescia: Morcelliana, 1982); Augusto del Noce, *Il cattolico comunista* (Milan: Rusconi, 1981); Gianni Baget Bozzo, *L'intreccio: Cattolici e comunisti 1945–2004* (Milan: Mondadori, 2004); Rosanna M. Giammanco, *The Catholic-Communist Dialogue in Italy: 1944 to the Present* (New York: Praeger, 1989); David Kertzer, *Comrades and*

government of Benito Mussolini, a stance known as apolitical. Other sectors already veering to the left, like F.U.C.I., became instead leading forces opposing Fascism. While legitimately criticizing its secular character, they also attacked its anticommunist content. At its 26th National Conference held in Genoa in 1938, F.U.C.I. addressed, from a leftist standpoint, the "moral duty of Christians to combat Fascism at this time."[337] A preferred target of communist penetration maneuvers, F.U.C.I. soon became a breeding ground for the far left.

In 1941, a group of F.U.C.I. members, including Adriano Ossicini and Franco Rodano, launched the "Manifesto of the Cooperativist Movement," proposing the adoption of a humanist Socialism in Italy. In 1943, the movement took the name, Movement of Catholic Communists (M.C.C.), and later Party of the Christian left. After the war, it was dissolved and its leaders joined the Communist Party. Most of its members joined center-left parties.

The term *Catho-communist* was coined in reference to this current. "We are staunch communists in politics but Catholic, absolutely and uncompromisingly Catholic in our religion," Franco Rodano proclaimed in 1944. "This means that the political problem of the Catholic world cannot be solved in Italy by the P.C.I. [Italian Communist Party] but by our country's entire working class."[338]

Palmiro Togliatti, head of the Communist Party, recommended that Catho-communists not join the Party. Moscow obviously preferred that they join the nascent Christian Democrats, strengthening their left wing and encouraging them to reach an understanding with the Communist Party, later called "the historic compromise." That compromise was the ultimate aim of the strategy of Alcide De Gasperi (1881–1954), who defined the Christian Democrats as "a centrist party that looks to the left." In other words, rather than having a few more comrades, the communists preferred to rely on a political machine that dragged Catholics to the left, thus weakening and emptying the sector of public opinion most likely to react. The Christian Democratic Party, Plinio Corrêa de Oliveira writes, "is an ideological and political device specifically made to drag right-wingers, and above all naive centrists, to the extreme left."[339]

The results exceeded all expectations. Unlike other countries where great revolutionary transformations were the work of the left, in Italy that was achieved by Christian Democrats. From the land reform program of 1950 to the divorce law of 1970, the new legislation on the family of 1975, the abortion law of 1978, and a long stream of etceteras, the Christian Democrats were the ones who implemented the socialist program, and, to some extent, also the communist one. The Law 194/78 on abortion is a paradigmatic example of this. In its own dreadful uniqueness, it is the only abortion law in the world to have been signed by six individuals, all of them Christian.[340]

The attempt to bring the left to power continued slowly but surely. Roberto de Mattei writes, "Collaboration with the socialists

was an essential step in the Christian Democrats' march to the left, which ended with their embracing the communists. De Gasperi's death prevented him from achieving this plan, taken up by his successors and particularly by Aldo Moro, the new secretary of the Christian Democrats."[341]

As F.U.C.I.'s national president from 1939 to 1942[342] and then leader of the Christian Democrats, Aldo Moro advocated the need for an alliance between his party and the Socialist Party. He later embraced the Communist Party as well. At the Christian-Democratic Conference of Naples in 1962, seeking to speed up the shift to the left, he managed to bring the party's entire leadership to that position. As prime minister, in 1963 he formed the first center-left government together with P.S.I., P.S.D.I., and P.R.I., a coalition that held together until 1968. From 1975, he sought to implement the third phase of the historic compromise, namely opening up to the Communist Party. His death at the hands of the Red Brigades, in May 1978, led to the failure of the historic compromise. In the 1979 elections, both Christian democrats and communists were defeated.

As happened in other countries and particularly in Latin America, under the auspices of LT, Catho-communist sectors steered so far to the left as to take up the armed struggle. Italy is no exception, as documented by Maria Vittoria Cascino and Lorenzo Podestà.[343]

Until not long ago the Red Brigades phenomenon was believed to have been born from a meeting held in August 1970 in the village of Pecorile, municipality of Vezzano sul Crostolo, in the province of Reggio Emilia. However, that was not the case, as Cascino and Podestà amply demonstrate. Making use of relevant parliamentary records, they tell of a meeting held in November 1969 by those who would soon form the strategic command of the Red Brigades.[344] According to those government documents, the gathering occurred in the Hotel Stella del Mare on Viale Enrico Millo, in Chiavari. The property was owned by the diocese, and was procured for the meeting by young men from the local Ligurian Catholic Action. Meeting participants included, among others, Renato Curcio and his wife Margherita "Mara" Cagol (later killed in a gun battle with police), Mario Moretti, and young men from the Student Movement, Catholic Action, Student Youth, and Worker Power.[345]

For lack of space we will skip over the participation of the left wing of Catholic Action in the May 1968 explosion in France and around the world, an upheaval that actually began at the Catholic

Christians: Religion and Political Struggle in Communist Italy (New York: Cambridge University Press, 1980).

337. Adriano Ossicini, *Un'isola sul Tevere: Il fascismo al di là del ponte* (Rome: Editori Riuniti, 1999), 66. See also Maria Cristina Giuntella, *La FUCI tra modernismo, partito popolare e fascismo* (Rome: Edizioni Studium, 2000).

338. Giovanni Tassani, *Agli origini del compromesso storico: I cattolici comunisti negli anni '50* (Bologna: Edizioni Dehoniane, 1978), quoted in Piero Vassallo, "Da Franco Rodano a Mario Monti," *Riscossa Cristiana*, Sept. 13, 2012.

339. Plinio Corrêa de Oliveira, preface to *Frei, o Kerensky chileno*, by Fábio Vidigal Xavier da Silveira, 2nd ed. (São Paulo: Editora Vera Cruz, 1967), 6.

340. Italy's President, Giovanni Leone, Prime Minister Giulio Andreotti, and cabinet ministers Tina Anselmi, Francesco Bonifacio, Tommaso Morlino, and Filippo

Maria Pandolfi.

341. de Mattei, *Il centro che ci portò*, 38–39.

342. On Moro's F.U.C.I. activities, see Renato Moro, *Aldo Moro negli anni della FUCI* (Rome: Studium, 2008); Tiziano Torresi, *L'altra giovinezza: Gli universitari cattolici dal 1935 al 1940* (Assisi: Cittadella Editrice, 2010).

343. See Maria Vittoria Cascino and Lorenzo Podestà, *Dalla croce alla stella: Novembre 1969, i fondatori delle Brigate Rosse nei locali della Curia Vescovile* (Turin: Bradipolibri Editore, 2009).

344. See Italian Parliament, "Notizie sul convegno di Stella Maris a Chiavari e suoi successivi sviluppi che in Liguria si sono registrati sul fenomeno dell'eversione," in Commissione Parlamentare D'Inchiesta Sulla Strage di via Fani Sul Sequestro e l'Assassinio di Aldo Moro e sul Terrorismo in Italia (Legge 23 novembre 1979, no. 597): Allegato Alla Relazione. Documenti, Legislatura VIII, Disegni di Legge e Relazioni, Documenti, vol. 27, doc. 23, no. 5:99–151 (Rome: Parlamento Italiano, 1988).

345. See Rino di Stefano, "Quei brigatisti che erano sempre in prima fila a Messa," *Il Giornale*, Aug. 30, 2009. Fr. Pino De Bernardis, director of the Chiavari diocesan Office for Education and Culture, and founder of the Chiavari Student Youth in 1964, denies that it was a real "convention" but admits that, in November 1969, "Curcio was lodged with his group at the Stella Maris inn."

University of the Sacred Heart in Milan as early as November 1967.[346] Joseph Cardinal Ratzinger writes:

> Characteristic of the whole situation was the fact that the turning, with a kind of rapturous fervor, to a Marxism that was at once anarchical and utopian not only bore within itself a religious pathos but was also supported primarily by student chaplains and student groups, who saw in it the dawning of a fulfillment of Christian hopes. The most outstanding event was that which occurred in France in May 1968. Dominicans and Jesuits stood on the barricades; the interdenominational communion that took place during the ecumenical Mass celebrated on the barricades was long regarded as a kind of salvation-historical event, as a revelation-event that introduced a new era of Christianity.[347]

While in 1969 a part of the Italian Catholic Action led by Vittorio Bachelet stuck to the so-called religious choice, i.e., keeping a distance from direct political involvement, other sectors eagerly joined the political struggles of the radical left, giving rise to the dissent of the seventies. These sectors of Catholic Action, says Valerio Gigante, "first through the experience of Christians for Socialism, and then through Proletarian Democracy partly merged into the Communist Refoundation and today are placed between the Federation of the Left and the Libertarian Left. Others ... joined the PSI ranks ... before switching in large numbers to the Democratic Party."[348] That was also the case with the Italian Christian Workers Associations (A.C.L.I.), which made the socialist choice between 1969 and 1970.[349]

d. From Un.E.C. to LT: Peruvian Catholic Action

LT was first introduced to the public in Peru, which can thus be considered its homeland. Beginning with Father Gutiérrez, all founding members of the movement came from Catholic Action.

The Peruvian Catholic Action's drift to the left was particularly visible in the university sector, organized in small cells called Comunidades Cristianas Universitarias [University Christian Communities]. In these communities, Peruvian historian Alfredo Garland Barrón explains, "Maritain's perspective on the 'New Christendom' quickly spread among the students and *Integral Humanism* was required reading."[350]

At the end of the fifties, proposing a more radical ideological commitment, the University Christian Communities created Un.E.C. (Union of Catholic Students) and appointed LT's founding father, Fr. Gustavo Gutiérrez Merino, as its chaplain. Garland explains: "Under the influence of Father Gutiérrez, these youth movements began to consider more seriously the possibility of political action."[351] That commitment materialized in 1963 with the formation of the Coordination of Christian Students' Social Fronts, which veered to the left in 1965, becoming

Izquierda Universitaria (University Left) and later the Organizing Revolutionary Committee, which officially espoused Marxist ideology and actively participated in the socialist revolution imposed at the time under the dictator Juan Velasco Alvarado, to whom Father Gutiérrez was an advisor.

In February 1968, in Cieneguilla, on the outskirts of Lima, Peru's capital, a closed-door meeting was held with Christian union leaders linked to M.O.S.I.C. (Christian Union Movement), chaplains and advisers of Catholic Action's youth groups (J.E.C., J.U.C., Un.E.C.), and progressive theologians, including Father Gutiérrez. The meeting was convened by Fr. Julián Salvador, the Peruvian Catholic Action leader, to define the role of Christians in Peru's revolutionary movement. During the meeting they decided to found the National Office for Social Information (O.N.I.S.), which in later years acted as a mainstay of the LT movement.[352] "The lay and priestly meeting at Cieneguilla," Garland states, "was the final outcome of the long road traveled by a sector of modern 'social Catholicism.'"[353] On March 9, 1968, O.N.I.S. published a manifesto supporting a proletarian revolution in Peru's leading newspapers.[354] LT was introduced to the public three months later, during an O.N.I.S. meeting in Chimbote, Peru.

e. Brazilian Catholic Action: From J.U.C. to the Communist Party

The case of the Brazilian Catholic Action is paradigmatic not only for the radical nature of its migration to the left, but also because its development gave rise to LT directly. That migration was particularly evident in J.U.C. (Catholic University Youth).

That migration had already started in the mid-forties, influenced especially by French progressive thinkers. J.U.C. leaders Haroldo Lima and Aldo Arantes recall, "JUC strove to imbibe avant-garde Catholic thinkers—Emmanuel Mounier, Teilhard de Chardin, Lebret, and others. Mounier's personalism had a considerable influence within JUC."[355] Former J.U.C. secretary Luiz Alberto Gomes de Souza likewise recalls, "The action of JUC militants ... was oriented by Mounier's thought, resulting in a commitment that gradually saw itself as personalist and socialist."[356]

J.U.C. enthusiastically greeted the 1959 Cuban revolution, which further accentuated its leftward dive. According to Lima and Arantes, "A better understanding of the structural problems in Brazil, the upsurge of the popular struggles and the triumph of the Cuban Revolution in 1959 opened JUC to the idea of a Brazilian revolution." This leftward turn deepened with J.U.C.'s involvement with the far-left U.N.E. (União Nacional dos Estudantes, National Union of Students). Lima and Arantes continue, "As a result of its militancy within the students' movement, JUC was pressed to define a broader political agenda for today's Christians. Thus, during its 1960 congress JUC approved a document ... affirming its adoption of 'democratic Socialism' and what it called a 'Brazilian revolution.'"[357]

During the leftist government of President João Goulart (1961–1964), a radical faction formed within J.U.C. Initially called the Grupão (Big Group), in 1962 this faction adopted the

---

346. To be precise, we should mention the strike at the Catholic University of Santiago, Chile, two months before Milan.

347. Joseph Ratzinger, *Principles of Catholic Theology: Building Stones for a Fundamental Theology*, trans. Mary Frances McCarthy (San Francisco: Ignatius Press, 1987), 387–88. See also Mario Bocci, "Un problema di identità? Alle origini della contestazione studentesca all'Università Cattolica," in *Dal "centrismo" al sessantotto*, ed. Marco Invernizzi (Milan: Edizioni Ares, 2007), 143–228; Julio Loredo, "Il '68 cattolico," *Tradizione Famiglia Proprietà* (June 2008), 19–21.

348. Valerio Gigante, "Cosa resta del Concilio? (Una mappa ragionata dell'altrachiesa)," *MicroMega*, no. 7 (2012), 4. Republished with permission.

349. See Carlo Felice Casula, *Le ACLI: Una bella storia italiana* (Rome: Anicia, 2008).

350. Alfredo Garland Barrón, *Como lobos rapaces: Perú: ¿una iglesia infiltrada?* (Lima: Servicio de Análisis Pastoral e Informativo, 1978), 61.

351. Garland Barrón, *Como lobos rapaces*, 61.

352. See Jeffrey L. Klaiber, *Religion and Revolution in Peru: 1824–1976* (Notre Dame, Ind.: University of Notre Dame Press, 1977).

353. Garland Barrón, *Como lobos rapaces*, 41.

354. O.N.I.S., "Declaración de los sacerdotes peruanos," *Oiga* (Lima), no. 265 (Mar. 22, 1968). See also Jo Young-Hyun, *Sacerdotes y transformación social en Perú, 1968–1975* (Mexico: Universidad Autónoma de México, 2005), 77–109.

355. Haroldo Lima and Aldo Arantes, *História da Ação Popular: Da JUC ao PC do B* (São Paulo: Editora Alfa-Omega, 1984), 27.

356. Luiz Alberto Gomes de Souza, *A JUC: Os estudantes católicos e a política* (Petrópolis, Brazil: Editora Vozes, 1984), 156.

357. Lima and Arantes, *História da Ação Popular*, 27–28.

name Ação Popular (A.P., Popular Action) and defined itself as socialist. Following the familiar pattern, A.P. quickly spawned its own specialized sectors, each of which absorbed the left wing of specialized Catholic Action movements.

In its 1963 conference, A.P. adopted its own bylaws, in which it "embraced Socialism and proposed the socialization of the means of production." The bylaws also praised the "leading role of the Soviet revolution" and pointed out "the decisive importance of Marxism, both in revolutionary theory and praxis."[358]

The leftward drift did not stop there. Influenced by the Cuban Revolution, at its 1968 national conference Ação Popular proclaimed itself Marxist-Leninist, changing its name to Marxist-Leninist Popular Action. Since nothing separated it from the Communist Party anymore, in 1972, A.P.M.L. was officially incorporated into the Partido Comunista do Brasil (P.C. do B., Communist Party of Brazil). Accordingly, in the late 1960s and early 1970s many J.U.C. activists ended up joining the armed struggle against Brazil's military rulers.

f. Argentina's Catholic Student Youth and the Montonero Terrorists

Argentina's J.E.C. (Catholic Student Youth) went through a similar process. Its radical sectors drifted so far left that a number of J.E.C. militants joined the communist guerrilla movement known as Montoneros. A J.E.C. chaplain, Fr. Alberto Carbone, was involved in the kidnapping and assassination of General Pedro Eugenio Aramburu in 1970.

11. The LT Movement Is Born from Catholic Action's Left Wing

The liberation theology movement was born from that leftward drift of Catholic Action in Latin America. The vast majority among the older generation of those involved with the LT movement took their first steps from within the ranks of Catholic Action. Peruvian Father Gutiérrez, as mentioned, the founding father of liberation theology, was chaplain of Un.E.C. Most Rev. Helder Câmara, the Brazilian red archbishop and sponsor of currents linked to the LT movement, was a Catholic Action chaplain. Fr. Ronaldo Muñoz, founder and mentor of Christians for Socialism, the mainstay of the Chilean LT movement, came from J.U.C. Brazilian Friar Betto (Carlos Alberto Libânio Christo), author of the much-publicized book *Fidel and Religion*, was national president of J.E.C. Belgian liberation theologian Fr. Joseph Comblin, expelled from Brazil in 1969 for subversive activities, began his ministry in the Belgian Catholic Action. Brazilian liberationist Luiz Alberto Gomes de Souza, who met Father Gutiérrez during a J.E.C. congress in France and later helped him draft his 1971 book, *A Theology of Liberation*—the cornerstone of LT—belonged to J.E.C. and even served a three-year stint as president of J.E.C.I. (Jeunesse Étudiante Chrétienne Internationale, Young Christian Students International). The list could go on.

Chilean liberation theologian Fr. Pablo Richard asserts that, in 1960, "Brazil already lived the effervescence of 'revolutionary Christianity'" that set the stage for liberation theology.[359] Luiz Alberto Gomes de Souza is even more explicit: "It was in Brazil, and more precisely in JUC, that many of the insights that would later coalesce into Latin American liberation theology began to take shape in the early 1960s."[360] Father Gutiérrez states that the developments that produced LT "began around 1960–62 among university movements of various South American countries."[361]

Retracing the roots of LT, Brazilians Leonardo and Clodovis Boff state, "Between 1959 and 1964 the Catholic left in Brazil produced a series of basic works ... linked to a popular action whose approach already foreshadowed liberation theology." They mention as mentors of this approach Frs. Almery Bezerra and Henrique de Lima Vaz, both J.U.C. chaplains.[362] Summarizing the issue, liberationist historian Samuel Silva Gotay affirms that liberation theology arose "out of the radicalization of the doctrines and practices of social Catholicism," and concludes that LT was made possible by "the passage from social Catholicism to revolutionary Christianity."[363]

358. Lima and Arantes, 37.

359. Pablo Richard, *Morte das cristandades e nascimento da Igreja: Análise histórica e interpretação teológica da igreja na America Latina* (São Paulo: Edições Paulinas, 1984), 155.

360. Gomes de Souza, *A JUC*, 9.

361. Gutiérrez, *A Theology of Liberation*, 120, no. 4.

362. Leonardo Boff and Clodovis Boff, *Como fazer teologia da libertação* (Petrópolis: Editora Vozes, 1986), 97.

363. Samuel Silva Gotay, "Origem e desenvolvimento do pensamento cristão revolucionário a partir da radicalização da doutrina social cristã nas décadas de 1960 e 1970," in *História da teologia na América Latina*, edited by C.E.H.I.L.A. (São Paulo: Edições Paulinas, 1981), 139.

Chapter 2:
From Liberal Catholicism to Liberation Theology:
The Story of an Error

In chapter 1 we sketched the story of the social action movement that started as social Catholicism and ended as Christian Socialism, from which liberation theology arose. In parallel to this development, there was another happening in philosophical and theological currents. Starting in the nineteenth century as liberal Catholicism, it gave rise to Modernism, and inspired what Pius XII called, in 1944, "Nouvelle Théologie," which in turn engendered LT. Like the confluence of two rivers, these social and liberal developments eventually merged into one inseparable whole.

Let us begin by analyzing liberal Catholicism in its two versions: the one akin to European Liberalism, particularly prevalent in France, and the seemingly more moderate one found in the Anglo-Saxon world. Consistent with our method, we will not analyze liberal Catholicism in depth, but only show how it gave rise to LT.[364]

A. Liberal Catholicism

1. The French Revolution and the Constitutional Church

The 1789 French Revolution was not only anti-monarchical, but also anti-Catholic. As much as it sought to destroy the throne, and with it the last vestiges of medieval order, it also moved to annihilate the Catholic Church. If the revolutionaries loathed all hierarchy and authority in the political sphere, they could not tolerate it in the spiritual realm. Their egalitarian hatred thus logically passed from the civil to the spiritual sphere. Hébert's infamous cry, "Peace will not reign in France until the last aristocrat is hanged with the entrails of the last priest," remains the paradigmatic statement of that twin hatred.[365]

A first step in this revolutionary assault in the religious sphere was the abolition of ecclesiastical privileges decreed by the National Assembly on August 4, 1789. This was closely followed by the confiscation of Church property on November 2. Three months later, the Assembly forbade monastic vows and suppressed the religious orders, completely disrupting the Church's organization. As the historian Adrien Dansette remarks, "The religious history of France has no precedent for such a violent and total destruction."[366]

The worst, however, was yet to come. On July 12, 1790, the National Constituent Assembly passed the Civil Constitution of the Clergy, a bill that attempted to revamp the Catholic Church according to the postulates of the Revolution. The document rested on the contention that, in the Church as in society, authority comes from the people. It thoroughly reorganized dioceses and parishes, severed the clergy from any obedience to Rome, decreed that all ecclesiastical charges would be elective from then on, and, in practice, turned the clergy into public functionaries, utterly dependent on the revolutionary government.

Furthermore, the Assembly ruled that all bishops and priests should take a public oath of allegiance to the Civil Constitution of the Clergy. While only seven bishops out of 160 bowed to the revolutionaries' heavy-handedness, a strong minority of the lower clergy took the oath. Historians agree that the absence of any guidelines from the Vatican played an important role in that setback.[367] Three months later, when Pope Pius VI finally pronounced himself, condemning the Civil Constitution, most priests recanted their oath and chose to face persecution. Thousands of them were killed, many as martyrs of the Faith.[368] Also, some thirty thousand sought shelter in other countries. During the Terror (1792–1794), the Revolution sought to de-Christianize France. The clergy was persecuted and all religious expression

---

364. On liberal Catholicism, see Barbier, *Histoire du catholicisme libérale*, vols. 1–2; M.G. Weill, *Histoire du catholicisme libérale en France 1828–1908* (Paris: Alcan, 1909); Anatole Leroy-Beaulieu, *Les catholiques libéraux de 1830 à nos jours* (Paris: Plon et Nourrit, 1885); Jules Morel, *Les catholiques libéraux* (Paris: E. Giraud, 1864); Angela Pietra, *Storia del movimento cattolico-liberale* (Milan: Vallardi, 1948). In Spain, a famous booklet by Fr. Félix Sardà y Salvany was published, *El liberalismo es pecado* (Barcelona: Librería y Tipografía Católica, 1884), commented in *Civiltà Cattolica*, no. 6 (1887), 525–48; no. 7 (1887), 38–61; no. 8 (1887), 346–50. See also Giacomo Martina, *La chiesa nell'età del assolutismo, del liberalismo, del totalitarismo: Da Lutero ai nostri giorni*, 4 vols. (Brescia: Morcelliana, 1970).

365. As often happens with *mots célèbres*, the authorship of this iconoclastic cry is disputed. It seems that the author was the French priest Jean Meslier (1664–1729). A revolutionary *avant la lettre*, he was a declared enemy of Church and monarchy, both guilty, in his opinion, of embodying hierarchy and authority. Anticipating some doctrines of modern liberal theology, Fr. Meslier attributed this hierarchical view to the idea of a personal and transcendent God, to which he opposed a kind of natural religion. From his immanentist idea of God, Fr. Meslier deduced an anarchist Communism supported by a materialist philosophy. His name was engraved on a plaque outside the Kremlin walls as one of the architects of Socialism. See Jean Meslier, *Oeuvres complètes*, edited by R. Desne, J. Deprun, and A. Soboul, 3 vols. (Paris: Editions Anthropos, 1970–1972). That dual hatred against altar and throne was a recurring theme during the Revolution. In a speech to the Convention in November 1793, the famous painter Jacques-Louis David, a Jacobin deputy at the time, railed against "the double tyranny of kings and priests." Geno Pampaloni, *Notre-Dame e la Sainte-Chapelle* (Novara: Istituto Geografico de Agostini, 1980), 4.

366. Dansette, *Religious History*, 1:49. The famous historian also notes: "[Such destruction] was accomplished with almost no effort on the part of the attackers, and without resistance from the defenders." Dansette, *Histoire religieuse*, 1:75. It is hard not to ask: In what condition was the leadership of the Church in France to allow itself to be swept away with one stroke without offering resistance? What would the battle's outcome have been if the Church were in different conditions when the Revolution struck? Is this state of mind not similar to the one displayed by some Church circles toward rising Protestantism two centuries earlier, and toward Communism two centuries later?

367. Historians set the percentage of juring priests at around 45%, though many swore *sub conditionem*, using formulas like "in the measure that the Roman, Catholic, and Apostolic faith permits." Many historians favorable to the ideals of 1789 believe that the Civil Constitution of the Clergy was the Revolution's greatest strategic blunder. By raising a problem of conscience among Catholics, it struck a hard blow at the soft and accommodating mood of a large part of the clergy, thus creating, by reaction, the cultural ground from which the Counter-Revolution came. According to Jean Leflon, "Even the historians most favorable to the National Constituent Assembly admit that the Civil Constitution of the Clergy was 'its greatest mistake.'" Jean Leflon, "La crise révolutionnaire 1789–1846," in *Histoire de l'église*, ed. A. Fliche and V. Martin (Paris: Bloud et Gay, 1951), 20:67.

368. See Havard de la Montagne, *Histoire de la démocratie chrétienne*, 14. Havard de la Montagne speaks of twelve thousand priests slaughtered. To these martyrs are added hundreds of guillotined religious, thirty-two of whom were beatified in 1925 by Pope Pius XI. See Augustin Gazier, *Études sur l'histoire religieuse de la révolution française, d'après des documents originaux et inédits, depuis la réunion des états généraux jusqu'au directoire* (Paris: A. Colin, 1887).

forbidden. The cult to the goddess Reason and to the Supreme Being was established.

While a majority of French Catholics may be blamed for a lack of a will to react, even though they were unsympathetic to the Revolution, a substantial minority adhered to the new ideas, sometimes enthusiastically. That minority established the so-called Constitutional Church, the starting point of liberal Catholicism.

At a 1791 sermon in Paris, Claude Fauchet, juring bishop of Calvados, expounded the basic ideas of that current:

> We adore God as the sovereign author of the [1789] Revolution that liberates us. ...
>
> Yes, my brethren, the true regime of Catholicism is that of universal liberty. ...
>
> ...What is the Catholic Church? It is the society of brothers under the government of legitimate pastors. And who are the legitimate pastors? Those freely elected by the brothers. ...
>
> ...There are no poor in a society that is so fraternal: there are only equals.[369]

The Constitutional Church held two national councils that approved a series of reforms in the Church's governance and liturgy which in some of their main aspects are not very different from those advocated by the progressive current in the 1960s.

2. Rome Condemns the Constitutional Church

Pope Pius VI (1775–1799) condemned the Constitutional Church and the doctrines of the French Revolution. In his brief *Quod aliquantum* of March 10, 1791, he stated,

> [The National Assembly] has established, as a natural right of man in society, this absolute liberty that not only assures him the right of not being disturbed in his religious opinions, but also of thinking, writing, and even publishing whatever he fancies about religion.
>
> It proclaims that these monstrosities derive and emanate from the equality and the liberty natural to all men. But who could think of anything more insane than to establish such equality and liberty among all, thus disregarding reason, with which nature has especially endowed the human race?[370]

In the Consistory of June 17, 1793, quoting the encyclical *Inescrutabile divinae sapientiae* of 1775, Pius VI further declared:

> "These most perverse philosophers endeavor to dissolve all links by which men are bound together and to their superiors and are held to the fulfillment of their duties. They say and proclaim ad nauseam that man is born free and subject to no one's authority ... and that, therefore, society is nothing more than a group of idiots whose imbecility bows to priests—who deceive them—and to kings—who oppress them—in such a manner that

concord between priesthood and empire is nothing but a monstrous conspiracy against man's innate liberty."
>
> To this false and deceptive word, Liberty, these arrogant masters of mankind have attached yet another equally fallacious word: Equality. As if among men gathered in society ... there should no longer be anyone with the necessary strength and authority to constrain, repress, and call back to duty those who fail.[371]

Condemned by Rome and ravaged by moral dissolution and heresy, the Constitutional Church disintegrated.[372] However, the desire to reconcile Catholicism with the revolutionary heritage of 1789—viewed by many as the wave of the future—continued well into the nineteenth century, giving rise to liberal Catholicism.

3. The Essence of Liberal Catholicism

a. The Liberal Spirit

In dealing with liberal Catholicism we must distinguish between underlying passional proclivities and doctrines properly speaking.[373] The first thing we find in liberal Catholics is a profound yearning for an egalitarian and permissive state of affairs. Their natural need to justify these leanings prompted in them specific ideological trends, fledgling ideas in the course of elaboration that initially collided with their own religious and social upbringing and habits. In some cases, this clash with the old doctrines and habits prevented the liberal Catholics' passional yearnings from producing its full consequences. In others, instead, the very dynamism of these leanings made fully explicit the revolutionary germs contained in them.

The degree of radicalism of the liberal Catholics' explicit doctrines depended on the outcome of this clash and on their caution to avoid a complete break with orthodoxy. Accordingly, several currents appeared within liberal Catholicism, some closer to orthodoxy, others expressing clearly erroneous doctrines. Nonetheless, all of them were moved by a liberal mentality tendentially opposed to all authority and, above all, basically optimistic regarding the new times ushered in by the 1789 Revolution.

In opposition to the double principle of hierarchy and authority, viewed as oppressive and offensive to human dignity, two notions express well the liberal spirit taken to its final consequences: "absolute equality, complete liberty." A person with a liberal mentality

subject to another's authority hates first of all the particular yoke that weighs upon him.

In a second stage, [he] hates all authority in general and all yokes, and, even more, the very principle of authority considered in the abstract.

---

369. Claude Fauchet, "Sermon sur l'accord de la religion et de la liberté," (Paris, Feb. 4, 1791), in *Collection intégrale et universelle des orateurs sacrés*, ed. Jacques Paul Migne (Paris: Ateliers Catholiques au Petit-Montrouge, 1855), 66:160, 169, 170. Among the juring bishops was A. Lamourette, of Rhône-et-Loire, whom some credit with having coined the expression "Christian democracy" in its modern meaning. See Hans Maier, *Revolution und kirche: Studien zur fruhgechichte der christlichen demokratie* (Freiburg: Rombach, 1959).

370. Pius VI, Brief "Quod Aliquantum" (Mar. 10, 1791).

371. Pius VI, "Allocution de notre très saint-père le pape Pie VI dans le consistoire secret du lundi, 17 juin, 1793 au sujet de l'assassinat de sa majesté très chrétienne Louis XVI," (Rome: l'Imprimerie de la Chambre Apostolique, 1793), 9. See Jacques Crétineau-Joly, *L'église romaine en face de la révolution*, 2 vols. (Paris: Henri Plon, 1859).

372. Of the 82 juring bishops, 10 died, 24 apostatized, 9 married, and 24 resigned. Of the roughly 27,000 juring priests, 22,000 resigned from their responsibilities, most renounced the priesthood, and several thousand—estimates vary—married. The head of the Constitutional Church, the apostate *abbé* Grégoire, died unrepentant in 1831. It is interesting to note that he exerted a considerable influence on Philippe Buchez, a father of Christian Socialism.

373. Here we follow Plinio Corrêa de Oliveira's well-known outline presented in *Revolution and Counter-Revolution*. The Brazilian thinker distinguishes three depths in the revolutionary process: in tendencies, ideas, and facts. See Corrêa de Oliveira, *Revolution and Counter-Revolution*, 26–28.

> Because he hates all authority, he also hates superiority of any kind. ...
>
> ...[Thus, the liberal spirit] can lead to the most radical and complete egalitarianism.[374]

Accordingly, in varying degrees of explicitness liberal Catholics propounded equality in the political sphere with the suppression or at least attenuation of inequality between the governing and the governed. The authority to govern, they claimed (with Hobbes, Locke, and Rousseau), does not come from God but from the people. The more consistent among them condemned monarchy and aristocracy as being intrinsically evil and acclaimed democracy as the only legitimate form of government. They also endeavored to establish equality in the structure of society, by attenuating differences derived from the right of property. Whence some clear tendencies toward collectivism.[375]

In sum, Liberalism implied a partial or total emancipation of man from the supernatural and moral orders, as well as a partial or total emancipation of the individual citizen from political authority. Both cases contained an affirmation of the sovereignty of the individual conscience. German Jesuit theologian Fr. Hermann Gruber writes, "A fundamental principle of Liberalism is the proposition: It is contrary to the natural, innate, and inalienable right and liberty and dignity of man, to subject himself to an authority, the root, rule, measure, and sanction of which is not in himself."[376]

b. Adapting to the Mindset of the Times

As we said, liberal Catholics presented their positions not so much as logical deductions from some theoretical postulates but as an unavoidable demand of the spirit of the times. In their view, some excesses notwithstanding, the 1789 Revolution had had the undeniable merit of sweeping away the "oppressive" structures of the Ancien Régime and opening the era of modernity under the aegis of liberty. This course of events, they contended, was irreversible, and the sooner the Church accepted the *fait accompli* and adapted herself to the new situation, the less traumatic would be her transition to modernity. In other words, a comprehensive Revolution had changed the civil sphere and was now imposing those changes on the Church.

Here lies, then, in all its dramatic force the problem of the relationship between the Church and the world, a problem as old as the Church herself and always at the heart of events that see the Bride of Christ carry out her salvific mission among men. While absolutely avoiding here the discussion of a topic as complex as it is delicate, we must nevertheless note that it has two aspects, a theoretical and a practical one. Theoretically: Is the Church the salt of the earth and the light of the world, or is the world the salt of the Church and her light? This is a theological and pastoral question which the Supreme Magisterium has often addressed.

For purposes of this study, however, the practical question is the more vital. The world in which nineteenth-century Catholics needed to operate had two conflicting types of influence. On the one hand, there were still important remnants of the medieval Christian order, like the "bruised reed ... and smoking flax" as it were (Matt. 12:20), although ever weaker and more marginal. On the other hand, like devastating cockle spoiling the good harvest of wheat (see Matt. 13:24–25), one had the new world resulting from centuries of revolutionary process of which the Revolution of 1789 was the most recent chapter.

In stark contrast to the destructive Revolution, for Catholics faithful to the Magisterium, relating to the world meant to defend, sustain, and restore the remnants of Christian civilization. Therefore, they conceived their apostolate in the world as essentially conservative and counter-revolutionary.[377] Far from allowing herself to be carried away by the revolutionary vortex produced by the father of lies, the Church established herself as the bulwark of order, teaching the unchanging truth to a humanity drifting away from the ways of God.

Liberal Catholics took a diametrically opposed position: The revolutionary process was essentially good and the Church should conform her teaching, structure, and liturgy to the modern world to avoid becoming anachronistic and a hateful obstacle to human progress.[378] Hence, the classical definition of liberal Catholicism as the party of those who wanted the Church to reconcile with the Revolution. As we will see, liberal Catholicism sought to baptize the Revolution of 1789, just as LT would later seek to baptize that of 1917.

"Catholics are inferior to their adversaries because they have yet to take sides with the great Revolution that gave birth to the new society, to the modern life of peoples," proclaimed Count Charles Forbes René de Montalembert (1810–1870) in his famous 1863 Malines speech:

> The future of modern society depends on two questions: correct democracy through liberty, and reconcile Catholicism with democracy. ...
>
> We accept, we invoke the principles and liberties proclaimed in 1789.[379]

The French Revolution was not the only event to influence liberal Catholicism. Striving to adapt the Church to the modern

---

374. Corrêa de Oliveira, 46–47.

375. Already in 1849, Pius IX warned that the abuse of liberty and equality can lead to Socialism. In the encyclical *Nostis et nobiscum,* the pope wrote, "As regards this [impious] teaching and these theories, [intended to tear the Italian people from their allegiance to Us and to this Holy See], it is now generally known that the special goal of their proponents is to introduce to the people the pernicious fictions of *Socialism* and *Communism* by misapplying the terms 'liberty' and 'equality.'" Pius IX, encyclical *Nostis et nobiscum* (Dec. 8, 1849), no. 18.

376. Hermann Gruber, S.J., s.v. "Liberalism," in *C.E.,* 9:212.

377. Plinio Corrêa de Oliveira writes:

> The Revolution attacks Christian civilization in a manner that is more or less like that of a certain tree of the Brazilian forest. This tree, the strangler fig *Urostigma olearia,* by wrapping itself around the trunk of another tree, completely covers it and kills it. In its "moderate" and low-velocity currents, the Revolution approached Christian civilization in order to wrap itself around it and kill it. We are in a period in which this strange phenomenon of destruction is still incomplete. In other words, we are in a hybrid situation wherein what we would almost call the mortal remains of Christian civilization, and the aroma and remote action of many traditions only recently abolished yet still somehow alive in the memory of man, coexist with many revolutionary institutions and customs.
>
> Faced with the struggle between a splendid Christian tradition in which life still stirs and a revolutionary action inspired by the mania for novelties to which Leo XIII referred in the opening words to the encyclical *Rerum novarum,* it is only natural that the true counter-revolutionary be a born defender of the treasury of good traditions, for these are the values of the Christian past that remain and must be saved. In this sense, the counter-revolutionary acts like Our Lord, Who did not come to extinguish the smoking wick nor to break the bruised reed. Therefore, he must lovingly try to save all these Christian traditions. (Corrêa de Oliveira, *Revolution and Counter-Revolution,* 78)

Revolutionary propaganda sometimes presented traditionalist Catholics, dubbed the "intransigent" back then, as blindly attached to the Ancien Régime and thus to a political system that history had made obsolete. Nothing could be more cartoonish.

378. Commenting on Vincenzo Gioberti (1801–1852), Gabriele de Rosa writes, "Gioberti needs as it were to spiritualize the Church in order to change its historical and institutional structure, modernize and adapt it to pressure from the national [unification movement], eradicate it from the context of long traditions. ...For Gioberti, the Church will thus avoid joining the revolution by the back door as part of a reluctantly accepted political compromise with the liberal world." De Rosa, *Il movimento,* 21.

379. Charles Forbes, count of Montalembert, *L'église libre dans l'état libre: Discours prononcés au congrès catholique de Malines par le comte de Montalembert* (Paris: Charles Douniol, 1863), 18, 70. On behalf of Pope Pius IX, Cardinal Antonelli wrote the French

world, more precisely to its revolutionary aspects, many European liberal Catholics were naturally attracted to the country that, in their view, represented modernity in its truer form: the United States of America. The great republic of America had found a constitutional framework in the liberal mold that should serve as a model for Europe while avoiding the excesses of radical Jacobinism.

By assuring non-interference by the State in religious affairs (First Amendment), the U.S. Constitution established a de facto separation between Church and State, and, therefore, religious freedom. While on the one hand the Catholic Church does not enjoy the patronage of the State, on the other hand she is entirely free to preach her beliefs. According to liberal Catholics, this situation was ideal as it enabled the Catholic Church to join the free market of religions and compete with other confessions for a niche in the hearts of Americans, free from the prejudices and parochial rivalries that haunted religious life in Europe.

In other words, the United States was the living proof that the liberal Catholic program was indeed feasible. It is no surprise, then, that in his inaugural address at the Académie Française in 1860, occupying the chair that used to belong to Alexis de Tocqueville, the liberal Catholic leader Father Lacordaire called the United States the "prophecy and vanguard of the future state of Christian nations."[380] This conception was wholly blind to the deleterious infiltration of the naturalist spirit inside the Church, a spirit later condemned by Pope Leo XIII as *Americanism*. On the other hand, it was founded on a unilateral interpretation of American reality, now refuted by modern historiography. We shall return to this issue later.[381]

4. Felicité de Lamennais

The beginnings of liberal Catholicism in France are inextricably linked to the figure of the apostate priest Felicité Robert de Lamennais (1782–1854), considered the father of the current. Father de Lamennais began his public life as a defender of Catholic dogma. In 1817, he published a book of apologetics, titled *Essai sur l'indifférence en matière de religion*, in which he made a vigorous plea for Catholicism against the rising tide of religious indifferentism. The work was widely acclaimed and earned the author instant fame. Alert spirits, however, already detected in it some disturbing trends.

Rejecting Cartesian rationalism, which he correctly perceived as sapping the foundations of the Christian Faith, Lamennais

embraced the opposite error. He disdained any rational argument and appealed instead to man's feelings and common sense, a trend later found in many currents of progressive theology. Revealing the first signs of the unquenchable pride that marked his public life and eventually led him to apostasy, Lamennais fancied himself founding a whole new philosophical school: "[He] thought that his philosophy was a *requiem* sung over that of the schoolmen."[382]

In 1824, Charles X, the last remaining brother of Louis XVI, ascended to the French throne. Catholic and conservative, he became an easy target of leftist forces, including liberal Catholics. The Ordinances of 1828 offered the pretext for an insurrection that culminated in the revolution of July 1830.[383]

Joining the insurrection, Lamennais published the book *Des progrès de la révolution et de la guerre contre l'église*, in which he formally broke with monarchy and put his hopes in a liberal republic: "An immense liberty is indispensable for the development of those truths which are to save the world."[384] Anarchy and destruction would follow, he conceded, but these were necessary for liberty to prevail. Meanwhile, continued Lamennais, the Church must cease to be a public entity so that liberty could reign. She must retreat from public activity and restrict her action to individual consciences and the private sphere. This book, condemned by the archbishop of Paris, Most Rev. Hyacinthe-Louis de Quélen, was aptly described by noted Jesuit historian Father Barbier as "the birth certificate of liberal Catholicism."[385] It was in the ensuing polemic that the expression *liberal Catholics* was coined to designate Lamennais and his followers.

5. The 1830 Revolution

The Revolution of 1830 swept away the Bourbon dynasty and with it the remnants of the traditional aristocracy. Historian Gabriele De Rosa writes, "After the Paris revolution of July 1830 ... the Restoration, with its cult of the Catholic legitimist tradition received a mortal blow whose effects were felt also in Italy."[386] The revolution brought to power a secular and positivist bourgeoisie.

---

nobleman a letter of rebuke for that speech, which he accepted "with resignation" but without changing his position. Cavour borrowed from Montalembert the motto of his liberal policy: "A Free Church in a Free State." See Angela Pelliciari, *Risorgimento anticattolico* (Casale Monferrato: Piemme, 2004), 178–86. See also *Lettre a M. le Comte de Cavour, président du conseil des ministres, a Turin, par le comte de Montalembert* (Paris: Charles Douniol, 1861).

380. Henri Lacordaire, "Discours de réception de Henri Lacordaire" (Jan. 24, 1861), Académie Française. Quoting de Tocqueville, Lacordaire stated: "Order in America is born from an equality accepted by all—that permeated customs as well as the law, true, sincere, candid freedom drawing all citizens closer in the same duties and rights." Lacordaire, "Discours."

381. The perception of liberal Catholics was indeed naive, to say the least. An unbiased historical appraisal shows a pattern of Protestant intolerance toward the Catholic Church lasting into the twentieth century. The Church was given freedom only to the extent that it did not oppose the liberal creed of the American Revolution. When she did, she was frequently subject to persecutions, as those epitomized by the Know Nothing Party and several other surges of Nativism. See A. James Reichley, *Religion in American Public Life* (Washington, D.C.: The Brookings Institution, 1985). Undoubtedly, the main factor in the spread of the American myth in Europe was the work by Alexis de Tocqueville, in which the author presents the United States as a model of ordered liberty. Modern authors, however, have corrected the work's central thesis, showing how Tocqueville mentions only the egalitarian and liberal aspects of the country, almost totally neglecting its traditional and hierarchical elements. See Alexis de Tocqueville, *Democracy in America*, trans. Harvey Mansfield and Delba Winthrop (Chicago: University of Chicago Press, 2002); Edward Pessen, *Riches, Class and Power Before the Civil War* (Lexington, Mass.: Heath & Co., 1973).

382. "Lamennais, Hugo Felicidad Roberto," *Enciclopedia Espasa-Calpe*, 29:410. This pretension was all the more ludicrous since Lamennais's scholarship was pitifully shallow. "This poor fellow doesn't even know his catechism!" exclaimed Fr. des Genettes at the time. Ibid. Even his disciple, Fr. Lacordaire, conceded that "[Lamennais] ignored some of the most elementary notions of theology." Lacordaire, "Letter to Foisset," (Dec. 23, 1858), in Joseph Crépon, ed. *Lettres du R.P.H.-D. Lacordaire a Théophile Foisset*, 2 vols. (Paris: Librairie Poussielgue Freres, 1886), 2:229. In addition to his runaway pride, Cardinal de Cabrières, bishop of Montpellier (1830–1921), points to another factor that may help explain Lamennais's explosive character, namely, his homosexuality. See Paul Lesourd and Claude Paillat, *Dossiers secrets: l'église de France de la révolution à nos jours* (Paris: Presses de la Cité, 1968), 2:185, quoted in Verbist, *Les grandes controverses*, 81.

383. It was on the eve of this revolution that Our Lady of the Miraculous Medal appeared for the first time to Saint Catherine Labouré (1806–1876), on the evening of July 18, 1830. Here are Our Lady's words: "My daughter, the times are very sad, serious disasters are going to hit France; the king will be overthrown, the whole world will be upset by calamities of all kinds." Like the words She uttered at La Salette on September 19, 1846, they reveal Divine Providence's negative view of the general course of human events in the nineteenth century, a judgment that contrasts painfully with the positive and optimistic one of liberal Catholics. For Our Lady, the diffusion of the liberal spirit with its moral, cultural, social, and political consequences ran counter to God's will. Our Lady's warning was a prophetic look over the next decades: "'There will come a time when the danger will be great and everything will seem lost, but take heart, for I will be with you.' With tears in her eyes the Virgin explained to Sister Catherine that many would die, including the archbishop of Paris, and that the Cross would be despised. ...'My child, the whole world will be in distress.'" Benoît Bemelmans, *La médaille miraculeuse: L'histoire vraie de la médaille donnée par la Sainte Vierge à sainte Catherine Labouré, racontée aux enfants* (Asnières-sur-Seine, France: Société française pour la défense de la Tradition, Famille et Propriété – TFP, 2003). Our Lady was referring to the series of revolutions that would scar the nineteenth century: 1830, 1848, and 1870—all supported by liberal Catholics. See René Laurentin and Michel Corteville, *Découverte du secret de la Salette* (Paris: Fayard, 2002).

384. Antoine Dégert, s.v. "Felicité Robert de Lamennais," *C.E.*, 8:764.

385. Barbier, *Histoire du catholicisme libéral*, 1:5. In his turn, Belgian theologian Fr. Henri Verbist calls Lamennais "the founder of liberal Catholicism and, maybe, also of social Christianism or Christian Socialism." Verbist, *Les grandes controverses*, 78.

386. De Rosa, *Il movimento*, 18.

While disapproving of some of the new regime's anticlerical tones, liberal Catholics nevertheless greeted it with enthusiasm. Father Lacordaire hailed the "people, triumphant over the ruins of a millennial monarchy, liberty victorious, and believing itself assured of a reign without end."[387] De Rosa rightly says, "This was the heyday of liberal Catholicism."[388]

Along with Father Lacordaire, Lamennais founded the newspaper *L'Avenir* (The Future). *L'Avenir* was read especially by the young clergy and inspired the formation of a movement that spread throughout the country with branches abroad, especially in Belgium and Italy. In a July 20, 1831 letter, Father Lacordaire acclaimed this Belgian branch calling it, "a sister, born from the same father and mother, namely, Christ and liberty."[389]

In that "heyday of liberal Catholicism" we can already see some key elements of the future progressivism that gave rise to LT.

a. Modern Revolutions Are the Work of God?

Running through liberal Catholicism we find an evolutionist view of history whereby, after the end of the Middle Ages, mankind set out on an inexorable process of breaking away from bondages perceived as proper to an infant age toward that complete emancipation characteristic of adulthood. Liberal Catholicism said that this liberating process was the work of Divine Providence. With the Revolution of 1789, France supposedly attained adulthood and should thus serve as a beacon for humanity.

"There are older siblings amidst the great family of nations," *L'Avenir* explained, in an oblique reference to France. "Therefore, in her we can better observe the evolution to which Providence has subjected mankind." France, however, was merely the forerunner. The social order heralded by the 1789 Revolution, continued the liberal publication, "will little by little penetrate ... all of Europe and even beyond."[390] For his part, Father Lacordaire stated that 1789 "opened the era of revolutions, and mankind cannot close it anymore."[391]

Introducing a dangerous confusion between religion and politics—one of the pillars upon which LT will rest—liberal Catholics tended to confound this purported progress of liberty with the redemption of mankind. They viewed the advance of revolutionary liberty as somehow having a religiously salvific meaning. With the revolutions of 1789 and 1830, affirmed *L'Avenir*, "A social order [the Ancien Régime] providentially 'struck with a sentence of reprobation is expiring amidst anguishing pains. ... But then, and only then, emerges the regenerating idea [liberty] that the Eternal has crowned as queen of a new universe. ... A new social era begins, and the world is saved.'"[392]

b. Christianity, the Driving Principle of the Revolutionary Process

Lamennais saw in Christianity the driving principle of this revolutionary process of liberation. He rationalized that, having freed the peoples from pagan slavery, the Church should now help them free themselves from the shackles of monarchy. He thus called on the Church to take up the banner of revolutionary causes: "It [Christianity] has laid the immutable and sacred foundations of

liberty. And from century to century, as it developed the social conscience, it proportionally developed liberty."[393]

Noting the "providential role *L'Avenir* attributed to revolutions," French theologian Fr. C. Constantin comments: "They [the liberal Catholics] proposed to the whole world the new political and social organization proclaimed by all the revolutions after 1789. ... They also asked that the Church assume the leadership of the movement that would overturn the thrones."[394] Fr. Gioacchino Ventura, a Roman Theatine, correctly affirmed that liberal Catholics "approved all past revolutions, and applauded in advance those to come."[395]

c. A Generalized and Disruptive Democracy

Used and abused by liberal Catholics, the term *liberty* became one of those "talismanic words" which Plinio Corrêa de Oliveira discusses. They are malleable concepts endowed with great propaganda value that arouse a large number of likes and phobias and are employed for the purposes of revolutionary propaganda. Susceptible of becoming highly radicalized, they subject people to an unperceived ideological transshipment.[396]

From demanding freedom for the Church, liberal Catholics went on to claim ever-expanding liberties in more and more fields until they reached, in some cases, wholly libertarian positions. *L'Avenir* writes, "Total, absolute freedom of opinion, doctrine, conscience and worship ... every civil liberty without privileges or restrictions. ... There must be full liberty for everyone."[397]

In the political field, this sweeping freedom was profoundly disruptive of the traditional order. Once the right to suffrage had been secured by the Revolution of 1789, liberal Catholics maintained that it had to be applied to all institutions of civil society: "[We must] extend the principle of free elections so it penetrates the very core of the masses to bring our institutions in line with [democracy]," *L'Avenir* proclaimed.[398] Asserting that "every private interest has the right to self-government,"[399] *L'Avenir* envisioned a sweeping decentralization of administrative and political powers, splintered into myriads of small units managed through direct democracy. It was only logical: Having dethroned the king, they would now unseat all other "kings" in society. This was precisely the stand adopted by the French Socialist Party as François Mitterrand launched self-managing Socialism in the 1980s.[400]

d. Liberation of the Proletariat

The developing social question naturally commanded part of the attention of liberal Catholics. By aligning themselves with the left wing of social Catholicism, they assumed the core of Marxist doctrine. Eighteen years before the *Communist Manifesto*, *L'Avenir* wrote, "After the latest revolution, all that is left ... are the bourgeoisie and the people, the class that buys labor and the class that sells it."[401] In its view, this condition was tantamount to servitude. As they struggled to end servitude in the political sphere through an increasing democratization of civil society, it

---

387. M. Foisset, *Vie du R.P. Lacordaire*, 2 vols. (Paris: Lecoffre Fils et cie., 1870), 1:151–52.

388. De Rosa, *Il movimento*, 18.

389. *Articles de l'Avenir*, 5:343, quoted in C. Constantin, s.v. "Libéralisme catholique," *D.T.C.*, 9–1e.:525.

390. *Articles de l'Avenir*, 5:162–63, 2:340–46, quoted in Constantin, 9–1e.:527.

391. Marc Escholier, *Lacordaire ou Dieu et la liberté* (Paris: Éditions Fleurus, 1959), 187.

392. *Articles de l'Avenir*, 2:83, quoted in Constantin, "Liberalisme catholico," *D.T.C.*, 9–1e.:527.

393. *Articles de l'Avenir*, 5:182, in Constantin, 9–1e.:532.

394. Constantin, 9–1e.:550, 558.

395. Letter of Fr. Ventura to Lamennais (Feb. 1831), quoted in Constantin, 9–1c.:550. On Fr. Gioacchino Ventura, see Mario Tesini, *Gioacchino Ventura: La chiesa nell'età delle rivoluzioni* (Rome: Studium, 1988).

396. See Corrêa de Oliveira, *Unperceived Ideological Transshipment and Dialogue.*

397. Constantin, "Libéralisme catholique," *D.T.C.*, 9–1e.:527.

398. *Articles de l'Avenir*, 1:384, quoted in Constantin, 9–1e.:533.

399. Constantin, 9:533.

400. See Corrêa de Oliveira, "What Does Self-Managing Socialism Mean for Communism."

401. *L'Avenir*, Oct. 19, 1830, in Constantin, "Libéralisme catholique," *D.T.C.*, 9–1e.:535.

was now only natural for liberal Catholics to feel attracted to the so-called emancipation of the proletariat.

According to *L'Avenir*, the evil lay in the capitalist system, perceived as being oblivious to the workers' plight and "solely preoccupied with determining the most favorable laws for the production of material wealth. ... subordinating the happiness of individuals and the welfare of workers to the splendor of the lords of fortune."[402] This situation could only produce a simmering class conflict. Thus, *L'Avenir* warned property owners of "implacable proletarian hatred gathering over their heads ... waiting only for them to slacken their vigilance in order to break loose."[403]

A populist spirit—that conceived the world as divided between "oppressors" and "oppressed"—thus began to creep into some strains of liberal Catholicism.

> Who crowded around Jesus to listen to him? [asked Lamennais.] The people...
> ...Who crucified him on Calvary between two thieves?
> The scribes, pharisees, doctors of the law ... the Roman government.[404]

Father Lacordaire likewise stated that Christ chose His apostles "not among the oppressors of the mind, but among the oppressed. ... Such were the first liberators of the human spirit."[405]

6. Gregory XVI Condemns Liberal Catholicism and Excommunicates Lamennais

Such troublesome tendencies could not fail to call the attention of Church authorities. In July 1832, fourteen French bishops issued a document condemning fifty-six propositions of liberal Catholicism. One month later, Pope Gregory XVI, in his encyclical *Mirari Vos*, formally condemned that current. The pope particularly rejected limitless freedom of conscience ("absurd and erroneous") and of opinion (stemming from "[t]his shameful font of indifferentism"). The sovereign pontiff solemnly denounced "teachings ... which attack the trust and submission due to princes," and warned that "the torches of treason are being lit everywhere."[406] The next day Cardinal Pacca sent Lamennais a letter explaining that he was the main target of the document.

Deeply grieved, but not in the least repentant, Lamennais refused to submit: "My conscience forces me to declare ... that, ... if on the religious plane a Christian must listen and obey, in the purely secular realm he remains entirely free in his opinions, words, and deeds vis-à-vis the spiritual power."[407] In other words, forced to choose between submission to the Church and liberalism, he chose the latter.

Now unrestrained, Lamennais slipped toward libertarian, agnostic, and socialist positions and his rupture with the Faith became inevitable. In 1833, he renounced his ecclesiastical functions and abandoned any outward profession of Faith. In 1834, he published the insolent book, *Paroles d'un croyant* [Words of a Believer]. Gregory XVI condemned the book, accusing him of "seeking to baptize the Revolution," and excommunicated him. Lamennais denounced "the conspiracy of kings and priests against the people" and, giving vent to his violent temper, called the

Vatican "the most dreadful cesspool that it has ever been the lot of man to look upon," and the pope, a "cowardly old imbecile."[408]

All his companions submitted, albeit relunctantly. Montalembert went so far as to define the encyclical *Mirari vos* "the most baleful event in the history of the Church in France."[409] *L'Avenir* closed down. Abandoned by his friends, Lamennais survived as a socialist deputy in the 1848 Constitutional Assembly and the 1849 National Assembly. He died in 1854 in poverty and isolation, refusing any consolation from the Church.

7. Fr. Henri Lacordaire

The more discerning disciples of Lamennais did not follow him to apostasy and were thus able to continue his work. Among them was Father Lacordaire, who played a central role in furthering liberal Catholic ideas in the ensuing years, serving as a bridge between the liberal Catholicism of 1830 and that of 1848.

After a brief career as a lawyer, Henri Lacordaire entered the seminary in 1824. In 1827, against the advice of his director, who perceived his rebellious nature, he was ordained a priest. A "spiritual son of the [1789] Revolution," as his biographer Marc Scholier defines him,[410] Father Lacordaire became the favorite disciple of Lamennais in 1830 and founded *L'Avenir* with him. A proud spirit, he fancied his mission as that of a great reformer. "I dare say that I have received from God the grace of understanding this century, which I have loved so much, and of giving truth a new color that will enable it to reach a larger number of people," he wrote.[411]

After the encyclical *Mirari vos*, Father Lacordaire prudently abandoned his master but explained that he submitted to the pope's decision "without, however, renouncing my liberal ideas."[412] He criticized Lamennais's haste but not his doctrine: "The Church had its profound reasons ... for refusing to go as fast as we would have liked."[413] He thus proposed a gradualist approach. In 1835, the archbishop of Paris offered him the pulpit of Notre Dame. His sermons, attended by the elite of Parisian society, became the main vehicle of liberal Catholic propaganda.

Father Lacordaire played yet another important role in the spread of revolutionary ideas in Catholic circles. He reestablished the Order of Preachers in France, outlawed since the 1789 Revolution. The move was opposed by many prelates, rightly fearing, as Father Lacordaire himself conceded, that "[the Order] could become a refuge for Lamennais's old friends."[414] Unfortunately, they were right. Many novices received from Father Lacordaire a formation heavily tinged with liberal ideas. Herein lies the onset of the progressive wing within the Dominican Order in France, which, in the twentieth century, developed the Nouvelle Théologie that served as the foundation for LT.

Having welcomed the revolution of 1830, Father Lacordaire naturally exulted in that of 1848, when he was elected to the Constitutional Assembly and sat with the republican left. He died in 1861, "a repentant Christian and an unrepentant liberal," to use his own words.

---

402. *Articles de l'Avenir*, 5:189, in Constantin, 9–1e.:535.

403. *Articles de l'Avenir*, 1:247, in Constantin, 9–1e.:535.

404. F. Lamennais, *Paroles d'un croyant: Le livre du peuple* (Paris: Garnier Frères, 1864), 55–56.

405. Henri Lacordaire, *Conférences de Notre-Dame de Paris*, 4 vols. (Paris: Sagnier et Bray, 1844), 1:38.

406. Gregory XVI, encyclical *Mirari vos* (Aug. 15, 1832), nos. 14, 17.

407. Barbier, *Histoire du catholicisme libéral*, 1:11.

408. Dansette, *Religious History*, 1:223.

409. Dansette, 1:223.

410. Escholier, *Lacordaire*, 112.

411. Escholier, 113.

412. Escholier, 91.

413. Escholier, 91.

414. Lacordaire, "Letter to Mme. de Prailly," Escholier, 141.

8. The 1848 Revolution

This is a crucial date in the history of the revolutionary process. A wave of liberal and socialist uprisings traversed Europe. In Italy, until today, "to do a forty-eight" means to create havoc, chaos, and confusion.

In France, the revolution overthrew King Louis Philippe I. Initially moderate, it gradually moved toward a Jacobin republic. The June barricades even projected the mirage of a proletarian dictatorship. The archbishop of Paris, Most Rev. Denis-Auguste Affre, took to the streets to calm tempers and was killed by the rebels as Our Lady had predicted to St. Catherine Labouré in the 1830 apparitions at Rue du Bac. The liberal Catholics supported the revolution, which they saw as a continuation of 1789 and 1830.

However, the socialist anarchy triggered a very strong reaction that led Prince Louis Napoleon to power, first as president and later as emperor. While Catholics faithful to tradition clung to the legitimist position, distancing themselves from the Second Empire, liberal Catholics joined the republican left to the point of supporting even the 1870 Commune.

In Italy, the 1848 riots unleashed by Masonry and the Carbonari, and romantically christened as the "springtime of peoples," were intertwined with the Risorgimento as part of the historical process leading to the foundation of the Kingdom of Italy with the House of Savoy. In chronological order, let us recall the Sicilian Revolution, the first to break out in Europe; the Five Days of Milan, during which pro-Piedmont patricians and moderate Democrats were also joined by Mazzini's Jacobins; the proclamation of the New Venetian Republic of Saint Mark led by the Masonic leader Daniele Manin, who unleashed an irreverent priest hunt through the streets of Venice; and, above all, the proclamation of the Roman Republic under the auspices of Mazzini and Garibaldi, who chased the Vicar of Christ from the Eternal City while freshly painted graffiti on church walls proclaimed, "Death to Christ! Long live Barabbas!"

Underlying it all was the complex phenomenon of the Italian Risorgimento, about which historian Marco Tangheroni writes, "The set of events that generally falls under the name 'Risorgimento' represents a moment in Italian history somehow similar to what the French Revolution represented for France. On the other hand, it has been linked to the latter and is often called the 'Great Revolution' from beyond the Alps."[415] Little wonder, then, that several authors refer to Risorgimento as a whole as the "Italian Revolution."[416]

This Revolution was done at the expense not only of the traditional States, lumped together into the Kingdom of Italy, but also of the pope, who became a prisoner in the Vatican. Despite the attempts by some liberal Catholics to baptize the Risorgimento by placing the pope as its guide,[417] it soon turned into a kind of all-out civil war unleashed against the Church at all levels:

ideological, military, political, and social. Ernesto Galli della Loggia is correct when he writes, "Italy is the only country in Europe (and not only in the Catholic area) whose national unity and liberation from foreign domination has taken place in an open and fierce contrast with its own national Church. In a sense, the incompatibility between the homeland and religion, between the State and Christianity is a foundational element of our collective identity as a nation state."[418] What an irony of history; the Catholic religion was the only thing uniting the peninsula states.

At the Parliament in Turin, Ferdinando Petruccelli della Gattina thundered, "The Catholic Church is an idea from the past, a corpse. Let the corpse dissolve by itself. ... Nothing but a mutual curse will remain between Italy and the nefarious tradition of the papacy. By seizing Rome by force, gentlemen, we have accomplished the greatest revolution of modern times. Henry VIII, Luther drove the pope out of their countries. We cast out the temporal papacy from the world and hung spirituality out to die. We have emancipated the human spirit from the authority of the papacy."[419]

In the Italian Revolution, two distinguishable things have been confused: the patriotic cause of national unity, theoretically legitimate, and the liberal and even Jacobin orientation of the historical process that carried it through. It is licit to ask to what degree, when supporting the former, liberal Catholics did not also yearn for the latter. "According to liberal Catholics," Gabriele De Rosa writes, "Italy's rebirth was inextricably linked to the history of the Church."[420]

For the Jacobins, the two things were obviously interweaved. Gabriele De Rosa speaks of "those who had seen the fall of the temporal power [of the pope] not so much as the culmination of the unification of Italy but as the first step toward the destruction of Catholicism." He recalls that one of the first public acts of the new government, on the occasion of the Voltaire death centennial, was to gather the Chamber of Deputies, the Senate, and the Municipality of Rome for a celebratory act. Posters affixed on every wall of the Eternal City praised the work of Voltaire: "It was war against superstition, religious prejudices, fanaticism, and religious intolerance. He had to declare war on religion, a merciless war every day and every hour. It was not the war of one man but of a whole century."[421]

The Italian Revolution divided both the country and the Church. While the liberal Catholic currents supported the Risorgimento, which they saw as a concrete opportunity to practice their beliefs, the ultramontane Catholics, following Pius IX, opposed it strenuously. Acts of open disobedience to the pope happened everywhere, such as the much-trumpeted 1862 referendum among the Venetian clergy on the unification of Italy, which turned into a plebiscite against Pius IX.[422] Under the influence of the 1848 revolution, a strong secularization process developed that was not that different from the one that hit the Church in the 1960s. Thousands of priests and religious left their churches and convents to "follow history." Moreover, in parallel

415. Marco Tangheroni, *Cristianità, modernità, rivoluzione: Appunti di uno storico fra "mestiere" e impegno civico-culturale,* ed. Oscar Sanguinetti (Milan: Sugarco Edizioni, 2009), 95. Antonio Socci writes: "[The idea] was to bring the Church to her knees before the world. ...For many, the [Revolution of] '48 was a decisive moment; many priests joined the liberals. Dark times began ...for those who remained faithful to the Church." Antonio Socci, *La dittatura anticattolica* (Milan: Sugarco, 2004), 98.

416. Massimo Viglione, *La rivoluzione italiana* (Rome: Minotauro, 2001). See also, Massimo Viglione, *Libera chiesa in libero stato? Il risorgimento e i cattolici: uno scontro epocale* (Rome: Città Nuova, 2005). In the wake of what had happened in France with its Constitutional Church, Italy saw an attempt to found a national church inspired by the Revolution. It was the Italian Evangelical Free Church, founded by Italian exiles in London in 1850. Among its main promoters was the apostate Barnabite priest Alessandro Gavazzi (1809–1889). See Giorgio Spini, *Risorgimento e protestanti* (Milan: Il Saggiatore, 1989).

417. This brings to mind Vincenzo Gioberti's *Del primato morale e civile degli italiani,* 2 vols. (Brussels: Meline, Cans, 1843), the starting point of the neo-Guelph unitarian current.

418. Ernesto Galli della Loggia, "Liberali che non hanno saputo dirsi cristiani," in *Il Mulino* 5/93, no. 349, 859. See also Angela Pellicciari, *Risorgimento da riscrivere: Liberali & massoni contro la chiesa* (Milan: Ares, 1998); Angela Pellicciari, *L'altro risorgimento: Una guerra di religione dimenticata* (Casale Monferrato: Piemme, 2000).

419. De Rosa, *Il movimento,* 101.

420. De Rosa, 19.

421. De Rosa, 101–2.

422. See Giovanni Azzolin, Gaetano De Lai, *"L'uomo forte di Pio X": Cultura e fede nel i novecento nell'esperienza del cardinale vicentino* (Vicenza: Accademia Olimpica, 2003), 28–36. See also Angelo Volpe, *La questione romana e il clero veneto* (Venice: Tip. della Gazzetta, 1862). In this booklet, Dom Angelo Volpe attacks the pope's powers and infallibility. See also Angelo Gambasin, *Il clero padovano e la dominazione austriaca 1859–1866* (Rome: Edizioni di Storia e Letteratura, 1967).

with events in the temporal sphere, liberal and revolutionary secret societies, such as the Most Holy Sodality of Padua, began to appear in Church circles.

9. The Malines Speech, a Manifesto of Liberal Catholicism

With a strong liberal Catholic presence, an International Catholic Congress convened in Malines, Belgium, in August 1863. Among others representing Italy was Giambattista Casoni (1830–1919), who would soon found in Bologna the Italian Catholic Association for the Defense of Church Freedom.[423] The high point of this Malines Congress was the speech given by Count Charles de Montalembert, a manifesto of liberal Catholicism.[424]

According to Montalembert, Catholics must quit dreaming of an alliance between altar and throne, and accept instead the modern liberties and the democratic institutions they inform. True, medieval Christendom had been a magnificent order, but it was dead and buried. Instead of foolishly clinging to a dead world, Catholics should accept the new order inaugurated by the French and American revolutions. The world was now on a new path: "The democratic flood is increasing and will eventually cover everything." Any attempt to stop this flood is utopian. Catholics, Montalembert concluded, must accept "these facts and realities" and discover the "Gospel values" in them.

The speech caused great malaise in Catholic circles. At the Congress itself, Nicholas Cardinal Wiseman and the papal envoy, Fr. Mieczyslaw Ledochowski, warned Montalembert. The pope's secretary of state, Giacomo Cardinal Antonelli, wrote the count a letter stating the pope's opinion that, given their opposition to the teachings of the Catholic Church, the speeches were reprehensible.

In April 1867, another Catholic Congress was held in Malines. This time, however, attendance was down and the tone cautious. For the purpose of our study, it is interesting to highlight the Congress's support of the nascent Christian Democratic movement and their intimate connection.[425]

10. Pius IX Condemns Liberal Catholicism

Very attentive to the dangers that could undermine the Faith, Pope Pius IX saw the liberal spirit as the most insidious enemy of the time.[426] He countered secularism, which denied any relevance of God and the Church, with the Catholic vision of a social and political order inextricably linked to the moral and religious one. For the pope, liberal Catholics were more dangerous than declared enemies since they fought the Holy City from within its very walls:

> Although the sons of this world be wiser than the sons of light, their snares and violence would undoubtedly have less success if a greater number of those who call themselves Catholics did not extend a friendly hand to them. Yes, unfortunately, there are those who wish to walk in agreement with our enemies, who try to establish an alliance between light and darkness, an agreement

between justice and iniquity by means of liberal Catholic doctrines, which, based on the most pernicious principles, adulate the civil power when it invades things spiritual and urge souls to respect, or at least tolerate the most iniquitous laws, as if it had not been written absolutely that no one can serve two masters. They are far more dangerous and pernicious than our declared enemies ... because maintaining themselves on the extreme limit of condemned opinions, they take on an appearance of integrity and irreproachable doctrine, beguiling the imprudent friends of conciliations and deceiving honest persons who would revolt against a declared error. For this reason, they bring about a dividedness of mind, rent the unity, and weaken the forces that should be gathered against the enemy.[427]

In 1862, as rumors had it that the pope was preparing a document condemning Liberalism, a group of liberal Catholics gathered secretly at Montalembert's castle in La-Roche-en-Breny, under the auspices of Most Rev. Félix Dupanloup, bishop of Orléans (1802–1878). That meeting's happening was discovered only years later when, during renovation works, a plaque came to light engraved with this Latin text: "In this oratory, Felix, bishop of Orleans, distributed the bread of the word and the bread of Christian life to a small group of friends who, long united in the struggle for a free Church within a free State, renewed the pact of dedicating the rest of their lives to God and liberty. October 12, 1862. Alfred, Count de Falloux, Teophile Foisset, Augustin Cochin, Charles Count de Montalembert, absent in body but present in spirit, Albert, Prince de Broglie."[428]

The use of the term *renewal* suggests the existence of a previous covenant linking the liberal Catholic leaders. At the heart of the liberal reaction against Pius IX was therefore an association whose contours remain obscure, a situation not very different from the modernists' reaction against St. Pius X, which he said, in 1910, was promoted by a *clandestinum foedus*, a secret league.

Pius IX's condemnation finally came in 1864 with the encyclical *Quanta cura* and the *Syllabus errorum*. While the former was a scathing analysis of the modern errors and the evils of contemporary civilization, which liberal Catholics loved and embraced so much, the latter was a detailed catalogue of liberal errors in the theological, philosophical, and sociopolitical fields. The blow was devastating. "The consternation was general," conceded the Prince de Broglie in his *Memoirs*.[429]

Unfortunately, the disarray did not last long. Sensing hesitation in some Catholic quarters to follow the pope in his crusade against the modern errors, Bishop Dupanloup published a commentary to Pius IX's documents, *La convention du 15 novembre et l'encyclique du 8 decembre*. The book sketched a line of defense that largely enabled liberal Catholics to circumvent the pope's condemnation, much like what Americanists and modernists did a few years later.

Bishop Dupanloup resorted to a crafty distinction between the thesis (doctrinal plane) and the hypothesis (concrete situations). The bishop of Orleans conceded that Rome had condemned doctrinal Liberalism (the thesis) and, thus, no Catholic could profess it. This notwithstanding, he continued, the Church

---

423. Severely persecuted by the Savoy government under the Crispi Law, the association was dissolved on May 14, 1866.

424. See Montalembert, "L'église libre dans l'état libre." On Montalembert, see L.R.P. Lecanuet, *Montalembert, d'après son journal et sa correspondance*, 3 vols. (Paris: Poussielgue, 1898–1902); Adolfo Tommasi, ed., *Montalembert* (Turin: Società Editrice Internazionale, 1928).

425. On relations between Catholics and liberal Christian Democrats, see Julio Menvielle, *De Lamennais a Maritain* (Buenos Aires: Ediciones Theoria, 1967).

426. On Blessed Pius IX, see Roberto de Mattei, *Pio IX e la rivoluzione italiana* (Siena: Cantagalli, 2012); Roberto de Mattei, *Pius IX*, trans. John Laughland (Leominster, Herefordshire, U.K.: Gracewing, 2004); Luigi Negri, *Pio IX: Attualità e profezia* (Milan: Ares, 2006); Giorgio Bouchard, *Pio IX, un papa contro il risorgimento* (Turin: Claudiana, 2001); David I. Kertzer, *Prigioniero del Vaticano: Pio IX e lo scontro tra la chiesa e lo stato italiano* (Milan: Rizzoli, 2005).

427. Pius IX, brief "To the president and young members of the Circle St. Ambrose of Milan" (Mar. 6, 1873), *La Civiltà Cattolica* 24, series 8, no. 547, 10:99–100.

428. Barbier, *Histoire du catholicisme libéral*, 1:32.

429. Albert de Broglie, *Mémoires*, 430, quoted in Constantin, "Libéralisme catholique," 9–1e.:592. Hurt to the quick by the documents of Pius IX, the liberals reacted angrily. The French government issued an official protest. In Italy, the publication of the two documents was prohibited until February 8, 1865.

had to face reality (the hypothesis), namely, the modern world molded by liberal attitudes and ideas. Two lines of conduct could be validly advanced, Bishop Dupanloup argued: Either leave the world and declare war against it; or, in the impossibility of defeating the world, learn to live with it and try to make the best within that compromise. This latter position, the liberal Catholic leader rationalized, did not necessarily imply an acceptance of the doctrines of Liberalism. It was a step imposed by circumstances.

That clever distinction enabled liberal Catholics to make a theoretical act of submission to the Church while continuing their endeavors in the 'real world.' By consigning the papal documents to the rarefied realms of abstract theory, liberal Catholics managed to make them largely irrelevant. Moreover, the distinction made it difficult to criticize liberal Catholics because concrete situations are so complex that they usually make decisions in this area subject to dispute.

Perhaps in no country did this distinction profit the liberal Catholics so much as in Italy. While very few people openly rose against the magisterium of Pius IX on doctrinal grounds (the thesis), in practical terms, many enthusiastically participated in various patriotic movements whose liberal, Masonic, and anti-Catholic inspiration they could not ignore. In this way, they supported in practice principles that they denied in theory.

On making that distinction, liberal Catholics overlooked an essential point. Consonant with her mission of saving souls, the Church must also strive to foster a sociopolitical order inspired by the Gospel. In other words, She must establish a Christian civilization. The Church can accept the trends of the times only when they do not run counter to revealed truth. Now, the dominant trends of the nineteenth century were gravely infected with revolutionary toxins. By saying that the Church should adapt to the world, liberal Catholics implicitly renounced the pursuit of a Christian civilization, thus betraying an important aspect of the salvific mission of the Church.

11. The First Vatican Council

On June 29, 1868, Pius IX convoked an ecumenical council at the Vatican, the twentieth in the history of the Church.[430] Many liberal Catholics greeted the step as a propitious occasion to spark a debate within the Church, which might give rise to substantial reforms. Some even likened the Council to the States General convoked by Louis XVI in 1788, the starting point of the French Revolution. Pius IX was no Louis XVI, though. He firmly made known his desire of holding a Council that would counter the errors of the time both in the dogmatic and pastoral fields. In the bull *Aeterni Patris* we read that the purpose of the Council was to "remedy the evils of the century in the Church and in society." In order to strike at the heart of the liberal mentality, Pius IX proposed the definition of the dogma of papal infallibility.

Initially, liberal Catholics seemed disconcerted. Montalembert charged the conservatives with "seeking to immolate justice and truth, reason and history to the idol they erected for themselves in the Vatican."[431] Some Council Fathers, unwilling to confront Pius IX head-on, decided to contest the dogma of infallibility on the sole ground that it was inopportune. In other words, they would not challenge the dogma in the thesis, but only in the hypothesis.

Others challenged the dogma also on doctrinal grounds. The reaction was particularly strong in Germany, where liberal Catholic leaders—mostly university professors—were deeply infected by the type of erudite rationalism dominant in German Protestant circles. The leading figure of this tendency was Fr. Johann Joseph Ignaz Döllinger (1799–1890), rector of the University of Munich and a participant in the Malines Congress. Under the pseudonym *Janus*, he published in the *Allgemeine Zeitung* of Augsburg a series of articles against the dogma, later collected in a volume titled *Der papst und das konzil*.[432] He was decisively refuted by Joseph Cardinal Hergenröther (1824–1890) in the book *Anti-Janus*. Döllinger ended his days excommunicated.

In France, the anti-infallibilist current was led by Bishops Dupanloup and Henri-Louis Charles Maret (1805–1884), the latter having been a former director, with Father Lacordaire, of *L'Ère Nouvelle*.[433] In England, the task befell Lord John Acton (1834–1902), director of *The Rambler*, mouthpiece of the liberal Catholic current. Opposed by many bishops and particularly by Cardinals Wiseman and Manning, Acton was forced to close down the monthly.

In Italy, at the initiative of Congressman Joseph Ricciardi, the Masons decided to respond to the pope by holding an anti-council in Naples. Among its first supporters was Giuseppe Garibaldi, who wrote Ricciardi from Caprera: "Overthrow the papal monster, build reason and truth upon its ruins. ... Conclusion: remove the priest-liar and sacrilegious teacher of God, and the primary obstacle to the moral unity of nations."[434]

In the end, despite the maneuvers of the liberal minority, the First Vatican Council closed with a victory of the conservative line. The States General of the Church dreamed of by the left would have to wait. Contrary to what readers might think, however, the conservative victory was quite painful. The liberal minority showed itself compact and combative at all times, bending only before the extreme firmness of Pius IX. As shown by some speeches at the Council, the process of infiltration of revolutionary errors was already very advanced even in the hierarchy. Writing to Fr. Josep Xifré, then Superior of the Claretian Congregation, St. Anthony Maria Claret (1807–1870) lamented, "I am ready to shed my blood, as I said at the Council. As I heard the errors and even blasphemies and heresies that were being uttered I was seized by such a great outrage and zeal that blood went to my head and produced a brain disorder."[435]

12. Leo XIII's Pontificate

Pope Leo XIII (1810, 1878–1903) continued his predecessor's anti-liberal work, giving it sound doctrinal foundations. We also owe him the first systematic exposition of the Church's social doctrine. In opposition to liberal and socialist doctrines, Leo XIII set forth the duties of men and institutions vis-à-vis God and the

430. On the First Vatican Council, see Theodor Granderath, *Histoire du concile du Vatican depuis sa première annonce jusqu'à sa prorogation d'après les documents authentiques*, 5 vols. (Brussels: Libraire Albert Dewit, 1913).

431. Lecanuet, *Montalembert*, 3:467.

432. See W.J. Sparrow-Simpson, *Roman Catholic Opposition to Papal Infallibility* (London: John Murray, 1909), 188–93, 205–6.

433. See Henri-Louis-Charles Maret, *Du concile générale et de la paix religieuse* (Paris: Henri Plon, 1869). He was opposed by Dom Prosper Guéranger in *De la monarchie pontificale: À propos du livre de Mgr. l'éveque de Sura* (Charleston, S.C.: Nabu Press, 2014). On Bishop Maret, see Claude Bressolette, *L'Abbé Maret: le combat d'un théologien pour une démocratie chrétienne, 1830–1851* (Paris: Beauchesne, 1977).

434. Rosario Francesco Esposito, *La massoneria e l'Italia dal 1800 ai nostri giorni* (Rome: Edizioni Paoline, 1979), 134, quoted in de Mattei, *Pio IX*, 207. See also Rosario Francesco Esposito, *Pio IX: La chiesa in conflitto col mondo; La S. Sede, la massoneria e il radicalismo settario* (Rome: Edizioni Paoline, 1979).

435. Giorgio Papasogli and Franco Stano, eds. *Antonio Claret, l'uomo che sfidò l'impossibile* (Vatican: Libreria Editrice Vaticana, 1963), 703. The great Spanish saint never recovered from the stroke and died in exile on October 24, 1870. A consistent minority opposed the dogma of infallibility during the First Vatican Council, showing how much revolutionary tendencies had spread among the hierarchy. According to progressive theologian August Bernhard Hasler, 130 out of 774 Council Fathers were staunchly anti-infallibilist, 500 were undecided, and about 50 were staunch supporters of infallibility. See August Bernhard Hasler, *Come il papa divenne infallibile* (Turin: Claudiana, 1982). Fifty-five Council Fathers abstained from the vote, and some left Rome to avoid supporting Pius IX.

Church. In his encyclical *Libertas praestatissimum* he condemned Liberalism even in its mild forms: "[M]an, by a necessity of his nature, is wholly subject to the most faithful and ever-enduring power of God; and that, as a consequence, any liberty, except that which consists in submission to God and in subjection to His will, is unintelligible. To deny the existence of this authority in God, or to refuse to submit to it, means to act, not as a free man, but as one who treasonably abuses his liberty; and in such a disposition of mind the chief and deadly vice of Liberalism essentially consists."[436]

In some aspects, however, Leo XIII's pastoral line diverged from that of Pius IX. While the latter consistently favored Ultramontanism and every form of opposition to the dominant revolutionary spirit, founded on a negative assessment of the historical moment, his successor preferred to attenuate the manifestations of antagonism. He did so in the hope that, seeing the Church's outstretched hand, her enemies would mellow and drop their anti-Catholic campaign. The most famous illustration of this policy was the so-called Ralliement with the French Republic, already discussed in the preceding chapter. Alec Vidler writes, "Leo XIII acquired the reputation of being a liberal pope ... due chiefly to the comparative difference between his policy and pontificate and those of his predecessor and of his successor."[437]

The new pastoral line was no longer intransigent but more accommodating. It corresponded to the modern Zeitgeist that was fashioning the world, a proof that events in the civil sphere almost always affect the Church. Leaving behind the horrors of the Franco-Prussian War of 1870, Europe had entered a period of great military, cultural, industrial, and technological development which would culminate in the Belle Époque. Between brilliant balls and lavish ceremonies, people gradually acquired a superficial and optimistic mentality and confidence in science and technology, symbolized by the Paris Universal Exposition of 1889. Some aspects of that mentality penetrated the Church to the point that theologian Fr. Jean Rivière spoke about the "optimism that characterized the pontificate of Leo XIII."[438] In short, although nothing in Church teaching had changed, the atmosphere in many Church circles was altogether different, more easy-going and relaxed, which, Father Rivière says, "risked encouraging imprudent or unwelcome initiatives."[439]

13. Liberal Catholicism and Christian Democracy

Toward the turn of the century, although some sectors still navigated what we may call the mainstream of liberal Catholicism, the more radical sectors advanced toward the logical consequences of their tendencies and ideas, gradually flowing into the modernist and Christian democratic currents.

"The paternity of Christian democracy belongs to Lamennais, originally the father of Catholic Liberalism," explains Robert Havard de la Montagne in his widely known history of Christian democracy.[440] In his speech to the Tenth Conference of the International Committee on Historical Sciences, held in Rome

in 1957, historian Jean Baptiste Durosselle asserts that "evidently, all the Christian democrats are liberal Catholics."[441] Summarizing the process, Jean-Yves Chevalier wrote, "In France, Christian democracy is the final result of a movement which had liberal Catholicism ... at its origin."[442]

B. Americanism

1. The Roots of the American Spirit

In the United States, the problem of liberal Catholicism presented itself somewhat differently. The question centered not so much upon trying to accommodate Catholic doctrine to the heritage of the French Revolution of 1789, but rather to a peculiar interpretation of the American Revolution (1765–1791). In its popular manifestations, this interpretation presented itself more as a way of life, a generalized mood, than as a body of structured and coherent doctrines. Studying this way of life is extremely important to analyze the development of liberal tendencies in the bosom of the Church.

We have already mentioned the fascination America exerted on European liberal Catholics in the nineteenth century, especially through the work of Alexis de Tocqueville. In the twentieth century, the influence of the Americanist mentality—more than its doctrine—turned out to be decisive. In fact, the world to which they claimed the Church had to adapt was shaped not only by socialist influences from Moscow (easily criticizable as coming from an ideology condemned by the Church), but also, and often preponderantly, by the influence of an Americanist mentality that exploded in the Roaring Twenties.[443] This mentality, all the more insidious because it was not easy to attack, became hegemonic in the West after the Second World War. It was the same mentality that penetrated large sectors of Catholic Action, weakening its fiber and opening it to the influence of the new theological doctrines.

The American Revolution was heir more to the Anglo-Scottish Enlightenment than the continental one, though the latter also played an important role.[444] The democratic and liberal principles born of this Revolution did not reveal the degree of revolutionary virulence shown by its French counterpart, although sharing a common lineage. The leading political currents in the early United States did not manifest the common European haste to draw out the extreme consequences of the revolutionary postulates. Rather, they preferred a cautious gradualness and prudent empiricism more congenial with the prevalent Anglo-Saxon

436. Leo XIII, encyclical *Libertas* (June 20, 1888), no. 36.

437. Alec R. Vidler, *The Modernist Movement in the Roman Church: Its Origins & Outcome* (New York: Gordon Press, 1976), 60.

438. Rivière, "Modernisme," col. 2016. The optimism shown in some Vatican circles contrasted conspicuously with Saint John Bosco's evaluation. In an interview to *Journal de Rome*, in April 1884, the reporter asked him, "What do you think about the present conditions in the Church and in Europe, in Italy, and their future?" The Turin saint answered, "No one but God knows the future. However, humanly speaking, one should think that the future will be dire. My predictions are very sad, but I fear nothing. God will always save His Church." Interview with *Journal de Rome*, April 25, 1884, quoted in Teresio Bosco, *Don Bosco: una biografia nuova* (Turin: Elledici, 1998), 415.

439. Rivière, "Modernisme," col. 2016.

440. Havard de la Montagne, *Histoire de la democratie chrétienne*, 123.

441. Jean Baptiste Durosselle, *Comitato Internazionale delle Scienze Storiche: Atti del X Congresso Internazionale* (Rome: 1957), quoted in Émile Poulat, *L'église, c'est un monde* (Paris: Les Éditions du Cerf, 1986), 102.

442. Jean-Yves Chevalier, *Revue des Deux Mondes*, May 1, 1968, 6–7, quoted in Poulat, *L'Église*, 102.

443. Plinio Corrêa de Oliveira defines this mentality as "a subconscious, and sometimes conscious state of the mind whereby enjoying life is raised up as the supreme human value, and one seeks to understand the universe and organize life in a voluptuous manner." Plinio Corrêa de Oliveira, "O coração do sábio está onde há tristeza," *Catolicismo*, no. 85 (Jan. 1985). "While Europe seemed to sink into chaos, America attained the zenith of Wilsonian splendor. The United States had reached its apogee." Plinio Corrêa de Oliveira, "A dinamite de Cristo," *O Legionário*, no. 321, Nov. 5, 1938.

444. Anglo-Saxon thinkers normally sustain that the Enlightenment started in England and Scotland, and only afterward expanded to the European continent, where it acquired a different tone. They thus distinguish between the Anglo-Scottish Enlightenment, prompted by Locke, Hobbes, and others, and the Continental one represented by Voltaire, Diderot, Rousseau, and the other French *philosophes*. They credit the former with having triggered the "Glorious Revolution" of 1688, the American Revolution, and the liberal-capitalist revolutions that followed in their wake. They fault the latter for having generated the French Revolution, Socialism, Communism, and anarchism. Thus, noted neo-conservative scholar Irving Kristol asserts, "Though the American Revolution was inspired by a rather casual intermingling of the two Enlightenments, it was the Anglo-Scottish Enlightenment that was, in the end, decisive." Irving Kristol, *Reflections of a Neoconservative: Looking Back, Looking Ahead* (New York: Basic Books, 1983), 142.

temperament and the common sense proper to the dominant capitalist-mercantilist mentality. We need only contrast George Washington's gentlemanly figure, measured countenance, and moral standards with the vulgar grimace, sanguinary agitation, and debauchery of Marat in order to grasp the sharp differences between the movements they typified.

In 1776, when the thirteen American colonies proclaimed their independence from the British crown, few residents doubted that a great nation was aborning. Expressions such as "providential mission," "manifest destiny," "great project," often employed in speeches at the time, conveyed the general yearning that the United States were destined to carry out a great mission in a not-so-distant future. Even the grandeur of its vast and grand geographical panorama seemed to mirror that destiny.

Most public men, and more broadly the population, saw this mission within the historical perspective that led to the independence of the United States, born from a liberal revolution. In breaking away from the mother country, the former colonies did nothing more than apply the postulates of Protestantism and the Enlightenment in the sociopolitical sphere. The confluence of both currents, along with significant remnants of British tradition still present on American soil, formed what we may call the original national spirit.

American Liberalism assumed, however, a different character from its European counterpart. While in continental Europe Liberalism showed above all its Jacobin, radical, and violent face represented by the French Revolution, in the United States it showed a somewhat smiling, optimistic, and moderate character, eminently pragmatic and averse to great ideological enthusiasm. It favored slow processes instead of sudden jerks.

This diversity also came from the respective historical contexts. While in Europe Protestantism and Liberalism still had to eradicate mighty remnants of medieval Christendom and impose themselves through bitter controversies and bloody revolutions, in the United States the ground was already prepared since a medieval Christendom had never existed there. Liberalism was thus able to prosper in peace and harmony, avoiding unnecessary haste, dampening religious and ideological disputes, and gradually shaping a broad consensus tending to a peculiar style of religious, moral, and philosophical relativism.

Moreover, the country's very governability required this kind of consensus. Indeed, in the political arena the United States formed a confederation of thirteen virtually independent states that did not always agree with one another. In the religious sphere, in addition to the minority Catholic Church, they incorporated a multitude of Protestant sects, none of which could boast hegemony. Furthermore, monarchist sectors were still strong enough to oppose significant reaction should the country slip too quickly to the left. Indeed, royalist feelings were so strong that the possibility of crowning George Washington as king was considered more than once.[445] His official title was "His Most Serene Highness, the President of the United States of America."[446]

Any conflict among Protestant sects, between them and the Catholic Church, or between different political or ideological

factions could compromise the fragile institutional stability of the young nation. Creating an atmosphere of mutual understanding, religious and political freedom, and prudence in governance was thus necessary for the maintenance of national unity, which in turn was a *conditio sine qua non* for the fulfillment of the great mission Americans saw for their country.

What resulted was not just a philosophy. Rather, it was an affable and welcoming way of life that saw clashing opinions from a distance as something typical of backward societies. It was an optimistic and irenic way of life that favored pragmatism and dodged theoretical disquisition as being always dangerous since it can easily give rise to absolute ideas and, thus, to pernicious ideological divisions. This way of life enabled the establishment of a climate of peaceful coexistence light years away from the European ambience, endemically ruptured by controversy and wars. Albeit bloody, the Civil War between North and South (1861–1865) was a parenthesis in this long history of national harmony.

Concessive by nature, this state of mind could easily degenerate into unbridled Liberalism susceptible to eliciting responses that could have dilacerated the national fabric, even if just by giving rise to counter-revolutionary movements. To avoid this, the State took on the defense of the Christian religion in general as the foundation of the moral and social order. Hence the paradox of a constitutionally nondenominational State which nevertheless openly proclaimed itself Christian to the point of incorporating a number of religious events into its public life. We are referring to the so-called civil religion.

Later, that way of life was enhanced by the Industrial Revolution precisely because it did not have to overcome the typical obstacles posed by Europe's traditional societies. It spread in the United States as in no other country, provoking a worship of the practical and a rejection of theoretical thought as being a non-movement and therefore a non-life.

2. A Unilateral Interpretation of the American Spirit

Much like French revolutionaries, however, progressive sectors spread the feeling that the entire "American proposition," to use the expression coined by the Jesuit Fr. John Courtney Murray (1904–1967),[447] contained the dawn of a new era for humanity as successor to the old, austere, and hierarchical European-style Christian civilization. This perception, in turn, gave rise to the idea that the manifest destiny of the United States was to usher

445. See Minor Myers, *Liberty Without Anarchy* (Charlottesville: The University Press of Virginia, 1983), 84. According to Pauline Maier, "The very word [republic] inspired confusion, such that John Adams, perhaps the country's most learned student of politics, complained that he 'never understood' what a republican government was and believed 'no other man ever did or ever will.'" Pauline Maier, *From Resistance to Revolution: Colonial Radicals and the Development of American Opposition to Britain, 1765–1776* (New York: W. W. Norton & Company, 1991), 287.

446. Having returned to Philadelphia, after his tenure as ambassador in Europe (1784–1789), Thomas Jefferson lamented, "I was astonished to find the general prevalence of monarchical sentiments insomuch that in maintaining those of republicanism, I

had always the whole company on my hands, never scarcely finding among them a single co-advocate in that argument." Arthur Meier Schlesinger, *New Viewpoints in American History* (New York: Macmillan, 1928), 82.

447. "It is classic American doctrine, immortally asserted by Abraham Lincoln," said Fr. John Courtney Murray, S.J., "that the new nation which our Fathers brought forth on this continent was dedicated to a 'proposition.'" Explaining the sense of the term, he continues, "It is an affirmation and also an intention. It presents itself as a coherent structure of thought that lays claim to intellectual assent; it also presents itself as an organized political project that aims at historical success." John Courtney Murray, S.J., *We Hold These Truths: Catholic Reflections on the American Proposition* (New York: Sheed & Ward, 1960), vii. Fr. Murray was secretary to the archbishop of New York, Francis Joseph Cardinal Spellman, and also a *peritus* at the Council, participating in the drafting of several documents, especially the declaration *Dignitatis humanae*, on religious freedom. In a 1963 article, Fr. Murray spoke about "the issue of religious liberty" as the Council's "American issue." John Courtney Murray, "On Religious Liberty: Freedom Is the Most Distinctively American Issue Before the Council," *America Magazine* 109 (Nov. 1963), 704. Fr. Murray was convinced that religious freedom was an American contribution to the world: "As it arose in America, the problem of pluralism was unique in the modern world, chiefly because pluralism was the native condition of American society. It was not, as in Europe and in England, the result of a disruption or decay of a previously existent religious unity. This fact created the possibility of a new solution; indeed, it created a demand for a new solution. The possibility was exploited and the demand was met by the American Constitution." Murray, *We Hold These Truths*, 27.

in this historic era, freeing the world from the oppression of dark centuries.[448]

The paradigm of this position, made explicit only by some Protestant millennialist strains but present in varying shades in many American liberal quarters, is the idea that America is the redeemer nation of humanity. According to this paradigm, the so-called Reformation brought freedom and equality in the religious sphere by proclaiming the sovereignty of the individual conscience, the free interpretation of Scriptures, and the end of the hierarchical priesthood. It thus liberated the world from the oppression of the "medieval" Catholic Church. Concomitantly, it inspired like revolutions in the secular sphere, thus liberating the world from the alleged oppression of the feudal order.

England was said to be the torchbearer of this revolution both in its religious and secular aspects, but had stopped short of full reform. It became America's manifest destiny to pick up the flare and carry it for the next sprint to complete the liberation (redemption) of mankind.[449]

Though this issue goes beyond the purpose of this book, we wish, however, to note that this peculiar interpretation of the American spirit is based on a unilateral vision of the country which has been corrected by recent historical and sociological research.[450] In particular, this research has shown how partial and propagandistic was the analysis done by Alexis de Tocqueville.[451]

3. The Manifest Destiny of American Catholicism

This general view, in varying degrees of explicitness, unfortunately also influenced many Catholics. In an 1895 speech, Most Rev. John Ireland, archbishop of Saint Paul, Minn. and leader of the liberal Catholic current at the time, stated, "Even as I believe that God rules over men and nations, so do I believe that a divine mission has been assigned to the Republic of the United States. That mission is to prepare the world ... for the universal reign of human liberty and human rights. America does not live for herself alone; the destinies of humanity are in her keeping."[452]

To that sentiment, the prelate added an ardent patriotism: "Republic of America, receive from me the tribute of my love and of my loyalty. ... I pray from my heart that thy glory be never dimmed.—*Esto perpetua.* [Be forever.] Thou bearest in thy hands the hopes of the human race. Thy mission from God is to show to nations that men are capable of highest civil and political liberty. ... Through thee may liberty triumph over the earth from the rising to the setting sun. *Esto perpetua.*"[453]

Fascinated by the manifest destiny of their country, it was inevitable that liberal American Catholics would likewise conceive a manifest destiny of American Catholicism. In its most explicit version, this conception posited that just as the United States needed to usher in a new era of freedom and equality for mankind, they also had to act as the Promised Land for the Church of the future, a religious version of the motto *novus ordo seclorum*.

4. The Americanization of the Church

This sentiment gave rise to a movement that called for an Americanization of the Catholic Church, that is, her conformance to American culture or, better, to its liberal and egalitarian strains. Its followers will be called here *Americanists*. We use the term sentiment purposefully. Rarely were the underlying assumptions of this movement made totally explicit or its final implications clearly explained. Some of its contours, however, can be easily traced. According to the more vocal partisans of Americanization, the Catholic Church had been enclosed in European civilization for too long and was too strongly influenced by it. Improperly transposing their peculiar interpretation of the American proposition, they maintained that this European Church could hardly have a place in such a liberal and rapidly changing country as the United States.

The underlying assumptions of this view can be summarized as follows:

—The dogmatic character of the Church's Magisterium and the strictness of her discipline were expressions of the authoritarian nature of European institutions; they were foreign to a country founded on the free consent of the governed and the enshrinement of individual freedom;

—The Church's hierarchical constitution was a transposition of the monarchical character of the European nations; it would have to be attenuated if the Church was to acclimate to a country that proclaimed the full equality of all citizens;

—The Church's care in relation to precise doctrinal definitions was the result of an unbalanced passion for abstract reasoning proper to the continental European mind; it was not normally welcomed among a people oriented more by common sense and pragmatism than by

---

448. Speaking on the floor of the U.S. Senate in 1897, historian Albert J. Beveridge (1862–1927) synthesized this position as follows: "God has not been preparing the English-speaking and Teutonic peoples for a thousand years for nothing but vain and idle self-contemplation and self-admiration. No. He made us master organizers of the world to establish system where chaos reigned. He has given us the spirit of progress to overwhelm the forces of reaction throughout the earth. ...Were it not for such a force as this the world would relapse into barbarism and night. And of all our race, He has marked the American people as His chosen nation to finally lead in the redemption of the world." Ernest Lee Tuveson, *Redeemer Nation: The Idea of America's Millennial Role* (Chicago: University of Chicago Press, 1968), vii. See also Conrad Cherry, *God's New Israel* (Englewood Cliffs, N.J.: Prentice-Hall, 1971); A. Frederick Mark, *Manifest Destiny and Mission in American History* (New York: Alfred A. Knopf, 1963). Conservative scholars, on the other hand, assume a markedly different position. See for example Mel E. Bradford, *A Better Guide Than Reason: Studies in the American Revolution* (La Salle, Ill.: Sherwood Sugden & Company, 1983); Mel E. Bradford, *Remembering Who We Are: Observations of a Southern Conservative* (Athens, Ga.: University of Georgia Press, 1985), 21–44.

449. Commenting on Milton, Tuveson remarks that the principal shortcomings of the English Revolution were "the failure to extinguish all the feudal institutions" and the "absence of toleration for the sects." Ernest Lee Tuveson, *Redeemer Nation*, 154. In other words, Britain carried out the great task but only up to a given point. The fulfillment of the mission would be up to another offshoot of the German race. In support of this thesis, some minority currents even claimed that the Anglo-Saxons were the spiritual heirs of the Chosen People, that is to say, the Hebrews, in whom all the prophecies of the Old Testament should be fulfilled. Englishman W.M. Milner writes, "Our King is the LORD'S *Anointed* [sic] both as Priest and King, *in each case by right of succession*, and in fulfilment of a like promise of perpetual ministry to the lines of David and of Aaron." W.M. Milner, *The Royal House of Britain: An Enduring Dynasty*, 15th ed., (London: The Covenant Publishing Co., 1991), 30. See also Herbert W. Armstrong, *The United States and the British Commonwealth in Prophecy* (Pasadena, Calif.: Radio Church of God, 1954); Hyrum L. Androus, Cleon W. Skousen and Robert R. Walton, "The Political Foundation of America," in *Freemen Digest* (Jan. 1984), 32–34; Hyrum L. Androus, Cleon W. Skousen and Robert R. Walton, "America's Anglo-Saxon Heritage of Freedom," *Freemen Digest* (Feb. 1984), 43–45; Hyrum L. Androus, Cleon W. Skousen and Robert R. Walton, "The Anglo-Saxon Connection," *Freemen Digest* (Apr. 1984), 29–31. This theory is not based on the slightest historical proof. On this point, conservative intellectuals also assume a clearly diverse position. See, for example, Hillaire Belloc, *Europe and the Faith* (London: Constable, 1920), especially chap. 5.

450. See Corrêa de Oliveira, *Nobility*, Part Two, "The United States: An Aristocratic Nation Within a Democratic State," 135–330, but especially "Alexis de Tocqueville: One Source of This Unilateral Vision," 146–49.

451. While lending itself to a liberal interpretation, de Tocqueville's work has also inspired several conservative thinkers. In praising the American liberal adventure, de Tocqueville nevertheless warned against going too fast. He particularly advocated the need to preserve religious and family values. For a conservative interpretation of de Tocqueville, see Kirk, *The Conservative Mind*, 178–95.

452. John Ireland, *The Church and Modern Society: Lectures and Addresses* (New York: D.H. McBride & Co., 1903), 1:192.

453. Ireland, *The Church and Modern Society*, 1:64.

philosophical inquest;

—The Church's predilection for ritual and solemnity were derived from European aristocratic pageantry; they were misplaced in a society where simplicity and candor were prized above all.

In short, these sectors warned that if the Church were to take root and flourish on American soil instead of being shunned as an alien graft, she would have to adapt her doctrines, structures, and very spirit to the liberal interpretation of the American one. Describing the crux of this sentiment, F. Deshayes explains in the authoritative *Dictionnaire de théologie catholique* that these sectors "dreamed of a system of mutual concessions [with American liberalism] in which the Roman Church would have to make the most concessions, which would bring, in the near future, the happy fusion between the Faith of our forefathers and modern civilization, amidst the final apotheosis of a cleansed, modernized, and renewed Catholicism: 'American Catholicism.'"[454]

Americanism was never presented as a school of thought, that is, a didactic synthesis of arguments and conclusions. It was rather a mood, a state of mind, a way of considering the American character and institutions, a set of naturalistic and liberal tendencies. It is not difficult, however, to identify its doctrinal foundation: It is none other than liberal Catholicism, though some nuances make it seemingly less sharp but no less dangerous than its European counterpart.

a. Liberalism

The first pillar upon which this Americanism rested was Liberalism. This resulted from an ingrained, if seldom violent, antipathy toward coercive authority and hierarchical order, be it religious, moral, intellectual, or political, an antipathy alleged to be well-suited to the American spirit of freedom. Thus, Americanists propounded an unwarranted extension of individual freedom to the point of breaking away from the constraints of the Church's legitimate authority. According to Americanists, the hour had come to carve a larger niche for individual liberty inside the Church and to restrain the directive power of the Church over individual consciences.

b. Democracy

The second pillar of this Americanism derived from the former. Rejecting any form of monarchical or aristocratic governance as intrinsically tyrannical, Americanists unilaterally extolled modern democracy—particularly American democracy—as the only system compatible with justice. "This is the era of democracy," trumpeted Bishop John Keane, then rector of the Catholic University of America. "The day of absolute government is over and never again will a nation's laws be made by one man, or set of men, other than the agents of the people."[455] Progressive writer Father Greeley comments that Americanists "were convinced that American democracy was the most noble work of polity that man has ever devised and that eventually the whole world would come to imitate this form of government."[456]

This repudiation of aristocracy was easily transposed to the ecclesiastical sphere. Accordingly, many Americanists tended to conceive the Catholic Church as they did their country. They propounded—in still mitigated terms—a democratization of her structures. This supposed a growing autonomy of local Churches vis-à-vis Rome, of the bishops vis-à-vis the Vatican, of the parishes vis-à-vis the dioceses, and of the faithful vis-à-vis their pastors—all this in the name of democratic self-government. This error already foreshadowed aspects of the modernist ecclesiology, and would be further developed by the Nouvelle Théologie and LT, as we shall see later.

c. Reconciliation With the Spirit of the Times

Americanists "had great sympathy ... for the spirit of the age,"[457] Father Greeley comments. In part, that sympathy was nourished by a fear of appearing insufficiently American. [Bishop John Ireland] "could not abide those Catholics who were opposed to the spirit of the times and especially to the boundless optimism." Father Greeley goes on to quote the bishop of Saint Paul:

> What! The Church of the Living God ... this Church not eager for the fray, not precipitating herself with love irresistible upon this modern world to claim it, to bless it, to own it for Christ.
> I preach the new, the most glorious crusade. Church and age! Unite them in the name of humanity, in the name of God.[458]

By rashly and optimistically proclaiming that the Church should conform to the spirit of the times, Americanists opened the Pandora's box of permanent revolution in the Church. Adapting to the spirit of the world prevalent at the close of the nineteenth century may appear moderate when compared to the absurdities we are witnessing today. However, adopting the spirit of the times as the dominant criterion to judge theological, moral, and ecclesiastical issues subordinated Catholic doctrine to a world in constant evolution. Just as the germs of modern revolutions would produce ever more extreme consequences, so the Church was expected to gradually evolve, adapting herself to an ever more revolutionary world.[459]

5. Leo XIII Condemns Americanism

Interpreting the pastoral line of Leo XIII in their own way, Americanists saw it as an incentive to continue on the path of Liberalism. "The title which above all others he has merited and which history will award is this—the pontiff of his age," Archbishop John Ireland commented. "The reconciliation of the Church with modern times is Leo's work."[460]

To dispel all doubt, in 1895 Pope Leo XIII wrote to American bishops the apostolic letter *Longinqua oceani*, in which, after expressing his joy at the growth of the Church in America, he expressed some concerns and advised pastors to be particularly vigilant.

The translation into French and subsequent dissemination in Europe of the life of Fr. Isaac Thomas Hecker (1819–1888), founder of the Paulist Fathers and a leading figure in the Americanist movement, revered by European liberal Catholics almost as a patron saint, led the Roman pontiff to act more resolutely. On January 22, 1899, he wrote the letter *Testem benevolentiae*, addressed to James Cardinal Gibbons, archbishop of Baltimore, and delivered to all the bishops of the United States.

Leo XIII condemns the view that "the Church should shape her teachings more in accord with the spirit of the age and relax

---

454. F. Deshayes, s.v. "Américanisme," *D.T.C.,* 1:1044.
455. Greeley, *The Catholic Experience*, 160.
456. Greeley, 181.
457. Greeley, 154.
458. Greeley, 155.
459. The most comprehensive study of Americanism remains Fr. Thomas McAvoy's *The Americanist Heresy in Roman Catholicism, 1895–1900* (Notre Dame, Ind.: University of Notre Dame Press, 1963).
460. Ireland, *Church and Modern Society*, 1:408, 423.

some of her ancient severity and make some concessions to new opinions." He went on to condemn the "opinion of the lovers of novelty, according to which they hold such liberty should be allowed in the Church, that her supervision and watchfulness being in some sense lessened, allowance be granted the faithful, each one to follow out more freely the leading of his own mind and the trend of his own proper activity." The Church, the pope states, cannot hide any aspect of her doctrine or discipline on the pretext of appearing more acceptable to modern man lest she risk losing her identity.

Touching a key part of the Americanist spirit, Leo XIII censures the prevalence of *active virtues* over *supernatural* or *passive* ones, and concludes, "We are not able to give approval to those views which, in their collective sense, are called by some 'Americanism.'"[461]

In Europe, the letter *Testem benevolentiae* was correctly interpreted as a condemnation of liberal Catholicism. Many bishops reproduced it in their diocesan publications. Almost all Americanist leaders wrote submissive letters to Leo XIII, beginning with Archbishop Ireland, whose letter was published in French in *L'Osservatore Romano* of February 24, 1899. In it the archbishop of Saint Paul speaks of mere "misunderstandings" and rebuffs the charge of "Americanism," calling it a "danger which was not understood by all the people of the United States" and which, according to him, is only attributable to the "astonishing confusion of ideas" created by "enemies of the Church in America." The prelate closes the letter protesting against his accusers: "We cannot but be indignant that such an injury has been done to us—to our bishops, to our faithful people, to our nation, in designating by the word 'Americanism' ... such errors and extravagances as these."[462]

The overly kind reception of such letters by Vatican authorities together with the lack of any disciplinary measures, conveyed the impression that the Americanist crisis had been overcome. That impression was further reinforced in a series of articles by democratic priest Fr. Pierre Dabry who, as Albert Houtin put it, "seems to have revived the courage of democratic Catholics."[463]

6. Americanism and Modernism

Americanism in the late nineteenth century served as a rallying banner for left-leaning people who, some years later, would show sympathy for modernist errors. Archbishop John Ireland's views, for example, were so dangerously close to those of Modernism that he fully expected to be condemned by St. Pius X during the modernist controversy of 1905–1914. Most Rev. John Lancaster Spalding (1840–1916), bishop of Peoria and founder of the Catholic University of America, also tended to modernist doctrines. "While Spalding stopped short of the modernists' attempts to reformulate dogma," historian Robert Cross comments, "he

shared their desire to destroy the sharp separation between secular and spiritual."[464]

In its theological implications, Americanism foreshadowed Modernism. If the Americanists' support for Modernism was not more vocal, it was due essentially to the cautiousness imposed on them by the letter *Testem benevolentiae*. In his 1907 encyclical *Pascendi Dominici gregis* condemning Modernism, St. Pius X pointed to an element common to the latter and Americanism: "With regard to morals, [the modernists] adopt the principle of the Americanists that the active virtues are more important than the passive."[465]

Describing the modernist controversy, Msgr. John Tracy Ellis, a historian of American Catholicism, quotes Daniel Rops of the Académie Française who affirms that "the *Americanism* of Archbishop Ireland and Fr. Hecker constitute[d] a practical prelude to Modernism."[466] For his part, Italian theologian Fr. Emanuele Chiettini also noted that Americanism contained in germ "many of the errors later condemned by Pius X under the generic name of Modernism."[467]

7. Repercussions of Americanism in Europe

Finally, we must note that Americanism exerted a notable influence on liberal European circles, not only on the Christian democratic movement, but also particularly on those theologians and intellectuals who were then laying the foundations of Modernism. Archbishop Ireland, Bishop Keane, and other representatives of the Americanist current made frequent lecture tours in Europe, where they were greeted and feted as brothers by liberals and Christian democrats, who saw in these lectures a valuable propaganda for their ideas. The example of the Catholic Church in America, fully accommodated to the republican regime and thriving in a liberal society, stood as a paradigm for European liberal Catholics and as a living vindication of their views. French Dominican Fr. Vincent Maumus mentions this in the closing pages of his 1898 book, *Les catholiques et la liberté politique*: "The gaze of European Catholics turns with admiration to the Church in America to learn from it what liberty can do."[468] He ends his book, however, with a cautionary note that a day will come when Catholics will be forced to choose between the Faith and the radical politics of liberty.

The same can be said of the Christian democratic current. Father Dabry writes, "Some fundamental differences notwithstanding, *Americanism and Christian Democracy beheld each other as brothers*, and exchanged many a sign of affection and esteem."[469]

European liberal Catholics not only beheld Americanists as brothers but as real saviors. Pius IX's magisterium, and particularly the First Vatican Council and the encyclicals of Leo XIII, had practically clipped their wings. They were understandably elated to watch similar ideas thrive on the other side of the Atlantic in a nation they saw as destined to be great and powerful. Should this

461. Leo XIII, apostolic letter *Testem benevolentiae* (Jan. 22, 1899).

462. John Ireland, *Letter to Leo XIII* (Feb. 22, 1899). We quote from a contemporaneous English translation. "Ireland to the Pope," *The New York Times*, Mar. 22, 1899.

463. M. Dabry, in *Vie catholique*, Mar. 14, 1899, quoted in Albert Houtin, *L'américanisme* (Paris: Librairie Émile Nourry, 1904), 369. An article published in *L'Italie* on March 6, 1899, sheds light on the story of the apostolic letter *Testem benevolentiae* by showing the extent to which liberal errors had penetrated high-ranking levels. The draft was written by Cardinals Satolli and Mazzella, both ultramontanes, and contained a clear condemnation of Americanism. Then, according to the French publication,

> fortunately, with his usual wit and secret sympathy for Americanism, the pope intervened.
> "Aided by Cardinal Rampolla, who also *quietly* favored the cause of Americanism, he introduced radical changes to the draft of Cardinals Satolli and Mazzella. They cut, expurgated, patched, changed it, and added pieces. The original document became absolutely unrecognizable." (Houtin, *L'américanisme*, 370–71)

464. Cross, *The Emergence*, 40.

465. St. Pius X, encyclical *Pascendi Dominici gregis* (Sept. 8, 1907), no. 38.

466. Daniel Rops, "Il y a cinquante ans, le modernisme," *Ecclesia Lectures Chrétiennes*, no. 77 (Aug. 1955), 13. See Msgr. John Tracy Ellis, "Les États-Unis depuis 1850," in *Nouvelle histoire de l'église* (Paris: Éditions du Seuil, 1975), 718.

467. Emanuele Chiettini, s.v. "Americanismo," *Enciclopedia cattolica* (E.C.) (Vatican: Ente per l'Enciclopedia Cattolica e per i Libro Cattolico, Soc. p. a., 1948), 1:1056. On the connection between Americanism and Modernism, see Margaret Mary Reher, "Americanism and Modernism: Continuity or Discontinuity?" *U.S. Catholic Historian*, no. 1 (1981): 87–103; R. Scott Appleby, "Modernism as the Final Phase of Americanism," *The Harvard Theological Review* 81, no. 2 (Apr. 1988): 171–92.

468. Vincent Maumus, *Les catholiques et la liberté politique* (Paris: Librairie Victor Lecoffre, 1898), 282.

469. M. Dabry, *Vie Catholique*, Mar. 14, 1899, quoted in Barbier, *Histoire du catholicisme libéral*, 3:263.

Americanist trend prevail, they surmised, their position would be vindicated. Writing in the *Courrier de Genève* on October 20, 1898, French modernist Auguste Sabatier (1839–1901) thus described the hopes of liberal Catholics:

> After the [First] Vatican Council, liberal Catholicism seemed to be altogether extinguished, and the Church of Rome was calm. ... This, however, was a delusive calm. Liberal Catholicism ... was not dead, it had emigrated. Transplanted to America, to a society free from any historical constraint and far from Rome's surveillance ... liberal Catholicism acquired an unprecedented strength, customs, and self-confidence. The old leaders of the liberal school ressurected in the new figures ... of Fr. Hecker, ... Archbishop Ireland, Cardinal Gibbons, Bishop Keane, Bishop O'Connell and so many others. ... Soon, this Liberalism crossed once again the ocean, returning to Europe under the name of *Americanism*. Archbishop Ireland became its apostle and came to France where, through his fiery speeches, he instantly rallied what was left of impenitent liberals.[470]

C. Modernism

1. A Multiform Current

The same revolutionary impulse that informed liberal Catholicism gave rise, toward the end of the nineteenth century, to a multiform current which St. Pius X later called *Modernism*. In a broad sense the term comprised several trends, found in both Catholic and Protestant circles, which sought radical changes in diverse fields. Whence one had theological Modernism, philosophical Modernism, historical Modernism, sociological Modernism, and so forth.[471]

In this item we will deal specifically with the modernist movement in the Catholic Church, composed of both priests and laymen whose object was to subvert traditional Catholicism on the pretext of adapting it to the modern world. "Well," wrote Antonio Fogazzaro in his novel *The Saint*, "there are many Catholics in Italy and outside of Italy who, with us, desire certain reforms in the Church ... [i]n religious instruction, in the ceremonies, in the discipline of the clergy, reforms even in the highest sphere of ecclesiastical government. ... Very probably a large number of pious and cultured people in the Catholic world feel as we do."[472]

The modernist undertaking was facilitated by the ambience of relative doctrinal tolerance that set in during the second half of Leo XIII's pontificate, contrasting with his predecessor's prudent watchfulness. "If the policy of Pius IX had been continued by his successor, it is unlikely that there would have been any modernist movement. ... Leo XIII, by modifying the intransigent policy of Pius IX, fostered the illusion that the modernist enterprise was worth attempting," writes Alec Vidler.[473]

A manifestation of Modernism *avant la lettre* were the doctrines of Ernest Renan (1823–1892), professor of Oriental studies at the Collège de France. A liberal and positivist, the apostate Renan introduced in France the method of historical criticism of the Holy Scriptures developed by German liberal Protestants.[474]

Renan's most famous work was *La vie de Jésus*, published in 1863. The first volume of this series was titled *Histoire des origines du christianisme*,[475] in which he sought to destroy the supernatural foundations of Christianity. The work was widely read in Italy. Gabriele de Rosa comments, "They sang the praise of the militant anticlericalism of Renan, who saw the papacy as a reactionary enemy of science, freedom, and modern thought, and dreamed of pulverizing the Roman Church. Reading Renan meant to be modern, nonconformist, open to new ideas."[476]

The book became a flag of the liberal current in Italy. There were even riots and popular uprisings with clashes of factions favorable and opposed to Renan. In Venice, after a solemn triduum celebrated in Saint Mark's Basilica, Patriarch Giuseppe Trevisanato condemned the book as "extremely evil" and it was burned on St. Zulian's Square.[477]

a. In France

The first signs of Modernism proper surfaced in the 1880s at the Institut Catholique of Paris under the aegis of Fr. Louis Duchesne (1843–1922). A professor of philosophy, Father Duchesne sought a profound renewal of biblical scholarship through the extensive use of historical criticism. In 1882, the Superior of Saint-Sulpice, Father Icard, forbade his seminarians (who made up the majority of Father Duchesne's students) to attend his lectures. Forced to suspend his teaching for a year, he profited by writing his *Liber pontificalis*, which was denounced by Cardinal de Luca and Bishop Charles-Émile Freppel as heterodox. In spite of the unfailing support of the rector, Msgr. Maurice d'Hulst (1841–1896), Father Duchesne had to quit the Institute in 1896. In 1912, his three-volume *Histoire ancienne de l'église* was included in the Index of Forbidden Books.

In 1880, Father Duchesne gathered a group of young disciples tuned to the latest developments in the theological field. Among his recruits was Fr. Alfred Loisy (1857–1940), who became the symbol figure of the modernist heresy. "We shall have to remove certain obstacles which separate us from the too scientific intellects of our contemporaries," explained Father Duchesne in 1881. "Theology, in its existing form, is finished; the old exegesis is played out."[478] On the pretext of making Catholicism relevant to contemporary scholarship, members of Father Duchesne's group set out to create a new exegesis[479] using the historical method regardless of the demolishing consequences to traditional Catholic theology.

Another representative of Modernism in France was Fr. Marcel Hébert (1851–1916), a Kantian philosopher and a close friend of Fathers Duchesne and Loisy. Father Hébert took the modernist postulates so far that he actually reached pantheism, outright denying that God was a Person. He broke with the Church in

---

470. Auguste Sabatier, *Courrier de Genève*, Oct. 20, 1898, quoted in Barbier, 3:259.

471. Pius XI assumes this meaning. "There is a species of moral, legal, and social Modernism which We condemn, no less decidedly than We condemn theological Modernism." Pius XI, encyclical *Ubi arcano*, no. 61. On Modernism, see Jean Rivière, *Le modernisme dans l'église* (Paris: Letouzey et Ané, 1929); Émile Poulat, *Histoire, dogme, critique dans la crise moderniste* (Paris: Casterman, 1962).

472. Antonio Fogazzaro, *The Saint* (Il Santo), trans. M. Prichard-Agnetti (New York: G.P. Putnam's Sons, 1906), 52.

473. Vidler, *The Modernist Movement*, 60. We speak of "impression," while Rev. Vidler says "illusion." Just as we had earlier distinguished between Leo XIII's magisterium and his pastoral line, we now must distinguish between the latter's reality and the

impression it caused in the liberal camp. "Perception is reality," Lee Atwater said. When it comes to favoring the revolutionary process in the Church, sometimes perception counts for more than reality.

474. The historical-critical method is understood as the set of principles and criteria proper to philology and exegesis that endeavors to trace the original form and meaning of a text by appealing to different sciences. Applied to the Holy Scriptures by liberal Protestants, the method was later used by the currents of thought that developed Modernism.

475. See Ernest Renan, *La vita di Gesù*, ed. F. Grisi (Rome: Newton Compton, 1994).

476. De Rosa, *Il movimento*, 28.

477. See *Gazzetta Ufficiale di Venezia*, Nov. 23, 1863.

478. Vidler, *The Modernist Movement*, 72.

479. Exegesis: the branch of theology that investigates and expresses the true sense of Sacred Scripture.

1903 and joined the socialist ranks. Apostate priest Albert Houtin (1867–1926) was the movement's historian. There were also some moderates called *modernizers* to distinguish them from modernists, like the Dominican priest Fr. Marie-Joseph Lagrange (1855–1938), Msgr. Pierre Batiffol (1861–1929), and George Fonsegrive (1852–1917).

b. In Italy

The founding of the magazine *Studi Religiosi* [Religious Studies] in January 1901, directed by Fr. Salvatore Minocchi (1869–1943), is usually given as the starting point of Modernism in Italy. In 1907, another magazine joined the current, Milan's *Il Rinnovamento* [Renewal], directed by Antonio Aiace Alfieri (1880–1962). In Italy, the modernist movement formed a small group of intellectuals and priests such as Tommaso Gallarati Scotti (1878–1966), Stefano Jacini (1886–1952), Alessandro Casati (1881–1955), Antonio Fogazzaro (1842–1911), Giovanni Semeria (1867–1931), and Giovanni Genocchi (1890–1926). The more notable are Ernesto Buonaiuti (1881–1946), the first professor of Church history at the Apollinae Seminary and then from 1915 at the University La Sapienza of Rome, and Romolo Murri, one of the main leaders of the Christian Democrats. Both were excommunicated.[480]

c. In Britain

Modernism in England was represented chiefly by the Irish Jesuit Fr. George Tyrrell (1861–1909). A restless and rebellious spirit, Father Tyrrell began to show his liberal leanings in the early 1890s, when he set forth to destroy scholastic theology on the pretext of vindicating a "liberal-minded and sympathetic" Aquinas.[481] According to Tyrrell, what made Aquinas dislikable was the excessive use of reason to draw overly linear and logical conclusions. "God's spirit working outside the Church is preparing for Himself an acceptable people; and we within must co-operate and go forward to meet this movement, by purging out of our midst any remnant of the leaven of rationalism," he pondered.[482] Between 1897 and 1899 he published three books—*Nova et vetera*, *Hard Sayings*, and *External Religion*—which broached modernist topics. These works attracted the attention of Baron Friedrich von Hügel (1852–1925), an Austrian gentleman born in Florence and living in London, who was dubbed "the lay bishop of Modernism" for his role in coordinating the movement across Europe.[483] Tyrrell refused to accept what he insolently called "the Vatican heresy" and died excommunicated.

d. In Germany

In Germany there existed a long tradition of liberal Catholicism, evolving around the University of Tübingen under the aegis of Fr. Johann Adam Möhler (1796–1838), and the University of Munich under the aegis of Father von Döllinger. This strain was strongly influenced by liberal Protestantism, particularly by the

doctrines of Friedrich Schleiermacher (1768–1834), the father of theological Modernism. These schools laid many of the theological foundations of Modernism even though, as it often happens with German thought, the French were the ones to translate and market it. Döllinger was excommunicated in 1871 and died unrepentant. Later modernist trends were represented by Hermann Schell (1850–1906), who had several books condemned by the Holy See, and by Franz-Xavier Krauss (1840–1904), whose teachings inspired the so-called *Reformkatholizismus* movement.

We should point out that until the publication of the anonymous *Program of the Modernists* in November 1907, presumably written by Ernesto Buonaiuti, the movement's doctrines had never been expounded by their mentors in a systematic fashion. They worked independently, developing particular aspects of the modernist creed, and at times even diverging on some secondary points. One of the great merits of the encyclical *Pascendi* was to put these scattered and apparently unconnected doctrines into an intelligible whole.

e. In the United States

The tendency toward Modernism in the United States had been dampened, if not altogether squelched, by Leo XIII's apostolic letter *Testem benevolentiae* in which he condemned Americanism. There was, therefore, no modernist theologian of any prominence in America, although there were underlying modernist trends running through liberal sectors. In a general way, we may say that the same impulse which led many liberals to accept Americanist principles propelled them to sympathize with Modernism. It is telling of these underlying modernist trends that the American edition of Antonio Fogazzaro's book *The Saint* (condemned by the Holy See) sold 14,000 copies in just seventeen days.

The most vocal adherent of Modernism in the United States was undoubtedly Paulist Fr. William Lawrence Sullivan (1872–1935). Some vain pretensions to the contrary, Father Sullivan was far from being a theologian. An unimaginative thinker, he merely echoed transatlantic developments. He was more preoccupied with issues closely related with American Liberalism—like freedom of conscience and representative government within the Church—than with the kind of biblical criticism and philosophical questions that characterized European Modernism. His Modernism appears rather like a radicalized version of Americanism, of which, indeed, he was a fervent partisan.

His ecclesiology, which partly foreshadowed that of liberation theology, merits a short notice. His exalted democratism having led him astray, Father Sullivan fancied the primitive Church as a fraternal association of people gathered in self-governing communities. According to the Paulist priest, ecclesiastical authority arose through a process of usurpation of the people's power by the clergy, completed at the close of the Middle Ages. The rise of liberal Catholicism in the nineteenth century, Father Sullivan further claimed, sounded the beginning of the demise of this clerical encroachment and opened a period of transition which would return power to the people, that is, the laity. Modernism would be an expression of this trend.

In 1910, Father Sullivan published his venomous *Letters to His Holiness Pope Pius X, by a Modernist*, in which the arrogance of tone is only equaled by the shallowness of scholarship. Insolently referring to the Vatican as "the regnant autocracy at Rome,"

> This world-regenerating idea, democracy, is, as it were, worshipped by this modern age. ... There is no bound or limit to the sacrifices we would make for it. ... We demand

480. On Modernism in Italy, see Michele Busi, Roberto de Mattei, Antonio Lanza, and Flavio Peloso, *Don Orione negli anni del modernismo* (Milan: Jaca Book, 2002); Lorenzo Bedeschi, *Il modernismo italiano: Voci e volti* (Cinisello Balsamo, Italy: San Paolo, 1995); Pietro Scoppola, *Crisi modernista e rinnovamento cattolico in Italia* (Bologna: Il Mulino, 1961).

481. George Tyrrell, letter to Baron von Hügel (Dec. 6, 1897), quoted in Vidler, *The Modernist Movement*, 147.

482. George Tyrrell, "A Perverted Devotion," in *Essays on Faith and Immortality*, arr. M.D. Petre (New York: Longmans, Green and Co., 1914), 171.

483. Hügel was also a writer. To him are due: *The Mystical Element of Religion as Studied in Saint Catherine of Genoa and Her Friends*, 2 vols. (London: J.M. Dent, 1909); *Eternal life: Study of Its Implications and Applications* (Edinburgh: T. & T. Clark, 1912); and *Essays and Addresses on Philosophy of Religion* (London: J.M. Dent, 1921). The collection of his *Selected Letters*, published by B. Holland in 1927, is very important for the history of Modernism.

that the papacy give us an accounting of its attitude toward democracy, toward representative government, toward the sense of popular rights and national self-respect which liberty, the mistress of the modern world, has taught us. ...

[Fr. Sullivan disparaged papal government as] the most exclusive despotism, the most absolute autocracy, the most humiliating tyranny. ...

[In short, he proposed that the hierarchical Church be substituted by] a representative government, autonomous local synods, and home-rule generally, [that would] supersede the present Italian and papal despotism.[484]

In other words, he sought to democratize the Church along Americanist lines.

This process of liberation, according to the American modernist, was particularly visible in the United States, which would thus have the divinely appointed mission of ushering in this new Church. According to Father Sullivan, in the words of his biographer John Ratté, "The American Catholic Church ... was alone qualified to rescue the rest of the Church from the ... primitive (from a democratic point of view) institutions to which papal rule had bound it."[485]

Father Sullivan spared ecclesiastical authorities the grief of a condemnation by abandoning the Paulist order in late 1910, and apostatizing to Unitarianism shortly afterward.[486] It is indicative of the diffusion of modernist ideas within the Paulist order that several members left it after the papal condemnations of Modernism. Along with these Paulists, two other priests broke with the Church altogether: John R. Slattery, American Provincial of the Society of Saint Joseph, and Thomas J. Mulvey of Brooklyn.

2. The Doctrines of Modernism

a. Infatuation With the Modern World

Modernists displayed an almost childish infatuation with the modern world and an overweening pride of being *enlightened* men, in synchrony with the spirit of the times, coupled with a haughty contempt for anyone who remained faithful to the Magisterium. We read in the *Program of the Modernists*:

We simply want to be Christians and Catholics living in harmony with the spirit of our time. ...

...We have pursued our century, we have sought to speak its language, to think in terms of its thought.[487]

Mesmerized by the reigning intellectual fads, they assumed even their contradictions, slyness, and ambivalences, gladly trading in the rock-solid soundness of traditional philosophy.

According to Alfred Loisy, "So-called modernists form ... a fairly definite group of men united in the common desire to adapt Catholicism to the intellectual, moral, and social needs of today."[488] Specifying the scope of this adaptation, he stated that the goal of Modernism was to accommodate the Church, "her constitution, doctrines, and rites" to the "modern spirit, science, and society."[489]

From the various trends of the moment, modernists particularly assumed:

a) The agnostic thinking stemming from Kantian-type idealism, manipulated to challenge the Aristotelian-scholastic philosophy traditionally adopted by the Church;[490]

b) The historical Biblical criticism developed by liberal Protestantism and applied to question the historical foundations of revelation;[491]

c) The so-called philosophy of action, developed by Maurice Blondel and others, with which they denied that religious truth could be expressed in formulas valid to all, considering it instead as a stirring of life itself;

d) Darwinism, as an affirmation of an all-encompassing evolutionary process that should also be applied to the Church.

b. A Subversion of Catholic Doctrine

Since there was total incompatibility between the traditional Catholic Church and this kind of modern thinking, accommodating the former to the latter could only be done through a complete subversion of her doctrine, institutions, and discipline. "Deep down," wrote Father Loisy, "all Catholic theology, even in

---

484. William Lawrence Sullivan, *Letters to His Holiness Pope Pius X, by a Modernist* (Chicago: Open Court Publishing Company, 1910), 4, 60–61, 188.

485. John Ratté, *Three Modernists: Alfred Loisy, George Tyrrell, William L. Sullivan* (New York: Sheed and Ward, 1967), 291. See also William Lawrence Sullivan, *The Priest: A Tale of Modernism in New England* (Boston: Beacon Press, 1914); William Lawrence Sullivan, *Under Orders: The Autobiography of William Lawrence Sullivan* (New York: Richard R. Smith, 1945).

486. Unitarian Association (today the Unitarian Universalist Association), a liberal Protestant sect tracing its roots to the late sixteenth century and, indirectly, to the anti-Trinitarian heresies of early Christianity. In the United States, modern Unitarianism arose in the late eighteenth century as a liberal dissidence of Puritanism. Along the nineteenth century, the rebellious libertarianism that lay at the core of the Unitarian Association fomented an increasingly radical "revision" of Christianity by the sect's leaders. One after another, the most elementary tenets of Christian faith fell victim to the iconoclastic animosity, until Unitarianism was effectively emptied of any Christian content, subsisting merely as a vague deism. In its extreme versions, Unitarianism denies Our Lord's divinity, the inspiration of the Bible, and even the need of any visible Church. Conceiving God not as a transcendent Person, but as a divine impregnation in nature and history, nineteenth-century Unitarianism became in the words of French theologian Fr. Léon Cristiani, "a sort of mystical and poetic pantheism." L. Cristiani, s.v. "Unitariens," *D.T.C.*, 15-2e.:2170. Thus, Unitarianism constituted the extreme left wing of Protestantism.

487. Anonymous (presumably Ernesto Buonaiuti), *Il programma dei modernisti: Risposta all'enciclica di Pio X "Pascendi Dominici gregis"* (Turin: Fratelli Bocca, 1911), 7, 10. In the encyclical *Pascendi* against Modernism, St. Pius X described this pride as follows: "Pride sits in Modernism as in its own house, finding sustenance everywhere in its doctrines and an occasion to flaunt itself in all its aspects. ...There is no road which leads so directly and so quickly to Modernism as pride" (no. 40).

488. Alfred Loisy, *Simples réflexions sur le decret du Saint Office* Lamentabili Sane Exitu, *et sur l'encyclique* Pascendi Dominici gregis (Ceffonds, près Montier-en-Der, Haute-Marne: self-published, 1908), 13. On Loisy, see Romolo Murri, *La religione di Alfredo Loisy* (Rome: Libreria Editrice Bilychnis, 1918); Ernesto Buonaiuti, *Alfredo Loisy* (Rome: A.F. Formiggini, 1925); and Adolfo Omodeo, *Alfredo Loisy, storico delle religioni* (Bari: Laterza, 1936).

489. Loisy, *Simples réflexions*, 276.

490. Immanuel Kant (1724–1804). We read in the *Program*:

Christian religiosity ... is capable of acquiring a new theoretical clothing based on the idealist postulates. These postulates are today at the source of the new attitudes in philosophy. ...

...We accept the criticism of pure reason done by Kant and Spencer. (Anonymous [pres. Buonaiuti], *Il programma dei modernisti*, 12, 98)

Loisy likewise acknowledged, "If the (Christological) problem ...is being raised anew ...it is ...because of the profound upheaval in ...modern philosophy." Alfred Loisy, *Autour d'un petit livre* (Paris: Alphonse Picard et fils, 1903), 128–29. This stance frontally denied the teaching of Leo XIII who, in the encyclical *Aeterni Patris* praising scholastic philosophy, had formally stated that the latter was "solemnly and authoritatively approved" by the First Vatican Council. Leo XIII, encyclical *Aeterni Patris* (Aug. 4, 1879), no. 8.

491. "Modernism ...is the critical method applied to the religious forms of mankind in general, and to Catholicism in particular." Anonymous (pres. Buonaiuti), *Il programma dei modernisti*, 23.

its fundamental principles, the general philosophy of religion, revelation, and the laws that govern our knowledge of religion are brought to judgment [by modernity]."[492] It is not hard to figure out his final verdict: "It may be that … the old ecclesiastical edifice is going one day to tumble down, that the gates of Paradise will prevail against it."[493]

In a less roundabout way, Father Tyrrell brazenly disclosed that he felt called to a prophetic mission: "I feel my work is to hammer away at the great unwieldy carcass of the Roman Communion and wake it up from its medieval dreams. Not that I shall succeed, but that my failure and many another may pave the way for eventual success."[494]

Across its more or less accidental variances, this iconoclastic hatred of traditional Catholic doctrine and the hierarchical Church was the trait that united the several strains of Modernism. At the movement's core lay a strong temperamental fermentation, a craving for an all-encompassing liberation from all things that embodied authority and hierarchy.[495] Commenting on this liberationist spirit, Belgian theologian Fr. Arthur Vermeersch, S.J., writes:

> The spirit of this plan of reform may be summarized under the following heads: (a) A spirit of complete emancipation, tending to weaken ecclesiastical authority; the emancipation of science, which must traverse every field of investigation without fear of conflict with the Church; the emancipation of the State, which should never be hampered by religious authority; the emancipation of the private conscience, whose inspirations must not be overridden by papal definitions or anathemas; the emancipation of the universal conscience, with which the Church should be ever in agreement; (b) A spirit of movement and change, with an inclination to a sweeping form of evolution, such as abhors anything fixed and stationary; (c) A spirit of reconciliation among all men through the feelings of the heart.[496]

c. Incoherence

Before delving further into the analysis of modernist doctrines we must forewarn the reader that he should not try to see them as a logically coherent system. These doctrines are avowedly confused and contradictory. Msgr. A. Farges commented upon this in his definitive essay "Synthèse du modernisme philosophique," "For the followers of this new school. … absurdity is no longer a sign of error. Quite the contrary. In their view, contradiction is the very stuff of reality in nature where everything is itself, and at the same time something different than itself, because everything is pure becoming … a perpetual contradiction between being and not being simultaneously."[497]

Does this seem exaggerated? Let us hear Édouard Le Roy (1870–1954), the foremost philosopher of Modernism: "The principle of non-contradiction is not universal and necessary. …

What is the becoming [*devenir*] of the universe if not a perpetual flight of blending contradictions?"[498]

At times, even St. Pius X despairs of trying to find logic in the modernists' *folly*, as he calls their thinking. Commenting on a particularly egregious incongruity, he asked, "By what legitimate process of reasoning … they proceed [from the premises to this conclusion?] … let him answer who can." Likewise, beholding the flimsiness of the modernist exegesis, the pope called it "a strange style of reasoning, truly."[499]

d. Anti-intellectualism and Agnosticism

In order to understand Modernism we must first analyze two philosophical systems that constituted its framework: *intuitionism*, developed by Henri Bergson (1859–1941); and its cognate, the *philosophy of action*, framed by Maurice Blondel (1861–1949), Édouard Le Roy (1870–1954), and Lucien Laberthonnière (1860–1932).[500] Some accidental divergences notwithstanding, these systems shared a fundamental anti-intellectualism that challenged the Aristotelian-scholastic philosophy. Both arose in the wake of the romantic reaction against the cold rationalism of the Enlightenment philosophy and were characterized by a bias against the reasoning intellect.[501] This disparaging of the intellect, conjugated with forms of voluntarism, resulted in a sweeping agnosticism leading to the destruction of the very foundations of logic.

Intuitionism takes its name from the theory that real knowledge does not consist in the abstract concepts of the reasoning intellect, but in the immediate apprehension of reality through intuition. Rational knowledge, Bergson contended, works through abstractions and concepts and does not actually know reality but constructs ideas about it. Reality itself remains out of reach and can be known only through intuition, which grasps the intimacy of reality directly and experimentally. Bergson explains, "The intellect … merely offers us … a transposition of life in terms of inertness. The intellect turns everything around; it elaborates a series of concepts about life from without, instead of penetrating it. *Intuition*, on the contrary, takes us to the very core of life."[502]

In Bergson's system, reality is a continuous "flow of life," a vital impulse (*élan vital*). Bergson defended the fantastic thesis that reality is a mere becoming (*devenir*); that being is not, it becomes. According to him, the flow of time (*durée*) is "the very fabric of reality."[503] To convey this absurdity, he even coined the expression

---

492. Loisy, *Simples réflexions*, 24.

493. Alfred Loisy, "Letter in 1900 to Fr. Marcel Hébert," quoted in Vidler, *The Modernist Movement*, 78.

494. George Tyrrell and M.D. Petre, *Autobiography and Life of George Tyrrell*, 2 vols. (London: Edward Arnold, 1912), 2:373.

495. "The spirit of Christ is a spirit of liberation," trumpeted *Rinnovamento*, the semi-official publication of the Italian modernists, sounding a slogan later adopted by liberation theology. Théodore Delmont, *Modernisme et modernistes: En Italie, en Allemagne, en Angleterre, et en France* (Paris: P. Lethielleux, 1909), 13.

496. Vermeersch, s.v. "Modernism," *C.E.*, 10:416.

497. Farges, "Modernisme: Synthèse du modernisme pilosophique," *D.A.F.C.*, 3:644.

498. Édouard Le Roy, *Revue de Métaphysique et de Morale* (1905), 203; (1901), 411, quoted in Farges, "Modernisme," 3:644.

499. St. Pius X, encyclical *Pascendi*, nos. 6, 9.

500. "On what philosophy is Modernism based?" asked the aforementioned Msgr. Farges. He answered, "On that 'new' philosophy called Bergsonism in France, which is obviously derived from the German and Lutheran philosophies of Hegel and Kant." Farges, "Modernisme," 3:640.

501. Their critique of the Enlightenment rationalism revolved around the contention that the discursive intellect, working through abstract concepts, does not encompass the whole gamut of reality. This argument is evidently sound and even a foundation of scholastic philosophy, which posits that knowledge comes through one's senses. However, by despising the rational intellect, modernists downplayed reason almost into nonexistence. Moreover, this rejection of reason and logic buttressed modernists' reformist designs. While it is not easy to refute the Magisterium starting from theological and philosophical principles, it is easy to undermine it by introducing the ever-changing flow of life as a criterion.

502. Henri Bergson, *L'évolution créatrice* (Paris: Presses Universitaires de France, 1948), 177–78. Bergson never sufficiently explained the nature of this intuition, limiting himself to describing it with vague expressions such as "auscultation," "knowledge by sympathy," "grasping reality from the inside," "identification with the original itself," etc. See Régis Jolivet, *Traité de philosophie* (Lyon-Paris: Emmanuel Vitte, 1949), 3:130–37.

503. Bergson, *L'évolution créatrice*, 4. We use the term *fabric* to follow Bergson's terminology. Bergson denies substance as a category and uses the terms *étoffe* (literally, fabric), and *durée* (the fabric of the universe). His preposterous theory of a pure becoming suppresses, in fact, the category of substance, whereas, in Catholic philosophy, being is the substance of the universe created by God.

"pure change": a change without anything changing, a movement without anything moving; in short, an accident without a substance! "There is change but there is nothing changing, change does not need a support. Movement does not imply that something moves," he awkwardly sustained in an Oxford Lecture.[504] Echoing his master, Le Roy likewise maintained that "becoming is the only concrete reality."[505] Not to fall behind, the *Program of the Modernists* also parroted that "existence is movement."[506]

Now, if the universe is an ever-flowing "ocean of life,"[507] what, then, are things? Bergson explains:

> Matter ... must be a flux rather than a thing. ...
> ... Things do not exist, there are only actions.[508]

In one of the most hermetic passages of his work, the French philosopher posited that

> our being ... was formed by a sort of local solidification [within the ocean of life]. ...
> ... We compare intelligence to a solid nucleus formed by condensation [of the surrounding fluid]. This nucleus does not differ substantially from the surrounding fluid.[509]

In Bergson's system, human intelligence is capable of knowing reality but in a way that actually falsifies it. Working through concepts, the reasoning intellect falsifies reality by fixing it in time, that is, by taking instants of this vital flow and artificially packaging them into concepts. Furthermore, it falsifies reality by fragmenting it, that is, by taking aspects of this continuum and encapsulating them into things. "Things," Bergson writes, "are constituted by an instantaneous partition operated by our intellect at a given moment, within the flux."[510] In other words, things do not exist in themselves but are created by our intellect. Bergson thus upheld the abstruse theory that the plurality of beings, that is, the distinction among individual beings, is merely an illusion due to the fragmentation (*morcellement*) of reality operated by the intellect.

This leads directly to Bergson's idea of intuition. Intuition can "experience reality from within" because there is no longer a distinction between a knowing subject and a known object. Both are fleeting solidifications of the vital flow. There is no longer "I," "you," and "them" but an all-encompassing "we," a kind of single cosmic consciousness which makes all beings immanent in one another. Bergson explained,

> Both intuition and intelligence are distinguished from each other against the same background, which we may call ... general consciousness, which must be coextensive with universal life. ...
> ...We exist, move, and live within the absolute. The knowledge we have of the absolute is undoubtedly incomplete, but it is not external or relative.[511]

Thus, at the core of Bergson's philosophy we find the type of immanentism that is the hallmark of the more up-to-date versions of LT.[512]

Bergson justified the reasoning intellect on merely practical grounds. Through intuition man grasps reality, he said, but cannot handle it for practical purposes, since no language can communicate the knowledge gained through it. Man must therefore create concepts which, although artificial, enable him to manipulate reality by fragmenting and fixing it in manageable forms. Concepts, then, would not be instruments of knowledge, but of action. For all its usefulness, however, the reasoning intellect remains lifeless. "Intelligence and instinct point in opposite directions. The former toward inert matter, the latter toward life," Bergson pontificated.[513]

Here we have a glimpse of another aspect of the modernist heresy: Philosophical and religious formulas are artificial symbols devised by men for practical purposes. They are all the more artificial to the extent that they pretend to be unchanging (such as, for example, Catholic dogma), since reality itself is fundamentally fluid and eludes any encapsulation.

Bergson verged on pantheism and, at times, he clearly crossed the line.[514] In the beginning, he said, there was god. This god was not a person, but a "pure becoming" containing such a superabundance of "vital flow" that it spontaneously exploded. From this explosion burst forth (*jaillit*) an unending flux of life which constituted the fabric (*étoffe*) of the universe. Thus conceived, the fabric of the universe is indistinguishable from god. Speaking of creation, he denies it was created by "a thing." Bergson writes, "I speak of a source, the source whence innumerable worlds burst forth like sparks from a great fire. However, I do not consider this source as a thing, but as a continuous flow. Thus defined, god did not do anything; he is unending life, action, freedom."[515]

This divine flux is the very cosmic consciousness. Through a long evolution—which Bergson never convincingly explicated in spite of the hundreds of pages he dedicated to the subject—this cosmic consciousness spawned the plurality of actions that form the universe. Finally, it produced human intelligence which, in turn, is capable of creating things through conceptualization. In Bergson's thinking, "Life [is] ... a continuing creation."[516] This evolution tends toward the reabsorption of the human intellect and, with it, the whole universe back into the initial cosmic consciousness: "Philosophy can only be an effort to melt ourselves back into this flux of life. By reintegrating itself back into its source, the intellect will relive its own genesis but in the opposite direction."[517]

In addition to Bergson's intuitionism, Modernism was also inspired by the philosophy of action developed by Blondel, Laberthonnière, and Le Roy. Blondel's thinking was so garbled as to admit a vast gamut of interpretations, which accounts for the widely diverging appreciations of his work.[518] "It cannot be

504. Henri Bergson, *Oxford Lecture*, 24, quoted in Farges, "Modernisme," 3:643.

505. Édouard Le Roy, "Sur quelques objections adressées à la nouvelle philosophie," *Revue de Métaphysique et de Morale* (1901), 418.

506. Anonymous (pres. Buonaiuti), *Il programma dei modernisti*, 11.

507. Bergson, *L'évolution créatrice*, 192.

508. Bergson, 187, 249.

509. Bergson, 193–94.

510. Bergson, 250.

511. Bergson, 187, 200.

512. Msgr. Farges comments, "As for the substantial immanence of beings, ones in the others, it is a sheer fantasy of pantheistic monism. Thus, when we hear Bergsonians announce that their intuition can offer a 'knowledge from within' ... something absolutely unheard of in the history of philosophy outside of occultism, we remain skeptical." Farges, "Modernisme," 3:652–53.

513. Bergson, *L'évolution créatrice*, 177.

514. In one of his last major works, Bergson tried to redress some of the more pointedly pantheistic features of his metaphysics, but this endeavor was clearly at variance with his life-long thinking. See Henri Bergson, *Les deux sources de la morale et de la religion* (Paris: Félix Alcan, 1932).

515. Bergson, *L'évolution créatrice*, 249.

516. Bergson, 179.

517. Bergson, 193.

518. His college tutor, Prof. Paul Janet, confided to Blondel, "Your thought is obscure and your way of writing makes it even more impenetrable. I spend one hour on each of your pages and often cannot understand it. I figured it would take me forty-five days to read your thesis. ... I gave up on reading it properly." Christian democrat leader Naudet

denied," Alec Vidler rightly points out, "that it was an adaptation or interpretation of his philosophy ... that gave rise to the Modernism of Laberthonnière and Le Roy."[519]

Philosophy of action denied that reality can be known simply through intellectual processes. Rational knowledge, said Blondel, is incomplete; the attainment of truth involves the activity of our whole being: intellect, will, and sensibility. Blondel termed this integral activity *action*, and identified it with the very operations of life. In order to grasp reality in its fullness, he continued, man must not only think about it but actually experience it. Blondel thus spoke of a "vital assimilation" of reality which produced a "communion with things" in a "universal interdependence of all beings."[520]

Blondel disapproved of the notional knowledge as inadequate and false because it fragments reality and works with concepts, which are "as dead as mummies." Conversely, he stressed action as something dynamic and fruitful. Action corresponds to reality because the latter is fluid and evolving, a "perpetual impulse." Beings, said Blondel, are never complete but always in the making, through action.

Consequently, no fixed truth can exist. The classical definition of truth as the adequation of the intellect of the knower to the thing that is known (*adequatio intellectus et rei*) becomes meaningless because reality is perpetually in motion, making any definitive adequation impossible. "We must replace the abstract and chimeric *adaequatio rei et intellectus*," Blondel wrote, "with *adaequatio realis mentis et vitae*."[521] For his part, Lucien Laberthonnière writes, "The immanence method implies ... a philosophy of life and of action as dynamic as life and action themselves. It is opposed to intellectualism, which is a philosophy of idea[s] which aspires to fixity and immobility without ever attaining them."[522]

What is this reality that can only be known through vital assimilation? Beyond the individuality of things, Blondel saw an element common to all, a non-material constituent, the "being of beings." In one of the most controversial aspects of his system, he esoterically called this subjacent element "non-thinking thought" and "cosmic thought."[523] This cosmic thought, according to Blondel, is a process in continuing evolution. It produced the beings in successive strata (*palier*) and finally yielded a "thinking thought"—man. This evolution unswervingly advances toward a final synthesis that would end the dichotomy between the cosmic unity and the plurality of beings by reabsorbing the latter into the former. It is no wonder that Catholic scholars charged Blondel with upholding a radical immanentism dangerously close to pantheism.[524] In 1924,

the Holy Office condemned twelve theses defended by Blondel, including his concept of truth, mentioned earlier.

e. Immanentism

These and other influences stemming from Kantian-type idealism made up one of the foundations of the modernist heresy: agnosticism.[525] For modernists, human knowledge is entirely confined within the field of sensible phenomena, that is to say, to things that appear and in the manner in which they appear, being incapable of knowing any general, supersensible, and unchanging reality. According to this extravagant theory, man experiences phenomena whose substance remains out of his reach. He is confined to registering impressions that come and go, being unable to know if they adequately express the reality of the things he perceives. He is utterly enclosed within his own consciousness.

However, if the individual cannot know with certainty anything beyond his own impressions, any objective foundation for religion is suppressed. How, for example, could modernists account for the belief in God? The answer had to be sought within the individual through the theory of *vital immanence*.

Deep within himself, the modernists claim, man feels the need of an enduring hope; he has an instinctive yearning for something higher, an innate sensibility for the infinite and mysterious. This impulse is at first obscure and hidden. Once perceived, it reveals to the soul the intimate presence of "superior energies," of the *élan vital* flowing within him: behold god is stirring inside. "We find god within ourselves," wrote Laberthonnière; "anything else is but a means to help us delve deeper within ourselves for him. It is in us, in our innermost self that spiritual union with god is achieved through his immediate action upon us. ... One needs to delve into oneself to find god. ... The action that basically constitutes our life is supernaturally animated by god. Thus, if we follow the expansion and development of human action we will see come out all that was within man: god is always there."[526]

Thus, while not explicitly denying that God is a Person (only Father Hébert did so), the modernists treated Him rather as a principle of life stirring in man and in the universe, an energy which man *feels* rather than *knows*. We read in the *Program of the Modernists*:

> Religious knowledge is the actual experience of the divine operating within us and in everything. ...
> ...We find in ourselves that "inferring sense" ... that enables us to grasp, in its ineffable mystery, the presence of superior energies with which we are in direct contact.[527]

---

likewise despaired, "I find Mr. Blondel's books horribly difficult to read. In spite of vigorous efforts, I have never understood his system." Barbier, *Histoire du catholicisme libéral*, 3:229. For his part, Fr. M. Flori, S.J., observes, "The Blondelian terminology is so paradoxical that, if one does not stretch benevolence very far it would hardly escape the accusation of being ambiguous and incoherent." M. Flori, S.J., "Intorno al Blondelismo," *La Civiltà Cattolica* 86, vol. 4, no. 2050 (Nov. 16, 1935), 301.

519. Vidler, *The Modernist Movement*, 186.

520. Scholastic philosophy also teaches that all of man's activity, including his thinking, is action (i.e., something he does). The term, however, took on a sensibly different meaning in Blondel's system. By disparaging rational thinking as fundamentally flawed, and stressing action instead, Blondel ended up conceiving the latter in voluntarist terms. Taking it a step further, and compounding this with particular Marxist postulates on the relationship between theory and praxis, liberation theology claims that theology is to be pursued in praxis.

521. Maurice Blondel, *Annales de philosophie chrétienne* (June 15, 1906), 235, quoted in Réginald Garrigou-Lagrange, O.P., "La Nouvelle Théologie, où va-t-elle?" *Angelicum*, no. 23 (1946), 129.

522. Lucien Laberthonnière, *Essais de philosophie religieuse* (Paris: Éditions du Seuil, 1966), 164–65.

523. Blondelian philosopher Argerami writes: "This rational element, inconceivable, intangible, and intrinsic to the cosmos is what we call *cosmic thought*." Omar Argerami, *Pensar y ser en Maurice Blondel* (Buenos Aires: Editorial Guadalupe, 1967), 87.

524. See Flori, "Intorno al Blondelismo," 300.

525. In a general sense the term agnosticism designates a philosophical theory that denies human reason the possibility of gaining true knowledge of supersensible things, limiting its field to sensible phenomena. In its most radical expression, agnosticism maintains that human thought cannot know anything external to it, being utterly confined to knowing its own ideas. It is thus a subjective and idealistic theory. Édouard Le Roy writes, "Something 'beyond' or 'outside' thought is by definition something unthinkable. ...When our thought searches an absolute object, it finds nothing but itself. ...[Thus,] a particular idealism seems imperative." Le Roy, *Revue de Métaphysique et de Morale* (1907), 488, 495, quoted in Farges, "Modernisme: Synthèse du modernisme philosophique," *D.A.F.C.*, 3:648. In its turn, the *Program of the Modernists* asserts, "Recent criticism of the various theories on knowledge leads us to conclude that in the field of knowledge, everything is subjective and symbolic." Anonymous (pres. Buonaiuti), *Il programma dei modernisti*, 112.

526. Laberthonnière, *Essais de philosophie religieuse*, 150–51.

527. Anonymous (pres. Buonaiuti), *Il programma dei modernisti*, 96–98.

Far from hiding their immanentism, the modernists flaunted it.

> Our postulates are inspired in immanentist principles.
> ... [proclaimed the *Program*.]
> We are immanentists.[528]

Alfred Loisy writes, "The evolution of modern philosophy tends ever more to the idea of an immanent god who has no need for intermediaries to act in the world and in man."[529]

Taken to its final consequences, immanentism paved the road for pantheism. "Disciples took their symbolism and immanentism much farther than Tyrrell, and came ultimately to the verge of a pantheism," Canon Roger Aubert reports.[530] Édouard Le Roy, for example, affirmed, "For us god is not; he becomes, his becoming is our own progress."[531] He called this position "an orthodox pantheism."[532] Alfred Loisy was also overt on this point. "Christ," he wrote, "has even less importance in my religion than he does in that of liberal Protestants; for I attach little importance to the revelation of God the Father for which they honor Jesus. If I am anything in religion, it is more pantheist-positivist-humanitarian than Christian."[533]

One person who took the modernist postulates in this field to their last logical consequences was Father Hébert. "Should the old belief in a transcendent God give way to the idea of a divine immanence?" he inquired. For him, god was a mere "metaphor," an "image," a "figment of the imagination." He proposed the destruction of this "pagan idol" to have "god" replaced with a vague "divine" immanent in man and in the world.[534] Commenting on this egregious doctrine, Jesuit theologian Fr. Albert Valensin wrote, "Ceasing to be understood as a personal being, God would be identified with the sensation man believes he has of Him, and which he calls divine."[535]

f. The Modernist Religion

The movement of the heart man has in response to his deep yearnings, which the modernists call *religious sense*, is allegedly at the origin of religion. Led by this sense, man tries to adopt toward that 'immanent divine' an attitude that would satisfy his yearnings. He continuously gropes and searches through the very operations of life for stances that will satisfy him. This search constitutes the soul's religious experience. Some men are more successful than others in this endeavor. Some privileged men even attain particularly strong religious experiences. Such a man was, for example, Jesus of Nazareth. "Religion," the *Program of the Modernists* says, "appears as a spontaneous result of unquenchable yearnings of the human spirit whose satisfaction is provided by the internal emotional experience of the divine present in us."[536] Modernism thus transferred religion from the realm of reason and

historical fact, verifiable by rational criteria, to that of individual experience, changeable by definition.

According to modernists, the religious sense, at first rudimentary, gradually emerges almost formless from the subconscious and matures during life. All religions are mere expressions of the religious sense. They are adequate to the degree that they offer a suitable vehicle for this sense, able to translate the person's religious experience and assuage his yearnings. "Even fetishism is a sign of the divine presence," Loisy wrote.[537]

g. An Immanent and Continuing Revelation

The Church's Magisterium teaches that man can know God through the lights of his natural reason. However, due to its limited capacity and the deterioration of original sin, natural reason is easily subject to error. So God, in His infinite mercy, revealed Himself to man, directly teaching him truths that his limited reason would never have known. This is public revelation—constituting the deposit of the faith—and is entirely contained in Holy Scriptures and Tradition.[538]

Not so for the modernists. Their *Program* reads, "In addition to the concept of inspiration, [modernist] criticism forces us to change that of revelation, not in its essence as we also believe that revelation is god's message to man, but as to the manner in which the divine message is transmitted to man."[539] In a less roundabout way, Loisy wrote, "The common idea of revelation is pure childishness."[540]

Enclosed in their subjectivist immanentism, modernists eschewed the idea of an external revelation and were forced to look for God's Word within man himself. French theologian Fr. Jules Lebreton states:

> Modernists understand revelation very differently; every man feels it directly in his soul. It is not the divine manifestation of a truth, but an emotion, a surge of the religious sense that, at times, surfaces from the depths of the subconscious and in which the person discerns a divine touch. ...
>
> ...While for a Catholic revelation is essentially the communication of a truth, for modernists it is essentially the exaltation or excitation of the religious sense.[541]

In other words, the modernists reduced revelation to the person's awareness of his religious sense, that is, to his perception of the divine immanence. "Revelation," Loisy writes, "is nothing else than the awareness that man acquires of his relationship with god."[542] The *Program of the Modernists* likewise asserts, "We conceive god's voice as an irresistible interior force. ... God cannot be the direct object of our sensations."[543] For his part, George Tyrrell affirmed that

> Revelation belongs rather to the category of impressions than to that of expressions. ...
> ... Revelation is not statement but experience.[544]

528. Anonymous, 98, 105.

529. Loisy, *Autour d'un petit livre*, 153–54.

530. Roger Aubert, s.v. "Modernism," *Sacramentum Mundi: An Encyclopedia of Theology*, ed. (New York: Herder and Herder, 1969), 4:101.

531. Édouard Le Roy, "Comment se pose le problème de Dieu," *Revue de Métaphysique et de Morale* (1907), 509.

532. Édouard Le Roy, *Dogme et critique,* 6th ed. (Paris: Librairie Bloud et Cie., 1907), 145.

533. Alfred Loisy, *Mémoires*, 3:397, quoted in Ratté, *Three Modernists*, 120.

534. Marcel Hébert, "La dernière idole: Étude sur la personnalité divine," *Revue de Métaphysique et de Morale* (1902): 397, 403–404, quoted in Albert Valensin, s.v. "Immanence (Doctrine de l')," *D.A.F.C.*, 2:575. On Fr. Hébert, see Houtin, *Un prêtre symboliste: Marcel Hébert* (Paris: F. Rieder et Cie., 1925).

535. Valensin, "Immanence (Doctrine de l')," *D.A.F.C.*, 2:575.

536. Anonymous (pres. Buonaiuti), *Il programma dei modernisti*, 99.

537. Ratté, *Three Modernists*, 70.

538. We will deal with this subject in chapter 3.

539. Anonymous (pres. Buonaiuti), *Il programma dei modernisti*, 42.

540. Alfred Loisy, *Quelques lettres sur des questions actuelles et sur des événements récents* (Ceffonds, près Montier-en-Der, Haute-Marne: self-published, 1908), 162.

541. Jules Lebreton, s.v. "Modernisme: L'encyclique et la théologie moderniste," *D.A.F.C.*, 3:676–77.

542. Loisy, *Autour d'un petit livre*, 195.

543. Anonymous (pres. Buonaiuti), *Il programma dei modernisti*, 43–44.

544. George Tyrrell, *Through Scylla and Charibdis*, 280, 285.

What becomes, then, of the Biblical narrations that record public revelation? The modernists simply brush them aside as mere literary devices. Their *Program* reads, "The biblical narrations give these communications an external form, but is this a mere literary device or an exact expression of reality?"[545] What do they think about the existence of miracles? "Too bad if the idea of miracle is unintelligible and false," contended Alfred Loisy. "I am close to believing that miracles and prophecies are ancient forms of religious thought bound to disappear."[546]

This notion of revelation is consistent with modernist immanentism, tending toward pantheistic monism. The person's awareness of his religious sense is tantamount to divine revelation because in the modernist system this sense is a manifestation of divine immanence. There is no longer a clear boundary between individual consciousness and divine substance, such that the operations of the former are taken as manifestations of the latter. Loisy writes, "The conscious individual can be seen almost alternatively as God's consciousness in the world by an incarnation of God in humanity and as the world's consciousness subsisting in God by a concentration of the universe in man."[547]

The Church teaches that public revelation closed with the death of the last apostle. Not so for modernists. Le Roy writes, "As far as psychology and history are concerned, revelation appears as a gradual blossoming [*épannouissement*] without any sudden hiatus or external intrusion; it appears as a continuous progress that resembles experience, life itself."[548] Indeed, if revelation is the awareness men have of their religious sense, and if this sense matures throughout history in the modernists' evolutionist worldview, then revelation is also in the process of being completed. "Biblical criticism has dissolved the belief in the formal tradition of a primitive revelation" boasts the *Program*. "[In Religion we discover] a principle of life ... that tends toward an ever more perfect expansion."[549]

h. The Modernist Dogma

Philosophically, truth consists in the conformity of the idea with its object. In the Catholic concept, a dogmatic formula supplies us with a correct knowledge of the object it represents, namely, some point of divine revelation. Since this object is invariable, the formula itself is always adequate. For the modernists, this makes no sense. According to them, a dogma is a mere symbol that tells us nothing of an objective truth. A dogma is not an expression of truth but an attempt to represent the feelings of the religious experience in human thought and language. From this agnostic and evolutionist perspective, for example, the dogma of the divinity of Christ is not correct because it corresponds to a fact, but because it serves as a tool for Christians to describe the religious experiences stirred up by the memory of that extraordinary personage called Jesus of Nazareth.

"The great Christian dogmas," Alfred Loisy contends, "are semi-metaphysic poems where a superficial philosopher will see nothing but a somewhat abstract mythology. They were useful to guide the Christian ideal, and this is their merit. However, as scientific definitions of religion—which is what they pretend to

be—they are necessarily outmoded. For today's science, they are the work of ignorance."[550]

The raison d'être of dogmas would be their usefulness in expressing and upholding the religious sense, and in satisfying its momentary needs. If so, they can only survive as long as they fulfill this role. Thus, for example, it would be absurd to preserve today all the dogmas defined by the Council of Trent (1545–1563), that might have expressed the religious sense of sixteenth-century Catholics but no longer reflect that of our times. According to the modernists, if religious formulas are to be truly religious and not merely intellectual constructions, they ought to be living and always changing as life itself is. Thus we find in the modernist heresy a sweeping evolutionism as regards dogmas that is in fact their negation. "Are there eternal and necessary truths? We doubt it," acknowledged Édouard Le Roy.[551] Similarly, Loisy maintained that "truth, as a human value, is not more immutable than man himself. Truth evolves with him, in him and through him."[552]

In the modernist system, the Church cannot define dogmas in God's name. The ecclesiastical authority is to be but an interpreter of the collective conscience. Indeed, if revelation is subjective, how can the faithful accept an external authority?

i. The Modernist Ecclesiology

Thus, from error to error, we arrive at the modernist ecclesiology. According to it, man is a social being; he feels the need to communicate his faith to others, particularly when he has had some strong religious experience. When a number of people coincide in this need, they put their faith in common and form a society to guard, promote, and propagate this faith. They constitute a church. Such were, for example, the early Christians, whose faith had been aroused by the messianic preaching of Jesus of Nazareth. Thus, in the modernist folly, the Church is the product of the collective consciousness, that is to say, the association of individual consciousnesses sharing their religious experiences. In short, the Church is a vital emanation of the collectivity of Christians, not a supernatural society directly founded by Our Lord Jesus Christ.

The modernists denied, as will liberation theologians decades later, that Our Lord consciously and explicitly established a Church. He merely preached the imminent coming of an eschatological "kingdom" and galvanized a number of followers. Loisy writes, "It may be said that Jesus, in the course of His ministry, neither prescribed nor practised any external rite of worship which would have characterized the gospel as religion. Jesus no more decided the form of Christian worship beforehand than He laid down the constitution and dogmas of the Church. ... The thought of Jesus was bent, as always, on the idea of realizing the kingdom of Heaven rather than the direct idea of founding a new religion and a Church."[553] The same doctrine is found in George Tyrrell: "The notion of a complete ecclesiastical organism produced abruptly by a divine fiat on the day of Pentecost belongs to the same sort of philosophy as the Mosaic cosmogony."[554]

However, when it became obvious that the kingdom would not come instantly, Christ's followers felt the need to form themselves into a society in order to safeguard the eschatological yearning and keep alive Christ's memory, that is, the reverberation of His

---

545. Anonymous (pres. Buonaiuti), *Il programma dei modernisti*, 43.

546. Loisy, *Quelques lettres*, 59, 61.

547. Loisy, 150.

548. Le Roy, *Dogme et critique*, 307. See also A. Firmin (Alfred Loisy), "L'idée de la révelation," *Revue du Clergé Français* 21 (Jan. 1900), 250ff; Edward Schillebeeckx, "Il concetto di verità e i problemi conessi—La toleranza," in *Grandi temi del concilio* by Frans Alphons Maria Alting von Geusau, et al. (Rome: Edizione Pauline, 1965), 851–53.

549. Anonymous (pres. Buonaiuti), *Il programma dei modernisti*, 110–11.

550. Loisy, *Quelques lettres*, 71. For an in-depth analysis of the modernist doctrines regarding faith and dogma, see Cristiano Pesch, S.J., *Fede, dogma e fatti storici: Studio su le dottrine moderniste* (Rome: Libreria Pontificia di F. Pustet, 1909).

551. Le Roy, "Comment se pose le problème de Dieu," 167.

552. Loisy, *Autour d'un petit livre*, 192.

553. Alfred Loisy, *The Gospel and the Church*, trans. Christopher Home (New York: Charles Scribner's Sons, 1904), 230–31.

554. Ratté, *Three Modernists*, 197.

preaching in their collective consciousness. "Jesus foretold the kingdom, and it was the Church that came," is one of Loisy's most quoted phrases.[555]

j. The Modernists' Historical Criticism

Catholic doctrine teaches that the Bible was written under direct inspiration from the Holy Spirit and contains the public revelation.[556] Indeed, the Bible is the paramount objective foundation of the Faith. This contradicts the very kernel of Modernism, for which religion is something internal and subjective. One of the pivots of the modernist heresy was the demolition of traditional Catholic exegesis through the extensive use of the so-called historical method of biblical criticism. Once the historical sources of revelation are demolished, the whole edifice of the Magisterium collapses.

For modernists, the Scriptures should be subjected to the relentless scrutiny of science, and what could not be scientifically corroborated had to be eliminated no matter what the Magisterium said. It was a purely naturalist approach.[557]

In modernist hands, this method was anything but scientific and constituted, deep down, the application of their peculiar philosophy to the realm of exegesis.[558] Undergirding the method was the agnostic postulate that the only realm accessible to our knowledge is that of sensible phenomena and therefore we cannot pass any judgment beyond it. History would thus be restricted to observable facts. Accordingly, for the modernists, God and any intervention of God in human affairs cannot be treated as historical facts and should be relegated to the domain of individual faith.

Applied to Our Lord Jesus Christ, for example, this implies that we can only know the historical personage: a man called Jesus of Nazareth, son of Joseph and Mary, born in the reign of Caesar Augustus, who preached in Galilee and Judea and was crucified in 33 A.D. by the Roman governor Pontius Pilate, leaving behind him a number of followers. These are the data offered to us by historical testimony. Now, was this man God, as the Gospels affirm? According to the modernist theory, this problem is beyond the sphere of historical fact and therefore is not an object of knowledge. A person may choose to believe that Jesus was God, but this is a construction of *his* individual faith, not an observable historical fact. Consequently, a critic has nothing to say about it. This is what the encyclical *Pascendi* meant when it charged the modernists with separating the historian from the believer.[559]

According to modernists, the most that can be said about Jesus is that he was a mystic and a seer, an extraordinary man with a unique destiny. Loisy, for example, declared that "Jesus lives in humanity to an extent and in a way never experienced by any other human being."[560] Applying this type of criticism to Scriptures, and discarding those points of faith which in his judgment were not warranted by historical testimony, Loisy arrived at this conclusion: "I did not accept ... any article of the Catholic creed, except that Jesus had been 'crucified under Pontius Pilate.'"[561] At the end of his life, Loisy even denied the very existence of God, all in the name of historical criticism.

Regarding the very facts narrated in the Bible, modernists distinguished those objectively documented from those they claimed were added by faith. For example, founded on many biblical passages analyzed by sound theology, traditional Christology has always attributed omniscience, that is, universal and infinite knowledge, to Jesus of Nazareth. This attribution necessarily derives from His divine nature. For modernists, though, this cannot be empirically verified. Accordingly, this attribution must be considered a mere transfiguration of the person of Jesus, that is, something extraordinary the evangelists attributed to Him to conform the biblical narration to the enthusiastic faith of the first Christians.

Modernists distinguished between the "Christ of history" and the "Christ of faith," the former being the real Christ, the latter His transfiguration. Sensing a particularly substantial religious experience in the historical Jesus, the faith of Christians elevated the personage above His true conditions, clothing Him with divine attributes. The *Program of the Modernists* reads, "We admit that, from the gnoseological standpoint the historical facts that serve as base for the faith underwent an intense elaboration by which they assumed a character they did not possess in the beginning. The Christ of faith, for example, is undoubtedly very different from the Christ of history."[562]

In the modernist heresy, the divinity of Our Lord was heavily veiled. Stripped of all the transfigurations of faith, Jesus's mission boiled down to the preaching of a messianic kingdom. Christ, then, was the Messias solely in that sense. Only much later did

---

555. Loisy, *The Gospel and the Church*, 166.

556. "The Church has always venerated the Scriptures as she venerates the Lord's Body. ...In Sacred Scripture, the Church constantly finds her nourishment and her strength, for she welcomes it not as a human word, 'but as what it really is, the word of God.'" *Catechism of the Catholic Church*, nos. 103–4.

557. The Magisterium has gradually authorized the use of the method by Catholic exegetes, although controversies remain about its limitations and dangers. In the preface to a document of the Pontifical Biblical Commission on the interpretation of the Bible in the Church, Cardinal Ratzinger warns:

> In the history of interpretation the rise of the historical-critical method opened a new era. With it, new possibilities for understanding the biblical word in its originality opened up. Just as with all human endeavor, though, so also this method contained hidden dangers along with its positive possibilities. The search for the original can lead to putting the word back into the past completely so that it is no longer taken in its actuality. It can result that only the human dimension of the word appears as real, while the genuine author, God, is removed from the reach of a method which was established for understanding human reality.
>
> The application of a "profane" method to the Bible necessarily led to discussion. ...
>
> ...Fifty years later, however, because of the fertile work of great Catholic exegetes, Pope Pius XII, in his encyclical *Divino Afflante Spiritu* of Sept. 30, 1943, was able to provide largely positive encouragement toward making the modern methods of understanding the Bible fruitful. The Constitution on Divine revelation of the Second Vatican Council, *Dei Verbum*, of Nov. 18, 1965, adopted all of this. It provided us with a synthesis, which substantially remains, between the lasting insights of patristic theology and the new methodological understanding of the moderns. (Joseph Cardinal Ratzinger, preface to "The Interpretation of the Bible in the Church" by Pontifical Biblical Commission [Apr. 23, 1993])

558. The scientific soundness of the modernist criticism must be taken with a grain of salt. On some points it is downright flimsy, in others it offers arguments far inferior to those of traditional exegesis, and still in others it has been disproved by more recent scholarship.

559. Saint Pius X teaches:

> We will take an illustration from the Person of Christ. In the person of Christ, they say, science and history encounter nothing that is not human. Therefore, in virtue of the first canon deduced from agnosticism, whatever there is in His history suggestive of the divine, must be rejected. Then, according to the second canon, the historical Person of Christ was *transfigured* by faith; therefore everything that raises it above historical conditions must be removed. Lately, the third canon, which lays down that the person of Christ has been *disfigured* by faith, requires that everything should be excluded, deeds, and words, and all else that is not in keeping with His character, circumstances, and education, and with the place and time in which He lived. (St. Pius X, encyclical *Pascendi*, no. 9)

560. Loisy, *The Gospel and the Church*, 125.

561. Vidler, *The Modernist Movement*, 90.

562. Anonymous (pres. Buonaiuti), *Il programma dei modernisti*, 115. This is how Tyrrell understood Christ: "What are the categories and concepts of Jesus to us? Are we to frame our minds to that of a first-century Jewish carpenter, for whom more than half the world and nearly the whole of its history did not exist; to whom the stellar universe was unknown; who cared nothing for art or science or history or politics or nine-tenths of the interests of humanity but solely for the Kingdom of God and His righteousness?" George Tyrrell, *Christianity at the Cross-Roads* (London: Longmans, Green and Co., 1910), 270.

the Christians transform this historical Christ into the Second Person of the Holy Trinity.[563]

What, then, is the Bible? For modernists, the Bible does not record purely historical facts but rather the transfiguration of these facts operated by the Jewish People and the early Christian communities. According to Loisy, the Gospels are

> an echo, necessarily weakened and a little confused, of the words of Jesus, the general impression He produced upon hearers well disposed toward Him. ...
>
> ...We know Christ only by the tradition, across the tradition, and in the tradition of the primitive Christians.[564]

Modernists thus reduced the Bible to an anthology of stories written by Jewish authors and early Christians to record their own religious experiences.

Did those stories contain divine revelation? Yes, said the modernists, to the extent that all religious experiences manifest the immanent divine. Living in a privileged time of divine immanence, its authors had notably strong religious experiences and captured the divine immanence better.[565] Thus, Loisy could write, "The Gospel is the highest manifestation of the human conscience in the pursuit of happiness in justice."[566]

However, since revelation continues in history in the religious experience of the faithful, nothing prevents writings produced within a new kairos from being considered a continuation of Holy Scriptures. This is the type of reasoning, for example, with which liberation theologians say they are writing the Newest Testament.[567]

3. The Condemnation of Modernism

The audacity of the modernist onslaught in the field of Biblical criticism had prompted Leo XIII to publish in 1893 the encyclical *Providentissimus Deus*, in which he warned against "the grave error of rationalism" and reaffirmed the traditional exegesis of the Church. The document, however, avoided explicitly condemning persons and books. Besides, as Vidler notes, "It required no great ingenuity to find loopholes in the encyclical."[568]

The situation came to a head during the pontificate of Pope St. Pius X (1835, 1903–1914), who immediately manifested his resolve to stop the heresy. In his first encyclical, *E supremi apostolatus*, he warned against "the snares of a certain new and fallacious science, which ... with masked and cunning arguments strives to open the door to the errors of rationalism and semi-rationalism."[569] Two months later, the Holy Office put four of Loisy's books and one of Albert Houtin on the Index, triggering a chain of similar measures that struck all the modernists. A series of actions followed, both by the Vatican and diocesan bishops, condemning modernist periodicals and interdicting their publishing houses. These measures climaxed in 1906 with the encyclical *Pieni l'animo*,

in which St. Pius X vehemently censured the innovating tendencies. All this, however, was but a presage of the great battle to come.

In 1907, the pope began a series of measures to thwart the modernist endeavor. In the consistorial allocution of April 17 that foreshadowed *Pascendi*, the pope castigated the modernists and denounced "this assault that constitutes not only a heresy, but the synthesis, the venomous essence of all heresies." On July 3, the Holy Office published the decree *Lamentabili sane exitu*, containing a syllabus of 65 condemned modernist propositions covering six areas: authority of the Church's Magisterium in biblical exegesis (1–8), inspiration and historicity of the Sacred Scriptures (9–19), the concepts of revelation and dogma (20–26), Christ (27–38), the sacraments (39–51), and the constitution of the Church (58–65).

Finally, on September 8, St. Pius X published the encyclical *Pascendi Dominici gregis*, formally condemning the modernist heresy. The pope defined Modernism as "the synthesis of all heresies" (no. 39) and called its partisans "the most pernicious of all the adversaries of the Church" (no. 3). Decrying "these audacious, these sacrilegious assertions" (no. 10), the pope lamented that "these are not merely the foolish babblings of infidels. There are many Catholics, yea, and priests too, who say these things openly; and they boast that they are going to reform the Church" (no. 10). Modernists, the pope further noted, "lay the axe not to the branches and shoots, but to the very root, that is, to the faith and its deepest fires. And having struck at this root of immortality, they proceed to disseminate poison through the whole tree, so that there is no part of Catholic truth from which they hold their hand, none that they do not strive to corrupt" (no. 3).[570]

The encyclical also contained a detailed examination of modernist philosophical and theological errors. It closes prescribing concrete measures to put an end to the expansion of heresy, including the establishment of a vigilance committee in every diocese.

St. Pius X further stigmatized Modernism in his consistorial allocution of December 16, when he accused the modernists of having "renounced the oath of fidelity taken in their Baptism," and condemned it once again in his 1910 motu proprio *Sacrorum antistitum*, where he instituted the anti-modernist oath, and demanded its swearing by bishops, priests, and professors of theology.

Realizing that Modernism had put together an ample support network in liberal Catholic circles and had even established a secret society that extended its web in the clergy and laity, St. Pius X also attacked it as a sect, carrying out an ample and well-structured plan to disrupt the revolutionary plot. He also supported the activities of the Sodalitium Pianum, better known as the Sapinière (Pine Grove), an information network on Modernism organized by Msgr. Umberto Begnini (1862–1934), an official in the Vatican Secretariat of State.[571]

In the aftermath of *Pascendi*, an anonymous Italian modernist, presumably Ernesto Buonaiuti, insolently published *Il programma dei modernisti: Risposta all'enciclica di Pio X 'Pascendi Dominici gregis'*. Evincing the high degree of clandestine articulation the movement had attained, this manifesto was quickly translated and published in several countries under the sponsorship of a mysterious International Religious Society. Pope Pius X forbade its reading under pain of mortal sin and excommunicated its

563. In the decree *Lamentabili*, St. Pius X condemned the following modernist proposition: "In all the evangelical texts the name 'Son of God' is equivalent only to that of 'Messias.' It does not in the least way signify that Christ is the true and natural Son of God." St. Pius X, decree *Lamentabili sane exitu* (July 3, 1907), no. 30.

564. Loisy, *The Gospel and the Church*, 13.

565. "According to the principles of the modernists, they [the Sacred Books] may be rightly described as a collection of *experiences*, not indeed of the kind that may come to anybody, but those extraordinary and striking ones which have happened in any religion." St. Pius X, encyclical *Pascendi*, no. 22.

566. Alfred Loisy, *Quelques lettres*, 71. In the modernist system, "inspiration ...is distinguished only by its vehemence from that impulse which stimulates the believer to reveal the faith that is in him by words or writing." St. Pius X, encyclical *Pascendi*, no. 22.

567. See chapter 4.

568. Vidler, *The Modernist Movement*, 88.

569. St. Pius X, encyclical *E supremi apostolatus* (Oct. 4, 1903), no. 11.

570. *"Illud definimus, ut omnium haereseon collectum esse affirmemus."* St. Pius X, encyclical *Pascendi*, nos. 39, 3, 10. Writing in 1990 in the magazine *Renovatio*, the periodical of the archdiocese of Genoa, Luigi Guglielmo Rossi states, "Modernism is the gravest insult to history, it desecrates Christianity, blasphemes the Holy Spirit. It has the curse of a harrow." Luigi Guglielmo Rossi, "Il modernismo," *Renovatio* (July–Sept. 1990), 401.

571. On the *Sodalitium Pianum*, see de Mattei, *The Second Vatican Council*, 5, 204.

authors and advertisers. The pope further established that, should there be a priest among them, he was suspended *a divinis* for life.

The supreme pontiff carried on this anti-modernist crusade with such coherence and vigor that the well-known traditionalist, British author Hillaire Belloc (1870–1953), exulted, "The blow was mortal! Modernism is dead!"[572] Alas! Belloc was crying victory much too soon. The modernist movement was not dead at all; it just dropped its label and lowered its profile even more.

As early as 1908, George Tyrrell had written to a Roman confidant, "As I look around, ... I'm forced to concede that the wave of modernist resistance is spent and has exhausted all its forces for now. ... We must wait for the day in which, through a silent and secret work, we shall have gained for us a far greater proportion of the Church's troops for the cause of liberty."[573]

St. Pius X's crusade against Modernism also reached America. In 1909, for example, the archbishop of New York closed the *The New York Review*, a Catholic bi-monthly periodical with a dubious position in the modernist controversy. The *Review*'s editor, Francis Gigot, merited a formal censure; and Fr. James Driscoll, a contributing editor and rector of Saint Joseph Seminary, was dismissed. Fr. Joseph Bruneau of Saint Mary's Seminary in Baltimore, and Fr. Cornelius Clifford of Immaculate Conception Seminary in South Orange, N.J., were also embroiled with Church authorities because of their modernist sympathies. Both were dismissed from their teaching posts and transferred to small parishes.[574]

4. The Catholic Freemasonry

A feature of the modernist movement, as indeed all modern heretical movements, was secrecy. In the novel *The Saint*, published in 1905 in the form of literary narrative, Antonio Fogazzaro dealt with very relevant issues of the modernist adventure, including the need to operate secretly by forming a Catholic Freemasonry.

Having brought the main players together in order to "unite for joint action," the author, in the person of character Abbé Marinier, states:

> "Therefore, before initiating this catholic freemasonry, I think it would be wiser to come to an understanding respecting these reforms. I will go even farther; I believe that, were it possible to establish perfect harmony of opinion among you, it would still be inexpedient to bind yourselves together with visible fetters, as Signor Selva proposes. My objection is of a most delicate nature. You doubtless expect to be able to swim in safety, below the surface, like wary fishes, and you do not reflect that the vigilant eye of the Sovereign-Fisherman, or rather Vice-Fisherman, may very easily spy you out, and spear you with a skilful thrust of the harpoon. Now I should never advise the finest, most highly flavoured, most desirable fishes to bind themselves together. You will easily understand what might happen should one be caught and landed. Moreover, you know very well that the great Fisherman of Galilee put the small fishes into his vivarium, but the Great Fisherman of Rome fries them." ...
>
> [In response to that speech, another character, Minucci, snaps:] "That is true! We have no human fears.

... We wish to be united, all of us, from many lands, and to regulate our course of action. Catholic freemasonry? Yes; the freemasonry of the Catacombs."[575]

Who took part in that Catholic Freemasonry? "His true name is Legion," Fogazzaro revealed at a 1907 lecture in Paris. "He lives, thinks, and works in France, England, Germany, America, and Italy as well. He wears a cassock, uniform, or toga. He shows up in universities. He hides in seminaries. He fights in the press. He prays in the depths of the cloisters. ... He is an exegete and historian, theologian and scholar, journalist and poet."[576]

Struck in the heart by Saint Pius X, this Catholic Freemasonry had to admit defeat in order to regroup even more secretly for future battles. Writing to a Roman confidant on August 24, 1908, George Tyrrell reveals the dominant feeling in the modernist camp: "I am afraid that we must admit that the interest raised by the novelty of the modernist insurrection has weakened and the public is a bit tired."[577]

Such machinations could not but draw the Roman pontiff's attention. In 1910, he published the motu proprio *Sacrorum antistitum*, in which he accused the modernists of having grouped into a secret society (*clandestinum foedus*), and "not having abandoned their plan to disturb the peace of the Church."[578]

In the following decades, that secret society carried on the "silent and secret work" proposed by Tyrrell and inspired most of the errors that plagued the Church in the twentieth century. "Reduced to a kind of clandestine life, modernists continued to operate underground, inspiring much of the religious dispute that now explodes in the Church," affirmed in 1972 the French Dominican theologian Fr. Albert-Marie Besnard.[579]

The progressives themselves confirm this. Looking back at the work of this secret society, Swiss theologian Fr. Hans Küng wrote in 1968:

> We have every reason to respect the Christian commitment of those lonely heroes in a struggle for a new truthfulness, a future of the Church which seemed then to have very little prospect. They groaned under the untruthfulness, weakness, obscurity, and unholiness of the holy Church of God for which all their work was done—but they did not leave her. ...They were suspected, hindered, disavowed, calumniated, persecuted, and exiled, by fellow-Christians, by bishops, and theologians in the Church—but they continued to work as best they could. They were considered dangerous, extremist, too radical, heretical-revolutionary; but they went on, as far as they were allowed to go and sometimes beyond this: doggedly patient, fearless, and bold against all fear. ...
>
> ...And it became clear that those pioneers of a new truthfulness were not outsiders, but the vanguard

572. Vincent Yzermans, ed., *All Things in Christ: Encyclicals and Selected Works of Saint Pius X* (Westminster, Md.: The Newman Press, 1954), 88.

573. Buonaiuti, *Le modernisme catholique*, 148–49, quoted in Rivière, s.v. "Modernisme," 10:2042.

574. See John Tracy Ellis, "Les États-Unis depuis 1850," in *Nouvelle histoire de l'église*, vol. 5, *L'Église dans le monde moderne* (Paris: Seuil, 1975), 304.

575. Fogazzaro, *The Saint*, 62, 67–68.

576. Delmont, *Modernisme et modernistes*, 24. Fogazzaro's biographer, Tommaso Gallarati-Scotti, comments: "The frequent duplicity of the modernists is one of the dark sides the future historian will have to deal with. To an impartial eye, the sheer phenomenon of anonymity certainly does not appear in a sympathetic light. For it is not without profound humiliation that man masks his name, and Modernism has tolerated this lie in its most complicated forms." Tommaso Gallarati-Scotti, *Vita di Antonio Fogazzaro* (Milan: Baldini & Castoldi, 1920), 496.

577. Ernesto Buonaiuti, *Le modernisme catholique*, 148–49, quoted in Rivière, s.v. "Modernisme," 10:2042.

578. St. Pius X, motu proprio *Sacrorum antistitum* (Sept. 1, 1910).

579. Albert-Marie Besnard, in *Les religions: Les dictionnaires du savoir moderne*, ed. Jean Chevalier (Paris: Centre d'étude et de promotion de la lecture, 1972), 306.

of a main force, following indeed slowly but at heart willingly.[580]

The work of the modernists was facilitated by considerable complicity within the Church itself. Suffice it to mention the strong reactions, even by bishops, against the motu proprio *Sacrorum antistitum*. Pope St. Pius X was highly respected but not always followed. In April 1912, he lamented and prophetically confided to his friend Most Rev. Alfonso Archi, bishop of Como (1864–1938): *"De gentibus non est vir mecum!"* [from the peoples no one was with me] (Isa. 63:3). "The danger lies precisely within the veins and bowels of the Church."[581] "Loneliness, and disobedience by many bishops, even within the Sacred College" was his lot, records French historian Émile Poulat.[582]

Once again we feel with our hands how the current Church crisis did not start in the sixties. Already at the beginning of the twentieth century the situation of the Church was so dire that the Vicar of Christ felt abandoned by everyone.

D. Nouvelle Théologie

1. A New Climate

St. Pius X died on August 20, 1914, distraught that he was unable to stop the "useless slaughter," as his successor defined the First World War. Covered by the roar of cannon, the neo-modernist secret society continued, without too many problems, to pull the Church in an opposite direction to the one intended by the deceased sovereign pontiff.

His successor, Benedict XV (1854, 1914–1922), reiterated more than once the doctrinal condemnation of Modernism. In the encyclical *Ad beatissimi apostolorum principis*, of November 1, 1914, he denounced "the monstrous errors of 'Modernism,' which Our Predecessor rightly declared to be 'the synthesis of all heresies,' and solemnly condemned. We hereby renew that condemnation in all its fullness, Venerable Brethren. ... Nor do We merely desire that Catholics should shrink from the errors of Modernism, but also from the tendencies or what is called the spirit of Modernism."[583]

Nevertheless, Rome was basking in the warmth of a new climate. While still criticizing Modernism on a doctrinal level, the supposed excesses in the anti-modernist struggle began to be condemned. It is in this context that the derogatory term *intégriste* (integrist, integralist) arose to describe the anti-modernist party. The new Roman pontiff made it known that the excesses had to end. He promised Pietro Cardinal Maffi, "The era of accusations is over."[584] Pope St. Pius X's closest collaborators were driven away, and many modernists affected by sanctions were rehabilitated.

The Dominican Father Chenu was then a young seminarian in the process of becoming the key figure of what would be called the Nouvelle Théologie. In 1975, recalling that change in climate, he states,

> Benedict XV represented a different trend. Today we would call him a liberal. So much so that Pius X had

refused to create him cardinal even though he was archbishop of Bologna. ...
> Benedict XV immediately sent away [Cardinal] Merry del Val [secretary of state under St. Pius X] and replaced him with Cardinal Gasparri. ... A real palace revolution! Cardinal Gasparri reinstated in their teaching posts young Italian priests and theologians previously suspected or even condemned, for the repression in Italy had been very tough.[585]

In a letter to Paul Sabatier, Fr. Giovanni Genocchi is even more explicit: "We are already seeing some good effects of the new pope's wisdom. He does not want to show the iconoclastic air of his predecessor. We are breathing better. ... Msgr. Duchesne is no longer the nemesis. Father Lanzoni ... has been made monsignor. Many victims of madness and fanaticism ... are already rehabilitated, and others are on the way."[586]

2. The Modernizers

The situation had changed. No longer able to speak as Catholics, the excommunicated modernists had lost all influence over the faithful. We can apply to them the words of Most Rev. Bernard McQuaid, bishop of Rochester, commenting on the possible excommunication of Fr. Edward McGlynn: "Then he steps out of the Church and loses his influence and power to hurt. He will soon find out what a small man he is outside of the Church!"[587]

These modernists, though, were just the tip of the iceberg, the vanguard of a much wider movement. A majority of them remained within the Church and were able to carry forward the "silent and secret work" Tyrrell had proposed. To distinguish them from the broader movement, members of the latter are sometimes called modernizers or *third party*. While generally coinciding with the modernists' theological approach, they stopped short of its last consequences. Above all, they were extremely careful to avoid formulations that had the flavor of heterodoxy. For the historian Émile Poulat, the years of neo-modernism (1930–1950) are largely due to the work of these modernizers.[588] The modernizing trends later gave rise to the Nouvelle Théologie, LT's forerunner.

The main focus of the modernizing trends was the Saulchoir, a theological college of the French Dominican province.[589] "Saulchoir was the center of attraction of the younger generation," Father Chenu recalls. "Sometimes the future takes shape without us noticing it. For me it all started in that first Saulchoir."[590] The Spanish Jesuit Fr. Joaquín Salaverri, opposed to Father Chenu, also stated, "The Saulchoir Dominican convent is one of the two main centers from which the movement to renew theology

580. Hans Küng, *Truthfulness: The Future of the Church*, trans. Edward Quinn (New York: Sheed and Ward, 1968), 155–56.

581. Mentioned by Most Rev. Alfonso Archi in his June 1914 pastoral letter (p. 11), quoted in Émile Poulat, *Intégrisme et catholicisme intégrale* (Paris: Casterman, 1969), 101.

582. Poulat, *Intégrisme*, 101.

583. Benedict XV, encyclical *Ad beatissimi apostolorum principis* (Nov. 1, 1914), no. 25.

584. From a Sept. 5, 1914, letter of Filippo Crispolti to his wife, quoted in Poulat, *Intégrisme*, 601.

585. Duquesne, *Un théologien en liberté*, 33. On Rafael Cardinal Merry del Val y Zulueta, secretary of state under St. Pius X, see Cenci, *Il Cardinale Raffaele Merry del Val*.

586. Giovanni Genocchi, "Letter to Paul Sabatier" (Dec. 28, 1914), quoted in Poulat, *Intégrisme*, 601. Genocchi refers to Fr. Francesco Lanzoni (1862–1929), a priest from Faenza, and a leading figure of the modernist movement.

587. Zwierlein, *Life and Letters of Bishop McQuaid*, 3:15.

588. See Ratté, *Three Modernists*, 27–28. For an interesting first-hand account of the modernizers' vicissitudes between doctrinal boldness and strategic prudence, see Cécile de Corlieu, *Carnets d'une chrétienne moderniste* (Toulouse: Privat, 1970).

589. After the French anticlerical government's 1903 suppression of Catholic congregations, the French Dominicans took refuge in the outskirts of Tournai, Belgium. In 1904, they transferred their theological college to an old Cistercian abbey called Saulchoir, "the forest of willows." Returning to France in 1939, they first established themselves at Étiolles, close to Évry, but retained the name Saulchoir until they moved to the Saint-Jacques convent in Paris, now called the Saulchoir Study Center. See André Duval, "Aux origines de l'Institut historique d'études thomistes du Saulchoir," *Revue des Sciences Philosophiques et Théologiques* (1991). See also Michael Quisinsky, "Congar avec Chenu et Féret au Saulchoir des années 1930," *Transversalités—Revue de l'Institut Catholique de Paris*, no. 98 (Apr.–Jun. 2006): 3–35.

590. Duquesne, *Un théologien en liberté*, 46–47.

originated."[591] Interestingly, the Dominicans of Saulchoir reckoned they were the "spiritual children of Lacordaire."

Those were years of great theological ferment. Fr. Yves Congar (1904–1995), another key figure of the Nouvelle Théologie, wrote about the "great revival of the years 1928–1938."[592] To Saulchoir was later added the Jesuit theological college of Fourvière (Lyons), another promoter of the new trends.[593]

The work done in those centers was very peculiar. As we will see, it was to adapt Catholic doctrine to the new trends of the twentieth century while avoiding the kind of all-too-clear formulations that had caused the downfall of the modernists. In a long interview in 1975 with Jacques Duquesne evoking the adventures of the Nouvelle Théologie, Father Chenu explains how an important aspect of their theological work was to search for "beautiful formulas" not easy to understand, which said one thing while appearing to say another. Maybe we can find here the origin of the art, later widespread in theological circles, of coming up with ambiguous formulations that can have an orthodox interpretation but which insiders always interpret their way.

Their success was also due to shrewdness in publicizing the new doctrines. While usually presenting more moderate formulations in books and magazines, they circulated extremist views in mimeographed samizdats, especially in seminaries and universities. Pius XII denounced this dual stratagem when condemning the Nouvelle Théologie in 1950:

> These new opinions ... are not always advanced in the same degree, with equal clarity nor in the same terms. ... Theories that today are put forward rather covertly by some, not without cautions and distinctions, tomorrow are openly and without moderation proclaimed by others more audacious, causing scandal to many, especially among the young clergy and to the detriment of ecclesiastical authority. Though they are usually more cautious in their published works, they express themselves more openly in their writings intended for private circulation and in conferences and lectures.[594]

If in hindsight the ultimate goal of this doctrinal development now seems quite clear given the disastrous consequences it has caused, it is easy to understand how its stealth may have deceived some contemporaries. This is all the more true since some original aspects of this thought might have been valid and made a contribution to modern theology had they not been misled. Hence, for example, the distinction made by the Spanish Jesuit Fr. Joaquín Salaverri, a staunch opponent of the new doctrines, between some of their originally "healthy aspects" and the "extremist" ones, which unfortunately prevailed.[595] Pius XII himself recognized that some new theologians were moved by "laudable motive" while others were led by a "reprehensible desire of novelty."[596] Clearly, in this study we refer exclusively to tendencies leading to LT.

In this way, the extremists developed a Nouvelle Théologie that was both an heir to Modernism and a forerunner of LT. "The change of perspective painfully and tragically initiated with Modernism was taken up and repeated by the Nouvelle Théologie," says Fr. Germano Pattaro (1925–1986), professor of theology at the Patriarchal Seminary of Venice.[597] Here is the contaminated wellspring from which most modern theological errors flow.

3. Initial Steps: The Theological Problem

Still under St. Pius X, the first tests of a new theology were attempted by the likes of the Dominican Fr. Ambroise Gardeil (1859–1931), superior of Saulchoir, and the Jesuit Fr. Pierre Rousselot (1878–1915). Influenced by Blondel's philosophy, they tried to bring theology closer to man's concrete existence and break with what they called the excessive intellectualism of the dominant Catholic theology.[598]

While both Fathers Gardeil and Rousselot raised issues that already prefigured some aspects of Nouvelle Théologie and even LT, their attempt was clearly premature in view of the doctrinal and disciplinary barriers that St. Pius X had erected. That did not prevent Alfred Loisy, in 1916, from saluting "a new and more profound modernist crisis."[599]

The first relevant manifestations of the neo-modernist current appeared in the 1930s with the so-called theological problem raised by some theologians of Saulchoir, including Fathers Chenu and Louis Charlier (1898–1981).[600] In the wake of an anti-intellectualism of obvious modernist inspiration, the mentors of this current held that theology had been excessively rational until then, striving to draw theological conclusions from the *depositum fidei* through syllogistic constructions. This method, they contended, distances us from true revelation, which is something alive and ever expanding. There was even talk of an "anti-scholastic revolt."

Several theologians stood up to refute these errors, including the renowned Spanish theologian Father Salaverri. He pondered that this approach assumes that "reason cannot arrive at an understanding of dogma through notions that are certain, and thus, the theological process does not consist in the rational deduction of true conclusions, but only in a likely explanation of the dogmas defined by the Church."[601]

The mentors of the theological problem shunned the *depositum fidei* as the proper source of theology, looking for it in the *experience* of the Church and thus in history. Father Salaverri continues, "Father Chenu taught that the immediate source of theology is the present life and daily experience of the Church, and that, therefore, history is the essential nourishment of the theologian. The theological progress consists, therefore, in the living perception of the faith."[602]

591. Joaquín Salaverri, "Satisfacción a los padres de Saulchoir," *Estudios Eclesiásticos* 25, no. 96 (Jan.–Mar. 1951), 84.

592. Yves Congar, *Journal d'un théologien 1946–1956*, ed. Etienne Fouilloux (Paris: Editions du Cerf, 2001), 57, quoted in Michael Quisinsky, "Congar avec Chenu et Féret," 3.

593. For an interesting overview of the penetration of the Nouvelle Théologie in Italy, see Agnès Esmazières, "Agostino Gemelli e gli intellettuali cattolici francesi nel secondo dopoguerra: La 'nouvelle théologie' vista da Milano (1946–1951)," *Annali di storia moderna e contemporanea*, no. 13 (2007), 159–92.

594. Pius XII, encyclical *Humani generis* (Aug. 22, 1950), no. 13.

595. Salaverri, "Satisfacción a los padres de Saulchoir," 85.

596. Pius XII, encyclical *Humani generis*, no. 13.

597. Germano Pattaro, *Corso di teologia dell'ecumenismo* (Brescia: Queriniana, 1985), 344.

598. See Ambroise Gardeil, *La crédibilité et l'apologétique* (1908); Ambroise Gardeil, *Le donné révelé et la théologie* (1915); Pierre Rousselot, *Les yeux de la foi* (1910); Pierre Rousselot, *L'intellectualisme de Saint Thomas* (1912). Fr. Gardeil was the first Superior of the Saulchoir. According to Fr. Congar, his book on revelation was a manual for the Dominicans of that Institute: "He was [our] teacher." Jean Puyo, *Une vie pour la verité: Jean Puyo interroge le père Congar* (Paris: Le Centurion, 1975), 47.

599. Alfred Loisy, *Mémoires*, 3:323, quoted in Émile Poulat, *Modernistica: horizons, physiognomies, débats* (Paris: Nouvelles Éditions Latines, 1982), 223. See also Duquesne, *Un théologien en liberté*, 37ff.

600. See Marie-Dominique Chenu, *Une école de théologie: Le Saulchoir* (Kain-lez-Tournai: Le Saulchoir, 1937). See also Louis Charlier, *Essai sur le problème théologique* (Ramgal Thuillies, 1938).

601. Joaquín Salaverri, "El problema de la 'nueva teología,'" *Sal Terrae* 38 (1950): 145. See also Jesús Iturrioz, "Nueva teología: Actitud de la iglesia," *Razón y Fé* 50, vol. 142 (July–Dec. 1950), 492.

602. Salaverri, "El problema de la 'nueva teología,'" 145.

The representatives of this school tended to consider theology not as an intellectual inquiry into revealed truths, but rather as a sort of psychological experience of the divine at work within the faithful. In a lecture in Bilbao, Spain, in 1952 on the genesis of the New Theology, Most Rev. Casimiro Morcillo, bishop of Bilbao, and later cardinal and archbishop of Madrid, commented, "As we have seen, rationalism, so often condemned, affirms the prevalence of human reason, thus giving purely natural philosophical principles an absolute and exclusive value in the field of theology. With their method issue, the mentors of the 'theological problem' fall on the opposite extreme by denying the capacity of reason to understand divine things ... and seek them instead in a psychological experience, both individual and collective."[603]

For his part, Father Salaverri writes, "Charlier adds that a strictly scientific theological conclusion is impossible because it would assume that the intellect can attain a true understanding of the revealed concepts."[604]

In February 1942, the main works of Fathers Chenu and Charlier were placed on the Index.[605]

4. The Years of Intense Fermentation

The theological problem proved to be merely the opening volley of a fight that was only beginning.[606] In the 1930s a new decisive factor intervened that would have substantially changed the rules of the game: The rise of Catholic Action, or rather, of some of its sectors.

In addition to their loquacity, the downfall of the modernist clique had been marked by their lack of influence over the general public. However important at the theological level, Modernism always remained an intellectual elite phenomenon. Ernesto Buonaiuti said,

> I myself was vaguely surprised several times by the existing disharmony between the radically renewing purpose of the modernist movement and the nature of its propaganda, so aristocratically intellectual. ...
>
> ...That broad popular consensus, saturated with messianic enthusiasm, which should be the main concern of a religious movement, has been constantly missing up till now and may instead be reserved for Modernism in the near future.[607]

Initially, even the new theologians resented this dearth. The situation changed substantially in the early 1930s. As mentioned in the previous chapter, many areas of Catholic Action had proven receptive to new trends almost from the start. Such openness came from a deep change of mentality, resulting from the infiltration in Catholic circles of the dominant revolutionary tendencies in society. In those sectors of Catholic Action, novelties spread far and wide, contaminating large parts of the faithful. Many of the

new theologians were ecclesiastical assistants to Catholic Action. They were thus able to count on something their modernist forefathers had lacked: A mass movement that would enable a concrete application of their doctrines, triggering a shock wave within the Church that erupted in force in the 1960s.

To this must be added the spread of those doctrines and trends in the clergy. Successive classes of seminarians influenced by the samizdats denounced by Pius XII were becoming priests and climbing the ranks of the hierarchy. Father Chenu himself recounts an example of how complicity with such doctrines and trends had arrived at the top. After his book *Une école de théologie* was condemned, he was summoned to the archdiocesan offices in Paris. "Cardinal Suhard ... tried to comfort Chenu with the remark that within twenty years everybody would echo his teachings."[608] Apparently, for the archbishop of Paris the future of the progressive movement was very clear: Sooner or later it was destined to win. Accordingly, he refused to publish the decree of condemnation in the diocesan paper, *Semaine Religieuse*.

"The years 1944–1946 in France were a time of intense fermentation," recalls Father Congar, himself an agent of that fermentation.[609] The new ideas found fertile ground in both clergy and laity, spreading particularly through three collections published under the direction of Frs. Jean Daniélou (1896–1974), Henri de Lubac, and Claude Mondésert (1906–1990) of the Jesuit college of Fourvière, which triggered the New Theology controversy. The collections were: *Sources Chrétiennes*, a commentated selection of patristic texts in which the authors strived to pitch the Church Fathers against Scholasticism; *Théologie*, a series of essays exploring the new theological perspectives; and *Unam Sanctam*, which developed the foundations of a new ecclesiology. "These publications were seen as the expression of a concerted effort, and the first fruit of a 'new theology,'" Father Congar remarked.[610]

Coordinated or not, the fact is that we find behind these collections some names which later dominated the theological landscape of the twentieth century: Henri de Lubac, Jean Daniélou, Marie-Dominique Chenu, Yves Congar, Hans Urs von Balthasar, Karl Rahner, Henri Bouillard, Theodore Camelot, and others. Religious authorities did not remain indifferent to the publication of these works. In particular, two books caught Rome's attention: Henri Bouillard's *Conversion et grâce chez Saint Thomas d'Aquin* (1944) and Henri de Lubac's *Surnaturel: Études historiques* (1945).[611]

While favored by the general flow of events and complicity even in high places, the rise of the Nouvelle Théologie was far from smooth. The new theologians ran into strong resistance from very authoritative theologians. In Spain, the Jesuits Joaquín Salaverri, Miguel Nicolás, Timoteo Zepelena, E. Sauras, Jesús Iturrioz, and others stood out.[612] In France, two names quickly come to mind:

603. Casimiro Morcillo, "Introducción al estudio de la encíclica," in *Comentarios a la encíclica* Humani generis, by Publicaciones del Obispado de Bilbao (Bilbao: Ediciones Desclée de Brouwer, 1952), 13. Spanish Jesuit Fr. Timoteo Zepelena published a decisive four-part rebuttal to Fr. Charlier. See T. Zepelena, "Problema theologicum," *Gregorianum*, 24 (1943), 23–47, 287–326; 25 (1944), 38–73, 247–82.

604. Salaverri, "El problema de la 'nueva teología,'" 145–46.

605. See Jürgen Mettepenningen, "Truth as Issue in a Second Modernist Crisis? The Clash Between Recontextualization and Retrocontextualization in the French-Speaking Polemic of 1946–1947," in *Theology and the Quest for Truth*, ed. M. Lamberigts, L. Boeve, and T. Merrigan (Louvain: Leuven University Press, 2006), 119–42.

606. According to Fr. Salaverri, the "theological problem" and the New Theology were "twin brothers, born from the same womb, nourished in identical ambiances and tending toward the same goal." Salaverri, "El problema de la 'nueva teología,'" 143.

607. Ernesto Buonaiuti, *Lettere di un prete modernista* (Rome: Libreria Editrice Romana, 1908), 140–41.

608. Hans Schwarz, *Theology in a Global Context: The Last Two Hundred Years* (Grand Rapids, Mich.: William B. Eerdmans Publishing Company, 2005), 427. Emmanuel Cardinal Suhard (1874–1949) was notorious for his progressive ideas. See Émile Poulat, *Cardinal Emmanuel Suhard archevêque de Paris (1940–1949): Temps de guerre, temps de paix, passion pour la mission* (Paris: Les Éditions du Cerf, 2011).

609. Yves Congar, *Situation et tâches présentes de la théologie* (Paris: Éditions du Cerf, 1967), 12.

610. Congar, *Situation et tâches*, 12.

611. The Spanish Jesuit Fr. Angel Perego commented: "Suffice it to see how often Henri de Lubac quotes from Blondel in his book *Surnaturel* to realize the great influence the French philosopher had over the theologians of the new theology." Angel Perego, "La teología nueva," *Ciencia y Fe* (Jan.–Mar. 1949): 11. De Lubac's book caused scandal. The Superior General of the Jesuits removed him as teacher and had his books, deemed "dangerous," withdrawn from schools and training institutes. Some of his book's propositions were condemned in the encyclical *Humani generis*.

612. For a pretty complete bibliography of publications for and against the Nouvelle Théologie (386 titles) see *Revista Española de Teología* 9, no. 35 (Apr.–June 1949): 303–18; 10, no. 36 (July–Sept. 1949): 527–46. See also M.J. Nicolas and R.L. Bruckberger, *Dialogue théologique: Pièces du débat entre la Revue Thomiste d'une*

Dominican Fathers Michel Labourdette and Réginald Garrigou-Lagrange, perhaps the most eminent theologian of his time.[613] They were immediately joined by Dominican friars linked to the province of Toulouse and its publication, the *Revue Thomiste*. In Italy, it is impossible not to recall the work of Fr. Mariano Felice Cordovani (1883–1950), chair of theology at the Catholic University of Milan and later rector of the Angelicum in Rome.[614] At the time, rumor had it that he was behind Father Chenu's condemnation. More recent but no less important was the work of Fr. Cornelio Fabro (1911–1995), another authoritative critic of the Nouvelle Théologie, above all in the field of philosophy.

The fact that these names remained largely unknown outside specialized circles while those of the new theologians are now stars of contemporary theology is telltale of the role played by a particular propaganda machine to spread the new doctrines and glorify its standard-bearers while downplaying traditional theology and relegating its representatives to oblivion. This raises another disturbing question: To what extent was this machine linked or identified with that which propelled revolutionary transformations in society?[615]

With his usual sharpness, Father Garrigou-Lagrange summarized the apprehensions of Church authorities and traditional theologians vis-à-vis the New Theology and warned his colleagues:

> Where is this new theology heading, with the new teachers that inspire it? Where is it heading, if not toward skepticism, fantasy, and heresy?. ...
>
> It is a strict obligation of conscience for traditional theologians to answer [this challenge]. For otherwise they would seriously fail their duty and will have to render an account to God for it. ...
>
> *Conclusion.* Where is the new theology heading? It is returning to Modernism.[616]

Still shrouded in some secrecy, the new theologians replied to Father Labourdette's criticism with an anonymous essay mocking traditional theologians and accusing them for "imagining a heretical monster emerging before our eyes."[617] Shortly afterward, however, replying to Father Garrigou-Lagrange, Msgr. Bruno de Solages (1895–1983), rector of the Institut Catholique of Toulouse, cited many names and clearly proclaimed their goals: *to change the very foundations of the Church.*[618]

5. Some Doctrines of the Nouvelle Théologie

As was the case with Modernism, the New Theology did not present itself as a school but rather as a motley current of philosophers and theologians, tackling seemingly unconnected questions and even diverging among themselves on one or another secondary point. However, some dominant trends and key issues can be recognized, as well as a clearly established *esprit de corps*. The new theologians themselves admitted it: "We do not deny the existence of fraternal links among us, nor do we deny that a common vocation, mentors, and apostolic goals can give us something of a family look."[619]

In line with the purpose of the present study, we will not attempt here to make a thorough or overall analysis of the New Theology, but simply highlight some points that set the groundwork for LT. An in-depth analysis will be made in subsequent chapters to show how LT doctrines are a radicalization of New Theology's.

a. Adapting to the Spirit of the Times

At the risk of sounding repetitive, we find in the New Theology the same pretext already found in all the heterodox currents we have been dealing with, namely, the concern of adapting Catholic doctrine, supposedly to make it relevant to the modern world and understandable to contemporary man. "In our view, the New Theology is more a question of a psychological attitude than a body of systematic doctrines," pondered Spanish theologian Fr. Jesús Iturrioz, S.J. "The theological errors [of the New Theology] ... are the consequence of something more profound,"[620] namely, the craving for accommodation with the modern world. That concern would be acceptable and even commendable as such if it were to meet the legitimate aspirations of modern man. However, that was not the angle adopted by new theologians, who sought instead to adapt Catholic doctrine to secularizing trends.

It would also be acceptable if it were to correct, with respect, some shortcomings of neo-scholastic theology. A joke circulated in academic circles at the time: You had first to read St. Thomas Aquinas in order to understand his commentators. While obviously malicious, the joke nevertheless contained a kernel of truth. In the laudable aim of defending dogma against any counterfeiting attempt, some had become entrenched in a sort of theological algebra, losing not only the broad original perspective of the Angelic Doctor but also the horizons of the Augustinian tradition, which prove increasingly relevant as the world advances toward the "civilization of the image" mentioned by Paul VI.

The New Theology threw away the baby with the bathwater. Its advocates claimed that Catholic doctrine was framed in rigid Aristotelian-scholastic intellectual categories, perhaps appropriate to the Middle Ages but no longer intelligible to modern man because they are too abstract and distant from everyday life. In order to make it relevant to people today, theology had to be translated into current terms of the thought in vogue. A book that helps understand this attitude is *Razing the Bastions* (1952), in which Swiss theologian Fr. Hans Urs von Balthasar strongly affirms the need for the Church to abandon its entrenchment and destroy the defensive walls that keep it separate from the modern world and its culture.

b. Existentialism

The philosophical fad of the time was the existentialism developed by Søren Kierkegaard (1813–1855), Martin Heidegger (1889–1976), Karl Jaspers (1883–1969), Gabriel Marcel

part, les RRPP de Lubac, Daniélou, Bouillard, Ferrand et von Balthasar d'autre part (Toulouse: St. Maximin, 1947).

613. See Michel Labourdette, "La théologie et ses sources," *Revue Thomiste* (Jan.–Mar. 1946): 353–71; Garrigou-Lagrange, "La Nouvelle Théologie où va-t-elle?" 126–45.

614. See Mariano Cordovani, "Per la vitalità della teologia," *Angelicum* 17 (1940): 385–96; Mariano Cordovani, "Verità et nouveauté en thèologie," *La Documentation Catholique* (Apr. 1948), 525–28; Mariano Cordovani, "Il primato della teologia," *Angelicum*, no. 26 (1946): 105–14. On Father Cordovani, see Raimondo Spiazzi, *P. Mariano Cordovani dei frati predicatori* (Rome: Belardetti, 1954).

615. According to Benedict XVI, this point is of paramount importance. In his celebrated February 14, 2013, speech in Rome denouncing the media's reporting on the works of the Second Vatican Council, he stated, "It was obvious that the media would take the side of those who seemed to them more closely allied with their world." (Benedict XVI, "Meeting with the Parish Priests and the Clergy of Rome," (Feb. 14, 2013).

616. Garrigou-Lagrange, "La Nouvelle Théologie où va-t-elle?" 134–35, 143.

617. Anonymous, "La théologie et ses sources: Réponse aux études critiques de la *Revue Thomiste*," *Recherches de Science Religieuse*, no. 33 (1946): 387. That anonymous piece was particularly intended as a response to Michel Labourdette's article titled, "Études critiques: La théologie et ses sources," *Revue Thomiste*, 46 (1946): 353–71.

618. See Bruno de Solages, "Pour l'honneur de la théologie," *Bulletin de Littérature Ecclésiastique*, no. 48 (1947): 65–84. For his part, Garrigou-Lagrange answered with "Verité et immutabilité du dogme," *Angelicum*, no. 24 (1947): 124–39.

619. Anonymous, "La théologie et ses sources," 387.
620. Iturrioz, "Nueva teología," 485–86.

(1905–1973), and others. "Theology," wrote Fr. Bernard Lonergan, S.J., "has become largely empirical. ... The Aristotelian analyses, concepts, words ... almost suddenly in the twentieth century have gone out of fashion. With equal rapidity the vacuum is being filled with ... ideas worked out by historicist, personalist, phenomenological, and existential reflection."[621]

Existentialists turn classical metaphysics on its head by maintaining that the essence of a thing is not what gives meaning to its existence. For them, what matters is not what a thing is in itself (its essence), but its concrete existence in space (the world) and time (history). While for classical metaphysics being is transcendent to both the world and history, that is, it does not depend on them, existentialists sustain that worldliness and historicity are the fundamental attributes of being, ontologically conditioning it. They end by suppressing the category of essence, and with it the very possibility of an objective truth. A being has no existence independent from place and time, but is defined as a "being in the world" (*in-der-Welt-sein*) and a "being in time" (*in-der-Zeit-sein*), or simply as "being there" (*dasein*), to use the terminology developed by Heidegger especially in the second part of *Dasein und zeitlichkeit* (1927).

On the pretext of addressing concrete realities, not abstract situations, existentialist analysis rejects the very idea of a transcendent order and restricts itself to phenomenological descriptions of historical situations. According to Father Garrigou-Lagrange, the New Theology "discards all metaphysics, all ontology, and tends to replace the philosophy of being with a philosophy of the phenomenon, or of a becoming."[622] For his part, Father Labourdette states, "Relativism is the pseudo-philosophy that unconsciously inspires historical methods ... [which] replace the metaphysical notion of speculative truth with the more modest one of historical truth as the more or less complete expression of the mentality and human experience of an epoch or human group. The very idea that our mind is capable of grasping a subsisting truth becomes unthinkable."[623]

c. Historicism

The introduction of worldliness and historicity as privileged categories for theological thinking is the very *leit motiv* of the New Theology. Mentors of this current maintained that traditional theology dealt exclusively with incorporeal realities, bearing little relevance to people's real life. Obsessed with transcendent realities and absolute truths, traditional theology forgot that man does not exist in the abstract but in a particular social and historical context that conditions him. Conversely, the new theologians stressed the historicity of man, dogma and religion, grace and the Church. At first glance their affirmations in this sense sound obvious, like that of Father Chenu reminding us that "man is a being-in-the-world."[624]

However, scratching beneath the surface one begins to perceive the unwholesome influence of existentialist thought, evident in the contention that the analysis of historical circumstances is not only important or necessary but actually decisive. For example, Father Chenu states, "Man is a historical reality. His nature includes a reference to time as an essential characteristic. He is within time.

Man's historicity is not only a psychological phenomenon, it is ontological."[625] Therefore, conditions of time and place would be part of man's essence, not his accidents, as traditional theology affirms. Elsewhere, Father Chenu wrote, "Time must be considered as a co-essential value, a value that modifies life and existence not only in its mechanisms but in its very substance. It is the whole problem of man's historicity."[626]

Now if man's historicity is ontological, that is, part of the human essence, then human nature would be in continuous mutation due to its dependence on the evolving historical circumstances. Religious, social, moral, and theological notions would also be conditioned by historical evolution. In its more radical versions, historicism affirms that these realities are fleeting expressions of a given historical situation.

The new theologians strived to apply historicist thinking to theology and religion. Thus, for example, Father de Lubac pretended to construct a "historical theology" that would not start from revelation but from the history of theology itself, that is, from the historical circumstances that shaped the development of theology. The central contention is that, contrary to what traditional Catholic doctrine asserted, theology itself was a fruit of a historical context, and not an abstract reflection that could arrive at particular conclusions. Likewise, Fr. Karl Rahner, S.J., strove to develop a much too drawn out and often obscure "transcendental anthropology." "Dogmatic theology today," he said, "must become a theological anthropology. This 'anthropocentrism' is necessary and fruitful."[627] For his part, Father Chenu introduced the so-called "theology of earthly realities" in which the object of theology is no longer the *depositum fidei,* but historical events, conceived as mediating divine revelation.

The new theologians thus continued shifting the object of theology from revelation, contained in the Holy Scriptures and Tradition, to historical processes and worldly situations. In this way, they tended to invert the process of theological research. It no longer started from revelation and deduced from it a theology to shed light on reality, but instead, it studied social, political, economic, and cultural realities and proposed to develop a theology from that. This visualization, wrote Father Chenu, "will oblige theology not to occupy itself solely with ontological relations and with definitions of essences, but to be primarily a reflection on a becoming, on a plan of salvation."[628]

This inversion of the theological process, and the introduction of history as a privileged source of theological reflection, was the major doctrinal breakthrough that enabled the development of liberation theology a few years later. As a transitional movement, as Pius XII defined it, the New Theology did not defend the exclusivity of historicist thinking, but simply claimed to introduce it by steering a fragile half-way path between scholasticism and existentialism. In fact, the tendency was all for abandoning the former in favor of the latter. "Theories that today are put forward rather covertly by some, not without cautions and distinctions, tomorrow are openly and without moderation proclaimed by others more audacious," Pius XII taught.[629]

621. Bernard Lonergan, S.J., "Theology in Its New Context," in *Renewal of Religious Thought: Proceedings of the Congress on the Theology of the Renewal of the Church Centenary of Canada, 1867–1967,* ed. L.K. Shook (New York: Herder and Herder, 1968), 39. We did not mention Jean Paul Sartre, because his brand of existentialism was so outspokenly anti-Catholic as to render it useless to Catholic theologians.

622. Garrigou-Lagrange, "La Nouvelle Théologie où va-t-elle?" 131.

623. Labourdette, "La théologie et ses sources," 362.

624. Marie-Dominique Chenu, "Les signes des temps," *Nouvelle Revue Théologique* 87, no. 1 (Jan. 1965): 30.

625. *La Documentation Catholique,* no. 997 (Aug. 17, 1947), 1060–61.

626. Chenu, "Les signes des temps," 29.

627. Karl Rahner, "Théologie et anthropologie," in *Théologie d'aujourd'hui et de démain,* ed. Patrick Burke (Paris: Les Éditions du Cerf, 1967), 99.

628. Marie-Dominique Chenu, "The History of Salvation and the Historicity of Man in the Renewal of Theology," in *Renewal of Religious Thought,* ed. L.K. Shook, (New York: Herder and Herder, 1968), 159.

629. Pius XII, encyclical *Humani generis,* no. 13.

d. A Revelation That Is Immanent in History

Behind this introduction of history as a privileged theological category lay also a shift of the *locus revelationis*, the source of public revelation. Since we will deal with this issue in greater depth in the next chapter, let us just say that the public revelation closed with the death of the last apostle, and is entirely contained in Holy Scripture and Tradition. From this *depositum fidei*, theology rationally explains, deduces, makes explicit, and develops the truth contained therein, "bring[ing] forth from [its] treasure new things and old" (Matt. 13:52) by employing instruments proper to theology and, secondarily, also from other disciplines. The historical circumstances in which the theological analysis takes place can add accidental nuances to the way of considering the *depositum fidei*. However, it will never touch its substance, made up of unchanging truths that are valid always and anywhere. Any blurs in this very sensitive field can easily destroy the very idea of *depositum fidei*.

The game of the New Theology was played precisely on this field. "Did not the problems and difficulties raised ... in the years 1944–1946 revolve mainly around the notion of revelation?" Father Congar asks.[630] Some versions were simply intended to develop a theology, and then a religion, more accessible and relevant to the concrete life of twentieth-century man. Other versions, however, argued that historical circumstances affect our understanding of revelation to such a point that we can never have a definitive understanding of it, but only approximations that vary throughout history. In this light, the dogmas are not unchangeable. Instead, they are merely provisional formulas, valid for the length of the historical circumstances in which they arose.

Thus, while admitting in principle a closed public revelation, these versions of New Theology argued that it had to be continuously reinterpreted or reread in the light of current historical circumstances. "We are not at all concerned with an 'adaptation' of the Word of God preconceived in abstract purity," declared Father Chenu. "We are not dressing up or stripping dogmatic formulas. It is a rereading of Scripture that progressively reveals its appropriate significance in each generation. ... It is a permanent reinterpretation within the regulating community."[631] In fact, this permanent reinterpretation easily reached the foundations of revelation, destroying its immutability and turning it into something evolving.

In this way, history became the hermeneutical (i.e., interpretative) principle of revelation, rather than the other way around. According to Prof. Germano Pattaro, the New Theology "highlights the 'historicity' of revelation, certainly in the sense that it occurred in history, but more radically, in the sense that historicity is its very hermeneutical principle."[632]

Some new theologians ultimately claimed that historical circumstances provide not only new criteria to interpret revelation, but a whole new understanding of it. This new understanding goes beyond accidental aspects, modifying the previous understanding in such a way that it actually constitutes a new revelation. History is not only the hermeneutical principle of revelation, but its very vehicle. In other words, revelation happens not only in history, but through history.

From this standpoint, the revelation contained in Holy Scriptures must no longer be considered a universal and definitive acquisition, but above all a fruit of given historical circumstances. "The realities of the Old Testament were provisional," wrote Fr. Jean Daniélou. "We should not try to preserve them when their time has passed."[633] He deemed history a "progressive economy."[634] Extreme versions of the New Theology took up one of the central points of Modernism: the idea of a continuing revelation.[635]

The New Theology rejected that public revelation was closed and treated it instead as an ongoing process. "Contrary to the prevailing doctrine that says that it stopped with Christ and the death of the last apostle, sacred history continues," Father Chenu wrote.[636] While the modernists turned to the interior of the soul in search of an immanent and continuing revelation, the new theologians considered historical events—particularly transformative processes in the secular sphere—to be the place where this immanent revelation should be preferentially found. "God speaks by events," insisted Father Chenu. "Such, then, is the economy of revelation in the old and in the new covenant: not a history in which a revelation occurred, but a history itself revealing."[637]

While not all new theologians were as candid as Father Chenu in this passage, they generally used ambiguous language that tended to blur the distinction between God and history. "God ... reveals himself through history. Or rather, God inserts himself in history," Father de Lubac wrote.[638] The God of New Theology is a God Himself made history. Father Von Balthasar writes, "In Jesus Christ, the Logos is no longer the realm of ideas, values, and laws which governs and gives meaning to history, but is himself history."[639] Taking this stance to its last consequences, Father Chenu writes, "God is immersed in history. ... My representations of God are not eternal, static, a-temporal. Mine is a God within time."[640]

Developing such ideas, the more radical people within New Theology developed a conception of God as immanent in historical events. This led to a sort of divinization of history by considering God not so much as a personal and transcendent being—"the jupiterian power of an exterior God" to use Father Chenu's disparaging expression[641]—but as a force acting inside historical processes. This is the essence of historicist immanentism, discussed in depth in chapter 4.

e. A Revolutionary View of History

Scrutinizing the historical events of their time in search of an immanent revelation, the new theologians might consider some positive signs. Take, for example, the consecration of the world to the Immaculate Heart of Mary made by Pius XII on December 8, 1942, which contributed to a vast movement of spiritual awakening known in France as *Le Grand Retour*. They could consider the imposing *Santas Misiones* undertaken by the Spanish bishops to revive the faith of the people after the horrors of the Civil War. They could study the *Rosenkranz-Sühnekreuzzug*, the Holy Rosary crusade of reparation the Capuchin Father Petrus Pavlicek launched in Austria, which involved the whole country.

630. Congar, *Situation et tâches*, 16.

631. Chenu, "The History of Salvation," 160.

632. Pattaro, *Corso di teologia dell'ecumenismo*, 346. On the historicity of revelation, see Henri de Lubac, *La postérité spirituelle de Joachim de Fiore*, 2 vols. (Paris: Le Sycomore, 1979–1981). See also Yves Congar, *La parole et le souffle* (Paris: Desclée, 1983), 96–101.

633. Jean Daniélou, *Essai sur le mystère de l'histoire* (Paris: Seuil, 1953), 13.

634. Daniélou, *Essai sur le mystère*, 13.

635. See Congar, *Situation et tâches*, 16.

636. Duquesne, *Un théologien en liberté*, 70. Although Fr. Chenu shrewdly speaks of "sacred history"—that is, the history of salvation—the context, as well as the very formula used in the phrase, shows that he is referring to public revelation.

637. Chenu, "The History of Salvation," 158–59.

638. Henri de Lubac, *Catholicism: A Study of Dogma in Relation to the Corporate Destiny of Mankind*, trans. Lancelot C. Sheppard (New York: Sheed and Ward, Inc., 1958), 83.

639. Hans Urs von Balthasar, *A Theology of History* (New York: Sheed and Ward, 1963), 18.

640. Duquesne, *Un théologien en liberté*, 82.

641. Chenu, "Les signes des temps," 33.

Above all, they could listen to the words of Our Lady at Fatima in 1917, indeed a real revelation in history.

However, for the new theologians, none of these events constituted revelation in history. Which events, then, attracted their attention? Father Chenu enumerates them: "[t]he progressive socialization of different areas of human life. ... [t]he development of the working class, the social activism of women, the organization of the international consciousness, the liberation of peoples under colonial rule."[642] To this Father Congar adds the "socioeconomic liberation" of workers, "the liberation of colonized peoples," "the liberation of women, whom Marx called 'the proletarians of men,'" and "sexual liberation." As an example of the liberation of peoples, Father Congar mentions "Wars of liberation. The liberation of Vietnam!"[643]

In other words, in search of an immanent revelation the new theologians looked exclusively for events with strong revolutionary content, showing a unilateral and ideological view of history that raises a big question mark on their resulting 'theology.' Moreover, it is interesting to note that Father Congar sees the liberation of women and sexual liberation as "signs of the times," paving the way for the latest versions of LT, which we will cover later on.

f. An Engaged Theology

Relegating Faith, the practice of virtue, and obedience to the Church's Magisterium to a secondary plane, the new theologians saw religion as historical awareness attentive to the "signs of the times." Fr. Urs von Balthasar wrote, "The essence of Christianity is history itself, where God has entered."[644] It is up to the community to grasp the meaning of these "signs of the times." However, in the community there are persons with a special insight, the "prophets." According to Father Chenu,

> The prophets are important not so much for their theoretical analyses ... but for their loving communion with the aspirations of the people. The 'signs' are the point of impact of their perceptions. ...
> ...The prophet is more realistic than the doctor because he reads in history.[645]

In this light, a theologian is no longer someone who studies revelation and rationally explains or makes explicit the truths contained in it, but someone who is attentive to historical processes. "The theologian," according to Father Chenu, "observes the Word of God at work within the community, a community situated in history. He perceives the Word of God as expressed in history."[646]

In order to "listen to the world on the move" the theologian must submerge himself in it.

> [He] must submerge himself in the movement of history. ...
> ...Theology is not a knowledge that falls from heaven and is fixed in concepts that obey a magisterium. Theology is immersed in the life of the People of God, linked to the world.[647]

Thus, as distinguished from a scholarly theology, the idea of an engaged theology began to emerge. While the former is supposedly developed in some silent library without any contact with reality, the latter is made in the heat of transformative social processes. The activist theologian is the one who participates in historical processes. This implied a revolutionary view of history and ongoing participation in revolutions by the new theologians.

This is also one of the key concepts of LT. For example, using almost identical terms to Father Chenu's, liberation theologians Leonardo and Clodovis Boff write, "The liberation theologian is not an armchair intellectual. Rather, he is ... a 'militant theologian' who positions himself within the march of the People of God. ... Yes, he keeps one foot in a center of reflection and another in the community's life. This, indeed, is his right foot."[648]

g. A Confusion of Planes

As a direct consequence of their historicist-immanentist stance, the new theologians also tended to blur the distinction between the natural and supernatural orders, nature and grace, the secular and the religious. According to Catholic theology, grace is not required by nature as such but is a gratuitous gift from God. The *Catechism of the Catholic Church* reads, "The grace of Christ is the gratuitous gift that God makes to us of his own life, infused by the Holy Spirit into our soul to heal it of sin and to sanctify it."[649] Angels and men were created in the natural order and only elevated to the supernatural sphere afterward. Thus, the distinction between grace and nature is both logical and ontological. Although they normally operate concurrently, they are essentially independent. "The distinction between the order of grace and that of nature [is] not contingent, but necessary," wrote Fr. Reginald Garrigou-Lagrange, refuting Father de Lubac.[650]

According to the new theologians, this distinction was artificially introduced by post-medieval scholars. Indeed, it was the central thesis of Father de Lubac's book, *Surnaturel*, in which he contended that nature as such requires the supernatural, thus dangerously veiling the latter's gratuity and paving the way for immanentism. "That non-gratuitousness of the supernatural order—for each case—easily leads to a sort of cosmic monism [i.e., pantheism]," the archbishop of Genoa, Giuseppe Cardinal Siri (1906–1989) correctly observed, criticizing Father de Lubac's theses.[651]

While usually maintaining the theoretical distinction between grace and nature, without which they would fall into pantheism explicitly, many new theologians tended to blur their ontological independence. They argued that, in the existential reality—the only one that truly commanded their attention—nature and grace form one indivisible whole. In short, nature would be inevitably immersed in the supernatural and inseparable from it. Father Rahner coined the expression "existential supernatural" to describe the supernatural element said to exist in nature.[652]

However, if there is no longer a purely natural order, then all human actions, even those exclusively within the civil sphere,

642. Chenu, 33.
643. Yves Congar, *Un peuple messianique: Salut et libération* (Paris: Les Éditions du Cerf, 1975), 165–66. This is a seminal book in which Fr. Congar proposes many basic ideas of LT, showing how they naturally derive from postulates of the New Theology.
644. Hans Urs von Balthasar, *Aux croyants incertains* (Paris: Lethielleux, 1980), 22.
645. Chenu, "Les signes des temps," 33–34.
646. Duquesne, *Un théologien en liberté*, 22.
647. Duquesne, 23, 68.
648. Boff and Boff, *Como fazer teologia da libertação*, 34.
649. *Catechism of the Catholic Church*, no. 1999. On St. Thomas Aquinas's doctrine on this issue, see Camillo Ruini, *La trascendenza della grazia nella teologia di San Tommaso d'Aquino* (Rome: Università Gregoriana Editrice, 1971).
650. Garrigou-Lagrange, "La nouvelle théologie où va-t-elle?" 132.
651. Joseph Cardinal Siri, *Gethsemane: Reflections on the Contemporary Theological Movement* (Chicago: Franciscan Herald Press, 1981), 60. The scandal caused by *Surnaturel* forced Fr. de Lubac to publish a second book, *Le mystère du surnaturel*. In this regard, Cardinal Siri comments, 'De Lubac explains some insufficiencies of expression of his first book "Supernatural", but he still maintains the same thesis." Siri, *Gethsemane*, 61.
652. See Karl Rahner, *Relations de la nature et de la grâce: Écrits théologiques* (Paris: Desclée de Brouwer, 1963), 3:9–33.

acquire a supernatural content. This view opened the way for all sorts of political theologies that consider man's political endeavors, and particularly revolutionary activism, as having an intrinsically religious character. Revolutionary militancy was thus likened to religious practice.[653] Once again, this later became one of the pillars of liberation theology.

Another aspect of this confusion of planes was the blurring of the distinction between sacred and profane history, that is, between the history of salvation—essentially supernatural—and the history of men in their secular life. Since, from this New Theology perspective, all human actions have an intrinsically religious significance, there is only one history, simultaneously religious and secular. "Profane history enters into sacred history," wrote Father Daniélou. "Because sacred history is really the total history, in which profane history is situated."[654] In this sense, for example, political acts are also acts of salvation *per se*.

The revolutionary consideration of sociopolitical activism as being part of the history of salvation led to the confusion between secular liberation and supernatural redemption, that is, to the idea that the emancipation from social, political, and economic "oppression" has a supernaturally redemptive character.[655] In short, new theologians were beginning to confuse the Revolution with the Redemption, precisely as LT would do a little later.

Facts like the independence of the African colonies, the rise of the Third World, the consolidation of the urban proletariat, the 'liberation' of women, and modern technological progress were all considered by new theologians to be "signs of the times" that manifested God's redemptive work.[656] As a result of these successive emancipations, they maintained, the world was advancing toward an era of widespread justice and peace which they tended to represent as the Kingdom of God on earth. Any step toward this secular utopia was also considered a step toward the Kingdom, and thus an act of salvation *per se*. We need not stress how this also constitutes a central tenet of liberation theology.

Father Congar mentions the Vietnam War as an example of the liberation of peoples. In other words, this Dominican theologian saw the imposition of Communism in Vietnam as a salvific "sign of the times"!

h. A New Ecclesiology

The New Theology also laid the foundations of a new ecclesiology entirely at variance with that of the Magisterium. Taken to extreme consequences and used in conjunction with Marxist errors, this ecclesiology will later serve as the groundwork for that of LT, analyzed in chapter 5. On the pretext of correcting an overly ethereal view of the Church, the new theologians began to belittle her supernatural and divine elements, without denying them

outright, emphasizing her human and mundane aspects instead. "We must fully recognize the *historicity* of the world and of the Church, distinct from the world but linked to it nevertheless," Father Congar writes.[657] For his part, Father Küng states, "The 'essence' of the Church is expressed in changing historical forms. Rather than talking about an ideal Church situated in the abstract celestial spheres of theological theory, we shall consider the *real* Church as it exists in our world, and in human history."[658]

So as not to tumble straight into existentialism, the new theologians distinguished between a subsisting core of supernatural origin, and its "historical incarnations." They claimed they wished to preserve the former while drawing attention to the latter in order to redress what they called a lack of balance in traditional ecclesiology. In practice, however, they dealt less and less with the core and concentrated on demonstrating that the Church always suffers from the historical context, that is, from social, political, economic, and cultural circumstances. Traditional ecclesiology, they maintained, often took as divinely ordained an institution that was in fact the product of historical circumstance. Much of what the traditional ecclesiology assumed to be essential and perennial, they concluded, was in fact a medieval and Tridentine incarnation of the Church no longer suited to the twentieth century.

Father Daniélou writes, "Christianity ... is in history. It really incarnates itself in history. Just as Christ belonged to a determined country, civilization, and time, so also does the Church. The Church incarnates herself in successive civilizations. And these incarnations participate in the decrepitude of such civilizations." To illustrate his perspective, the French theologian assumes the Marxist categories of "structure" and "superstructure": "When Marx sees the original Christianity as a reflection of the economic conditions of the first-century Galilee, Byzantine Christianity as an image of the theocracy of the Byzantine emperors, the Reformation as an expression of the economic expansion of the Renaissance and the collapse of medieval society, we can say that he is describing subsequent Christianities which, to employ Marxist language in reverse, are deciduous and changing super-structures but not the infra-structure which is the permanent Church in its incorruptible reality."[659]

A central contention of this ecclesiology was that the world was witnessing the rise of a new civilization, the proletariat, in which the Church should "incarnate" by shedding many of her ancient and now obsolete structures. Father Daniélou writes, "Christianity has been incarnate in the bourgeois civilization over the last four centuries. ... But today the world is going through a crisis of civilization the likes of which have seldom been seen in history. The whole old world, that of bourgeois civilization, is falling apart. ... It is the agony of a civilization and also the agony of that Church bonded to that civilization. Bourgeois Christianity is now obsolete." According to Father Daniélou, the new world in which the Church of the twentieth century was to incarnate was "the workers' world, full of authentic values that overwhelm the obsolete structures and manifest God's action."

Protecting his flank from possible heterodox implications, the future cardinal warns, "On the other hand there is the danger

---

653. "I understand political theology, first of all, to be a critical correction of present-day theology inasmuch as this theology shows an extreme privatizing tendency (a tendency, that is, to center upon the private person rather than 'public,' 'political' society). At the same time, I understand this political theology to be a positive attempt to formulate the eschatological message under the conditions of our present society." Johannes B. Metz, *Theology of the World*, trans. William Glen-Doepel (New York: Herder and Herder, 1969), 107.

654. Daniélou, *Essai sur le mystère*, 33. Using almost identical language, Fr. Gutiérrez enunciates the liberation theology position on this point as follows: "There are not two histories, one profane and one sacred, 'juxtaposed' or 'closely linked.' Rather there is only one human destiny, irreversibly assumed by Christ, the Lord of history." Gutiérrez, *A Theology of Liberation*, 153.

655. See, for example, Marie-Dominique Chenu, "Libération politique et messianisme religieux," *Parole et Mission*, no. 19 (Oct. 15, 1962): 529–42. Fr. Chenu proclaimed: "We must live the Gospel politically and live politics the Gospel way." Marie-Dominique Chenu, introduction to *Quando un gruppo diventa chiesa*, by Antonio Fallico (Rome: La Roccia, 1974), 9.

656. As we saw, among the emancipation events opened to the theologians' consideration, Fr. Congar mentions socioeconomic and sexual liberation, and the liberation of women and colonized peoples. See Congar, *Un peuple messianique*, 165–66.

657. Yves Congar, *Informations Catholiques Internationales*, Nov. 15, 1964, quoted in Chenu, "Les signes des temps," 30. (Emphasis in original.)

658. Hans Küng, *The Church*, trans. Burns and Oates, Ltd. (Garden City, N.Y.: Image Books, 1976), 23. (Emphasis in original.)

659. Daniélou, *Essai sur le mystère*, 30–31. As is generally the case with the New Theology, these arguments admit an acceptable intellection. However, within an ambiance rife with historicist thinking, they easily led to the relativization of the doctrines concerning the Church's organic constitution. Such outcome is further facilitated by the general course of the new theologians' doctrinal elaboration.

of Modernism, which is to abandon the essential together with the transient, taking adaptation so far as to sacrifice the deposit of faith."[660] Thus, while some espoused a narrow adaptation, others called for a broad one that left precious little of the traditional Church still standing.[661] In any case, they never denied the imperious, categorical need to *adapt* the Church to the modern world. Since the prevailing view of history in these environments was revolutionary—the world was moving toward increasingly liberal, democratic, and socialist ways—the concrete adaptation they proposed also went in that direction.

On the other hand, if we must talk about the real life and not about abstract doctrines, we need to consider not so much the books containing such doctrines, but their practical use in circles of progressive hotheads. While minimalist, narrow interpretations were used mostly to protect the new theologians from possible condemnations, broad ones spread in the Church like wildfire, especially among the younger generations of progressive clergy and laity, creating conditions for the great explosion of the 1960s.

i. The Church as the People of God

The new theologians also shifted the focus from the Church as the Mystical Body of Christ to being the "People of God." "All of the other definitions of Church, including 'mystical body,' are mere images. 'People of God' is the only exact and justified definition of Church," wrote Dutch Dominican Fr. Edward Schillebeeckx.[662]

The expression is perfectly legitimate, indeed traditional. In the triumphal arch of the Basilica of Saint Mary Major in Rome we read this inscription dedicated to Pope Sixtus III (432–440): "*Xystus episcopus plebi dei,*" Sixtus, Bishop of the People of God. In defining the Church, the *Catechism of the Catholic Church* calls her "People of God, Body of Christ, Temple of the Holy Spirit."[663]

However, in an environment overheated by progressivism and eager to adapt the Church to the revolutionary tendencies of the moment, the expression could easily appear at variance with the Magisterium. Abandoning the *theological* concept of "people," that is, the ensemble of the baptized faithful who become citizens of the Kingdom of Heaven through sanctifying grace, new theologians espoused *sociological* concepts arising from democratic doctrine (popular sovereignty) and from Marxist theory (the proletariat). The application of these concepts to the Church gave rise to an egalitarian ecclesiology entirely foreign to Tradition. "My vision of the Church challenges the pyramidal, hierarchical, and juridical system established by the Counter-Reformation," Father Congar stated. "My ecclesiology is that of the 'people of God.'"[664]

This abuse of the "Church people of God" formula was linked to LT precisely by Joseph Cardinal Ratzinger, who denounced it in the year 2000:

> In the first phase of the Council's implementation, the theme of collegiality and the concept of people of God dominated. From the general linguistic use of the word people, the latter was quickly understood in the domain of liberation theology in the Marxist sense of people distinguished from the ruling classes and,

even more broadly, in the sense of popular sovereignty, which would finally be applied to the Church. In turn, this gave rise to broad debates about her structures, interpreted, according to the situation in the Western world, as "democratization," or in the eastern sense of "people's democracy."[665]

6. Pius XII Condemns the New Theology

In 1943, the stand on ecclesiology taken by new theologians led Pope Pius XII to publish the encyclical *Mystici Corporis Christi*. According to Prof. Plinio Corrêa de Oliveira, then president of the Archdiocesan Council of Catholic Action in São Paulo, the document "filled with enthusiasm all of us who longed for an authoritative clarification that would put an end to the multiple and dangerous errors that circulate about the matter."[666] The Vatican itself took care of translating it into different languages, a sign that no linguistic manipulation would be tolerated. Moreover, it was dated June 29, feast of Saints Peter and Paul, a symbolic date.

At the very beginning, the pope warns, "We must confess that grave errors with regard to this doctrine [on the Church] are being spread among those outside the true Church, and that among the faithful, also, inaccurate or thoroughly false ideas are being disseminated which turn minds aside from the straight path of truth."[667] The pope goes on to reiterate the traditional doctrine on the Church: The Church *is* the Mystical Body of Christ, one, undivided, visible, organically and hierarchically established.

In his allocution to the Jesuit Fathers gathered for their 29th General Congregation on September 17, 1946, the Roman pontiff warned very clearly on the dangers of the "new theology": "Let no one weaken or upset that which should never change. Much has been said in a light manner about the 'new theology,' according to which Catholic theology should evolve following the general evolution of things and be in perpetual progress, without ever being firmly anchored. Were one to assume such an opinion, what would become of the immutable dogmas of the Catholic Church? What would become of the unity and stability of the faith?"[668]

Five days later, the sovereign pontiff manifested similar apprehensions to the Dominican Friars, gathered in Rome for their General Chapter. Notably, he cautioned against impugning "the very foundations of the perennial philosophy and of theology."[669]

Perhaps emboldened by the increasing acceptance of their doctrines in Catholic ranks, even among the hierarchy, new theologians ignored the pope's warnings, pretending that they were of no concern. In particular, Father Rahner published an impertinent essay in which he claimed that the pope's allocutions made no reference to the modernist peril in the New Theology.[670] In sum, despite the pope's clear intentions, his interventions had a somewhat limited effect. "The pope's words did not stop the

660. Daniélou, 31, 75, 32.

661. For an example of broad adaptation see Yves Congar, *True and False Reform in the Church*, trans. Paul Philibert (Collegeville, Minn.: Liturgical Press, 2011). The Vatican banned this book's second edition. Fr. Congar attributes a central role in the spreading of the new revolutionary tendencies to Catholic Action. His testimony on this is noteworthy.

662. Edward Schillebeeckx, "I laici nel popolo di Dio." In *I.D.O.C.*, ed., *La fine della chiesa come società perfetta* (Verona, Italy: Arnoldo Mondadori, 1968), 197.

663. *Catechism of the Catholic Church*, part 1, sec. 2, art. 9, par. 2.

664. Puyo, *Une vie pour la verité*, 102.

665. Joseph Ratzinger, "Intervento del Cardinale Joseph Ratzinger sull'ecclesiologia della costituzione 'Lumen Gentium' al convegno internazionale sull'attuazione del Concilio Ecumenico Vaticano II promosso dal comitato del grande giubileo dell'anno 2000," (Feb. 27, 2000).

666. Plinio Corrêa de Oliveira, "Mystici Corporis Christi," *O Legionário*, no. 585 (Oct. 24, 1943).

667. Pius XII, encyclical *Mystici Corporis Christi* (June 29, 1943), no. 8.

668. Pius XII, "Allocution to the Jesuit Fathers on the occasion of their 29th General Congregation" (Sept. 17, 1946). See also *La Documentation Catholique*, no. 978 (Nov. 24, 1946), 1317–18. The expression "new theology" had already been used in 1941 by a consultant to the Holy Office regarding the doctrines of Frs. Charlier and Chenu. See Salaverri, "Satisfacción a los padres del Saulchoir," 88.

669. Pius XII, "Allocution to the Dominican Friars on the occasion of their General Chapter" (Sept. 22, 1946). See also Salvador Muñoz Iglesias, ed., *Doctrina pontificia: Documentos biblicos* (Madrid: Biblioteca de Autores Cristianos, 1955), 595.

670. Karl Rahner, S.J., "Richtungen der neuen theologie," *Orientierung* (Switzerland), Dec. 20, 1947.

innovating movement completely," the *Revista Española de Teología* admitted at the time.[671]

In 1947, the pope promulgated the encyclical *Mediator Dei*, which amounted to a condemnation of New Theology in the liturgical field. Finally, on August 12, 1950, he issued the encyclical *Humani generis*, specifically aimed at the New Theology. In it, the pope condemned those who "audaciously support the monistic and pantheistic opinion that the world is in continual evolution."

> [He likewise decried] the new erroneous philosophy which, rivaling idealism, immanentism and pragmatism, has assumed the name of existentialism, since it concerns itself only with existence of individual things and neglects all consideration of their immutable essences.
>
> ...[The Roman pontiff further censured] a certain historicism, which attributing value only to the events of man's life, overthrows the foundation of all truth and absolute law, both on the level of philosophical speculations and especially ... Christian dogmas.[672]

Humani generis had the undeniable effect of temporarily curbing some of the most daring manifestations of New Theology and inducing its spokesmen into some caution. Some years later, Father Chenu himself admitted, "The atmosphere was becoming unbreathable."[673] However, it did not totally stem the rising tide. The absence of an accompanying document that catalogued and anathematized the condemned theses—like Pius IX's *Syllabus* and Pius X's *Lamentabili*—and the overall restrained tone of the encyclical permitted mainstream commentators to minimize its rebukes while stressing its equanimity.

A typical example was an article by Msgr. René Fontenelle in *La Croix*: "The attentive and serene reading of the full text of the encyclical *Humani generis* has dissipated some apprehensions raised by the first communiqués, which presented the document as a new *Syllabus*. Really, it is a doctrinal document of the utmost importance, but it is, on the whole, an affectionate warning more than a harsh condemnation."[674]

On the other hand, new theologians insidiously manipulated some passages of the encyclical. Asked in 1975 if *Humani generis* had barred the spread of New Theology, Father Chenu observed, "Obviously, as was the case with all these documents, there was always a footnote, a hidden phrase, a small paragraph that left a loophole that enabled us to continue our work. Father de Lubac took advantage of that loophole and wrote a very nice book, *The Splendour of the Church [Méditation sur l'église]*."[675]

The disciplinary measures that followed the encyclical also had limited effects. While some mentors of New Theology were censored by their religious superiors and Rome, the time of excommunications was gone. In 1941, for example, Rome reprimanded five Jesuit theologians of Fourvière and simply ordered them to take a sabbatical. Among the censured scholars were Fathers de Lubac and Bouillard, subsequently rehabilitated.

One of the most publicized episodes was the abrupt trip of Fr. Emanuel Suárez, the Dominican Master General, to France in 1943. Father Suárez summarily dismissed the three provincials of the Order (Paris, Lyon, and Toulouse) and disapproved four Saulchoir theologians (Fathers Chenu, Boisselot, Congar, and Féret), who were forced to quit the faculty for some time. The move was hailed as a firm brake on the innovating movement. However, the spectacular nature of the affair and the easiness with which Father Suárez muzzled his usually loquacious confrères soon raised some eyebrows. It turned out that several bishops had filed complaints in Rome against these priests, and a canonical process had been opened in the Holy Office. With his instant action, the Dominican Master General preserved the independence of the Order vis-à-vis Curia agencies and probably spared his confrères from a formal condemnation. Historian Adrien Dansette comments, "The success of Fr. Suárez was easy and complete. The French Dominicans understood that their General was sparing them from the worse."[676]

Some theologians, such as Father Congar, were temporarily forbidden to teach. No other action was taken against representatives of this current, while books placed on the Index safely returned to the shelves of Catholic libraries and even seminaries. The do-good, dialoguing, and reforming trend, later called the "spirit of the Council," grew stronger and stronger and in practice banned any punishment, seen as stern and uncharitable.

"The pontificate of John XXIII (1958–1963) would rapidly change the situation," said Rosino Gibellini in his famous history of theology in the twentieth century.[677] He quotes Father Congar: "In a few short weeks John XXIII created a new ecclesial climate in the church, and then came the council. This most significant breakthrough came from on high. All of a sudden, forces for renewal which had scarcely had room to breathe found ways to be expressed."[678]

For the most part the new theologians, fully rehabilitated now, participated in the Second Vatican Council as *periti*. "The crisis has now passed, if there ever was a real crisis," pondered Father Congar in 1967.[679] Four of New Theology's leaders were eventually created cardinals: Fathers Daniélou, de Lubac, Congar, and von Balthasar. The last, once in the vanguard of the movement, adopted a milder stance from the mid-1960s on. He died before receiving the hat.

E. Liberation Theology

1. The Launching

The perception that Latin American liberation theology is in many respects a radical and politicized version of European new theology is well founded. Most liberation theologians were educated in New Theology hotbeds in Europe. In the sixties, the University of Louvain in Belgium welcomed a whole generation of Latin American students who later formed the backbone of the LT movement. Among them was the Colombian priest Camilo Torres Restrepo (1929–1966), who, precisely in Louvain, consolidated his decision to join the armed struggle in the ranks of E.L.N. (National Liberation Army). He was killed in a shootout with the army. After studying at Louvain, the Peruvian Father

671. A. Avelino Esteban, "Nota bibliográfica sobre la llamada 'teología nueva,'" *Revista Española de Teología*, no. 36 (July–Sept. 1949): 528.

672. Pius XII, encyclical *Humani generis*, nos. 5–7.

673. Duquesne, *Un théologien en liberté*, 131.

674. René Fontenelle, "Honneur au magistère," *La Croix*, Sept. 7, 1950, in *La Documentation Catholique*, no. 1079 (Oct. 8, 1950), 1295. For his part, well-known Catholic writer André Brissaud wrote that the encyclical was "nuanced, it is more a warning than a formal condemnation." André Brissaud, "Après l'encyclique de Pie XII, le dialogue avec les catholiques est-il encore possible?" *Combat*, Aug. 24, 1950, in *La Documentation Catholique*, no. 1079, 1299. André Fontaine likewise remarked in *Le Monde* that the encyclical "has neither the tone nor the scope [of a *Syllabus*.]" André Fontaine, "En face de certaines tendances doctrinales, l'encyclique *Humani generis* réaffirme l'autorité du magistère de l'église," *Le Monde*, Aug. 24, 1950, in *La Documentation Catholique*, no. 1079, 1298.

675. Duquesne, *Un théologien en liberté*, 131.

676. Dansette, *Destin du catholicisme français*, 288.

677. Rosino Gibellini, *La teologia del XX secolo* (Brescia: Queriniana, 1992), 184.

678. Congar, *True and False Reform*, 2.

679. Congar, *Situation et tâches*, 15.

Gutiérrez graduated from the Jesuit college at Fourvière under the tutorship of Father de Lubac. In his book, *A Theology of Liberation*, Father Gutiérrez acknowledges the seminal role played by New Theology and even quotes at length Father Chenu's book, *Une école de théologie*.[680]

Browsing through the footnotes of books by Latin American liberation theologians is sufficient to realize just how heavily they draw on their European masters, particularly French and German.[681] They simply built on modernist and neo-modernist principles, compounded them with Marxist ideology, and applied the resulting mixture to the concrete situation of their continent in the sixties, which they saw as a new kairos that should revolutionize theological discourse.

LT's immediate roots can be found in the meeting of theologians held in Petrópolis, Brazil, in March 1964, even as the third session of the Second Vatican Council was being held in Rome. The coincidence is not accidental, given the way liberation theologians read the Council. Diego Facundo Sánchez writes in his history of LT:

> For the Church's 'being and doing', the Second Vatican Council is a Copernican revolution. ...
>
> A historical period was being closed ... and another, radically new, was being opened.[682]

For his part, Spanish-Salvadoran theologian Fr. Jon Sobrino stated that the Second Vatican Council and the 1968 C.E.L.A.M. Medellín meetings

> were profound ruptures ... in the history of the Church. ...
>
> ...Another Church, another faith, another Christianity was possible.[683]

In fact, the entire LT movement developed in the post-conciliar period. The future liberation theologians said they were encouraged by some expressions used in the preparation of the Council, such as John XXIII's reference to a "Church of the poor" in his radio message of September 11, 1962.[684]

The Petrópolis meeting was attended by the theologians who would become the core of the LT movement in the ensuing years: Frs. Juan Luis Segundo, Gustavo Gutiérrez, Lucio Gera, Leonardo Boff, Clodovis Boff, and Hugo Assmann, the layman Enrique Dussel, and others. "The Petrópolis meeting ... is fundamentally important. ... It marks a beginning, a new path," writes Claudinei Jair Lopes, of the Pontifical Catholic University of Rio de

Janeiro.[685] It was followed by a series of preparatory workshops, notably the one held in July 1965 in Havana, Cuba, under the aegis of Fidel Castro, who stated, "For the revolution in Latin America, liberation theology is more important than Marxism."[686]

The expression "theology of liberation" was first used in 1960 by the Uruguayan theologian Fr. Juan Luis Segundo (1925–1996) and was launched by Father Gutiérrez during a national conference of the O.N.I.S. priestly movement held in Chimbote, Peru, in July 1968.[687] A parish priest in a popular Lima neighborhood and later professor of theology at the Pontifical Catholic University of Peru, Father Gutiérrez developed his thesis with three successive texts.[688] Finally, in 1971, he published *Una teología de la liberación*, which became a reference point for the liberationist current.[689]

In the shock wave that followed the C.E.L.A.M. (Latin American Bishops' Conference) Assembly in Medellín, Colombia, tempers in Latin America were overheated. The Second General Assembly of C.E.L.A.M. was held there in August 1968. The presence of Pope Paul VI made the meeting more authoritative, and it was called "the Second Vatican Council of the Latin American Church." Many liberation theologians participated in its preparatory commissions, and later as periti, managing to shape its conclusions.[690] That success enabled them to present themselves not only as being in good standing, but as heralds of a new Latin American Church. Costa Rican liberationist Victorio Araya appropriately comments that "in Medellín, liberation theology received its own ID card."[691] No wonder many people consider Medellín the birthplace of liberation theology.

The assembly is regarded as a watershed event in the history of the Church in Latin America, which supposedly finally broke with its *medieval* past by jumping onto the progressive bandwagon. In addition to the actual content of the documents, the "spirit of Medellín" began to blow very strongly, moving vast ecclesiastical sectors more and more to the left. This ecclesiastical '68 was part of a revolutionary political process which, under the influence

---

680. See Gutiérrez, *A Theology of Liberation*, 8.

681. Fr. Congar is the most quoted author in Fr. Gutiérrez's aforementioned book. He returned the compliment in 1975, "I envy those who, like Gustavo Gutiérrez, Joseph Comblin and others, strive for the same synthesis from within an onerous, effective, and concrete commitment within the movements of liberation." Congar, *Un peuple messianique*, 8. The second most quoted theologian is Jürgen Moltmann, followed by Frs. Chenu, Rahner, Metz, and Schillebeeckx.

682. Diego Facundo Sánchez, *Teología de la liberación: En el derrotero hacia otro modelo de iglesia* (final thesis, Escuela Universitaria de Teología, 2009), 2, 6. On the inspiration that liberation theologians drew from the Council, see Gustavo Gutiérrez, "La recepción del Vaticano II en Latinoamérica," in *La recepción del Vaticano II*, ed. Giuseppe Alberigo and Jean-Pierre Jossua (Madrid: Cristiandad, 1987).

683. Jon Sobrino, interview in "O absoluto é Deus, e o coabsoluto são os pobres," by Graziela Wolfart and Luís Carlos Dalla Rosa, trans. Moisés Sbardelotto, *IHU online* 12, no. 404 (Oct. 5, 2012), 6. Fr. Sobrino returned to the spotlight when, bypassing normal procedures, Pope Francis unblocked the beatification process of the controversial Most Rev. Oscar Arnulfo Romero (1917–1980), archbishop of San Salvador, and a disciple of Fr. Sobrino.

684. That call inspired the formation in Rome of the "Forum of the Poor," in which progressive Latin American Council Fathers participated under the auspices of Most Rev. Helder Câmara (1909–1999), then auxiliary bishop of Rio de Janeiro.

685. Claudini Jair Lopes, *A relevância teologica da história e a relevância histórica da teologia na teologia da libertação latino-americana* (doctor's thesis, Pontifícia Universidade Católica do Rio de Janeiro, 2009), 150. For a summary of the meeting's conclusions, see Roberto Oliveros, *Liberación y teología: Génesis y crecimiento de una reflexión, 1966–1976* (Lima: C.E.P., 1977), 52–57. See also Pablo Richard, ed. *Materiales para una historia de la teología en América Latina* (San José, Costa Rica: D.E.I., 1981).

686. Leonardo Boff, "A originalidade da teologia da libertação em Gustavo Gutiérrez," *Revista Eclesiástica Brasileira* 48, no. 191 (Sept. 1988): 550.

687. The acronym stands for *Oficina Nacional de Información Social* [National Bureau of Social Information], founded in 1967. See chapter 1.

688. See Gustavo Gutiérrez, *La pastoral de la iglesia en América Latina* (Montevideo: J.E.C.I., 1968); *Hacia una teología de la liberación* (Montevideo: J.E.C.I., 1969); and *Notas hacia una teología de la liberación* (Lima: mimeographed, 1969).

689. See Gustavo Gutiérrez, *Una teología de la liberación* (Lima: Centro de Estudios y Publicaciones, 1971). Fr. Segundo comments: "Contrary to the most common assumption, Latin American theology, without any precise title, began to have clearly distinctive features at least ten years before Gustavo Gutiérrez's well-known book, *A Theology of Liberation*. This was a kind of baptism, but the baby had already grown old." Juan Luis Segundo, *The Shift Within Latin American Theology: Lecture Given at Regis College Toronto 22 March 1983* (Toronto: Regis College Press, 1983), 2. In 1971, Fr. Gutiérrez's lecture was given in Switzerland at a meeting organized by SODEPAX. See "Notes on theology of liberation," in *In Search of a Theology of Development: A SODEPAX Report* (Lausanne: Committee on Society, Development and Peace, Ecumenical Centre, Publications Department, 1969), 116–79.

690. C.E.L.A.M.'s Second General Assembly approved fifteen documents: Justice, Peace, Family and Demography, Education, Youth, People's Pastoral, Pastoral of Elites, Catechesis, Liturgy, Lay Movements, Priests, Religious, Church Poverty, Joint Pastoral, and Means of Social Communication. See Consejo Episcopal Latinoamericano, *La iglesia en la actual transformación de América Latina a la luz del concilio* (Bogotá: Secretariado General del C.E.L.A.M., 1968). See also Hernán Parada, *Crónica de Medellín: Segunda conferencia general del episcopado latinoamericano* (Bogotá: Indo-American Press Service, 1975).

691. Victorio Araya, "La teología de la liberación: Aproximación histórica," in *Teología de la liberación: Documentos sobre una polémica*, by Joseph Ratzinger, et al. (San José, Costa Rica: Departamento Ecuménico de Investigaciones, 1987), 108.

of Cuba, saw a number of Latin American countries move into the Soviet orbit. In countries with non-communist governments, liberation theologians called on Catholics to oppose the authorities, even through armed struggle.

In the wake of Medellín, the LT movement spread throughout Latin America. The first Symposium on Liberation Theology was held in Bogotá, Colombia, in March 1970, with the participation of five hundred people.[692] The most recent was held in October 2012 in São Leopoldo, Brazil, and was called to reexamine LT's situation fifty years after the Council.[693]

In July 1972, Latin American liberation theologians met with their Spanish confrères in El Escorial, Spain, for the conference titled, "Christian Faith and Social Change in Latin America." This conference marked the official onset of the LT movement in the Old Continent, though several theologians, like Italian Fr. Giulio Girardi and Belgian Fr. François Houtart had already been promoting similar doctrines since the early 1960s.[694] In 1975, the Theology in the Americas conference convened in Detroit with the participation of hundreds of liberation theologians and activists. This gathering marked the beginning of a dialogue between Latin American liberation theologians and their American counterparts.[695] A second inter-American conference was held in 1981, also in Detroit.[696] The movement's internationalization culminated in 1978, with the formation of the Ecumenical Association of Third World Theologians (E.A.T.W.O.T. in English, A.S.E.T.T. in French).

Tracing LT's history, Rosino Gibellini distinguishes three phases: the "preparatory phase," from the Second Vatican Council to the 1968 C.E.L.A.M. Medellín conference; the "formative phase," from 1968 to 1975; and the "systematizing phase," from 1976 onward.[697]

2. A Heretical Pedigree

The preceding pages have outlined the immediate roots of LT. In fact, although presenting it as the wave of the future, liberation theologians boasted much more remote roots, harking back all the way to pauperist, utopian, and heretical currents that arose at the end of the Middle Ages.

Analyzing LT's philosophical and theological roots, American feminist theologian Rosemary Radford Ruether comments on the role played by the fourteenth-century followers of monk Joachim of Fiore (1130–1202) who "declared the advent of a Third Age, the

Reign of the Spirit, which would supersede the clerical church."[698] According to the feminist theologian,

> This radical apocalyptic or millennialist tradition was carried on by the left-wing sectarians of the Reformation, such as the Anabaptists in the sixteenth-century Continental Reformation ... Seekers, Levellers, and Fifth-Monarchy men of left-wing Puritanism in the seventeenth-century English Civil War. ...
>
> ...The Enlightenment [Ruether continues,] secularized the Joachite language about the Third Age of the Spirit by looking forward to a new age of the triumph of reason. ... Militant deist or atheistic Liberalism in eighteenth-century France ... would be taken over into Marxism. ...
>
> ...By the mid-nineteenth century various groups of Christian socialists began to reclaim these secular traditions of social reform and revolution for Christian faith. ... Twentieth-century Liberation Theology, [Ruether concludes,] is basically a third world rediscovery of this same project.[699]

In her book, *The Anarchist Dimension of Liberation Theology*, Linda Damico traces the roots of LT all the way to the Gnostic heresy in early Christianity:

> The Gnostic movement is a good example of the anarchist development of early Christianity. In their claims of immanent divinity and direct access to God, the Gnostics posed a serious threat to later attempts at Church centralization and hierarchical authority. ...
>
> ...The Carpocratians of Alexandria in the second century; the Beghards, Waldenses, and Albigenses of the twelfth and thirteenth centuries; the Adamites and the Hussites of the fifteenth century; and the Anabaptists and early Quakers of the sixteenth and seventeenth century have all been part of a subterranean stream of anarchism reacting against domination.[700]

The anarchist yearnings that inspired these movements, Damico concludes, were carried on by the utopian strains within Socialism in the nineteenth and twentieth centuries, and were finally assumed by liberation theology.

692. See Gustavo Gutiérrez, et al. *Liberación: Opción de la iglesia en la década del 70* (Bogotá: Editorial Presencia, 1970); Camilo Moncada, ed., *Aportes para la liberación: Simposio teología de la liberación* (Bogotá: Editorial Presencia, 1970).

693. See Agenor Brighenti, ed., *La teología de la liberación en prospectiva*, 2 vols. (Montevideo: Amerindia, 2012).

694. On the LT movement in Spain, see "La teología de la liberación en España," *Iglesia Mundo* (Madrid), nos. 305–306 (Oct. 1985); Ricardo de la Cierva, *La teología de la liberación desenmascarada* (Barcelona: Plaza y Janés, 1986); Ricardo de la Cierva, *Oscura rebelión en la iglesia* (Barcelona: Plaza y Janés, 1987).

695. See Sergio Torres and John Eagleson, eds., *Theology in the Americas: Detroit 1975* (Maryknoll, N.Y.: Orbis Books, 1976), Reprinted by permission of Orbis Books; Manfred K. Bahmann, *A Preference for the Poor: Latin American Liberation Theology from a Protestant Perspective* (Lanham, Md.: University Press of America, 2005), 33–37; Paul E. Sigmund, *Liberation Theology at a Crossroads: Democracy or Revolution* (New York: Oxford University Press, 1990), 64–65.

696. See Cornel West, Caridad Guidote, and Margaret Coakley, eds. *Theology in the Americas: Detroit II Conference Papers* (Maryknoll, N.Y.: Orbis Books, 1982).

697. Rosino Gibellini, *The Liberation Theology Debate*, trans. John Bowden (Maryknoll, N.Y.: Orbis Books, 1988), 1–2. See Rosino Gibellini, *O debate sobre a teologia da libertação* (São Paulo: Edições Loyola, 1987), 8–9. For a history of the progressive movement in Brazil, see Oscar Beozzo, *A igreja do Brasil, de João XXIII a João Paulo II, de Medellín a Santo Domingo* (Petrópolis: Editora Vozes, 1994).

698. In March 2010, Pope Benedict XVI warned against the doctrine of Joachim of Fiore:

> As I have already said, among St. Bonaventure's various merits was the ability to interpret authentically and faithfully St. Francis of Assisi, whom he venerated and studied with deep love. In a special way, in St. Bonaventure's day a trend among the Friars Minor known as the "Spirituals" held that St. Francis had ushered in a totally new phase in history and that the "eternal Gospel," of which Revelation speaks, had come to replace the New Testament. This group declared that the Church had now fulfilled her role in history. They said that she had been replaced by a charismatic community of free men guided from within by the Spirit, namely the "Spiritual Franciscans." This group's ideas were based on the writings of a Cistercian Abbot, Joachim of Fiore, who died in 1202. In his works he affirmed a Trinitarian rhythm in history. He considered the Old Testament as the age of the Father, followed by the time of the Son, the time of the Church. The third age was to be awaited, that of the Holy Spirit. The whole of history was thus interpreted as a history of progress: from the severity of the Old Testament to the relative freedom of the time of the Son, in the Church, to the full freedom of the Sons of God in the period of the Holy Spirit. This, finally, was also to be the period of peace among mankind, of the reconciliation of peoples and of religions. (Benedict XVI, "General Audience" [Mar. 10, 2010])

699. Rosemary Radford Ruether, "Political Theologies in the Churches: Does God Take Sides in Class Struggle?" in *Churches in Struggle: Liberation Theologies and Social Change in North America*, ed. William K. Tabb (New York: Monthly Review Press, 1986), 24.

700. Linda H. Damico, *The Anarchist Dimension of Liberation Theology* (Eugene, Ore.: Wipf and Stock Publishers, 1987), 5–6.

Chapter 3:
The Foundations of Liberation Theology

A. What Is Catholic Theology?

In the previous chapters we sketched the historical roots of LT, offering some doctrinal insights into the philosophical and theological errors that paved the way for its outbreak in the sixties. We will now begin a systematic exposition of its doctrinal foundations, contrasting them with Catholic theology.

In analyzing the foundations of liberation theology, we must begin by saying that it is not really a theology at all. If we apply the traditional and etymological meaning to the term—*Theo logos,* the study of God—LT fails the test.

Theology is traditionally defined as "the science of God and of divine things."[701] The object of theological inquiry is always and can only be God, and creation as related to God.

Man can come to know God and His divine perfections through natural reason. Although flawed by original sin, the human intellect is capable of knowing God by its own natural lights, both syllogistically and through the contemplation of the natural order (i.e., creation). The whole universe reflects the divine perfections. "The heavens show forth the glory of God, and the firmament declareth the work of His hands," says the Psalm.[702] This study of God is called natural theology.[703]

However, the human intellect has a limited capacity and, due to original sin, is subject to error. So God, in His infinite mercy, revealed Himself to man, confirming by His Divine authority some truths that man might already have come to know and teaching him truths that his intellect would never have grasped. This is supernatural revelation. The study of God and of divine things founded on supernatural revelation is called theology, properly speaking. Theology is the most perfect and certain way of knowing God, because it is based on God's Word—Truth itself.

From the standpoint of its sources, it is less subject to the frailty of the human intellect.

Theological inquiry may use other sciences as instruments (philosophy being the most important), but it always takes the revealed Truth, accepted by faith on God's authority, as its source and starting point.[704] Theology rationally explains, deduces, makes explicit, or develops the truths contained in this *depositum fidei,* bringing forth new things and old (Matt. 13:52).

B. What Is Liberation Theology?

Liberation theologians claim that they have not really developed a new theology, but rather a "new way of doing theology," or a "new hermeneutical approach."

1. LT Does Not Have God as Its Object

According to the Spanish Dominican theologian Fr. Victorino Rodríguez (1926–1997), liberation theologians "do not treat of God as their primary and defining *object* [for their reflections], nor even of man in the theological perspective of his origin, end and fulfillment, but rather of the movement of sociopolitical emancipation of men in an oppressed society."[705]

Phillip Berryman, a onetime Maryknoll priest with ample experience with the so-called people's church in Central America, is quite clear: "[Liberation theology] arises out of a revolutionary praxis; it is centered not on the church but on society." To corroborate this statement, Berryman quotes the words of the Colombian guerrilla priest Camilo Torres, a precursor of LT: "I discovered Christianity as a life centered totally on love of neighbor. ...It was later that I understood that in Colombia you can't bring about this love simply by beneficence. There was needed a whole change of political, economic, and social structures. That love was intimately bound up with revolution."[706]

---

701. *"Theologia est scientia de Deo et de rebus divinis."* Michaele Nicolau and Ioachim Salaverri, *Introductio in theologiam: De revelatione christiana; De ecclesia Christi—De sacra scriptura.* Vol. 1, *Sacrae theologiae summa* (Madrid: Biblioteca de Autores Cristianos, 1958), 15. Msgr. Livi states: "Theology is true only if it respects in the intentions, and above all in the facts, the epistemological statute of that science which after the event of the Incarnation may be called 'science of the faith' and consists of a systematic and methodologically consistent reflection on the revealed truth. Therefore, theology relates to what God has said of Himself. As the Canadian theologian Rene Latourelle aptly put it, theology is the 'science of revelation.'" Mauro Faverzani, "I falsi teologi del neomodernismo—Intervista a mons. Antonio Livi," *Radici Cristiane,* no. 79 (Nov. 2012), 4. See Antonio Livi, *Vera e falsa teologia: Come distinguere l'autentica "scienza della fede" da un'equivoca "filosofia religiosa"* (Rome: Casa Editrice Leonardo da Vinci, 2012).

702. Ps. 18:2. Benedict XVI often dealt with the knowledge of God through the contemplation of creation. See, for example, Benedict XVI, general audience at Castelgandolfo (Aug. 31, 2011). The topic was also the object of a Vatican document. See Pontifical Council for Culture, *Via pulchritudinis* (Mar. 28, 2006). See Plinio Corrêa de Oliveira, *Innocenza primordiale e contemplazione sacrale dell'universo* (Siena: Cantagalli, 2013).

703. The Magisterium explicitly teaches the possibility of knowing God through reason. The First Vatican Council established: "The same Holy Mother Church *holds and teaches* that God, the source and end of all things, can be known with certainty from the consideration of created things, by the natural power of human reason." First Vatican Council, Dogmatic Constitution *Dei Filius,* sess. 3 (Apr. 24, 1870), chap. 2, 1.

704. In a general sense, faith is the intellectual acquiescence to some truth founded on the authority of those who manifest that truth. Theology, founded on God's revelation, presupposes the belief that the Holy Scriptures and Tradition truly contain the Word of God. Therefore, as Msgr. Livi stated, "Theology relates to what God has said of Himself. ... Logically, only those who unreservedly believe in the Christian revelation can practice this type of science." Faverzani, "I falsi teologi del neomodernismo," 4.

705. Victorino Rodríguez, "Godless 'Theology' and Enslaving 'Liberation': A Theological Analysis of 'Liberation Theology.'" *TFP Newsletter* (Nov. 1984), 12. On Fr. Victorino Rodríguez, see Santiago Cantera Montenegro, "Fray Victorino Rodríguez, O.P., Un teólogo clarividente: A los diez anos de su muerte," *Verbo* (Madrid), no. 453–454 (2007), 207–17.

706. Phillip E. Berryman, "Latin American Liberation Theology," in *Theology in the Americas: Detroit 1975,* ed. Sergio Torres and John Eagleson (New York: Orbis Books, 1976), 20. Liberation theologians employ the term *praxis*—action or activity, from the Greek verb *prássein* (πράσσειν: do, operate, act)—in the Marxist sense of changing society in a revolutionary direction. We shall return to this topic. Camilo Torres Restrepo (1929–1966) was a Colombian priest, guerrilla fighter, and revolutionary. He was an LT precursor and a member of the National Liberation Army, a fighting unit of "Marxist-Leninist-Christian" inspiration. He promoted a *rapprochement* between revolutionary Marxism and Catholicism.

2. LT Inverts the Theological Process

Liberation theology inverts the process of theological inquiry. It does not start from revelation and deduce a theology to shed light on reality; instead, it studies social, political, economic, and cultural realities, and then proposes to develop a theology from that.

Brazilian liberation theologian and secularized priest Hugo Assmann, one of the movement's founders, affirms that

> the contextual starting point of a 'theology of liberation' is the historical situation of dependence and oppression in which the people of the 'Third World' find themselves. ...
> ...The theology of liberation takes a decisive step ... when it admits that the concrete fact of the praxis ...is its fundamental reference, its contextual starting point.[707]

Fr. Gutiérrez is also very clear in this regard: "The theology of liberation. ...is a reflection that begins from the historical praxis of man."[708] The Brazilian Jesuit Fr. Henrique Cláudio de Lima Vaz, philosophical mentor of a whole generation of liberation theologians, states that "liberation theology presents itself as the first school of theological thought that resolutely proceeds from the profane to the sacred, or, if we wish, from history to revelation, reversing the theological process consecrated for a millennium."[709]

All this marks a profound break with Catholic theology and explains why LT is sometimes referred to as *contextual* or *process theology*. It is not a theology based on a transcendent, personal, and unchanging God, a theology based on being, but rather a theology based on concrete historical situations in constant evolution.[710] Fr. Edwin Garvey, C.S.B., former professor of philosophy at the University of St. Thomas in Houston, Texas, aptly points out that "by making [historical] evolution, not God, the object of faith, Christian theology is turned upside down."[711]

3. A Continuing Revelation

LT turns Catholic theology on its head by manipulating the concept of revelation. The Church teaches that public revelation ended with the death of the last apostle. This revelation—the *depositum fidei*, deposit of the faith—is contained in its entirety in Holy Scriptures and in Tradition.[712] Our Lord Jesus Christ instituted a Church that legitimately and authoritatively interprets this revelation.

Not so for LT, which denies that public revelation closed with the apostles, and maintains that it continues throughout history. According to liberation theologians (assuming modernist errors),[713] the interior movements of the soul and great social, political, economic, and cultural revolutionary movements of modern times may constitute revelation. While the original versions of LT were more centered on revolutionary mass movements, its latest ones exploit man's inner movements and even, as we shall see later, the movements of nature.

Ambiguously lumping together private and public revelation as "Christian revelation," the Jesuit Fr. Thomas Clarke, of the Woodstock Theological Center of Washington, D.C., in an essay on the use of LT by Basic Christian Communities in the United States, writes,

> The key notion here will be that of divine revelation as mediated through human experience. ...
> The key term, I believe, is *revelation*. For many years at Woodstock I simply assumed the truth of the thesis that Christian revelation had ceased with the death of the last apostle. ...Yet, if we take the mission of the Holy Spirit seriously, we must *also* say that God continues to be revealed in us—to Christians and to every human being.[714]

---

of Trent, "Decree Concerning the Canonical Scriptures." The same doctrine is found in the *Catechism of the Catholic Church*:

> 76 In keeping with the Lord's command, the Gospel was handed on in two ways: —orally "by the apostles who handed on, by the spoken word of their preaching, by the example they gave, by the institutions they established, what they themselves had received—whether from the lips of Christ, from his way of life and his works, or whether they had learned it at the prompting of the Holy Spirit"; —in writing "by those apostles and other men associated with the apostles who, under the inspiration of the same Holy Spirit, committed the message of salvation to writing. ...
> 78 This living transmission, accomplished in the Holy Spirit, is called Tradition, since it is distinct from Sacred Scripture, though closely connected to it. (*Catechism of the Catholic Church*, nos. 76, 78)

In addition to the public revelation, there are also private revelations. The *Catechism of the Catholic Church* teaches:

> 67 Throughout the ages, there have been so-called "private" revelations, some of which have been recognized by the authority of the Church. They do not belong, however, to the deposit of faith. It is not their role to improve or complete Christ's definitive revelation, but to help live more fully by it in a certain period of history. Guided by the Magisterium of the Church, the sensus fidelium knows how to discern and welcome in these revelations whatever constitutes an authentic call of Christ or his saints to the Church.
> Christian faith cannot accept "revelations" that claim to surpass or correct the revelation of which Christ is the fulfilment. (*Catechism of the Catholic Church*, no. 67)

Likewise, a document by the Congregation for the Doctrine of the Faith reads as follows:

> The teaching of the Church distinguishes between 'public revelation' and 'private revelations.' The two realities differ not only in degree but also in essence. The term 'public revelation' refers to the revealing action of God directed to humanity as a whole and which finds its literary expression in the two parts of the Bible: the Old and New Testaments. ...[This] revelation came to an end with the fulfillment of the mystery of Christ as enunciated in the New Testament. ...
> ...'[P]rivate revelation' ...refers to all the visions and revelations which have taken place since the completion of the New Testament. (Congregation for the Doctrine of the Faith, *The Message of Fatima* [June 26, 2000])

---

707. Hugo Assmann, *Opresión-liberación: Desafío a los cristianos* (Montevideo: Tierra Nueva, 1971), 50, 65.

708. Gustavo Gutiérrez, "Praxis de libertação e fé cristã," appendix to Gustavo Gutiérrez, *Teologia da libertação* (Petrópolis, Brazil: Editora Vozes, 1975), 267.

709. Henrique Cláudio Lima Vaz, S.J., introduction to *Teologia da libertação: Política ou profetismo? Visão panorâmica e crítica da teologia política latino-americana* by Alfonso García Rubio (São Paulo: Edições Loyola, 1977), 3. He should have said "for two millennia," that is, from the beginning of the Church.

710. For an interesting analysis of the switch from a theology founded on being to one founded on process, leading to LT, see the insightful study by Enrique T. Rueda, *The Marxist Character of Liberation Theology* (Washington, D.C.: The Free Congress Research and Educational Foundation, 1986), 1–3.

711. Edwin C. Garvey, C.S.B., *Process Theology and Secularization* (Houston: Lumen Christi Press, 1973), 2.

712. See N. Iung, s.v. "Révelation," *D.T.C.*, 26:2581. See also Ioannis Bapt. Franzelin, *Tractatus de divina traditione et scriptura* (Rome: Typis S.C. de Propaganda Fide, 1870). Here, the term "Tradition" is employed in its technical theological sense, that is, "The set of revealed truths concerning faith and morals, not recorded in Scripture but orally delivered by God to the Church and transmitted by it." J.M. Hervé, *Manuale theologiae dogmaticae* (Paris: Berche et Pagis, 1957), 1:532. Canon Hervé reiterates the doctrine of the Council of Trent: "[T]his truth and discipline are contained in the written books, and the unwritten traditions which, received by the apostles from the mouth of Christ himself, or from the apostles themselves, the Holy Ghost dictating, have come down even unto us, transmitted as it were from hand to hand." Council

713. In the decree *Lamentabili*, St. Pius X condemned the following modernist error: "Revelation, constituting the object of the Catholic faith, was not completed with the apostles." St. Pius X, *Lamentabili*, no. 21.

714. Thomas E. Clarke, S.J., "A New Way: Reflecting on Experience," in *Tracing the Spirit: Communities, Social Action, and Theological Reflection*, ed. James E. Hug, S.J. (New York: Paulist Press, 1983), 15, 19. Republished with permission. This proposition is a modernist error condemned by St. Pius X in his encyclical *Pascendi* (no. 8). Indeed, Fr. Clarke assumes the legacy of Modernism: "I had been brought up ...to view the

Commenting on this doctrine, Fr. James E. Hug, S.J., writes,

> A great breakthrough took place in the recent history of Christian spirituality when we affirmed that interior moods, emotions, movements—the energies that move within us—should be understood as important signs from God. ...We recognized that we must learn to 'read' these signs to discern the revelation that God was offering us through them. ...
>
> ...God is present and is revealed in our interior movements.[715]

Because of its collectivist nature, LT preferentially scrutinizes "interior moods, emotions, [and] movements" occurring both in individuals and in human masses in constant evolution, that is to say, in historical processes. According to LT, one must listen to historical processes and interpret their profound meaning to discover the "signs of the times," that is, the voice of God, in a revelation immanent in history. Father Gutiérrez comments: "Theologically speaking, 'signs of the times' means the conviction that the God in whom we believe is a God of history, who speaks to and challenges us through history."[716]

Liberation theology especially emphasizes as 'bearers of revelation' those movements and processes that foster reforms in society, understood as the great revolutionary movements in modern history.

> Our interior movements are bearers of revelation [says Father Hug], so too are the exterior, social ones. ...
>
> ...The social institutions and movements of our times, are presented to us as a privileged place of revelation. God is active and moving in our world, revealing to us, inviting us, calling us through social movements and major institutional reform movements in the public arena. ...
>
> ...[These major reform movements, concludes Father Hug,] are privileged sources of revelation.[717]

This doctrine that public revelation is continuing and mediated through historical movements is derived from an error called historicist immanentism, the doctrinal core of LT, amply covered in the next chapter.

Thus, LT does away with the idea of a completed deposit of faith and of an infallible Magisterium that interprets it. Instead, it turns to an ever-changing human consciousness and to evolving sociopolitical realities. From this perspective, as we shall see,

revelation is transformed into an ever-evolving "truth" that man constructs in every epoch through "liberating praxis," which thus becomes the criterion for truth.

James Cone, the principal exponent of so-called Black Theology, speaks of the "divine dimensions of the reality." Explicitly denying the immutability of revelation, he writes, "We do not begin our theology with a reflection on divine revelation. ...We do not believe that revelation is a deposit of fixed doctrines or an objective Word of God that is then applied to the human situation. On the contrary, we contend that there is no truth outside of, or beyond, the concrete historical events in which people are engaged as agents."[718]

Following the same line, Father Assmann does not consider revelation to be a deposit of absolute and immutable truths. According to him, God's Word proceeds from revolutionary involvement as interpreted in each epoch by the agents of sociopolitical transformations:

> The word of God is no longer a fixed absolute, an eternal proposition we receive before analyzing social conflicts and before committing ourselves to the transformation of historical reality. ...God's word today, grows from the collective process of historical awareness, analysis and involvement, that is, from praxis. ...
>
> ...This kind of historical hermeneutics may destroy the false security of the word of God given once for all, the absolute of the word of God in itself.[719]

This view of history as the paramount source of truth instead of God and His revelation marks precisely the break of modern theology with traditional Catholic theology. "The *historicization* of Western thought," writes Samuel Silva Gotay, a professor at the University of Puerto Rico, "is the key to understanding the theological transformation that occurred in Europe, which in turn reverberated in Latin America, where the historicization of religious thought was taken to its final consequences [by LT]."[720]

4. The Poor and Oppressed, Main Locus Theologicus[721]

According to LT, this revelation immanent in history manifests itself preferentially—we would say almost exclusively—through one aspect of reality, namely, the "poor" and "oppressed" engaged in "subversive praxis."

"The theology of liberation," says Father Gutiérrez, "is an attempt to understand the faith from within the concrete historical, liberating, and subversive praxis of the poor of this world—the exploited classes, despised ethnic groups, and marginalized cultures."[722] In other words, the poor, that is, any class seen as oppressed, despised, or marginalized, are LT's privileged and practically only locus theologicus, especially when engaged in a liberating and subversive

---

Modernism of the turn of the century as a subjectivistic and Protestantizing camel's nose under the Catholic tent. But eventually my exposure to the 'new theology' of the post–World War II period made me see in it a new and irrepressible wave of the consciousness that had surfaced unsuccessfully through the modernists." Clarke, "A New Way," 17.

Such explicit adoption of modernist theses is not uncommon among American liberation theologians. To indicate the gravity of the fact, we recall the excommunication by St. Pius X in his motu proprio *Praestantia*: "We do by our apostolic authority repeat and confirm both that decree of the Supreme Sacred Congregation [*Lamentabili*] and those encyclical letters of ours [*Pascendi*], adding the penalty of excommunication against their contradictors, and this We declare and decree that should anybody, which may God forbid, be so rash as to defend any one of the propositions, opinions, or teachings condemned in these documents he falls, ipso facto, under ...the excommunications *latae sententiae*, simply reserved to the Roman pontiff." St. Pius X, motu proprio *Praestantia scripturae* (Nov. 18, 1907).

715. James E. Hug, S.J., and Rose Marie Scherschel, *Social Revelation* (Washington, D.C.: Center of Concern, 1987), 19–20.

716. Gustavo Gutiérrez, opening talk at the "Twenty Years After Medellín" conference, São Paulo (Oct. 25, 1988). Recordings of proceedings. T.F.P. archive. See also Clodovis Boff, O.S.M., *Sinais dos tempos: Principios de leitura* (São Paulo: Edições Loyola, 1979).

717. Hug and Scherschel, *Social Revelation*, 20, 22.

718. Cone, "Black Theology: Its Origin," 39.

719. Hugo Assmann, "Statement," in *Theology in the Americas: Detroit 1975*, ed. Sergio Torres and John Eagleson (New York: Orbis Books, 1976), 299.

720. Silva Gotay, "Origem e desenvolvimento," 145.

721. *Locus theologicus*: expression coined in the sixteenth century by Spanish Dominican theologian Melchior Cano (1509–1560), meaning source or spring of theological knowledge. See Nicolau and Salaverri, *Sacrae theologia summa*, 1:20–22. See Melchior Cano, *De locis theologicis* (Salamanca: n.p., 1562), ed. Juan Belda Plans (Madrid: Biblioteca de Autores Cristianos, 2006). Cano's work was clearly intended at innovation as it paved the way for the historicization of theology. Disavowed by ecclesiastical authorities, Cano was designated bishop in the faraway Canary Islands by Philip II, but Pope Paul IV did not approve.

722. Gustavo Gutiérrez, *The Power of the Poor in History: Selected Writings*, trans. Robert R. Barr (Maryknoll, N.Y.: Orbis Books, 1983), 37.

historical praxis, that is, when acting as agents of revolutionary transformations by peaceful or violent means.

On this point, Spanish liberation theologian Fr. Jon Sobrino, S.J., one of the movement's principal figures, writes,

> The Spirit of Jesus is in the poor. ...The history of God advances indefectibly by way of the poor ...the Spirit of Jesus takes historical flesh in the poor ...the poor show the direction of history that is in accord with God's plan. ...
> ...The poor are the authentic *theological source* for understanding Christian truth and practice.[723]

In a paper for the world conference of liberation theologians held in Brazil in September 2012, Father Sobrino goes further by stating, "The absolute is God, and the co-absolute are the poor," a philosophically absurd phrase one is surprised to hear from a Jesuit theologian who graduated from the Hochschule in Frankfurt.[724]

In LT's original versions, liberation theologians spoke preferentially of the poor, but this term should not be understood in its literal meaning, that is, in reference to the materially deprived. In LT's logic, poor is anyone who somehow feels oppressed, alienated, or discriminated against, a victim of inequality. Adopting this broad meaning, the aforementioned Black theologian James Cone says that "God's revelation comes to us in and through the cultural situation of the oppressed."[725]

From the above quotations, it is clear that not all of the poor are sources of revelation. Those involved in some subversive praxis to overcome oppression are, but those who are resigned and peaceful are not. These are the ones best (or exclusively) able to hear and interpret the voice of the "God hidden in history." This is what liberation theologians mean by the awkward expression "hermeneutical privilege of the oppressed," an expression coined by the Uruguayan theologian Fr. Juan Luis Segundo.[726] Mind you, not all poor, but only the *struggling* poor.

From this perspective, only struggling revolutionaries, partisans of subversive doctrines, and disseminators of rebellious animosities can aptly interpret God's voice in history. Their subversive activities become a "privileged" locus of revelation, the raw material of liberation theology. This approach forcibly rejects serenity of mind and psychological detachment from events, essential conditions for a balanced and objective interpretation of reality. Liberation theologians are not interested in objectivity. Theirs is an avowedly biased view. For Jesuit Fr. Alfred Hennelly, of the Woodstock Theological Center, liberation theology must be born from a "precious tincture of rage."[727]

Needless to say, such attitudes are diametrically opposed to the Church's social teaching. A call to peace is found at the very heart of the Christian message. By their very nature, rational beings ardently yearn for peace. This supposes a loving attitude toward neighbor, which is part and parcel of being Christian. Upon these basic truths, the Church has built a social doctrine supported by the concepts of order, harmony, and balance: inner harmony in people, harmony in the family, harmony between institutions, harmony between social classes, harmony among nations. The Church rejects systems based on hatred, envy, division, and confrontation.

Seemingly mischievous, at this point a question arises that really touches the heart of the problem: What happens when the poor do not fight? Are they still a source of revelation? The answer is: no, not at all!

Fr. Juan Luis Segundo and his colleague Fr. Alfred Hennelly point out that the poor are a privileged source of revelation only when they act as revolutionary agents. Conversely, when they lose their hermeneutical privilege, Father Hennelly laments, "I agree with [Fr. Segundo] that the theologian must remain critical regarding the theological views of the poor. ...In my years working in the Third World, I had ample—almost daily—experience of the frequency with which very poor people internalize the dominating beliefs of their oppressors, and also of the depth and the tenacity with which those views are defended."[728] Apparently, for liberation theologians these deeply ingrained conservative attitudes do not constitute revelation.

In a lecture delivered at the Eighth Conference of Theology held in Madrid in September 1988, Italian liberation theologian Father Girardi bemoaned the lack of revolutionary fervor of the poor, a fact he slyly attributes to discouragement rather than to the main factor, namely, a conservative mentality widespread among the people: "One of the most dramatic findings is that this [liberation] perspective is considered impossible by the people themselves, the very working class that according to our perspectives should be the axis of the transformations. Often times they do not believe that this prospect [of liberation] is achievable."[729]

In the written version of his lecture, he expressed even greater pain: "To pursue the popular utopia ...means above all and perhaps this is its most dramatic aspect, to give oneself to the cause of the people even without their massive support, let alone their recognition ...feeling like a stranger in one's own ambience."[730] So here we have the real face of liberation theologians: strangers in their own ambience. In other words, they are not the people's champions and interpreters of their aspirations, but lack their support and are even suspicious of them.

5. Marxism as a Theological Instrument

Inverting Catholic theology, liberation theologians do not take revelation as the starting point of their analysis, but propose to study the concrete social, political, economic, and cultural situation of the poor and "oppressed" struggling for their "liberation" and the historical processes resulting therefrom. Now, liberation theologians say, since neither Scripture nor traditional Catholic doctrine offer scientifically valid criteria for social analysis, these must be sought elsewhere. They could have chosen the social

723. Jon Sobrino, *The True Church and the Poor,* trans. Matthew J. O'Connell (Maryknoll, N.Y.: Orbis Books, 1984), 93. (Emphasis in the original.)

724. Sobrino, "O absoluto é Deus e o coabsoluto são os pobres," 7.

725. James H. Cone, *A Black Theology of Liberation* (Maryknoll, N.Y.: Orbis Books, 1987), 28.

726. See Juan Luis Segundo, *The Liberation of Theology* (Maryknoll, N.Y.: Orbis Books, 1976). In a book recalling his years as head of the Congregation for the Doctrine of the Faith, former pope Benedict XVI denounced LT's manipulation of the "poor," stating:

> It was the common opinion, be it in Europe or in North America, that it was about support to the poor and, therefore, a cause that should certainly be approved. But it was an error.
> Poverty and the poor were without a doubt put forth as topics of the Theology of Liberation but in a very specific perspective. ... It was not a question of aid or reform, it was said, but of a great upheaval from which a new world would spring. The Christian faith was being used as the engine for this revolutionary movement, thus transforming it into a kind of political force. (Benedict XVI, "Il ricordo del pontefice emerito," 17–18)

727. Alfred Hennelly, *Theology for a Liberating Church: The New Praxis of Freedom* (Washington, D.C.: Georgetown University Press, 1989), 6.

728. Hennelly, *Theology for a Liberating Church*, 64–65.

729. Giulio Girardi, lecture "Utopía popular y esperanza cristiana," taken from the taped proceedings, Eighth Conference of Theology, Madrid (Sept. 7–11, 1988). T.F.P. Archive.

730. Giulio Girardi, "Utopía popular y esperanza cristiana," in *Utopia y profetismo: VIII Congreso de Teología*, ed. José María González Faus (Madrid: Evangelio y Liberación, 1989), 104.

doctrine of the Church taught by the popes since Leo XIII or the criteria proposed by the sociological schools in vogue. However, they chose historical materialism, namely Marxism. This is understandable because the core of their analysis is the dialectical struggle between the "oppressed" and their "oppressors."

In this regard, the well-known American liberation theologian Robert McAfee Brown remarks, "Those in the church who are sharing in the liberation struggle draw on another kind of resource for understanding their world and their faith, the resource of *social analysis*. Theology does not provide tidy plans for action; nor does the Bible provide all the tools needed for understanding the contemporary world. ...Some of the insights for this descriptive analysis come from Marxism, and the point needs to be addressed."[731] Elsewhere he states that "it would be foolish to pretend that there is not a lot of Marxist analysis in the way the liberation theologians look at the world."[732]

Adopting Marxist analysis—an essential point in the Holy See's 1984 criticism of LT—is not done for economic or circumstantial reasons but from a particular ideological choice. After listing LT's compounded philosophical legacy, Father Gutiérrez explains its main tenet: "To these factors can be added the influence of Marxist thought, focusing on praxis and geared to the transformation of the world. ...In recent times, its cultural impact has become greater. Many agree with Sartre that Marxism, as the formal framework of all contemporary philosophical thought, cannot be superseded." The Peruvian theologian puts this choice within a broader context: "Contemporary theology does in fact find itself in direct and fruitful confrontation with Marxism, and it is to a large extent due to Marxism's influence that theological thought, searching for its own sources, has begun to reflect on the meaning of the transformation of this world and the action of man in history."[733]

Brazilian liberation theologian Luiz Alberto Gomes de Souza goes so far as to state, "Presently, for liberation theology there is no better theoretical reflection than Marxism, which is immersed in the praxis of reality. ...It is a theoretical option that we must assume as mediation, discipline, and effective tactic."[734] Leonardo Boff, one of the movement's foremost representatives, is equally clear: "What we propose is not to put theology into Marxism, but to put Marxism—historical materialism—into theology."[735]

Thus, liberation theologians take Marxist analysis and its principles, apply them to a social and historical reality, and then label their conclusions—obviously tainted by the method of analysis—as "theology"!

Again, this is not a merely circumstantial choice, but a consciously ideological one. Joseph Holland—former director of PILLAR (Pallotine Institute for Lay Leadership and Apostolic Research) of New Jersey, and a key figure in the American LT movement—and Jesuit Fr. Peter Henriot, state:

> Social analysis [used by LT] is not value-free. This point is extremely important. Social analysis is not a neutral approach, a purely "scientific" and "objective" view of reality. ...
> ...We always choose an analysis that is implicitly linked to some ideological tradition.[736]

The ideological tradition liberation theologians chose when they first developed their doctrines was none other than Marxism.

Liberation theologians flaunt this reliance on Marxism, like the late Spanish Jesuit Fr. Ignacio Ellacuría, former rector of the Universidad Centroamericana Simeón Cañas, assassinated in 1989. He considered that the impact of Marxism on today's Church has had some "highly positive and profoundly Christian" consequences. He notes, "It would not be correct to deny the influence of Marxism when we need to justify why we should historically stand with the poor. ...In general, we could say that theoretical and practical Marxism ...has had an important influence on something highly positive and profoundly Christian as such, namely, the redefinition of the social place of the Church, and its preferential option for the poor."[737]

Some liberation theologians try to disguise their exclusive use of Marxist analysis by claiming it is one method among others. For example, Father Gutiérrez says, "As theologians, we do not intend to shed new light on reality. We resort, therefore, to social, political and economic analysis, including Marxist analysis."[738] In fact, it is difficult and even impossible to figure out a method of sociopolitical analysis used by liberation theologians that is not centered on the dialectical struggle between the "oppressed" and the "oppressors." Father Girardi clearly states that "[LT's] methodological premise is that reflection on the religious reality, and in particular on the Christian reality, can and must be done with the materialist method, that is, in light of the dialectical struggle between oppression and liberation."[739]

6. Other Theoretical Instruments

This heavy and in fact exclusive reliance on Marxist analysis among liberation theologians was obvious during the first phase of its development (1960s–1970s). The situation led some otherwise meritorious critics to pay inordinate attention to the role played by Marxism in LT while missing other analytical criteria employed

731. Robert McAfee Brown, "The 'Preferential Option for the Poor' and the Renewal of Faith," in *Churches in Struggle: Liberation Theology and Social Change in North America*, ed. William K. Tabb (New York: Monthly Review Press, 1986), 15. Other major works by McAfee Brown are: *Theology in a New Key: Responding to Liberation Themes* (Philadelphia: Westminster Press, 1978); *Unexpected News: Reading the Bible With Third World Eyes* (Philadelphia: Westminster Press, 1984); *Spirituality and Liberation: Overcoming the Great Fall* (Philadelphia: Westminster Press, 1988); *Gustavo Gutiérrez: An Introduction to Liberation Theology* (Maryknoll, N.Y.: Orbis Books, 1990); *Liberation Theology: An Introductory Guide* (Philadelphia: Westminster Press, 1993).

732. Robert McAfee Brown, preface to *Theology in the Americas: Detroit 1975*, ed. Sergio Torres and John Eagleson (New York: Orbis Books, 1976), xvii.

733. Gutiérrez, *A Theology of Liberation*, 9. To corroborate his thesis, the Peruvian theologian quotes Roger Garaudy, *Perspectives de l'homme: Existentialisme, pensée catholique, marxisme* (Paris: Presses Universitaires de France, 1960); Erich Kellner, ed., *Christentum und marxismus heute* (Vienna: Europa Verlag, 1966); Giulio Girardi, *Marxismo e cristianesimo* (Assisi: Cittadella, 1977); Georges Cottier, O.P., *Chrétiens et marxistes: Dialogue avec Roger Garaudy* (Tours: Mame, 1967).

734. Roger Veckemans, S.J., "Expansión mundial de la teología de la liberación latinoamericana," in *Socialismo y socialismos en América Latina*, ed. C.E.L.A.M. (Bogotá: Secretariado General del C.E.L.A.M., 1977), 276. Veckemans also quotes Manuel Velásquez, then director of the Social Secretariat of the Mexican Bishops' Conference: "The faith cannot become truth without the necessary mediation of an ideology. ... In the case of liberation theology, this mediation necessarily would be Marxism."

735. Leonardo Boff, O.F.M., "Marxismo na teologia," *Jornal do Brasil*, Apr. 6, 1980, Especial, p. 2.

736. Holland and Henriot, *Social Analysis*, 16–17.

737. Ignacio Ellacuría, "El auténtico lugar social de la Iglesia," in *Desafíos Cristianos*, ed. Misión Abierta (Madrid: Loguez Ediciones, 1988), 81–82. The assumption of Marxist analysis and its inevitable consequences are precisely one of the main criticisms of LT found in the 1984 Pastoral Instruction *Libertatis nuntius*, issued by the Congregation for the Doctrine of the Faith. As mentioned before, quoting Paul VI, the document states, "[I]t would be illusory and dangerous to ignore the intimate bond which radically unites them, and to accept elements of the Marxist analysis without recognizing its connections with the ideology, or to enter into the practice of class-struggle and of its Marxist interpretation while failing to see the kind of totalitarian society to which this process slowly leads." (*Instruction on Certain Aspects*, VII, no. 7).

738. Fr. Gutiérrez, in a lecture at the Hotel del Portal, during the so-called "parallel conference" of liberation theologians held at the 1979 C.E.L.A.M. conference in Puebla, Mexico. Frei Betto [Carlos Alberto Libânio Christo], *Diário de Puebla* (Rio de Janeiro: Civilização Brasileira, 1979), 94.

739. Giulio Girardi, "Possibilità di una teologia europea della liberazione," *IDOC Internazionale* (Rome) 1 (1983), 41.

in its more recent versions. A consequence of that excessive attention is the view, widespread today even among high-ranking prelates, that LT's problem is simply Marxism. Remove Marxism and you're done! As a result, rather than an *erroneous* LT, we will have a *correct* one.[740] Nothing could be more simplistic.

We have just finished demonstrating how LT turned to Marxism as a theoretical tool to discover and analyze situations of supposed oppression, poverty, and marginalization. This use of Marxism comes from the fact that, unlike in developed countries, in Latin America the demagogic manipulation of actual poverty has played a much more important role triggering revolutions than moral, cultural, and other grievance factors that have only recently gained some importance in that vast area of the world.

Back in 1975, Gregory Baum, a secularized German-Canadian Augustinian priest and Vatican Council II *peritus* (expert), as well as one of the most conspicuous figures in the North American LT movement, noted that Latin American liberation theologians "focus almost exclusively on economic injustices." According to Baum, that was because in Latin America "the economic factor dominates all others—the political order, the cultural trends, the ecclesiastical system, etc. All expressions of society are reflections of the economic order. In this situation, the class domination becomes the key for understanding the misery in which people live and the form which social sin has taken."[741] According to Marxist doctrine, class domination is founded on economics.

The economic factor is far from being the only one to cause oppression, however, especially in developed countries where it is not easy to manipulate situations of economic distress. "The structures of domination in North America," says Baum, "undoubtedly include the injustices implicit in the economic system, but they also also include other significant factors as independent variables: institutionalized racism, the growing immobility of bureaucratic centralization, the devastation of natural resources through industrial expansion, the exclusion of women from public life, etc."[742]

To Baum's list of "oppression" factors that should interest an LT hand-tailored for the First World, the Jesuit Father Hennelly adds others: "chauvinism and militarism in dealing with other nations ...consumerism and selfish individualism."[743]

Liberation theologians also use other theoretical instruments to analyze factors of oppression in order to develop a particular "theology." Always utilized by their counterparts in the developed world, such instruments are increasingly being used in updated versions of LT in Latin America. They employ Freudianism to probe into what they call psychological factors of oppression; Marcusianism, to uncover oppression by the industrial society; Black Power ideology (or Indigenism), to demagogically denounce racist domination; environmentalism, to mourn the destruction of nature; and myriads of similar doctrines which, properly assessed,

can manifest an even more radical virulence than Marxism. The latter was itself a rationalization carefully crafted to bring more wood to the fire of the revolutionary process in mid-nineteenth century Europe.

In the eighties, real Socialism and its revolutionary praxis found themselves in crisis. This had a profound impact on LT, which, like many a revolutionary reality, had to adapt to new horizons. "The epochal collapse of the Soviet bloc in 1988, which dragged Marxist ideology in its disastrous fall was a mortal blow for liberation theologians," writes Battista Mondin in his history of contemporary theology. "They finally realized that the philosophical and methodological support of their theology was unsustainable."[744]

While the role played by Marxist dogma kept on shrinking, that of new doctrines proportionally increased, giving LT a new look which developed in parallel to the new look of the Revolution itself. We will discuss this in detail later. We now need to see how LT developed historically (and how it still subsists in some circles) with its heavy emphasis on Marxist doctrine.

7. Revolution, a Source of Divine Revelation

According to liberation theology, the "poor" or "oppressed" engaged in "subversive praxis" are the principal source of theological reflection, the main aspect of reality through which God's revelation is made manifest to man. Their actions, that is, revolutionary struggles, become locus theologicus par excellence. The Chilean Fr. Sergio Torres, leader of Christians for Socialism, categorically states, "The struggles of the oppressed are a privileged place where the true God can be discovered."[745]

The same idea is expressed by Nicaraguan Jesuit theologian Fr. Juan Hernández Pico, professor at the Catholic University of Managua: "*The conflictive reality in history of a struggle between good and evil, between justice and injustice, being waged by the poor in our countries ...is a* locus theologicus *where God is breaking into history*."[746] Applying this postulate to the revolutionary struggles of the Blacks in the United States, deemed an "oppressed" category seeking "liberation," theologian James Cone is even clearer: "*Revelation*," he says, "*is a black event*—it is what blacks are doing about their liberation."[747]

Therefore, when liberation theologians state that God must be found in history, they mean that God is to be found inside revolutionary processes. An international manifesto supporting the Nicaraguan revolution, published in 1983 by 44 top liberation and progressive theologians from all over the world, including several Americans, illustrates this idea: "From within the Sandinista revolutionary process, you have discovered the God that heeds the cry of the oppressed and decides to liberate them (see Exod. 3:7)."[748]

In other words, the real locus theologicus of liberation theologians is not the poor as they demagogically purport, but

740. See "Il fattore decisivo: Intervista al prefetto della Congregazione per la Dottrina della Fede Gerhard Ludwig Müller," *L'Osservatore Romano,* July 26, 2013.

741. Gregory Baum, *Religion and Alienation: A Theological Reading of Sociology* (New York: Paulist Press, 1975), 214. Excerpt from *Religion and Alienation: A Theological Reading of Sociology* by Gregory Baum, Copyright © 1975 by Gregory Baum, published by Paulist Press, Inc., New York/Mahwah, N.J. Reprinted by pemission of Paulist Press, Inc. www.paulistpress.com. Gregory Baum was born in Berlin in 1923. After the war, he moved to Canada, where he was ordained an Augustinian priest in 1954. He was professor of theology at the University of Toronto and at McGill University. A conciliar *peritus* with the Secretariat for Ecumenism, Baum took part in the drafting of the conciliar documents *Dignitatis humanae, Nostra aetate,* and *Unitatis redintegratio.* For many years he was a member of the editorial board of the journal *Concilium.* He subsequently joined the LT movement, which he strove to import into North America. In 1976, he left the priesthood. Toward the end of his life, he publicly admitted his homosexuality.

742. Baum, *Religion and Alienation,* 216.

743. Hennelly, *Theology for a Liberating Church,* 3.

744. Battista Mondin, *Storia della teologia,* 4 vols. (Bologna: Edizioni Studio Domenicano, 2019), 4:1003.

745. Sergio Torres, "Opening Remarks," in *Theology in the Americas: Detroit II Conference Papers,* West, Guidote, and Coakley, eds. (Maryknoll, N.Y.: Orbis Books, 1982), 5.

746. Juan Hernández Pico, "Solidarity With the Poor and the Unity of the Church," in Jon Sobrino and Juan Hernández Pico, *Theology of Christian Solidarity,* trans. Phillip Berryman (Maryknoll, N.Y.: Orbis Books, 1985), 61. (Emphasis in the original.) See also Renny Golden and Michael McConnell, *Sanctuary: The New Underground Railroad* (Maryknoll, N.Y.: Orbis Books, 1986), 156. Fr. Girardi also affirms that "the praxis of liberation is a privileged locus of [theological] research and reflection." Girardi, "Possibilità di una teologia europea," 31.

747. Cone, *A Black Theology,* 30.

748. Johannes B. Metz, "Carta de apoyo a la iglesia de los pobres que está en Nicaragua," no. 6, *Tierra Nueva,* 13–14, nos. 52–54 (Jan.–Apr. 1985), 102. The importance of this manifesto cannot be overstated as it seals the official support of LT in one of its most radical manifestations, by some of the main representatives of the New Theology and "liberation," which in their peculiar ideological bias means revolution. Some liberation theologians go so far as to contend that revolutionary struggles are not just a privileged locus theologicus, but in fact the only one. "I can believe only in a liberating God and a liberating revelation," proclaims Father Segundo.[749]

Further developing this point, Father Segundo explains, "In reality our God is known only with the movement and process of de-alienation [i.e., liberation], creation, and love. ...He is never known prior to, or outside of, that process. No heavenly sign points him out to those who do not scrutinize the [dialectic] ambiguity of history in search of their common liberation."[750]

Revolutionary situations vary greatly not only from one country or region to another, but also over decades. Revolutionary processes, always in motion, advance from one paroxysm to another driven by a dynamism of their own. Even seemingly calm periods are times of muted but profound fermentation that prepare new outbreaks.

The method of liberation theology is thus applied to different and ever-changing situations. Even if the method of analysis remains the same, the resulting conclusions are bound to vary. Consequently, they do not seek an absolute truth but merely endeavor to discern the revelation being mediated through a particular revolutionary process at a given time. For LT, truth itself is historical and constantly evolving.

In this sense, Latin American LT, as it was developed in the 1960s and 1970s, was but one of the many possible expressions. It results from the application of this methodology to a somewhat homogeneous group of countries in a concrete historical moment. It should also be noted that, just as revolutionary situations in Latin America evolved, this theology also changed, striving to adapt to the new circumstances.

8. LT: Revolutionary Praxis

a. "Liberation Theology Begins With ...Insurrection"

Referring to the "primacy of praxis," a criterion borrowed from Marxism, liberation theologians claim they do not start from theory but directly from action, revolutionary action.[751] For example, Father Hug states,

> God is revealing and being discovered in action. ...
> ...It [theological reflection] usually does not begin with Scripture study or research into the writings of the Christian tradition. It begins in action.[752]

However, not just any action will do, but only those aimed at transforming the world in an egalitarian and liberated sense. In typical Marxist jargon, Father Gutiérrez writes, "What we understand by 'praxis' is 'transforming action,' not simply any kind of action, but rather a historical transformation."[753]

Involvement in the revolutionary process thus precedes any theological endeavor. In other words, theology begins with revolution. "Liberation theology begins with the fact of insurrection," says Sharon Welch of the Harvard Divinity School, a self-defined "feminist liberation theologian."[754] This is why, as liberation theologian Gregory Baum notes, "Liberation theology supposes a revolutionary situation."[755] In fact, for liberation theologians, theology is revolutionary involvement. Father Gutiérrez is absolutely clear on this point. "Liberation theology as we understand it here involves a direct and specific relationship with historical praxis; and historical praxis is a liberation praxis. ...It involves immersion in the political process of revolution."[756]

This is an obvious conclusion that can be drawn from the premises expounded in previous sections. If God reveals Himself in revolutionary processes, the only way to heed that revelation would be by getting involved in them. Only those people actually engaged in some revolutionary activism would be in direct contact with so-called divine revelation and would thus be able to "do theology." "History is the locale where God reveals the mystery of his person," Father Gutiérrez writes. "His word will reach us to the extent that we immerse ourselves in the ongoing process of history, and that history is riddled with conflict. It is filled with ...bitter struggles for justice."[757]

b. Theology Comes After Revolution

For LT, revolutionary praxis is the fundamental activity; theological reflection comes afterward, as a second step. "Theology is not the first step. Involvement comes first, and theology is a reflection of that involvement," Father Gutiérrez writes.[758]

Brazilian theologians Leonardo and Clodovis Boff ask, "How do you do liberation theology?" They answer, "We must do liberation before doing theology. The first step in theology is pre-theological. It is to live the commitment of the faith, which in our case means participating somehow in the liberating process, taking the side of the oppressed."[759]

In other words, liberation theologians first want to get involved in revolutionary struggles and only afterward reflect on that involvement, according to revolutionary criteria. They then call this praxis/reflection "theology." This is why they speak of "doing theology," a meaningless expression if applied to traditional

of European progressive theology in general, implicitly acknowledging its paternity. Among the signers are Marie-Dominique Chenu, Johann Baptist Metz, Edward Schillebeeckx, Hans Küng, Jürgen Moltmann, Georges Cassalis, Giuseppe Alberigo, Christian Ducquoq, Norbert Greinacher, Jean-Pierre Jossua, Gregory Baum, Matthew Lamb, Rossino Gibellini, J. Pohier, Elisabeth Schüssler Fiorenza, François Houtart, and others. See *Servir* (Jalapa), no. 102 (1983): 307–31.

749. Hennelly, *Theology for a Liberating Church*, 63.

750. Juan Luis Segundo, *Our Idea of God* (Maryknoll, N.Y.: Orbis Books, 1974), 153.

751. The *Dizionario dei termini marxisti* (Dictionary of Marxist Terms) states that

> the praxis is the material activity of the transformation of reality. ...
> One of the central points of the Marxist interpretation of the praxis is the materialistic affirmation of the superiority, the priority of the concrete moment of the transformation of the world with regard to the theoretical interpretation. (Ernesto Mascitelli, ed., *Dizionario dei termini Marxisti* (Milan, Italy: Vangelista, 1977), 261–62, s.v. "Prassi o Pratica")

This is the classical Marxist statement on the problem. More recently, liberation theologians have been exploring the more elaborate insights of the so-called Frankfurt School of Marxism with regards to the relations between theory and praxis. See Matthew Lamb, *Solidarity With the Victims: Toward a Theology of Social Transformation* (New York: Crossroad, 1982), 61ff; Joseph Kroger, "Prophetic-Critical and Practical-Strategic Tasks of Theology: Habermas and Liberation Theology," *Theological Studies*, 46 (Mar. 1985): 3–20.

752. Hug, *Tracing the Spirit*, 2–3.

753. Gustavo Gutiérrez, statement in *Theology in the Americas: Detroit 1975*, ed. Sergio Torres and John Eagleson (New York: Orbis Books, 1976), 310.

754. Sharon D. Welch, *Communities of Resistance and Solidarity: A Feminist Theology of Liberation* (Maryknoll, N.Y.: Orbis Books, 1985), 35.

755. Gregory Baum, "La teologia de la liberación y lo sobrenatural," in Gregory Baum et al., *Vida y reflexión: Aportes de la teología de la liberación al pensamiento teológico* (Lima: Centro de Estudios y Publicaciones—C.E.P., 1983), 70.

756. Gustavo Gutiérrez, "Liberation Praxis and Christian Faith" in *Frontiers of Theology in Latin America*, ed. Rosino Gibellini, trans. John Drury (Maryknoll, N.Y.: Orbis Books, 1979), 24.

757. Gustavo Gutiérrez, "Liberation Praxis and Christian Faith," in *Lay Ministry Handbook*, by Diocese of Brownsville (Texas: Diocese of Brownsville, 1984; 3rd quarter), 21.

758. Gustavo Gutiérrez, "Hacia una teología de la liberación." Notes for a talk by Fr. Gutiérrez at the Second Gathering of Priests and Laymen held in Chimbote, Peru, July 21–25, 1968.

759. Boff and Boff, *Como fazer teologia da libertação*, 37.

Catholic theology. In this sense, to be involved in liberation struggles would be to do theology.

So much for the theory. In real life, liberation theologians are at times obliged to cast it aside and take an altogether different approach.

Brazilian liberation theologian Fr. Carlos Mesters, a theoretician of the Basic Christian Communities, admits how easily a group of people can be induced to first reflect "theologically" on a given reality and then involve them in revolutionary activism. In that case, Father Mesters says, liberation theologians simply dump their theory about the primacy of praxis and adopt the most expedient approach to advance liberation. They are clearly interested in revolution and will take any road that serves that purpose.

Fr. Alfred Hennelly writes, "It would be a very rare event for a group of Christians to engage in common action with no background of Christian symbols and reflection on them at all. Thus it may be a false question to ask whether action or reflection should come first." According to him, "the position of Mesters offers greater freedom to assess the strength and weakness of different communities and to adapt the method in a creative way."[760]

c. A Critical Reflection on Praxis

From this perspective, what is liberation theology?

Secularized Chilean priest Pablo Richard, a leading liberation theologian, defines LT as follows: "*Being a 'critical reflection on praxis,' liberation theology is defined as an integral part of a praxis of liberation*. It is inside praxis as a specific stage of that praxis. Theology is not reduced to praxis, neither is praxis to theology. But theology finds its origin and development entirely inside praxis as a specific part of a global historical process."[761]

Therefore, for liberation theologians, theology is not actually an inquiry but a stage of revolutionary militancy, concretely, the stage of critical reflection on that militancy. LT stems from and is oriented to revolutionary involvement ("praxis"), its main activity.

---

760. Hennelly, *Theology for a Liberating Church*, 85. More cognizant Marxists denounce the absurdity of the theory of the primacy of praxis, i.e., of action as a first step in revolutionary involvement, regardless of ideology. They show how a person commits himself to the socialist struggle thanks to previously adopted doctrines and principles. French Marxist philosopher Kostas Axelos, rightly observes that it is ridiculous to claim that proletarians conceive revolutionary ideas on their own: "The proletariat that commits itself to the task of suppressing alienation is unable to achieve it without the guidance of revolutionary ideas that illuminate its struggle. Where do those ideas come from? From bourgeois intellectuals who renounce their class and join the proletariat, the oppressed class." Kostas Axelos, *Marx: Penseur de la technique* (Paris: Les Éditions de Minuit, 1969), 157. Axelos recalls Lenin's phrase, "There is no revolutionary movement without a revolutionary theory" (Axelos, *Marx: Penseur,* 158) and goes on to quote him: "We have said that there could not have been Social-Democratic consciousness among the workers. It would have to be brought to them from without. The history of all countries shows that the working class, exclusively by its own effort, is able to develop only trade union consciousness, i.e., the conviction that it is necessary to combine in unions, fight the employers, and strive to compel the government to pass necessary labour legislation, etc. The theory of socialism, however, grew out of the philosophic, historical, and economic theories elaborated by educated representatives of the propertied classes, by intellectuals" (Vladimir Ilyich Lenin, *What Is To Be Done?* chap. 2).

Italian liberation theologian Fr. Girardi is of the same opinion. The former Salesian priest posits that praxis cannot be the criterion of truth because it presupposes a metaphysical position, a peculiar vision of the human being, society, and history:

> The concept of *praxis* itself gives way to another, more fundamental one. An action is successful if it reaches that toward which it is tending. This presupposes a value to which it is orientated, a value to be realized, an ideal. The concept of *praxis* is defined in relation to an ideal of humanity, namely, liberty in the ethical and economic sense. This is really the ultimate criterion of value and truth, and the key to the whole system. ...
> ...The same criterion of *praxis* cannot be adequately justified from *praxis* itself, nor from experience in general. ...
> ...The procedure, therefore, is not from a vision of reality to the affirmation of values, but vice versa, from the affirmation of values to a vision of reality which renders them attainable. (Giulio Girardi, *Marxism and Christianity*, trans. Kevin Traynor [New York: The Macmillan Company, 1968], 14–15)

761. Pablo Richard, *La iglesia latinoamericana entre el temor y la esperanza* (San José, Costa Rica: DEI, 1987), 24–25.

LT, according to the Spanish theologian Juan José Tamayo-Acosta, is "a moment in the process of transformation of the world."[762]

For a better understanding, let us say a word about the adjective critical. In LT jargon, "critical thinking" is an analysis opposed *a priori* to the established order. It is not intended to solicit an objective view of reality but rather to find cracks in the system to better attack it. It is an aggressive analysis aimed at the destruction of the present order of things. From LT's standpoint, a non-subversive reflection would not be critical and should therefore be dismissed as naive or childish. LT is based on a deliberately biased view concocted by activists struggling to achieve revolutionary goals. "Liberation precedes and judges theology," Father Hennelly says. "This statement is an act of faith."[763]

d. Militant Theologians

A liberation theologian "is...a 'militant theologian' who positions himself within the march of the People of God," Leonardo and Clodovis Boff explain.[764] LT is not, properly speaking, a school of theological thought, but a subversive praxis oriented by revolutionary postulates. LT's subversive nature can be seen, for example, in Robert McAfee Brown's promotional blurb for Father Gutiérrez's book *A Theology of Liberation*: "It is ...a solidly reasoned theological argument for radical changes in our social structures."[765]

In passing, we should point out that, as in the case of its socio-historical analysis, LT's praxis is also largely guided by Marxist principles. "Marxism is not only a useful descriptive tool," says McAfee Brown, "it also provides a basis for action."[766]

e. A Theology From the Streets

As a consequence of such views, liberation theologians sustain that the whole endeavor of the movement's scholars and thinkers to "do theology" is secondary. The fundamental "theological reflection" is the revolutionary action carried out by activists involved in radical praxis, especially by members of the Basic Christian Communities, the movement's vanguard in liberationist mythology. "The primary *situation* of theological reflection as an historical phenomenon is neither the seminary nor the university, but the basic Christian community," says Fr. Thomas Clarke.[767]

Father Hug adds, "The theological reflection we're considering here is coming from the streets, from shacks, from the living rooms where small communities and coalitions are being drawn together by the struggle for justice."[768]

f. Organic Intellectuals of Socio-Ecclesial Revolution

Liberation theologians maintain they are only "organic intellectuals," an expression coined in the early 1930s by Italian communist thinker Antonio Gramsci (1891–1937) and assumed by liberation theology in a slightly modified sense.[769] In contrast

---

762. Juan José Tamayo-Acosta, "Evolución histórica de los movimientos," *Misión Abierta* (Madrid) 77, no. 2 (Apr. 1984): 69. Born in 1946, Tamayo-Acosta became secretary general of the John XXIII Association of Theologians, which gathers the extreme left of Spanish and Latin American theologians. He is a professor at Madrid's Carlos III University and writes for the Geneva-based *MicroMega* magazine, directed by Paolo Flores d'Arcais.

763. Hennelly, *Theology for a Liberating Church*, 63.

764. Boff and Boff, *Como fazer teologia da libertação*, 34.

765. Gutiérrez, *A Theology of Liberation*, back cover.

766. McAfee Brown, "Preferential Option for the Poor," 16.

767. Clarke, "A New Way," 32.

768. Hug, *Tracing the Spirit*, 2.

769. See *Dizionario dei termini marxisti*, 170–71, s.v. "Organic and traditional intellectuals." In *Notebook from Prison 12*, Gramsci poses the question of whether famous intellectuals constitute an autonomous group or whether each social group has its own intellectual class. Gramsci distinguishes two different types of intellectuals coming from different historical traditions. On the one hand, each class produces

with armchair intellectuals, who elaborate their doctrines behind closed doors, completely detached from current revolutionary processes, the organic intellectuals of liberation theology would be those immersed and actually taking part in the liberation struggle. Their job would be merely to theorize on revolutionary struggles, which would be the fundamental activity and criterion of their theological endeavors.

"The liberation theologian," Leonardo and Clodovis Boff explain, "is not an armchair intellectual. Rather, he is an 'organic intellectual,' a 'militant theologian' who positions himself within the march of the People of God. ...*Yes, h*e keeps one foot in a center of reflection and another in the community's life. This, indeed, is his right foot."[770]

For his part, Robert McAfee Brown writes, "Liberation theology is a theology of the people, a by-product of the ongoing struggle of the poor to overcome oppression, rather than a theology of the experts crafted in quiet libraries and then offered to 'the masses.'"[771]

9. LT: A Collective Discernment of God's Actions

a. The Community's Experience, a Source of Theology

To close this analysis of the foundations of LT we should note that in its mentors' view, LT is not so much a task of individuals as a collective enterprise to be pursued by the community of faithful and, within this community, by those more actively engaged in revolutionary praxis. This is an extreme consequence of LT's egalitarian stance. Unwilling to recognize the least hierarchy among men, liberation theologians claim that it does not arise from the intellectual effort of learned individuals but from the praxis of an anonymous collectivity, the *community*. "Liberation theologies," observes Fr. Robert Schreiter, Dean of the Catholic Theological Union in Chicago,

> emphasize the role of the entire believing community in the development of a local theology.
> ...[He further explains that LT] mak[es] the community itself the prime author of theology.[772]

This "theology" is not an intellectual endeavor. Instead it would be the community's discernment of God's actions in its midst and in the historical processes it is involved in, as well as shared commentaries on such situations. The role of the professional theologians as organic intellectuals would be merely to help shape the commentaries.

Immanent divine action, liberation theologians contend, shapes the experience of the community, determining the interior life of its members and their sociopolitical involvement. By incorrectly taking that experience as public revelation, LT deems it an indispensable source of theology. Father Schreiter writes, "The whole community of faith, whose experience is the indispensable source of theology."[773]

b. The Role of Radical Minorities

In LT's egalitarian logic, that immanent divine action animates the entire community of faithful. Each individual believer would thus be able to theologize on his experience. However, that is not what happens in practice. Liberation theologians conceive history as an ongoing revolutionary process impelled by liberating struggles of the oppressed against oppressive structures, a process that inexorably advances toward an egalitarian and liberationist utopia. They claim that God reveals Himself primarily through these struggles, of which He is said to be the driving force.

This immanent revelation, therefore, would be particularly felt by those more radical activists in the vanguard of the revolutionary process. Their militant experience would be most in line with God's designs in history. They would thus play a preponderant role in shaping LT. Father Schreiter comments, "It is helpful to make a distinction between the role of the whole community of the faithful ...and the role of smaller groups within the community that actually give shape to that theology."[774]

c. Prophets, the Radical Minorities' Tip of the Spear

However, liberation theologians continue, within the radical minorities there are persons with greater fervor, a stronger revolutionary spirit, a clearer discernment of the revolutionary utopia, a more vibrant zeal in pursuing revolutionary struggles. Within the vanguard, they are the tip of the spear. In LT language, they are *prophets*.

They have a special charisma to understand the ways of the Revolution, that is, God's liberating actions in history. They are better able to capture the profound meaning of the community's experience and lead it toward utopia, playing a major role in shaping the community's theology. "More recent research into oral traditions indicates that it is individuals capturing the spirit of those communities who do the actual shaping [of theology]," Father Schreiter says. He concludes, "Is not the voice of the prophet and the praxis of the prophetic community all we need?"[775]

Thus, after having refused the public revelation, reneged on Tradition, and repudiated the Magisterium of the Church, finding themselves light years away from traditional theology, liberation theologians find their privileged locus theologicus in revolutionary struggles of radical minorities led by fanatical leaders, by mediums who galvanize and disseminate "liberating energies," and by gurus prized as bearers of special charismas and praised as prophets of the revolutionary utopia.

Quomodo obscuratum est aurum! (How is the gold become dim.)[776]

its own intellectuals, who play a specific role in the social and political hegemony of their class. Gramsci calls them "organic intellectuals." This contrasts with the position of intellectuals not directly linked to a class: writers, artists, philosophers, scientists. These, according to Gramsci, are "traditional intellectuals." See L. Tornatore, P.A. Ferrisi, and G. Polizzi, *La filosofia attraverso i testi: Profili, temi, autori* (Bologna: Loescher Editore, 1996), 3.2:606–20.

770. Boff and Boff, *Como fazer teologia da libertação*, 34.
771. Robert McAfee Brown, "After Ten Years," preface to *The Power of the Poor*, by Gustavo Gutiérrez (Maryknoll, N.Y.: Orbis Books, 1983), vi.
772. Robert J. Schreiter, C.PP.S., *Constructing Local Theologies* (Maryknoll, N.Y.: Orbis Books, 1985), 16–18, with a foreword by Fr. Edward Schillebeeckx, O.P. A similar view is expressed by the Cuban-American feminist liberation theologian Ada María Isasi-Díaz. "The community of struggle," she says, "is the one that does theology, and not individuals who are not intrinsic members of the community." Ada María Isasi-Díaz, "Mujeristas: A Name of Our Own," in *The Future of Liberation Theology: Essays in Honor of Gustavo Gutiérrez*, ed. Marc H. Ellis and Otto Maduro (Maryknoll, N.Y.: Orbis Books, 1989), 413.

773. Schreiter, *Constructing Local Theologies,* 17.
774. Schreiter, 17.
775. Schreiter, 17, 18.
776. Lam. 4:1.

Chapter 4:
The Doctrinal Core of Liberation Theology

A. Transcendence and Immanence

1. Defining Concepts

This chapter will deal with the doctrinal core of LT: immanentism. As the matter touches on delicate theological grounds, to facilitate the reading we must first define some basic concepts.

"Etymologically," the term *immanent* (from the Latin *in manere*, to stay inside), "means that which dwells or remains within something." Philosophically, it means that which resides in being and has its own beginning and end in itself. In everyday language, it is equivalent to *interior* or *inherent*.[777]

Philosophy distinguishes between immanent and transitive actions. An immanent action is "that which finds within the very subject in which it dwells its entire foundation, nourishment, and the outcome of its development."[778] In other words, it is an action that begins, develops, and ends entirely within the agent, without producing any external effect. For example, thinking. The opposite is a *transitive* action, that which produces an effect external to the agent. In other words, it is an action that begins within a being and passes to another. For example, hammering in a nail.[779]

The acts through which God the Father generates God the Son and Their loving relations produce God the Holy Spirit, that is, the Trinitarian circuminsession (*perichoresis*), are immanent actions because the Son and the Holy Spirit are one with the Father. On the contrary, the act through which God created the universe was a transitive action. He did not create the universe from His own substance or within Himself. He created it *ex nihilo*—out of nothing—and *ad extra*—externally.[780]

Likewise, something is said to be immanent to a being when it does not result from an external action; that is, when it is not caused by the intervention of an agent other than himself. When

there is an outside intervention, the cause is said to be transitive, that is, other in relation to the being upon which it acts. When this transitive cause is also superior, it is said to be *transcendent*.

2. God's Presence in Creation

Catholic doctrine teaches that God is both immanent to and transcendent from the created universe.

Something can be present in a being or place in three ways:

— by presence, vision, or knowledge: as students are present before the professor looking at them from his rostrum;

— by potentiality, influence, or power: when the influence of a being is felt even when it is not materially present, like a king's authority is present throughout the kingdom;

— by essence or substance: when something is really present in the place.

God is present in all creation in this triple way. By knowledge, because nothing escapes His attention; by potentiality, because everything is subject to His power; by essence, because He is in all things as the cause, governor, and sustainer of their being.[781]

St. Thomas devotes a whole section of the *Summa theologiae* to the *praesentia Dei in rebus*. He explains that "God is in all things; not, indeed, as part of their essence, nor as an accident, but as an agent is present to that upon which it works."[782] God not only created things out of nothing, that is, He gave them the totality of their being, but He also sustains them. Created things are beings *per accidens* and by participation in the Being *per se* (see Is. 45:5). They need to be constantly sustained by God so as not to revert into nothing. Since any action in God is indistinguishable from His essence, He is really present in all things through the divine action that maintains them in their existence.[783]

Similarly, God is really present in everything through the divine action that governs creation (Divine Providence). These two actions, as any *ad extra* action of God, are formally immanent but virtually transitive. There are also special forms of presence of God in the universe, as the renowned Spanish Dominican theologian Fr. Antonio Royo Marin explains:

— The hypostatic or personal presence that unites Our Lord's human nature to the second Person of the Holy Trinity;

— The sacramental or Eucharistic presence, by which God is really present in the Eucharistic species by virtue of the transubstantiation;

— The indwelling presence in the souls of the just through grace, which is a participation in the Divine life;

777. Centro di Studi Filosofici di Gallarate, *Enciclopedia filosofica*, 4 vols. (Venice-Rome: Istituto per la Collaborazione Culturale, 1957), 2:1276 and 4:128.

778. Valensin, s.v. "Immanence (Doctrine de l')," *D.A.F.C.*, 2:569.

779. In the *Summa theologiae*, the Angelic Doctor explains, "There is a twofold class of action; one which passes out to something beyond, and causes passion in it, as burning and cutting; and another which does not pass outwards, but which remains within the agent, as to feel, to understand, to will; by such actions nothing outside is changed, but the whole action takes place within the agent." Saint Thomas Aquinas, *Summa theologiae*, I, q. 54, a. 2. See André Lalande, *Vocabulaire technique et critique de la philosophie* (Paris: Presses Universitaires de France, 1956), 470–71; Abbé Bergier, *Dictionnaire de théologie* (Paris: Leroux et Jouby, n.d.), 348; J. Bricourt, ed., *Dictionnaire pratique des connaissances religieuses* (Paris: Letouzey et Ané, 1926), 3:920–21.

780. Scholastic theology qualifies the creative act (as indeed all *ad extra* acts of God) as formally immanent (*formaliter immanens*) and virtually transitive (*virtualiter transiens*). "Formally" refers to the form of the act, that is, the act itself. "Virtually" refers to that which is predetermined in God, even though it does not yet appear externally, and contains all the conditions proper to its action. See A. Michel, s.v. "Virtuel, virtuellement," *D.T.C.*, 15-2e:3097–98. In God, actions are identical to His essence, since it would otherwise mean He would have accidents. Thus the creative act is formally immanent; it is in itself identical to the divine essence. Now, as it had external effects, it must also be considered transitive. It cannot be formally transitive, since this would imply an emanation of the divine essence, passing from the agent (God) to the creatures through the creative act. It can, therefore, be only virtually transitive. See Réginald Garrigou-Lagrange, O.P., *Dieu: Son existence et sa nature* (Paris: Beauchesne, 1950), 465–68; H. Pinard, s.v. "Création," *D.T.C.*, 3–2e:2134–35.

781. See Aquinas, *S.T.*, I, q. 8. See also Antonio Royo Marín, O.P., *Dios y su obra* (Madrid: Biblioteca de Autores Cristianos, 1968), 81–86.

782. Aquinas, *S.T.*, I, q. 8, a. 1.

783. See Garrigou-Lagrange, *Dieu: Son existence*, 783–90.

—The presence of vision or manifestation, which is reserved to Heaven, where the saints contemplate God in the beatific vision.[784]

Notwithstanding this immanence of God in creation, Catholic doctrine teaches that, having created the universe from nothing, God remains infinitely different (other) and transcendent from creation. His substance can never be confused with that of the universe, nor can His actions be considered as immanent in it.[785]

Thus, Catholic theology defines God's transcendence as "the attribute whereby God is conceived as a personal Being, absolutely independent from the universe He created through an act of free will."[786]

The *Enciclopedia cattolica* explains this point: "God enjoys his perfect life in and of Himself (Trinity), before and without the creature (free creation in time), so that the distinction between the two lives, the divine and the human, between the finite and infinite perfection, is not quantitative, of degrees (one universal, in time and space, the other particular, in a limited area) but contains an absolute difference in quality (time-eternity, being by participation, being by essence)."[787]

Any confusion on this crucial point would blur the distinction between God and creation, leading to forms of immanentism, whereby God is conceived as immersed in history and indistinguishable from it (historicist immanentism), or (a deeper degree of immanentism) as immersed in and indistinguishable from the cosmos (pantheism).

B. The Rejection of Transcendence

It was precisely in this domain that the early twentieth century modernists worked hardest to alter Catholic theology, knowing that once this point was changed the whole edifice would implode. They created a slippery confusion surrounding the notion of immanence and its theological and philosophical implications by using the term in ever broader meanings without ever buttressing it with the classical scholastic distinctions, which they mocked as intellectualism. Fueled by its own internal dynamism, this confusion tended to blur the distinction between God and creation, ultimately paving the way for pantheism.[788]

In the encyclical *Pascendi*, against the modernists, St. Pius X distinguishes three degrees of immanentism:

Concerning *immanence* it is not easy to determine what modernists mean by it, for their own opinions on the subject vary. Some understand it in the sense that God working in man is more intimately present in him than man is even in himself, and this conception, if properly understood, is free from reproach. Others hold that the divine action is one with the action of nature, as the action of the first cause is one with the action of the secondary cause, and this would destroy the supernatural order. Others, finally, explain it in a way which savors of pantheism, and this, in truth, is the sense which tallies best with the rest of their doctrines.[789]

Liberation theologians resumed the modernists' ambiguity, going several steps further. Early versions of LT, notably the Latin American variety, fell into the second category of immanentism denounced by St. Pius X, particularly into historicist immanentism.[790] Other, more up-to-date versions take that error to its last consequences, broaching on the third degree, namely, pantheism.

As we saw in the previous chapter, LT eschews supernatural revelation and Tradition and turns instead to personal experience and evolving historical processes in search of "God's word."[791] It thus tends to erase the idea of a transcendent God, a God essentially extrinsic to creation.

"Classical conceptions of God," Robert McAfee Brown writes, analyzing LT,

depict Him ... as all-powerful, all-knowing, and far removed from earth—"transcendent" is the term usually used.

[Brown impugns this transcendent conception and proposes instead a God immanent in revolutionary struggles of the poor or oppressed.] By contrast, or at least by way of supplement, the God of those committed to a preferential option for the poor is a God unalterably committed to the cause of the poor. ...

... So if [liberation theologians] are asked, "Where is God to be found?" they will answer, "Look among the poor, look at where the oppressed are struggling for their liberation."[792]

This was a central issue at the Theology in the Americas Conference held in Detroit in 1975. For the first time ever, the conference gathered the most notorious Latin American liberation theologians with their American colleagues. It was the inaugural event of the Theology in the Americas Project, an ongoing movement seeking to develop new versions of liberation theology.

"What took place at the conference was a clash between two views of divine transcendence," comments Council peritus Gregory Baum. A conference participant, Baum thus describes the problem at hand: "Traditional piety ... visualized God as the supreme Lord over and above human history. This God was available to believers as they reached out to him, inwardly or upwardly, beyond the actual, historical situation in which they lived. God's transcendence was here unrelated to history. ... Contrary to this, the spirituality associated with many forms of contemporary theology holds that God's transcendence is mediated in and through history. ... The transcendent divine mystery is immanent in human life and the cosmos."[793]

By speaking of a divine immanence no longer only in human life and history but also in the cosmos, Baum shows how slippery

784. See Royo Marín, *Dios y su obra*, 86.

785. See Aquinas, *S.T.*, I, q. 3, a. 8.

786. Régis Jolivet, *Vocabulaire de la philosophie* (Paris: Emmanuel Vitte, 1946), 187.

787. Cornelio Fabro, s.v. "Immanenza," *E.C.*, 6:1675.

788. "Metaphysical immanentism strictly speaking is pantheistic in tendency" rightly observes Swiss Jesuit Fr. Peter Henrici. Peter Henrici, s.v. "Immanentism," *Sacramentum Mundi: An Encyclopedia of Theology* (New York: Herder and Herder, 1969), 3:107.

789. St. Pius X, encyclical *Pascendi*, no. 19.

790. In the sort of 1988 *mea culpa* Fr. Gutiérrez made trying to explain LT in the light of the Vatican documents *Libertatis Nuntius* and *Libertatis Conscientia*, he strongly defends himself from the accusation of immanence: "There is no slightest tinge of immanentism in this approach to integral liberation. But if any expression I have used may have given the impression that there is, I want to say here as forcefully as I can that any interpretation along those lines is incompatible with my position." Gustavo Gutiérrez, *A Theology of Liberation: History, Politics, and Salvation,* trans. and ed. by Caridad Inda and John Eagleson, rev. ed. with a new introduction (Maryknoll, N.Y.: Orbis Books, 1988), xxxix. Too bad, though, that written words remain. Without a precise disavowal of his original thesis, it is difficult for Fr. Gutiérrez to escape the charge of historicist immanentism.

791. Feminist liberation theologian Sharon Welch openly confesses, "I will not attempt an exploration of liberation theology's reliance on the authority of tradition and of scripture, but merely present my reasons for avoiding those authorities." Welch, *Communities of Resistance*, 25.

792. McAfee Brown, "Preferential Option for the Poor," 10–11.

793. Gregory Baum, "The Christian Left at Detroit," in *Theology in the Americas: Detroit 1975*, ed. Sergio Torres and John Eagleson (New York: Orbis Books, 1976),

historicist immanentism is, and how easily it leads to conceptions that broach on pantheism.

Impelled by their internal logic, some liberation theologians take their doctrines beyond historicist immanentism. For example, after asserting that God should be sought in "Black experience," "Black history," and "Black culture," almost as if He were an internal energy driving the liberation of the black people, James Cone, the ideologue of black liberation, admits the consequences of his doctrine: "I am aware of possible pantheistic distortion of my analysis. But this risk must be taken."[794]

To understand better LT's immanentist stance, it is well to take a quick look at its doctrinal core before analyzing the several areas in which this immanentism shows.

C. The Foundations of LT's Immanentism

Liberation theologians are skilled. Only rarely do they clarify the more controversial aspects of their views concerning immanentism. Gregory Baum, for one, offers some elucidating insights in his book *Religion and Alienation*: "Sociological tradition contains basic truth absent from philosophical and theological thought, truth that actually modifies the very meaning of philosophy and theology."[795]

1. LT Is Influenced by a Rejection of the Idea of a Transcendent and Personal God

Baum turns to "young Hegel"[796] for a basic "truth" said to have influenced some strains of modern theology: "The radicalism of the young Hegel, especially his analysis of religion and alienation, remains of lasting interest to contemporary theologians." Inspired by Hegel, Baum continues, "A growing number of them have come to speak of god, and listen to god, as the non-objectified and non-objectifiable mystery present in people's lives."[797]

What truth did contemporary liberation theologians learn from Hegel? It is precisely the refusal to consider God as a transcendent Being, replacing Him instead with the experience of an immanent god.

Baum contends that Hegel "anticipate[d] the radical rejection of extrinsicism in Christian theology"[798] and "anticipated modern theological literature, arguing against traditional theism, against the outsider God, the God over and above history, the God out there."[799] Of course, the refusal of a transcendent God is not exclusive to Hegel. He chose Hegel only because the German philosopher, in Baum's judgment, explains the roots of immanentism in a clear and logical way. One can almost say that Baum uses Hegel to expound some of the most profound principles of LT, of which he is a standard-bearer.

According to Baum, the idea of "an infinite being over and above the finite world, extrinsic to and apart from human life and history," would make God a "divine stranger in the heavens, who rule[s] the earth and its peoples from above."[800] This conception, he continues, is dangerous because it sees God as an object, that is to say, as an extrinsic Person, another, different, and transcendent in relation to man and creation.

2. Genesis of the Idea of a Transcendent God

What are, in Gregory Baum's view, the psychological foundations of this transcendent idea of God? What was its historical genesis? What is the origin of the "alienating" notion of God as a Person, a superior Being extrinsic to man, Creator, Ruler, and Model?

a. A Primitive Community Life of Reconciliation and Love

Baum espouses the idea of a mythic primeval stage of human history when men lived in perfect "reconciliation," which he interprets as the absence of "structures of domination" "and separation." In other words, a thoroughly egalitarian state of affairs in which men lived a communitarian life.

(i) Reconciliation With Human Instincts

In this mythical early stage, man felt no internal conflict with his natural instincts. He was "in touch with [his] own depth and ... reconciled to the sources of [his] vitality"[801] and in perfect harmony with them. In other words, man considered the spontaneous manifestation of his instincts as normal, without fearing the destructive consequences that the outflows of the passions normally produce. Man was not internally divided.

(ii) Reconciliation With One's Fellowmen

In Baum's view, primitive man was not only "reconciled" with himself and his physical vitality but also with his neighbor, in a relationship based on "love," which prevented the rise of "antagonistic groups and classes."[802] Primitive man manifested a naturally unselfish impulse to share. In that primitive society, perfect fraternity reigned within absolute equality. It was a sort of idyllic communist society.

(iii) Reconciliation With Nature

According to this myth, man was also "reconciled" with nature, over which he did not exert "domination" but a "creativity in nature inspired by confidence."[803] Man did not fear nature as he now does, nor did he wish to dominate it, using it for personal gain. He was nature's "brother" and lived in perfect harmony with it. He did not seek "the false self-elevation of man over nature."[804]

(iv) Rejection of Reason

Early man eschewed reason as discriminatory and divisive: "Reflection objectifies life and hence ... inevitably falsifies life and becomes estranged from it. ... Life must be lived, not thought. Thinking negates life."[805] According to this view, primitive man based his life not on a governing reason but on a unifying "love," on the free manifestation of communitarian yearnings stemming from his innermost instincts: "Human life [was] unified through loving."[806]

417–18.

794. Cone, *A Black Theology*, 30.

795. Baum, *Religion and Alienation*, 1. See also Gregory Baum, *Man Becoming: God in Secular Language* (New York: Herder and Herder, 1970), 170ff.

796. Baum, *Religion and Alienation*, 7. Georg Friedrich Hegel (1770–1831). Baum examines above all his *Theologische jugendscriften*, written in Frankfurt, between 1794 and 1800. It is interesting to note how Baum uses Hegel to justify the immanentism of some contemporary theological schools, and particularly LT. Baum says that he drew inspiration from the essay by P. Asveld, *La pensée religieuse du jeune Hegel: Liberté et aliénation* (Louvain: Publ. Universitaire de Louvain, 1953), and also from the book by B. Bourgeois, *Hegel à Francfort* (Paris: J. Vris, 1970). See also Paul Cobben and P. Crusyusberghis, eds., s.v. "Pantheismus," *Hegel-lexikon* (Darmstadt: Wissenschaftliche Buchgesellschaft, 2006), 345.

797. Baum, *Religion and Alienation*, 16.

798. Baum, 9.

799. Baum, 7.

800. Baum, 8.

801. Baum, 16.

802. Baum, 14.

803. Baum, 11.

804. Baum, 11.

805. Baum, 7.

806. Baum, 7.

b. The Sensation of an Immanent God

(i) God Found in the Depths of Man and Nature

Immersed in this idyllic community atmosphere, man experienced a profound sensation of communion and fraternity: communion with himself, communion with his fellow men, communion with nature. This overwhelming sensation gave him the experience of the existence of a "divine impulse"[807] that animated the whole cosmos. He identified this indefinable impulse, which consolidated love and reconciliation among beings, with god. Accordingly, god was "a mystery to be encountered in nature, in one's own depth, and in the human community."[808]

Primitive man conceived—or rather felt—god as the "supreme mystery operative within him as source of his life."[809] Man also found god in nature as "a common light shining through human life and the cosmos."[810]

(ii) The Experience of an Immanent God Gives Rise to a "Good Religion"

From this experience of an immanent god, continues Baum in his search for the "truth" contained in the works of young Hegel, arose a "good religion"[811] that did not produce "alienation," a religion for which "the divine is present in nature, present in one's own personal depth and in the community at large,"[812] a religion whose god "could never become the object of the mind"[813] but rather a sort of energy to be felt "in love, in action."[814]

c. "Original Sin" in Primitive Society

(i) A Mysterious Original Sin

At a given historical moment, which neither Baum nor Hegel specify, there would have been a deplorable "refusal to love and to live a reconciled life."[815] As a consequence of this mysterious pseudo-original sin in the primitive communitarian society, man was torn apart by a series of internal lacerations and disruptions in relations with his fellow men and nature. With the defeat of "love" and "communion," the "structures of domination" and "[those] of separation"[816] gradually prevailed. This disruptive process ultimately conditioned his very experience of god.

(ii) Internal Disruption

As a consequence of this pseudo-original sin, man felt "estranged from [his] own depth,"[817] unable to "look for an inner harmony."[818] In other words, he began to feel an internal conflict with his instincts. He became "estranged … from himself."[819]

(iii) Man Appeals to Reason

Internally torn apart, man felt the need to appeal to a coercive and ordering principle in order to prevent his own disintegration. He sought this principle in reason. "The inability to love," writes Baum, "made [man] regard reason as the highest faculty."[820] Man thus submitted his other faculties and instincts to the rule of this kind of interior divinity called reason. Referring to Hegel, Baum asserts that this recourse to reason "severs [man] from the sources of life."[821]

(iv) Disruption in Society

The "refusal to love and to live a reconciled life,"[822] according to this myth, made men selfish and hostile, divided into antagonistic classes and groups. The "freedom that unites [man] with others and with the world"[823] became unattainable. With this, fraternity within equality ended. Just as individual man was forced to appeal to the authority of reason to order himself interiorly, he had to appeal to the authority of lords and masters to establish order in society. Hierarchy thus appeared.

(v) Disruption in Man's Relationship With Nature

Having vanished from human relationships, "reconciliation" also disappeared from man's relations with nature. Instead of "exercising [a] creativity … inspired by confidence, people began to oscillate between the fear of nature and the desire to dominate it."[824] Man began trying to exert on nature the same domination that reason exerted internally on his passions and the ruling classes exerted externally on human society.

d. Disrupted Man Creates the Idea of a Transcendent God

(i) Man Appeals to the Ordering Power of a Transcendent God

Human reason, deformed by the dominion it exerted over the passions and by the emergence of a hierarchical society based on selfishness, then conceived the idea of a transcendent God. This God is said to play in the universe the ordering role that reason played in man's interior and which the ruling classes played in human society. In this way, man's pathological process of alienation would attain a climax.

Baum writes, men "no longer listen to the voice speaking within their lives. They turn to listen to the orders from a stranger who rules from afar. … The light is then sought outside of themselves."[825]

Consequently, Baum says, God was conceived as superior, transcendent, as a Person, Creator, Lord, and Legislator of the universe. Instead of feeling God as an immanent force within him, society, and nature, man "objectif[ied]" the divine."[826] He began to conceive God as "an infinite being over and above the finite world, extrinsic to and apart from human life and history."[827] God became a "stranger and object … *the* almighty supreme being in heaven … the totally other."[828] To Baum, the idea of a transcendent and personal God is nothing but "a human projection compulsively produced out of man's inability to love. Man projects the worst of himself … unto the cosmos."[829]

(ii) This Idea Creates a Bad Religion

The idea of a transcendent and personal God gave rise to a "bad religion,"[830] an alienating religion that legitimates all subjection.[831]

---

807. Baum, 16.
808. Baum, 15.
809. Baum, 9.
810. Baum, 10.
811. Baum, 16.
812. Baum, 16.
813. Baum, 8.
814. Baum, 9.
815. Baum, 13.
816. Baum, 16.
817. Baum, 12.
818. Baum, 12.
819. Baum, 13.
820. Baum, 13.

821. Baum, 7.
822. Baum, 13.
823. Baum, 12.
824. Baum, 11.
825. Baum, 12.
826. Baum, 13.
827. Baum, 8.
828. Baum, 8.
829. Baum, 13.
830. Baum, 13.
831. *Alienation* (in Marxist theory): subjection; a condition of workers in a capitalist economy, resulting from a sense of being subjected, controlled, or exploited.

"Surrounded by his enemies,"[832] writes the German-Canadian liberationist, "man creates for himself a harsh divinity who curses his foes and crushes their strength. He inscribes in his God the image of all his hatreds, and, by doing so, makes for himself a God who protects and promotes his wars, his dominations, his conquests."[833]

3. A Transcendent and Personal God Would Be Alienating and Legitimize Oppression

a. The Transcendent God, Supreme Source of Man's Multiple Alienations

According to Baum, this idea of a personal and transcendent God is "the supreme source of man's multiple alienation[s]."[834] In other words, this transcendent God would not only be an alienating, oppressor God who establishes a "master-slave relationship"[835] with man, but also the source of all other "oppressions" that befall man. He would be a "bad infinity"[836] sowing evil and sorrow throughout the universe. It is this bad infinity, Baum concludes, following the young Hegel, that gives rise to "the manifold alienations of human life."[837]

b. A Transcendent God Would Legitimize Oppression in Society

Thus, to conceive of God as an infinitely good Father would justify the authority of all fathers and, indeed, of any legitimate authority; to conceive of Him as an infinitely perfect Lord would uphold the position of legitimate overlords in every sphere; to conceive of Him as an infinitely wise legislator would sanction the legitimacy and necessity of law, coercion, and the punishment of transgressors. Baum highlights the political consequences of such theological views: "Alienating religion ... divides the human family into rulers and the ruled."[838] The division occurs not just in the religious sphere but also in the sociopolitical realm.[839] "The bad infinity," Baum explains, "undermines the unity of the human family. ... [p]rotects the failure of love."[840] He concludes, "God as object and stranger becomes the legitimating symbol for all regimes of domination."[841]

4. Liberation: Uprooting the Idea of a Transcendent God

a. Deliverance From the Transcendent God

If the idea of a transcendent and personal God is alienating and a consequence of previous alienations, the "liberation" sought by LT must necessarily entail the uprooting of this idea. Following Baum's logic and the latest versions of LT, the destruction of this transcendent concept of God will not come through a rational

endeavor but through the promotion of communitarian forms of life founded on love and reconciliation. "The deliverance from this projection," he writes, "is not offered by an effort of the mind ... but by a life of love, sacrifice and reconciliation."[842]

Man would then experience once more the feeling of a "good infinity [that] could not be conceptualized"[843] and would be sought "in a life dedicated to overcoming the contradictions in human existence."[844] Indeed, if God is not an extrinsic Being, a Person that man can rationally know, but rather an energy immanent in human life, nature, and the cosmos, then the way of "knowing" him would be through connaturality, feeling.

b. A Totally Liberated Society

When this sensation of an immanent god becomes part of people's mentalities, giving rise to a new religion and thus to a new society, in Baum's words it will produce "a breakthrough to a non-alienating human life,"[845] that is, to a society in which all "oppression" is finally destroyed. While traditional religion was a source of alienation in society, the new immanentist religion will save "people from the cleavages and contradictions of their society."[846] It is implied that the new society will necessarily be egalitarian and liberal, since all hierarchy and constraints are considered oppressive.

In search of complete liberation, some theologians have taken this "de-alienating"[847] logic to its ultimate consequences. For them, the quest for a "non-alienating human life"[848] includes not only sociopolitical and cultural structures but also moral patterns and examples. According to Baum, they seek to free people from "alienation ... from their body and sexuality."[849]

In other words, the present moral norms that "alienate," that is, estrange men from the licentious use of their own bodies and sexuality would have to disappear. The rules imposed by a morality founded on a transcendent and legislator God, as well as in nature itself, would no longer be understood by a humanity finally "liberated" from all "alienation," including sexual alienation. Thus, in the view of the former Augustinian friar, the idea of an immanent god would somehow lead to man's complete "liberation."

◆   ❖   ◆

In the preceding pages we outlined the foundations of LT's immanentism: the idea that a transcendent God is the result of a fundamental alienation that in turn legitimizes all "oppression." We analyzed LT's consequent call for a total "liberation" that entails the destruction of that idea. What exactly do liberation theologians understand by a non-alienating god, though? We shall answer this question first from the perspective of some up-to-date versions of LT and then expound the Latin American versions that preceded them.

---

832. Baum, *Religion and Alienation*, 11.

833. Baum, 11.

834. Baum, 8.

835. Baum, 15.

836. Baum, 8.

837. Baum, 8.

838. Baum, 15.

839. We find the same idea expressed by Belgian priest Fr. Joseph Comblin, a well-known figure in the international LT movement who was expelled from Brazil in 1969 for his subversive actions. He writes, "There is a certain monotheistic God who serves as the foundation and support of all kinds of domination: that of the father, the teacher, the master, the owner, the State, and the army. This God is a God of power, and He sacralizes all power. He is the God of the ego, the God which the ego discovers within as the source of a more expansive and bloated social ego or as the projection of an oppressive super ego." Joseph Comblin, "What Sort of Services Might Theology Render," in *Frontiers of Theology in Latin America*, ed. Rosino Gibellini, trans. John Drury (Maryknoll, N.Y.: Orbis Books, 1979), 70.

840. Baum, *Religion and Alienation*, 14.

841. Baum, 15.

842. Baum, 14.

843. Baum, 8.

844. Baum, 9.

845. Baum, 9.

846. Baum, 9.

847. Baum, 16.

848. Baum, 9.

849. Baum, 12.

D. God, an Energy Pulsating in the Cosmos

Gregory Baum's reflections above are from 1975, when the Theology in the Americas conference was held in Detroit. Since then, several LT currents have advanced further along these lines, developing more radical consequences from their immanentist postulates. Before speaking about ecofeminist and indigenous theologies, which are specifically addressed in chapter 8, we will see how, in their efforts to develop a liberation theology in the developed world, theologians like Frs. Matthew Fox, James Hug, Thomas Berry, and layman Joe (Joseph Edward) Holland have gone well beyond the historicist immanentism of early LT versions and taken positions bordering on pantheism.

1. Blurring the Idea of a Creation *Ex Nihilo*

In a pastoral handbook for use by American Basic Christian Communities, Father Hug, of Georgetown University's Woodstock Theological Center, director of the Center of Concern and a conspicuous promoter of LT in the United States, describes the universe as a never-ending pulsation of "human-divine energies" that make it difficult to distinguish god from the cosmos.

"At the beginning of the cosmos" he writes, "[there was] the unleashing of unbelievable energy. Energy expanding through spaces and periods of time that stretch the limits of human imagining. ... [Energy] flowing within us, around us, among us." Father Hug identifies this mysterious energy with god: "Energy ... is ... an active name for god."[850]

Echoing Bergson, Father Hug tends to efface the idea of a creation *ex nihilo* (out of nothing), and therefore *ad extra* (externally), suggesting the creation was the explosion and subsequent expansion of the divine essence, so that creatures have a divine origin. Indeed, not even the idea of an explicit creation is present here. For Father Hug, the beginning of the universe was merely the "unleashing of unbelievable energy," an energy which, as we shall see, he identifies at times with god, at other times with the cosmos.

The Jesuit theologian seems to assume—following schools of undeniable pantheistic savor[851]—that in the beginning there was a packet of unlimited energy. At a particular moment, this packet exploded, disintegrating into myriads of tiny particles that constituted individuated beings. The explosion also unleashed an "unbelievable energy," whose surges of expansion and contraction would account for the movements of the universe. In other words, all beings would be like cells enclosing a bit of divine substance, bearers of divine particles totally submerged in an ever-flowing energy also of divine origin, like drops of water in the ocean.

2. "Energy: The Soul of All That Is and Is Becoming"

According to Father Hug, this energy would be the very source of life, of dynamism and creativity in the universe, the soul of all that exists: "Energy, the dynamism of life, generating creativity and hope. Energy, the vibrant soul of all that is and is becoming."[852]

3. Energy: An Active Name for God

The American theologian identifies this mysterious energy with god: "Energy ... is ... an active name for god." God would be a sort of fluid circulating inside human beings, social processes, nature and, indeed, throughout the cosmos. This energy would be the driving force of history, the vector of all spiritual and social processes:

> Human history and contemporary society are the legacy of the convergencies and clashes of these energies. ...
> ... Our interior energies are integral to and inseparable from the energies and movements that constitute our universe.[853]

4. Creation Is Like "Sexual Communion"

In a paper presented at the Conference of Major Superiors of Men held in Atlanta in August 1984 and published one year later by the Center of Concern, Joe Holland—a leading promoter of LT, which he qualifies as postmodern theology—also delves into its immanentist aspects and touches upon the question of creation *ad extra*.[854]

Holland's approach to the problem of immanence begins with an analysis of the knowledge process. In the classical theory of knowledge, the subject intellectually apprehends the idea of the object he is knowing and stores it in his mind. The knowing subject is distinct from the known object. Philosophy calls this the subject-object split.[855]

According to Holland, however, this clear distinction between the knowing subject and known object is wrong and harmful because it sunders a supposed unity of all beings in the universe, which he calls "primeval communion." This split would be the root of all evil since it detaches man from the "natural community." Beings separate when some are treated as objects. Thus, knowledge becomes "structured in a model of domination," Holland concludes.[856] The knowing subject would dominate the known object, and any domination is bad.

These versions of LT take egalitarianism to an absurd degree. That a human being—the subject—can feel his otherness from the object of his knowledge and dominate it by comprehending its idea is labeled *oppression*!

Joseph Holland proposes a different path to knowledge that "is not an act of cognitive external dominance, a kind of master/slave relationship between the knowing and the known, but rather ... an act of loving communion." It would be knowledge by connaturality. The subject feels united to the object because somehow it is already inside him, and vice-versa.

Thus, knowing becomes more a discerning of the other's presence inside oneself than the actual intellectual apprehension of an extrinsic being. Holland likens this immanentist knowledge, where the subject is inside the object and vice-versa, to "sexual communion."[857] Applying this theory to creation, Holland affirms that the creative act was a sexual communion between god and his creatures. In other words, here, too, there is no subject-object split, no sharp differentiation between a creator god and his created

850. Hug and Scherschel, *Social Revelation*, 1.
851. It is not difficult to identify in Fr. Hug's writings, as well as those of other liberation theologians, the looming influence of the late French Jesuit Pierre Teilhard de Chardin (1881–1955), whose pantheistic doctrines were twice condemned by the Holy See. See the Holy Office's *Monitum* of June 30, 1962. Sacred Congregation of the Holy Office, "Warning Regarding the Writings of Fr. Teilhard de Chardin" (June 30, 1962). The French theologian stated, "I have always had a naturally pantheistic soul." Pierre Teilhard de Chardin, *Hymne de l'univers* (Paris: Éditions du Seuil, 1961), 56. That did not prevent Fr. de Lubac from publicly defending his confrere, defying the Holy See.
852. Hug and Scherschel, *Social Revelation*, 1.
853. Hug and Scherschel, 1, 20.
854. See Joe Holland, *The Post Modern Cultural Earthquake* (Washington, D.C.: Center of Concern, 1985).
855. See Holland, *Post Modern Cultural Earthquake*, 5.
856. Holland, 6, 5.
857. Holland, 6.

beings. Rather, the creatures are taken to be already somehow inside god's substance and vice-versa.[858]

5. "An Immanent Divine Mind": God's Governance of the Universe

In the wake of this extreme immanentism, postmodern liberation theologians obviously conceive God's governance of the universe in an erroneous way. For them, the universe is not ruled by an extrinsic Being that governs it through virtually transitive actions, without confounding Himself with it. Instead, the universe is self-governed by an immanent divine mind permeating the cosmos.

Holland admits that the order of the universe is not random but clearly shows the action of a mind. He refuses to identify that mind, however, with the One True God. According to him, this mind is not external to the universe: "[It is] not a mind outside matter, but a mind within matter. ... The universe is ... a great and creative thought."[859]

Following in the footsteps of Fr. Teilhard de Chardin, Holland sees the universe as a "living web." The cosmos is conceived as being animated by a divine mind of its own. God is not seen as a Person Whom man can rationally know, but as the immanent mind of the universe, a force to be felt, an energy flowing everywhere. "The mind is deeply immanent within the universe. ... We experience it not by going outside the world, but by going deeper into it."[860]

E. An Immanent Revelation

1. "God Is Found in the Depth of the World"

Holland's last sentence takes us back to the idea of an immanent revelation.

If god is an energy pulsating in the cosmos that propels psychological, social, and historical processes, then discerning that energy becomes revelation.[861] God, according to Holland, is revealed within the universe.

> We do not know god outside of creation; we know god through creation. ...
> God is found in the depth of the world.[862]

He calls this discovery of god in the depth of the world a sub-natural revelation: "We might describe the 'supernatural' revelation of Jesus in this sense as a sub-natural 'revelation.' It does not come from outside nature. Rather it comes from deeper within nature than nature itself."[863] He concludes that the deeper we delve into nature, the more we approach god.

2. The "Internal Arena of Revelation"

a. The Human Body as Source of Revelation

From this perspective, the human body becomes the first place to know, or rather, to feel god: "Our body ... is a primary place of the disclosure of the mystery."[864]

Elaborating on this point, in another paper Holland states, "We first know god's creative presence in the reality of our own bodies. ... Our own body is our first religious encounter with the mystery expressed in creation. ... [Our body is] our first and abiding encounter with the creative spirit."[865]

This process by which "the spirit does not come down from above to matter but rather the spirit comes out of matter," Holland calls *transcarnation*. It would be revelation "through the flesh, the emergence of the spiritual from the mystical depths of the flesh."[866]

Similar views are held by Franciscan Richard Rohr, head of the Center for Action and Contemplation of Albuquerque, N.M., and a well-known figure in liberationist American circles: "We cannot return to a healthy Jewish and incarnational view of reality until we accept that god has forever made human flesh the privileged place of the divine encounter."[867]

This idea of a revelation being mediated through the flesh, through bodily activity of any kind, has given rise to aberrant versions of LT that take sexual activity—heterosexual as well as homosexual—to be a privileged place where god can be encountered.[868] Here is one foundation of "ecofeminist theology" and "gay theology." Little wonder Holland exclaims, "It has been one of the blessings of the modern sexual revolution to recover our sense of sexual embodiment. Similarly, modern feminist spirituality ... celebrates embodiment."[869]

b. Interior Movements as Source of Revelation

According to this visualization, not only the body but also interior movements of the soul mediate revelation. Father Hug writes:

> God is present and is revealed in our interior movements. ...
> ... Our interior movements are bearers of revelation. ...
> ... [He calls this the] internal, affective, psychological arena of revelation.[870]

3. Ecological Revelation

Consistent with his view of creation as one sole community immersed in divine energy Holland affirms that all creation reveals god:

> All of life is but one living, throbbing organism of which we are a cell. ...
> The web is living. It glistens with life. ... It glistens with the religious mystery.[871]

---

858. See Holland, 6. Though an understandably unpleasant task, we must say a word on the metaphor used by Holland. Some contemporary theologians, the French priest J.M. Pohier among them, make long speculations on sexual symbolism, striving to extract images for theological and philosophical lucubrations. They often explain immanence through the symbolism of sexual contact, in which both partners interpenetrate ("one flesh") and yet maintain their own identity. Some theologians go so far as to explain the Holy Trinity in terms of a sexual relationship. God the Father would be the masculine element, Our Lord Jesus Christ the feminine, and the Holy Ghost the love that binds them, or—as some neo-modernist theologians maintain—the phallus that unites both. See, for example, J.M. Pohier, *Au nom du Père: Recherches théologiques et psychanalitiques* (Paris: Éditions du Cerf, 1972).

859. Holland, *Post Modern Cultural Earthquake*, 27.

860. Holland, 27.

861. Few liberation theologians explicitly deny that Holy Scriptures and Tradition contain revelation but, even when most of them theoretically admit the validity of these sources, they act as if the only revelation were the immanent one. Thus, for all practical purposes, this immanent revelation becomes the primary source for knowing god.

862. Holland, *Post Modern Cultural Earthquake*, 11.

863. Holland, 9.

864. Holland, 11.

865. Joe Holland, *The Spiritual Crisis of Modern Culture* (Washington, D.C.: Center of Concern, 1984), 12.

866. Holland, *Post Modern Cultural Earthquake*, 9.

867. Richard Rohr, "Pure Passion: The Holiness of Human Sexuality," *Sojourners* (Oct. 1982).

868. Fr. Rohr states, "At its core, therefore, sexuality is a constant expression of the spirit." Richard Rohr, "An Appetite for Wholeness: Living With Our Sexuality," *Sojourners* (Nov. 1982).

869. Holland, *Spiritual Crisis*, 12.

870. Hug and Scherschel, *Social Revelation*, 20–22.

871. Holland, *Post Modern Cultural Earthquake*, 10.

More recently, this visualization of nature as containing a divine reality with which man should be in full communion and in relation to which he should never assume an attitude of dominance has given rise to all types of ecological theologies. Indeed, with the fall of real Socialism, more than one Marxist liberation theologian has recycled into environmentalist liberation. We will return to this issue.

This ecological revelation, on the other hand, is squarely consistent with LT's egalitarian logic. Conceiving revelation as occurring merely within the human sphere—the human body, interior movements, and praxis, in other words, in history—would be arrogant anthropocentrism, a sort of human chauvinism, discriminating against the other realms of creation.[872]

4. Social, Cultural, and Historical Revelation
Finally, liberation theologians present the gamut of human activities—social, cultural, political, even recreational—as sources of revelation. Father Hug writes:

> The social institutions and movements of our times are presented to us as a privileged place of revelation. ...
> ... The socio-economic world with its institutions and movements [is a source of revelation].[873]

F. "God Becomes History"
Such radical immanentism—already bordering on pantheism—is increasingly creeping into LT's more recent versions. Historically, however, liberation theologians developed their doctrines emphasizing a more moderate version, namely, historicist immanentism.

Unlike the Catholic conception that man can know God through revelation and the contemplation of the natural order, LT's historicist immanentist conception holds that god is known in historical processes. He would be a kind of driving force pushing history to attain the "Kingdom." So in order to find revelation one would need to discern that impulse. According to the 1984 Instruction *Libertatis Nuntius*, issued by the Congregation for the Doctrine of the Faith and signed by Joseph Cardinal Ratzinger, for LT "history thus becomes a central notion. ... It is said that God Himself becomes history."[874]

The Spanish-Guatemalan Jesuit theologian Fr. Juan Hernández Pico writes, "The god of revolutionary Christians is a god hidden in history."[875] Explicitly referring to New Theology exponents dealing with "anthropological aspects of revelation," Father Gutiérrez states, "Human history ... is the location of our encounter with [god]."[876] This is what liberation theologians mean when they speak of the "lord of history."

It should be noted that, in liberationist parlance, the term *history* has a special meaning. It does not refer to the commonly accepted definition of history, that is, the "narration of past facts worthy of remembrance," in the perennial words of Herodotus. By history, liberation theologians understand the continuing revolutionary process that has been systematically destroying every tradition in the religious and civil domains from the late Middle Ages on, driven by the "liberating" action of revolutionary agents.[877]

G. Manipulating the Notion of the Kingdom of God
LT's historicist immanentism rests on an astute manipulation of the notion of "Kingdom of God." In order to better assess this distortion, we shall first explain Catholic doctrine on this matter.

1. Catholic Doctrine: The Kingdom of God Is Spiritual
In his authoritative *Manuale theologiae dogmaticae*, Canon Jean-Marie Hervé explains, "The announcement and establishment of the kingdom of God or the kingdom of Heaven occupies the primary place in the mission of Christ, the Envoy of God."[878] The expression "Kingdom of God" has several meanings, which are closely interrelated.

a. Kingdom of Heaven
The Kingdom of God, properly speaking, refers to the Kingdom of Heaven. After the second coming of Christ and the Last Judgment, God will reign forever amid the angels and saints. Those who die in the state of grace will merit this Kingdom. This is the eschatological element of the Kingdom.

b. Kingdom of God in Souls
This Kingdom has two phases: It begins here on earth and is completed in heaven. In other words, the Kingdom of God is already being constructed here on earth. It is first being built inside souls—"The Kingdom of God is within you," (Luke 17:21)—to the extent that the person has faith and opens himself to God's grace, thus creating the conditions here and now to enter the Kingdom of Heaven. It is the dominion of God over souls. This is the internal element of the Kingdom.

c. Visible Manifestations of the Kingdom of God
According to Catholic theology, the Kingdom of God is not merely eschatological and interior. It also has visible or exterior manifestations. This is true of the Catholic Church, said to be the Kingdom of God in the sense that Our Lord reigns in her in a special way through faith, grace, and virtues, as well as in the sense that she sanctifies and guides souls to eternal salvation, thus being the path to Heaven. The pope, supreme head of the Church, is the visible representative of the invisible King, Our Lord Jesus Christ. This is the social or visible element of the Kingdom.

d. The Essential Element of the Kingdom of God: Its Religious, Spiritual Nature
The essential characteristic of the Kingdom of God (present in the aforementioned senses) is, therefore, its religious and spiritual nature. By its origin and nature, the Kingdom of God is not of this world—"My Kingdom is not of this world" (John 18:36).

872. In this as in other points, more recent forms of LT depart from earlier versions, largely based on Marxism. See, for example, Martin Jay, *Marxism and Totality: The Adventures of a Concept from Lukács to Habermas* (Berkeley, Calif.: University of California Press, 1984), 170–71, 316–18.

873. Hug and Scherschel, *Social Revelation,* 20–22. (Emphasis in the original.)

874. Congregation for the Doctrine of the Faith, *Instruction on Certain Aspects,* no. IX 3. We translate in part from the document's original Latin version because the Vatican's official English translation misses the proper sense, rendering it as "God Himself makes history" (no. 3). For the correct sense see, for example, Fr. Boff: "Ever since the incarnation of the son and the presence of the spirit as a person within history, god is in history, or rather, god has become history." Leonardo Boff, "The Originality of the Theology of Liberation," in *The Future of Liberation Theology: Essays in Honor of Gustavo Gutiérrez,* ed. Marc H. Ellis and Otto Maduro (Maryknoll, N.Y.: Orbis Books, 1989), 44. See also Rodriguez, "Godless Theology and Enslaving Liberation," 12.

875. Juan Hernández Pico, "Convergencia entre iglesia popular y organización popular en centroamérica," *Dialogo* (Mexico) 10, no. 52 (Jun.–Jul.), 29.

876. Gutiérrez, *A Theology of Liberation,* 189. The Peruvian theologian quotes, among others, the essay by Charles Ducuoq, "Eschatologie et réalités terrestres," *Lumière et Vie,* no. 50 (1960): 4–25. See also André Dumas, *Une théologie de la réalité* (Geneva: Éditions Labor et Fides, 1968).

877. See Corrêa de Oliveira, *Revolution and Counter-Revolution,* part 1. We will return to this point in chapter 8.

878. Hervé, *Manuale theologiae dogmaticae,* 1:270. To prepare this chapter, in addition to consulting the classic manuals of theology, the author consulted theologians at the Real Colegio Universitario Maria Cristina, El Escorial (Madrid), from whom he received a written reply.

It must nonetheless grow in this world, inside souls, and also, in a visible way, in the Catholic Church.[879]

Can one speak of civil society as the Kingdom of God?

When fundamentally guided by Catholic doctrine and informed by the Catholic spirit, temporal society, in its various spheres (government, economy, culture, etc.), may be seen as a fruit of the Kingdom of God. If God fully reigns in people's souls, social institutions and customs will reflect it and one has a Christian civilization. In turn, a Christian civilization can contribute to the development of the Kingdom of God. It can protect and foster the social practice of virtue, thus influencing its practice by individuals; it can incorporate institutions according to the natural law and Christian principles to predispose citizens to virtue and enable the action of grace. In this sense, a Christian civilization will act as a forum, i.e., a preparation and pathway to the Kingdom of God, in the happy expression of Plinio Corrêa de Oliveira.[880] By itself, however, temporal society does not produce holiness, which is the condition and goal of the Kingdom of God. This is the work of divine grace in souls. Even when there is an obvious and profound connection, temporal society should not be confused with the Kingdom of God.

2. LT's Kingdom of God, a "Libertarian and Egalitarian Popular Utopia"

Liberation theologians introduce a fundamental confusion about the Kingdom of God. They do not present it as an eschatological horizon but as a "libertarian and egalitarian popular utopia," in the words of Father Girardi, that is, as a secular utopia identified with a communist and permissive society.[881]

a. The Kingdom of God, a Secular Utopia: Confusion Regarding the Eschatological Element

Some liberation theologians overtly deny the essentially spiritual nature of the Kingdom of God. During the Eighth Congress of Theology, held in Madrid in September 1988, Spanish theologian Juan Mateos stated, "Not so long ago the 'Kingdom of God' was identified with eternal bliss after death. However, nothing can be so distant from the teachings of the Gospel. The kingship of God must be exercised in history and the Kingdom of God is a reality in history."[882]

Most liberation theologians, however, while not explicitly denying the spiritual character of the Kingdom of God, usually remain silent about it, focusing instead on the Kingdom as a sociopolitical utopia to be realized in this world at an unspecified future point.

Spanish liberation theologian Fr. Ignacio Ellacuría explains what LT means by the expression *Kingdom of God*. "In the first place," he says, "the Kingdom of God has to do with historical reality, a structural reality that to some extent shapes individual destinies. Secondly, it has to do with a historical praxis that, without abandoning the personal dimension, affects strictly social dimensions. Thirdly, it has to do with an entire people on the march, and thus—at least as a goal—with the whole humanity. Finally, it has to do with the structural evil and the social sin which, because

of their historical nature, require social factors to be interpreted and overcome."[883]

For liberation theology, however, the "Kingdom of God" will be fully realized in history only when total "liberation" is achieved in the religious, social, political, economic, cultural, psychological spheres, etc. For LT, the Kingdom's eschatological element is the same as the secular utopia. On this point, Leonardo Boff writes, "[The] Kingdom ... is the utopia that is realized in the world, the final good of the whole of creation in god, completely liberated from all imperfection and penetrated by the divine. The Kingdom carries salvation to its completion. The *world* is the arena for the historical realization of the Kingdom."[884]

b. "To Build the Kingdom" Is to Fight Political, Social, Cultural, Racial, and Sexual Oppression

The specific mission of the Church is to lead souls to eternal salvation, that is to say, to the Kingdom of Heaven. Liberation theologians also say they want to "build the Kingdom." However, by merging the eschatological element of the "Kingdom" with an egalitarian and liberationist worldly utopia, in LT jargon this means something totally different, namely, the revolutionary struggle against "structures of oppression" (the "anti-Kingdom"). Leonardo Boff writes, "Presently the world is decadent and stained by sin; because of this, the Kingdom of God is [built] against the powers of the anti-Kingdom, engaged in the onerous process of liberation so that the world might accept the Kingdom itself and thus achieve its joyous goal."[885]

Developing "Kingdom Theology" (an attempt to establish LT in Great Britain), Peter Price, Anglican vicar in Croydon, Surrey, enumerates several types of oppression that have to be eliminated in order to establish the Kingdom:

> The Kingdom of God is political. ...
> ... [Jesus] identified the Kingdom of God with the basic struggles of humanity against political oppression; cultural, racist and sexist alienation; the destruction of the environment through industrialization.[886]

For his part, Father Gutiérrez asserts that "to place oneself in the perspective of the Kingdom means to participate in the struggle for the liberation of those oppressed by others."[887]

Spanish liberation theologian Fr. José María Díez-Alegría, president of the Asociación de Teólogos Juan XXIII, reminds us that the struggle for the Kingdom is both secular and ecclesial: "The Kingdom of God means liberation from the oppressive powers that, in order to survive, sacrifice the poor and oppress them with

879. See Cornelius a Lapide, *Commentaria in scripturam sacram*, in Acta Apostolorum 1:3; Acta Apostolorum 2:30; Lucam 1:33; Isaiam Prophetam 65:17; Danielem Prophetam 2:44.

880. See Plinio Corrêa de Oliveira, *Note sul concetto di Cristianità: Carattere spirituale e sacrale della società temporale e sua "ministerialità"* (Palermo: Thule, 1998); Plinio Corrêa de Oliveira, "The Twentieth Century Crusade."

881. Girardi, *Utopía popular*, 105.

882. Juan Mateos, "La utopía de Jesús," in *Utopía y profetismo*, ed. González Faus, 42.

883. Ellacuría, "El auténtico lugar," 80.

884. Leonardo Boff, *Church: Charism and Power; Liberation Theology and the Institutional Church*, trans. John W. Diercksmeier (New York: The Crossroad Publishing Company, 1986), 1.

885. Boff, *Church: Charism and Power*, 1–2. The verb "built" appears in the original Portuguese. See Leonardo Boff, *Igreja: Carisma e poder—Ensaios de eclesiologia militante* (São Paulo: Editora Ática, 1994), 20. This book, the keystone of LT's ecclesiology, has been condemned by the Congregation for the Doctrine of the Faith: "The Congregation also feels obliged to declare that the options of L. Boff analyzed here endanger the sound doctrine of the faith, which this Congregation has the task of promoting and safeguarding." Congregation for the Doctrine of the Faith, "Notification on the book 'Church: Charism and Power' by Father Leonardo Boff O.F.M," (Mar. 11, 1985), Conclusion. Unfortunately, as often happens with such otherwise laudable condemnations, the book continues to circulate freely, even in Roman seminaries.

886. Peter Price, *The Church as the Kingdom: A New Way of Being the Church* (Basingtoke, U.K.: Marshall Pickering, 1987), 15.

887. Gutiérrez, *A Theology of Liberation*, 203.

their harsh yoke. It also means, and not the least, liberation from religious oppressions."[888]

c. Confusion Regarding the Interior Element

For liberation theologians, the interior element of the Kingdom means the profound change a person undergoes when he opens his soul to the luring gleams of the liberationist utopia.

This is a profound change in beliefs, temperament, and even in the actual ways of feeling and living. He would be crushing the "interior structures of oppression," killing the "old man," and thus "building the Kingdom" in his soul, thereby giving birth to the "new man" who is egalitarian, communitarian, no longer rational but rather whimsically imaginative, a new man fully liberated from any constraint whatsoever, including those of logic.

Fr. Gustavo Gutiérrez writes, "It is not enough that we be liberated from oppressive socio-economic structures; also needed is a personal transformation by which we live with profound inner freedom in the face of every kind of servitude."[889] "At stake here is the construction of a new man. Not in the Pauline and theological sense of the expression, but as used in political philosophy and historical stances to emphasize that human coexistence requires, along with just structures, attitudes and mentalities that are not a mechanical product of like structures."[890]

Deeming any rational construction an obstacle to the free flow of vital energies (thus, an "oppression"), the LT-liberated man must freely satisfy the cravings of a superficial and whimsical creativity. Since any moral norm would be an obstacle to the free flow of vital impulses, the goal of human life would be for man to satisfy his instincts in a carefree way.

d. Confusion Regarding the Social or Visible Element

For liberation theologians, the social or visible element of the Kingdom is the revolutionary movement that leads to "liberation struggles" against the following:

(a) traditional society and particularly societal structures that perpetuate hierarchy and moral norms, and,

(b) the traditional Church, to establish the new, free, egalitarian, and "pneumatic church" dreamed of by extreme fringes of Catholic progressives.

This "liberation" is simultaneously temporal and religious, and intends to eliminate every "oppressive structure" in society and the Church.

e. Socialism, a Step Toward the Kingdom

From this perspective, intermediate stages of the revolutionary process, such as Socialism, would be steps toward the "Kingdom."

The Brazilian Dominican Friar Betto, a notorious figure in the LT movement, and Chilean theologian Father Richard affirm that Socialism "is only one stage of the Kingdom of God."[891] The same defense of Socialism as a stage en route to the "Kingdom" is found in a document drafted by C.O.N.I.P. (Spanish acronym for National Coordinating Body of Archbishop Oscar Romero's People's Church), an umbrella organization of the LT movement in El Salvador: "For us today, building the bases for Socialism is

the historical mediation and the concrete alternative that brings us closest to the Kingdom of God."[892]

Thus, the LT movement hailed the violent and clearly Marxist-inspired Sandinista revolution that seized power in Nicaragua in 1979 after years of bloody guerrilla warfare as a step toward the Kingdom of God. Father Richard says, "With the triumph of the popular forces, the people of Nicaragua find themselves now closer to the Kingdom of God."[893]

This is perfectly consistent with LT's doctrinal postulates that private property and the resulting social, political, cultural, and economic structures, which produce inequalities, are "oppressive" as such and constitute a collective sin. Accordingly, eliminating such structures and one of their foundations—private property—by establishing Socialism would be a collective "redemption" from sin and a step toward achieving the Kingdom of God on earth.

Not by chance did Father Gutiérrez proclaim, "Only by eliminating private ownership of the wealth created by human labor will we be able to lay the foundations for a more just society. This is why efforts to project a new society in Latin America are moving more and more toward Socialism."[894]

f. "Communism and the Kingdom of God Are … the Same Thing"

According to Marxist Socialism, Communism is the final stage of the revolutionary process. It is, therefore, understandable that Fr. Ernesto Cardenal, future Sandinista Minister of Culture, would proclaim:

> Communism and the kingdom of God on earth are one and the same thing. …
> … As Christians, we believe that we should be the first ones to spread Communism.[895]

In this sense, Communism does not mean the Soviet dictatorship of the proletariat, but the stage of the revolutionary process beyond State Socialism, in which the last traces of inequality and "alienation" would have been abolished.

To the extent that today's communist countries are in the process of achieving this goal, they are supposedly closer to the Kingdom. In 1987, three Brazilian liberation theologians, the brothers Leonardo and Clodovis Boff and Friar Betto, visited Cuba. It was not their first trip to the island-prison, nor would it be their last. Upon returning, Fr. Clodovis Boff wrote an unusual *Theological Letter on Cuba*, expounding LT's views on the Cuban revolution and lavishly praising Fidel Castro. Referring to the Kingdom, he states, "Speaking now as a theologian I would say that, although the presence of the Church is weak, that of the Kingdom seems strong. Indeed, one can see there the 'signs of the Messias,' that is, the fulfillment of the great evangelical values, especially the 'works of mercy,' translated into a political key. … The Kingdom of God [is] specifically written into the

888. José María Díez-Alegría, "¿Cristianismo profético y liberador?" *Misión Abierta* (Madrid) 77, no. 2 (Apr. 1984), 77.

889. Gutiérrez, new introduction ("Expanding the View") to *A Theology of Liberation* (1988 rev. ed.), xxxviii.

890. Gustavo Gutiérrez, new introduction "Mirar lejos," in *Teología de la liberación: Perspectivas*, 16th ed. (Salamanca: Ediciones Sigueme, 1999), 43. (Our translation.)

891. *Movimento* (Brazil), Mar. 3, 1980, quoted in Corrêa de Oliveira, et al., *Grassroots Church Communities*, 33.

892. *Iglesia de Jesucristo, iglesia del pueblo* (Lima, Perú: C.E.L.A.D.E.C., 1981), quoted in Roberto Jiménez, "Teología de la liberación: Proyecto histórico y tres de sus conceptos claves," *Paramillo* 5 (1986): 32. *Paramillo* is the magazine of the Center for Interdisciplinary Studies of the Catholic University of Táchira, San Antonio, Venezuela.

893. *Movimento*, Feb. 25, 1980, quoted in Corrêa de Oliveira, et al., *Grassroots Church Communities*, 33.

894. Gutiérrez, "Liberation Praxis and Christian Faith," Diocese of Brownsville, *Lay Ministry Handbook*, 22.

895. Fr. Ernesto Cardenal, interview "A igreja do padre Cardenal," *O Estado de S. Paulo*, Jan. 17, 1979, p. 6.

[Cuban] structures. I had the strong impression that Christ and His Kingdom are present there."[896]

Liberation theologians also saw 'signs of the Kingdom' in Soviet Russia. Some months after visiting Castro's Cuba, when Gorbachev's perestroika was still largely a hollow slogan, the aforementioned trio paid a visit to the Soviet Union. Narrating his impressions, Leonardo Boff praises

> the inestimable goods of the Kingdom which the Soviets knew how to build with Socialism. ...
> ... The socialist project is fundamentally ordained to something found in God's project. ...
> ... How is it possible that real Socialism contains significant goods of the Kingdom of God without having passed through any religious mediation?[897]

g. Toward an Enigmatic Liberation of the Cosmos

The utopia that liberation theologians identify with the "Kingdom" contains developments that go beyond Communism. Still largely implicit in LT's early formulations, such developments have now come to the fore as the collapse of State Socialism behind the former Iron Curtain profoundly changed the panorama. Describing the Kingdom as he conceives it, Leonardo Boff affirms that it implies "a total and global transformation of the old world that, through divine intervention, would become the new world where sin, sickness, hatred, and all of the alienating forces that affect both human life and the entire cosmos are defeated."[898]

For the Brazilian theologian, the coming of the Kingdom supposes the destruction of all "alienating forces" that cause subjection and obedience not only among men but in the whole cosmos. What does he mean by this reference to alienating forces that produce hierarchy in the universe? Is this inequality not a consequence of God's will? God created a hierarchical universe. He subjected all creatures to His law, and inferior creatures to superior ones.[899] What does this "liberation" of the "entire cosmos" propounded by liberation theologians imply? How does it characterize the "Kingdom"?

Some cues are visible in ecological currents that arose within the LT movement over the last few years. In the name of purported animal and even plant rights, these novel forms of liberationism challenge man's dominion over nature as an inadmissible

oppression, a kind of "species imperialism."[900] It is deemed unbearable or even worse than the sociopolitical and economic "imperialism" decried by earlier forms of LT in the name of human rights. Hence, they propose a liberation of the cosmos that puts an end to such dominion. Indeed, if the whole cosmos is animated by just one vital force, it becomes imperative for man to treat nature as his equal rather than subordinate it to his own ends.

Just what is this "liberation" of nature, an integral part of the "cosmic liberation" proclaimed by Boff? What are its implications for the modern industrial society? Should man renounce the industrial exploitation of natural resources and revert to some type of simpler life, perhaps inspired in primitive tribal models, as some spokesmen for the LT movement are suggesting?[901] In this case, what would a non-oppressive use of nature be like?

At least as a working hypothesis, can we imagine even more maximalist liberationist positions? Like mineral "rights"? Voices are already proclaiming the sacredness of the planet's water, demanding dedevelopment, "environmental justice," and the banning of human "exploitation" of natural resources. Unthinkable? A few years ago the mere idea of "animal rights," let alone "plant rights," would have been scoffed at as extravagant. Today, international agencies support them. Let us recall that in 1978, U.N.E.S.C.O. approved the Universal Declaration of the Rights of Animals. NGOs have been pushing for UN approval of others such as the Universal Charter of the Rights of Other Species, the Universal Declaration of Animal Welfare, and a similar charter on the rights of plants.[902]

This, after all, falls within the leveling logic of liberation theology. After having "liberated" all living nature, "alienation" would still be found in one realm: the inorganic mineral kingdom. By

---

896. Clodovis Boff, "Carta teológica sobre Cuba," *Revista Eclesiástica Brasileira* 46, no. 182 (Jun. 1986): 368.

897. Leonardo Boff, "O socialismo como desafio teológico," *Vozes* 81 (Brazil), no. 6 (Nov.–Dec. 1988), 692–93.

898. Boff, *Church: Charism and Power*, 146. Boff uses the term *alienation* in the Marxist sense, which is becoming increasingly commonplace today. Generically, alienation means the cession of something to someone else. Thus, in juridical language, the transfer of property to a new owner. In Marxist ideology, the term has a specific sense. Marx maintained that, by selling one's work to another, the proletarian became *alienated*: The product of his economic activity belongs to someone else. "Alienation appears," he wrote, "in the fact that my means of existence is that of another person." Gérard Bekerman, *Vocabulaire du marxisme* (Paris: Presses Universitaires de France, 1981), 27. Since for Marx work is the very "expression of life," the very "affirmation of life," (Bekerman, *Vocabulaire du marxisme*, 147), the activity through which man "creates" himself, then, when a person sells his work, he cedes something of his own existence, something of himself. In other words, part of himself becomes alienated to another. From this original Marxist sense, leftist thinkers later expanded the meaning of the term, pointing out that alienation occurs in more than just an economic form. For them, any circumstance creating dependence or hierarchy results in the alienation of the inferior to the superior. The vassal becomes alienated to his lord, the farmworker to the farmer, the employee to the employer, and even children to their parents. From this leftist viewpoint, any hierarchy would generate alienation and, therefore, oppression.

899. See St. Thomas Aquinas, *Summa contra gentiles* bk. 3, chap. 77; Aquinas, *S.T.,* I, q. 47, a. 2; q. 50, a. 4.; q. 96, a. 3; Corrêa de Oliveira, *Revolution and Counter-Revolution,* 47–50.

900. Since the 1930s, the perception that man's dominion over nature is something evil and harmful has been developed in avant-garde circles of the revolutionary intelligentsia. From this, a body of doctrines appeared that condemned not only the biblical concept of man as king of nature (see Ecclus. 17:3–4), but also the Enlightenment's eagerness to dominate nature through reason and science. Expanding further on these ideas, revolutionary currents during the 1950s and 1960s questioned industrial society in its entirety. This gave rise to the ecologist and anti-consumerist movements, which are intimately related. One of this tendency's main tenets is the idea of "species imperialism," meaning a purported "imperialism" of humanity over the animal and plant kingdoms. Prof. Martin Jay, of the University of California, offers an insightful history of the development of these ideas within neo-Marxist circles. See, for example, Jay, *Marxism and Totality*, 170–71, 186–87, 214–15, 261–63, 265–70 passim. See also Douglas Kellner, *Critical Theory: Marxism and Modernity* (Baltimore: The John Hopkins University Press, 1989), 27–28, 63, 85–98 passim.

901. There is a growing sector within the LT movement that presents primitive tribal life—as existing, for example, among the Amazon Indians—as the ideal model for human existence. In Joe Holland's words,

> The one to which we have to return for healing. ...
> ... Healing the destructiveness of late modern civilization. (Holland, *Post Modern Cultural Earthquake*, 10)

This would supposedly revert the alienating process outlined in item C. 3. b. of this chapter. These LT currents propose the return to this "primal stage" (Holland and Thomas Berry use this expression) as the way to total liberation. They see in tribal life the illusory synthesis of full freedom and absolute equality, with the consequent achievement of widespread fraternity, not only among men, but between man and nature. In the tribe, the individual "I's," with their peculiar and often conflicting ways of thinking, wills, and ways of being, are dissolved in a collective personality that generates strongly communitarian bonds. Thus, the structures of separation and alienation that oppress men and hinder the flow of the divine energies would be defeated, and the experience of an immanent god once again made dominant among men. This experience would give rise to a pentecostal type of religion (Berry calls it "shamanic"), in which the last vestiges of a structured Church, dogmas, and rituals would be obliterated, thus also achieving total liberation in the religious-ecclesiastical sphere. Among the most notorious figures of this tribalist current within the LT movement was the late Most Rev. Pedro Casaldáliga, bishop emeritus of São Félix do Araguaia, Brazil. An outspoken supporter of the now-defunct Sandinista government in Nicaragua, Bishop Casaldáliga considered the return to the tribal stage as the next logical step beyond Communism. See Plinio Corrêa de Oliveira, *Indian Tribalism: The Communist-Missionary Ideal for Brazil in the Twenty-First Century*, part 3.

902. Switzerland has had a law in this regard since 2008. "Plants have dignity and moral value," we read in the Declaration of the Federal Commission on Ethics for Genetic Engineering that paved the way for the law. Franco Zantonelli Lugano, "Ora per la legge svizzera hanno diritti e sentimenti," *La Repubblica*, Oct. 14, 2008.

subjecting things to their rule and establishing order in the universe, the laws that govern matter are instruments and symbols of the Supreme Legislator and Ruler. Would they also have to somehow yield to a "liberation" process? What, then, would become of the universe if even these basic elements of order were obliterated? What would this radical nihilism mean if not the ultimate destruction of any image of the transcendent God in creation?

Will liberation theologians take their iconoclastic frenzy to such extremes? It is not that far-fetched since extreme currents in modern thought, to which they always refer (even utopia has its extremists), propose a transmutation of nature that leads to the ultimate fusion of all beings, erasing all distinction among them and, therefore, the very possibility of any "alienation." Behold the old Gnostic dream rising to the forefront of modern thought.[903]

Based on the witness of Scriptures, the Church teaches that the point that divided the angels in Heaven was the refusal of some to obey, to subject ("alienate") themselves to their Creator. Satan and his followers voiced that quintessential revolutionary and "liberating" rebel cry: *Non serviam!*—I shall not serve! (Jer. 2, 20) I shall not be subject to You! They were cast into hell, whence they plot and strive to end all due subjection to God's law as a way of diminishing the glory owed to the Creator.

Once again we ask, what are the final implications of LT's liberation? Obviously, we do not intend to answer this question, which must be clarified by the liberation theologians themselves. What we point out is how the liberation they propose does not end with struggles of the proletariat against the bourgeoisie to establish Communism. This is merely a sociopolitical consequence of the liberation theologians' metaphysical position regarding the order of the universe.

3. Kingdom and History: Indistinguishable Realities?

At times, liberation theologians manipulate the notion of "Kingdom of God" in a sense that calls to mind its spiritual and transcendent meanings—the Kingdom of Heaven, man's spiritual destiny, man's religious life, and so forth. At other times, they intend it to mean the egalitarian and liberationist secular utopia. This introduces an essential ambiguity than runs through all LT and which the various mea culpas expressed after the Vatican's condemnation have done little to dispel.

By confounding the Kingdom of Heaven with the revolutionary utopia, LT ends by not distinguishing between the spiritual life and revolutionary activism, between the life of grace and political activism, between spiritual salvation and temporal liberation, between the supernatural and natural orders, between biblical accounts and ongoing revolutions. Both orders of reality become indistinguishable. Samuel Silva Gotay writes, "[Liberation theologians] see god as present in social revolution. ... The concept of transcendence is historicized, the historical future takes the place of heaven; the political nature of the acts of salvation is rediscovered ... the political nature of faith is emphasized, the

basic categories of Faith, salvation and grace are applied to the historical process. ..."[904]

Let us see some areas in which this ambiguity is highlighted.

H. LT Blurs the Distinction Between the Supernatural and Natural Orders

Based on a god indistinct from history, liberation theologians tend to blur, and in some cases even eliminate, the distinction between Creator and creatures, thus blurring the distinction between the supernatural and natural orders. Spanish theologian Victorino Rodríguez comments, "[In LT] the distinction between the natural and supernatural orders becomes meaningless on being diluted in this historicist immanentism of God and man."[905] Not all history, however, is a privileged place of revelation. According to LT, revelation is mediated preferentially, in fact almost exclusively, by a practical aspect of history, namely, revolutionary movements.

As a consequence of such confusions, liberation theologians consider revolutionary activism to be one and the same with the life of grace. Revolutionary activism acquires a religious meaning, and religion, a revolutionary one. Religious practice is politicized while political activism is sacralized. This is one of the criticisms the Vatican Instruction *Libertatis Nuntius* makes of LT: "One needs to be on guard against the politicization of existence which, misunderstanding the entire meaning of the Kingdom of God and the transcendence of the person, begins to sacralize politics and betray the religion of the people in favor of the projects of the revolution."[906]

In Latin America in the seventies and eighties, this fact was quite salient in LT's radical political activism. Clodovis Boff points out that "the faith-life union leads to a *fusion* between religious practices and political practices. ... A religious practice, such as listening to and sharing the Word as a community, acquires a political meaning. ... On the other hand, a political practice such as ... participation in a strike ... is animated fully by a faith motivation."[907]

Speaking on the same subject, Father Gutiérrez affirms, "Social praxis is gradually becoming more of the arena itself in which the Christian works out—along with others—both his destiny as man and his life of faith in the lord of history. Participation in the process of liberation is an obligatory and privileged *locus* for Christian life and reflection."[908]

From this view, man strives for his salvation not by having faith and practicing the Christian virtues, but by becoming involved in revolutionary causes. The unavoidable consequence is that any religious practice that does not lead to revolutionary action or at least to a revolutionary stance would be scorned as false and alienating.

One of the consequences of blurring the distinction between the natural and supernatural aspects of man's life is to eliminate that between the history of salvation and profane history, both of which

903. We already find this gnostic and pantheistic myth in Hegel, whose influence in modern revolutionary thought is all-pervasive. More recently, and not to speak of Fr. Teilhard de Chardin, this hatred of reality proper to the gnostic mentality is evident in avant-garde currents within Marxism and psychoanalysis, being represented by theoreticians like Norman Brown, Michel Foucault, and Jacques Lacan. See, for example, Daniel Bell, "Beyond Modernism: Beyond Self," in *The Winding Passage: Essays and Sociological Journeys,* by Daniel Bell, 275–354 (Cambridge, Mass.: Abt Books, 1980); Lionel Abel, "Important Nonsense," *Dissent* (Mar./Apr. 1968): 147–57; Richard W. Noland, "The Apocalypse of Normal O. Brown," *The American Scholar* (Winter 1968–1969): 59–68.

904. Gotay, "Origem e desenvolvimento," 146. Spanish LT adept Fr. Julio Lois comments on the same point: "The relation between the Kingdom and history, between transcendence and the immanent historical process has to be viewed as a strictly dialectical relationship. ... Thus, the eschatological aspect of the Kingdom, far from turning the historical process relative, links it with the absolute and, consequently, 'the [revolutionary] historical praxis of liberation acquires an eschatological value.'" Julio Lois, "Función crítica de la iglesia en la sociedad," in *Desafíos Cristianos*, ed. Misión Abierta (Madrid: Loguez Ediciones, 1988), 174.

905. Rodríguez, "Godless 'Theology' and Enslaving 'Liberation,'" 12.

906. Congregation for the Doctrine of the Faith, *Instruction on Certain Aspects*, XI, no. 17.

907. Clodovis Boff, O.S.M., "A influência política das comunidades eclesiais de base (CEBS)," *Sedoc* (Brazil) (Jan.–Feb. 1979): 802.

908. Gutiérrez, *A Theology of Liberation*, 49.

are obviously linked but essentially different.[909] As mentioned, for LT there is only one history. Father Gutiérrez writes, "There are not two histories, one profane and one sacred, 'juxtaposed' or 'closely linked;' rather, there is only one human destiny, irreversibly assumed by Christ, the lord of history."[910]

Fully assuming the consequences of this stance, Father Gutiérrez states outright, "We can no longer speak properly of a profane world." For him, "Salvation is not something otherworldly," it is something to be pursued in this world through the struggles for liberation.[911]

This immanent fusion of the two histories is one of the points explicitly condemned by the Holy See in the Instruction *Libertatis Nuntius*: "It will be added that there is only one history, one in which the distinction between the history of salvation and profane history is no longer necessary. To maintain the distinction would be to fall into 'dualism.' Affirmations such as this reflect historicist immanentism. Thus, there is a tendency to identify the kingdom of God and its growth with the human liberation movement, and to make history itself the subject of its own development, as a process of the self-redemption of man by means of the class struggle. This identification is in opposition to the faith of the Church."[912]

I. Redemption and Liberation

Another aspect of this "one history" approach is confusion between supernatural Redemption and sociopolitical "liberation."

1. Silence on the True Meaning of Redemption

To redeem means to regain possession of something by paying back a debt. It is the same as to ransom.[913] Our Lord paid back to God the Father the debt mankind had incurred with original sin, thus enabling man to enter Heaven. Only He could pay that debt. Since the offense was committed against the infinite God, only the Son of God, equally infinite, could redeem it. He was the Innocent Victim, the Lamb of God, Who, in a gratuitous act of pure love, expiated for the whole of mankind. This is the efficient cause of our Redemption, which unites God's infinite justice and His equally infinite mercy. His redeeming work attained an apex with His Passion and Death on the Cross.

Redemption was an authentic liberation, the liberation par excellence, as it freed mankind from the triple slavery of the devil, sin, and eternal death. Although having temporal (social, political, cultural) consequences, it was essentially a supernatural liberation, a gratuitous gift of divine mercy to which man corresponds through faith and good works.

This is not the doctrine of liberation theology. The aforementioned Instruction *Libertatis Nuntius* asserts that liberation theologians tend "to misunderstand the person of Our Lord Jesus Christ, true God and true man, and thus the specific character of the salvation He gave us, that is above all liberation from sin."[914]

Some liberation theologians openly deny the true meaning of Our Lord's Redemption. Father Ellacuría, for example, affirms

that "No mystic expiatory meaning appears [in Our Lord's death on the Cross]." The late Spanish theologian goes even further. After casting doubt on the accuracy of the Evangelists' narrative he denies that Our Lord Jesus Christ knew why He was dying: "Not even the evangelists, in their theological reinterpretations, felt authorized to put in Jesus's lips and in his manifest conscience a clear statement of the meaning of his death." For Father Ellacuría, the references to Our Lord's death found in the Gospels "do not mean that Jesus conceived of himself as the servant of Yahweh, accomplishing a messianic mission with an expiatory death."[915]

Most liberation theologians, however, while not openly denying the proper notion of the Redemption, subtly tend to eliminate it. They first relegate it to a secondary plane; then they begin to employ ambiguous language that confuses the essentially supernatural character of the Redemption with its temporal consequences. This confusion casts a shadow on the primacy of its supernatural aspects. In a more advanced stage, while keeping supernatural character on this secondary plane, they bring its temporal consequences to the fore. Finally, driven by the logic of their own doctrines, liberation theologians simply eliminate the supernatural character of Redemption from their considerations. It thus acquires a purely secular and human meaning, identified with man's struggles to "liberate" himself from any oppression or "alienation."

2. Slippery Confusion Between Supernatural Redemption and Revolutionary Liberation

This silence on the true meaning of Our Lord's Redemption enables liberation theologians to create a slippery confusion between supernatural Redemption and revolutionary liberation. Rarely do they speak of Redemption, a term with precise theological significance. Instead, they speak of "liberation," a term easily manipulated which, in common language, has strong revolutionary overtones imparted by the liberation theologians themselves.

They see Our Lord as a secular leader, put to death by the authorities for attempting to liberate His people from Rome's imperialism. It is precisely the image of Christ as "a revolutionary, as the subversive man from Nazareth," condemned by John Paul II in his 1979 Message at Puebla.[916]

The mission of Moses is seen almost exclusively as the sociopolitical liberation of the Jews from Egyptian oppression. Father

---

909. The expressions are technical. "History of salvation" designates all that which contributes to the salvation (or damnation) of men. It is, therefore, essentially supernatural. The expression "profane history" designates the history of men in their secular life.

910. Gutiérrez, *A Theology of Liberation*, 153.

911. Gutiérrez, 151.

912. Congregation for the Doctrine of the Faith, *Instruction on Certain Aspects*, IX, no. 3.

913. In the Old Testament, *redemption* usually indicates the ransom demanded. In the New Testament, it designates the "great price" (1 Cor. 6:20) that Our Lord paid for our liberation.

914. Congregation for the Doctrine of the Faith, *Instruction on Certain Aspects*, X, no. 7.

915. Ignacio Ellacuría, "Por qué muere Jesús y por qué lo matan," in *Desafíos Cristianos*, ed. Misión Abierta (Madrid: Loguez Ediciones, 1988), 35, 38. Fr. Ellacuría's reference to a supposed "reinterpretation" by the Evangelists merits a short explanation. The Spanish LT adept contends that Our Lord was not conscious of the redemptive character of His death. According to him, this notion was improperly introduced by the Evangelists, particularly Saint Luke, and reflected ideas circulating in Christian communities that were an interpretation of Our Lord's life, not an objective remembrance.

916. In Puebla, Mexico, during the Third General Conference of the Latin American Episcopate (C.E.L.A.M.), the sovereign pontiff stated that "this idea of Christ as a political figure, a revolutionary, as the subversive man from Nazareth, does not tally with the Church's catechesis." John Paul II, Address (Jan. 28, 1979), I, no. 4.
Liberation theologians repeat *ad nauseam* that Our Lord was a worker, the son of Joseph the carpenter and Mary, a woman from the people, the implication being that, having been born among the poor, Our Lord would have personally felt the "oppression" of His class. He would have developed a "class consciousness" (to use Marxist jargon), and waged a class struggle against the social order that divided people between rich and poor, and for which He would have been put to death by the power structure of His time. Accordingly, He would be a model for today's "struggling poor."
LT adepts forget that Our Lord Jesus Christ was born of the royal House of David. Through Our Lady, Jesus "was made to [God] of the seed of David, according to the flesh" (Rom. 1:3). St. Joseph, Our Lord's foster father, was also of the House of David (see Luke 1:27). The Archangel Gabriel solemnly proclaimed that "the Lord God shall give unto him [Jesus] the throne of David his father" (Luke 1:32). Far from being a symbol of struggle between social classes, Our Lord—prince and worker—is the hyphen that links them, the symbol of social unity and harmony. See Leo XIII, encyclical *Magnae Dei Matris* (Sept. 8, 1892), no. 7; Pius XII, "La risposta agli auguri della Guarda Nobile Pontificia" (Dec. 26, 1939), in *Discorsi del Summo Pontefice Pio XII* (Modena: Typografia Immacolata Concezione, 1942), 306; and Corrêa de Oliveira, *Nobility*, 469–73.

Gutiérrez writes, "The liberation of Israel is a political action. It is the breaking away from a situation of despoliation and misery and the beginning of the construction of a just and fraternal society."[917] All the prophets and patriarchs of old are viewed in this light.

There is a counterweight, however. If on the one hand liberation theologians understand Our Lord's Redemption primordially as a sociopolitical liberation, on the other hand they consider all revolutionary "liberation" struggles as having a religiously redemptive character. "The historical liberating praxis acquires an eschatological value," says Argentine liberation theologian José Míguez Bonino.[918]

In other words, revolutionary struggles somehow participate in and continue Our Lord's Redemption (liberation). They are instruments for the historical realization of that egalitarian people's utopia that liberation theologians call "Kingdom of God." "What meaning does Jesus's liberation or cause have in the conditions of economic, political, social and cultural oppression in which our fellow citizens live?" asks Spanish LT adept Juan José Tamayo-Acosta. He answers, "Jesus's liberation has historical meaning not if we attribute to it an autonomous eschatological character, but rather if it is implemented through liberating mediations, if this liberation is anticipated in the present situation."[919]

Giving a religious meaning to sociopolitical liberation, Tamayo-Acosta goes on to quote Leonardo Boff: "Political-economic liberation is not merely political-economic. Its implementation already constitutes the historical form that anticipates full liberation in time."[920] Therefore, sociopolitical "liberation" would be part of the history of salvation. According to Father Gutiérrez, "The liberating action of Christ ... is at the heart of the historical current of humanity; the struggle for a just society is in its own right very much a part of salvation history."[921]

Only in the light of such theology can one understand the shocking statements of Most Rev. Pedro Casaldáliga, then bishop of São Felix do Araguaia, Brazil. On February 28, 1980, in the theater of the Pontifical Catholic University of São Paulo, Brazil, a "guerrilla evening" was held under the patronage of Paulo Evaristo Cardinal Arns, archbishop of São Paulo. The meeting was part of the Fourth International Ecumenical Congress of Theology, which was attended by 160 bishops, priests, nuns, and lay people involved with the LT movement. The session culminated with lawyer Idibal Piveta presenting a military guerrilla uniform to Bishop Pedro Casaldáliga. Donning it, the prelate said,

> I will try to show with facts my gratitude for this sacrament of liberation that I now receive. ...
>
> I say that I will try to thank with facts, and, if need be, with blood (applause). ...
>
> For me, for all of us, today is a truly historic day.
>
> For the first time in Brazil, in the world, the faith of the Church thought out in theology ... is witnessed

by the practice, by the commitment of a charity that becomes social and political even to the death! ...

> Dressed as a guerrilla I feel vested like a priest (intense applause). The same celebration [the guerrilla fight and the Mass] drives us toward the same hope.[922]

J. A Biblical View of the Revolution—a Revolutionary Reading of Scripture

1. Writing the Newest Testament

As we saw, liberation theologians sustain that public revelation is mediated through men's internal experiences and historical processes. The whole gamut of human experiences thus becomes a source of revelation. "We revere our own experience as God's revelation too—our personal experience, the experience of our contemporaries," writes the Jesuit theologian Fr. Thomas Clarke.[923] Accordingly, there would be no difference between biblical narration, which records public revelation, and accounts of present-day history. Today's radical activism would be as much a part of biblical narration as the Old and New Testaments.

Explaining the use of liberation theology in American B.C.C.s, Father Hug says that their militants are "discovering 'our story within the Scriptures and Scripture within our story.'"[924] The story of the subversive struggles of the poor and oppressed and their liberating activities in any field—religious, economic, political, social, cultural, moral, psychological—are considered as biblical narration. A document drafted by Brazilian B.C.C.s spells out this view:

> The Old Testament was written by an oppressed people. The New Testament was written with the very life of Jesus, a poor man of Nazareth. ... We, today's poor, are writing the Newest Testament with our lives.
>
> We are doing the New Gospel ... with our deeds.*
> The word of God, contained in the Bible ... is also revealed through the history of the people.†[925]

2. A Marxist Reading of Holy Scripture

As a consequence of this biblical view of revolutionary activism, liberation theologians treat the Holy Scriptures as a sort of revolutionary manual for today. The Bible is reread, hence reinterpreted, on the basis of sociopolitical, cultural, and moral categories which usually coincide with revolutionary ideologies: Marxism, Freudianism, phenomenology, feminism, environmentalism, and so on. Spanish theologian Fr. Casiano Floristán clearly states that B.C.C. militants give the Scriptures "a 'materialist' (or Marxist) reading."[926]

917. Gutiérrez, *A Theology of Liberation*, 155.

918. Lois, "Función crítica," 174.

919. Juan José Tamayo-Acosta, "Las comunidades cristianas populares," in *Desafíos Cristianos*, ed. Misión Abierta (Madrid: Loguez Ediciones, 1988), 163.

920. Leonardo Boff, "¿Qué es hacer teología desde América Latina?" in *Liberación y cautiverio: Debates en torno al método de la teología en América Latina—Encuentro latinoamericano de teología, México, agosto 1975*, ed. Enrique D. Dussel and Enrique Ruiz Maldonado (Mexico: n.p., 1976), 143, quoted in Tamayo-Acosta, "Las comunidades cristianas populares," 163.

921. Gutiérrez, *A Theology of Liberation*, 168.

922. Plinio Corrêa de Oliveira, "Na 'noite sandinista': o incitamento à guerrilha," *Catolicismo* (Brazil), nos. 355–356 (July–Aug. 1980), 15.

923. Clarke, "A New Way," in *Tracing the Spirit*, ed. Hug, 11.

924. Clarke, 1.

925. "Mensagem da igreja de Goiás," *Sedoc* (Nov. 1976): 515*, and *Sedoc* (Oct. 1976): 447–48†, quoted in Gustavo Antonio Solimeo and Luiz Sergio Solimeo, *As CEBs, das quais muito se fala, pouco se conhece: A TFP as descreve como são; Comentários e documentação totais* (São Paulo: Editora Vera Cruz, 1982), 45. We find the same idea in Argentine theologian José Severino Croatto. After saying that revelation is a "cycle" that is repeated throughout history, the professor emeritus of Hebrew Scriptures and Phenomenology of Religion at Buenos Aires' I.S.E.D.E.T. University Institute writes, "The Bible is the faith reading of the paradigmatic successes in the history of salvation, and the paradigmatic reading of a history of salvation which is still not over." José Severino Croatto, *Hermenêutica bíblica: Para uma teoria da leitura como produção de significado* (São Paulo: Paulinas-Sinodal, 1986), 65.

926. Casiano Floristán, *La comunidad cristiana de base*, rev. ed. (San Antonio: Mexican American Cultural Center, 1976), 17.

This contrasts head-on with the message of John Paul II to the General Conference of the Latin American Episcopate in Puebla, in which he condemned

> "re-readings" of the Gospel ...
> ... [that purport] to show Jesus as politically committed, as one who fought against Roman oppression and the authorities.[927]

3. The Proliferation of Prophets

Liberation theologians single out excerpts of the Bible as especially appropriate to be used as lessons in revolutionary struggle. The Book of Exodus, for example, is reinterpreted as the great saga of the Jewish People's political liberation from the pharaoh's imperialist yoke.[928] Other episodes of Sacred History "reread" in this sense are Easter, Jesus's first lecture at the Synagogue (Luke 4:18–19), and the Magnificat (Luke 1:46–55). Today's poor are raised to the category of biblical personages, while the latter are reduced to the struggling poor. LT sacralizes politics while desacralizing the Sacred Scriptures. Old Testament prophets are reduced to revolutionary leaders, and the latter are promoted to prophets. For example, Leonardo Boff writes that "some of the distinguished representatives of modern liberation were Jews: Marx, Freud, Marcuse, Einstein. They carried with them the liberating wisdom of the Old Testament prophets."[929]

4. Modern Revolutions: Prophetic Movements

Under the suggestive title, *A Post-Secular Prophetic Model*, Spanish leftist writer José Luis López Aranguren exploits the possibility of "a prophetic model of society." His essay appears in a 1988 book in which leading LT representatives assess future possibilities for their movement facing the collapse of real Socialism. He states that "the Prophet is God, he is the Sense, he is Hope speaking to men through a man's lips." He enumerates several "prophetic movements" of our times: "Have there been prophetic movements of this secular type in our times? Certainly. Without going back to the Revolution par excellence, the French Revolution, and to those that it inspired, we have Marxism. After Marxism, Jean Paul Sartre saw [such a movement] in the beginnings of the Cuban revolution. ... Finally, not to speak of the little-known and non-Western Chinese cultural revolution, the last manifestation of this sort, at least for the time being, was the preparation in the United States and in Germany, and later the outbreak in Paris, of the May 1968 revolution."[930]

In this light we understand how the term *prophetic* is used today by some theologians to designate the feminist, homosexual, and environmental movements. They are the tip of the spear, the cutting edge of history, understood as revolutionary process.

5. Prophetism and Collective Conscience

However, there is a difference between today's revolutionary prophets and those of the Old Testament. Consistent with LT's egalitarian and communitarian inspiration, liberation theologians understand modern prophetism as something collective, albeit often existing in persons who become focal points of the people's revolutionary energies.

They turn revolutionary leaders into prophets, enlightened charismatic leaders who carry out God's work in their liberating struggles. In LT's communitarian and immanentist view, these leaders are not clairvoyant individuals endowed with a God-given mission to galvanize and guide the people. Rather, they know how to interpret and channel particular "movements of the spirit" at work within the people, motivating them toward the Kingdom. Thus, divine action would be exercised not so much upon individuals but upon the collective conscience of the people, often made explicit by the voice of the prophet.

Writing about "prophetism and collective conscience," José Luis López Aranguren comments, "prophetism is always communitarian. The secularized prophetism of our times is eminently communitarian. The contemporary prophet, or better, prophets, as there are always several, lend their voices and articulate the yearnings of the community. We mention the example of the last great prophecy ... the Revolution that seemed to arrive in 1968. Was it not much more the collective action of the youth of that time than the prophetic action of some particular mentor?"[931]

LT thus presents revolutionary movements as spontaneous events rising from the deep yearnings of the people and impelled by liberating energies from the Spirit, rather than the result of a "carefully-planned plot carried out by professional revolutionaries" (using Lenin's expression).[932]

K. A New Religion

Putting together all these errors present in LT's various currents to a greater or lesser degree, it is difficult to escape the impression that we are facing a new religion.

1. A New Concept of Virtue and Sanctity

Liberation theologians propose an entirely new concept of virtue and sanctity. A virtuous person is not someone who has the strength (virtue) to keep God's commandments, but someone who ardently commits to the liberating process, namely revolutionary activity. Also in this case, while not denying that virtue entails fighting one's own defects, they highlight instead the fight against "oppressive structures." Leonardo Boff writes, "The base communities have created the possibility for another type of holiness, that of the militant. Beyond fighting against one's own passions, the militant fights [politically] against exploitation and exclusive accumulation of wealth in an effort to build more communitarian and balanced social structures."[933]

2. A New Concept of Sin

Referencing Saints Augustine and Thomas Aquinas, the *Catechism of the Catholic Church* defines sin as "an utterance, a deed, or a desire contrary to the eternal law."[934] Mortal sin supposes

927. John Paul II, Address to the Third General Conference of the Latin American Episcopate, no. I.4.

928. Fr. Gutiérrez writes, "The Exodus experience is paradigmatic. ... It remains vital and contemporary due to similar historical experiences which the People of God undergo." Gutiérrez, *A Theology of Liberation*, 159. With this game of smoke and mirrors, liberation theologians identify oppressed citizens with the people of Israel and the pharaoh with the government they seek to overthrow.

929. Leonardo Boff, *Francis of Assisi: A Model for Human Liberation*, trans. John W. Diercksmeier (Maryknoll, N.Y.: Orbis Books, 2006), 74. Reprinted by permission of Orbis Books.

930. José Luis López Aranguren, "Un modelo profético post-secular," in *Desafíos Cristianos*, ed. Misión Abierta (Madrid: Loguez Ediciones, 1988), 333, 331. Boff writes, "Liberation theology is understood in the thread of these great movements of emancipation that characterize the modern age." Boff, *Francis of Assisi*, 74.

931. Aranguren, "Un modelo profético," 334.

932. Analyzing the strategy of the Russian Revolution, Lenin maintains that the proletarian revolution was carried out by a vanguard, the Communist Party, made up mainly of "professional revolutionaries," that is, men and women who dedicate their lives to the communist cause. See Lenin, *What Is to Be Done?*

933. Boff, *Church: Charism and Power*, 123. The term *politically* was included as it appears in the original Brazilian edition. See Boff, *Igreja: Carisma e poder*, 206.

934. See *Catechism of the Catholic Church*, no. 1849. (St. Augustine, *Contra Faustum* 22: *PL* 42, 418; Aquinas, *ST* I-II, q. 71, a. 6). Completing the definition, the *Catechism* states:

> 1849 Sin is an offense against reason, truth, and right conscience; it is failure in genuine love for God and neighbor caused by a perverse attachment to

grave matter, as well as full knowledge of the evil and full deliberation to carry it out. Venial sin occurs when one of these conditions is missing. Sin can only be practiced by persons. Only a person can assume moral responsibility for his deeds, words, desires, thoughts, and omissions.

One may speak of social or structural sin only in an analogical sense, as John Paul II recalled in his homily closing the Sixth General Assembly of the Synod of Bishops on October 29, 1983: "We can and should speak of social sin and even of structural sin in an analogical sense, since properly speaking, sin is a personal act."[935]

In LT the concept of sin is changed to a different, predominantly secular concept, losing the meaning of a person's moral action and assuming a collective and social meaning: the existence of "oppressive structures."

Mainstream liberation theologians downplay the notion of personal sin and stress social sin instead. "In the liberation approach," Father Gutiérrez writes, "sin is not considered as an individual, private, or merely interior reality—asserted just enough to necessitate a 'spiritual' redemption which does not challenge the order in which we live. Sin is regarded as a social, historical fact. ... When it is considered in this way, the collective dimensions of sin are rediscovered." The Peruvian liberation theologian concludes by stating, "Sin is evident in oppressive structures, in the exploitation of man by man, in the domination and slavery of peoples, races and social classes. Sin appears, therefore, as the fundamental alienation, the root of a situation of injustice and exploitation."[936]

Some more radical liberation theologians—more consistent with their tenets—openly deny the concept of personal sin. The Spanish theologian Father Rodríguez, writes, "Liberation theology propounds an exclusively sociological concept of sin." He goes on to quote Father Assmann: "We must switch from an individualist concept of sin to a social and structural one."[937]

Calling it "the best depiction I have found of the profound primary evil of social sin," Jesuit Father Hennelly quotes a text by Zambian theologian Fr. Laurenti Magesa, a professor at the Catholic University of East Africa in Nairobi: "The worst type of sin, in fact the only 'mortal sin' which has enslaved man for the greater part of his history, is the institutionalized sin."[938]

It is only logical that the confusion liberation theologians make about the true nature of sin should also affect their concept of original sin. Gregory Baum, for example, decries, "At one time theologians linked this inherited distortion [of original sin] to Adam's transgression in a literal sense and saw in it a quasi-ontological legacy." After affirming that the concept of original sin dogmatically taught by the Church was "an embarrassing doctrine for many Christians," the German-Canadian liberationist proposes the doctrine of LT: "Contemporary theologians ... have tended to identify the inherited sin with what the Bible calls 'the sin of the world'—that is, the structure of evil, built into society."[939]

3. A New Concept of Conversion

In Catholic doctrine, *conversion* has several meanings, all of which evolve around the idea of an interior change of heart and thought producing a new, correct relationship with God. So does the passage from a false religion to the Catholic faith, from a sinful life to a virtuous one, and so forth.[940]

Now if sin has a predominantly social nature, then the concept of conversion also changes. For LT, conversion is the elimination of oppression. First, it means shedding interior oppression by adopting a new mentality that rejects the alienating dominant culture.

Secondly, conversion implies discarding a bourgeois or indifferent attitude by making an earnest commitment to fight social oppression. Father Gutiérrez writes, "Conversion means a radical transformation of ourselves; it means thinking, feeling and living as Christ—present in exploited and alienated man. To be converted is to commit oneself to the process of the liberation of the poor and oppressed, to commit oneself lucidly, realistically, and concretely."[941]

Progressive American theologian Phillip Berryman writes,

> Liberation theology emphasizes the collective nature of sin. ...
> As a consequence, we must say that liberation from sin cannot be direct but must be mediated through political and historical liberation.[942]

Commenting on LT's tortuous views, noted conservative Cuban-American scholar Fr. Enrique Rueda writes, "What in traditional Catholic thought is sin, in Liberation Theology is collective alienation. Grace ceases to mean an integral transformation of the individual soul and becomes a collective and external phenomenon which favors the advent of Socialism; the concept of man is collective rather than individual and evangelization means the promotion of the Revolution. Conversion has a political meaning rather than a religious sense since religion is absorbed by politics."[943]

4. A New Concept of Truth

a. The Catholic Concept of Truth

Catholic doctrine considers truth from three points of view: theological, philosophical, and moral. From the theological point of view, it is said that God is the substantial and sovereign truth. "I am the way, the truth, and the life," Our Lord said (Mark 14:17). Being Truth itself, God is the first cause and measure of all truth. From the philosophical standpoint, "truth is the conformance of our judgments to the reality of things" (*adaequatio intellectus et rei*), Father Rodríguez explains. "When our judgments correspond to reality, we have truth; when they do not correspond to reality, we have error."[944]

From the moral point of view, truth becomes the virtue of veracity, sincerity, or frankness, coupled with the virtue of justice. It is "the quality that consists in presenting oneself [as] truthful in everything one does, and in speaking truthfully in everything one says."[945]

certain goods. It wounds the nature of man and injures human solidarity. ...
1850 Sin is an offense against God. ... Sin sets itself against God's love for us and turns our hearts away from it. Like the first sin, it is disobedience, a revolt against God. ... Sin is diametrically opposed to the obedience of Jesus, which achieves our salvation. ... (*Catechism of the Catholic Church*, nos. 1849–1850)

935. John Paul II, Homily at Sixth General Assembly of the Synod of Bishops (Oct. 29, 1983), no. 3.
936. Gutiérrez, *A Theology of Liberation*, 175.
937. Victorino Rodríguez, O.P., "Pecado individual y pecado colectivo," *Iglesia Mundo* (Madrid) (Dec. 1, 1984), 10.
938. Hennelly, *Theology for a Liberating Church*, 114.
939. Baum, *Religion and Alienation*, 199.

940. Conversion, the *Catechism of the Catholic Church* teaches, is "the movement of a 'contrite heart,' drawn and moved by grace to respond to the merciful love of God" (no. 1428).
941. Gutiérrez, *A Theology of Liberation*, 205.
942. Berryman, "Latin American Liberation Theology," 46.
943. Rueda, *The Marxist Character*, 38.
944. Victorino Rodríguez y Rodríguez, O.P., "The Liberating Truth," *TFP Newsletter* (Special Issue, 1985), 11.
945. A. Michel, s.v. "Vérité, véracité," *D.T.C.*, 15–2e.:2683.

b. The Marxist Concept of Truth

As we have seen, LT does not accept the theological concept of an absolute truth manifested in Divine revelation. Since it is not a rational inquiry, it does not even seek a philosophical truth. Liberation theologians seek truth in praxis. Leonardo Boff says, "It is not thought out truth that saves us, but the truth that is done and realized in a praxis."[946] This is but the transposition of the Marxist concept of truth to the domain of theology: Truth is neither something subsistent, an intellectual value, nor is it objective. According to Marx, truth is the efficaciousness of the revolutionary praxis, one that actually yields results.

Liberation theologians confer inordinate importance to what they call the "epistemological break" realized by Karl Marx, that is, the break with traditional criteria for philosophical and moral judgments.[947] Father Gutiérrez writes, "For people today truth is what we make true. ... In his penetrating and finely chiselled *Theses on Feuerbach*, Marx starts from that perspective to lay the epistemological bases of his own contribution to a scientific understanding of history."[948]

This epistemological break is said to be contained in Marx's "Theses on Feuerbach."

The eleventh thesis asserts, "The philosophers have only interpreted the world, in various ways; the point is to change it."[949] In order to change it the philosopher or thinker must prove in praxis—revolutionary action—the transformative power of his ideas. He should not try to conceive a reality isolated from praxis. Marx further develops this in the second thesis: "The question whether objective truth can be attributed to human thinking is not a question of theory but is a practical question. Man must prove the truth—i.e. the reality and power, the this-sidedness of his thinking in practice. The dispute over the reality or non-reality of thinking that is isolated from practice is a purely *scholastic* question."[950]

Marxism—and with it liberation theologians—totally rejects the idea of an objective truth. For Marx, the question of whether a person understands a specific reality correctly or erroneously, whether his understanding corresponds or not to the objective world, is meaningless. What matters is whether the person can actually change society in a revolutionary sense by putting his conceptions into practice. The criterion of truth becomes the actual effectiveness of revolutionary action. Whatever helps the revolutionary process is true and good; whatever hinders it is false and bad.

As a corollary, the question of morals is also made relative and subordinated to the effectiveness of revolutionary action. Here is how Lenin considered this issue: "[For] us there is no such thing as a morality that stands outside human society; that is a fraud. [For] us morality is subordinated to the interests of the proletariat's class struggle."[951] Who determines what the "interests of the proletariat are"? Why, the Communist Party, a group of revolutionaries, or even a community of "committed Christians." In other words, the Revolution replaces the absolute, the Divine Law.

c. LT Assumes the Marxist Concept of Truth

"The criterion of a true theology," writes Uruguayan liberation theologian Father Segundo, "consists not in an orthodoxy elaborated by the theology itself, but in a real, and even material, success in a historical liberation."[952] Along the same line, U.S.–educated Brazilian liberation theologian Rubem Alves asserts, "Truth is the name given by the historical community to those historical acts that were, are, or will be efficacious for the liberation of man."[953]

Illustrating the LT method, Father Hennelly writes, "Liberation theology's greatest achievement and its major contribution to the world church has been precisely to overcome this truncated and profoundly alienating understanding of theology. And it has achieved this by creating a method of doing theology which is intimately linked not only with orthodoxy but also with orthopraxis, that is, the liberating action which will provide the ultimate test of orthodoxy." He quite agrees with Fr. Matthew Lamb, who sees "orthopraxy as the foundation of orthodoxy," upending Catholic theology.[954]

In LT, revolution replaces the absolute. Just as it makes no sense for liberation theologians to ask whether a particular thought or action is objectively true, so also it makes no sense to ask whether it is according to God and His law or whether it corresponds to something in the divine essence. For them, historical liberation, and not God, is the measure of truth. Feminist theologian Sharon Welch is clear: "The referent of the phrase 'liberating God' is not primarily God but *liberation*. That is, the language here is true not because it corresponds with something in the divine nature but because it leads to actual liberation in history."[955]

If truth is conceived as effective revolutionary praxis, it is something man builds while pursuing revolutionary objectives. "The notion of truth ..." Father Assmann says, "is identified with the notion of efficacious praxis."[956] Truth is a concept that depends purely on the current conveniences of the revolutionary situation. This is why liberation theologians do not speak of orthodoxy but orthopraxis.

5. A New Concept of Faith

Faith, in the theological sense, is an act of the intellect commanded by the will to believe in the revelation founded on the authority of God's word, that is, divine truth.[957] This concept of faith has no place in LT.

Liberation theologians conceive faith as praxis. Father Gutiérrez writes,

> Evangelical truth, truth as the gospel sees it, is something that is done. ...
> More and more, then, faith surfaces as a liberation praxis.[958]

Under the title, "Faith as Praxis," Father Assmann states that "faith should be fundamentally understood as praxis in the strong sense of historical praxis and not simply religious practice." The

946. Boff, "Qué es hacer teología desde América Latina?" 140, quoted in Roberto Jimenez, "Teología de la liberación, Proyecto histórico y tres de sus conceptos claves," 74.

947. Epistemological: literally "referring to the sciences," from the Greek *episteme*, "science." In modern philosophy it refers to that part of Logic known as *critique* or *criteriology*.

948. Gutiérrez, "Liberation Praxis and Christian Faith," 19. See also Gutiérrez, *A Theology of Liberation*, 29.

949. Karl Marx, "Theses on Feuerbach," no. 11, Marxists.org.

950. Marx, no. 2.

951. Vladimir I. Lenin, "The Tasks of the Youth Leagues," (Speech delivered at the Third All-Russia Congress of the Russian Young Communist League), Oct. 2, 1920.

952. Juan Luis Segundo, "Statement," in *Theology in the Americas: Detroit 1975*, ed. Sergio Torres and John Eagleson (New York: Orbis Books, 1976), 281.

953. Rubem Alves, "Apuntes para una teología del desarrollo," quoted in Assmann, *Opresión liberación*, 90.

954. Hennelly, *Theology for a Liberating Church*, 37, 47.

955. Welch, *Communities of Resistance*, 7.

956. Assmann, *Opresión liberación*, 90.

957. See Aquinas, *S.T.*, II–II, q. 4, aa. 2, 5.

958. Gutiérrez, "Liberation Praxis and Christian Faith," 20.

Brazilian liberation theologian concludes that "faith is conceived as praxis, and praxis as faith."[959]

6. A Warning on LT's Duplicitous Language

At the time of Saint Pius X, one of the causes that led modernists to ruin was their frankness. In order to circumvent any condemnations, their successors endeavored to develop a new, wily, and slippery language which, while able on the one hand to have an orthodox interpretation, contained on the other innovative doctrines (their real, intended meaning). Faithful heirs to modernism, liberation theologians often use doublespeak as well.

Writing about her colleagues, American feminist theologian Sharon Welch confirms this point: "Their language is that of traditional theology—God, Christ, salvation, sin, grace—but the meanings of these traditional terms are distinctly nontraditional. Liberation theology uses the same symbols that are found in traditional theology, but they are interpreted by different criteria."[960]

---

959. Assmann, *Opresión liberación*, 97.
960. Welch, *Communities of Resistance*, 34.

Chapter 5:
The Ecclesiology of Liberation Theology

A. Introduction

1. A Completely Revamped Catholic Doctrine

The Brazilian liberation theologian Leonardo Boff correctly points out that the "theology of liberation represents a new lens through which the whole content of Christianity may be considered."[961]

This upheaval touches the very structure of the Church. "Ecclesiology is the theological discipline developed in greatest detail in liberation theology," Fr. Sergio Torres stated in an international conference of liberation theologians in Detroit.[962] Indeed, such is the role this new ecclesiology plays in liberationists' lucubrations that one is almost tempted to say they developed their theology in view of their peculiar ecclesiology, rather than vice-versa.

2. "A New Communitarian Model of Church"

This new ecclesiology is not reformist but revolutionary. Well-known B.C.C. theoreticians James and Evelyn Whitehead of the Institute of Pastoral Studies at Loyola University Chicago assert, "Minor adjustments—such as ordaining married men to a permanent diaconate—are not sufficient. Major adjustments—such as allowing women to join a hierarchy of clerical leaders—will not suffice. A reimagining of the Christian community itself [i.e., the Church] is required."[963]

Liberation theologians do not hide the fact that this metamorphosis entails the end of the Catholic Church as it was known for two thousand years, and the emergence of a new church. "We are seeing the rising of a new church, born in the heart of the old Church, in the form of *comunidades de base*," proclaims Leonardo Boff, the person who has best systematized the ecclesiology of liberation theology.[964]

The new church dreamed of by liberation theology would not have the structure of the Church founded by Christ. Rather, it would be an amorphous, fluid conglomerate of grassroots communities united by bonds of fraternity and a prophetic commitment. "What we want," Spanish liberation theologian Juan José Tamayo-Acosta says, "is a new communitarian model of the Church." This "communitarian church," he continues, can only be built upon the ruins of the present Church: "The primary goal is to ... turn the Church into a community of communities, destroying the whole bureaucratic framework that hinders the achievement of this objective."[965]

A handbook on how to develop Basic Christian Communities, published by the National Federation of Priests' Councils, quotes Joseph Holland, with the Center of Concern, in Washington, D.C.:

> It is becoming increasingly clear that the hierarchical structures of the pre–Vatican II Church are not adequate. ... Today, however, we need new structures. ...
>
> ... We are entering ... a whole new form of the Church, altering elements dominant since the time of Constantine. ... [It] is not simply a short term transitional strategy but a profound shift ending Constantinian Christianity. ...
>
> ... [This new Church would take the form of] a de-centralized network of small groups nourished by personal faith-sharing, spontaneous prayer, a biblical rootedness, and a prophetic social outreach.[966]

What could be the *notae ecclesiae* (marks of the Church) of the new church longed-for by liberation theologians? Let us hear the Spanish theologian Juan García-Nieto:

> *A fraternal and non-authoritarian community.* In other words, more horizontal than vertical. ...
>
> *A "community of communities" church.* In other words, universal and not exclusively Roman. ...
>
> *A much more service-oriented than ecclesiocentric church.* ...
>
> *A church with democratic structures.* In other words, one that is committed to revamping all its structures. ...
>
> *A church without sexist or other discriminations* [thus, unopposed to women's ordination]. ... Liberation ... demands that the Church suppress ... the discrimination between a teaching and a learning church.
>
> *A borderless ecumenical church.* ...
>
> *A church "on" the side of the poor.* Not just "at" the side of the poor ... with all that this implies regarding the rupture with the current society. [A church that assumes class analysis]. ...
>
> *A free church.* ... without any privilege. ... that renounces any kind of confessionalism and power, as well as any form of "Christendom." [A church that proclaims all freedoms.][967]

---

961. Leonardo Boff, "Statement," in *Theology in the Americas: Detroit 1975*, ed. Sergio Torres and John Eagleson (New York: Orbis Books, 1976), 294.

962. Sergio Torres, "Goals of the Detroit Conference," in *Theology in the Americas: Detroit 1975*, ed. Sergio Torres and John Eagleson (New York: Orbis Books, 1976), 258.

963. James D. Whitehead and Evelyn Eaton Whitehead, *The Emerging Laity: Returning Leadership to the Community of Faith* (New York: Image/Doubleday and Company, 1988), 25.

964. Boff, *Church: Charism and Power*, 62.

965. Tamayo-Acosta, "Las comunidades cristianas populares," 164–65.

966. James Ratigan, introduction to *Developing Basic Christian Communities: A Handbook*, edited by National Federation of Priests' Councils (Chicago: National Federation of Priests' Councils, 1979), 1–3. See also Holland and Henriot, *Social Analysis*, 85.

967. Juan Garcia-Nieto Paris, "Proyecto de una sociedad y una iglesia en clave de utopía," in *Utopia y profetismo*, ed. González Faus, 149–51. Phrases between brackets correspond to the recorded proceedings from the Eighth Congress of Theology organized by the Theological Association John XXIII, held in Madrid on Sept. 10, 1988. T.F.P. Archive.

3. The Complete Destruction of the Catholic Church

The changes sought by liberation theologians are so profound and encompassing, so utterly self-demolishing, one cannot help but ask what would be left of the Church should they be implemented. Italian liberationist Luigi de Paoli, a psychiatrist and former national coordinator of the "We Are Church" movement, describes in detail the ecclesiastical revolution pursued by liberation theology. "We cannot speak of a profound and radical transformation ... unless we simultaneously influence and modify the whole ecclesiastical system in its three *coordinates: the conceptual framework, the socio-economic structures, and the personality of each one of its members*."

a. A New Doctrine

In the first place, according to Paoli, the entire deposit of Catholic doctrine must be abolished. "The conceptual apparatus of the Church contains not only truths of the faith and their interpretation, but also subjective views of the world, determined by the subconscious structure of the faithful." The whole conceptual system of the Church "is *the product of intellectuals and not of the working class ... in other words, it is Western and not Eastern, machoist and not feminist, rational instead of sentimental, moralistic instead of scientific, old and not young. ... A conceptual* and theoretical overhaul is required."

b. New Structures

In the second place he proposes the demolition of the present structures of the Church and their replacement. "The communitarian structure is radically different from the centuries-old one of the institutions."

c. A New Man

Finally, Paoli writes, "*This 'metanoia' requires not only a change in people's logic-conceptual and socioeconomic structures but also in the psycho-libidinal structures*."[968]

Obviously, the transformations propounded by liberation theologians go much beyond establishing a new church. They intend to create a new man fitting that church, with a new psychological structure, a new sensibility, new patterns of volition and behavior, and even a new libido.

4. "Reinventing the Church"

"Reinvention" is the buzzword used to describe this immense upheaval. Liberation theologians want nothing less than to "reinvent" the Church. "The best conceptualization of this [LT] experience," Leonardo Boff writes, "is in the frequently heard expression 'reinvention of the church.' The church is beginning to be born at the grassroots"[969] —as if the Church had not existed for the past 2,000 years!

What are the foundations of this new church proposed by LT? On what points does it depart from the Church founded by Our Lord Jesus Christ? Presenting them alongside the traditional Catholic doctrine will help to highlight the contrast.

*In this next section, for the reader's greater ease in accompanying the analysis, each numbered point of the characteristics of the Catholic Church as founded by Our Lord Jesus Christ is presented with a **T** (for **True**).*

*For better contrast, the equivalent numbered point in LT's new church is shown with an **F** (for **False**), and the text expounding on LT's doctrinal errors is shaded in gray.*

B. Contrasting the Catholic Church Founded by Christ with LT's New Church

1T. Our Lord Willed to Found a Church and He Founded the Holy Roman Catholic Church

In his 1910 motu proprio *Sacrorum antistitum*, issued "to promulgate some laws in order to check the modernist peril," St. Pius X teaches that "the Church, the guardian and teacher of the revealed word, was personally instituted by the real and historical Christ when he lived among us."[970] We find the same doctrine in the *Catechism of the Catholic Church*[971] and in the Constitution *Lumen gentium*.[972]

Explaining the reasons why Our Lord founded a Church, the dogmatic Constitution *Dei Filius*, of the First Vatican Council, teaches,

> 10. So that we could fulfill our duty of embracing the true faith and of persevering unwaveringly in it, God, through his only begotten Son, founded the Church, and he endowed his institution with clear notes to the end that she might be recognized by all as the guardian and teacher of the revealed word.
>
> 11. To the Catholic Church alone belong all those things, so many and so marvelous, which have been divinely ordained to make for the manifest credibility of the Christian Faith.[973]

1F. Christ Did Not Want to Found a Church, but Only to Preach a Kingdom

a. Our Lord Did Not Found a Church

Liberation theologians openly deny that Our Lord Jesus Christ founded a Church. Reaffirming modernist errors, they hold that Our Lord simply preached the imminent coming of the "Kingdom of God" and never wanted to found a Church. Leonardo Boff agrees with Swiss theologian Father Küng, who peremptorily states: "During his lifetime, *Jesus did not found a church*."[974] To buttress this thesis, Boff does not hesitate to cite the condemned Loisy: "Alfred Loisy ... the modernist, stated the problem well when he wrote, somewhat

968. Luigi de Paoli, "Camino y propuesta hacia una iglesia nazarena," in *Desafíos Cristianos*, ed. Misión Abierta (Madrid: Loguez Ediciones, 1988), 146–48. (Emphasis in the original.)

969. Leonardo Boff, *Ecclesiogenesis: The Base Communities Reinvent the Church*, trans. Robert R. Barr (Maryknoll, N.Y.: Orbis Books, 1986), 23. Condemning this position, Benedict XVI stated, "Indeed, we know that after the Second Vatican Council some were convinced that everything was new, that there was a different Church, that the pre-Conciliar Church was finished and that we had another, totally 'other' Church, an anarchic utopianism!" Benedict XVI, General Audience (Mar. 10, 2010), "Saint Bonaventure," no. 3.

970. St. Pius X, motu proprio *Sacrorum antistitum* (Sept. 1, 1910).

971. "The Lord Jesus inaugurated his Church." *Catechism of the Catholic Church*, no. 763.

972. "The Catholic Church was founded as necessary by God, through Christ." Second Vatican Council, Dogmatic Constitution *Lumen Gentium*, no. 14. (Our translation from the Latin.)

973. First Vatican Council, *Dei Filius*, sess. 3 (Apr. 24, 1870), chap. 3, 10–11.

974. Boff, *Ecclesiogenesis*, 50.

disconcertedly, 'Christ preached the Kingdom of God, and the Church appeared instead.'"[975]

b. The Church Was Instituted by the Apostles as a Substitute for the Kingdom

The Church, according to liberation theology, was instituted by the apostles when it became clear to them that the Kingdom would not come in their time. The Church would be a transitory substitute for the original design of Jesus, a historical accident without its own raison d'être. Leonardo Boff states,

> [Christ] did not preach the Church but rather the Kingdom of God. ... In his preaching and practice of the Kingdom of God, Christ introduced elements that later would form the basis for the Church, such as the gathering of the twelve apostles, the institution of baptism, and the eucharistic supper. But these elements do not constitute the entire reality of the Church. The Church exists only because the Kingdom was not accepted by the Jewish people and Jesus was rejected by them. If the Kingdom preached by Christ had been realized, there would be no need for the Church. Essentially, the Church substitutes for the Kingdom. ...
>
> The Church as institution is not based on the incarnation of the Word but rather in the faith in the power of the apostles inspired by the Holy Spirit.[976]

2T. The Church Is Immutable in Her Organic Constitution

The organic constitution of the Church is immutable by divine ordinance. The Church does adapt to times and places in secondary and accidental aspects, but she cannot suffer any substantial change. If, *ad absurdum*, she were to modify her organic constitution she would cease to be the true Church of Christ. In the decree *Lamentabili*, St. Pius X condemned this modernist proposition: "The organic constitution of the Church is not immutable. Like human society, Christian society [i.e., the Church] is subject to a perpetual evolution."[977] Likewise, the *Catechism of the Catholic Church* teaches, "The Lord Jesus endowed his community with a structure that will remain until the Kingdom is fully achieved."[978]

2F. The Church Is Built Throughout History, Following Socioeconomic Evolution

a. Not a Harbinger but an Obstacle

As mentioned, for liberation theology the Church was flawed at birth. Instead of fulfilling Our Lord's original design (the "project of Jesus," in LT's awkward jargon), the Church was born as a substitute for the messianic utopia. This replacement, shaped by historical circumstances, later acquired a rigid and permanent structure totally alien to the fluid nature of the Kingdom. The Church thus betrayed Christ's messianic utopianism. Instead of being a harbinger of the Kingdom, the Church became an obstacle to its realization.

According to liberation theology, history is a revolutionary process inexorably advancing toward the fulfillment of the egalitarian and permissive utopia described in the preceding chapters and identified as the Kingdom of God. In its secular manifestation, this revolutionary process advances by establishing Communism in the fight against traditional society. Parallel to and reflecting this development, the real church is built throughout history in the fight against the traditional Church.

We will retrace these false and arcane doctrines in slow motion.

b. The Church Depends on the Kingdom

For liberation theologians, the Church has no intrinsic reason for being but is conceived in function of the Kingdom of God, which they identify with the egalitarian and liberationist utopia. The Magisterium does teach that the Church is directed toward the Kingdom of God. Liberation theologians, however, manipulate this truth to relativize the Church and make her substantially evolutionary.

Argentine liberation theologian José Míguez Bonino explained this point during an international conference on LT ecclesiology organized in 1980 in Brazil by the Ecumenical Association of Third World Theologians: "The ultimate point of reference for the Christian faith is not the church but the Kingdom of God. The church is *relative* to that horizon; it must be seen in that perspective. In that sense, the church is relativized."[979]

According to LT, the Church is nothing but an assembly of faithful animated by utopian aspirations. Their mission would be to labor to establish the Kingdom. "They fight for a free, just, egalitarian and fraternal society and for a church, community of communities, in the service of the Kingdom," as Spanish liberationist José Antonio Pérez Tapias states.[980]

c. The Kingdom and the Church Are Built Throughout History

The Church is thus relative to the Kingdom, and the Kingdom is built throughout history in revolutionary struggles for liberty, equality, and fraternity. "The Kingdom," Leonardo Boff comments, "is certainly the Christian utopia that lies at the culminaton [*sic*] of history. But it must be repeated that this Kingdom is found in the process of history wherever justice and fraternity are fostered and wherever the poor are respected and recognized as shapers of their own destiny. All individuals, institutions, and activities directed toward those ideals favored by the historical Jesus are bearers of that Kingdom."[981]

The Church envisioned by liberation theology is thus gradually built throughout history. Boff writes,

---

975. Boff, 49–50.

976. Boff, *Church: Charism and Power*, 146–47. To buttress his thesis, Boff quotes Erik Peterson, *Theologische traktate* (Munich: Kösel-Verlag, 1951), the chapter on the Church, 409–24; and Joseph Ratzinger, "Zeichen unter den völkern", in *Wahrheit und zeugnis*, M. Schmaus and A. Lapple, eds. (Düsseldorf: Patmos Verlag, 1964), 456–66.

977. St. Pius X, decree *Lamentabili*, no. 53.

978. *Catechism of the Catholic Church*, no. 765.

979. José Míguez Bonino, "Fundamental Questions in Ecclesiology," in *The Challenge of the Basic Christian Communities*, ed. Sergio Torres and John Eagleson (Maryknoll, N.Y.: Orbis Books, 1981), 146.

980. José A. Pérez Tapias, "Balance prospectivo," *Misión Abierta* (Madrid) 77, no. 2 (Apr. 1984): 59. A professor at the University of Granada, Pérez Tapias became a congressman for the Spanish Socialist Workers Party (P.S.O.E.).

981. Boff, *Church: Charism and Power*, 10.

This Church is being built day by day. ...
Today we are witnessing a true ecclesiogenesis. ... [The Church] never judges itself to be complete but [is] always [in the making, becoming] what it should be, that is, the sacrament of Christ and of the Spirit.[982]

d. The Church Is Built According to Changes in the Modes of Economic Production

Many liberation theologians, particularly Latin Americans, anchor this evolutionist conception of the Church in Marxist ideology.

Marxists hold that the religious, social, political, and cultural structures are consequences ("superstructures") of the mode of economic production.[983] Thus, historic evolution toward ever more socialized forms of production and ownership would automatically bring about evolution toward more egalitarian social, political, cultural, and religious structures. Communism—the stage beyond the dictatorship of the proletariat—would be the final stage of this process. According to LT, the Church is shaped by prevailing sociopolitical structures, which in turn are shaped by the prevailing mode of economic production. Leonardo Boff writes:

The Church does not operate in a vacuum, but in a society which is situated in history. This means that the Church, like it or not, is limited and shaped by a social context. ... The religious-ecclesiastical realm is a part of the social realm, which influences it in a dialectical manner. ... The organization of a society revolves around its means of production. ...

This organization is infrastructural, and the rest of society is built upon it. ... The Church is also conditioned, limited, and oriented by a specific means of production.[984]

The Church, thus, would accompany the evolution of the system of economic production. Boff writes, "The ecclesiastical-religious dimension [of the Church] is not a given, ready-made structure of practices, actors, institutions, and discourses having to do with God, Christ, and the church as sacrament. It is the result of a production process, the product of a structuring effort in which two productive forces are at work. One productive force is society with its specific mode of production. The second productive force is the Christian experience with its content of divine revelation. In other

words, the church is not born ready made in heaven. It, too, is the fruit of a specific history."[985]

3T. The Church Is a Perfect Society With a Visible Structure

a. A Visible Structure

Our Lord Jesus Christ founded His Church as a perfect society with a visible structure governed by a legitimate authority instituted by Him.

God desired that the Church have a visible structure so all men, even the unlearned, could unmistakably recognize her through her appearance. Leo XIII taught, "If we consider the chief end of [Christ's] Church and the proximate efficient causes of salvation, it is undoubtedly *spiritual*; but in regard to those who constitute it, and to the things which lead to these spiritual gifts, it is *external* and necessarily visible."[986]

b. A Perfect Society

The Church is a society because she possesses all the characteristics of a society:
—a body of members: the faithful;
—an authority providing the moral union among the members and directing them toward a common end: the pope and bishops;
—a common end: eternal salvation;
—common means to attain that end: profession of the same faith, participation in the same sacraments, and obedience to the same authority.

This society is perfect because it possesses all necessary means to attain its end and thus enjoys full autonomy within its proper sphere. In other words, the Church does not depend on any outside authority to attain its own end. Pius XI taught, "The Church [is] a society of the supernatural order and of universal extent; a perfect society, because it has in itself all the means required for its own end, which is the eternal salvation of mankind; hence it is supreme in its own domain."[987]

c. The Church Is the Mystical Body of Christ

The *Catechism of the Catholic Church* reiterates the perennial doctrine: "The Church is ... the Mystical Body of Christ."[988]

Explaining this truth, Leo XIII teaches,

Precisely because it is a body is the Church visible. ...
... The Church is a society *divine* in its origin, *supernatural* in its end and in means proximately adapted to the attainment of that end; but it is a *human*

---

982. Boff, 62. The words in brackets are the author's translation from the original Portuguese. See Boff, *Igreja: Carisma e poder*, 114.

983. Marx introduces the concept of "superstructure" in his January 1859 preface to *A Contribution to the Critique of Political Economy*:

In the social production of their existence, men inevitably enter into definite relations, which are independent of their will, namely relations of production appropriate to a given stage in the development of their material forces of production. The totality of these relations of production constitutes the economic structure of society, the real foundation, on which arises a legal and political superstructure and to which correspond definite forms of social consciousness. The mode of production of material life conditions the general process of social, political, and intellectual life. It is not the consciousness of men that determines their existence, but their social existence that determines their consciousness. (Karl Marx, *A Contribution to the Critique of Political Economy*, trans. S.W. Ryazanskaya, Marxists.org)

984. Boff, *Church: Charism and Power*, 110–11.

985. Leonardo Boff, "Theological Characteristics of a Grassroots Church," in *The Challenge of the Basic Christian Communities*, ed. Sergio Torres and John Eagleson (Maryknoll, N.Y.: Orbis Books, 1981), 126–27. See Leonardo Boff, "Notas teológicas da igreja na base," in *A igreja que surge da base*, ed. Sergio Torres (São Paulo: Edições Paulinas, 1982), 210.

986. Leo XIII, encyclical *Satis cognitum* (June 29, 1896), no. 3.

987. Pius XI, encyclical *Rappresentanti in terra* (Dec. 31, 1929), no. 13. Much has been written about the concept of the Church as a perfect society, often in a manipulative and misleading way. We are led to believe that the term *societas perfecta* refers to the fact that, before Vatican II, the Church was thought to be unstained and thus needed no reform. Not so. It is a technical expression that designates a society that possesses all the means to attain its own end and has no need to resort to any other society to attain it. In this sense, there are two perfect societies: the Church and the State. All other societies, such as the family, are imperfect in that they require other societies to fully attain their end. See Mario Cuminetti, ed., *La fine della chiesa come società perfetta* (Milan: I.D.O.C.-Mondadori, 1968).

988. *Catechism of the Catholic Church*, nos. 771, 779.

community inasmuch as it is composed of men. For this reason we find it called in Holy Writ by names indicating a perfect society. ... Finally it is the *body of Christ*—that is, of course, His *mystical* body, but a body living and duly organized and composed of many members.[989]

3F. The Church Is a Fluid Community Animated by the Spirit

a. The Church Is Not a Perfect Society

For LT, the Church is not a perfect society, nor even a visible one. LT's more authentic versions posit that the Church should have no formal juridical structure. The Spanish liberation theologian Father Floristán, former president of the Asociación de Teólogos Juan XXIII and professor at the Mexican American Cultural Center in San Antonio, Texas, takes issue with the definition of the Church as a perfect society. Adopting the hermeneutic of discontinuity and rupture denounced by Benedict XVI, he states, "The Second Vatican Council marked an important turning point. The church does not define itself with juridical categories—a perfect society hierarchically organized—but highlights its essentially communitarian and historical reality. In other words, it is the communion of believers called together by God, animated by the Spirit."[990]

b. A Pneumatic Church Defined in Terms of Energy and Charisms

In defining the new church they envisage, liberation theologians reject the traditional and dogmatic doctrine of the Church as being the mystical body of Christ. A body, they say, connotes structure, and thus hierarchy. They eschew this concept and speak instead of the church in terms of spirit, a fluid reality that shuns any structure.

After strongly rejecting the traditional Magisterium, and particularly criticizing the encyclicals *Satis cognitum* of Leo XIII and *Mystici Corporis Christi* of Pius XII, Leonardo Boff writes, "The expression of the Church as the body of Christ must be carefully defined. ... The Church must be thought of in terms of the risen Christ, identified with the Spirit, rather than in terms of the carnal Jesus. The Church has a christological origin; it also has, in particular, a pneumatological one (pneuma-Spirit) ... It has a dynamic and functional dimension; it is defined in terms of energy, charism, and the progress of the world."[991]

c. LT's Ultimate Goal: A Pneumatic and Cosmic Church

(i) A Church Guided by a Mysterious Immanent Power

Boff's words introduce two concepts: *pneumatic church* and *cosmic church*, which are increasingly used in LT's latest versions as the Marxist-flavored people's church loses historical relevance.

The pneumatic church would be a fluid assembly of people who receive inspirations directly from the "Spirit" in the form of specific internal movements and charisms. These pentecostal stirrings are shared by the community through rituals akin to those popular in New Age ambiences. This would be the source of authority and ministry in the new church. According to James and Evelyn Whitehead,

> This benevolent power was not addressed as a person. ... God's leadership is portrayed here not ... [as] a patriarch or lord but as a stirring of power within the group itself.[992]

(ii) Indistinguishable From the Cosmos

The pneumatic church would know no limits, possess no fixed doctrine or established liturgy, structure, or visible authority. To belong to this church it would suffice to follow the inspirations of the Spirit that blows anywhere it wills. One would no longer need to obey any hierarchy, believe in dogmas, nor—it seems—even be baptized.

Under the title "The Cosmic Church as the Body of the Risen Christ" Leonardo Boff explains LT's doctrine on this point:

> The pneumatic character of the Church is best seen by analyzing the expression "The Church is the body of Christ." ... This expression will lead to theological confusion if the term body is taken in its carnal sense rather than in its pneumatic meaning. ... Christ became spiritual, rather than carnal, through the resurrection (cf. 1 Cor. 15:45); that is, his nature of body, soul, and divinity is no longer limited to a particular place or time but is [in arcane language, he draws out the ultimate implications of this statement], as Spirit, free of all these earthly constraints and acquires a cosmic dimension, open to the totality of all reality. His is a "spiritual body" (1 Cor. 15:44). As such, he is present in all things. He is "all in all things" (Col. 3:11) and nothing that exists is far from his presence. As an ancient text stated, "quoting" the risen Christ: "lift a stone and I am under it; split a log and I am within it. I will be with you until the end of time." The risen Christ tore down all barriers.[993]

According to the Brazilian theologian, Christ is not made of flesh but is rather pneumatic and cosmic, an immanent presence indistinguishable from the universe, an energy flowing inside all things. The Church as the body of Christ, then, has the dimensions of the pneumatic Christ, that is, it is boundless: "If the pneumatic (risen) Christ knows no limitations, neither may his body, the Church, confine itself to the limitations of its own dogma, its rituals, its liturgy, or its canon law. The Church has the same boundaries as the risen Christ; and these dimensions are cosmic in nature." Who belongs to that cosmic Church? Boff answers, "All people of faith, in the Holy Spirit, must be members of the church. ... No one is outside of the church because there is no longer an 'outside,' because no one is outside of the reality of God and the risen Christ."[994]

What exactly do liberation theologians mean by this pneumatic or cosmic church they envision as the final goal of their liberating struggles in the ecclesiastical realm, a church that seems to embrace not only all men, but even inorganic

---

989. Leo XIII, encyclical *Satis cognitum*, nos. 3, 10.

990. Floristán, *La comunidad cristiana de base*, 69. This book contains the outline of the course on B.C.C.s that Fr. Floristán used to give at the Mexican American Cultural Center, in San Antonio, Texas.

991. Boff, *Church: Charism and Power*, 145–46.

992. Whitehead and Whitehead, *The Emerging Laity*, 21–22.

993. Boff, *Church: Charism and Power*, 151.

994. Boff, 152.

things, a church not governed by a visible authority but by an immanent power stirring within the community and not seen as a person? These extremely delicate questions remain unanswered, at least in their published works. On the other hand, we ask, would this pneumatic church still bear any resemblance to the Catholic Church?

Liberation theologians must explain themselves.

4T. The Church Is a Hierarchical Society

a. A Hierarchy That Teaches, Governs, and Sanctifies

Our Lord Jesus Christ founded His Church as a hierarchical society. He instituted a visible head for this society when He conferred on Simon Peter the power of the keys: "Blessed art thou Simon Bar-Jona. ... And I say to thee: That thou art Peter; and upon this rock I will build my Church, and the gates of hell shall not prevail against it. And I will give to thee the keys of the kingdom of heaven. And whatsoever thou shalt bind upon earth, it shall be bound also in heaven; and whatsoever thou shalt loose on earth, it shall be loosed also in heaven" (Matt. 16:18–19).

This is the doctrine of the Church, immutably taught to this day, for example, by the *Catechism of the Catholic Church*: "The Lord made Simon alone, whom he named Peter, the 'rock' of his Church. He gave him the keys of his Church and instituted him shepherd of the whole flock."[995] This echoes the conciliar constitution *Lumen Gentium*, which states, "In virtue of his office, that is as Vicar of Christ and pastor of the whole Church, the Roman pontiff has full, supreme, and universal power over the Church. And he is always free to exercise this power."[996]

Our Lord instituted a hierarchy in His Church when He chose twelve apostles from among His many followers, and instructed them in a special way. The apostles were consecrated bishops. Our Lord gave them both a mandate and the necessary powers to carry it out.[997] This mandate is the mission of teaching, sanctifying, and governing, which they must exercise in union with Peter. Citing the constitution *Lumen Gentium*, the *Catechism of the Catholic Church* is very clear: "'Just as the office which the Lord confided to Peter alone, as first of the apostles, destined to be transmitted to his successors, is a permanent one, so also endures the office, which the apostles received, of shepherding the Church, a charge destined to be exercised without interruption by the sacred order of bishops.' Hence, the Church teaches that 'the bishops have by divine institution taken the place of the apostles as pastors of the Church, in such wise that whoever listens to them is listening to Christ and whoever despises them despises Christ and him who sent Christ.'"[998]

The apostles did not receive their mandate and powers from the early faithful but directly from Our Lord Jesus Christ. They were not elected by the people, they were chosen by God. Thus, the hierarchy of the Church was divinely instituted.

The apostles (bishops) received the plenitude of priesthood and constituted the first degree of the ecclesiastical hierarchy instituted by God. The second degree is made up by presbyters (priests), who only partially share the bishops' mandate and powers. The third degree is composed by deacons, ordained by the apostles to help with specific pastoral duties.[999] The transmission of power takes place in a personal way, by the laying on (imposition) of hands.

These are the degrees of Holy Orders in the Church hierarchy, a doctrine taught from the early times, as attested by the *Letter to the Corinthians* of Pope Saint Clement I, written in the year 96,[1000] and the letters to Cyprian of Carthage and Fabius of Antioch, written by Pope Saint Cornelius in 251.[1001] Reiterating this teaching the Council of Trent decreed, "If anyone says that in the Catholic Church there is not instituted a hierarchy by divine ordinance, which consists of bishops, priests, and ministers, let him be anathema."[1002]

Then there are lay people who, while being part of the Church through Baptism, do not participate in the sacrament of Holy Orders.

b. Two Different Categories: Shepherds and Flock

Whence the traditional division of the Church into *Ecclesia docens* or hierarchy, with the power to teach, govern, and sanctify; and *Ecclesia discens* or laity, with the duty to be taught, governed, and sanctified. "All the Christian faithful have the duty and right to work so that the divine message of salvation more and more reaches all people in every age and in every land," mandates the Code of Canon Law,[1003] but this must never be confused with lay participation in the powers of the hierarchy.

With extreme clarity, St. Pius X summarizes this doctrine:

> The Scripture teaches us, and the tradition of the Fathers confirms the teaching, that the Church is the mystical body of Christ, ruled by the *Pastors* and *Doctors*—a society of men containing within its own fold chiefs who have full and perfect powers for ruling, teaching, and judging. It follows that the Church is essentially an *unequal* society, that is, a society comprising two categories of persons, the Pastors and the flock, those who occupy a rank in the different degrees of the hierarchy and the multitude of the faithful. So distinct are these categories that with the pastoral body only rests the necessary right and authority for promoting the end of the society and directing all its members toward that end; the one duty of the multitude is to allow themselves to be led, and, like a docile flock, to follow the Pastors.[1004]

The *Catechism of the Catholic Church* reaffirms this doctrine.[1005]

---

995. *Catechism of the Catholic Church*, no. 881.
996. Second Vatican Council, constitution *Lumen Gentium*, no. 22.
997. See Matt. 28:18–20.
998. *Catechism of the Catholic Church*, no. 862.
999. See Acts, 6:6, 13:3.
1000. See St. Clement I, *Letter to the Corinthians*, trans. John Keith, in *Ante-Nicene Fathers*, vol. 9, ed. Allan Menzies (Buffalo, N.Y.: Christian Literature Publishing Co., 1896), rev. ed. for New Advent by Kevin Knight.
1001. See D.H., 108–9. In addition to the papal documents dating from the early centuries, there is a vast patristic literature showing how the hierarchical view of the sacrament of Holy Orders was part of the Magisterium from the first centuries. See, for example, A. Carpin, *Il sacramento dell'Ordine: Dalla teologia isidoriana alla teologia tomista* (Bologna: E.S.D., 1988), 9–74.
1002. Council of Trent, sess. 23 (canon on the sacrament of Holy Orders), can. 6, in D.H., 1776.
1003. *Code of Canon Law*, can. 211.
1004. St. Pius X, encyclical *Vehementer nos* (Feb. 11, 1906), no. 8.
1005. "The very differences which the Lord has willed to put between the members of his body serve its unity and mission. For 'in the Church there is diversity of ministry but unity of mission. To the apostles and their successors Christ has entrusted the office of teaching, sanctifying and governing in his name and by his power. But the laity are made to share in the priestly, prophetical, and kingly office of Christ; they

4F. The Church Is Thoroughly Democratic and Egalitarian

a. LT Obliterates the Distinction Between Ecclesia Docens and Ecclesia Discens

Driven by their egalitarian and revolutionary mentality, liberation theologians tend to obliterate all hierarchy in the Church, beginning with the distinction between *Ecclesia docens* and *Ecclesia discens*. In his book, *Charism and Power*, Leonardo Boff devotes a whole chapter to the topic. He writes:

> First Thesis: The entire Church (communitas fidelium) is the Ecclesia discens. ...
>   ... The entire Church is the *Ecclesia discens*. ...
>   ... *Docens* and *discens* are two aspects of the one community. They are not two nouns that split the community.[1006]

b. Papal Authority, a Dictatorship

Updating theses already proposed by the modernists and by some extreme followers of the Nouvelle Théologie, liberation theologians claim—without any historical foundation—that the hierarchical constitution of the Church is a result of the Edict of Milan (313), with which Constantine declared Christianity a *religio licita*, and of the Edict of Thessalonica (380), with which Theodosius imposed it as the official religion of the Empire. Betraying the Church's original "fraternal nature," the papacy then assumed the features of the Roman Empire, a process said to have been completed in the Middle Ages, especially with St. Gregory VII.

Criticizing the fact that "the supreme pontiff thus took up the legacy of the Roman Empire and established himself as the absolute power, joining in his person both priesthood and kingdom," Boff rejects the "dictatorship of the papacy," contemptuously dismissing "the ideology of the so-called 'cephalization.'"[1007] This stance is perfectly consistent with LT's egalitarianism. Could Boff accept hierarchy in the Church while rejecting it in society?

c. The Church vs. The People of God: The People Confer Power on the Clergy

During the First National Conference of Brazilian Basic Christian Communities, held in 1975 in Vitória (State of Espírito Santo), Leonardo Boff presented a paper with a diagram of the new ecclesiology:

[Traditional Theology]	[Liberation Theology]
God	*Christ-Holy Spirit*
⇓	
Christ	⇓
⇓	
Apostles	*Community-People of God*
Bishops	⇓
⇓	
Priests	*Bishop-priest-coordinator*
⇓	
Faithful [1008]	

Boff explains, "All services are rendered to the People of God, in the People of God, for the People of God. The services come second. The community comes first. Style: fraternal-communitarian, flexible."[1009] In this conception, the community holds powers through a "direct sharing" in Christ and bestows these powers on the bishops, priests, and coordinators (that is, B.C.C. facilitators). To round off their devious conceptions, liberationists downplay the bishop's laying on of hands during the sacrament of Holy Orders (though recorded in the Bible) as a symbolic gesture that merely approves or confirms the election and empowerment by the community.

d. The Community Is Sovereign

The central tenet of LT's ecclesiology (and all progressive ecclesiology) is a peculiar understanding of the "people of God" which is at variance with the Magisterium. It is an almost literal application to the Church of Rousseau's revolutionary doctrine of popular sovereignty.[1010] According to this visualization, the Church would be constituted by a substantially undifferentiated body of faithful, all equally "people of God." Being sovereign, the People of God should

---

have therefore, in the Church and in the world, their own assignment in the mission of the whole People of God." *Catechism of the Catholic Church*, no. 873.

1006. Boff, *Church: Charism and Power*, 138–39.

1007. Boff, *Igreja: Carisma e poder*, 98. The published English translation does not include "dictatorship of the papacy." See Boff, *Church: Charism and Power*, 52.

1008. Boff, *Church: Charism and Power*, 133.

1009. Boff, *Igreja: Carisma e poder*, 222. Once more, the U.S. edition differs slightly from the original Portuguese. The author did his own translation from the latter. See Boff, *Church: Charism and Power*, 133.

1010. According to Jean-Jacques Rousseau (1712–1778), the *volonté générale* (general will) of the people originates from the community established by the social contract into a genuine political body and determines their actions as a sovereign people. The people, as a community characterized by a precise will, is the sole and exclusive repository of sovereignty. That sovereignty can only belong to the people and it is neither divisible nor alienable. This view is so egalitarian as to deny even the ability to delegate sovereignty to representative bodies. See Jean-Jacques Rousseau, *The Social Contract*. According to Rousseau, hierarchies are not derived from nature but appeared when society was formed, and are, therefore, both illegitimate and harmful. Rousseau also foreshadows Marx in identifying private property as the cause of social inequalities, and advocates for its abolition. See Jean-Jacques Rousseau, *Discourse on Inequality: What Is the Origin of Inequality Among Men, and Is It Authorised by Natural Law?* trans. G.D.H. Cole.

To the unrealistic concept of people which exists in the imagination of revolutionary philosophers, the Church opposes a vision of people as a historical reality resulting from a social, political, and religious context, with rights, duties, and concrete customs stemming both from their inherent natural and supernatural dignity, and their organically formed temporal context. See Pius XII, "Christmas Radio Message" (Dec. 24, 1944). Likewise, the theological notion of the Church as the People of God in no way implies equality among its members: "The body's unity does not do away with the diversity of its members." *Catechism of the Catholic Church*, no. 791.

not recognize any human authority, but simply allow themselves to be guided by "movements of the Spirit." Father Floristán writes,

> Authority (service, not power) comes from Christ to the community, not in a pyramidal way, through successive 'mediations.'

The base communities emphasize the charisms: movements of the Spirit, gratuitous graces stemming from local needs or concrete situations.[1011]

e. The Democratization of the Church

Applying Rousseau's myth to the Church leads to her democratization, that is, to the dissolution of her divinely ordained hierarchical constitution. "The doctrinal affirmation that *every* member of the People of God ... *shares in the triple function of Christ* [king, priest, prophet] leads to the recognition of the *ministerial nature of the whole Church*," Spanish theologian Fr. Joaquín Losada affirms. He continues, "This recognition opens the way for everybody's real participation in the life of the Church. This participation may find its concrete forms in the models offered by modern democratic society. From this perspective, based on the conciliar ecclesiology, we must speak about the urgency of a process of *democratization of the Church*."[1012]

f. A Communal Church

The understanding of democracy in the writings of liberation theologians is very different from that of Pope Leo XIII in his encyclicals *Diuturnum illud* and *Immortale Dei*, and rather akin to the one minted by the French Revolution.[1013]

In this sense, according to Fr. David Killian, C.S.P., former chairman of the National Federation of Priests' Councils Task Force on Basic Christian Communities, democratization entails a communal model of Church: "These communities are a grassroots expression of the new vision of Church. ... They attempt to live out the theology of the Church as the 'People of God' on pilgrimage in the world. This model of Church is not predominantly hierarchical or authoritarian, but rather is communal and ordered to service."[1014]

Thus, Irish theologian Fr. James O'Halloran asserts that LT ecclesiology "presupposes a community vision of the Church, a series of communities rippling out in ever-widening concentric circles."[1015] In this communal church composed by concentric circles rather than hierarchies, the charisms and movements of the Spirit working within the people of God would spur a new and mysterious communal life sustained by special mystic and perhaps parapsychological phenomena still unclarified by LT theoreticians. These phenomena would

somehow be shared by all the faithful, enabling the new Church to subsist fraternally, dispensing with fixed structures. It would be, then, an anarchical church in the etymological sense of the word, a church without a visible government.

This democratization is consistent with the idea of a god immanent in the community. "When the priest or bishop was pictured exclusively as the representative of a transcendent God," write B.C.C. theoreticians James and Evelyn Whitehead, "it made sense to place him above and apart from the community."[1016] However, if god is conceived as an "immanent power" in the people of god, this hierarchical differentiation no longer makes sense.

g. Hierarchy or Different Functions? LT's Fictional Narrative

Liberation theologians do not speak of hierarchy. Rather, they speak of different functions within the "people of God." They contend these functions are not powers stemming from the sacrament of Holy Orders, nor do they generate any type of hierarchy. They are services to be rendered to the community, the real holder of Our Lord's mandate.

According to LT, the powers to teach, sanctify, and govern were not given to individuals but to the early Church as a whole, as a community. Our Lord did not establish the apostles as bishops. Leonardo Boff writes, "Now we can say that Jesus did not select the Twelve as founders of future churches. *Jesus established the Twelve as a community: as messianic, eschatological church.* The apostles are not to be understood first and foremost as individuals, but precisely as the *Twelve*. ... This community then broadened and gave rise to other apostolic communities."[1017]

We can apply to liberation theologians St. Pius X's accusation against the modernists: "the vagaries devised by the Modernist school concerning the Church."[1018] In LT's fictional narrative, in the early Church there was "a rich and splendid confusion of ministries." These ministries were exercised by men and women indiscriminately, but, "as an apocalyptic expectation of an end of the world waned, ... Christians began the process, which still continues, of authorizing specific forms of ministry and leadership to meet the needs of the times."[1019]

Accordingly, communities were gradually organized and some ministries developed to meet their needs, like administering sacraments and "presiding over" the Eucharist. The communities gradually empowered (one of LT's buzzwords) bishops, priests, and deacons to perform these duties. So, what the traditional Church calls a divinely instituted hierarchy would really be a set of particular functions originating from local necessities of the communities.

Not knowing what to call those new ministries, the faithful came up with titles such as *elder* and *supervisor*, merely metaphors or images devised to label those services. In time, authority became concentrated in the hands of a few, as "Christians began to picture their leaders as priests."[1020] The presbyters separated from the communities and the elders became priests, while the supervisors became bishops. The administering of the sacraments, up to then done by the community, emerged as a privilege of the clergy. Women were

1011. Floristán, *La comunidad cristiana de base*, 78.

1012. Joaquín Losada, "El posconcilio: El problema de la transformación de la iglesia," in *Desafíos Cristianos*, ed. Misión Abierta (Madrid: Loguez Ediciones, 1988), 89. (Emphasis in original.)

1013. The Magisterium of the Church, inspired by St. Thomas Aquinas (see *La política dei principi cristiani* [Siena: Cantagalli, 1981], I, chap. 2, 19–21) and others, accepts three forms of government as legitimate: monarchy, aristocracy, and democracy. Provided that the common good is served, there is no reason why a Catholic cannot choose one form or another. However, the Church condemns both the revolutionary (egalitarian) conception of democracy and the claim that this form of government is the only legitimate one. See St. Pius X, *Notre charge apostolique*. For an ample discussion on the topic, see Corrêa de Oliveira, *Nobility* ("Forms of Government), 391–418.

1014. David Killian, introduction to *Basic Christian Communities: The United States Experience*, edited by National Federation of Priests' Councils (Chicago: National Federation of Priests' Councils, 198x), 1.

1015. James O'Halloran, *Living Cells: Developing Small Christian Community* (Dublin: Dominican Publications, 1984), 25.

1016. Whitehead and Whitehead, *The Emerging Laity*, 24.

1017. Boff, *Ecclesiogenesis*, 28.

1018. St. Pius X, encyclical *Pascendi*, no. 23.

1019. Whitehead and Whitehead, *The Emerging Laity*, 141.

1020. Whitehead and Whitehead, 145.

gradually excluded and the clergy began to adopt celibacy. Finally, in the Middle Ages, an ecclesiology was spawned to justify that process of decadence totally alien to the original intent of Our Lord.

b. Fraternity and Egalitarianism

Liberation theologians often speak of *fraternity* giving the impression they are referring to brotherly love among men, particularly among Our Lord's followers. In fact, for them the term fraternity has a peculiar meaning. Man, in their view, can only love when he does not treat his neighbor as a superior or inferior but as someone equal to him. Inequality would bring oppression and exploitation, prompting rebellion from the oppressed. Fraternity, then, would be the sentiment uniting equals. In the secular realm, fraternity would thus imply a classless society. In the ecclesiastical sphere, it would entail a thoroughly egalitarian Church.

Under the title "Toward a People's Fraternity," Spanish liberation theologian Juan José Tamayo-Acosta explains LT's understanding of fraternity: "True fraternity is realized only when built, managed, and participated in by the whole people. And this will only be possible ... in a classless society, where all exploitation of man by man disappears."[1021]

5T. The Church Is Divided Into Clergy and Laity

a. The Sacrament of Holy Orders Produces a Substantial Differentiation in the Church

Bishops and priests are ordained ministers. They do not receive the sacrament of Holy Orders from the community of the faithful but from Our Lord Jesus Christ, Whose priesthood is unique, sufficient, and unrepeatable (see Heb. 7:27). There is, thus, a substantial distinction in the Church between clergy and laymen, who do not receive the sacrament of Holy Orders.[1022]

b. It Is Heretical to Affirm That the Community of the Faithful Confers Priestly Powers

In his encyclical *Pascendi* (1907), St. Pius X renewed this condemnation issued by Pius VI in the constitution *Auctorem fidei* (Aug. 28, 1794) against the heretical Synod of Pistoia: "The proposition which states 'that power has been given by God to the Church, that it might be communicated to the pastors who are its ministers for the salvation of souls;' if thus understood that the power of ecclesiastical ministry and of rule is derived from the COMMUNITY of the faithful to the pastors,—heretical."[1023]

c. The Priesthood of the Laity

Through Baptism, Christians become members of the Mystical Body, whose head is Christ, the Supreme Priest, and thus somehow participate in His triple ministry: royal, prophetic, and priestly, but not all baptized Christians are equally priests. The priesthood of the faithful, called common or baptismal, is substantially different from that derived from the sacrament of Holy Orders, called sacramental, ministerial, or hierarchical.

In the encyclical *Mediator Dei*, Pius XII warns against

those who ... teach that in the New Testament by the word "priesthood" is meant only that priesthood which

applies to all who have been baptized; and hold that the command by which Christ gave power to His apostles at the Last Supper to do what He Himself had done, applies directly to the entire Christian Church, and that thence, and thence only, arises the hierarchical priesthood. Hence, they assert that the people are possessed of a true priestly power, while the priest only acts in virtue of an office committed to him by the community.

... [Pius XII explains the substantial difference between the two priesthoods:] The priest acts for the people only because he represents Jesus Christ, who is Head of all His members and offers Himself in their stead. Hence, he goes to the altar as the minister of Christ, inferior to Christ but superior to the people. The people, on the other hand, since they in no sense represent the divine Redeemer, and are not mediator between themselves and God, can in no way possess the sacerdotal power.[1024]

The same doctrine is found in the *Catechism of the Catholic Church*: "The ministerial or hierarchical priesthood of bishops and priests, and the common priesthood of all the faithful participate, 'each in its own proper way, in the one priesthood of Christ.' While being 'ordered one to another,' they differ essentially."[1025]

5F. The Whole People of God Has Priestly Powers

a. Our Lord Was Not a Priest and Did Not Ordain Priests

Countering the dogmatic teaching of the Church, James and Evelyn Whitehead peremptorily state, "Jesus was emphatically *not* a priest—either in the then contemporary sense of a Jewish high priest or in the modern sense of ordained Catholic clergy." They deride the traditional understanding that "Jesus ordained the apostles as priests."[1026] According to them, "In the first century of Christian life no distinction of clergy and lay had yet emerged."[1027]

b. Group Priesthood

Liberation theologians introduce a slippery confusion regarding priesthood. By proclaiming that every member of the people of God receives powers directly from Christ, liberation theologians speak of a baptismal priesthood which they improperly magnify to liken it to the priesthood of the clergy. Leonardo Boff writes, "Whole and entire, [the community] is priestly, and directly priestly—the mediation of ordained minister aside—just by the fact of its faith and its baptism. Thus the faithful are grafted onto Christ, and Christ with all his powers becomes present and active in the community."[1028]

1021. Tamayo-Acosta, "Las comunidades cristianas populares," 166.
1022. See *Catechism of the Catholic Church*, no. 1536ff.
1023. Denz. 1502. See St. Pius X, *Pascendi*, no. 24.
1024. Pius XII, encyclical *Mediator Dei* (Nov. 20, 1947), nos. 83–84.
1025. *Catechism of the Catholic Church*, no. 1547.
1026. Whitehead and Whitehead, *The Emerging Laity*, 142.
1027. Whitehead and Whitehead, 5.
1028. Boff, *Ecclesiogenesis*, 71.

Liberation theologians propose the concept of community priesthood. Father Floristán writes,

> The division between clergy and laity is a social parallel of the distinction between the aristocracy and popular class.
>
> The Christian community demands a new type of presbyter and a new style of ministry. Maertens defines the new ministry as follows: "The Christic animation of a gathering of the local church on the basis of its faith in Jesus Christ, in order to inspire its activities in the world."...
>
> In these communities a new type of declericalized ministry is established, a ministry oriented toward group priesthood.[1029]

There is no need to explain how this doctrine is light years away from the Magisterium.

Liberation theologians, however, remain cautious. They do not wish this concept of group priesthood to be immediately implemented. It can provoke reactions. Rather, they envision a long process whereby laymen would progressively assume priestly functions until the difference between clergy and laity is obliterated. The laity would be gradually empowered, supposedly recovering long-neglected communitarian elements of early Christianity.

Brazilian theologian Carlos Mesters, a theoretician of those communities, describes it as follows:

> The people will gradually assume priestly functions, though not with a "clerical" vision. ...
>
> If we manage to start this process, I think the people will enter the core of priesthood little by little (which is presently closed to them by canon law), and will be able to perform sacramental "services" as a function of their own. ... [This, Mesters continues, will not come about without a liberating struggle.] This will not be a gift freely offered to the people by the hierarchy, mitigating canon law. It will be a conquest of the people.[1030]

C. Additional Characteristics of LT's New Church

1. The People's Church

Having briefly outlined the contrast between traditional Catholic doctrine and LT ecclesiology, we close this chapter with a quick discussion of the idea of a people's church proposed by liberation theologians. Of Latin American origin, the idea of a people's church has now permeated progressive circles even in Europe. In October 2012, for example, a conference was held in Genoa to present a special issue of *MicroMega*, a magazine directed by Paolo Flores d'Arcais and dedicated to "The Second Vatican Council and the popular church." Various speakers, including Fr. Andrea Gallo, highlighted the contrasts between the "hierarchical Church" and the "church of God."

a. Liberating the Church

LT's goal in the religious sphere is to establish a pneumatic, cosmic, fraternal, and communitarian Church without structures or fixed dogmas. That church can only be born through a "painful process of liberation" (Leonardo Boff), that is, a revolutionary struggle against the traditional Church. Two thousand years of hierarchical constitution, dogmatic Magisterium, solemn liturgy, and strict moral discipline cannot simply wither away. A liberating struggle is necessary, therefore, to put an end to oppression and pave the way for the new church.

Thus, one of the immediate tasks of the Latin American LT movement is to organize the "oppressed" in the Church to wage a dialectical struggle against oppressive ecclesial structures. This association is referred to by liberation theologians as the people's church or the Church of the poor.

According to Father Sobrino, this Church of the poor goes beyond the ecclesiology of the "people of God" taught by the Second Vatican Council:

> The Church of the poor may not without qualification be identified with Vatican II's description of the Church as the people of God. This description was a major advance, and an extremely important one. It served to counterbalance the excessive weight given to an ecclesiology of the "mystical" body by giving the body a historical existence and dimension. It served also to counterbalance the hierarchical conception of the Church by giving the worldwide base of the Church priority over the apex of the pyramid. It served to eliminate a monopolistic view of the faith by locating it first and foremost in the whole body of the faithful. ...
>
> ... The thinking of Vatican II was extremely important in that it approached the idea and reality of a Church of the poor, but this idea and reality were only virtually present in the Council.[1031]

b. A Church Made Up of the Oppressed

Liberation theologians do not use the term "people of God" in its traditional meaning, that is, Church members, but rather in the Marxist sense of proletariat, that is, the oppressed. The concept has changed from theological to ideological. Leonardo Boff writes, "A Church as People of God: The term 'people' is not taken in the sense of nation, lumping everyone together indiscriminately and thus hiding internal differences, but rather in the sense of people/lower class, defined as those who are excluded from participation in society and reduced to the mass."[1032]

Broadening the concept of *poor*, the Final Document of the Ecumenical Theology Congress on the Ecclesiology of the Basic Christian Communities, held in São Paulo, Brazil, in 1980, states, "[The poor] are the exploited classes, the oppressed races, people whom some would hope to keep anonymous or absent from human history."[1033] The concept of poor adopted by avant-garde sectors of the LT movement encompasses all those who somehow feel oppressed: women, homosexuals, Blacks, Indians, and so forth.

1029. Floristán, *La comunidad cristiana de base,* 79, 87.

1030. Carlos Mesters, *O futuro de nosso passado,* 167, quoted in Solimeo and Solimeo, *As CEBs: Comentários e documentação totais,* 62.

1031. Sobrino, *The True Church and the Poor,* 91–92.

1032. Boff, *Church: Charism and Power,* 117.

1033. Ecumenical Theology Congress on the "Ecclesiology of the Basic Christian Communities," "Final Document," in *The Challenge of the Basic Christian Communities,* ed. Sergio Torres and John Eagleson (Maryknoll, N.Y.: Orbis Books, 1981), 232.

c. A Substantial Novelty: A New Church

Liberation theologians do not hide the fact that this Church of the poor they are building is a new church. Jon Sobrino writes,

> The poor have given rise to a new form of Church that is distinct from the previous form and more in accord with the Church's beginnings. ...
> ... The spirit of Jesus is in the poor and, with them as his point of departure, he re-creates the entire Church.[1034]

2. The Marxist Character of This Ecclesiology

As in other points, particularly in its Latin American versions, LT ecclesiology on the people's church borrows some doctrinal foundations from Marxism.

a. The Marxist Concept of Alienation

In its general lines, Marxism assumes the Rousseauean myth of a primeval, quasi-paradisiacal society in which all men were equal and free, property was held in common, and themes of general interest were decided on by consensus.[1035] According to Marx, in this kind of primitive Communism, there reigned overall happiness because the main cause of friction and conflict among men—covetousness—had no place; everything belonged to everyone equally.

In the passage from a nomadic to a sedentary life based on agriculture and sheep herding—the myth continues—some men appropriated the means of production for their personal advantage—land, herds, and agricultural implements. This dealt a fatal blow to the primeval egalitarian society, creating conflict. According to Marx, the dispossessed were then forced to sell their work to the owners, thus becoming dependent, that is "alienated." They lost not only their economic freedom but with it their individual freedom and even a part of their own being.[1036]

Concomitantly, the owners' newly acquired economic power enabled them to amass political, social, and cultural power, further alienating the dispossessed. From then on society was sundered into two antagonistic classes: a summit or vertex, composed of those who owned the means of production; and a base, composed of those who had none and must sell their work to the former. From a Marxist perspective, this dependence implies not only exploitation and oppression, but also a prostitution of human dignity.

b. LT Adapts These Marxist Concepts to the Church

(i) The Early Church Was Egalitarian and Had No Power Structure

Adapting the Rousseauean-Marxist fable to the ecclesiastical sphere, liberation theologians posit that the early Church was nothing but a gathering of faithful, the people of God, with neither hierarchies nor power structure. Enthusiasm and fraternal joy reigned precisely because everything belonged to everyone.

(ii) A Hierarchy Arose and Appropriated the "Ecclesiastical Means of Production"

At a given point, however, some designing individuals appropriated church powers and privileges ("ecclesiastical means of production"), establishing themselves as a hierarchy. Then they elaborated an *ad hoc* ecclesiology in order to justify their privileged situation, much as, in Marxist doctrine, the bourgeoisie shapes the dominant culture to justify its privileges.

(iii) The Church Was Split Between Summit and Base

The institutionalization of the Church (i.e., the imagined dispossessing of the laity by the hierarchy) occurred during the early centuries of the Christian era and was consummated by the fourth century. In this regard, Leonardo Boff writes,

> The primitive Church, until the fourth century, with the advent of the age of Constantine (313 A.D.), was made up largely of the poor. ...
> Beginning with Constantine and Theodosius, the Church is led to accept the hegemonic spread of Western culture. This implies taking the place of political power. From a base, the Church is transformed into a cupola, introducing a division between the simple faithful (*plebs christiana*), who continue to be the base, and the ecclesiastical hierarchy, who are transformed into a body of dignitaries (*nobiles*), the cupola.[1037]

Continuing his tale, Boff goes on to explain that the Church later spawned an *ad hoc* theology to justify that division:

> Power was gradually concentrated in the hands of the clergy, civil as well as religious power. Beginning with the eighth century, they were beginning to be a sociological phenomenon, starting to achieve complete domination under Gregory VII and Innocent III, at the time of Saint Francis [of Assisi]. This is when clericalism, the total concentration of sacred power in the hands of the clergy, emerged. The clergy monopolized the goods of salvation and became the exclusive holders of that competence necessary to produce and reproduce symbolic capital. *Pari passu* [the clergy] achieved a growing disappropriation of the laity, until they were reduced to the mere mass of the faithful, attending the rites, lacking the means to produce their own religious goods. ...
> Alongside these practices, under the sign of clericalism there developed a corresponding theology (ideology) that justified them.[1038]

1034. Sobrino, *The True Church and the Poor*, 95, 93.

1035. Marx wrote:

> The first prerequisite of this earliest form of landed property appears as a human community, such as emerges from spontaneous evolution [*naturwuchsig*]: the family, the family expanded into a tribe. ... We may take it for granted that pastoralism, or more generally a migratory life, is the first form of maintaining existence, the tribe not settling in a fixed place but using up what it finds locally and then passing on. ... Hence the tribal community, the natural common body, appears not as the consequence, but as the precondition of the joint (temporary) appropriation and use of the soil. ...
> ... The earth is the great laboratory, the arsenal which provides both the means and the materials of labor, and also the location, the *basis* of the community. Men's relations to it is naive; they regard themselves as its *communal proprietors*. (Karl Marx, *Pre-Capitalist Economic Formations* [1857–1858], trans. Jack Cohen)

1036. For a discussion on the Marxist concept of *alienation*, see chap. 4, n. 831.

1037. Boff, *Francis of Assisi*, 47–48.

1038. Boff, 94–95.

(iv) The Hierarchical Constitution of the Church Explained in Marxist Terms

Here is how the Spanish theologian Father Floristán, a theoretician of the Basic Christian Communities, summarizes the dispossessing of the base (the laity) by the hierarchy:

1.What is "the base"?
It is the opposite of "the summit" or "peak."...
1.1. Negative characteristics of the base

1.1.1 Economic
"The summit" appropriates the means of production. ...
The base is the sector deprived of its goods. ...

1.1.2 Political
"The summit" concentrates in its hands the government of the res publica. ...
The base is the sector deprived of power. ...

1.1.3 Cultural
The summit has the monopoly of knowledge. ...
The base is the sector deprived of knowledge. ...

The problem is not that the base
— is poor
— does not have political power
— and is ignorant.
but that it has been dispossessed by means of:
— exploitations
— oppressions
— dominations. ...

2.1.2 Institutional ecclesiology
Clearly distinguishes between a Church of the clergy and that of the laity:
A teaching and a learning Church (knowledge) [is taken away from the base].
A sanctifying and a sanctified Church (ownership) [is taken away from the base].
A governing and a governed Church (power) [is taken away from the base].[1039]

c. The Institutional Church Allies Itself With the Oppressors

According to LT, the hierarchy consolidated its power when Christianity became the official religion of the Roman Empire in the fourth century. Liberation theology interprets this as a villainous alliance between the ecclesiastical hierarchy (the oppressors in the Church) and the elite of the Roman State (the oppressors in society). From that point on—says LT—the institutional Church always sided with the oppressors: It sided with the power structure of the Roman Empire, then with the feudal lords and kings during the Middle Ages, and so on up to our days, when it sides with the capitalist bourgeoisie.

3. Base vs. Hierarchy

a. Class Struggle in the Church, Class Struggle in Society

Marxism conceives society as being split into two antagonistic classes: the bourgeoisie and the proletariat. Similarly, for LT, the Church is divided into two antagonistic classes: the hierarchy and the base. Both divisions would be manifestations in two realms (Church and society) of one and the same evil: *inequality*. For both Marxism and LT, inequality means oppression, so both Church and society would express the oppressor/oppressed contradiction. We read in the final document of the 1975 Christians for Socialism conference held in Quebec, Canada:

> We also reflected on the situation of our Churches, nationally and internationally, and on the emergence of a Christianity of a proletarian and popular character capable of emancipating itself from the tutelage of the dominant bourgeois ideology. We thus see with hope the emergence of a liberating evangelization and the seeds of a popular Church. ...
>
> ... A truly new type of Church can only take shape fully within a society that has broken the structural relations of domination.[1040]

Class struggle would remedy such situations of oppression both in the Church and in society. For Italian liberation theologian Father Girardi, "Class struggle also means struggle inside the church."[1041]

b. Liberation in the Church, Liberation in Society

According to LT, the process of liberation of the ecclesial base began in the nineteenth century with liberal Catholicism, continued in the last century with the modernist movement, and attained maturity in the sixties with the emergence of the people's church thanks to a particular interpretation of the Council. The rise of Church grassroots coincided with a stepped-up proletarian struggle in the sociopolitical field, especially in Latin America, where, for the first time, one could foresee a communist takeover.

In LT's interpretation these two processes are aspects of a single "irruption of the poor in history,"[1042] which manifests itself in the ecclesiastical field with a dialectical struggle for the destruction of the institutional Church and a victory of the people's church, and, in the civil sphere, with a dialectical struggle for the destruction of traditional society and a socialist victory. In both cases the historical subjects, that is, the protagonists of the liberation struggle, would be the same.

Leonardo Boff writes:

> This is the phenomenon that is taking place with the base ecclesial communities in Latin America: a true ecclesiogenesis, the genesis of a new Church ... taking place in the base of the Church and in the grassroots of society, that is, among the lower classes who are religiously as well as socially deprived of power. This novelty must be understood analytically; these communities mean a break with the monopoly of social and religious power

---

1039. Floristán, *La comunidad cristiana de base*, 38–40.

1040. Christians for Socialism, "Final Communiqué," International Conference of Christians for Socialism (Quebec, April 13, 1975), nos. 2, 25, Yves Vaillancourt, "La première rencontre internationale des chrétiens pour le socialisme," *Relations* 35, no. 405 (June 1975), 174–76. A first conference of Christians for Socialism was held in Santiago, Chile, in 1972, with the participation of delegates from 23 countries. See "Clausurado el encuentro de cristianos para el socialismo," *El Mercurio*, May 2, 1972. It was the apex of the Marxist government of Salvador Allende, a close ally of Fidel Castro's Cuba and of Peru's Juan Velasco Alvarado. The assembly sought to reiterate the support of Christians for Socialism to the process of communization of Latin America. For reports on the conference, see articles on Cristians for Socialism in *Revista Mensaje* (Chile), no. 209 (June 1972).

1041. Giulio Girardi, *Amor cristiano y lucha de clases* (e-version, 2000), 13.

1042. See Gustavo Gutiérrez, "The Irruption of the Poor in Latin America and the Christian Communities of the Common People," in *The Challenge of the Basic Christian Communities*, ed. Sergio Torres and John Eagleson (Maryknoll, N.Y.: Orbis Books, 1981), 107ff.

and the inauguration of a new religious and social process
for restructuring both the Church and society, with a
different social division of labor as well as an alternative
religious division of ecclesiastical labor.[1043]

According to Father Gutiérrez, LT should inspire both liberations: "The break with an unjust social order and the search for
new ecclesial structures—in which the most dynamic sectors of
the Christian community are engaged—have their basis in this
ecclesiological perspective."[1044]

4. B.C.C.s and Catholic Dissent

We have come to a very important topic which, for lack of
space, we can just outline: the Basic Christian Communities
as the leading edge of the Revolution both in the religious and
temporal spheres.

In Latin America, B.C.C.s' involvement in socialist revolutions
came to a climax in the seventies. Nicaragua is perhaps the paradigmatic case, in which thousands of B.C.C. militants joined
the armed struggle alongside the communist guerrillas of the
Sandinista National Liberation Front.[1045]

In the U.S., a large sector of the B.C.C.s merged with the
so-called populist left inspired by Saul Alinsky through the
Industrial Areas Foundation and its network of peoples' orga-
nizations. In this way, many a B.C.C. became part of the radical
American left, sometimes even its protagonists, such as during
Barack Obama's electoral campaigns.[1046]

B.C.C.s joined the struggles of the extreme left in Italy as well.
"*Among the realities of dissent*," Valerio Gigante writes, "the Basic
Christian Communities movement deserves a prominent place,
born spontaneously within Catholic groups and communities in
the sixties and seventies, to try to live a faith not disembodied from
contradictions, challenges, and dramas of the contemporary world."

He continues, "In forty years of life, the Basic Christian
Communities have followed different paths albeit with a national
coordination and common path agreed on at national meetings of
discussion and study in which they built their trove of fixed points:
commitment against the Concordat and ecclesiastical privileges,
de-clericalization of liturgies and community life, political and
social commitment with strongly leftist overtones, secularism and
openness on all major issues of the contemporary debate, from
abortion to euthanasia, from same-sex marriage to immigration."

The mention of abortion, same-sex "marriage," and immigration
is telltale of how Italian B.C.C.s have accompanied the unfolding
revolutionary process, whose focus has switched from Marxism
to the moral and cultural revolution. Here Gigante mentions the
B.C.C.s' "closeness to the homosexual and transsexual world"
without forgetting experiments with "new forms of horizontality"
and "participatory democracy" in the Church itself.[1047]

Among more recent developments we can mention the Piagge
community in Florence, led by Fr. Alessandro Santoro, who openly
declares, "We are inspired by liberation theology."[1048] Father
Santoro made news headlines in 2008 for having joined in religious
marriage a man and a transsexual woman. Punished by Most Rev.
Giuseppe Betori, then archbishop of Florence and now a cardinal,
he was rehabilitated shortly afterward.

1043. Boff, *Church: Charism and Power*, 116.

1044. Gutiérrez, *A Theology of Liberation*, 261.

1045. See Corrêa de Oliveira, "Na 'noite sandinista.'"

1046. See Raffaelle Citterio, "Hillary, Obama e il maestro Alinsky," *Radici Cristiane*, no. 32 (Feb.–Mar. 2008).

1047. Gigante, *Cosa resta del concilio*, 7.

1048. Fr. Alessandro Santoro, "Il Vaticano deve sparire," *MicroMega*, no. 7 (2012), 117.

Chapter 6:
A Preferential Option for the Poor, or for Poverty? LT's Lead-Filled Life Jacket

A. Liberation Theology and Soviet Communism: What the Kremlin Was Saying Back Then

Everyone knows the expression *fellow travelers*, as used by Lenin to designate members of the bourgeoisie whom Communism would use as temporary allies and then discard once the proletarian revolution was established.[1049] By extension, the expression means any temporary ally of Communism. Among the fellow travelers of international Communism in its long march through the twentieth century, perhaps no current has been as useful as liberation theology, especially in Latin America.

Indeed, Latin America is an overwhelmingly Catholic continent. In the sixties, the percentage of Catholics easily exceeded 90% of the population. The communist mentality would hardly have been able to penetrate, especially into the lower classes, without the contribution of the Catholic left.[1050] Soviet analysts themselves say so. Two papers published in the eighties by the Academy of Sciences of the U.S.S.R. shed light on this matter.

The first is an essay published in the journal Вопросы философии (*Problems of Philosophy*), dedicated to the study of Marxist-Leninist philosophy in its relations with other contemporary systems of thought. Written by V.M. Pacika, the study analyzes the theology of liberation in depth, considering it an important development for the advancement of the Marxist revolution in Latin America.

Pacika begins by observing that "the most significant change in Christian ideology in recent decades has been the emergence of new 'germinative theologies' [*sic*] preferentially oriented toward the interpretation of the historical process and the solution of social problems." The most obvious example of these new theologies is "liberation theology, [which] emerged as an independent current in the late sixties and early seventies in the wake of the national liberation movements in Latin America."

The Soviet analyst welcomes the fact that liberation theologians have recourse to Marxist analysis and get involved in revolutionary struggles: "The class struggles in which these theologians participate as ideologues and politicians are laden with radical and anti-bourgeois political significance. This forces them to reconsider their own theoretical assumptions and to turn instead to the study of Marxism not only in its social and political manifestations, but also in its philosophy."

"The representatives of liberation theology," Pacika continues, "do not see Marxism as a system of thought to be countered by developing a Christian alternative, but rather as a theory of social

development which Christianity is lacking and from which they can and must take advantage."

It is interesting to note how the Marxist scholar also recognizes the importance of LT's theological foundations. Pacika praises the fact that liberation theologians abandoned the traditional theological method, which starts from revelation, and adopted historical and social analysis instead. "What is more important, social praxis or the word of God? Which one takes precedence?" Pacika rhetorically asks. He answers, "According to the theology of liberation, praxis is more important. Liberation theology does not accept the word of God as such, but always in the context of a faith in continuous evolution and verified by concrete praxis. As Father Gutiérrez says, theology starts with praxis."

This epistemological break with traditional theology, the Soviet writer continues, implies a restructuring of Catholic doctrine that draws it close to Marxism: "The need to take social praxis as a starting point for theological elaboration, and the understanding of theology as historically conditioned implies a true reconstruction of the very foundations of Christian ideology. Liberation theologians undertake this reconstruction without hesitation."

As Pacika rightly observes, such reversal of Catholic theology could not happen without a lot of preparation: "We must admit in all justice that the determining factor that has allowed the rise of liberation theology was the evolution of Christian thought in recent decades." Showing a good knowledge of contemporary theology, Pacika specifically mentions the role played by Emanuel Mounier, Jacques Maritain, Pierre Teilhard de Chardin, Marie-Dominique Chenu, Yves Congar, and other theologians associated with the Nouvelle Théologie.

The Soviet scholar concludes by recognizing the role LT has played in spreading Marxism. "As a rule, the theology of liberation seeks a sincere rapprochement with Marxism and considers it an ally. By taking Marxism as a method of analysis, liberation theology stimulates its study and thus contributes to its spread in large sectors of the population."[1051]

Another interesting document is an essay published by *América Latina*, a Spanish-language magazine published by the Institute for Latin America of the Academy of Sciences of the U.S.S.R. Written by Valentina Andronova, the essay examines the role of the Basic Christian Communities in the revolutionary process. "The emergence of the Basic Christian Communities is a phenomenon of fundamental importance," Andronova writes. "By adopting a new religious practice full of democratic and revolutionary content, these base communities bring their religious concepts to the revolutionary process. ... They propose a collective action

---

1049. V.I. Lenin, "On the Road," in *Selected Works: In Three Volumes* (Moscow: Progress Publishers, 1970), 1:585.

1050. See Julio Loredo, "Cattolicesimo e comunismo in America Latina," *Tradizione Famiglia Proprietà* (Dec. 2003); Julio Loredo, "La Waterloo del comunismo," *Tradizione Famiglia Proprietà* (Oct. 2008), 70–76.

1051. V.M. Pacika, "Dialettica dello sviluppo sociale e della lotta ideologica: La teologia della liberazione nella sua versione radicale latino-americana," *Problemi di Filosofia*, no. 1 (1985): 92–100. On K.G.B. involvement in spreading LT, see Ion Mihai Pacepa, "A cruzada religiosa do Kremlin," *Mídia Sem Máscara*, Apr. 30, 2013. Pacepa, a two-star Romanian general, was the highest-ranking military officer ever to desert from the Soviet bloc.

aimed at the liberation of the poor. ... The old religion, founded on obedience and submission is relegated to a secondary plane. The faithful replace it with a new religion linked to their struggle for liberation."

The Soviet analyst also praises liberation theologians' manipulation of the Bible: "The new interpretation of the Bible facilitates the development of social consciousness among believers, resulting in activities geared toward creating a fraternal society, i.e., a classless society."

Andronova concludes that LT's new church becomes an integral part of the communist system: "In the areas liberated by the guerrillas, where a socialist regime is in force the Basic Christian Communities function as a new church, in complete solidarity with the armed struggle and with Socialism."[1052]

It does not get any clearer.

B. The Perfect Fellow Traveler

It is impossible to recount LT's saga in Latin America in a few pages. Suffice it to say that, where possible, liberation theologians behaved as perfect fellow travelers of the communist revolution even in its metamorphosis. Fidel Castro was right when he declared, "Liberation theology is more important for the revolution in Latin America than Marxism."[1053] The guerrilla leader Ernesto "Che" Guevara (1928–1967) thought likewise: "When Christians decide to give a full revolutionary testimony, the Latin American revolution will be invincible."[1054]

Let us give a few examples, in a necessarily brief fashion.

1. Brazil

Politically, Communism in Brazil is a marginal phenomenon. In the 2010 general election, the openly communist parties received a meager 2.8% of the vote. The Catholic left, however, is much more insidious. "Brazil is a viscerally Catholic country," Plinio Corrêa de Oliveira writes. "If the Church opposes one of her enemies, he will hardly manage to seize power, let alone keep it."[1055] Unfortunately, since the 1940s, far from opposing the enemies of Catholicism, important segments of the Brazilian clergy have favored them, drifting to the left to the point of forming what Plinio Corrêa de Oliveira called a "Fifth Power," often more decisive than the other four, favoring the country's socialization.[1056]

Under the auspices of prelates like Most Rev. Helder Câmara (1909–1999), the "red archbishop" of Olinda-Recife,[1057] that Fifth Power gradually became the most influential force of the left in Brazil, systematically promoting socialist reforms while opposing any conservative reaction.[1058] In the sixties and seventies, the Fifth Power promoted liberation theology and its militant arm, the Basic Christian Communities, which intended to carry out "a real revolution."[1059] It is no coincidence that some of LT's most radical manifestations arose in Brazil.

Here is one example among thousands: In 1968, the "Comblin Document," a text written by the Belgian priest Fr. Joseph Comblin, a theoretician of the Basic Christian Communities and professor at the Theological Institute (seminary) of Olinda-Recife, was published in Brazil. The document outlined the stages of a popular revolt, with a final round of violence destined to establish a socialist dictatorship with revolutionary courts to eliminate opponents. The priest was expelled from Brazil for subversive activities, but this did not prevent some bishops from expressing solidarity with him, implicitly endorsing armed insurrection.[1060]

The Marxist-inspired Partido dos Trabalhadores (P.T., Workers Party), in power in Brazil from 2003 until 2016, was founded and developed under the auspices of LT and the Basic Christian Communities. The P.T. was established on February 10, 1980, in the convent of the Sisters of Our Lady of Sion in São Paulo, with the advice of leading liberation theologians, including the Dominican Friar Betto, the ideological mentor of P.T.'s secretary-general and later two-term president Luiz Inácio "Lula" da Silva.[1061] Although his original program ("We will transform Brazil into a second Cuba") received a setback after the fall of the Iron Curtain in 1989, his party nevertheless continued trying to move the country as much as possible to the left.

Luiz Inácio da Silva, known as "Lula," limelighted by international propaganda as leader of the new Latin American Socialism together with the late Hugo Chávez (1954–2013), is a typical product of the LT movement, which launched him as a union leader in 1980, during strikes in the São Paulo industrial area, the starting point of his political career. It was also the LT movement that pushed him to found P.T. Lula has always shown gratitude to his mentors. In his message, already as Brazil's president, which he addressed to the participants in the B.C.C.s' 11th Interecclesial Encounter in 2005, he said:

> Dear male and female comrades attending the 11th Interecclesial Encounter of the Basic Christian Communities. ...
>
> ... I understand the importance of your meeting as representatives of the most popular and committed grassroots of our country. ...
>
> You know how much I love the B.C.C.s and recognize the role the Basic Christian Communities have played in resisting the military dictatorship, forming the Popular

1052. Valentina Andronova, "Las comunidades cristianas de base: Nueva forma de protesta social para los creyentes," *América Latina* (Moscow) (Apr. 1985).

1053. Boff, "A originalidade da teologia da libertação," 550.

1054. Mario Amorós, "La iglesia que nace del pueblo: Relevancia histórica del movimiento Cristianos por el Socialismo," 20.

1055. Plinio Corrêa de Oliveira, *A igreja frente a escalada da ameaça comunista: Apelo aos bispos silenciosos* (São Paulo: Editora Vera Cruz, 1977), 55.

1056. See Corrêa de Oliveira, et al., *As CEBs*, 46ff. Obviously, this definition does not apply to the whole Brazilian clergy but only to its progressive sectors, which nevertheless hold the reins of ecclesiastical power by controlling the National Conference of Brazil's Bishops (C.N.B.B.) and its main pastoral agencies. For a history of the leftward drift of the Church in Brazil, see Leo Alting von Geusau, "Revolution and Religion: The Radical Church in Brazil," *Dialectical Anthropology* 3, no. 1 (Feb. 1978): 21–42; Margaret Patrice Todaro, *Pastors, Prophets and Politicians: A Study of the Brazilian Catholic Church, 1916–1945* (doctoral thesis, Columbia University, 1971); Thomas C. Bruneau, *The Political Transformation of the Brazilian Catholic Church* (Cambridge: Cambridge University Press, 1974); Scott Mainwaring, *The Catholic Church and Politics in Brazil 1916–1985* (Stanford: Stanford University Press, 1986).

1057. On the role played by Most Rev. Helder Câmara, see de Mattei, *Crusader of the 20th Century*, 90ff; Introvigne, *Una battaglia nella notte*, 102ff.

1058. See Corrêa de Oliveira, *A igreja frente a escalada*; Corrêa de Oliveira, *Indian Tribalism*; Corrêa de Oliveira, "Na 'noite sandinista'"; Plinio Corrêa de Oliveira and Carlos Patricio del Campo, *Sou católico: Posso ser contra a reforma agrária?* (São Paulo: Art Press, 1981); Plinio Corrêa de Oliveira, *A propriedade privada e a livre iniciativa no tufão agro-reformista* (São Paulo: Editora Vera Cruz, 1985); Plinio Corrêa de Oliveira and Carlos Patricio del Campo, *No Brasil, a reforma agrária leva à miséria ao campo e à cidade* (São Paulo: Editora Vera Cruz, 1986). See also *Meio século de epopéia anticomunista*, Abel de Oliveira Campos, ed. (São Paulo: Editora Vera Cruz, 1980).

1059. Corrêa de Oliveira, et al., *As CEBs*, 42.

1060. See *Revista Eclesiástica Brasileira* (Sept. 1972), 697.

1061. Commenting on the creation of P.T., a Brazilian socialist weekly explains, "The help of Friar Betto, the Dominican who spread and coordinated the work of the Grassroots Church communities in São Paulo and who is today a kind of adviser and shield bearer of Lula, was greatly valued." The leftist journalist José Neumane Pinto reports, "Friar Betto became a kind of eminence of the strike [from which the PT arose]. A personal friend and confidant of Lula, he went to live in the house of the worker leader. ... Friar Betto is known for his tactical instructions and, according to a union militant, 'he is the one who pushes Lula on. . .'" Corrêa de Oliveira, et al., *Grassroots Church Communities*, 75.

Movements, and supporting the trade union movement and particularly the PT.

I believe that the link between faith and social commitment, between faith and political activism has produced very valuable fruits for our people. ...

God bless ... your struggle![1062]

"In short," Plinio Corrêa de Oliveira writes, "the communist onslaught in [Brazil] had nothing to fear from the Bishops' Conference and those who follow it. It took no serious blow from those prelates. Indeed, it has only benefited from several of their omissions and attitudes. In doctrinal matters, Communism has drawn support now and then from notables belonging to the Bishops' Conference or those who follow it."[1063]

2. Chile

Led by Raúl Cardinal Silva Henríquez (1907–1999), archbishop of Santiago, almost all the Chilean bishops and a considerable part of the clergy supported the socialist reforms of the Christian Democratic government of Eduardo Frei Montalva (1964–1970), leading many Catholics to follow his drift toward the left.[1064] Then the clergy facilitated the rise of the Marxist candidate Salvador Allende Gossens (1908–1973) to the presidency,[1065] strenuously supporting his government even when it became unpopular. In 1973, when Allende fell, the clergy preached reconciliation with the communists and tried to save and rally together the remnants of the communist regime, while threatening with excommunication anyone who dared to oppose their maneuver. Clergy support of the extreme left went so far as to host, on church premises, M.I.R. (Movement of the Revolutionary Left) guerrilla thugs hiding from the police, and even to conceal their weapons in altar tabernacles.

This is clearly shown in the well-documented 1976 book, *The Church of Silence in Chile: The TFP Proclaims the Whole Truth*.[1066] Based on over 200 documents, the work went through three printings in less than a month. The ensuing controversy reached behind the Iron Curtain. Radio Moscow devoted four broadcasts to defend progressive Chilean bishops while attacking the book's authors.[1067] Even *L'Unità*, mouthpiece of the Italian Communist Party, took the field in their defense.[1068] A curious case of wolves howling in the defense of shepherds...

For large sectors of the Chilean clergy, to defend the Allende government was all the more incomprehensible because, lacking popular support, the left itself was organizing armed insurrection. "The people's power must arm itself," headlined the daily *La Segunda* of July 3, 1973, reporting: "Radical groups of the CP, MIR and PS are giving out weapons in factories and working class neighborhoods."[1069] In May 1973, along with Luis Corvalán, head of the Communist Party, and Carlos Altamirano, leader of the Socialist Party, General Carlos Prats, the Army commander in chief, traveled to the U.S.S.R. On the margins of official negotiations, secret conversations were held in which the general committed to deliver Army weapons to extreme leftist groups to terrorize the reaction and establish a workers' government.

A telegram recently discovered in German archives by Chilean historian Victor Farías, written by East German agent Harry Spindler and dated July 11, 1973, offers a harrowing picture of the situation. Spindler reported that "the M.I.R. [subversive movement] has proposed to prepare for armed struggle along with the Communist Party and the Socialist Party." He continued, "In a conversation with the First Secretary of the Socialist Party, Altamirano, they said that resorting to armed confrontation is necessary to further the development of the revolutionary process in Chile." According to him, "a battle between the [communist-infiltrated] Army and the reactionaries will occur. In that case, General Prats will take advantage of these clashes to fulfill his promise to distribute weapons to the working class and ally the Army to them. For his part, Altamirano promotes establishing a monolithic MIR-socialist-communist front. The youth of the Communist and Socialist parties are also preparing for the decisive confrontation."[1070]

Also of great interest is a report by the Chilean communist leader Volodia Teitelboim to Hermann Axen, a member of the Central Committee of East Germany's Socialist Party, dated August 9, 1973. Teitelboim discusses possible secret arms shipments and informs that the Chilean Communist Party was making military preparations "*in complete lawlessness*."[1071] Finally, there is a report by Soviet ambassador A.V. Basov recounting a conversation with the Secretary General of the Chilean Communist Party, Luis Corvalán: "In a dialogue at the Soviet embassy, Comrade Corvalán said: ... 'What chance do we have to get out of this crisis? ... In any event, the socialists want to take up arms. ... If we could count on sufficient militants with weapons, and their support by the Army, the result could be positive.'"[1072]

The insurrectionist drift of the Chilean left was well known to the Catholic leaders who, nevertheless, continued to shore up the Allende government.

It was precisely during Salvador Allende's government that LT developed the most in Chile as a theological justification of Catholic support for the socialization of the country. In April 1972, the First Latin American Encounter of Christians for Socialism was held in Santiago with the participation of 400 delegates. It was chaired by Most Rev. Sergio Méndez Arceo, bishop of Cuernavaca, Mexico, who stated, "For our underdeveloped world there is no alternative but to Socialism."[1073]

The meeting of Christians for Socialism in Santiago marked a decisive point in the history of LT in Latin America. Nicaraguan

---

1062. "Carta de Lula às CEBs," *CNBB*, Jul. 19, 2005.

1063. Corrêa de Oliveira, *A igreja frente a escalada*, 79.

1064. See Vidigal Xavier da Silveira, *Frei, o Kerensky chileno*. This book predicted, three years in advance, that President Frei's socialist policies would pave the way for Communism in Chile. It compared Frei to Aleksandr Fëdorovič Kerenskij (1881–1970), who prepared Lenin's rise. The prophecy was fulfilled in 1970, with the election of Marxist Salvador Allende. See also Plinio Corrêa de Oliveira, *Il crepuscolo artificiale del Cile cattolico* (Piacenza: Cristianità, 1973).

1065. After Allende's death on September 11, 1973, the left worldwide mythified him. Today this myth is collapsing thanks to recent discoveries in the archives of former East Germany, which show that Salvador Allende subscribed to Nazi-type eugenic theories that promoted the sterilization of the mentally ill, was anti-Semitic, and an ally of Adolf Hitler. Documents also emerged showing how the U.S.S.R. was preparing a bloodbath in Chile in 1973. See Julio Loredo, "Allende: il crollo di un mito," *Tradizione Famiglia Proprietà* (May 2007).

1066. See Chilean Society for the Defense of Tradition, Family, and Property (Studies Commission), *The Church of Silence in Chile: The TFP Proclaims the Whole Truth* (New York: Lumen Mariae Publications, 1976).

1067. See Chilean T.F.P., "Verdugos de los católicos rusos se levantan en favor de la jerarquía eclesiástica chilena" ["Butchers of Russian Catholics Rise in Favor of the Ecclesiastical Hierarchy in Chile"], *Las Ultimas Noticias* (Santiago), Feb. 28, 1976.

1068. See Alceste Santini, "È più aspro il contrasto fra stato e chiesa in Cile," *L'Unità*, Mar. 21, 1976, 17.

1069. *La Segunda* (Santiago), July 3, 1973.

1070. Víctor Farías, *Salvador Allende: El fin de un mito—El socialismo entre la obsesión totalitaria y la corrupción; Nuevas revelaciones*, 3rd ed. (n.p.: Editorial Maye Ltda., 2007), 178–79.

1071. Farías, *Salvador Allende*, 186. (Our emphasis.)

1072. Farías, 192.

1073. *El Siglo* (Santiago), Apr. 27, 1972. For the conference's written proceedings, see Gonzalo Arroyo, et al., *Los cristianos y el socialismo: Primer encuentro latinoamericano* (Buenos Aires: Siglo XXI, 1973). For a story on Christians for Socialism with ample bibliography, see Amorós, *La iglesia que nace del pueblo*.

Franciscan friar Uriel Molina, who later played an important role in the communist insurrection in his country, states:

> In Chile I was able to observe liberation theologians closely, and hear their case. ...
> ... The meeting of Christians for Socialism had a huge influence on us. ... [As did] the liberation theology of Gustavo Gutiérrez.[1074]

3. Uruguay

In November 1976, a bombshell book shook Uruguay. Its title said everything: *Progressivism in the Church, 'Fellow Traveler' of Communism in Its Long Adventure of Failures and Metamorphoses*.[1075] Based on nearly four hundred documents, the work showed that while the country was torn apart by the Tupamaro guerrillas,[1076] almost all the bishops and a considerable part of the clergy failed their sacred duty by leaving their flock exposed to the communist offensive, hindering any healthy reaction, and, even worse, sowing confusion by aiding and abetting the Marxist cause in many ways. Once Tupamaro terrorists had been defeated, instead of alerting the faithful to possible new dangers, a large sector of the clergy promoted reconciliation with the guerrillas and spread a relativist and feel-good stance vis-à-vis the communists, a prelude to their hostile attitude toward anti-communists. At the same time, the clergy allowed revolutionary trends and ideas to infiltrate Catholic organizations, creating a vast constituency for the extreme left.[1077] All of that took place under the auspices of liberation theology, which had in Uruguay some of its earliest manifestations, with the theologian Father Segundo.

4. Colombia

Colombia has a long and troubled history of communist guerrilla violence, still not completely eradicated. Insurgency was precisely the route chosen by the Golconda Priestly Movement. Founded in 1968, in 1969 it held a national conference in Buenaventura under the patronage of Bishop Gerardo Valencia Cano, who later stated, "I proclaim myself a socialist and a revolutionary."[1078] Attendees included Most Rev. Raúl Zambrano Camader, bishop of Facatativá, and fifty-three priests. The Final Document reads, "Our strong rejection of neocolonial capitalism ... makes us direct our actions and efforts toward the establishment of a socialist type of social organization."[1079]

Golconda honored the memory of the guerrilla priests Camilo Torres Restrepo, Domingo Lain, Manuel Pérez Martínez, and others who fought in the ranks of the National Liberation Army (E.L.N.) guerrilla group founded in 1964, which recruited their militants mainly from LT–inspired Basic Christian Communities. In her history of the E.L.N., Marxist Chilean writer Marta Harnecker writes, "The Christian movement of the Basic Ecclesial Communities went on to form a true Christian mass movement with revolutionary willpower and commitment. Consequently, in the seventies the [E.L.N.] organization began to pay much attention to this phenomenon and even created structures to work within the Basic Ecclesial Communities. In addition, many priests, like the Franciscan Diego Cristóbal Uribe Escobar, joined the guerrillas."[1080]

5. Nicaragua

A small Central American country, Nicaragua will go down in history as a textbook case in which the LT movement actually succeeded in seizing power in an alliance with the communist forces of the F.S.L.N. (Sandinista National Liberation Front).

In January 1966, Fidel Castro hosted in Havana the Tricontinental Conference, a gathering of revolutionary organizations from around the world, in order to create a global subversive movement. It was on that occasion that "Che" Guevara called for "two, three or many Vietnams."[1081] The conference gave a strong boost to guerrilla movements in Latin America, including Nicaragua's Frente Sandinista de Liberacion Nacional. Born as a nationalist insurrection against U.S. presence, the F.S.L.N. gradually became Marxist-Leninist. Its fighters were trained in the Middle East by Yasser Arafat's P.L.O., then in collusion with the U.S.S.R.[1082]

They applied the classic communist ploy: Well-trained minorities took advantage of tense situations in cities and countryside to create a growing discontent, resulting in a people's revolution. The hated dictatorship of Anastasio Somoza Debayle (1925–1980) seemed to offer an ideal climate. Nevertheless, a few years later, the Sandinista offensive ran aground, bereft of popular support. Nicaragua's deeply Catholic people showed themselves refractory to Marxist preaching.

At that point, however, a new factor intervened: LT–inspired Basic Christian Communities. Using conscientization techniques,[1083] the B.C.C.s managed to turn many Catholics into revolutionaries and send them to the F.S.L.N. Johannes Van Vugt explains, "The Nicaraguan Revolution succeeded because of ... Christian Base Communities. By membership in these organizations, a mobilization network was provided which raised the consciousness of the masses in opposition to the [Somoza] regime, offered a revolutionary ideology compatible with the Catholic faith, and provided leaders, members and a network for the militant revolutionaries or guerrillas known as the Sandinistas."[1084] The result was F.S.L.N.'s military victory in July 1979.[1085]

As had happened with the 1959 Cuban revolution and Allende's rise in 1970, the Sandinista victory galvanized the Latin American left. A guerrilla evening was held on February 28, 1980, in the theater of the Pontifical Catholic University of São Paulo, Brazil,

1074. Uriel Molina, *El sendero de una experiencia*, quoted in Jiménez, "Teología de la liberación," 29–30.

1075. See Sociedad Uruguaya de Defensa de la Tradición, Familia y Propiedad (Comisión de Estudios), *Izquierdismo en la iglesia, "compañero de viaje" del comunismo en la larga aventura de los fracasos e de las metamorfosis* (Montevideo: T.F.P., 1976).

1076. Between 1967 and 1973, that terrorist organization robbed four banks, nearly 200 hundred stores, and countless citizens, stealing over U.S. $10,000,000, and killing forty-five soldiers and policemen.

1077. This infiltration yielded its bitterest fruits in 2010 with the election of the former Tupamaro guerrilla fighter José Alberto Mujica Cordano to the presidency, with leftist Catholic support.

1078. *I.C.I.*, no. 356 (1970): 16, quoted in Enrique Dussel, *Historia de la iglesia en América Latina* (Barcelona: Editorial Nova Terra, 1974), 309. However, Bishop Valencia Cano, did not unreservedly support the use of violence.

1079. *El Colombiano* (Medellín), Feb. 1, 1969. For the full text of the Buenaventura Document, see Conferencia Episcopal de Acción Social (C.E.A.S.), ed., *Signos de renovación: Recopilación de documentos post-conciliares de la iglesia en América Latina (1966–1969)* (Lima: C.E.A.S., 1969), 107–14.

1080. Marta Harnecker, *Colombia ELN: Unidad que multiplica* (Havana: Rebelión, 1988), 7–8.

1081. Ernesto "Che" Guevara. "Message to the Tricontinental" (Apr. 16, 1967), Marxists.org.

1082. See U.S. Department of State, *The Sandinistas and Middle Eastern Radicals* (Washington, D.C.: U.S. Department of State, 1985).

1083. See chap. 1, n. 281.

1084. Johannes Van Vugt, "Christian Base Communities," *The Ecumenist* (Ottawa) 24, no. 1 (Nov.–Dec. 1985): 1; see Johannes P. Van Vugt, *Democratic Organization for Social Change: Latin American Christian Base Communities and Literacy Campaigns* (New York: Bergin & Garvey, 1991).

1085. See Carlos Alberto Libânio Christo, *Nicaragua livre: O primeiro passo* (Rio de Janeiro: Civilização Brasileira, 1980); Hernández Pico, *Convergencia entre iglesia popular*. President Carter significantly contributed to the Sandinista victory by withdrawing U.S. support for Anastasio Somoza on the pretext of defending human rights. Somoza was murdered in Asunción, Paraguay, in 1980 by a terrorist commando.

under the patronage of Paulo Evaristo Cardinal Arns, archbishop of São Paulo. The meeting was part of the Fourth International Ecumenical Congress of Theology, which was attended by 160 bishops, priests, nuns, and lay people involved with the LT movement in Latin America. Guests of honor at the event were Sandinista guerrillas led by Nicaraguan President Daniel Ortega accompanied by the Franciscan Uriel Molina, who was presented as the guerrilla chaplain, and David Chavarría, a "Christian guerrilla man." The Sandinistas sought to teach Brazilian Catholics the formula of their success so they could replicate it. It was an open incitement to armed struggle.

The next day, the archdiocesan newspaper headlined, "Nicaragua Is Just a Beginning!" In an interview, Cardinal Arns disclosed that, under archdiocesan auspices, successive cohorts of B.C.C. activists were traveling to Nicaragua to receive training in the revolutionary struggle. "This is just a beginning!" His Eminence enthusiastically exclaimed.[1086]

One could do a full tour of Latin America telling similar stories. In short, wherever the LT movement found a revolutionary process in place, it joined it and became one of its driving forces. It was a strategically vital force because it enlisted in the revolutionary cause sectors of the population that otherwise would have been contrary to leftwing propaganda. LT already existed as praxis and was launched as theology only in 1971 with Father Gutiérrez's book. We may say that LT arose as a theological justification for a revolutionary praxis already largely in place.

In addition to the scandalous Catholic collaboration with a reality the Magisterium of the Church defines as "intrinsically wrong,"[1087] we must highlight a fact that stands out as LT's most glaring contradiction. While proclaiming themselves defenders of the poor, liberation theologians advocate systems that generate poverty. It almost seems that their preferential option is not one for the poor but rather for poverty as such. As aptly expressed by Indro Montanelli, "The left loves the poor so much that every time it comes to power it increases their number."

C. The "Shame of Our Time"

1. Poverty, a "Value of the Kingdom"

The twentieth century saw the clash of two socioeconomic systems, one based on private property, the free market, and development; the other, on their denial. As for material well-being, we have to admit that history has shown the former to be right. While the West attained the highest economic and technological level ever achieved by a society in history, the communist world plunged into such squalor as to lead Cardinal Ratzinger to call

it, in a document issued by the Congregation for the Doctrine of the Faith, the "shame of our time."[1088]

The failure of real Socialism in the East was so obvious that not even its top leaders could hide it any longer. "Sooner or later the U.S.S.R. would be over," Mikhail Gorbachev stated. "It was impossible to continue living that way. We were becoming increasingly weak against the West. The country was not developing and there was huge discontent. In that way the Soviet Union would not last more than two decades."[1089] The wall of silence began to crumble along with the Soviet system. After decades of having repeated the opposite and hidden the misery behind the euphemism *maloo-bespechennost* (малообеспеченность: low-income), in 1989, the Soviet authorities had to admit that as many as "20 percent of the population" lived in extreme poverty, a Third World figure.[1090]

In Cuba—the tropical U.S.S.R.—the average salary is still only U.S. $ 21.00 per month, the lowest in Latin America, "insufficient to meet the most basic needs of the population," as President Raúl Castro admitted in a speech at the National Assembly. Let us add that 43% of the population has to make do with an income lower than the minimum wage. The food products that make up the *canasta normada* (food basket the government guarantees to every household) only cover 41.2% of the daily calories recommended by health authorities. Recently published data by economist Raúl Sandoval, of the University of Havana, show that 70% of Cuban homes are dilapidated.[1091]

The story was pretty much the same in Chile during the government of Salvador Allende. In three years of Marxist government (1970–1973) the economy deteriorated to the point that food rationing had to be imposed, as in times of war. That was handled by J.A.P. (Juntas de Abastecimiento y Precios), a network of neighborhood soviets which also acted as political commissars. A mere suspicion that a person opposed the regime was enough for him to be denied a *tarjeta* (card) and doomed to hunger. Let us see a few figures.

In the period 1970–1973, the Chilean G.D.P. fell from +8.0% to -4.3%; annual inflation increased from 22.1% to 5,605.1%; the annual change to median income went from +22.3% to -25.3%; and the trade balance plunged from +$114 to -$112 million dollars.[1092] It came down to what the economist Carlos Guerrero, of the University of Chile, defined as "total collapse": The number of citizens below the poverty line increased by as much as 33%.[1093]

Still, liberation theologians presented that very misery as a model!

In 1985, a trio of liberation theologians went to Cuba—brothers Leonardo and Clodovis Boff, along with the Dominican

1086. "Nicarágua é apenas um começo," *O São Paulo*, Mar. 1, 1980. For a complete report on the guerrilla evening, see Corrêa de Oliveira, "Na 'noite sandinista.'"

1087. "See to it, Venerable Brethren, that the Faithful do not allow themselves to be deceived! Communism is intrinsically wrong, and no one who would save Christian civilization may collaborate with it in any undertaking whatsoever. Those who permit themselves to be deceived into lending their aid toward the triumph of Communism in their own country, will be the first to fall victims of their error. And the greater the antiquity and grandeur of the Christian civilization in the regions where Communism successfully penetrates, so much more devastating will be the hatred displayed by the godless." Pius XI, encyclical *Divini Redemptoris* (Mar. 19, 1937), no. 58. On Socialism, the pope teaches, "Whether considered as a doctrine, or an historical fact, or a movement, Socialism, if it remains truly Socialism ... cannot be reconciled with the teachings of the Catholic Church." Pius XI, encyclical *Quadragesimo anno* (May 15, 1931), no. 117.

1088. Congregation for the Doctrine of the Faith, *Instruction on Certain Aspects*, XI, no. 10.

1089. Beatriz Silva, "La Unión Soviética, tal como existía, no habría sobrevivido más de 20 años," *El Mercurio* (Santiago), Dec. 8, 2006, p. A4.

1090. New York Times News Service, "Poverty Exists for Millions of Soviets, USSR Admits," *Chicago Tribune*, Jan. 30, 1989. See L. Zubova, N. Kovalena, and L. Khakhulina, "Poverty in the U.S.S.R.: The Population's Point of View," *Problems of Economic Transition* 34, no. 10 (Feb. 1992): 85–98.

1091. See Raúl A. Sandoval Gonzalez, "La pobreza en Cuba," *AucaLatinoAmericano*, Mar. 30, 2012; Carmelo Mesa Lago, *Cuba en la era de Raúl Castro: Reformas económico-sociales y sus efectos* (Madrid: Editorial Colibrí, 2011); Jorge Mario Sánchez Egozcue and Juan Triana Cordoví, "Un panorama actual de la economía cubana, las transformaciones en curso y sus retos perspectivos," *Boletín Elcano* (June 2008).

1092. See data from the Central Bank of Chile, C.I.E.P.L.A.N., and O.D.E.P.L.A.N., quoted in Carlos Guerrero, "Economía chilena en la época de Salvador Allende," *Rincón del Vago*.

1093. Guerrero, "Economía chilena." See also Patricio Meller, *Un siglo de economía política chilena (1890–1990)* (Santiago: Editorial Bello, 1996). For a rather complete report on the misery caused by the regime of Salvador Allende, see Cosme Beccar Varela, hijo, et al., *Allende et sa voie chilienne pour la misère* (Paris: Tradition Famille Propriété, 1974).

Friar Betto. Their impressions of the Fidel Castro regime were reported in an unusual "Theological Letter on Cuba," written by Friar Clodovis: "Although the presence of the Church is weak, that of the Kingdom seems strong. ... The Kingdom of God [is] specifically written into the [Cuban] structures."[1094] Unable to deny the extreme poverty besetting the former Pearl of the Antilles, Friar Clodovis tried to give it a spiritual character: "The general impression Cuba gave me was that of an immense community of religious. ... What they have there is great sobriety or austerity. ... I liked this life reduced to essentials. For me, austerity is not an economic policy to weather crises but an ideal for life in society."[1095]

The "Theological Letter on Cuba" was followed by an equally bizarre "Theological Letter on the U.S.S.R.," resulting from a 1987 journey by the trio to the Soviet Union. There, too, the liberation theologians saw "values of the Kingdom." Leonardo Boff writes:

> The Socialist Revolution of October 1917 opened a new chapter in the history of humanity. It was influenced by the [Holy] Spirit. ...
> This is particularly true for Soviet real Socialism. If we find values of the Kingdom there...[1096]

Fr. Clodovis Boff emphasized the poverty: "Being a friar, it was impossible not to compare Soviet society to an immense monastery where no one lacks the necessary and everyone lives a sober life."[1097]

To complete their tour of communist dictatorships, the trio also went to Mao's China and praised the "modest and restrained life" of the Chinese under Socialism. "Socialism is not to be seen as synonymous with wealth," Friar Betto remarked.[1098]

2. Preferential Option for Poverty

As we have already said, it seems that LT's preferential option is not so much for the poor but for poverty. Now, poverty is an evangelical value when lived by an individual who specifically elects to lead a religious life, but is undesirable when imposed on an entire society. Liberation theologians take their apology of poverty to unbelievable extremes.

The 10th International Conference of Theology was held in Madrid in September 1990 on the initiative of the John XXIII Association of Theologians. Its topic was the future of liberation theology facing the collapse of Socialism. After acknowledging the "profound failure of Socialism in the countries of central and eastern Europe," the Final Message stated, "This constitutes a challenge for us: how to go beyond Socialism." In order to overcome the failure of the real Socialism so dear to them, liberation theologians proposed nothing less than to establish "a society guided by the principle of poverty."

The idea was no longer to criticize the capitalist society because it does not fully achieve the ideal of progress and material well-being or benefits only a few; it was no longer to make a preferential option for the poor in the sense of elevating them, inviting them to share from the horn of plenty; it was no longer to criticize excessive luxury and consumerism. Instead, it was to make a critique of wealth, abundance, and consumption as such, deeming them alienating and distorting for the human person.

Spanish theologian Father Sobrino explains:

> The option that imposes itself in today's world is no longer one between rich and poor, but ... between two conflicting principles: that of wealth and that of poverty. ...
> ... We must make an option for poverty; we must take the principle of poverty as the foundation of everything.[1099]

He concluded by proposing an austere society, beyond consumption.

The most applauded report was undoubtedly the one by Sister Mari Conchi Puy, of the Little Sisters of Charles de Foucauld, who proclaimed radical poverty as an ideal and "an alternative to the consumer society."[1100]

It fell to Alberto Giráldez, in the conference's final report, to unveil the goal of liberation theologians. According to him, the Kingdom of God is realized only "in a society completely devoid of money. ... without economic exchange not even in the form of barter." Such society, he argued, requires "a radical change of mentality, even in our neurons." The "communal production of goods" must replace the "ownership-usufruct interest." Only this society would bring "that freedom, so greatly sought." Giráldez concluded by proposing large tribes as a model. "In large tribes there is no economic exchange. Everything belongs to everyone."[1101] The subject was not new. Two years earlier, at their 8th Conference, Spanish liberation theologian Father Ellacuría had focused his speech on the "civilization of poverty."[1102]

The defense of primitive societies as a model of evangelical poverty is a constant in some LT currents. During LT's International Conference held in Brazil in 2012, a rapporteur proposed, "The austerity of life in many indigenous peoples, especially nomads, offers contemporary society examples on how you can live well with the bare minimum. It is not necessary to consume or accumulate goods. ... Only austere lifestyles like those of indigenous peoples are sustainable for the future."[1103]

More recently, we have seen the overt support liberation theologians gave to Amazonian tribalism during the Pan-Amazon Synod held in Rome in October 2019.

3. Defending Dictatorship and Poverty

An uncontrolled lust for revolution can perhaps explain two glaring contradictions in liberation theologians. They proclaim themselves the defenders of freedom but enthusiastically support dictatorships provided they are communist or socialist. They proclaim themselves the champions of the poor but obstinately reject an economic system that has proven capable of producing great material well-being. Instead, they propose a failed system that only produces misery and oppression. Able to choose development and wealth, they prefer revolution and poverty.

LT was originally developed precisely to counter the theory of development. "We speak of social revolution, not reform; of liberation, not development; of socialism, not modernization,"

1094. Boff, *Carta teológica sobre Cuba*, 368.

1095. Boff, 349.

1096. Leonardo Boff, "O socialismo como desafio," *Revista de Cultura Vozes*, no. 6 (Nov.–Dec. 1987): 691–92.

1097. Clodovis Boff, "Carta teológica sobre a URSS," *Revista de Cultura Vozes*, no. 6 (Nov.–Dec. 1987): 653

1098. Frei Betto, *A igreja na China* (São Paulo: C.E.P.I.S., 1988), 133.

1099. Julio Loredo, "Rumbo al socialismo ecológico: Apología de la pobreza en el X Congreso de Teología Juan XXIII," *Covadonga Informa* 12, no. 148 (Nov. 1990), 8.

1100. Loredo, "Rumbo al socialismo ecológico," 9.

1101. Loredo, 10.

1102. T.F.P. Covadonga, "Teología de la liberación, ¿libertad o pobreza?" *Covadonga Informa*, 6.

1103. Graziela Wolfhart, "O bem viver e uma teologia indígena," *IHU Online* 12, no. 404 (Oct. 5, 2012): 33.

Father Gutiérrez proclaimed.[1104] "The concept of 'liberation' was used to overcome the concept of 'development,'" Father Sobrino recalls.[1105]

A careful country-by-country analysis of Latin America clearly shows that whenever policies proposed by liberation theologians were implemented, the result was a significant increase in poverty and discontent. Conversely, when the socioeconomic policies they abhor were applied, the result was a general increase in well-being. Even today, in socialist regimes allied to the ideals of liberation theologians such as Venezuela and Argentina, the social and economic situation is increasingly grim. In contrast, in Chile, Peru, Colombia, Mexico, where opposite policies were applied, the economy roared ahead, and with it all the social indicators.

Let us take a case in point: Peru, the homeland of Father Gutiérrez and our own.

On October 3, 1968, a military coup led by General Juan Velasco Alvarado overthrew the democratic government of Fernando Belaúnde Terry (1912–2002), establishing a "revolutionary, social-ist, and nationalist" military dictatorship, as Velasco stated in one of his early speeches. The new Revolutionary Government of the Armed Forces set out on an ambitious project (the Inca Plan) to subvert the country to its foundations.

While a land reform bill confiscated rural property holdings by transferring ownership to cooperatives modeled after Soviet kolkhozes, a law for the industrial sector established worker self-management, and education legislation imposed a unique government-dictated curriculum while banning foreign textbooks. Another bill nationalized all media in order to stifle any dissent. The absurdity went so far that a government decree banned the image of Santa Claus, accused of being a "foreigner." A ministry of propaganda called S.I.N.A.M.O.S. (National System to Support Social Mobilization) was created to shore up the regime and was entrusted to Marxist Hugo Neira, who wanted to turn Peru into a "new Cuba."[1106]

The result did not take long. Prisons filled with political oppo-nents even as supermarket shelves emptied. Who could forget the long waits to buy a pound of sugar or rice? There was a ban on eating meat for fifteen days a month. The use of fishmeal for food became widespread. With the prohibition of imports, high quality products disappeared from the market, and the standard of living dropped considerably. Except, of course, for the *nomenklatura*, whose members benefited from exclusive shops. The country went into a state of economic and psychological prostration from which it did not recover for many years.

Undoubtedly, land reform, imposed to tear down the hated landowner class, was the regime's crown jewel. In a short time, that reform became precisely its worst failure.

An exhaustive study conducted in 1980 by the Marxist-oriented Institute of Peruvian Studies, therefore unsuspected of harboring any bias against the regime, reported:

> Ten years later, the land reform program was already paralyzed. ...
> ... Among the 1,388 rural cooperatives examined, sixty-eight percent had no managment. Forty-seven

percent lacked accounting records ... seventy-eight percent had labor shortages. ...

> ... Given their previous achievements, positive results could have been expected from the large sugar production cooperatives. On the contrary, from 1976 on their balance sheets showed deficits. These went from S/1,659 million Peruvian soles that year to S/2,758 million in 1977, and over S/3,000 million soles in 1978.[1107]

In short, it was a catastrophe.

The LT movement rose precisely during the years of Velasco Alvarado's pro-communist dictatorship as an expression of the Catholic left's support for the revolutionary process underway. Liberation theologians kept supporting the government even after the so-called *Limazo* of February 1975, when the dictatorship drowned in blood a popular protest in the capital of Lima. The repression left 86 dead, 155 wounded, and 1,012 imprisoned. The military dictatorship defended Father Gutiérrez, who was considered one of its key supporters.

Velasco was replaced in 1975 by General Francisco Morales Bermúdez, who, given the failure of the regime, was forced to call elections in 1980. Finally, as a new Constitution was approved in the mid-nineties, Peru was able to exorcise the demons of Velasco's Socialism and resume its development. The results are there for anyone who wants to see. In two decades, per capita income more than doubled, poverty was halved, and wealth distribution greatly improved.[1108] The Peruvian economy keeps growing almost at a Chinese pace, peaking at 9.8% in 2008. In 2013, even amid the global crisis, Peru grew by 5.9%. I.M.F. forecasts 6.1% growth for 2014. The biggest beneficiaries are the people, the very people that liberation theologians would seek to push back into the clutches of socialist misery.

Uruguayan Jesuit Fr. Horacio Bojorge is right when, criticizing Father Segundo, he accuses liberation theologians of offering the poor a "lead-filled life jacket."[1109]

One such example is Venezuela. A country rich in oil resources, in the seventies it was thriving so bountifully as to be likened to a "South American Florida." Today, as Prof. Roberto Rigobon stated at the "Perspectives 2013" forum held in Caracas by Instituto de Estudios Superiores de Administración, it has been reduced by Chavista Socialism to the economic situation of "a country at war."[1110] The country was impoverished even when oil prices were steady at around $100 a barrel. According to the latest report by C.E.P.A.L. (Economic Commission for Latin America and the Caribbean), every year the percentage of Venezuelan families whose income fails to cover their needs rises by 3%. Inflation is the highest in the continent. Yet liberation theologians keep obstinately defending the Bolivarian Socialism that has caused such misery. As a matter of fact, one of the government's main advisors is the Jesuit theologian Fr. Jesús Gazo, chaplain of the Catholic University of Táchira.[1111]

1104. Gutiérrez, *The Power of the Poor*, 45.
1105. Sobrino, "O absoluto é Deus," 10.
1106. Hugo Neira, *Il Perù può diventare una nuova Cuba?* (Rome: Samonà e Savelli, 1969).

1107. José Matos Mar and José Manuel Mejia, *La reforma agraria en el Perú* (Lima: Instituto de Estudios Peruanos, 1980), 337–38. For an analysis of the economic disaster experienced during the Velasco years, see Rex A. Hudson, ed., *Peru: A Country Study* (Washington, D.C.: Federal Research Division, Library of Congress, 1992).
1108. See Gobierno del Perú/Presidencia del Consejo de Ministros, *Evolución de la pobreza en el Perú al 2010*, Aníbal Sanchez Aguilar, ed. (Lima: Instituto Nacional de Estadística e Informática, 2012).
1109. Bojorge, *Teologías deicidas*, 9.
1110. "Por la escasez, 'Venezuela parece un país en guerra,'" *Infobae América*, Mar. 1, 2013.
1111. See Ferenc Dosza, "Teologia e populismo," *Tradizione Famiglia Proprietà* (June 2013).

Another example is Ecuador, also rich in oil resources, yet forced in 2008 to default on its foreign debt, becoming unable to find international credit lines. In 2013, China had to fly to its support and buy its entire oil production.[1112]

4. Socialist and Confiscatory Land Reform

To close this chapter, let us briefly comment on an issue which has lent itself to much demagoguery: land reform, i.e., the expropriation of rural properties to distribute land to peasants. Some propaganda, and not just from the left, keeps denouncing what is seen as an unfair distribution of land ownership in many Latin American countries due to alleged oppression and exploitation. Accordingly, they propose land reform to divvy up the land. In Latin America, land reform has always been the main battle horse of both Communism and LT. Paradoxically, it was also the wrongheaded battle horse of U.S. foreign policy through Alliance for Progress, a project of John F. Kennedy, which conditioned U.S. aid to the implementation of structural reforms, and primarily land reform.[1113]

To avoid misunderstandings, let us immediately clarify that land reforms were never carried out to improve the situation of peasants, that is, for economic reasons, but rather to destroy a specific social system for ideological reasons. British historian Eric Hobsbawm writes,

> For the [revolutionaries] the case for land reform was political ... ideological ... and sometimes economic. ...
> The strongest economic case for land reform rests not on productivity but on equality.[1114]

This opinion is shared by Jacques Chonchol, Salvador Allende's Agriculture Minister and one of the main ideologues of land reform in Latin America: "Undoubtedly, the fundamental objective [of land reform] was to do away with the system of slavery in which peasants have lived for generations. It was not a productive goal, but a social one."[1115]

C.E.L.A.M. (Latin American Episcopal Conference) was right when it stated, in a 1976 document, "Latin America was born under the sign of the Council of Trent. ... Our original substance is medieval Catholicism."[1116] The social and cultural structure built by medieval Catholicism was still strong in the twentieth century, especially in the countryside. It still retained many elements of organic society, which the left dismissed as paternalistic.[1117] In

order to establish Communism in Latin America, its mentors first had to demolish that Catholic society through structural reforms, beginning with land reform. It is no coincidence that the first step a leftist government would take was always to implement land reform legislation.

There is no need for land reform in Latin America. Unlike Europe, in Latin America there is no lack of arable land. One example is Brazil, with an area of more than 3.28 million square miles (larger than the 48 contiguous U.S. states), 42% of which is still pristine. With adverse possession of just two years, anyone can become a landowner. Studies also show that the system of private property has proven capable of attaining productivity indexes equal to those in highly developed countries.[1118]

A large number of scientific studies demonstrate the total failure of land reform programs in Latin America. The stark fact is that no land reform has ever been able to improve the situation of peasants—quite the contrary. Without exception, while ideologues imposed land reform with great fanfare destroying the organic society, its implementation was an economic failure, producing poverty and neglect. Leftist Peruvian analyst Antonio Zapata comments,

> Forty years later, based on its results, land reform is still very ambiguous. It was partially successful. But from many standpoints it was a complete failure. On the one hand it freed Peruvian peasants from the bondage of landowners. ... But its production proposals were utopian and senseless, leading to a serious shortfall in agricultural productivity. ...
> Economic failure was the consequence. ... Food production diminished.[1119]

The collapse of agricultural production, with consequent situations of hunger and poverty, has forced millions of peasants to migrate to the cities in complete poverty.

As for Brazil, it is interesting to look at the data presented in April 2012 by an analyst beyond suspicion, Francisco Graziano Neto, a former president of I.N.C.R.A. (National Institute for Agrarian Reform and Colonization), the department responsible for implementing land reform. Here are some passages from his speech:

> Brazil has implemented the world's largest land reform program. ...
> According to data provided by INCRA, from 1994 to 2011, 1,176,813 families were settled across an area of two hundred and seventeen million acres. ...[1120]
> ... Let me recall that the area cultivated in France is seventy-four million acres.
> If there was a world ranking of agricultural reforms Brazil would undoubtedly be the winner by size but the last for results. Here is the problem. The land reform

1112. See "La bandiera cinese piantata sull'Ecuador: Il gigante asiatico compra tutto il greggio" ["The Chinese Flag Planted in Ecuador: The Asian Giant Buys All Its Oil"] *Corriere della Sera*, Sept. 30, 2013.

1113. See Hernando Agudello Villa, *La revolución del desarrollo: Origen y evolución de la Alianza para el Progreso* (México, D.F.: Editorial Roble, 1966).

1114. Eric Hobsbawm, *Age of Extremes: The Short Twentieth Century 1914–1991* (London: Abacus, 1995), 355–56. Furthermore, Karl Marx himself had proposed land reform as the first and indispensable step to establish Socialism. See Wolfang Leonhard, *Die dreispaltung des marxismus* (Vienna: Econ Verlag, 1975), 59.

1115. Angela Cousiño Vicuña and María Angélica Ovalle Gana, *Reforma agraria chilena: Testimonios de sus protagonistas* (Santiago: Memoriter, 2013), 89.

1116. C.E.L.A.M., "Igreja e religiosidade popular na América Latina," *Sedoc* (July 10, 1977), 20, 23.

1117. Here is a description of landlord-peasant relations in Chile, which is valid for most of the continent: "The peasant was a tenant of sorts who had a house, some land, animals, and enjoyed specific benefits such as electricity, running water, and food. In exchange for that, he provided labor on the owner's farm and also received a daily stipend for this work. In this scheme, the owner was an authority that ... governed the property and regulated work, imposing order and taking care of the education and health [of his peasants]." Cousiño Vicuña and Ovalle Gana, *Reforma agraria chilena*, 23. Here a careful observer will notice elements of feudal relations, and this is precisely what infuriated the left, as such a scheme is inherently "alienating" no matter how beneficial it may be to the peasant. On the situation of peasants in a feudal regime, see Marc Bloch, *La società feudale* (Turin: Einaudi, 1949); Marc Bloch, *La servitù nella società medievale* (Florence: La Nuova Italia, 1975) [our translation].

1118. See Geraldo de Proença Sigaud, Antonio de Castro Mayer, Plinio Corrêa de Oliveira, and Luiz Mendonça de Freitas, *Reforma agrária, questão de consciência* (São Paulo: Ave Maria, 1960); Carlos Patricio del Campo, *Is Brazil Sliding Toward the Extreme Left? Notes on the Land Reform Program in South America's Largest and Most Populous Country* (Pleasantville, N.Y.: The American Society for the Defense of Tradition, Family, and Property, 1986); Carlos Patricio del Campo, "Posso e devo ser contra a Reforma Agrária: Considerações econômicas," in Corrêa de Oliveira and del Campo, *Sou católico*; Corrêa de Oliveira and del Campo, *No Brasil*.

1119. Antonio Zapata, "¿Fracasó la reforma agraria?" *La República* (Lima), Aug. 26, 2009.

1120. The Brazilian land reform program gathers peasants in *assentamentos*, that is, settlements, which work as self-managing rural cooperatives. The peasants in this situation are called *assentados*, settlers.

[program] appears to be the worst failure of public policy in our country. Apart from the usual exceptions, all settlements have become rural shantytowns.

A 2010 survey by INCRA collected information on the way of life, production, and income of families living in the settlements. The questionnaires were completed by a sample of 16,153 beneficiaries, involving 1,164 land reform projects. Only 32.6% of homes have electricity; 57% of the settlements have no access roads; public health barely covers 56% of households; on average. ...

The government's inability to support the new producers, along with the inability of most settled families is reflected in earnings. In the State of Ceará, 70% of the peasants have a total annual income no greater than two minimum wages, with the aggravating circumstance that 44% of that income comes from state welfare programs. A rural tragedy in the Northeast. ...

However, most surprising of all for the analysts who discovered the "black hole" of land reform is the impossibility of knowing with certainty the amount of agricultural production coming from the settlements. Incredible as it may seem, there are no general statistics on the production volume of cereals, fruits, vegetables, and even cattle to quantify the settlements' contribution to the national harvest. This seems almost a joke. ...

... There is no government data from the countryside that allow us to assess the land reform program in terms of production. We know that cost-benefit analysis has never been the forte of agrarian populism. As if mere land distribution were a passport to eternal happiness.[1121]

Thus, an I.N.C.R.A. president himself stated that land reform appears as "the worst failure of public policy in our country." Graziano then speaks of "rural shantytowns," a notion reiterated by Minister Gilberto Carvalho: "Many land reform settlements have become rural shantytowns."[1122] The term was coined in 1996 by journalists Nelson Ramos Barreto and Paulo Henrique Chaves in a landmark book titled, *Land Reform Sows Settlements, Peasants Harvest Misery and Desolation*.[1123] After visiting hundreds of settlements the authors found that most had been reduced to the situation of "rural shantytowns." "We all miss the good times of the owners!" was the general comment among settlers.

Yet, the Brazilian Bishops' Conference fiercely defended these rural shantytowns through its Pastoral Commission on Land, and liberation theologians supported the Landless Workers Movement.

A book recently published in Chile devotes five hundred pages, including statistical data and interviews with participants, to analyze the land reform program in that important country.[1124] Again, land reform was implemented "to eliminate large estates ... without worrying ... about productivity indexes."[1125] In fact, productivity was its primary victim. While the Frei government

(1964–1970) had maintained an annual agricultural G.D.P. growth rate of 2%, the same rate dropped to -4.6% under Allende and climbed to 8.7% with Pinochet, who implemented diametrically opposed policies.[1126] Then there was the mass exodus to the cities. Today, forty years after the land reform law, only 10% of beneficiaries remain as farmers in the countryside; 90% had to migrate in order to survive, gathering in poor neighborhoods.

The same Jacques Chonchol recently had to admit, "From the social point of view [land reform] was a big thing. From the point of view of production, it was not that great."[1127] It would have been more honest to say that it was a disaster, a disaster wanted and advocated by liberation theologians. Obviously, they prefer peasants starving to death, but "free" from owner "oppression" to well-nourished farm workers "alienated" by a "paternalist system."

1121. Xico Graziano (Francisco Graziano Neto), "Reforma agrária de qualidade," *O Estado de S. Paulo*, Apr. 17, 2012, p. 2. Republished with permission.

1122. Fernando Odila, "Política agrária federal criou 'favelas rurais', diz ministro," *Folha de S. Paulo*, Feb. 9, 2013.

1123. See Nelson Ramos Barreto and Paulo Henrique Chaves, *Reforma agrária semeia assentamentos: Assentados colhem miséria e desolação; Reportagem da TFP revela a verdade inteira* (São Paulo: Sociedade Brasileira de Defesa da Tradição, Familia e Propriedade, 1996). See also Nelson Ramos Barreto, *Reforma agrária: O mito e a realidade* (São Paulo: Artpress, 2003). On the failure of land reform in Colombia, see Absalón Machado Cartagena, *Reforma agraria: Una ilusión que resultó un fracaso* (Bogotá: Biblioteca Virtual del Banco de la República, 2005).

1124. See Cousiño Vicuña and Ovalle Gana, *Reforma agraria chilena*.

1125. Vicuña and Gana, 67.

1126. See Rafael Yrarrázaval, "Reforma agraria en Chile," *Ciencia e investigación agraria* 6, no. 1 (Jan.–Mar. 1979), 7–9, quoted in Vicuña and Gana, 76.

1127. Vicuña and Gana, 90.

Chapter 7:
One Door Leaf Closed, the Other Wide Open

A. The Puebla Conference

As mentioned in chapter 2, the Second General Assembly of C.E.L.A.M. was held in Medellín, Colombia, in August 1968. The presence of Pope Paul VI gave more authority to the meeting, which many began to call the "Second Vatican Council of the Latin American Church." Many liberation theologians participated in its preparatory committees and later as experts during the proceedings, managing to shape some of its conclusions. In addition to the actual content of its documents, the "spirit of Medellín" began to blow very strongly, moving vast ecclesiastical sectors more and more to the left. In the wake of that conference, the liberationist movement had a strong expansion.

C.E.L.A.M.'s Third General Assembly was held in Puebla, Mexico, in January 1979, with the presence of Pope John Paul II. This time, however, the climate was quite changed. Argentine socialist Diego Facundo Sánchez writes, "It was clear with the pope's opening speech that a completely different phase was beginning for the Latin American Church in general and LT specifically."[1128] From his first lines, Pope John Paul II forcefully insisted that the politicization of the Church in Latin America under LT's auspices had been a serious mistake:

> It is a great consolation for the universal Father to note that you come together here not as a symposium of experts, not as a parliament of politicians, not as a congress of scientists or technologists, however important such assemblies may be, but as a fraternal encounter of Pastors of the Church. And as Pastors you have the vivid awareness that your principal duty is to be Teachers of the Truth. Not a human and rational truth, but the Truth that comes from God, the Truth that brings with it the principle of the authentic liberation of man: 'you will know the truth, and the truth will make you free' (John 8:32); that Truth which is the only one that offers a solid basis for an adequate "praxis." ....
>
> ... [Referring to LT's biblical method, the pope condemned] "re-readings" of the Gospel, the result of theoretical speculations rather than authentic meditation on the word of God and a true commitment to the Gospel.
>
> They cause confusion by diverging from the central criteria of the faith of the Church, and some people have the temerity to pass them on, under the guise of catechesis, to the Christian communities. ...
>
> [The pope went on to criticize LT's Christology:] In other cases people claim to show Jesus as politically committed, as one who fought against Roman oppression and the authorities, and also as one involved in the

class struggle. This idea of Christ as a political figure, a revolutionary, as the subversive man from Nazareth, does not tally with the Church's catechesis. ...

> ... [Quoting Pope John Paul I, and dismantling LT's very core, he said,] "It is wrong to state that political, economic and social liberation coincides with salvation in Jesus Christ, that the *Regnum Dei* is identified with the *Regnum hominis*." ...
>
> ... [Also, countering LT's socialist tendencies, the supreme pontiff defended private property, about which he mentioned] the vigorous teaching of Saint Thomas Aquinas, repeated so many times.[1129]

It seemed to be a serious repudiation of LT both in its doctrinal foundations and political practice. However, with passages that admitted different interpretations, and silence on some aspects of the revolutionary creed, coupled with the lack of a true and formal condemnation, despite being basically positive the papal message failed to completely block the way for LT. "The message closed only one of the door leaves," Plinio Corrêa de Oliveira commented at the time, manifesting the hope that future documents would close the other leaf as well.[1130]

Entering through the door leaf left open, C.E.L.A.M. approved a *Final Document* in which, in the words of Diego Facundo Sánchez, "concessions were made to the church of liberation due to the evangelical style of its ... pastoral proposals. ... The method used to present the topics and the document as a whole showed continuity with Medellín."[1131] That was, for example, the position of Father Sobrino, who believed that Puebla was "a serene affirmation of Medellín."[1132] In particular, the document reiterated the use of the "preferential option for the poor" as a Latin American pastoral policy criterion. That was the open door leaf through which LT managed to slip through.

Submitted to the scrutiny of Rome, which made some alterations, Puebla's *Final Document* was published by bishops' conferences only in November and in a rather strange format: It was full of comments stressing its progressive aspects while downplaying changes the Holy See had opposed. "The comments interpret the text of the document to bring more water to the mill

---

1128. Sánchez, *Teología de la liberación,* 33.

1129. John Paul II, "Address of His Holiness," Puebla, Mexico (Jan. 28, 1979).

1130. "In the face of Communism, the message neither blocked its way entirely (as was direly needed), nor left the way entirely open. As I said, it closed only one of the door leaves (which helps some)." Plinio Corrêa de Oliveira, "'Hipoteca social': Só grava a propriedade? A mensagem de Puebla: Notas e comentários—V (final)," *Folha de S. Paulo,* May 19, 1979.

1131. Sánchez, *Teología de la liberación,* 34.

1132. Jon Sobrino, "Puebla, serena afirmación de Medellín," *Diakonía* (Managua) no. 9, 27–56.

of liberation theology, censured by John Paul II. ... And no one moves," Plinio Corrêa de Oliveira lamented.[1133]

At any rate, it was quite clear that the climate was beginning to change. LT opponents had to operate in a substantial magisterial vacuum. While it is true that in the General Audience of October 21, 1970, Paul VI had censured the "theology of revolution," he did not seem to consider a 1968 message signed by more than two million Latin Americans asking him to intervene in order to stem communist infiltration in Catholic circles.[1134] He even protected some LT leaders.[1135] Instead, the address by John Paul II in Puebla seemed to mark the beginning of a turnaround, further strengthened by the appointment of bishops not aligned with LT.

B. The Instructions *Libertatis Nuntius* and *Libertatis Conscientia*

On August 6, 1984, the Congregation for the Doctrine of the Faith published the *Instruction on Certain Aspects of the Theology of Liberation, Libertatis Nuntius*, widely believed to be a true and formal condemnation of LT.[1136] It was signed by Joseph Cardinal Ratzinger with the approval of Pope John Paul II. The document opens by challenging a fundamental point of LT:

> Liberation is first and foremost liberation from the radical slavery of sin. Its end and its goal is the freedom of the children of God, which is the gift of grace. ...
>
> ... Sin is the greatest evil, since it strikes man in the heart of his personality. The first liberation, to which all others must make reference, is that from sin (IV, no. 12). ...
>
> 14. Consequently, the full ambit of sin, whose first effect is to introduce disorder into the relationship between God and man, cannot be restricted to "social sin" (IV, no. 14). ...
>
> 15. Nor can one localize evil principally or uniquely in bad social, political, or economic "structures" as though all other evils came from them so that the creation of the "new man" would depend on the establishment of

different economic and sociopolitical structures (IV, no. 15).

Defining Communism as the "shame of our time" (XI, no. 10), the document criticizes LT's lack of critical examination of the Marxist analysis, pointing out that the latter is not at all scientific but ideological: "The thought of Marx is such a global vision of reality that all data received from observation and analysis are brought together in a philosophical and ideological structure, which predetermines the significance and importance to be attached to them. ... If one tries to take only one part, say, the analysis, one ends up having to accept the entire ideology" (VII, no. 6).

This ideology, Cardinal Ratzinger continues, is LT's poisoned core: "In fact, the ideological core borrowed from Marxism, which we are referring to, exercises the function of a 'determining principle'" (VIII, no. 1). A whole string of errors incompatible with Church doctrine follow: "This all-embracing conception thus imposes its logic and leads the 'theologies of liberation' to accept a series of positions which are incompatible with the Christian vision of humanity" (VIII, no. 1).

It is an error to conceive the truth as revolutionary praxis: "The truth is a truth of class: there is no truth but the truth in the struggle of the revolutionary class" (VIII, no. 5). By conceiving the truth as praxis, one blurs the distinction between good and evil: "In particular, the very nature of ethics is radically called into question because of the borrowing of these theses from Marxism. In fact, it is the transcendent character of the distinction between good and evil, the principle of morality, which is implicitly denied in the perspective of the class struggle" (VIII, no. 9). This dialectical vision easily results in violence, which is also incompatible with a Catholic vision.

"History thus becomes a central notion. It will be affirmed that God Himself makes history. It will be added that there is only one history, one in which the distinction between the history of salvation and profane history is no longer necessary. To maintain the distinction would be to fall into 'dualism.' Affirmations such as this reflect historicist immanentism" (IX, no. 3). LT's hermeneutics is condemned as well: "The new 'hermeneutic' inherent in the 'theologies of liberation' leads to an essentially 'political' re-reading of the Scriptures" (X, no. 5).[1137]

Showing the profound affinity between the two schools, European theologians linked to extreme versions of the Nouvelle Théologie—including Fathers Congar, Chenu, Metz, Schillebeeckx, and Küng—rebelled against the Vatican, and rose up in defense of LT.

The chagrin of progressive theologians stood in sharp contrast with the satisfaction of Latin American Catholics. Prof. Plinio Corrêa de Oliveira welcomed the *Instruction* as "a jet of fresh and beneficial water gushing from a fire hydrant. As President of the National Council of the Brazilian T.F.P. ... it is a duty of justice for me to manifest my joy, gratitude, and above all the hope I feel on experiencing this relief amid the fire." However, even on this occasion the road was still not completely blocked: "While I believe that only one jet of water does not suffice to put out a fire, this does not prevent me from welcoming it as a relief. Especially since we cannot prove that this gush of water will remain the only

---

1133. Plinio Corrêa de Oliveira, "Raio, vaga-lume, silêncio," *Folha de S. Paulo*, Dec. 29, 1979.

1134. Brazilian T.F.P., "Reverente e filial mensagem a Sua Santidade o Papa Paulo VI," *Catolicismo*, nos. 212–214 (Aug.–Oct. 1968).

1135. On his return from Rome in 1976, the archbishop of São Paulo, His Eminence Paulo Evaristo Cardinal Arns, rejecting criticisms by Brazilian Catholics against Most Rev. Pedro Casaldáliga, bishop of São Félix do Araguaia and openly aligned with Marxist-Sandinist guerrillas, stated, "I heard from Paul VI himself that messing with Bishop Pedro Casaldáliga is like messing with the pope." *O São Paulo*, Jan. 6, 1976.

1136. In an interview, recalling his years as head of the Congregation for the Doctrine of the Faith, the former pope offers interesting insights on the reasons that prompted him to publish the *Instruction*. He states:

The first great challenge we addressed was the Theology of Liberation, which was spreading in Latin America. It was the common opinion, be it in Europe or in North America, that it was about support to the poor and, therefore, a cause that should certainly be approved. But it was an error.

Poverty and the poor were without a doubt put forth as topics of the Theology of Liberation but in a very specific perspective. ... It was not a question of aid or reform, it was said, but of a great upheaval from which a new world would spring. The Christian faith was being used as the engine for this revolutionary movement, thus transforming it into a kind of political force. ...

... It was necessary to oppose such a falsification of the Christian faith precisely for the sake of the poor and the service that should be rendered to them.

Based on his experience in his Polish homeland, Pope John Paul II gave us essential explanations. On the one hand he had lived the enslavement by Marxist ideology, which became the godmother of liberation theology. Based on his painful experience, it was clear that one had to fight that kind of "liberation." ...

That is what we tried to say in the two Instructions. (Benedict XVI, "Il ricordo del pontefice emerito," 17–18)

1137. Congregation for the Doctrine of the Faith, *Instruction on Certain Aspects*.

one." The illustrious thinker concluded, saying, "It is our duty to hope that such [doctrinal and practical] barriers are erected."[1138]

While liberation theologians trudged on, manipulating some loopholes left in the *Instruction*, it has been a stumbling block for LT supporters.[1139]

Moreover, the *Instruction* was not universally applied. In May 1988 John Paul II made his second apostolic visit to Peru for the closure of the Eucharistic and Marian Conference of Bolivarian Nations.[1140] Visibly upset at the lack of concrete measures, the pope stated in his message to the Peruvian bishops:

> Your mission as pastors and teachers of the faith includes the obligation to discern, clarify and propose solutions in view of deviations that may arise. You should not hesitate to exercise this duty ... against positions that contradict the faith and the Church's teachings. ...
>
> ... [Having recalled the figure of Saint Toribio de Mogrovejo (1538–1606), archbishop of Lima, who] loved those who erred but never shrunk from combating error. ... [he called the bishops to their duty.] You must implement a solid, clear, and courageous teaching to apply the directives of the Instructions on Liberation Theology from the Congregation for the Doctrine of the Faith.[1141]

In 1986, two years after *Libertatis Nuntius*, a companion document came to light: the *Instruction on Christian Freedom and Liberation, Libertatis Conscientia*.[1142] As the Introduction explains, "Between the two documents there exists an organic relationship. They are to be read in the light of each other." Its tone, however, was very different. Abandoning any direct censorship of LT, the new document emphasized instead positive aspects of contemporary man's "modern liberation process" (I, I) deeming its achievements "positive" for humanity: "The advances of freedom and equality in many societies are undeniable" (no. 8). While admitting some "ambiguities" in this process (no. 10), the new Instruction stated that "Awareness of man's freedom and dignity, together with the affirmation of the inalienable rights of individuals and peoples, is one of the major characteristics of our time. But freedom demands conditions of an economic, social, political and cultural kind which make possible its full exercise. A clear perception of the obstacles which hinder its development and which offend human dignity is at the source of the powerful aspirations to liberation which are at work in our world" (no. 1).

The mission of the Church is basically liberating. It implies first of all liberation from "sin, the root of human alienation" (no. 38). Since man is a social being, this also means liberation from the "structures of exploitation and slavery" (no. 42). Thus, in the "liberating mission of the Church" (no. 61), the "eschatological hope" goes hand in hand with the "commitment for temporal liberation" (no. 60). Such liberation, nevertheless, must take truth and justice into account.

With a sentence very much commented on by liberation theologians, the 1986 Instruction concludes, "A theology of freedom and liberation ... is something needed by the times in which we are living" (no. 98). The LT–inspired Basic Christian Communities also receive a friendly nod: "The new basic communities or other groups of Christians which have arisen to be witnesses to this evangelical love are a source of great hope for the Church" (no. 69).[1143]

The changed tone in relation to the earlier document was interpreted as a softening, an outstretched hand to LT. Liberation theologians were the first to make such a reading:

> [The document] marks a thaw. . . . The attitude is constructive, more open to dialogue, and the positions are more nuanced. ...
>
> The Instruction sees the main theoretical and practical aspects of the [LT] subject in a positive light. ...
>
> This second C.D.F. document shows an obvious influence from LT's theological and pastoral movement. ...The Congregation for the Doctrine of the Faith thus assumes examples, patterns, and concepts that make up the specific discourse of LT. The second Instruction was a positive outcome for LT in that it leaves some room for the exercise of a responsible LT. ...
>
> It made a favorable assessment of the BCCs. ... Clearly, the second document's tone is much more optimistic and was seen as a step toward reconciliation with LT.[1144]

Emphasizing reconciliation, on April 9, 1986, the pope sent the Brazilian bishops a letter in which he stated, "Liberation theology is not just timely but useful and necessary." He asked, nevertheless, that it be inserted in the wake of Catholic theology: "[LT] must mark a new stage—in close connection with earlier ones—of that theological reflection which began with the Apostolic Tradition and continued with the great Fathers and Doctors, with the ordinary and extraordinary magisterium and, in more recent times, with the rich patrimony of the social doctrine of the Church."[1145]

C. Condemnations, Mea Culpas, and Diversionary Maneuvers

The Instructions by the Congregation for the Doctrine of the Faith were accompanied by some disciplinary measures. We will briefly mention two.

1. The Case of Then-Father Leonardo Boff

In March 1984, Cardinal Ratzinger condemned the main theses of the book by then-Father Leonardo Boff, *Church: Charism and Power*, and summoned him to Rome for clarification. The Franciscan theologian, a former student of Cardinal Ratzinger in Tübingen, landed in the Eternal City flanked by Their Eminences Cardinals Ivo Lorscheiter, archbishop of Fortaleza, and Paulo Evaristo Arns, archbishop of São Paulo. The latter had written

---

1138. Plinio Corrêa de Oliveira, "A mangueira, o desejo e o dever," *Folha de S. Paulo*, Dec. 10, 1984.

1139. Overlooking the fact that the *Instruction* had been submitted previously to John Paul II, the then-prefect of the Congregation for the Doctrine of the Faith dismisses the document as "Joseph Ratzinger's personal affirmations." Gerhard Ludwig Müller, "'Vagliate ogni cosa e tenete ciò che è buono.' A 25 anni dall'istruzione *Libertatis Nuntius*," in *Dalla parte dei poveri*, by Gustavo Gutiérrez and Gerhard Ludwig Müller, 181.

1140. By *Bolivarian Nations*, organizers meant Bolivia, Colombia, Ecuador, Peru, and Venezuela.

1141. John Paul II, Address to the Peruvian Episcopal Conference (May 15, 1988), no. 5.

1142. See Congregation for the Doctrine of the Faith, *Instruction on Christian Freedom and Liberation* (Mar. 22, 1986).

1143. Congregation for the Doctrine of the Faith. As we saw earlier, in n. 1136, the former pontiff offered a new key to interpret that document: It was intended to prevent Latin American countries from falling into communist "slavery" falsely presented as liberation.

1144. Sánchez, *Teología de la liberación*, 40–41.

1145. John Paul II, "Letter to the Brazilian Bishops Conference" (Apr. 9, 1986), no. 5.

to the secretary of state, Agostino Cardinal Casaroli, declaring himself responsible for the sins of Leonardo Boff.[1146]

The Brazilian newspaper *O Estado de S. Paulo* commented that the presence of Cardinals Arns and Lorscheiter weighed heavily in high-ranking Vatican circles to make what initially seemed an interrogation become a cordial chat.[1147] Years later, Boff disclosed that Cardinal Arns had confronted the Congregation prefect, pointing out that the Brazilian bishops would be displeased by a possible condemnation.[1148] Thus, what had seemed a looming condemnation became a mere slap on the wrist. At any rate, one year of "obsequious silence" was imposed on the liberation theologian.[1149] That was enough for seventeen Brazilian bishops, in May 1985, to state they were in "complete disagreement" with the Holy See. They accused the pope of showing "a less than evangelical attitude." Schism was in the air. Cardinal Ratzinger himself said he gave up on condemnations because they attracted greater publicity for those censured.

In 1992, Leonardo Boff left the Franciscan order and asked to be dispensed from his vows. Without that dispensation, already in 1981 he joined Marcia Monteiro da Silva Miranda, a divorced mother of six, with whom he maintained a secret relationship.[1150]

His younger brother, Friar Clodovis Boff, O.S.M., who until then had been very close to him, did not follow him. Instead, he wrote a long article in the *Revista Eclesiástica Brasileira* denying some of LT's fundamental points. According to him, the fatal error is that

> God is no longer the first operative principle of theology, the poor are. ... It is an error of principle, and thus, of perspective. It is grave, fatal even. ...
>
> What happens with the faith and its doctrine on the level of theology and pastoral policy when the poor acquire the status of epistemological "primum"? ...
>
> The inevitable result is the politicization of the faith ... ... and the consequent social, political, and ideological [abuse] of the faith.
>
> ... The "pastoral of liberation" becomes one among the many arms of the "people's movement." The Church becomes something similar to an NGO and is physically emptied: it loses workers, militants, and faithful. Those "outside" feel little attraction for a "Church of liberation" because, as militants, they already have NGOs, while from the standpoint of religious experience they need much more than a simple social liberation.[1151]

2. The Case of Fr. Gustavo Gutiérrez

On March 13, 1983, the Congregation for the Doctrine of the Faith sent the Peruvian Bishops' Conference a letter titled, "Ten observations about the theological thought of Gustavo Gutiérrez," containing articulated critiques of his doctrine. Although "Gutiérrez's answers were rather evasive," as theologian Battista

Mondin reported,[1152] from then on the Peruvian theologian began a normalization process which led him to soften his positions without denying his past. After three years of talks, not always serene, between Rome and the Peruvian Bishops' Conference, they came to a compromise. The liberation theologian was asked to make a "clarification" to be added as an introduction to his book, *A Theology of Liberation*. Titled "Expanding the View," the essay appears in the book's more recent editions.[1153]

As a mea culpa, the step is somewhat curious. Almost nothing was changed in the original, theoretically condemned book. His defense of Marxism remained untouched. He added some Council texts to his Marxist sources to make for a more *spiritual* and less *political* reading. He attributes his problems with the Vatican merely to "reasons that eventually pass away" and announces that "the theological labor must continue."[1154]

So as not to appear completely insensitive to Vatican criticism, in the new introduction the Peruvian theologian makes distinctions by stating, for example, that "the first ... phase of theological work is the lived faith that finds expression in prayer and commitment,"[1155] thus distancing himself from the Marxist theory of truth as praxis, which he still intimately clings to. He also reiterates his total fidelity to the Church by describing liberation theology's development as an "ecclesial function,"[1156] and defends himself from various charges such as upholding "immanentism."[1157]

Nevertheless, the Peruvian theologian reaffirms the core of LT: "Ever since Medellín, ... liberation theology in Latin America has been accompanied by a continual awareness that we have entered into a new historical stage in the life of our peoples. ..."[1158] "A new historical era to be characterized by a radical aspiration for integral liberation. ... The vision is still valid."[1159] The movement's worldwide adepts long "for liberation from every form of servitude."[1160] Father Gutiérrez recognizes, however, that "in the years since Medellín there has been an inevitable clarification of this theological undertaking."[1161] Later, he adds, "A process of maturation has been under way."[1162] This maturation has caused LT to stop being "simplistic"[1163] and to become "complex."[1164]

Complexity derives from a broadened concept of liberation (the topic we will deal with in the next chapter). Father Gutiérrez writes:

> Within the different Christian confessions and their respective traditions, thinkers have adopted the liberation perspective. ...
>
> [These include] Black, Hispanic, Amerindian theologies in the United States ... and the especially fruitful thinking of those who have adopted the feminist perspective.[1165]

1146. See *Folha de S. Paulo*, Sept. 5, 1984, p. 6.

1147. See *O Estado de S. Paulo*, Sept. 8, 1984, p. 9, and Sept. 19, 1984, p. 9.

1148. See *Caros amigos* (Brazil) 1, no. 3 (June 1997).

1149. Boff claims that it was John Paul II himself who, on Holy Saturday 1986, eleven months after the admonishment, personally suspended it. Boff said that he received a phone call informing him that "the pope says you are now free and may speak again." Leonardo Boff, Interview, Marina Amaral, et al., "A igreja mente, é corrupta, cruel e sem piedade," *Caros amigos* 2 (Brazil), no. 18 (Sept. 1998). A letter from the Vatican secretary of state followed. It praised his stance and affirmed that "In this way one can build an authentic theology of liberation." Amaral, "A igreja mente."

1150. See Lucia Boldrini, "Confissões amorosas de um padre," *Revista da Folha* (Nov. 21, 1993): 17–21.

1151. Clodovis Boff, "Teologia da libertação e volta ao fundamento," *Revista Eclesiástica Brasileira* 67, no. 268 (Oct. 2007): 1001–22. Republished with permission.

1152. Mondin, *Storia della teologia*, 4:979.

1153. See Gutiérrez, new introduction ("Expanding the View") to *A Theology of Liberation* (1988 rev. ed.), xvii–xlvi.

1154. Gutiérrez, xviii.

1155. Gutiérrez, xxxiv.

1156. Gutiérrez, xxxiii.

1157. Gutiérrez, xxxix.

1158. Gutiérrez, xviii.

1159. Gutiérrez, xvii.

1160. Gutiérrez, xliv.

1161. Gutiérrez, xviii.

1162. Gutiérrez, xix.

1163. Gutiérrez, xviii, xxiii, xxv.

1164. Gutiérrez, xxi, xxiii, xxv, xl.

1165. Gutiérrez, xix.

This was possible because the concept of poverty was broadened: "The socioeconomic dimension is very important but we must go beyond it. ... Diverse factors [psychological, racial, cultural, etc.] are making us aware of the different kinds of opposition and social conflict that exist in the modern world."[1166]

To analyze these new situations of so-called oppression Father Gutiérrez says we need new tools of analysis, "new sources of knowledge from the human sciences: psychology, ethnology, anthropology," and so on.[1167] Father Gutiérrez thus issues a call: "Attention to cultural factors will help us to enter into mentalities and basic attitudes that explain important aspects of the reality with which we are faced. The economic dimension itself will take on a new character once we see things from the cultural point of view."[1168] The result is not a theology of liberation, but a plethora of liberation theologies whose natural synergy will lead humanity toward "total liberation," in which he includes deliverance from sin, "the very source of social injustice and other forms of human oppression."[1169]

So, instead of revising his theological postulates, discarding the erroneous ones, Father Gutiérrez simply broadens them to include a variety of subjects and social situations while retaining LT's dialectical core. He argues the need to develop this perspective and to continue with LT's orientation.

Continuing his normalization process, Father Gutiérrez has produced more recent writings such as "The Situation and Tasks of Liberation Theology Today"[1170] and "Where Will the Poor Sleep?"[1171] Other than reaffirming new horizons in theology such as Indian, black, feminist, and so on, the most recent works by the Peruvian theologian have little if any flavor. It seems that, unable to reassert his old doctrines and unwilling to recant them, he has been reduced to the sad situation of a top turning round and round. This is the feeling conveyed, for example, by his Rome speech in February 2016 at the launching of Cardinal Müller's book. After warm applause he went on for twenty dull minutes making an exegesis on the parable of the Good Samaritan. That still did not prevent some media from presenting him as the icon of a LT that was cleared at last.

1166. Gutiérrez, xxiv.

1167. Gutiérrez, xxiv.

1168. Gutiérrez, xxiv–xxv.

1169. Gutiérrez, xxxviii.

1170. See Gustavo Gutiérrez, "Situación y tareas de la teología de la liberación," *Páginas* (Lima), no. 161 (Feb. 2000), as "Situation and Tasks of Liberation Theology Today," in *On the Side of the Poor: The Theology of Liberation*, by Gustavo Gutiérrez and Gerhard Ludwig Cardinal Müller, trans. Robert A. Krieg and James B. Nickoloff (Maryknoll, N.Y.: Orbis Books, 2015), 32–53.

1171. See Gustavo Gutiérrez, *¿Dónde dormirán los pobres?* (Lima: I.B.C.-C.E.P., 2002), as "Where Will the Poor Sleep?" in *On the Side of the Poor* by Gutiérrez and Müller, 83–133.

Chapter 8:
Beyond Marxism: Liberation Theology's Ultimate Horizons

A. LT, a Phase in a Centuries-Old Revolutionary Process

As has become clear in the previous chapters, liberation theology did not rise as a response to a concrete situation of poverty and oppression in Latin America in the sixties. Liberation theologians themselves place their movement within the much broader framework of a revolutionary process that broke out in the fifteenth century and is still advancing toward more and more extreme horizons. Only in the perspective of this centuries-old revolutionary process are we able to grasp the breadth and scope of LT.

Fr. Gustavo Gutiérrez explains:

> To characterize the situation of the poor countries as dominated and oppressed leads one to speak of economic, social and political liberation. But we are dealing here with a much more integral and profound understanding of human existence and its historical future.
>
> A broad and deep aspiration for liberation inflames the history of mankind in our day, liberation from all that limits or keeps man from self-fulfillment, liberation from all impediments to the exercise of his freedom.[1172]

This liberationist aspiration did not surface yesterday: "What is at stake ... is the possibility of enjoying a truly human existence, a free life, a dynamic liberty which is related to history as a conquest. We have today an ever-clearer vision of this dynamism and this conquest, but their roots stretch into the past."[1173]

According to Leonardo Boff, we have to go back at least five centuries to discover the roots of this process: "The theme of liberation is not new, though it certainly is the strongest impulse in modern culture. Generally, we can state that the history of the past five centuries centers in large part on the process of emancipation."[1174]

According to liberation theologians, what are the roots of this centuries-old liberation process to which they claim to be heirs and successors? What are its historical stages? Its ultimate goals?

1. Medieval Christendom, Vilified as the Apex of Oppression

The starting point in LT's history is the thesis that the Middle Ages, that is, medieval Christendom, was the apex of oppression in every aspect of life. Medieval man was subjected to "oppressive structures" that conditioned his personal, social, and religious life: ecclesiastical and secular powers, religious practices, moral principles, cultural norms. First of all, according to Father Gutiérrez, the Church was dominated by a bad "Christendom mentality." The Peruvian writes, "The Church is regarded substantially as the exclusive depository of salvation. ... Because of this exclusiveness, notwithstanding certain qualifications which do not change the overall picture, the Church feels justified in considering itself as the center of the economy of salvation and therefore presenting itself as a powerful force in relation to the world. This power will spontaneously and inevitably seek to express itself in the political arena."[1175] Then there was the temporal power, that is, feudal society, made up of a complex, hierarchically structured web of rights and obligations. For LT, that society was the very image of injustice and oppression.

2. Decadence of the Middle Ages and Birth of Modernity

In the fifteenth century, liberation theologians say, one could begin to see in Christian Europe a change of mentality which became increasingly clear in the sixteenth century. The transformation was so profound and fraught with consequences in every aspect of life that it marked the beginning of a new historical era. "The medieval synthesis of classical Catholic Christendom ... was disrupted and eventually displaced by the rise of what we call the modern world," Joseph Holland writes.[1176]

Father Gutiérrez writes, "The fifteenth and sixteenth centuries are important milestones in man's understanding of himself." Those centuries, he continues, mark a clear break with previous history, so that "man abandoned his former image of the world and himself," that is, the medieval mentality.[1177] Applying Marxist criteria, Father Gutiérrez explains this huge transformation as the result of scientific discoveries: "[Man's] relationship with nature changed substantially with the emergence of experimental science and the techniques of manipulation derived from it." As a result of scientific advances, man changes his philosophical premises: "Gilson expresses this idea in a well-known phrase: 'It is because of its physics that metaphysics grows old.' Because of science man took a step forward and began to regard himself in a different way."[1178] Father Gutiérrez therefore reduces a complex, eminently spiritual, cultural, and psychological phenomenon to a mechanical relationship between the Marxist categories of structure and superstructure.[1179]

What huge transformation was this? Emerging from within the human soul, made temperate and gentle by Christianity, was a craving, a deep aspiration for liberation, a new "awareness of freedom" along with a belief that freedom would be attained through liberating struggles. According to Father Gutiérrez, that craving for liberty grew to become the driving force of modern history: "Through the lord-bondsman dialectic ... the historical

---

1172. Gutiérrez, *A Theology of Liberation*, 27.
1173. Gutiérrez, 28.
1174. Boff, *Francis of Assisi*, 73.

1175. Gutiérrez, *A Theology of Liberation*, 53.
1176. Joseph Holland, "Linking Social Analysis and Theological Reflection," in *Tracing the Spirit: Communities, Social Action and Theological Reflection*, edited by James E. Hug, S.J., (New York: Paulist Press, 1983), 177.
1177. Gutiérrez, *A Theology of Liberation*, 28.
1178. Gutiérrez, 28.
1179. On the concepts of *structure* and *superstructure*, see chap. 5, n. 983.

process will then appear as the genesis of consciousness and therefore of the gradual liberation of man. ... The driving force of history is the difficult conquest of freedom, hardly perceptible in its initial stages."[1180]

Leonardo Boff also sees this craving for liberty as the "strongest impulse in modern culture." According to him, when that craving began to guide the most profound tendencies in Western history it unleashed an uninterrupted and still unfolding "process of emancipation" strongly marked by that craving.[1181] The liberty impulse thus marked modernity. "If there is a key word throughout the rise of the modern world, it has been 'freedom,'" Joseph Holland opines.[1182]

Showing its power through the ages, that craving for liberty produced new lifestyles, cultural trends, religious concepts, social structures, philosophical schools, and political doctrines. Finding its roots in the deepest problems of the soul—from whence it spread to all of man's personality and activities, eroding all aspects of human life—this craving rebelled against the institutions that formed medieval Christendom, emerging from the field of tendencies to that of ideas and then to that of facts.

What are the stages of this process? Joseph Holland responds, "This [process] meant historical freedom from the chains of the past for the sake of a better future. Successively it came to mean cultural freedom (humanism), religious freedom (Protestantism), political freedom (democracy), and economic freedom (capitalism and later Socialism)."[1183]

We see this process step by step, in the writings of some liberation theologians.

3. Humanism: Liberation of Reason

"The first significant emergence," Leonardo Boff writes, "came with Galileo Galilei and the liberation of *reason* from within the religious totality that impeded the free flight of thought in the discovery of the working mechanisms of the world."[1184]

Catholic doctrine teaches that man is able to know many truths and practice various virtues using only his natural powers. However, it is impossible for him to know the whole truth or to persevere in the practice of all the commandments without faith and the help of grace. A pure and humble man accepts these limits and willingly submits his personal judgment to the authority of the Church instituted by Our Lord, and likewise subjects his passions

to the dictates of morality. However, a proud and sensual man, agitated by the craving for liberty, will try to shake off the yoke of religion and morality by claiming he is free to decide what is true and good.

Finally, the proud man will devise new doctrines to justify his unruly passions, proclaiming the liberation of human reason from any constraint. As mentioned earlier, "One must live as one thinks, under pain of sooner or later ending up thinking as one has lived."[1185] That is what happened with Humanism, which liberation theologians see as their ancestor. "The rise of humanism and the emancipation of science in the Renaissance were an initial sign of the new culture, as the human dimension began to take primacy," says Joseph Holland.[1186]

4. Protestantism: Liberation of the Individual Conscience

Protestantism, almost absent in the writings of Latin American liberation theologians as a stage of the revolutionary process, is nevertheless studied by their Anglo-Saxon colleagues. "The Protestant Reformation further weakened the old culture by heightening the sense of the individual (private conscience), undercutting the power of the institutional Church, and orienting religious energies more toward history," Holland writes.[1187] Preaching that everyone was free to interpret Holy Scripture on their own, Luther proclaimed the autonomy of the individual conscience in the theological sphere, liberating it from the Magisterium of the Church. Not surprisingly, feminist liberation theologian Rosemary Radford Ruether says LT comes from the Protestant left.[1188]

5. Enlightenment: Freedom of Thought

Medieval thought was oriented by scholastic philosophy, founded on the testimony of a reality perceived through the senses and developed with intellectual rigor according to the principles of logic and ontology, and primarily that of non-contradiction.[1189] Hence, it was known as the "philosophy of common sense" or "perennial philosophy." In modern man, however, the craving for liberty caused an increased weakening of the will to follow what his intellect indicated as good, and an increasing tendency of the intellect itself to justify the craving even at the cost of denying the evidence of his senses and the fundamental principles of logic. Without such blurring it would be difficult to explain the rise of philosophical schools so contrary to the true, the good, and the beautiful.[1190]

In this regard, Father Gutiérrez borrows from two philosophers, René Descartes (1596–1650) and Immanuel Kant (1724–1784). According to the Peruvian theologian, Descartes and Kant contributed to the advance of the revolutionary process by breaking

---

1180. Gutiérrez, *A Theology of Liberation*, 29.

1181. Boff, *Francis of Assisi*, 73.

1182. Holland, "Linking Social Analysis," 178.

1183. Holland, 178. Conversely, this view coincides with the classical scheme of the counter-revolutionary school, which sees modern history as a succession of three revolutions: Protestantism, the French Revolution, and Communism. See Corrêa de Oliveira, *Revolution and Counter-Revolution*, 15–18. Likewise, Cardinal Ratzinger writes:

> At the Renaissance, it was thought that by a return to antiquity in philosophy and through the natural sciences man would be able to gain freedom of thought and action, thanks to his knowledge and control of the laws of nature.
>
> Luther, for his part, basing himself on his reading of Saint Paul, sought to renew the struggle for freedom from the yoke of the Law, which he saw as represented by the Church of his time. But it was above all in the Age of the Enlightenment and at the French Revolution that the call to freedom rang out with full force. (Congregation for the Doctrine of the Faith, *Instruction on Christian Freedom*, no. 6)

1184. Boff, *Francis of Assisi*, 73. Whether Galileo really thought that way is another matter. It is interesting to note the use (or abuse) liberation theologians make to justify the historical process of which they proclaim themselves heirs. On Galileo, see Bernard Vinaty, et al., *Galileo Galilei: 350 anni di storia (1633–1983): Studi e ricerche*, ed. Paul Poupard (Rome: Piemme, 1984); Mario d'Addio, *Considerazioni sui processi a Galileo* (Rome: Herder, 1985); W. Brandmüller and E.J. Greipl, eds., *Copernico, Galilei e la chiesa: Fine della controversia (1820) gli atti del sant'uffizio* (Florence: Olschki, 1992); Walter Brandmüller, *Galilei e la chiesa, ossia il diritto ad errare* (Vatican: Libreria Editrice Vaticana, 1992).

1185. Bourget, *Le démon du midi*, 2:375.

1186. Holland, "Linking Social Analysis," 177. On relationships between faith and science, see Joseph Ratzinger/Benedict XVI, *Fede e scienza, un dialogo necessario: Un'antologia*, ed. Umberto Casale (Turin: Lindau, 2010).

1187. Holland, "Linking Social Analysis," 177.

1188. See Ruether, "Political Theologies in the Churches," 24–25.

1189. Saint Thomas calls the principle of non-contradiction the first and supreme principle of human thought. Battista Mondin writes,

> "The basic principle of all knowledge is the principle of non-contradiction, which states that it is impossible to say that one thing is and is not under the same aspect. ...
>
> Following the example of Aristotle, St. Thomas shows that the principle of non-contradiction is a very solid and most certain principle, naturally known to everyone." Battista Mondin, *La metafisica di S. Tommaso d'Aquino e i suoi interpreti* (Bologna: Edizioni Studio Domenicano, 2002), 234.

1190. The cornerstone of revolutionary psychological warfare is precisely to cause man to lose the sense of contradiction as a first step toward Liberalism and relativism. For an in-depth analysis of the consequences of losing the principle of non-contradiction, see T.F.P. Covadonga, *España anestesiada sin percibirlo, amordazada sin quererlo, extraviada sin saberlo: La obra del PSOE* (Madrid: Editorial Fernando III el Santo, 1986), 31–50.

with the realism and common sense proper to scholastic philosophy and thus freeing human thought from the "oppression of objective reality."

Descartes rejected the evidence of the senses as unreliable and placed the subjective construction of ideas as a criterion of truth, opening the way for subjectivist and idealistic currents. Father Gutiérrez writes, "Descartes is one of the great names of the new physics which altered man's relationship to nature. He laid the cornerstone of a philosophical reflection which stressed the primacy of thought and of 'clear and distinct ideas,' and so highlighted the creative aspects of human subjectivity."[1191] Systematically obliged to be wary of evidence, man lost his serenity to think and felt a sense of distress and insecurity that corroded his certainties. In such conditions, it became easy to take him on a frantic ride of increasingly absurd doctrines and tendencies.

For his part, Kant laid the foundations of idealism, according to which man can simply discard outward evidence and follow only his thoughts. "For [Kant] our concept ought not to conform to the objects," says Father Gutiérrez. As a consequence, the human mind would no longer be forced ("oppressed") to follow the evidence of the senses and would be able to lucubrate freely. Kant's subjectivist philosophy, Father Gutiérrez says, "leads to a 'new method' of thought, to a knowledge which is critical of its foundations and thus abandons its naiveté and enters an adult stage."[1192] For the Peruvian theologian, therefore, to believe in the adjustment of the intellect to reality is a childish naiveté from which man should liberate himself.

6. French Revolution: Political Liberation

The profound action of Humanism and the Enlightenment did not cease to unfold in a growing chain of consequences. Closely akin to Protestantism, the French Revolution carried out in the political sphere a work symmetrical in every way to that of the Protestant Reformation in the religious sphere. As noted by Prof. Corrêa de Oliveira, the French Revolution was simply the transposition of the leveling and liberalizing reforms carried out by Protestant sects in the religious field (within the Church) to the political one (within the State).

"Then, there was the liberation of the *citizen* from the absolutism of the kings, to see the citizen as the real bearer and delegate of political powers, as Rousseau thought," writes Leonardo Boff, continuing the history of the revolutionary process that culminates in LT.[1193] Joseph Holland concurs: "The American and French revolutions, along with the general rise of liberal nation states, began a national centralization of diffused communities, weakening the overarching imperial culture tied to the heritage of the Roman Empire and advancing the modern stress on progress and freedom."[1194] Father Gutiérrez also mentions the French Revolution as the next stage of the revolutionary process: "This historical event had vast repercussions, for it proclaimed the right of every man to participate in the direction of the society to which he belongs."[1195]

7. Communism: Economic Liberation

That brings us to Communism, the third great revolution liberation theologians present as part of the historical process whose

legacy they claim. Two characters come to the fore here, Friedrich Hegel and Karl Marx (1818–1883).

Hegel is invoked to proclaim the unlimited freedom of the spirit, said to be in continuous evolution. Leonardo Boff writes, "With [Hegel's] writings, there was the liberation of *spirit* alienated in physical matter by way of the transfiguration of absolute Spirit."[1196] Father Gutiérrez also analyzes Hegel to present an evolutionary conception of man and of history. According to the Peruvian theologian, Hegel introduced a "dynamic and historical conception of man" implying the idea that human nature is not immutable but under construction in history through dialectic: "Through the dialectical process man constructs himself ... he liberates himself."[1197]

Assuming Hegel's evolutionary conception, Karl Marx turned it upside down by not applying it to the spirit but to matter. His is the so-called dialectical materialism, the philosophical foundation of Socialism that proclaims the liberation of the proletariat from so-called oppression by owners and employers. Father Gutiérrez writes, "Marx deepened and renewed [Hegel's] line of thought in his unique way." Marx's great contribution to the revolutionary process, according to him, was his "'epistemological break' ... with previous thought," by which man should no longer be satisfied to know the world; he should seek to transform it through class struggle.[1198]

Also Leonardo Boff mentions Marxism as a historic stage in the liberation process that results in LT: "With Marx, attention turned to the liberation of the *proletariat* from capitalist economic domination with the aim of arriving at a socialist society without class distinctions."[1199]

8. Liberation of the Instincts

Leonardo Boff indicates a rebellion of instincts against the "oppression" of reason and moral precepts as the next stage of the historical process of liberation, invoking in his support the figure of Friedrich Nietzsche (1844–1900): "With Nietzsche, there was the liberation of *life*, shortened and suffocated by the sophistication of metaphysics, morals, and culture."[1200]

Undoubtedly one of the bad teachers of the twentieth century, Nietzsche claimed that man should not submit to any precept, but indulge in the free expansion of his vital impulses, the "Dionysian spirit" made up of sensuality, excitement, and enthusiasm. Any kind of precept—religious, moral, rational, social, political—inevitably weakens and enslaves man. By announcing the "death of God," seen as the archetype of all "oppression," Nietzsche proposed the ideal of a completely free man: the *overman*.[1201]

9. Freudianism: Psychological Liberation

Having destroyed the philosophical, religious, political, social, and economic situations of "oppression" supposedly burdening

---

1191. Gutiérrez, *A Theology of Liberation*, 28.

1192. Gutiérrez, 28.

1193. Boff, *Francis of Assisi*, 73.

1194. Holland, "Linking Social Analysis," 177–78.

1195. Gutiérrez, *A Theology of Liberation*, 28–29.

1196. Boff, *Francis of Assisi*, 73. The use of "his" in the published U.S. version suggests that Boff is speaking of Rousseau. In the Portuguese original, however, it is clear that Boff means Hegel.

1197. Gutiérrez, *A Theology of Liberation*, 32, 29.

1198. Gutiérrez, 29. On the "epistemological break," see chap. 4.

1199. Boff, *Francis of Assisi*, 73.

1200. Boff, 73.

1201. Through the mouth of Zarathustra, Nietzsche states:

Behold, I teach you the overman! ...
   I appeal to you, my brothers, remain true to the earth, and do not believe those who speak to you of otherworldly hopes! Poisoners are they, whether they know it or not.
   Despisers of life are they, decaying and poisoned themselves, of whom the earth is weary: so let them pass away!
   Once sin against God was the greatest sin; but God died, and with him these sinners. (Friedrich Nietzsche, *Thus Spoke Zarathustra*, ed. Bill Chapko, Feedbooks, 13–14)

man, the craving for liberty would lash out at the last remnants of order: interior "oppression," that is, man's internal hierarchy whereby Faith enlightens one's intellect, the latter guides the will, which in its turn dominates one's sensibility. "Modern man's aspirations," affirms Father Gutiérrez, "include not only liberation from *exterior* pressures which prevent his fulfillment as a member of a certain social class, country, or society. He seeks likewise an *interior* liberation, in an individual and intimate dimension; he seeks liberation not only on a social plane but also on a psychological [one]. He seeks an interior freedom. ... [i]n relation to the real world of the human psyche as understood since Freud."[1202]

To explain one aspect of this inner liberation, liberation theologians appeal to the figure of Sigmund Freud (1856–1939). Leonardo Boff writes, "Freud developed a whole plan for the liberation of the *psyche* from its interior bonds."[1203]

According to Freud, the libido, i.e., sexual drive, already present at a young age, is the driving force of human development. However, the requirements of civilization force man to repress that impulse, causing a neurosis that stays with him throughout life, affecting society. Libido repression attains an apex with religion, which Freud sees as an obsessive infantile neurosis. To eliminate the neurosis Freud proposed the total liberation of the sexual instinct even in its perverse manifestations.

Undeniably, Freud's doctrines have social and even political consequences. A Freud disciple, Herbert Marcuse, writes, "Freud's individual psychology is in its very essence social psychology. Repression is a historical phenomenon. The effective subjugation of the instincts to repressive controls is imposed not by nature but by man. The primal father, as the archetype of domination, initiates the chain reaction of enslavement, rebellion, and reinforced domination which marks the history of civilization."[1204]

For the founder of psychoanalysis, the institutions that shape our civilization—family, property, morals, authority—force man to renounce sexual pleasure, suppressing the main factor of psychological development and alienating him from the innermost sources of happiness. Psychoanalysis would be a practice to free man from any psychological constraint and allow him to develop as an individual and in society. In his works, Freud presents the destruction of the oppressive structures of society as a condition for man to reach sexual maturity, but despairs over the concrete feasibility of establishing a non-repressive civilization.

Fr. Gustavo Gutiérrez assumes the core of the Freudian vision: "A new frontier was in effect opened up when Freud highlighted the unconscious determinants of human behavior, with repression as the central element of man's psychic makeup. Repression is the result of the conflict between instinctive drives and the cultural and ethical demands of the social environment."[1205]

The external aspects of "liberation"—social, political, economic—are somehow coupled with interior ones—moral, cultural, and psychological. Quoting the well-known theoretician of anti-psychiatry, David Cooper, Father Gutiérrez states: "If we are to talk of revolution today our talk will be meaningless unless we effect some union between the macro-social and micro-social, and between 'inner reality' and 'outer reality.'"[1206]

10. Marcuse and the Non-repressive Society

Freud never sketched the ultimate consequences of his doctrines, trying to reconcile the demands of the libido with those of civilization. According to Marcuse, "The notion that a non-repressive civilization is impossible is a cornerstone of Freudian theory."[1207] Some of his disciples, including Marcuse, took up the task of bringing his doctrines to fruition, foreseeing a total destruction of modern civilization and its replacement with a perfectly egalitarian and liberated non-repressive society in which the last remnant of oppression will have been effaced. This is the so-called Freudian-Marxist current that inspired the student revolution of 1968, the fourth great stage of the revolutionary process which liberation theologians claim as their heritage.

Father Gutiérrez writes, "In this area, Marcuse's attempt, under the influence of Hegel and Marx, to use the psychoanalytical categories for social criticism is important. Basing his observations on a work [by Freud], *Civilization and Its Discontents*, Marcuse analyses the *over-repressive* character of the affluent society and envisions the possibility of a non-repressive society. ... In order to achieve this non-repressive society, however, it will be necessary to challenge the values espoused by the society which denies man the possibility of living freely."[1208]

Leonardo Boff also mentions the philosopher of 1968: "Marcuse launched the manifesto of the liberation of industrial man, reduced to only one dimension by assembly-line production."[1209]

B. The Role of LT in the Revolutionary Process

So here is a brief outline of the revolutionary historical process of which the liberation theologians claim to be heirs and successors. In that case, what would be the specific role played by LT?

1. An Integral Part of the Revolutionary Process

We cannot understand LT except as an integral part of the revolutionary process. Leonardo Boff writes, "Liberation theology is understood in the thread of these great movements of emancipation that characterize the modern age."[1210]

2. Providing Theological Meaning to the Revolutionary Process

LT's primary role would be to give the revolutionary process a theological and religious meaning. Boff writes, "Fundamentally, liberation theology deals with two principal tasks: first, to point out the theological relevance of freedom movements. ... This perspective allows the rereading of the liberation movements of the past centuries and of the secular culture resulting from them as theologically relevant. ... Christian faith ... makes it possible to read with a theological key the emancipatory processes."[1211]

3. Reinterpreting Religion in a Liberated Sense

"Second," Boff continues, "the theology of liberation deals with emphasizing the liberating aspects that are present in the

---

1202. Gutiérrez, *A Theology of Liberation*, 30.

1203. Boff, *Francis of Assisi*, 73.

1204. Herbert Marcuse, *Eros and Civilization: A Philosophical Inquiry into Freud* (Boston: Beacon Press, 1966), chap. 1.

1205. Gutiérrez, *A Theology of Liberation*, 30. We speak of core Freudian doctrines and not of their totality. In fact, the Peruvian theologian notes some ambiguities and points to be clarified, at times even making critical comments. In general, however, he treats Freud with obvious sympathy, considering him a valuable member of the profound and broad aspiration for freedom that characterizes modernity.

1206. Gutiérrez, *A Theology of Liberation*, 31.

1207. Marcuse, *Eros and Civilization*, chap. 1.

1208. Gutiérrez, *A Theology of Liberation*, 31.

1209. Boff, *Francis of Assisi*, 73.

1210. Boff, 74.

1211. Boff, 75.

Gospel, in the life and praxis of Jesus, and in the great tradition of the Church."[1212]

4. Creating the New Man Through a Permanent Cultural Revolution

A non-repressive society would be unworkable without major changes in human nature itself, without creating that new man dreamed of by all revolutionary currents. This is the third role played by LT according to the Brazilian theologian: To help create the new, socialist, egalitarian, and liberated man. "It has to do with a liberating evangelization, urging a Christian practice that implies also a transformation of society, helping to form a new humanity. ... This, fundamentally, is what is proposed by liberation theology."[1213]

Fr. Gustavo Gutiérrez devotes an entire section of his main work to the topic: "The goal is not only better living conditions, a radical change of structures, a social revolution; it is much more: the continuous creation, never ending, of a new way to be a man, a *permanent cultural revolution*."[1214]

5. Cultural Revolution

We thus arrive at what we have called LT's new look. Abandoning Marxism, swallowed by the vortex of history, liberation theologians now subscribe to the new post-Marxist tendencies that broke out in 1968, including the generic term *cultural revolution*, the stage of the revolutionary process that we are in today.[1215] "[LT's] utopian project," American liberation theologian Fr. Phillip Berryman comments, "demands an economic and political liberation: the taking of power by the people and the socialization of the means of production, the abolition of class privileges, and an organization of the economy in function of the majorities. All this is essential but insufficient: These things alone could lead to other abuses. Needed is the creation of the New Man who lives for others (Che Guevara). This utopian liberation is the object of the cultural revolution."[1216]

C. From the Third to the Fourth Revolution

1. The Fourth Revolution Planned by the Communists

LT was born and initially developed as part of the Third Revolution, the communist one, with which it entered into an intimate symbiosis. However, this is not the final and definitive stage of the revolutionary process. The very idea of process indicates something that moves forward. An integral part of this essentially evolutionist ideology is the idea of a permanent revolution, i.e., an ever evolving history toward the egalitarian and liberated utopia.[1217] Just as Socialism, first utopian and then scientific, was born from the French Revolution, Communism was also supposed to open the way for more radical horizons. This is not

a hypothesis, but a topic which the communists explicitly deal with. Prof. Plinio Corrêa de Oliveira explains:

> Neither Marx nor the generality of his most notorious followers (whether orthodox or heterodox) considered the dictatorship of the proletariat to be the final phase of the revolutionary process. This dictatorship is, according to them, nothing but the most refined, dynamic aspect of the universal Revolution. And, in the evolutionist mythology inherent to the thinking of Marx and his followers, just as evolution will develop to infinity over the centuries, so also the Revolution will be endless. From the First Revolution, two other revolutions have already been born. The third, in its turn, will generate another. And so on ...
>
> It is impossible to predict within the Marxist perspective what the Twentieth or Fiftieth Revolution would be like. However, it is possible to predict what the Fourth Revolution will be like. This prediction has already been made by the Marxists themselves.
>
> This revolution will necessarily be the overthrow of the dictatorship of the proletariat as a result of a new crisis. Pressured by this crisis, the hypertrophic state will be victim of its own hypertrophy. And it will disappear, giving rise to a scientist and cooperationist state of things in which—so the communists say—man will have attained a heretofore inconceivable degree of liberty, equality, and fraternity.[1218]

Moreover, the collapse of the proletarian dictatorship was envisaged in the preamble of the Soviet Constitution: "The supreme goal of the Soviet state is the building of a classless communist society in which there will be communist social selfgovernment."[1219] F.V. Konstantinov, of the Soviet Academy of Sciences, explains this passage:

> The development of socialist democracy strengthens the power of the State and at the same time paves the way for its extinction along with a step to a social regime in which society may be run without the need for a political apparatus or state coercion. ...
>
> From the standpoint of dialectics, the problem of the extinction of the state is the problem of the transformation, from the socialist State, into the communist self-management of society.[1220]

Engels had already proposed the dissolution of the State in his *Origin of the Family, Private Property and the State*, written in 1884. In it he presents the tribal society of North American Indians as a model: "A wonderful constitution it is, this gentile constitution, in all its childlike simplicity! No soldiers, no gendarmes or police, no nobles, kings, regents, prefects, or judges, no prisons, no lawsuits—and everything takes its orderly course ... yet there is no need for even a trace of our complicated administrative apparatus." He augurs a similar development for Europe: "The State, therefore, has not existed from all eternity. There have been societies which have managed without it, which had no notion of

---

1212. Boff, 75.

1213. Boff, 76.

1214. Gutiérrez, *A Theology of Liberation*, 32.

1215. See Corrêa de Oliveira, *Revolution and Counter-Revolution* ("The Aborning Fourth Revolution"), 156–65.

1216. Berryman, "Latin American Liberation Theology," 47.

1217. *Permanent revolution*: This was an expression used mainly by Leon Trotsky, but is found in the writings of Marx and Engels, for example, in the directives to the League of Communists in the aftermath of 1848. More recently, it is interesting to see works by Ernst Bloch such as, for example, *Geist der utopie* (Munich: Verlag von Duncker & Humblot, 1918); and *Das prinzip hoffnung*, 3 vols. (Frankfurt: Suhrkamp Verlag, 1954–1959).

1218. Corrêa de Oliveira, *Revolution and Counter-Revolution*, 157–58.

1219. Boris Topornin, *The New Constitution of the USSR*, trans. Murad Saifulin (Moscow: Progress Publishers, 1987), 259.

1220. Fedor Vasilevich Konstantinov, *Fundamentos de la filosofia marxista*, trans. Adolfo Sánchez Vázquez and Wenceslao Roces, 2nd ed. (Mexico: Editorial Grijalbo, 1965), 514–15.

the State or state power. ... [The social classes] will fall as inevitably as they once arose. The State inevitably falls with them."[1221]

2. The Failure of Marxism-Leninism

That step, however, was based on a premise: the creation of the "new socialist man" whose natural tendency to provide for his own needs and those of his family would be replaced by a "collectivist consciousness" through which he would not seek his own good but that of the community. The coercive apparatus of the dictatorship of the proletariat would have to be kept in place until such a man should arise.

For Marx, the oppression of the bourgeoisie on the proletariat derived from the private ownership of the means of production. The economy, or more precisely relations of production, would be the fundamental reality ("structure"). All other spheres—legal, political, social, cultural, moral, religious—would be only consequences ("superstructure"). Human consciousness itself would be a superstructure, that is, an emanation of the relations of production: "The mode of production of material life conditions the general process of social, political and intellectual life. It is not the consciousness of men that determines their existence, but their social existence that determines their consciousness."[1222]

Consistent with this view, Marx assumed that a change in the relations of production would automatically result in a change in the human consciousness. In other words, the new socialist man would simultaneously rise to the dictatorship of the proletariat. More realistic, in his famous 1902 work *What Is to Be Done?* Lenin called for abandoning the primitive approach based solely on the mechanical nature of dialectical laws or on the spontaneity of revolutionary enthusiasm to organize a revolutionary party led by professional revolutionaries in order to seize power by force and use it to build the new man.

Nevertheless, after over seventy years of real Socialism, not even a shadow of the new socialist man has appeared. ... No sooner had the U.S.S.R. collapsed than a consumer rush as vigorous as any in the West spread in many former communist countries. Although communists in the West relied on the greatest propaganda machine in history, no Communist Party has ever been able to rise to power through the electoral process. The failure of Marxism-Leninism to create the new man and move the revolutionary process forward was already obvious to farsighted communists in the aftermath of the Bolshevik revolution.

3. Cultural Revolution

Striving to overcome the impasse, the Institut für Sozialforschung (Institute for Social Research) of the Johann Wolfgang Goethe University in Frankfurt, Germany, came up with a line of reasoning currently known as the "Frankfurt School" even after its representatives had moved, first to France and then to the United States.[1223] Exploring different and not necessarily coinciding paths, the scholars associated with that school proposed to draw up an overall critique of modern society in order to plot a revolution that could unhinge it and thus move beyond Communism.

Its main representatives include Theodor Adorno (1903–1969), who developed a radical critique of the society resulting from advanced capitalism; Max Horkheimer (1895–1973), who formulated a theory on the "logic of domination" incorporating social, political, and cultural elements; Herbert Marcuse (1898–1979), philosopher of the 1968 revolution; Erich Fromm (1900–1980), who applied Freud's theories to the revolution, emphasizing the role of ambiences in the formation of mentality; Jürgen Habermas (1929–), who explored the linguistic and epistemological aspects of oppression; and many others we are unable to list for lack of space. From their efforts was born so-called Freudian-Marxism, which fit into the work of Wilhelm Reich (1897–1957), author in 1936 of *The Sexual Revolution*. Various other trends arose which were incorporated into Marxist Humanism.[1224]

Another line of reasoning to overcome the impasse was brought forward by Antonio Gramsci, one of the founders of the Italian Communist Party. To explain why the communist revolutions Marx had predicted had taken place in non-industrialized countries, Gramsci studied the concept of *hegemony*, broadening it to include its cultural variety. In his book, *Marxism and Literature* (1977), Raymond Williams, a professor at Oxford and Cambridge and a member of the English new left, deems the concept of cultural hegemony as the focal point of revolutions in the twentieth century: "It is in just this recognition of the wholeness of the process that the concept of 'hegemony' goes beyond 'ideology.' What is decisive is not only the conscious system of ideas and beliefs, but the whole lived social process as practically organized by specific and dominant meanings and values. Ideology ... is a relatively formal and articulated system of meanings, values, and beliefs, of a kind that can be abstracted as a 'world view.'"[1225]

According to this concept, culture is an instrument of oppression far more treacherous than the economic one because it takes possession of the very consciousness of the oppressed. "The group in power can promulgate its views as 'objective reality,'" writes liberation theologian Father Elizondo. "These cultural stereotypes hide the real violence of the ongoing oppression and exploitation of the weak."[1226]

4. Total Revolution

Thus, the idea of a total revolution gradually formed, that is to say a movement aimed at the simultaneous destruction of all oppression in every field. French Marxist thinker Pierre Fougeyrollas (1923–2008) explains:

> The psycho-sexual revolution currently taking place among the youth is a decisive force to implement the total revolution. ...
>
> ... The expression "cultural revolution" means a revolution in the ways of feeling, acting, and thinking, a revolution in the way we live, individually and collectively, in short, a revolution in civilization.[1227]

1221. Friedrich Engels, *Origin of the Family, Private Property and the State*, trans. Alick West, chap. 9, 94, Marxists.org.

1222. Marx, *A Contribution to the Critique of Political Economy*, preface, Marxists.org.

1223. On the Frankfurt School, see Francesco Apergi, *Marxismo e ricerca sociale nella scuola di Francoforte* (Florence: La Nuova Italia, 1977); Giuseppe Bedeschi, *La scuola di Francoforte* (Rome-Bari: Laterza, 1987); Rocco Buttiglione, *Dialettica e nostalgia: La scuola di Francoforte e l'ultimo Horkheimer* (Milan: Jaca Book, 1978); Rocco Buttiglione, *La crisi dell'economia marxista: Gli inizi della scuola di Francoforte* (Rome: Studium, 1979); Umberto Galeazzi, *La teoria critica della scuola di Francoforte: Diagnosi della società contemporanea e dialogo critico con il pensiero moderno* (Naples: Edizioni Scientifiche Italiane, 2000).

1224. On Marxist humanism, see Tone Stres, "Il marxismo e la domanda sull'uomo," in *CSEO Documentazione*, no. 11 (Nov. 1976): 314–24; and Giuseppe Saragat, *L'umanesimo marxista* (Milan: Dalai Editore, 1999).

1225. Raymond Williams, *Marxism and Literature* (Oxford, U.K.: Oxford University Press, 1977), 108–9.

1226. Virgilio P. Elizondo, *Mestizaje: The Dialectic of Cultural Birth and the Gospel, a Study in the Intercultural Dimension of Evangelization*, 3 vols in 2 (San Antonio: Mexican American Cultural Center, 1978), 1–2:272.

1227. Pierre Fougeyrollas, *Marx, Freud et la révolution totale* (Paris: Anthropos, 1972), 367, 390.

Herbert Marcuse was even more explicit. At a May 23, 1968 talk at the University of California San Diego, he stated: "The traditional idea of the revolution, and the traditional strategy of the revolution are out. They are outdated."[1228] Later that year, on December 5, speaking at the Fillmore East concert hall in New York City for the twentieth anniversary of the *Guardian*, he said, "What we have to envisage is some kind of diffused and dispersed disintegration of the system."[1229]

5. The New Proletariat

The growing scope of action of the Revolution produced a broadening of the concept of proletariat. According to the old Marxist script, the revolution should be driven mainly by peasants and industrial workers in revolt against employers and the capitalist society. In the Fourth Revolution, this proletariat is joined by a new, diverse and sociocultural one consisting of those categories of individuals that feel discriminated against in any field—moral, cultural, psychological, racial, religious, and so on—regardless of their economic or social situation.

Accordingly, feminists feel discriminated against by the "macho culture"; homosexuals, by the natural law and Christian morality; immigrants, by "xenophobia"; drug addicts, by current legislation; prostitutes, by society's rejection; persons of color, by white so-called racism; young people, by the constraints of a society still not completely liberated; nudists, by bourgeois prejudices, and so on. According to the new script, each category of the marginalized must shake off the oppressive factors imposed on it by initiating a liberating struggle. The synergy resulting from these various liberations would lead to total revolution.

The modes of revolution also change. While the mentors of Communism advocated social and political confrontation, those of the Fourth Revolution want it to advance playfully whenever possible, that is, in a happy and carefree fashion. In fact, no ideological preparation or party militancy is required to participate in this revolution. Just surrender to the unruly passions in the name of "it is forbidden to forbid." The carnival atmosphere of homosexual Pride parades is an example.

This radical change in the mode of revolution also implies transforming the structures that promote it. In the new perspective, the Communist Party is obsolete as a political, dogmatic, and rigidly structured organization. The new revolutionary forces are not organized in political parties but lobbies or pressure groups active in social and cultural fields. The homosexual movement is a typical example of this. The role of such lobbies is to exacerbate ethnic, moral, cultural, and social tensions to liberate the revolutionary energy latent in discriminated groups and coordinate their disruptive effects to completely destroy any remnants of Christian civilization.

D. LT in the Era of the Fourth Revolution

Liberation theologians were not surprised at the collapse of real Socialism in 1989 and the subsequent disappearance of the praxis they had been engaged in for nearly three decades. In February 1988 they held a worldwide conference in Maryknoll, New York at the Maryknoll headquarters. Its central theme was how to move beyond Marxism, which had not only become obsolete but definitely uncomfortable after the Vatican condemnation.[1230] It was during this meeting that Father Gutiérrez presented a first draft of his introduction, "Expanding the View," mentioned in the previous chapter.

Having accompanied the revolutionary process in the communist phase, liberation theologians also follow it in the post-communist one.

LT's fundamental concept from top to bottom is that of liberation, i.e., an interior and exterior movement tending to emancipate individuals and societies from particular situations deemed oppressive or discriminatory. Confusing this earthly liberation with the eternal salvation offered by God, liberation theologians give it a religious character. Now, in order to propose such liberation, the current's theoreticians must first analyze situations of oppression or discrimination from which they intend to liberate themselves. Two questions arise: What do they mean by *oppression*, and, consequently, what *liberation* do they concretely propose? The two concepts are extremely flexible and allow for a wide range of meanings.

In Marxism, oppression was basically economic and would be resolved by eliminating private ownership of the means of production. This is precisely the sense which liberation theologians espoused in the beginning. Father Gutiérrez proclaimed, "This discovery [of the world of the other—the poor, the oppressed, the exploited] is made only in a revolutionary struggle. ... It insists on a society in which private ownership of the means of production is eliminated."[1231] Liberation would consist, therefore, of a proletarian revolution to establish Socialism.

In the wake of the Fourth Revolution, liberation theologians switched from this rather raw vision to more nuanced analyses of oppression. Chilean liberation theologian Father Torres explains:

> The concept of liberation has widened a lot. ... At first, one spoke about the liberation of the poor, understood as the factory workers in the continent's large cities. The concept of poor has been subsequently enriched. The poor are all those who are excluded, marginalized, ... discriminated against. ...
>
> Today there is no single theology of liberation. There is a theological pluralism that is open but still faithful to some of the basic intuitions and principles of the early liberation theology.[1232]

Race is the first domain the new theologies of liberation analyze. In this case, the poor are those ethnic groups deemed to be marginalized: blacks, Chicanos (Mexican-Americans), indigenous peoples, and so on. By applying to these new historical subjects

1228. Herbert Marcuse, "Talk at University of California San Diego" (May 23, 1968), in "Herbert Marcuse and the Student Revolts of 1968: An Unpublished Lecture," *Jacobinmag.com*, Mar. 31, 2021. See also Herbert Marcuse, *La sociedad carnívora*, trans. Miguel Grinberg (Buenos Aires: Ediciones Godot, 2011), 59.

1229. Herbert Marcuse, "Talk at Fillmore East Concert Hall, New York, for Twentieth Anniversary of the *Guardian* (Dec. 5, 1968)," in Carl Oglesby Papers, Radical Perspectives, University of Massachusetts at Amherst, 33:52 to 33:59. See also Marcuse, *La sociedad carnívora*, 69. On total revolution, see Jacques Ellul, *Changer de révolution: L'inéluctable prolétariat* (Paris: Seuil, 1982); André Gorz, *Réforme et révolution* (Paris: Seuil, 1969); Richard Gombin, *Les origines du gauchisme* (Paris: Seuil, 1971).

1230. See Marc H. Ellis and Otto Maduro, eds., *The Future of Liberation Theology: Essays in Honor of Gustavo Gutiérrez* (Maryknoll, N.Y.: Orbis Books, 1989).

1231. Gutiérrez, *The Power of the Poor*, 37.

1232. Moisés Sbardelotto, "'A teologia da libertação pode ajudar a interpretar o mal-estar global de hoje.' Entrevista especial com Sergio Torres," *Instituto Humanitas Unisinos*, Oct. 22, 2011. The final message of the 33rd Conference of Liberation Theologians held in Madrid in September 2013 reads, "Liberation theology is historical and contextual, and is reformulated in the new processes of liberation through the emerging subjects of transformations: women discriminated against who become conscious of their own revolutionary potential; destroyed cultures that affirm their identity; peasant communities that are mobilized ... young people who are outraged ... at their blocked future; the plundered nature ... that suffers and rebels ... abused migrants ... the indigenous religions ... that are reborn after centuries of silence." "La teología de la liberación, hoy," Juan G. Bedoya, "Mil teólogos piden al papa que rehabilite a los castigados por Ratzinger," *El País* (Madrid), Sept. 8, 2013.

the same dialectical criteria (oppression-liberation) earlier applied to the poor, liberation theologians have built a plethora of new liberation theologies based on race and culture. While black and Chicano liberation theology appeared in the United States, indigenous liberation theology made its way in Latin America.

1. Black Liberation Theology

Some American Marxist thinkers, including W.E.B. Dubois (1868–1963), adding racial and cultural factors to class analysis, already treated blacks as proletarians oppressed by the white middle class. In the wake of the book *Black Religion*, written by sociologist Joseph R. Washington in 1964,[1233] and applying the categories of Latin American LT, several Protestant theologians worked to impart theological value to the struggle of American blacks then in full bloom with the Civil Rights Movement, which the left saw as revolutionary praxis.[1234] Thus was born the Black Theology of Liberation. Its birth certificate was the "Statement on Black Theology," launched in 1969.[1235]

Among the admirers of the Black Theology of Liberation is none other than former President Barack Obama. In 1985, the Industrial Areas Foundation (I.A.F.) founded in Chicago by Saul Alinsky, the guru of the American populist left, made a job offer to Obama. They were recruiting him to organize blacks in Chicago's South Side. Obama attended the training course as a community organizer and went to work at the Developing Communities Project, tied to I.A.F. Obama himself considered his years as community organizer "my 'best education.'"[1236]

His work as a community organizer put him in contact with the reality of religious progressivism and he ended up converting to the black Christianity preached by Rev. Jeremiah Wright, who became his spiritual mentor. Wright is pastor of Trinity United Church of Christ, a predominantly Afro-American congregation.

He is also a follower of the Black Theology. In a 2008 speech at the National Press Club, Wright declared,

[I speak] as a pastor and a professor who comes from a long tradition of what I call the prophetic theology of the black church. ...

Liberation theology. ... [s]tarted from the vantage point of the oppressed.[1237]

2. Theology of Chicano Liberation

The Chicanos are Americans of Mexican ancestry residing primarily in parts of the U.S. that belonged to Mexico until 1848. Midway between the Latin and Anglo-Saxon cultures the Chicanos have always been a social group disputed by conflicting trends. In the seventies, the LT movement identified this group as a potential historical subject to be dialectically maneuvered against the American system. Then, LT–inspired Hispanic religious associations arose such as PADRES (Padres Asociados para Derechos Religiosos Educativos y Sociales) and Hermanas (Sisters).[1238] A dense network of Hispanic Basic Christian Communities was then created, coordinated by the Secretariat for Hispanic Affairs of the U.S. Bishops' Conference, then led by Pablo Sedillo, a fervent LT follower.[1239] Sharing these revolutionary goals, this B.C.C. network was integrated, especially in Texas, with the network of People's Organizations inspired by Saul Alinsky's Industrial Areas Foundation.[1240]

A Chicano Theology[1241] perfectly integrated into the Latin American LT movement was simultaneously developed. One of its important figures was the late liberation theologian Father Elizondo, a former participant at the 1968 C.E.L.A.M. conference in Medellín and later director of the Mexican American Cultural Center in San Antonio, Texas.[1242]

3. Indigenous Liberation Theology

More important both in number of adepts, and above all for its ecclesial and political implications, is indigenous liberation theology. At a lecture in Madrid in 1991, Chilean liberation theologian Father Richard explained, "We often have the impression that liberation theology is dead. ... Far from it! We can reconstruct liberation theology and the basic ecclesial communities today but they must be adapted to a new historical juncture. ... This is what we are doing. ... My task is the indigenous theme ... indigenous theology."[1243]

1233. See Joseph Washington, *Black Theology: The Negro and Christianity in the United States* (Boston: Beacon Press, 1964).

1234. While it is hard not to empathize with some aspects of the civil rights movement, namely the end of racial discrimination, the left saw the movement as a revolutionary praxis, i.e., not as an end in itself but as a means to promote revolution in the United States. As mentioned, Martin Luther King himself deemed it "part of [an] overall movement in the world in which oppressed people are revolting against ... imperialism and colonialism." King, "The Legitimacy of the Struggle" Statement, quoted in Cone, "Martin Luther King, Jr., and the Third World," in *The Future of Liberation Theology*, edited by Ellis and Maduro, 347. It is perhaps no coincidence that some of King's closest aides were linked to the Communist Party U.S.A. Moreover, most of those who formed the LT movement in the U.S. took part in the civil rights movement. Also stemming from this movement were the 1964 Berkeley riots, the starting point of the 1968 student revolution in France. See Barbara Harris Combs, *From Selma to Montgomery: The Long March to Freedom* (New York: Routledge, 2013).

1235. See National Committee of Black Churchmen, *Black Theology: Statement by the National Committee of Black Churchmen* (June 13, 1969), in *Black Theology: A Documentary History, 1966–1979*, ed. James Cone and Gayraud S. Wilmore, 2nd ed. rev. (Maryknoll, N.Y.: Orbis Books, 1993), 37–39. See Gibellini, *La teologia del XX secolo*, 411–45. In addition to the long Black Theology bibliography quoted by Gibellini, see Dwight N. Hopkins and Edward P. Antonio, eds., *The Cambridge Companion to Black Theology* (Cambridge: Cambridge University Press, 2012); Cone, *A Black Theology*; James H. Cone, *God of the Oppressed* (Maryknoll, N.Y.: Orbis Books, 1997); James H. Cone, *The Spirituals and the Blues: An Interpretation* (Maryknoll, N.Y.: Orbis Books, 1992); Cone and Wilmore, *Black Theology*; Dwight N. Hopkins, *Introducing Black Theology of Liberation* (Maryknoll, N.Y.: Orbis Books, 1999); Jamie T. Phelps, ed., *Black and Catholic: The Challenge and Gift of Black Folk; Contributions of African American Experience and Thought to Catholic Theology* (Milwaukee: Marquette University Press, 1997); and J. Deotis Roberts, *Liberation and Reconciliation: A Black Theology* (Maryknoll, N.Y.: Orbis Books, 2004).

1236. Edward Sisson and William Dembski, "My 'best education,'" *World*, Oct. 10, 2008. See also Ryan Lizza, "The Agitator: Barack Obama's Unlikely Political Education," *The New Republic*, Mar. 9, 2007; David Moberg, "Obama's Third Way," *National Housing Institute*, no. 49 (Spring 2007).

1237. "Transcript. Reverend Wright at the National Press Club," *New York Times*, Apr. 28, 2008.

1238. See Richard Edward Martinez, *PADRES: A study of revolutionary Chicano priests* (Graduation thesis, University of Michigan, 2002).

1239. See Stevens Arroyo, *Prophets Denied Honor*. On Hispanic B.C.C.s in the United States, see Secretariat for Hispanic Affairs, *Basic Christian Communities: An Experience in the United States* (Washington, D.C.: N.C.C.B., 1982); Frank Ponce, "Building Comunidades Eclesiales de Base," in *Developing Basic Christian Communites: A Handbook* (Chicago: National Federation of Priests' Councils, 1979), 27–36. In 2007, the Secretariat for Hispanic Affairs was incorporated into the Office of Cultural Diversity in the Church. See Joan Faraone, *The Evolution of the Secretariat of Hispanic Affairs of NCCB/USCCB and Its Contribution to Catechesis of Hispanos/Latinos in the United States* (Washington, D.C.: graduation thesis, Catholic University of America, 2009).

1240. See Julio Loredo, "The 'Catholic Left' on the Border: Adding Fuel to the Fire," *TFP Newsletter* 4, no. 22, 4–6.

1241. See Andrés González Guerrero, *A Chicano Theology* (Maryknoll, N.Y.: Orbis Books, 1987); Mario T. Garcia, *Chicano Liberation Theology: The Writings and Documents of Richard Cruz and Católicos por la Raza* (Dubuque: Kenall Hunt, 2009); Virgilio Elizondo, *Christianity and Culture* (San Antonio: Mexican American Cultural Center, 1983); Elizondo, *Mestizaje*. See also Rodolfo Acuña, *Occupied America: The Chicano's Struggle Toward Liberation* (San Francisco: Cantfield Press, 1972).

1242. See, for example, Virgilio Elizondo, *Galilean Journey: The Mexican-American Promise* (Maryknoll, N.Y.: Orbis Books, 2000). Some of LT's main theologians such as Frs. Gustavo Gutiérrez, Jon Sobrino, and Casiano Floristán are found among the teachers at the Mexican American Cultural Center.

1243. Julio Loredo, "Teología indígena," *Covadonga Informa* 15, no. 162 (Mar. 1992), 5. On indigenist theology, see: Josef Estermann, ed., *Teología andina*, 2 vols. (La Paz: Instituto Superior Ecuménico Andino de Teología (I.S.E.A.T.)/Plural

One of its pioneers was Most Rev. Leonidas Proaño (1910–1988), bishop of Riobamba, Ecuador. Here is how he explains its goal: "'The only way left to the peoples of Latin America to change the so-called established order is a genuine revolution ... global, radical, quick.' As Bishop Proaño would have it, "the indigenous peoples would be the champions of that global revolution."[1244] LT has had an important indigenous component from its inception. Not surprisingly, Father Gutiérrez's main work is dedicated to José María Arguedas (1911–1969), a Peruvian ethnologist and anthropologist who was a standard-bearer of the indigenist current. Already in 1977, Plinio Corrêa de Oliveira denounced the indigenist doctrines that inspired the pastoral policy of the Brazilian Bishops' Conference.[1245]

At the heart of this theology we find the thesis that primitive Andean and Amazonian indigenous societies contain values more precious than those of Western culture, so that we should learn from them. Devoid of the sense of *I*, the Indian is said to lack even the notion of *mine*. Thus, a perfect fraternity, founded on equality and the absence of private property. "The Indians already live the beatitudes," we read in a document by the Brazilian bishops. "They do not know private property, profit or competition. They possess an essentially communitarian life in perfect balance with nature. They live in harmony. ... The Indians are a prophecy for the future."[1246] The starting point is, therefore, a rejection of the evangelizing and civilizing work of the Church in the New World. According to these theologians, the missionaries committed a historic mistake by assimilating the indigenous peoples to Catholicism and Western culture, as they had superior religions and traditions. "The Indian," Father Richard stated, "had ancient religions in which there was faith much before the arrival of Christopher Columbus and his boys. ... They were very profound and pure religions. There was impressive sanctity and spiritual depth."[1247]

In contact with Indians, missionaries should not preach the doctrine of Our Lord Jesus Christ but join their tribes to learn their wisdom. "Indigenous communities must be received as evangelizers, a model for our society that has much to learn from them," stated Most Rev. Fernando Gomes, archbishop of Goiânia.[1248] Father Richard adds, "Sometimes I go to the mountain with my Bible and do not know where to put it. I am ashamed. How can I speak of Saint Paul and Moses to people who have two thousand years of tradition. ... We must open the way for a new, liberating evangelization starting from the ancient religions of our indigenous peoples."[1249]

It is in this light that can be understood the shocking statements by Most Rev. Tomás Balduino, bishop emeritus of Goiás, Brazil, at a conference held in Rome in 2009: "The profound conviction of missionaries today is that these indigenous peoples are the true evangelizers of the world. We must not go to them as one who brings a doctrine or gospel given and entrusted to us by Christ. We have to go to the Indians knowing that Christ has anticipated us in their midst and that seeds of the Word are there. We have the conviction that the Indians already live the beatitudes. It is we that must convert to their cultures."[1250]

How can one say that Our Lord has preceded the Church among the Indians?

According to these theologians, there is a primitive revelation inherent in nature. This revelation should not be understood as the manifestation of a transcendent Being but as vitality inherent in nature. Religious experience is a direct perception of this vitality. At a given time, considering himself superior to nature, man lost contact with this vital immanence. At that point there was a second revelation, the one recorded in the Holy Scriptures so men could intellectually understand part of what we had first perceived by connaturality. Therefore, Holy Scriptures would be a substitute necessarily inferior to primitive revelation. The Bible should be interpreted in the light of primitive revelation. Father Richard explained, "God has written two books. God's first book is the cosmos, culture, the indigenous religion. *This is the fundamental book of God*. God has also written another book, the Bible, but only to help us understand the first."[1251] Reasoning of this kind draws indigenous theology closer to postmodern trends borrowed from cosmic pantheism, about which we will talk later.

In order to develop indigenous theology, "Continental Encounters on Indian Theology" are held periodically, organized by A.E.L.A.P.I. (Latin American Ecumenical Network of Indigenous Pastoral). The latest one was held in Tolé, Panama, February 10–14, 2020.

4. Homosexual, Lesbian, Queer Liberation Theology

In addition to racial and cultural analyses, the new liberation theologies also exploit moral and psychological factors, taking on new homosexual, feminist, and gender-oriented trends. The homosexual cause is an important element of the Fourth Revolution. Mario Mieli (1952–1983), founder of F.U.O.R.I. (Italian Revolutionary Homosexual United Front) explains, "The gradual liberation of repressed erotic tendencies will further strengthen the revolutionary movement. ... We cannot imagine the importance of the contribution made to the revolution and to human emancipation by the progressive liberation of sadism, masochism, pederasty, gerontophilia, zooerastia, autoerotism, fetishism, scatology, undinism, exhibitionism, voyeurism, etc."[1252]

The homosexual horizon is not new in LT. Canadian Guy Ménard, professor of religious studies at the University of Quebec, was undoubtedly a pioneer in this regard. In 1980, he wrote *De Sodome à l'Exode: Jalons pour une théologie de la libération gaie.*[1253] Some groups of "Catholic" homosexuals, including the European Forum of Homosexual Christians, attended the international conference of liberation theologians held in Madrid in September 1989. A round table was devoted to "groups and sectors marginalized in the Church." The idea was to find new marginalized groups

Editores, 2006); Nicolás Sarmiento, *Caminos de la teología india* (Cochabamba: Verbo Divino, 2000); Juan José Tamayo-Acosta and Juan Bosch, eds., *Panorama de la teología latinoamericana* (Estella: Verbo Divino, 2001); Juan José Tamayo-Acosta and Raul Fornet, eds., *Interculturalidad, diálogo interreligioso y liberación* (Estella: Verbo Divino, 2005). Diego Irarrázaval is an indigenist theologian often cited in Europe. See Diego Irarrázaval, "Interculturalidad y teología: Interrogantes latinoamericanos," *Nación Juvenil*, Jan. 5, 2012.

1244. Loredo, "Teología indígena," 1, 4.

1245. See Corrêa de Oliveira, *Indian Tribalism*.

1246. Conferência Nacional dos Bispos do Brasil—C.N.B.B., "1ª Assembléia Nacional de Pastoral Indigenista: Em debate a situação indígena em nível nacional," *Boletim do CIMI* 4, no. 22 (Jul.–Aug. 1975), 7. This idyllic vision obviously does not correspond to reality.

1247. Loredo, "Teología indígena," 5.

1248. "Iniciado curso sobre a integração dos índios," *O Popular* (Goiânia), July 13, 1976. For his part, Diego Irarrázaval states: "For me, it [interreligious dialogue] means to divest oneself, to humbly approach the small religious traditions like those of the Indians ... to approach them to grow together, to share wisdoms and spiritual energies." Hernán Ingelmo, "Entrevista a Diego Irarrázaval," *C.E.T.R.*, May 3, 2008.

1249. Loredo, "Teología indígena" 5.

1250. "Mons. Romero, Martin Luther King, Don Diana: Quando la parola diventa microfono dei senza voce," *Adista Notizie*, no. 40, Apr. 11, 2009. The conference took place at the Di Liegro Room of the Rome Province. See also Victor Madrigal Sanchez, "Teología india," in *Trabajos Científicos*, vol. 1, *La teología de la liberación en prospectiva* (Montevideo: Fundación Amerindia, 2012), 131–42.

1251. Loredo, "Teología indígena," 6.

1252. Claudia Pilato, "Dall'omosessualità alla pedofilia: sullo scivolo della rivoluzione sessuale," *Tradizione Famiglia Proprietà* (Oct. 2013), 18.

1253. Guy Ménard, *De Sodome à l'exode: Jalons pour une théologie de la libération gaie* (Montréal: L'Aurore/Univers, 1980).

to replace the old LT's "poor," including homosexuals, now seen as "moral proletarians." The main lecture was delivered by the priest Emili Boils, who stated, "I am homosexual by nature and by the grace of God. ... I am a priest because I am homosexual." The priest went on to denounce "the twenty centuries of social and religious marginalization, of oppression of every kind which my people have suffered." He closed with a threat: "We must prepare for war, our own intifada."[1254]

In subsequent years, by applying LT categories to homosexuals and lesbians—deemed oppressed and in need of liberation—Catholic and Protestant theologians developed gay, lesbian, and queer liberation theology. The expression *queer theology* was coined in 1994 by Robert Goss in his book *Jesus Acted Up: A Gay and Lesbian Manifesto*.[1255] Queer theology rests on the assumption that gender nonconformity and homosexual conduct are a constant in history. What is needed is to discover the structures of oppression that have historically weighed upon these categories, proclaiming their liberation.[1256]

In the United States we may also mention Carter Heyward, an ordained Episcopal minister, professor of theology at the Episcopal Divinity School, Cambridge, Mass., and a lesbian feminist liberation theologian.[1257]

This theology has its own revolutionary praxis: the homosexual movement, now rapidly expanding around the world, which includes a large Catholic component. In 2003, the Coordination of Christian Homosexual Groups in Italy (C.O.C.I.) was established to network the various groups of Christian homosexuals active in that country. Several "Catholic" homosexual groups such as Ali d'Aquila and L.G.B.T. Christians take part in homosexual Pride parades. "If one does not overcome the barriers of the mind, those of the heart will have a hard time. That is why for many centuries our church found it hard to accept homosexual love," declared theologian Vito Mancuso at the Forum of Homosexual Christians held in May 2012 in Albano (Rome) at the congregation of the Somaschi Fathers at the request of volunteers of the Gionata Project.[1258]

5. Feminist and Ecofeminist Liberation Theology

A widespread feminist theology is that developed, for example, by Elizabeth Schüssler Fiorenza, Rosemary Radford Ruether, Mary Daly, and, in Italy, Elizabeth Green. Initially on the basis of the old LT, some liberation theologians began to explore more subtle factors of oppression and found their revolutionary praxis in the feminist movement, entering into a symbiosis with it. Feminist theology is widespread, especially in feminine religious orders. Belgian theologian Alice Dermience writes:

Theologians happily recognize the positive impact [of feminist theology] on ... contemporary theological reflection. ...

... [She quotes David Tracy and continues:] "Feminist thought has been the major stimulant in several disciplines including philosophy and theology." ... Today it is not possible to do a serious work ... while ignoring gender issues.[1259]

What are the foundations of this feminist theology?

a. Patriarchal Society

This theology revolves around the denunciation of patriarchalism, i.e., men's domination over women in every field. Brazilian feminist theologian Ivone Gebara writes,

Patriarchy is ... this kind of "original sin" that we have carried on our backs for six thousand years now. ...

... Despotism, authoritarianism, militarism ... are the legitimate "children" of religious patriarchalism powerfully transmitted by Christianity.[1260]

By denouncing patriarchalism, feminist theologians intend to strike at none other than the hierarchical principle of the universe. "A particular reading of this foundational text [Genesis] has given Western culture the fundamental idea that the universe is a hierarchy: a system of order imposed by spiritual power from above, an order to which we owe obedience," Irish feminist theologian Anne Primavesi writes. "This totalitarian view of our relationship with God permeates our perception of power. It is conceived of as power over those lower than oneself on whatever scale of being is in question."[1261]

b. Deconstruction

The whole Magisterium of the Church and the theology that sustains it are said to have been shaped by men and therefore to reflect a patriarchal mentality. Consequently, the first step of feminist theology is to deconstruct the Magisterium, i.e., delete the truths of faith that the Church has taught us, thereby destroying also the myths of patriarchal society. "The women's revolution is not only Anti-Church. It is a postchristian spiritual revolution," Mary Daly proclaims.[1262]

c. Ecology

Along with oppressing women, men also subjected Mother Earth—Gaia—without realizing that it is a source of life, energy, and revelation. In this way feminist theology engages

1254. Julio Loredo, "Homosexualidad y teología de la liberación," *Covadonga Informa* (Madrid, May 1990), 8–9. For the written proceedings of the conference, see Ruiz-Gimenez, Joaquín, ed., *Iglesia y derechos humanos: IX Congreso de teología* (Madrid: Evangelio y Liberación, 1989).

1255. See Robert E. Goss, *Jesus Acted Up: A Gay and Lesbian Manifesto* (San Francisco: Harper, 1994).

1256. See John J. McNeil, *Scommettere su Dio, teologia della liberazione omosessuale* (Casale Monferrato: Edizioni Sonda, 1994); Patrick S. Cheng, *Radical Love: An Introduction to Queer Theology* (New York: Church Publishing, 2011); Robert E. Goss, *Take Back the Word: A Queer Reading of the Bible* (Boston: The Pilgrim Press, 2000); Gary David Comstock, *Gay Theology without Apology* (Eugene, Ore.: Wipf & Stock, 2009); J. Michael Clark, *A Place to Start: Toward an Unapologetic Gay Liberation Theology* (Monument, Colo.: Monument Publishing, 1989).

1257. See "Rev. Dr. Carter Heyward—Profile," *LGBTQ Religious Network Archive*.

1258. Pasquale Quaranta, "Chiesa e omosessualità, intervista a Vito Mancuso" Liberstef.myblog.it, May 8, 2012. For the complete text of Mancuso's speech, see Progetto Gionata, "Il teologo Mancuso e le prospettive teologiche sull'amore omosessuale e il suo esercizio mediante l'affettività," *Progetto Gionata*, Apr. 27, 2012.

1259. Alice Dermience, "Théologie de la femme et théologie feministe," *Révue Théologique de Louvain*, no. 31 (2000), 520–21. On feminist theology, see Elizabeth E. Green, *Filo tradito: Vent'anni di teologia femminista* (Turin: Claudiana, 2011); Elizabeth E. Green, *Il Dio sconfinato: Una teologia per donne e uomini* (Turin: Claudiana, 2007); Juan Antonio Montes Varas, *Desde la teología de la liberación a la teología eco-feminista: Una revolución enquistada en la iglesia, intenta destruir la civilización y la moral cristiana* (Santiago, Chile: Acción Familia, 2011); L. Russelli, *Teologia femminista* (Brescia: Queriniana, 1977); Mary Daly, *Per una filosofia della liberazione della donna* (Rome: Editori Riuniti 1990).

1260. Ivone Gebara, prologue to *Del cielo a la tierra: Una antología de teología feminista*, ed. Mary Judith Ress, Ute Seibert, and Lele Sjorup (Santiago: Sello Azul, 1997), 15, 18. Gebara comes from the LT movement and was a teacher at the Recife Theological Institute for many years under the aegis of Archbishop Helder Câmara. In 1993, the Vatican condemned her for defending abortion as a woman's right. See Ivone Gebara, *Teologia ecofeminista: Ensaio para repensar o conhecimento e a religião* (São Paulo: Olho d'Água, 1997); Ivone Gebara, *O que é teologia feminista* (São Paulo: Olho d'Agua, 2007).

1261. Anne Primavesi, *From Apocalypse to Genesis: Ecology, Feminism and Christianity* (Minneapolis: Fortress Press, 1991), 203, 198.

1262. Mary Daly, "The Qualitative Leap Beyond Patriarchal Religion," *Quest* 1, no. 4 (Spring 1975): 21.

the environmentalist variety, giving rise to ecofeminist theology. "Ecofeminism," Rosemary Radford Ruether explains, "brings together these two explorations of ecology and feminism, in their full, or deep forms, and explores how male domination of women and domination of nature are interconnected both in cultural ideology and in social structures."[1263] It supposedly behooves women, who have in their body the secrets of the Earth's fertility and thus can empathize with it, the task of freeing the Earth from male oppression, and liberating themselves in the process.

d. Sexuality and Genitality

A central point of feminist theology is precisely the emphasis on the woman's body as a place in which god reveals himself, not by communicating transcendental truths but rather a feeling of his immanence. Maryknoll Sister Mary Judith Ress explains: "All of this brings me to a new definition of myself. I am no longer an individual called Judy. I'm trying to connect with my ecological being, in which the boundaries of my being dissolve and blend with the other, with the sea, the forest, the starry night."[1264] The way to connect with one's ecological being would be through eastern meditation techniques, now widespread in convents of nuns, along with massage and physical stimulation techniques that enable a woman to explore her own body and those of others, even in their genitality, to discover god therein.

For the 10th anniversary of the Con-spirando Collective in Santiago, Chile, in 2002, Ivone Gebara wrote:

> Once again, the body has emerged as a place of action and reflection. ... We dared to talk about god and female genitalia, or the female genitalia and god. ... The holy spirit, by coming into the flesh of female genitalia, strongly and unexpectedly imposes himself in our conversations. ...
>
> ... In our genital reality we also discover ourselves as opressed genitality and we discover the connection between this form of oppression and all the others.[1265]

This discovery of women as "genital subjects" and the consequent liberation of "oppressed genitality" is said to be accomplished through specific rituals proposed by ecofeminists as a new spirituality, which we reproduce here with an obvious note of rejection. Here is how ecofeminist theologian Doris Muñoz describes one of these rituals, practiced in feminist Catholic circles:

> Keeping our circle, we looked for a suitable place in the room to connect with the Earth. ...
>
> ... I invited everyone to undress. ...
>
> Slowly, silently, we strip ourselves of all the rags on us, turning our pelvis to the beat of the music and connecting with the unfiltered energy of Baubo. ...
>
> At this point we pass from hand to hand two small bottles with perfumed oil. ... I invited everyone to spread it on their [private parts] ... each of us was free to feel this act as a blessing and/or a cure.[1266]

Feminist theology has ravaged American religious life. Still fresh in our memory is the rebellion of the Leadership Conference of Women Religious (L.C.W.R.), an organization representing 80% of U.S. nuns. In August 2012, nearly a thousand L.C.W.R. delegates met in St. Louis and voted a motion of repudiation of the Magisterium of the Church on issues such as abortion, homosexuality, euthanasia, and women's ordination, responding to direct intervention by the Vatican with the document titled "Doctrinal Assessment." The Vatican accused L.C.W.R. of "radical feminism" and condemned its "commentaries on 'patriarchy' [which] distort the way in which Jesus has structured sacramental life in the Church."[1267]

6. A Theology Without Religion

From liberation to liberation, some liberation theologians end up freeing themselves from religion, seen as inherently oppressive. Such was the theme of a recent world conference of Eatwot (Ecumenical Association of Third World Theologians), an international forum of liberation theologians founded in 1976. "The time has come for a post-religious theology without dogmas and doctrines, secular, simply human," the Adista news agency headlined.[1268] They call it "pluralist liberation theology" and their creed has been illustrated by the Brazilian liberation theologian Dominican Friar Betto:

> I believe in the god freed from the Vatican and from all religions that exist and will exist. The god who precedes all baptisms, pre-exists the sacraments, and is beyond all religious doctrines. Free from theologians. ...
>
> I believe in the god who has no religion, creator of the universe, giver of life and faith, fully present in nature and in humanity.[1269]

7. Ecotheology: Liberation of Nature

Environmentalism is undoubtedly a trend of our time both in its rather acceptable manifestations (the protection of nature) and in its controversial ones such as the so-called deep ecology, which has clearly pantheistic implications. Liberation theologians on the Fourth Revolution bandwagon would never pass it up so as to ride the crest of the wave. "To the cry of the poor we must add the cry of the Earth," announced Leonardo Boff. Thus, ecological liberation theology, or ecotheology, emerged. "Ecology is the new paradigm born from the cry of the poor and the cry of the Earth, and taking cosmocentrism, i.e., the centrality of ecology, which replaces anthropocentrism, to the core of theological reflection," Emerson Sbardelotti Tavares wrote in his report on the international theological Congress held in Brazil in 2012.[1270]

The starting point of ecotheology is the consideration of the Earth as a living entity, which also includes human life: "The

---

1263. Rosemary Radford Ruether, *Gaia & God: An Ecofeminist Theology of Earth Healing* (New York: HarperCollinsPublishers, 1994), 2.

1264. Mary Judith Ress, ed. *Lluvia para florecer: Entrevistas sobre el ecofeminismo en América Latina* (Santiago, Chile: Colectivo Conspirando, 2002), 35.

1265. Ivone Gebara, "Haciendo las conexiones: Encuentro con teólogas eco/feministas," *Con-spirando* 40, no. 2 (June 2002), 46–47.

1266. Doris Muñoz, "Experimento entonces mi cuerpo como fuente de plenitud," *Con-spirando* 53, no. 6 (Aug. 2006), 43.

1267. Congregation for the Doctrine of the Faith, "Doctrinal Assessment of the Leadership Conference of Women Religious" (Apr. 18, 2012), II. See also Giacomo Galeazzi, "Il Vaticano rilancia il dialogo con le religiose della LCWR che avevano messo in discussione la dottrina cattolica," in *Vatican Insider-La Stampa*, April 16, 2013. Other than the document mentioned, the Vatican took no disciplinary measure regarding L.C.W.R.

1268. Adista, "È giunto il tempo di una teologia post-religioni: Senza dogmi e dottrine, laica, semplicemente umana," *Adista Documenti*, no. 24 (Mar. 20, 2010). See José María Vigil, Luiza Tomita, and Marcelo Barros, eds. *Per i molti cammini di Dio*, vol. 3, *Teologia latinoamericana pluralista della liberazione* (Rimini: Pazzini Editore, 2010).

1269. Frei Betto, "Um novo credo," *Correio da Cidadania*, Apr. 23, 2007.

1270. See Emerson Sbardelotti Tavares, "Ecoteologia: Do grito dos pobres ao grito da Terra na perspectiva da Teologia da libertação de Leonardo Boff," in *Trabajos Científicos*, vol. 1, *La teología de la liberación en prospectiva* (Montevideo: Fundación Amerindia, 2012), 235. See, at the same conference, the report by Willian Kaizer de Oliveira, titled "Ecoteologia: Perspectivas de novas temáticas da teologia latinoamericana," in *Trabajos*

Earth is not just a planet on which life exists. It is alive. It is a living superorganism that the Andeans called 'Pacha Mama' and people today refer to as 'Gaia,' the Greek name for the living Earth." Leonardo Boff writes.[1271] Considering himself rather distinct and superior, man supposedly mistreated the Earth, exploiting it for his own purposes, just as bosses exploit workers. It is time to proclaim the liberation of nature. Other than the extravagance, to say the least, of treating the Earth as a theological subject in need of liberation, one is struck by the ability of this theology to descend into unfathomable abysses.

A source of inspiration for ecotheology is the work of American Dominican theologian Matthew Fox, father of so-called Creation Spirituality.[1272] Quoting Fr. Bede Griffiths, O.S.B. Cam. Fox's homepage reads: "[Matthew Fox's] creation spirituality is the spirituality of the future, and his theology of the Cosmic Christ is the theology of the future."[1273] Working on the heels of Fr. Teilhard de Chardin, seasoned with New Age elements, Fox came to clearly pantheistic positions. Censured by the Vatican, expelled from the Dominican Order, in 1994, Fox became a minister of the Episcopalian Church in California.

8. The Postmodern Paradigm

As Belgian historian Fr. François Houtart (close to the LT current) explains, "As Leonardo Boff says. ... the technical-scientific paradigm of modernity is neither universalizable nor integral. Leonardo Boff is opposed to an optimistic view of endless progress ... and develops a holistic vision of the living universe."[1274] According to Father Houtart, today we are seeing the crisis of our civilization and the rise of a new paradigm. The modern paradigm, he claims, is now exhausted and is being replaced by the postmodern one. What are its key elements?

a. End of the Economy of the Logos

What marks the transition to the postmodern paradigm is the abandonment of reason as the driving force of history. Leonardo Boff writes:

> Everything points to the fact that we are arriving at the end of this long process [the economy of the Logos], not at the end of reason ... but at the end of its total rule. ...
>
> ... In this sense, [we are] at the beginning of a new cultural dawning, we may dream of the beginning of a new reign, that of Eros and Pathos. ...
>
> ... The Greek Logos is at the root of our culture, and the Cartesian Cogito at the origin of modernity. ... [But] reason does not explain or touch upon everything. ... From below there emerges something older, deeper, more elementary and primitive—affectivity. From above

... an experience that beyond the concrete there are ... gratifying feeling, sympathy and tenderness.[1275]

Commenting on these doctrines, American sociologist Daniel Bell notes that "impulse and pleasure alone are real and life-affirming; all else is neurosis and death."[1276]

Together with Eros is Pathos, that is, feeling, emotions: "The base experience is feeling. Not the *cogito, ergo sum* (I think, therefore I am), but the *sentio, ergo sum* (I feel, therefore I am), not Logos but Pathos." According to this theology, knowledge is no longer intellectual learning resulting in the formation of a concept, but direct knowledge through sympathy. According to Boff, "Ancient man, before the hegemony of reason, lived a mystical union with all realities, including god; he felt umbilically linked with the surrounding world and with his own intimacy. ... He lived the truly archaic structure of life."[1277]

b. An Immanent Revelation

We thus find, at the heart of the postmodern religion, an immanent revelation. God is an energy pulsating in the cosmos that we need to discern. We find god, first of all, in our body. "Our body, therefore, is a primary place of the disclosure of the Mystery ... our body as a place where we first know god," Joseph Holland writes.[1278] "We first know god's creative presence in the reality of our own bodies: flesh, blood, breath, posture, digestion, sexuality, psyche, etc."[1279] God is to be found in "the mystical depths of the flesh." Then god reveals himself in our psychological and temperamental movements. That would be the interior, emotional field of revelation. Finally, god is revealed in nature through an ecological revelation.[1280]

c. A Ludic Society

Another central element of the postmodern paradigm would be its ludic, that is, playful character. Quoting Hans-George Gadamer, Gibson Winter explains, "Gadamer's point of departure is the notion of play, itself being dialectical, an expression of the to-fro movement of life and nature. ... Gadamer sees play as the way of being of bios and cosmos. ... In this sense, art is rooted in the character of life itself as play."[1281] Whereas the classic human type is *homo sapiens*, and the modern one *homo faber*, the postmodern human type would be *homo ludens*.

As man's more natural and spontaneous activity deriving from the free flow of his energies and imagination rather than from the disciplining action of the intellect, the *ludus* would be the best way to grasp the divine energies circulating in the cosmos, the best mediation through which this god-energy manifests himself to men. The ludus makes the bios and the cosmos accessible to the world of meaning.

The way of moving the revolution forward also changes substantially. Proletarian insurrections are no longer promoted. "History presents itself as a game. ... A free, inventive, joyful game ... that we hope will be the future," explained the Spaniard Eugenio Fernández at an international conference of liberation theologians.[1282]

Científicos, vol. 1, *La teología de la liberación en prospectiva* (Montevideo: Fundación Amerindia, 2012), 668–80. See also Marcelo Barros and Frei Betto, O *amor fecunda o universo: Ecologia e espiritualidade* (Rio de Janeiro: Agir, 2009); Leonardo Boff, *Ecologia, grito da terra, grito dos pobres* (Petropolis: Vozes, 1996); Luis Carlos Susin and Joe Marçal dos Santos, *Nosso planeta, nossa vida: Ecologia e teologia* (São Paulo: Paulinas, 2011); José María Vigil, "Desafío de la ecología a las religiones," *Revista Vinculum* (Bogotá), no. 238 (2010).

1271. Leonardo Boff, "A terra não é um planeta em que há vida, ela é um organismo vivo," *O Tempo*, Apr. 4, 2014.

1272. See, for example, Matthew Fox, *The Coming of the Cosmic Christ, The Healing of Mother Earth and the Birth of a Global Renaissance* (San Francisco: Harper, 1988); Matthew Fox, *Creation Spirituality: Liberating Gifts for the Peoples of the Earth* (San Francisco: Harper, 1991).

1273. "About Matthew Fox," accessed May 13, 2021, www.matthewfox.org.

1274. François Houtart, "L'état actuel de la théologie de la libération en Amérique latine," *RisalInfo*, Sept. 14, 2006.

1275. Boff, *Francis of Assisi*, 7–9.

1276. Daniel Bell, *The Cultural Contradictions of Capitalism* (New York: Basic Books, Inc. Publishers, 1976), 51.

1277. Boff, *Francis of Assisi*, 9.

1278. Holland, *Post Modern Cultural Earthquake*, 11.

1279. Holland, *Spiritual Crisis*, 12.

1280. See Holland, *Post Modern Cultural Earthquake*, and Holland, *Spiritual Crisis*.

1281. Gibson Winter, *Liberating Creation: Foundations of Religious Social Ethics* (New York: Crossroad, 1981), 12.

1282. Eugenio Fernández, "La historia: Un juego que va en serio," in *Desafíos Cristianos*, ed. Misión Abierta (Madrid: Loguez Ediciones, 1988), 195.

In this playful society, the imagination plays a primary role, just as advocated by the Sorbonne student revolution of 1968. "Imagination is ... the attunement of the human to the creative processes of bios and cosmos," Winter writes.[1283] By freeing the imagination one would open that privileged channel through which the god-energy would manifest himself.

d. Liberation of Dreams

Thus, the emphasis on the liberation of dreams. We read in a training manual for Basic Christian Communities, "It is a dream that originates in god; it is a way of life that god is dreaming into reality."[1284] Any factor that inhibits dream-wandering is considered oppressive. This will erase any distinction between imagination and reality, and imagination will reign supreme. Having arrived at this point, liberation theology would have attained its end by freeing man from the last oppression: that of reality itself.

Will the standard-bearers of the liberationist current take it all the way there? It is difficult to say, but the future is a cause for concern. While the original LT vitally depended on a stage of the revolution with a predictable decline—real Socialism—these new theologies ride a cultural revolution that has nothing but worsened year after year without any significant barriers being raised on the Catholic side. Here we touch a nerve.

In the preface to a recent book on the homosexual revolution by Gianfranco Amato, president of Jurists for Life, His Excellency Most Rev. Luigi Negri, then-bishop of Ferrara-Comacchio, warns,

> As bishops, as a Church, we cannot just watch passively the tragedy that is before us.
> As I recently stated, in the judgment of future historians the continuing silence of the Church about this revolution will somehow render us conniving.[1285]

This deafening silence on the part of many ecclesiastical authorities facing this terrible, ongoing revolution is perhaps the most apocalyptic aspect of the current situation.

1283. Winter, *Liberating Creation*, 111.
1284. Evelyn Eaton Whitehead and James D. Whitehead, *Community of Faith: Models and Strategies for Building Christian Communities* (New York: Seabury Press, 1982), 105.
1285. Luigi Negri, preface to *Omofobia o eterofobia: Perché opporsi a una legge ingiusta e liberticida,* by Gianfranco Amato (Verona: Fede & Cultura, 2014).

Conclusion
An Invitation to Engage in the Battle for Holy Mother Church

The threat of liberation theology continues to our days. Its philosophies, methods, and dialectics have infiltrated into our society and the Church. Reading this dramatic history of the liberation theology movement should open our eyes to the processes of the Revolution and chaos that afflict our times. It should invite us to reflect on how we might fight against it more efficaciously.

I have therefore listed five conclusions for my American audience that I feel will help readers engage in the fight for the Church and America. These conclusions can guide our actions and help us develop strategies to oppose this cancerous growth inside the Church.

First Conclusion: See the Big Picture

In this book, I have tried to bring clarity to the present-day scene. This is not a small skirmish spanning a few decades. We are in the extreme throes of a struggle between the Church and a centuries-old process of decadence and apostasy, which Prof. Plinio Corrêa de Oliveira called the Revolution. This Revolution (with a capital "R") did not begin in the sixties, nor was it triggered by the Second Vatican Council. It began centuries ago. To trace the roots of today's heresies and deviations, I went back to the French Revolution (1789). I could have gone back much further. Indeed, liberation theologians trace the beginning of their movement to the fifteenth century.

Thus, instead of seeing the Second Vatican Council as the cauldron of all evils plaguing the Church in our days, we must see the big picture—this Revolution with a capital "R." If, by a miracle, we managed to return to the pre-conciliar framework of the fifties, the dynamism of this revolutionary process would bring our whole nightmare back in a few short years. The only way to reverse the crisis in the Church is to take an axe to the roots—all of them. Do not spare a single one. I have endeavored to point out those roots.

Second Conclusion: Be Aware of the Importance of Civil Society

We have seen how all the heresies that have infected Holy Mother Church over the past few centuries came from the civil sphere. From there, they penetrated the Mystical Body of Christ. The common theme of liberal Catholicism, Modernism, Nouvelle Théologie, liberation theology, and the more recent postmodern theologies is a desire to "adapt the Church to modern times." That is to say, the philosophical errors of civil society found in modern times gave rise to these heresies in the Church. The Council and the Novus Ordo Missae, for example, were two attempts to adapt the Church to modernity.

While the defense of the traditional Latin Mass is a necessary and noble endeavor, it will not succeed unless we crush the Revolution at its roots in temporal society. We must deal with causes, not consequences. The Revolution infects both the religious and civil spheres, making these crises intimately intertwined.

Third Conclusion: The Cultural Revolution Is Important

Much has been written about the doctrines and events of the great upheavals that have marked contemporary history, eventually affecting the Church. However, little or nothing is said about a prior and more profound aspect: the cultural element manifested through ambiances, music, clothes, art styles, and human types. Prof. Corrêa de Oliveira referred to this cultural upheaval as a *tendential revolution*. He affirmed that the disordered tendencies inside the soul serve as a hotbed that later gives rise to bad doctrines. Just as plants thrive in the carefully prepared environment of a greenhouse, so also revolutions develop and spread in cultures tendentially ready to foment bad doctrines that justify the fermenting of unruly passions.

If we are to fight the crisis in the Church, we cannot forget this tendential cultural battle. Just refuting erroneous doctrines and confronting evil events is not enough. We need to rid the culture of the disordered tendencies and unbridled passions that give rise to these errors and evils.

Fourth Conclusion: Never Lose Hope

By presenting the big picture, we also realize just how fleeting this Revolution is. Our Holy Mother Church has existed for two thousand years, and she will continue her journey until the end of the world. She has Our Lord's promise that the gates of Hell will never prevail against her. As Prof. Corrêa de Oliveira states:

> The Revolution and the Counter-Revolution are extremely important episodes in the history of the Church, for they constitute the very drama of the apostasy and the conversion of the Christian West. Even so, they are mere episodes.
>
> The mission of the Church does not lie only in the West, nor is it bound by time to the length of the revolutionary process. Amid the storms through which she passes today, she could proudly and tranquilly say: "*Alios ego vidi ventos; alias prospexi animo procellas*" ("I have already seen other winds, I have already beheld other storms"). The Church has fought in other lands, against adversaries from among other peoples, and she will undoubtedly continue to face problems and enemies quite different from those of today until the end of time.[1286]

1286. Corrêa de Oliveira, *Revolution and Counter-Revolution*, 114–15.

Fifth and Final Conclusion: Engage in the Battle

This book would not be complete without a final call to action. This is a read-and-do book.

These pages have shown how Holy Mother Church is being assailed by a revolutionary process that seeks to destroy her. As faithful children of the Church, we cannot simply stand by, analyzing the situation as if it were an abstract matter. Anyone who seriously loves the Church is called to fight for her in this extreme moment. Our baptismal vows and the Sacrament of Confirmation demand our Christian militancy. This duty implies bearing witness to Christ before men, confronting those attacking His Mystical Body, and battling those who seek to destroy His work of salvation.

We are not alone in this battle. Our Lady is at our side. Nay, she is leading the charge. In singing her praises, the Church says "thou alone hast destroyed all heresies." In Fatima, she promised us much more than just victory when she said, "Finally, My Immaculate Heart will triumph!"

Bibliography

Abel, Lionel. "Important Nonsense." *Dissent* (Mar./Apr. 1968): 147–57.

Abell, Aaron I. *American Catholicism and Social Action: A Search for Social Justice, 1865–1950.* Notre Dame, Ind.: University of Notre Dame Press, 1963.

— ed. *American Catholic Thought on Social Questions.* Indianapolis: The Bobbs-Merrill Company, 1968.

Acuña, Rodolfo. *Occupied America: The Chicano's Struggle Toward Liberation.* San Francisco: Canfield Press, 1972.

Adista. "È giunto il tempo di una teologia post-religioni: Senza dogmi e dottrine, laica, semplicemente umana." *Adista Documenti,* no. 24 (Mar. 20, 2010). https://www.adista.it/articolo/46989.

Advielle, M. Victor. *Histoire de Gracchus Babeuf et du babouvisme d'après de nombreux documents inédits.* 2 vols. Paris: self-published, 1884.

Agnes, Mario, ed. *Giovanni Acquaderni: Ricordi ai suoi amici.* Rome: AVE, 1977.

Agudello Villa, Hernando. *La revolución del desarrollo: Origen y evolución de la Alianza para el Progreso.* Mexico City: Editorial Roble, 1966.

à Lapide, Cornelius. *Commentaria in scripturam sacram.* In Acta Apostolorum I:3; In Acta Apostolorum II:30; in Lucam I:33; in Isaiam Prophetam LXV:17; in Danielem Prophetam II:44. Accessed Apr. 9, 2021. http://www.catholicapologetics.info/scripture/newtestament/Lapide.htm.

Alberigo, Giuseppe, and Jean-Pierre Jossua, eds. *La recepción del Vaticano II.* Madrid: Cristiandad, 1987.

Alinsky, Saul D. *"Playboy* Interview: Saul Alinsky: A Candid Conversation With the Feisty Radical Organizer." *Playboy* (Mar. 1972): 59–78, 150, 169–173, 176–78. Accessed Oct. 10, 2021. https://documents.theblackvault.com/documents/fbifiles/100-BA-30057.pdf.

— *Reveille for Radicals.* New York: Random House, 1969.

— *Rules for Radicals: A Practical Primer for Realistic Radicals.* New York: Vintage Books, 1989. Accessed Oct. 10, 2021, https://archive.org/details/RulesForRadicalsSaulAlinskyOCR/page/n9/mode/2up.

— "The Professional Radical: Conversations with Saul Alinsky," *Harper's Magazine* (June 1965): 37–47.

Amorós, Mario. *La Iglesia que nace del pueblo: Relevancia histórica del movimiento Cristianos por el Socialismo.* Accessed Mar. 29, 2021. http://www.rebelion.org/docs/75701.pdf.

Anderson, Theo. "What Is Actually Radical About Bernie Sanders' Democratic Socialism Isn't the Socialism." *In These Times* 39, no. 12 (Dec. 2015). https://inthesetimes.com/article/saul-alinsky-and-bernies-sanders-vision-of-democracy.

Andreotti, Giulio. *Intervista su De Gasperi.* Edited by Antonio Gambino. Bari: Laterza, 1977.

Androus, Hyrum L. "The Anglo-Saxon Connection." *Freemen Digest* (Apr. 1984): 29–31.

— "The Political Foundation of America." *Freemen Digest* (Jan. 1984): 32–34.

— Cleon W. Skousen, and Robert R. Walton. "America's Anglo-Saxon Heritage of Freedom." *Freemen Digest* (Feb. 1984): 43–45.

Anonymous. "La théologie et ses sources: Réponse aux études critiques de la Revue Thomiste." *Recherches de Science Religieuse,* no. 33 (1946): 384–91.

Anonymous (presumably Ernesto Buonaiuti). *Il programma dei modernisti: Risposta all'enciclica di Pio X "Pascendi Dominici Gregis."* Turin: Fratelli Bocca, 1911.

Apergi, Francesco. *Marxismo e ricerca sociale nella scuola di Francoforte.* Florence: La Nuova Italia, 1977.

Appleby, R. Scott. "Modernism as the Final Phase of Americanism." *The Harvard Theological Review* 81, no. 2 (Apr. 1988): 171–92.

Aquinas, St. Thomas. *La politica dei principi cristiani.* Siena: Cantagalli, 1981.

— *Summa contra gentiles.* Accessed Mar. 23, 2021. https://isidore.co/aquinas/english/ContraGentiles.htm.

— *Summa theologiae.* Accessed Mar. 23, 2021. https://www.newadvent.org/summa/.

Araya, Victorio. "La teología de la liberación: Aproximación histórica." In *Teologia de la liberación: Documentos sobre una polémica* by Joseph Ratzinger, et al. San José, Costa Rica: Departamento Ecuménico de Investigaciones, 1987.

Argerami, Omar. *Pensar y ser en Maurice Blondel.* Buenos Aires: Editorial Guadalupe, 1967.

Ariovaldo da Silva, José. *O movimento liturgico no Brasil.* Petrópolis: Editora Vozes, 1983.

Armstrong, Herbert W. *The United States and the British Commonwealth in Prophecy.* Pasadena, Calif.: Radio Church of God, 1954.

Arroyo, Gonzalo, et al. *Los cristianos y el socialismo: Primer encuentro latinoamericano.* Buenos Aires: Siglo XXI, 1973.

Asociación de Teólogos/as Juan XXIII. "Mensaje del 33 Congreso de Teología" (Sept. 8, 2013). *Atrio.* Accessed Mar. 30, 2021. https://www.atrio.org/2013/09/mensaje-del-33-congreso-de-teologia/.

Assmann, Hugo. *Opresión-liberación: Desafío a los cristianos.* Montevideo: Tierra Nueva, 1971.

— "Statement." In *Theology in the Americas,* edited by Sergio Torres and John Eagleson, 299–303. Maryknoll, N.Y.: Orbis Books, 1976.

Aubert, Roger. "Modernism." *Sacramentum Mundi: An Encyclopedia of Theology,* 99–104. New York: Herder and Herder, 1969.

Axelos, Kostas. *Marx: Penseur de la technique.* Paris: Les Éditions de Minuit, 1969.

Azzolin, Giovanni. *Gaetano De Lai, "L'uomo forte di Pio X": Cultura e fede nel I Novecento nell'esperienza del cardinale vicentino.* Vicenza: Accademia Olimpica, 2003.

Baget Bozzo, Gianni. *L'intreccio: Cattolici e comunisti 1945–2004.* Milan: Mondadori, 2004.

Bahmann, Manfred K. *A Preference for the Poor: Latin American Liberation Theology from a Protestant Perspective.* Lanham, Md.: University Press of America, 2005.

Balthasar, Hans Urs von. *A Theology of History.* New York: Sheed and Ward, 1963.

— *Aux croyants incertains.* Paris: Lethielleux, 1980.

Bandera, Armando. *Paulo Freire: Un pedagogo.* Caracas: Universidad Católica Andrés Bello, 1981.

Barbier, Emmanuel. *Histoire du catholicisme libéral et du catholicisme social en France: Du concile du Vatican à l'avénement de S.S. Benoît XV (1870–1914).* Bordeaux: Imprimerie Y. Cadoret, 1924.

Barreto, Nelson Ramos. *Reforma agrária: O mito e a realidade.* São Paulo: Artpress, 2003.

— and Paulo Henrique Chaves. *Reforma agrária semeia assentamentos: Assentados colhem miséria e desolação; Reportagem da TFP revela a verdade inteira*. São Paulo: Sociedade Brasileira de Defesa da Tradição, Familia e Propriedade, 1996.

Barros, Marcelo, and Frei Betto. *O amor fecunda o universo: Ecologia e espiritualidade*. Rio de Janeiro: Agir, 2009.

Baum, Gregory. "La teologia de la liberación y lo sobrenatural." In Gregory Baum et al. *Vida y reflexión: Aportes de la teología de la liberación al pensamiento teológico*. Lima: Centro de Estudios y Publicaciones—C.E.P., 1983.

— *Man Becoming: God in Secular Language*. New York: Herder and Herder, 1970.

— *Religion and Alienation: A Theological Reading of Sociology*. New York: Paulist Press, 1975.

— "The Christian Left at Detroit." In *Theology in the Americas*, edited by Sergio Torres and John Eagleson, 399–429. Maryknoll, N.Y.: Orbis Books, 1976.

Beccar Varela, hijo, Cosme, et al. *Allende et sa voie chilienne pour la misère*. Paris: Tradition Famille Propriété, 1974.

Bedeschi, Giuseppe. *La scuola di Francoforte*. Roma-Bari: Laterza, 1987.

Bedeschi, Lorenzo. *Il modernismo italiano: Voci e volti*. Cinisello Balsamo, Italy: San Paolo, 1995.

— *Le origini della gioventù cattolica dalla caduta del governo pontificio al primo congresso cattolico di Venezia su documenti inediti d'archivio*. Bologna: Cappelli, 1959.

— *Murri, Sturzo, De Gasperi: Ricostruzione storica ed epistolario (1898–1906)*. Cinisello Balsamo, Italy: San Paolo, 1994.

Bedoya, Juan G. "Mil teólogos piden al papa que rehabilite a los castigados por Ratzinger." *El País* (Madrid), Sept. 8, 2013. Accessed Dec. 19, 2021. https://elpais.com/sociedad/2013/09/08/actualidad/1378670585_242867.html.

Bekerman, Gérard. *Vocabulaire du marxisme*. Paris: Presses Universitaires de France, 1981.

Bell, Daniel. *The Cultural Contradictions of Capitalism*. New York: Basic Books, Inc. Publishers, 1976.

Bell, Stephen. *Rebel, Priest, and Prophet: A Biography of Dr. Edward McGlynn*. New York: Devin Adair, 1937.

Belloc, Hillaire. *Europe and the Faith*. London: Constable, 1920.

Bemelmans, Benoît. *La médaille miraculeuse: L'histoire vraie de la médaille donnée par la Sainte Vierge à sainte Catherine Labouré, racontée aux enfants*. Asnières-sur-Seine, France: Société française pour la défense de la Tradition, Famille et Propriété – TFP, 2003.

Benedict XV. Encyclical *Ad beatissimi apostolorum* (Nov. 1, 1914). http://w2.vatican.va/content/benedict-xv/en/encyclicals/documents/hf_ben-xv_enc_01111914_ad-beatissimi-apostolorum.html.

Benedict XVI. *Fede e scienza, un dialogo necessario: Un'antologia*. Edited by Umberto Casale. Turin: Lindau, 2010.

— General Audience (Mar. 10, 2010). https://w2.vatican.va/content/benedict-xvi/en/audiences/2010/documents/hf_ben-xvi_aud_20100310.html.

— General Audience at Castelgandolfo (Aug. 31, 2011).

— Incontro con i parroci e il clero di Roma (Feb. 14, 2013). http://w2.vatican.va/content/benedict-xvi/en/speeches/2013/february/documents/hf_ben-xvi_spe_20130214_clero-roma.html.

Benedict XVI (emeritus). "Il ricordo del pontefice emerito." In *Accanto a Giovanni Paolo II: Gli amici & i collaboratori raccontano*, edited by Wlodzimierz Redzioch. Rome: Ares, 2014.

Beozzo, Oscar. *A igreja do Brasil, de João XXIII a João Paulo II, de Medellín a Santo Domingo*. Petrópolis: 1994.

Bergier, L'Abbé. *Dictionnaire de théologie*. Paris: Leroux et Jouby, nd.

Bergon, Frank, and Murray Norris. *Delano, Another Crisis for the Catholic Church*. Fresno, Calif.: Rudell Publishing Company, 1968.

Bergson, Henri. *Les deux sources de la morale et de la religion*. Paris: Félix Alcan, 1932.

— *L'évolution créatrice*. Paris: Presses Universitaires de France, 1948.

Berryman, Phillip. "Latin America: 'Iglesia que nace del pueblo.'" *Christianity and Crisis* 41, no. 14 (Sept. 21, 1981): 238–42. Accessed Nov. 27, 2021. https://archive.org/details/sim_christianity-and-crisis_1981-09-21_41_14.

— "Latin American Liberation Theology." In *Theology in the Americas*, edited by Sergio Torres and John Eagleson, 20–83. Maryknoll, N.Y.: Orbis Books, 1976.

Berthre de Bourniseaux, Pierre Victor Jean. *Histoire des guerres de la Vendée et des chouans, depuis l'année 1792 jusqu'en 1815*. Paris: Brunot-Labbe, 1819.

Betto, Frei [Carlos Alberto Libânio Christo]. *A igreja na China*. São Paulo: C.E.P.I.S., 1988.

— *Diário de Puebla*. Rio de Janeiro: Civilização Brasileira, 1979.

— *Nicaragua livre: O primeiro passo*. Rio de Janeiro: Civilização Brasileira, 1980.

— "Um novo credo." *Correio da Cidadania*, Apr. 23, 2007. https://www.correiocidadania.com.br/colunistas/frei-betto/187-23-04-2007-um-novo-credo.

Bianchi, Enrico Ciro. *Pobres en este mundo, ricos en la fe: La fe vivida en el cristianismo popular latinoamericano en la obra 'El cristianismo popular según las virtudes teologales' de Rafael Tello*. Master's thesis, Universidad Católica Argentina (Buenos Aires), 2011.

Billot, Louis. *Les principes de '89 et leurs conséquences*. Paris: Téqui, 1989.

Bloch, Ernst. *Das prinzip hoffnung*. 3 vols. Frankfurt: Suhrkamp Verlag, 1954–1959.

— *Geist der utopie*. Munich: Verlag von Duncker & Humblot, 1918.

Bloch, Marc. *La servitù nella società medievale*. Florence: La Nuova Italia, 1975.

— *La società feudale*. Turin: Einaudi, 1949.

Bocci, Mario. "Un problema di identità? Alle origini della contestazione studentesca all'Università Cattolica." In *Dal "centrismo" al sessantotto*, edited by Marco Invernizzi, 143–228. Milan: Edizioni Ares, 2007.

Boff, Clodovis. "A influência política das comunidades eclesiais de base (C.E.B.S.)." *Sedoc* (Brazil) (Jan./Feb. 1979): 797–818.

— "Carta teológica sobre a URSS." *Revista de Cultura Vozes*, no. 6 (Nov.–Dec. 1987): 645–75.

— "Carta teológica sobre Cuba." *Revista Eclesiástica Brasileira* 46, no. 182 (Jun. 1986): 348–71.

— *Sinais dos tempos: Principios de leitura*. São Paulo: Edições Loyola, 1979.

— "Teologia da libertação e volta ao fundamento." *Revista Eclesiástica Brasileira* 67, no. 268 (Oct. 2007): 1001–22. Accessed Jan. 19, 2022. https://revistaeclesiasticabrasileira.itf.edu.br/reb/article/view/1490.

Boff, Leonardo. "A originalidade da teologia da libertação em Gustavo Gutiérrez." *Revista Eclesiástica Brasileira* 48, no. 191 (Sept. 1988): 531-43.

— "A terra não é um planeta em que há vida, ela é um organismo vivo," *O Tempo*, Apr. 4, 2014. Accessed Feb. 3, 2022. https://www.otempo.com.br/opiniao/leonardo-boff/a-terra-nao-e-um-planeta-em-que-ha-vida-ela-e-um-organismo-vivo-1.818479.

— *Church: Charism and Power; Liberation Theology and the Institutional Church*. Translated by John W. Diercksmeier. New York: The Crossroad Publishing Company, 1986.

— *Ecclesiogenesis: The Base Communities Reinvent the Church*. Translated by Robert R. Barr. Maryknoll, N.Y.: Orbis Books, 1986. Accessed Nov. 25, 2021. https://archive.org/details/ecclesiogenesisb00boff/page/n9/mode/2up.

— *Ecologia, grito da terra, grito dos pobres*. Petrópolis: Vozes, 1996.

— *Francis of Assisi: A Model for Human Liberation*. Translated by John W. Diercksmeier. Maryknoll, N. Y.: Orbis Books, 2006. Reprinted by permission of Orbis Books.

— *Igreja: Carisma e poder—Ensaios de eclesiologia militante*. São Paulo: Editora Ática, 1994.

— Interview. *Caros amigos* (Brazil) 1, no. 3 (June 1997).

— Interview. Marina Amaral, et al. "A igreja mente, é corrupta, cruel e sem piedade." *Caros amigos* (Brazil) 2, no. 18 (Sept. 1998). Accessed Dec. 19, 2021. https://web.archive.org/web/20071008204003 /http://carosamigos.terra.com.br/outras_edicoes/grandes_entrev /boff2.aspisc-latam.html.

— "Marxismo na teologia." *Jornal do Brasil*, Apr. 6, 1980, Especial, p. 2. Accessed Dec. 17, 2021. http://memoria.bn.br/DocReader /DocReader.aspx?bib=030015_10&hf=bndigital.bn.gov .br&pagfis=4715.

— "Notas teológicas da igreja na base." In Sergio Torres, ed. *A igreja que surge da base*, 207–235. São Paulo: Edições Paulinas, 1982.

— "O socialismo como desafio teológico." *Vozes* 81 (Brazil) 6 (Nov.–Dec. 1988): 687–98.

— "¿Qué es hacer teología desde América Latina?" *Liberación y cautiverio: Debates en torno al método de la teología en América Latina—Encuentro latinoamericano de teología, México, agosto 1975*, edited by Enrique D. Dussel and Enrique Ruiz Maldonado, eds., 129–54. Mexico: n.p., 1976.

— *São Francisco de Assis: Ternura e vigor*. Petrópolis: Editora Vozes, 1985.

— Statement. In *Theology in the Americas*, edited by Sergio Torres and John Eagleson, 294–98. Maryknoll, N.Y.: Orbis Books, 1976.

— "Theological Characteristics of a Grassroots Church." In *The Challenge of the Basic Christian Communities*, edited by Sergio Torres and John Eagleson. Maryknoll, N.Y.: Orbis Books, 1981.

— "The Originality of the Theology of Liberation." In *The Future of Liberation Theology*, edited by Marc H. Ellis and Otto Maduro, 38–48.

— and Clodovis Boff. *Como fazer teologia da libertação*. Petrópolis: Editora Vozes, 1986.

Bojorge, Horacio. *Teologías deicidas: El pensamiento de Juan Luis Segundo en su contexto—Reexamen, informe crítico, evaluación*. 2nd ed. Montevideo: Centro Cultural Católico, 2011. Accessed Nov. 28, 2021. https://fdocuments.ec/reader /full/horacio-bojorge-teologias-deicidas.

Boldrini, Lucia. "Confissões amorosas de um padre." *Revista da Folha* (Nov. 21, 1993): 17–21. https://acervo.folha.com.br// leitor.do?numero=12249&anchor=5677787&pd=3c02bcb 9636944ce5e90c62aaaf92363.

Bonino, José Míguez. "Fundamental Questions in Ecclesiology." In *The Challenge of the Basic Christian Communities*, edited by Sergio Torres and John Eagleson. Maryknoll, N.Y.: Orbis Books, 1981.

Bosco, Teresio. *Don Bosco: una biografia nuova*. Turin: Elledici, 1998. Accessed Dec. 28, 2021. http://donboscowest.org/sites/default/files /resources/Don_Bosco_Una-Biografia-Nuova_Teresio -Bosco_SDB.pdf.

Bouchard, Giorgio. *Pio IX, un papa contro il risorgimento*. Turin: Claudiana, 2001.

Bourget, Paul. *Le démon du midi*. Paris: Librairie Plon, 1914.

Boyte, Harry C. *The Backyard Revolution: Understanding the New Citizen Movement*. Philadelphia: Temple University Press, 1981.

Bradford, Mel E. *A Better Guide Than Reason: Studies in the American Revolution*. La Salle, Ill.: Sherwood Sugden & Company, 1983.

— *Remembering Who We Are: Observations of a Southern Conservative*. Athens, Ga.: University of Georgia Press, 1985.

Brandão, Carlos Rodrigues. *O que é o método Paulo Freire*. São Paulo: Editora Brasiliense, 1981.

Brandmüller, Walter. *Galilei e la chiesa, ossia il diritto ad errare*. Vatican: Libreria Editrice Vaticana, 1992.

— and E.J. Greipl, eds. *Copernico, Galilei e la chiesa: Fine della controversia (1820) gli atti del sant'uffizio*. Florence: Olschki, 1992.

Braudel, Fernand. *The Perspective of the World*. Vol. 3, *Civilization and Capitalism 15th–18th Century*. Translated by Sian Reynolds. New York: Harper & Row Publishers, 1984.

Braunthal, Julius. *Geschichte der internationale*. Berlin-Bonn: Dietz Nachf Verlag, 1978.

Brazilian Society for the Defense of Tradition, Family, Property—T.F.P. "Reverente e filial mensagem a Sua Santidade o Papa Paulo VI." *Catolicismo*, nos. 212–214 (Aug./Oct. 1968). Accessed Apr. 4, 2021. https://pliniocorreadeoliveira.info/1968_212 -214_CAT_Reverente_e_filial_mensagem.htm.

Brazzoli, Luigi. *Papa Paolo VI: Tormento e grandezza di un'anima*. Milan: C.O.G.E.D., 1978.

Brentano, Lujo. *Die christlich soziale bewegung in England*. Leipzig: Dunke & Humboldt, 1883.

Bressolette, Claude. *L'Abbé Maret: le combat d'un théologien pour une démocratie chrétienne, 1830–1851*. Paris: Beauchesne, 1977.

Bricourt, J., ed. *Dictionnaire pratique des connaissances religieuses*. Paris: Letouzey et Ané, 1926.

Brighenti, Agenor, ed. *La teología de la liberación en prospectiva*. 2 vols. Montevideo: Amerindia, 2012.

Brissaud, André. "Après l'encyclique de Pie XII, le dialogue avec les catholiques est-il encore possible?" *Combat*, Aug. 24, 1950. In *La Documentation Catholique*, no. 1079 (Oct. 8, 1950), 1299–301.

Broderick, Francis L. "John A. Ryan." In *New Catholic Encyclopedia*. 2nd ed. 12:445–46. Accessed Oct. 10, 2021, https://cvdvn.files .wordpress.com/2018/05/new-catholic-encyclopedia-vol-12.pdf.

— *Right Reverend New Dealer: John A. Ryan*. New York: The Macmillan Company, 1963.

Brophy, Mary Liguori. *The Social Thought of the German Roman Catholic Central Verein*. Washington, D.C.: The Catholic University of America Press, 1941.

Browne, Henry J. *The Catholic Church and the Knights of Labor*. New York: Arno Press, 1976.

Bruneau, Thomas C. *The Political Transformation of the Brazilian Catholic Church*. Cambridge, U.K.: Cambridge University Press, 1974.

Buonaiuti, Ernesto. *Alfredo Loisy*. Rome: A.F. Formiggini, 1925.

— *Lettere di un prete modernista*. Rome: Libreria Editrice Romana, 1908. Accessed Feb. 2, 2022. https://archive.org/details/MN5173ucmf_7 /mode/2up.

Buonarroti, Filippo. *Gracchus Babeuf et la conspiration des égaux*. Paris: Armand le Chevalier, 1830.

Burke, Edmund. *Reflections on the Revolution in France*. N.p.: n.p., 1790. Accessed Sept. 19, 2021, https://socialsciences.mcmaster.ca/econ /ugcm/3ll3/burke/revfrance.pdf.

Busi, Michele, Roberto de Mattei, Antonio Lanza, and Flavio Peloso. *Don Orione negli anni del modernismo*. Milan: Jaca Book, 2002.

Buttiglione, Rocco. *Dialettica e nostalgia: La scuola di Francoforte e l'ultimo Horkheimer*. Milan: Jaca Book, 1978.

— *La crisi dell'economia marxista: Gli inizi della scuola di Francoforte*. Rome: Studium, 1979.

Cano, Melchor. *De locis theologicis*, edited by Juan Belda Plans. Madrid: Biblioteca de Autores Cristianos, 2006. Accessed Apr. 4, 2021. https://www.documentacatholicaomnia.eu/03d/1509-1560 ,_Cano_Melchior,_De_Locis_Theologicis,_LT.pdf.

Cantera Montenegro, Santiago. "Fray Victorino Rodríguez, O.P., Un teólogo clarividente: A los diez anos de su muerte." *Verbo* (Madrid), nos. 453–454 (2007): 207–17.

Cardenal, Fr. Ernesto. Interview "A igreja do padre Cardenal." *O Estado de S. Paulo*, Jan. 17, 1979, p. 6. Accessed Oct. 7, 2021. https://acervo .estadao.com.br/pagina/#!/19790117-31854-nac-0006-999 -6-not/.

Carpin, A. *Il sacramento dell'ordine: Dalla teologia isidoriana alla teologia tomista*. Bologna: E.S.D., 1988.

Cascino, Maria Vittoria, and Lorenzo Podestà. *Dalla croce alla stella: Novembre 1969, i fondatori delle Brigate Rosse nei locali della Curia Vescovile*. Turin: Bradipolibri Editore, 2009.

Castellani, Armando. *Il beato Leonardo Murialdo*. 2 vols. Rome: Tipografia S. Pio X, 1966–1967.

Casula, Carlo Felice. *Cattolici comunisti e sinistra cristiana 1938–1945*. Bologna: Il Mulino, 1976.

— *Le ACLI: Una bella storia italiana*. Rome: Anicia, 2008.

Catechism of the Catholic Church. Accessed May 13, 2021. https://www .vatican.va/archive/ENG0015/_INDEX.HTM.

Cavagna, Alfredo Maria, ed. *La parola del papa su l'Azione Cattolica*. 3rd ed. Milan: Società Editrice Vita e Pensiero, 1936.

Cenci, Pio. *Il cardinale Raffaelle Merry del Val*. Rome-Turin: Roberto Berruti Editore, 1933.

Centro di Studi Filosofici di Gallarate. *Enciclopedia filosofica*. 4 vols. Venice-Rome: Istituto per la Collaborazione Culturale, 1957.

Charlier, Louis. *Essai sur le problème théologique*. Ramgal Thuillies, 1938.

Cheng, Patrick S. *Radical Love: An Introduction to Queer Theology*. New York: Church Publishing, 2011.

Chenu, Marie-Dominique. Introduction to *Quando un gruppo diventa chiesa*, by Antonio Fallico. Rome: La Roccia, 1974.

— "Les signes des temps." *Nouvelle Revue Théologique* 87, no. 1 (Jan. 1965): 29–39.

— "Libération politique et messianisme religieux." *Parole et Mission*, no. 19 (Oct. 15, 1962): 529–42.

— "The History of Salvation and the Historicity of Man in the Renewal of Theology." In *Renewal of Religious Thought: Proceedings of the Congress on the Theology of the Renewal of the Church Centenary of Canada, 1867–1967*, edited by L.K. Shook, C.S.B., 153–66. New York: Herder and Herder, 1968.

— *Une école de théologie: Le Saulchoir*. Kain-lez-Tournai: Le Saulchoir, 1937.

Cherry, Conrad. *God's New Israel*. Englewood Cliffs, N.J.: Prentice-Hall, 1971.

Chevalier, Jean, ed. *Les religions: Les dictionnaires du savoir moderne*. Paris: Centre d'étude et de promotion de la lecture, 1972.

Chiettini, Emanuele. "Americanismo." In *E.C.*, 1:1054–56. Accessed Nov. 26, 2021. https://archive.org/details/enciclopedia -cattolica-vol.-1/page/n643/mode/2up.

Chilean Society for the Defense of Tradition, Family, and Property (Studies Commission). *The Church of Silence in Chile: The TFP Proclaims the Whole Truth*. New York: Lumen Mariae Publications, 1976.

— "Verdugos de los católicos rusos se levantan en favor de la jerarquía eclesiástica chilena." *Las Ultimas Noticias* (Santiago), Feb. 28, 1976.

Chossat, S.J., Marcel. "Modernisme: Foi et dogme." *D.A.F.C.*, 3:618–37. Accessed Nov. 26, 2021. https://archive.org/details /dictionnaireapol03aluoft/page/313/mode/2up.

Christians for Socialism. Final communiqué, International Conference of Christians for Socialism (Quebec, April 13, 1975). Yves Vaillancourt, "La première rencontre internationale des chrétiens pour le socialisme." *Relations* 35, no. 405 (June 1975), 174–76. Accessed Nov. 30, 2021. https:// mcsq.ca/a/public/mcsq/fichiers/202012/relations1975 chretienssocialisme.pdf.

Citterio, Raffaelle. "Hillary, Obama e il maestro Alinsky." *Radici Cristiane*, no. 32 (Feb.–Mar. 2008), 12–14.

Civardi, Luigi. *Compendio di storia dell'Azione Cattolica italiana*. Rome: Coletti, 1956.

Clark, J. Michael. *A Place to Start: Toward an Unapologetic Gay Liberation Theology*. Monument, Colo.: Monument Publishing, 1989.

Clarke, S.J., Thomas E. "A New Way: Reflecting on Experience." In *Tracing the Spirit: Communities, Social Action, and Theological Reflection*, edited by James E. Hug, S.J., 13–37. New York: Paulist Press, 1983.

Cleary, J.M. *Catholic Social Action in Britain 1909–1959: A History of the Catholic Social Guild*. Oxford: Catholic Social Guild, 1961.

Clement I, Saint. *Letter to the Corinthians*, trans. John Keith. In *Ante-Nicene Fathers*, vol. 9, ed. Allan Menzies. Buffalo, N.Y.: Christian Literature Publishing Co., 1896. Rev. ed. for New Advent by Kevin Knight. Accessed May 5, 2021. http://www .newadvent.org/fathers/1010.htm.

Cobben, Paul, and P. Crusyusberghis, eds. *Hegel-lexikon*. Darmstadt: Wissenschaftliche Buchgesellschaft, 2006.

Comblin, Joseph. "What Sort of Service Might Theology Render." In *Frontiers of Theology in Latin America*, edited by Rosino Gibellini. Translated by John Drury, 58–78. Maryknoll, N.Y.: Orbis Books, 1979.

Comby, Jean. "Liberdade, igualdade, fraternidade: Princípios para uma nação e para uma igreja." *Concilium* 221, no. 1 (1989).

Comstock, Gary David. *Gay Theology Without Apology*. Eugene, Ore.: Wipf & Stock, 2009.

Cone, James H. *A Black Theology of Liberation*. Maryknoll, N.Y.: Orbis Books, 1987.

— "Black Theology: Its Origin, Method and Relation to Third World Theologies." In *Churches in Struggle: Liberation Theology and Social Change in North America*, edited by William K. Tabb, 32–45. New York: Monthly Review Press, 1986.

— *God of the Oppressed*. Maryknoll, N.Y.: Orbis Books, 1997.

— "Martin Luther King, Jr., and the Third World." In *The Future of Liberation Theology: Essays in Honor of Gustavo Gutiérrez*, edited by Marc H. Ellis and Otto Maduro, 346–57. Maryknoll, N.Y.: Orbis Books, 1989.

— *The Spirituals and the Blues: An Interpretation*. Maryknoll, N.Y.: Orbis Books, 1992.

— and Gayraud S. Wilmore, eds. *Black Theology: A Documentary History, 1966-1979*. 2nd ed. rev. Maryknoll, N.Y.: Orbis Books, 1993.

Conferencia Episcopal de Acción Social (C.E.A.S.), ed. *Signos de renovación: Recopilación de documentos post-conciliares de la iglesia en América Latina (1966–1969)*. Lima: C.E.A.S., 1969.

Conferencia Episcopal Peruana. *Constructor de la civilización del amor: Mensajes de S.S. Juan Pablo II, 14–16 de mayo de 1988, Lima-Perú*. Lima: Conferencia Episcopal Peruana, 1988.

Conferência Nacional dos Bispos do Brasil—C.N.B.B. "1ª Assembléia Nacional de Pastoral Indigenista: Em debate a situação indígena em nível nacional." *Boletim do CIMI* 4, no. 22 (Jul.–Aug. 1975).

Congar, Yves. *Journal d'un thèologien 1946–1956*. Edited by Etienne Fouilloux. Paris: Editions du Cerf, 2001.

— *La parole et le souffle*. Paris: Desclée, 1983.

— *Situation et tâches présentes de la théologie*. Paris: Éditions du Cerf, 1967.

— *True and False Reform in the Church*. Translated by Paul Philibert. Collegeville, Minn.: Liturgical Press, 2011.

— *Un peuple messianique: Salut et liberation*. Paris: Les Éditions du Cerf, 1975.

Congregation for the Doctrine of the Faith, Sacred. *Doctrinal Assessment of the Leadership Conference of Women Religious* (Apr. 18, 2012). http://www.vatican.va/roman_curia /congregations/cfaith/documents/rc_con_cfaith _doc_20120418_assessment-lcwr_en.html.

— *Instruction on Certain Aspects of the Theology of Liberation* (Aug. 6, 1984). www.vatican.va/roman_curia/congregations/cfaith /documents/rc_con_cfaith_doc_19840806_theology -liberation_en.html.

— *Instruction on Christian Freedom and Liberation* (Mar. 22, 1986). http://www.vatican.va/roman_curia/congregations /cfaith/documents/rc_con_cfaith_doc_19860322_freedom -liberation_en.html.

— "Notification on the book 'Church: Charism and Power' by Father Leonardo Boff O.F.M." http://www .vatican.va/roman_curia/congregations/cfaith/documents /rc_con_cfaith_doc_19850311_notif-boff_en.html.

— *The Message of Fatima* (June 26, 2000). http://www.vatican.va /roman_curia/congregations/cfaith/documents/rc_con_cfaith _doc_20000626_message-fatima_en.html.

Consejo Episcopal Latinoamericano. *La iglesia en la actual transformación de América Latina a la luz del concilio*. Bogotá: Secretariado General del C.E.L.A.M., 1968.

Constantin, C. "Libéralisme catholique." In *D.T.C.*, 9:506– 629. Accessed Nov. 26, 2021. https://archive.org/details /dictionnairedet09vaca/page/252/mode/2up.

Cooper, David, ed. Introduction to *Dialectics of Liberation*, by S. Carmichael, et al., 9–10. London: Verso Books, 1968.

Cordovani, Mariano. "Il primato della teologia." *Angelicum*, no. 26 (1946): 105–14.

— "Per la vitalità della teologia." *Angelicum* 17 (1940): 385–96.

— "Veritè et nouveauté en thèologie." *Documentation Catholique* (Apr. 1948): 525–28.

Corrêa de Oliveira, Plinio. "A dinamite de Cristo." *O Legionário*, no. 321 (Nov. 5, 1938). Accessed Apr. 23, 2021. https://pliniocorreadeoliveira .info/LEG_381105_Jackson_de_Figueiredo.htm#.YIM76R9KiUk.

— *A Igreja frente a escalada da ameaça comunista: Apelo aos bispos silenciosos*. São Paulo: Editora Vera Cruz, 1977. Accessed Dec. 21, 2021. https://www .pliniocorreadeoliveira.info/Escalada_197606_igreja_silencio_chile .htm#.YcJFZ8nMKUk.

— "A mangueira, o desejo e o dever." *Folha de S. Paulo*, Dec. 10, 1984. Accessed May 8, 2021. https://www.pliniocorreadeoliveira.info /FSP_841210_teologia_da_libertacao.htm#.YJbuMR9KiUk.

— *A propriedade privada e a livre iniciativa no tufão agro-reformista*. São Paulo: Editora Vera Cruz, 1985.

— Gustavo Antonio Solimeo, and Luiz Sergio Solimeo. *As CEBs, das quais muito se fala, pouco se conhece: A TFP as descreve como são*. São Paulo: Editora Vera Cruz, 1982.

— *Autogestion socialiste: Les têtes tombent à l'entreprise, à la maison, à l'école*. Paris: Tradition Famille Propriété, 1983.

— "'Hipoteca social': Só grava a propriedade? A mensagem de Puebla: notas e comentários—V (final)." *Folha de S. Paulo*, May 19, 1979. Accessed May 8, 2021. https://www.pliniocorreadeoliveira.info /FSP%2079-05-19%20A%20mensagem%20V.htm#.YJbs9x9KiUk.

— *Il crepuscolo artificiale del Cile cattolico*. Piacenza: Cristianità, 1973.

— *In Defense of Catholic Action*. Spring Grove, Penn.: The American Society for the Defense of Tradition, Family, and Property, 2006. Accessed Apr. 19, 2021. http://www.pliniocorreadeoliveira.info /UK_1943_INDEFENSEOFCATHOLICACTION.pdf.

— *Indian Tribalism: The Communist-Missionary Ideal for Brazil in the Twenty-First Century*. Accessed May 1, 2021. https://www.tfp.org/indian-tribalism-the-communist-missionary -ideal-for-brazil-in-the-twenty-first-century/.

— *Innocenza primordiale e contemplazione sacrale dell'universo*. Siena: Cantagalli, 2013.

— "Kamikaze." In *Folha de S. Paulo*, Feb. 15, 1969. Accessed Apr. 21, 2021. https://pliniocorreadeoliveira.info/FSP%20 69-02-15%20Kamikaze.htm.

— "Mystici Corporis Christi." *O Legionário*, no. 585 (Oct. 24, 1943). Accessed Apr. 26, 2021. https://pliniocorreadeoliveira .info/LEG%20431024_MysticiCorporisChristi.htm.

— "Na 'noite sandinista,' incitamento à guerrilha dirigido por sandinistas 'cristãos' à esquerda catolica no Brasil e na América espanhola." *Catolicismo* (Brazil), 355–356 (July–Aug. 1980). Accessed May 6, 2021. https://www.pliniocorreadeoliveira .info/Noite%20Sandinista_198008.pdf.

— *Nobility and Analogous Traditional Elites in the Allocutions of Pius XII: A Theme Illuminating American Social History*. York, Penn.: The American Society for the Defense of Tradition, Family, and Property, 1993. http://www.tfp.org/tfp-home/books /nobility.html. — *Note sul concetto di cristianità: Carattere spirituale e sacrale della società temporale e sua "ministerialità."* Palermo: Thule, 1998.

— "O coração do sábio está onde há tristeza." *Catolicismo*, no. 85 (Jan. 1985). Accessed Dec. 21, 2021. https://www .pliniocorreadeoliveira.info/1958_085_CAT_O _cora%C3%A7%C3%A3o_do_s%C3%A1bio.htm.

— "Pela grandeza e liberdade da Ação Católica." *O Legionário* (São Paulo), no. 331, Jan. 15, 1939. Accessed Apr. 21, 2021. https:// pliniocorreadeoliveira.info/LEG%20390115_PELAGRANDEZAE LIBERDADEDAA%C3%87%C3%83OCAT%C3%93LICA .htm.

— Preface to *Frei, o Kerensky chileno*, by Fábio Vidigal Xavier da Silveira, 3–6. 2nd ed. São Paulo: Editora Vera Cruz, 1967. Accessed Nov. 28, 2021. https://www.pliniocorreadeoliveira.info/PRE_67_Frei_o _Kerenski_chileno.htm#.YaQDjVXMKUk.

— "Raio, vaga-lume, silêncio." *Folha de S. Paulo*, Dec. 29, 1979. Accessed May 8, 2021. https://www.pliniocorreadeoliveira.info /FSP_791229_raio_vaga_lume_silencio.htm#.Yb5Eo8nMKUk.

— *Revolution and Counter-Revolution*. 3rd ed. York, Penn.: The American Society for the Defense of Tradition, Family, and Property, 1993. Accessed Apr. 8, 2021. https://www.tfp.org /revolution-and-counter-revolution/.

— "The Twentieth Century Crusade." Accessed Apr. 30, 2021. https:// pliniocorreadeoliveira.info/UK_195101_TheTwentiethCentury Crusade.htm.

— *Unperceived Ideological Transshipment and Dialogue*. Accessed Apr. 7, 2021. http://www.tfp.org/tfp-home/books/unperceived -ideological-transshipment-and-dialogue.html.

— *What Does Self-Managing Socialism Mean for Communism: A Barrier? Or a Bridgehead?* http://www.tfp.org/tfp-home/books/the-double -game-of-french-socialism-gradual-in-strategy-radical-in-goal .html.

— and Carlos Patricio del Campo. *No Brasil: A reforma agrária leva a miséria ao campo e à cidade—TFP: informa, analisa, alerta*. São Paulo: Art Press, 1986.

— *Sou católico, posso ser contra a reforma agrária?* São Paulo: Art Press, 1981.

Cort, John C. *Christian Socialism: An Informal History*. Maryknoll, N.Y.: Orbis Books, 1988.

Cottier, Georges. *Chrétiens et marxistes: Dialogue avec Roger Garoudy*. Tours: Mame, 1967.

Council of Trent. Canon on the sacrament of Holy Orders. In D.H. (no. 1776).

— *Decree Concerning the Canonical Scriptures and the Traditions to be Upheld*. Accessed Apr. 26, 2021. https://en.wikisource.org/wiki/Canons_and_Decrees_of_the_Council_of_Trent/Session_IV/Canonical_Scriptures. In D.H. (no. 1501).

Courtois, Stéphane, Nicolas Werth, Jean-Louis Panné, Andrzej Paczkowski, Karel Bartošek, Jean-Louis Margolin, eds. *The Black Book of Communism: Crimes, Terror, Repression.* Translated by Jonathan Murphy and Mark Kramer. Cambridge, Mass.: Harvard University Press, 1999.

Cousiño Vicuña, Angela, and María Angélica Ovalle Gana. *Reforma agraria chilena: Testimonios de sus protagonistas*. Santiago: Memoriter, 2013.

Cox, C.B. *Education: The Next Decade*. London: Conservative Political Centre, 1981.

Crépon, ed., Joseph. *Lettres du R.P.H.-D. Lacordaire a Théophile Foisset*. 2 vols. Paris: Librairie Poussielgue Freres, 1886. Accessed Feb. 5, 2022. https://archive.org/details/lettresdurphdlac02laco/mode/2up.

Crétineau-Joly, Jacques. *Histoire de la Vendée militaire*. 5 vols. Paris: Pays & Terroirs, 1895.

— *L'église romaine en face de la révolution*. 2 vols. Paris: Henri Plon, 1859.

Cristiani, L. "Unitariens." In *D.T.C.*, 15-2e.:2162–72. Accessed Nov. 26, 2021. https://archive.org/details/dictionnairedetv15pt2vaca.

Croatto, José Severino. *Hermenêutica bíblica: Para uma teoria da leitura como produção de significado*. São Paulo: Paulinas-Sinodal, 1986.

Cross, Robert D. *The Emergence of Liberal Catholicism in America*. Chicago: Quadrangle Paperbacks, 1968.

Cuminetti, Mario, ed. *La fine della chiesa come società perfetta*. Milan: I.D.O.C.-Mondadori, 1968.

Dabry, Pierre. *Les catholiques républicains*. Paris: Chevalier et Rivière, 1905.

d'Addio, Mario. *Considerazioni sui processi a Galileo*. Rome: Herder, 1985.

d'Alès, Adhémar, ed. *Dictionnaire apologétique de la foi catholique* (*D.A.F.C.*). 5 vols. Paris: Gabriel Beauchesne, 1922.

Dal Pane, L. "Antonio Labriola e Romolo Murri." In *Scritti di sociologia e politica in onore di Luigi Sturzo*, edited by Istituto Luigi Sturzo. 3 vols. Bologna: Nicola Zanichelli Editore, 1953.

Dal Toso, Paola, and Ernesto Diaco. *Mario Fani e Giovanni Acquaderni: Profilo e scritti dei fondatori dell'Azione Cattolica*. Rome: AVE, 2008.

Daly, Mary. *Per una filosofia della liberazione della donna*. Rome: Editori Riuniti, 1990 .

— The Qualitative Leap Beyond Patriarchal Religion." *Quest* 1, no. 4 (Spring 1975): 20–40.

Damico, Linda H. *The Anarchist Dimension of Liberation Theology*. Eugene, Ore.: Wipf andStock Publishers, 1987.

Daniélou, Jean. *Essai sur le mystère de l'histoire*. Paris: Seuil, 1953.

Dansette, Adrien. *Destin du catholicisme français 1926–1956*. Paris: Flammarion, 1957.

— *Histoire religieuse de la France contemporaine. De la révolution à la troisième république*. Paris: Flammarion, 1948.

— *Religious History of Modern France*. Translated by John Dingle. 2 vols. New York: Herder and Herder, 1961.

da Silva, Luiz Inácio "Lula". "Carta de Lula às CEBs." *CNBB*, Jul. 19, 2005. Accessed Jan. 15, 2022. https://www.cnbb.org.br/carta-de-lula-as-cebs/.

Day, Dorothy. Preface to *Camilo Torres: Priest and Revolutionary; Political Programme and Messages to the Colombian People*. Edited by John Alvarez Garcia and Christian Restrepo Calle. Translated by Virginia M. O'Grady. London: Sheed and Ward, 1968.

Day, Mark. *Forty Acres: Cesar Chavez and the Farm Workers*. New York: Praeger Publishers, 1971.

De Antonellis, Giacomo. *Storia dell'Azione Cattolica dal 1867 a oggi*. Milan: Rizzoli, 1987.

de Bortoli, Ferruccio. "Benedetto XVI non è una statua: Partecipa alla vita della Chiesa." *Corriere Della Sera*. Mar. 4, 2014. https://www.corriere.it/cronache/14_marzo_04/vi-racconto-mio-primo-anno-papa-90f8a1c4-a3eb-11e3-b352-9ec6f8a34ecc.shtml.

de Corlieu, Cécile. *Carnets d'une chrétienne moderniste*. Toulouse: Privat, 1970.

de Fabrègues, Jean. *Le Sillon de Marc Sangnier: Un tournant majeur du mouvement social catholique*. Paris: Libraire Académique Perrin, 1964.

Dégert, Antoine. "Félicité Robert de Lamennais." *The Catholic Encyclopedia*. Vol. 8. New York: Robert Appleton Company, 1910. Accessed Apr. 18, 2021. http://www.newadvent.org/cathen/08762a.htm.

de la Brière, Yves. "Pouvoir pontifical dans l'ordre temporel." In *D.A.F.C.*, 4:94–115. https://gallica.bnf.fr/ark:/12148/bpt6k5730049r/f1.item.

de la Cierva, Ricardo. *La teología de la liberación desenmascarada*. Barcelona: Plaza y Janés, 1986.

— *Oscura rebelión en la Iglesia*. Barcelona: Plaza y Janés, 1987.

Delassus, Henri. *La condamnation du modernisme social dans la censure du Sillon*. Cambrai: Desclée de Brouwer, 1910.

— *L'esprit familiale dans la maison, dans la cité et dans l'état*. Lille: Desclée de Brouwer, 1910.

de la Tour du Pin, René. *Vers un ordre social chrétien*. Paris: Éditions du Trident, 1987.

de la Tour du Pin Gouvernet, Lucie. *Mémoires de la marquise de la Tour du Pin*. Paris: Mercure de France, 1979.

Delatte, Dom Paul. *Dom Guéranger: Abbé de Solesmes*. Paris: Plon-Nourrit, 1909.

del Campo, Carlos Patricio. *Is Brazil Sliding Towards the Extreme Left? Notes on the Land Reform Program in South America's Largest and Most Populous Country*. Pleasantville, N.Y.: The American Society for the Defense of Tradition, Family, and Property, 1986.

de Lella, Cayetano. *Cristianismo y liberación en América Latina*. Mexico City: Ediciones Nuevomar, 1984.

Delmont, Théodore. *Modernisme et modernistes: En Italie, en Allemagne, en Angleterre, et en France*. Paris: P. Lethielleux, 1909. Accessed Dec. 16, 2021. http://www.liberius.net/livres/Modernisme_et_modernistes_000000717.pdf.

del Noce, Augusto. *Il cattolico comunista*. Milan: Rusconi, 1981.

de Lubac, Henri. *Catholicism: A Study of Dogma in Relation to the Corporate Destiny of Mankind*. Translated by Lancelot C. Sheppard. New York: Sheed and Ward, Inc., 1958. Accessed Dec. 5, 2021. https://archive.org/details/catholicismstudy0000luba/mode/2up.

— *La posterité spirituelle de Joachim de Fiore*. 2 vols. Paris: Le Sycomore, 1979–1981.

de Mattei, Roberto. *Il centro che ci portò a sinistra*. Rome: Edizioni Fiducia, 1994.

— *Il concilio Vaticano II. Una storia mai scritta*. Turin: Lindau, 2010.

— *Pio IX e la rivoluzione italiana*. Siena: Cantagalli, 2012.

— *Pius IX*. Translated by John Laughland. Leominster, Herefordshire, U.K.: Gracewing, 2004.

— *The Crusader of the 20th Century:* Plinio Corrêa de Oliveira. Leominster, Herefordshire, U.K.: Gracewing Publishers, 1998.

— *The Second Vatican Council: An Unwritten Story*. Fitzwilliam, N.H.: Loreto Publications, 2012.

Dembski, William, and Edward Sisson. "My 'best education.'" *World*, Oct. 10, 2008. https://world.wng.org/2008/10/my_best_education.

de Menezes Neto, Antonio Julio. *A ética da teologia da libertação e o espírito do socialismo no MST*. Belo Horizonte: F.M.G., 2012.

de Moly, H. "La règlementation du travail en France et les catholiques," *La Réforme sociale* 10 (May 16, 1890): 585–606 in *La Réforme Sociale*, 2e. serie, vol. 9, year 10 (Jan.–Jun. 1890). Paris: Secrétariat de la Société d'Économie Sociale, 1890. Accessed Apr. 12, 2021. https://gallica.bnf.fr/ark:/12148/bpt6k415087t/f604.item.r.

de Mun, Albert. *1888-1891*. Vol. 4, *Discours et Écrits Divers du Comte Albert de Mun*. Paris: Librairie Ch. Poussielgue, 1895.

— *Ma vocation sociale: Souvenirs de la fondation de l'Oeuvre des Cercles Catholiques d'Ouvriers*. Paris: P. Lethielleux, Libraire-Éditeur, 1950. Accessed Aug. 22, 2021. https://gallica.bnf.fr/ark:/12148/bpt6k55600v.pdf.

— *Questions sociales*. Vol. 1 of *Discours du Comte Albert de Mun*. Paris: Librairie Poussielgue Frères, 1888.

de Oliveira Campos, Abel, ed. *Meio século de epopéia anticomunista*. São Paulo: Editora Vera Cruz, 1980.

de Paoli, Luigi. "Camino y propuesta hacia una iglesia nazarena." In *Desafíos Cristianos*, edited by Misión Abierta, 144–55. Madrid: Loguez Ediciones, 1988. Accessed Jan. 29, 2022. https://cupdf.com/document/mision-abierta-desafios-cristianos.html.

Dermience, Alice. "Théologie de la femme et théologie feministe." *Révue théologique de Louvain*, no. 31 (2000): 492–523. Accessed Dec. 27, 2021. https://www.persee.fr/docAsPDF/thlou_0080-2654_2000_num_31_4_3117.pdf.

De Rosa, Gabriele. *Il movimento cattolico in Italia: Dalla restaurazione all'età giolittiana*. Bari: Editori Laterza, 1988.

Deshayes, F. "Américanisme." In *D.T.C.*, 1:1043–49. Accessed Nov. 26, 2021. https://archive.org/details/dictionnairedet01vaca/page/522/mode/2up.

de Solages, Bruno. "Pour l'honneur de la théologie." *Bulletin de Litterature Ecclesiastique*, no. 48 (1947): 65–84.

de Tocqueville, Alexis. *Democracy in America*. Translated by Harvey Mansfield and Delba Winthrop. Chicago: University of Chicago Press, 2002.

de Toledano, Ralph. *Little Cesar*. New York: Anthem Books, 1971.

de Vesins, Bernard "XIIIe congrès d'Action française—Déclarations de Bernard de Vesins, Président de la Ligue d'Action française," *L'Action Française*, Nov. 24, 1926. Accessed Feb. 4, 2022. https://www.retronews.fr/journal/l-action-francaise/24-novembre-1926/4/502269/1.

Díez-Alegría, José María. "¿Cristianismo profético y liberador?" *Misión Abierta* (Madrid) 77, no. 2 (Apr. 1984): 77–82.

Doherty, Robert E. "Thomas Haggerty, the Church, and Socialism." *Labor History* (Winter, 1965): 39–54.

Dombrowski, James. *The Early Days of Christian Socialism in America*. New York: Octagon Books, 1966.

Dosza, Ferenc. "Teologia e populismo." *Tradizione Famiglia Proprietà* (June 2013).

Ducuoq, Charles. "Eschatologie et réalités terrestres." *Lumière et vie*, no. 50 (1960): 4–25.

Dumas, André. *Une théologie de la réalité*. Geneva: Éditions Labor et Fides, 1968.

Duquesne, Jacques. *Un théologien en liberté: Jacques Duquesne interrogue le père Chenu*. Paris: Le Centurion, 1975.

Duroselle, J.B. *Les débuts du catholicisme social en France, 1822–1970*. Paris: Presses Universitaires de France, 1951.

Dussel, Enrique. *Historia de la iglesia en América Latina*. Barcelona: Nova Terra, 1974.

Duval, André. "Aux origines de l'Institut historique d'études thomistes du Saulchoir." *Revue des Sciences philosophiques et théologiques* (1991).

— *Lacordaire et Buchez*, "Idéalisme révolutionnaire et réveil religieux en 1849." *Revue des sciences philosophiques et théologiques* 45 (1961): 422–55.

Echeverria Ruiz, Bernardino Cardinal. "Plinio Corrêa de Oliveira: Distinguished Apostle, Ardent and Intrepid Polemist." TFP.org, Nov. 12, 1995. https://www.tfp.org/plinio-correa-de-oliveira-distinguished-apostle-ardent-and-intrepid-polemist/.

Ecumenical Theology Congress on the "Ecclesiology of the Basic Christian Communities." "Final Document." In *The Challenge of the Basic Christian Communities*, edited by Sergio Torres and John Eagleson. Maryknoll, N.Y.: Orbis Books, 1981.

Elizondo, Virgilio P. *Christianity and Culture*. San Antonio: Mexican American Cultural Center, 1983.

— *Galilean Journey: The Mexican-American Promise*. Maryknoll, N.Y.: Orbis Books, 2000.

— "Mestizaje as a Locus of Theological Reflection." In *The Future of Liberation Theology*, edited by Marc Ellis and Otto Maduro, 358–74.

— *Mestizaje: The Dialectic of Cultural Birth and the Gospel, a Study in the Intercultural Dimension of Evangelization*. 3 vols. in 2. San Antonio: Mexican American Cultural Center, 1978.

Ellacuría, Ignacio. "El auténtico lugar social de la iglesia." In *Desafíos Cristianos*, edited by Misión Abierta, 77–85. Madrid: Loguez Ediciones, 1988. Accessed Jan. 29, 2022. https://cupdf.com/document/mision-abierta-desafios-cristianos.html.

— "Por qué muere Jesús y por qué lo matan." In *Desafíos Cristianos*, edited by Misión Abierta, 31–40. Madrid: Loguez Ediciones, 1988. Accessed Jan. 29, 2022. https://cupdf.com/document/mision-abierta-desafios-cristianos.html.

Ellis, John Tracy. "Les États-Unis depuis 1850." In *Nouvelle histoire de l'église*. Vol. 5, *L'église dans le monde moderne*. Paris: Seuil, 1975.

Ellis, Marc H. "Liberation Theology and the Crisis of the Western Society." In *Liberation Theology: The Challenge to U.S. Public Policy*, edited by Richard L. Rubenstein and John K. Roth, 48–70. Washington, D.C.: The Washington Institute Press, 1988. Accessed Nov. 29, 2021. https://archive.org/details/politicsoflatina00rube.

— and Otto Maduro, eds. *The Future of Liberation Theology: Essays in Honor of Gustavo Gutiérrez*. Maryknoll, N.Y.: Orbis Books, 1989. Accessed Jan. 16, 2022. https://archive.org/details/futureofliberati0000unse.

Ellul, Jacques. *Changer de révolution: L'inéluctable prolétariat*. Paris: Seuil, 1982.

Engels, Friedrich. *Origin of the Family, Private Property and the State*. Translated by Alick West. Accessed Mar. 24, 2021. https://www.marxists.org/archive/marx/works/download/pdf/origin_family.pdf.

— "The Movements of 1847." In *Marx and Engels 1845–48*. Vol. 6, *Collected Works*, by Karl Marx and Frederick Engels, 520–29. Lawrence & Wishart Electric Book, 2010. Accessed Sept. 19, 2021. http://www.koorosh-modaresi.com/MarxEngels/V6.pdf.

Ente per l'Enciclopedia Cattolica e per i Libro Cattolico, Soc. p. a. *Enciclopedia cattolica*. 12 vols. Vatican: Ente per l'Enciclopedia Cattolica e per i Libro Cattolico, Soc. p. a., 1948–1954.

Escholier, Marc. *Lacordaire ou Dieu et la liberté*. Paris: Éditions Fleurus, 1959.

Esmazières, Agnès. "Agostino Gemelli e gli intellettuali cattolici francesi nel secondo dopoguerra: La 'nouvelle théologie' vista da Milano (1946–1951)." *Annali di storia moderna e contemporanea*, no. 13 (2007): 159–92.

Esposito, Rosario Francesco. *Pio IX: La chiesa in conflitto col mondo—La S. Sede, la massoneria e il radicalismo settario*. Rome: Edizioni Paoline, 1979.

Esteban, A. Avelino. "Nota bibliográfica sobre la llamada 'teología nueva." *Revista Española de Teología*, no. 36 (July–Sept. 1949): 527–46.

Estermann, Josef, ed. *Teología andina*. 2 vols. La Paz, Bolivia: Instituto Superior Ecuménico Andino de Teología (I.S.E.A.T.)/ Plural Editores, 2006.

Fabro, Cornelio. "Immanenza." In *E.C.*, 6:1673–80. Accessed Nov. 26, 2021. https://archive.org/details/enciclopedia-cattolica-vol.-6/page /n971/mode/2up.

Falconi, Carlo. *Gedda e l'Azione Cattolica*. Florence: Parenti, 1958.

Fanello, Gabriella. *Storia della FUCI*. Rome: Editrice Studium, 1971.

Faraone, Joan. *The evolution of the Secretariat of Hispanic Affairs of NCCB/USCCB and its Contribution to Catechesis of Hispanos/ Latinos in the United States*. Graduation thesis, Catholic University of America, 2009.

Farges, A. "Modernisme: Synthèse du modernisme philosophique." In *D.A.F.C.*, 3:637–65. Accessed Nov. 26, 2021. https://archive.org /details/dictionnaireapol03aluoft/page/323/mode/2up.

Farías, Víctor. *Salvador Allende: El fin de un mito—El socialismo entre la obsesión totalitaria y la corrupción; Nuevas revelaciones*. 3rd ed. N.p.: Editorial Maye Ltda., 2007. Accessed Feb. 3, 2022. https://issuu.com/memoriahistoricachile/docs /el_fin_de_un_mito._edicion_final_1.

Fauchet, Claude. "Sermon sur l'accord de la religion et de la liberté" (Paris, Feb. 4, 1791). In *Collection intégrale et universelle des orateurs sacrés*, edited by Jacques Paul Migne, 66:159–74. Paris: Ateliers Catholiques au Petit-Montrouge, 1855. Accessed Dec. 15, 2021. https://archive.org/details/collectionintgra66mign/mode/1up.

Faverzani, Mauro. "I falsi teologi del neomodernismo—Intervista a mons. Antonio Livi." *Radici Cristiane*, no. 79 (Nov. 2012). Accessed Apr. 4, 2021. https://www.radicicristiane.it/2012/11 /attualita-politica-societa/i-falsi-teologi-del-neomodernismo/.

Fernández, Eugenio. "La historia: Un juego que va en serio." In *Desafíos Cristianos*, edited by Misión Abierta, 185–95. Madrid: Loguez Ediciones, 1988. Accessed Jan. 29, 2022. https://cupdf .com/document/mision-abierta-desafios-cristianos.html.

Ferrari, Francesco Luigi. *L'Azione Cattolica e il "regime."* Florence: Parenti, 1952.

Ferrari, Liliana. *L'Azione Cattolica in Italia dalle origini al pontificato di Paolo VI*. Brescia: Editrice Queriniana, 1982.

Fesquet, Henri. "La crise de l'A.C.J.F. repose le problème du rôle des laïcs dans l'église." *Le Monde*, Nov. 27, 1956. In *La Documentation Catholique*, no. 1237 (Oct. 28, 1956), 1398–99.

Finks, P. David. *The Radical Vision of Saul Alinsky*. New York: Paulist Press, 1984.

First Vatican Council. Dogmatic Constitution *Dei Filius*. Accessed Apr. 26, 2021. https://www.papalencyclicals.net/councils /ecum20.htm.

Fisher, Robert. *Let the People Decide: Neighborhood Organizing in America*. Boston: Twayne Publishers, 1984.

Fisichella, Domenico. *La democrazia contro la realtà: Il pensiero politico di Charles Maurras*. Rome: Carocci Editore, 2006.

Fitzsimons, John, and Paul McGuire, ed. *Restoring all Things: A Guide to Catholic Action*. New York: Sheed & Ward, 1938. Accessed Dec. 10, 2021. https://archive.org/details/restoringallthin0000unse/page /n5/mode/2up.

Flori, M. "Intorno al Blondelismo." *La civiltà cattolica* 86, vol. 4, no. 2049 (Nov. 2, 1935): 177–88, and no. 2050 (Nov. 16, 1935): 299–307.

Floristán, Casiano. *La comunidad cristiana de base*. Rev. ed. San Antonio: Mexican American Cultural Center, 1976.

Fogazzaro, Antonio. *The Saint*. Translated by M. Prichard-Agnetti. New York: G.P. Putnam's Sons, 1906. https://archive.org/details /cu31924027679673/page/52/mode/2up.

Foisset, M. *Vie du R.P. Lacordaire*. 2 vols. Paris: Lecoffre Fils et cie., 1870. Accessed Feb. 6, 2022. https://archive.org/details /viedurplacordai00foisgoog/mode/2up.

Foner, Philip Sheldon. *The AFL in the Progressive Era, 1910–1915*. Vol. 5 of *History of the Labor Movement in the United States*. New York: International Publishers, 1980.

Fontaine, André. "En face de certaines tendences doctrinales, l'Encyclique *Humani Generis* réaffirme l'autorité du magistère de l'Église," *Le Monde*, Sept. 2, 1950, in *La Documentation Catholique*, no. 1079 (Oct. 8, 1950), 1297–99.

Fontenelle, René. "Honneur au magistère." *La Croix*, Sept. 7, 1950, in *La Documentation Catholique*, no. 1079 (Oct. 8, 1950), 1295–96.

Fougeyrollas, Pierre. *Marx, Freud et la révolution totale*. Paris: Anthropos, 1972.

Fox, Mary Harrita, and Peter E. Dietz. *Labor Priest*. Notre Dame: University of Notre Dame Press, 1953. Accessed Oct. 9, 2021. https://archive.org/details/peteredietzlabor0000foxm/page /n5/mode/2up.

Fox, Matthew. *Creation Spirituality: Liberating Gifts for the Peoples of the Earth*. San Francisco: Harper, 1991.
　　— *The Coming of the Cosmic Christ, The Healing of Mother Earth and the Birth of a Global Renaissance*. San Francisco: Harper, 1988.

Francis, Pope. "La ricchezza è un bene se aiuta agli altri." Preface to *Povera per i poveri: La missione della Chiesa*, by Gerhard Ludwig Mueller, 5–12. Vatican: Libreria Editrice Vaticana, 2014.

Franzelin, Ioannis Bapt. *Tractatus de divina traditione et scriptura*. Rome: Typis S.C. de Propaganda Fide, 1870.

Frazer, Hamish. "Jacques Maritain and Saul Alinsky: Fathers of Christian Revolution." *Approaches* (1981).

Freire, Paulo. *L'educazione come pratica della libertà*. Milan: Mondadori, 1974.
　　— *Pedagogia dell'autonomia: saperi necessari per la pratica educativa*. Turin: E.G.A., 2004.
　　— *Pedagogy of the Oppressed*. Translated by Myra Bergman Ramos. New York: Continuum, 1982
　　— *Teoria e pratica della liberazione: Testi scelti*. Rome: AVE, 1974.

F.U.C.I. *Coscienza universitaria, fatica del pensare, intelligenza della fede*. Milan: San Paolo, 1996.

Fumet, Stanislas. "Jacques Maritain." *I.C.I.*, no. 432 (May 15, 1973).

Funck-Brentano, Frantz. *The Old Regime in France: The Social Institutions and Traditions of the Eighteenth Century and Their Influence on the Government of the Monarchy*. Translated by Herbert Wilson. London: E. Arnold & Co., 1929.

Fundación Amerindia, ed. *Teología de la liberación en perspectiva*. 2 vols. Montevideo: Amerindia-Doble Clic Editoras, 2012.

Fustel de Coulanges, Numa Denis. *The Ancient City: A Study on the Religion, Laws, and Institutions of Greece and Rome*. Translated by Willard Small. Boston: Lee and Shepard, 1877. Accessed Jan. 18, 2022. https://archive.org/details/cu31924100532054 /page/n3/mode/2up.

Gaiotti de Biase, Paola. *Le origini del movimento cattolico femminile*. Brescia: Morcelliana, 1963.

Galante Garrone, Alessandro. *Filippo Buonarroti e i rivoluzionari dell'ottocento (1828–1837)*. Turin: Einaudi, 1972.

Galeazzi, Umberto. *La teoria critica della scuola di Francoforte: diagnosi della società contemporanea e dialogo critico con il pensiero moderno.* Naples: Edizioni Scientifiche Italiane, 2000.

Gallarati-Scotti, Tommaso. *Vita di Antonio Fogazzaro.* Milan: Baldini & Castoldi, 1920. Accessed Dec. 26, 2021. https://archive.org/details /lavitadiantonio00scotgoog/mode/2up.

Galli della Loggia, Ernesto. "Liberali che non hanno saputo dirsi cristiani," *Il Mulino* 5/93, no. 349: 855–66.

Gambasin, Angelo. *Il clero padovano e la dominazione austriaca 1859–1866.* Rome: Edizioni di Storia e Letteratura, 1967.

Garaudy, Roger. *Perspectives de l'homme: Existentialisme, pensée catholique, marxisme.* Paris: Presses universitaires de France, 1960.

Garcia, Mario T. *Chicano Liberation Theology: The Writings and Documents of Richard Cruz and Católicos por la Raza.* Dubuque: Kenall Hunt, 2009.

Garcia-Nieto Paris, Juan. "Proyecto de una sociedad y una iglesia en clave de utopía." In *Utopia y profetismo,* edited by José Ignacio Gonzales-Faus, 128–54.

Gardeil, Ambroise. *La crédibilité et l'apologétique.* 1908.
— *Le donné révélé et la théologie.* 1915.

Garland Barrón, Alfredo. *Como lobos rapaces: Perú: ¿una iglesia infiltrada?* Lima: Servicio de Análisis Pastoral e Informativo, 1978.

Garrigou-Lagrange, O.P., Réginald. *Dieu: Son existence et sa nature.* Paris: Beauchesne, 1950.
— "La nouvelle théologie, où va-t-elle?" *Angelicum,* no. 23 (1946): 126–45. Accessed Dec. 16, 2021. https://archive.org/details /7NouvelleThologieRefutationsInAngelicum/mode/1up.
— "Verité et immutabilité du dogme." *Angelicum,* no. 24 (1947): 124–39.

Garvey, C.S.B., Edwin C. *Process Theology and Secularization.* Houston: Lumen Christi Press, 1973.

Gaxotte, Pierre. *La révolution française.* Paris: Arthème Fayard, 1962.

Gazier, Augustin. *Études sur l'histoire religieuse de la révolution française, d'après des documents originaux et inédits, depuis la réunion des états généraux jusqu'au directoire.* Paris: A. Colin, 1887.

Gearty, Patrick W. *The Economic Thought of Monsignor John A. Ryan.* Washington, D.C.: The Catholic University of America Press, 1953.

Gebara, Ivone. "Haciendo las conexiones: Encuentro con teólogas eco/feministas." *Con-spirando* 40, no. 2 (June 2002), 46–48.
— *O que é teologia feminista.* São Paulo: Olho d'Agua, 2007.
— Prologue to *Del cielo a la tierra: Una antología de teología feminista,* 15–20. Edited by Mary Judith Ress, Ute Seibert, and Lele Sjorup. Santiago, Chile: Sello Azul, 1997.
— *Teologia ecofeminista: Ensaio para repensar o conhecimento e a religião.* São Paulo: Olho d'Agua, 1997.

Gedda, Luigi. *18 aprile 1948: Memorie dell'artefice della sconfitta del Fronte Popolare.* Milan: Mondadori, 1998.

Geusau, Leo Aalting von. "Revolution and Religion: The Radical Church in Brazil." *Dialectical Anthropology* 3, no. 1 (Feb. 1978): 21–42.

Giammanco, Rosanna M. *The Catholic-Communist Dialogue in Italy: 1944 to the Present.* New York: Praeger, 1989.

Gibbons, James Cardinal. *A Retrospect of Fifty Years.* 2 vols. Baltimore: John Murphy Company, 1916.

Gibellini, Rosino, ed. *Frontiers of Theology in Latin America.* Translated by John Drury. Maryknoll, N.Y.: Orbis Books, 1979.
— *La teologia del XX secolo.* Brescia: Queriniana, 1992.
— *The Liberation Theology Debate.* Translated by John Bowden. Maryknoll, N.Y.: Orbis Books, 1988. Accessed Dec. 5, 2021. https://archive.org /details/liberationtheolo0000gibe/mode/2up.

Gigante, Valerio. "Cosa resta del concilio? (Una mappa ragionata dell'altrachiesa)." *MicroMega,* no. 7 (2012): 3–16.

Gioberti, Vincenzo. *Del primato morale e civile degli italiani.* 2 vols. Brussels: Meline, Cans, 1843.

Giocanti, Stéphane. *Maurras: Le chaos et l'ordre.* Paris: Flammarion, 2006.

Girardi, Giulio. *Amor cristiano y lucha de clases.* E-version, 2000. Accessed Dec. 23, 2021. https://www.ensayistas.org/critica/liberacion/TL /documentos/girardi.pdf.
— *Educare: per quale società?* Udine: Forum, 2008.
— Lecture "Utopía popular y esperanza cristiana." Taped proceedings of Eighth Conference of Theology, Madrid (Sept. 7–11, 1988). T.F.P. Archive.
— *Marxism and Christianity.* Translated by Kevin Traynor. New York: The Macmillan Company, 1968.
— *Marxismo e cristianesimo.* Assisi: Cittadella, 1977.
— "Possibilità di una teologia europea della liberazione." *IDOC Internazionale* (Rome) 1 (1983): 30–48.
— "Utopía popular y esperanza cristiana." In *Utopía y profetismo,* edited by José María González Faus.

Giuntella, Maria Cristina. *La FUCI tra modernismo, partito popolare e fascismo.* Rome: Edizioni Studium, 2000.

Gobierno del Perú/Presidencia del Consejo de Ministros. *Evolución de la pobreza en el Perú al 2010.* Edited by Aníbal Sanchez Aguilar. Lima: Instituto Nacional de Estatística e Informática, 2012.

Golden, Renny, and Michael McConnell. *Sanctuary: The New Underground Railroad.* Maryknoll, N.Y.: Orbis Books, 1986.

Gombin, Richard. *Les origines du gauchisme.* Paris: Seuil, 1971.

Gomes de Souza, Luiz Alberto. *A JUC: Os estudantes católicos e a política.* Petrópolis: Editora Vozes, 1984.

Gonzalez, Marcelo. *La reflexión teológica en la Argentina, 1962–2004: Apuntes para un mapa de sus relaciones y desafíos hacia el futuro.* Córdoba: Universidad Católica de Córdoba, 2005.

González Faus, José María, ed. *Utopia y profetismo: VIII Congreso de Teología.* Madrid: Evangelio y Liberación, 1989.

González Guerrero, Andrés. *A Chicano Theology.* Maryknoll, N.Y.: Orbis Books, 1987.

Gorz, André. *Réforme et révolution.* Paris: Seuil, 1969.

Goss, Robert E. *Jesus Acted Up: A Gay and Lesbian Manifesto.* San Francisco: Harper, 1994.
— *Take Back the Word: A Queer Reading of the Bible.* Boston: The Pilgrim Press, 2000.

Gramsci, Antonio. *Il Vaticano e l'Italia.* Edited by Elsa Fubini. Rome: Editori Riuniti, 1974.

Granderath, Theodor. *Histoire du concile du Vatican depuis sa première annonce jusqu'à sa prorogation d'après les documents authentiques.* 5 vols. Brussels: Librarie Albert Dewit, 1913.

Gras, Yves. *Castelnau ou l'art de commander.* Paris: Delanoël, 1990.

Graziano Neto, Francisco (Xico). "Reforma agrária de qualidade." *O Estado de S. Paulo,* Apr. 17, 2012, p. 2. https://acervo.estadao.com .br/pagina/#!/20120417-43281-nac-2-opi-a2-not.

Greeley, Andrew M. *The Catholic Experience: An Interpretation of the History of American Catholicism.* Garden City, N.Y.: Doubleday & Company, 1967.

Green, Elizabeth E. *Filo tradito: Vent'anni di teologia femminista.* Turin: Claudiana, 2011.
— *Il Dio sconfinato: Una teologia per donne e uomini.* Turin: Claudiana, 2007.

Gregory XVI. Encyclical *Mirari vos* (Aug. 15, 1832). PapalEncyclicals.net. Accessed Apr. 23, 2021. https://www.papalencyclicals.net/greg16 /g16mirar.htm.

Greteau, Jean-Jacques. *Marc Sangnier: Le semeur d'espérances.* Paris: L'Harmattan, 2009.

Gruber, S.J., Hermann. "Liberalism." In *The Catholic Encyclopedia* (New York: Robert Appleton Company, 1910), 9:212. *NewAdvent.org*. Accessed Apr. 22, 2021. http://www.newadvent.org/cathen/09212a.htm.

Guéranger, Dom Prosper. *De la monarchie pontificale: À propos du livre de Mgr. l'évêque de Sura*. Charleston, S.C.: Nabu Press, 2014.

Guerrero, Carlos. "Economía chilena en la época de Salvador Allende." *Rincón del Vago*. Accessed Apr. 4, 2021. http://html.rincondelvago.com/economia-chilena-en-la-epoca-de-salvador-allende.html.

Guevara, Ernesto "Che." "Message to the Tricontinental" (Apr. 16, 1967). Marxists.org. Accessed Apr. 4, 2021. https://www.marxists.org/archive/guevara/1967/04/16.htm.

Guizot, François. *Mémoires pour servir à l'histoire de mon temps*. 8 vols. 2nd ed. Paris: Michel Lévy Frères, 1858–1872. Accessed Dec. 14, 2021. https://archive.org/details/mmoirespourser01guizuoft/mode/2up.

Gutiérrez, Gustavo. *A Theology of Liberation: History, Politics, and Salvation*. Maryknoll, N.Y.: Orbis Books, 1973.

— *A Theology of Liberation: History, Politics, and Salvation*. Rev. ed. with a new introduction. 15th anniv. ed. Translated and edited by Caridad Inda and John Eagleson. Maryknoll, N.Y.: Orbis Books, 1988.

— *¿Dónde dormirán los pobres?* Lima: I.B.C.-C.E.P., 2002.

— Foreword to *La iglesia latinoamericana entre el temor y la esperanza,* by Pablo Richard. San José, Costa Rica: DEI, 1987.

— "Hacia una teología de la liberación." Notes for a talk by Fr. Gustavo Gutiérrez at the Second Gathering of Priests and Laymen held in Chimbote, Peru, July 21–25, 1968. Accessed Dec. 17, 2021. https://www.ensayistas.org/critica/liberacion/TL/documentos/gutierrez.htm.

— *La recepción del Vaticano II en latinoamérica*. In *La recepción del Vaticano II*. Edited by Giuseppe Alberigo and Jean-Pierre Jossua. Madrid: Cristiandad, 1987.

— "Liberation Praxis and Christian Faith." In Diocese of Brownsville, *Lay Ministry Handbook*. Brownsville, Tex.: Diocese of Brownsville, 1984 (3rd quarter).

— "Liberation Praxis and Christian Faith." In *Frontiers of Theology in Latin America*, edited by Rosino Gibellini. Translated by John Drury, 1–33. Maryknoll, N.Y.: Orbis Books, 1979.

— "Notes on theology of liberation." In *In Search of a Theology of Development: A SODEPAX Report*, by Sodepax (Society, Development and Peace Committee), 116–79. Lausanne: Committee on Society, Development and Peace, Ecumenical Centre, Publications Department, 1969.

— Opening talk at "Twenty Years After Medellín" Conference in São Paulo (Oct. 25, 1988). Recording of proceedings. T.F.P. Archive.

— "Praxis de libertação e fé cristã." Appendix to Gustavo Gutiérrez. *Teologia da libertação*. Petrópolis, R.J.: Editora Vozes, 1975.

— "Signos de liberación." Appendix to Gustavo Gutiérrez. *Teologia da libertação*. Petrópolis, R.J.: Editora Vozes, 1975.

— "Situación y tareas de la teología de la liberación." *Páginas* (Lima), no. 161 (Feb. 2000).

— "Statement." In *Theology in the Americas*, edited by Sergio Torres and John Eagleson, 309–13. Maryknoll, N.Y.: Orbis Books, 1976.

— "The Irruption of the Poor in Latin America and the Christian Communities of the Common People." In *The Challenge of the Basic Christian Communities*, edited by Sergio Torres and John Eagleson. Maryknoll, N.Y.: Orbis Books, 1981.

— *Teologia da libertação*. Petrópolis, R.J.: Editora Vozes, 1975.

— *Teologia de la liberación: Perspectivas*. 16th ed. Salamanca: Ediciones Sigueme, 1999.

— *The Power of the Poor in History: Selected Writings*. Translated by Robert R. Barr. Maryknoll, N.Y.: Orbis Books, 1983.

— *Una teología de la liberación: Perspectivas*. Lima: Centro de Estudios y Publicaciones, 1971.

— and Gerhard Ludwig Mueller. *On the Side of the Poor: The Theology of Liberation*. Translated by Robert A. Krieg and James B. Nickoloff. Maryknoll, N.Y.: Orbis Books, 2015.

— Salvador Blanco Piñán, Aníbal Muñoz Duque, Franz Hinkelammert, and Jorge Rios Dalenz. *Liberación: Opción de la iglesia en la década del 70*. Bogotá: Editorial Presencia, 1970.

Guzzetti, Giovanbattista. *Il movimento cattolico italiano dall'unità ad oggi*. Naples: Edizioni Dehoniane, 1980.

Handy, Robert T. "Christianity and Socialism in America 1900–1920," *Church History* 21 (Mar. 1982): 39–54.

Harnecker, Marta. *Colombia ELN: Unidad que multiplica*. Havana: Rebelión, 1988.

Harris Combs, Barbara. *From Selma to Montgomery: The Long March to Freedom*. New York: Routledge, 2013.

Hasler, August Bernhard. *Come il papa divenne infallibile*. Turin: Claudiana, 1982.

Havard de la Montagne, Robert. *Histoire de la démocratie chrétienne de Lamennais à Georges Bidault*. Paris: Amiot-Dumont, 1948.

Healey, S.J., Cletus. *Battle for the Vineyards*. New York: Twin Circle, 1969.

Hellman, John H. *Emmanuel Mounier and the New Catholic Left*. Toronto: University of Toronto Press, 1981.

Hennelly, Alfred. *Theology for a Liberating Church: The New Praxis of Freedom*. Washington, D.C.: Georgetown University Press, 1989. Accessed Jan. 15, 2022. https://archive.org/details/theologyforliber0000henn/mode/2up.

Henrici, Peter. "Immanentism." *Sacramentum Mundi: An Encyclopedia of Theology*, 107–8. New York: Herder and Herder, 1969.

Hernández Pico, Juan. "Convergencia entre iglesia popular y organización popular en centroamérica." *Dialogo* (Mexico) 10, no. 52.

— "Solidarity With the Poor and the Unity of the Church." In *Theology of Christian Solidarity,* by Jon Sobrino and Juan Hernández Pico, 43–98. Translated by Phillip Berryman. Maryknoll, N.Y.: Orbis Books, 1985.

Hervé, J.M. *Manuale theologiae dogmaticae*. Paris: Berche et Pagis, 1957. Accessed Dec. 7, 2021. https://archive.org/details/manualetheologid0000herv/mode/1up.

Hobsbawm, Eric. *Age of Extremes: The Short Twentieth Century 1914–1991*. London: Abacus, 1995. Accessed Feb. 4, 2022. http://libcom.org/files/Eric%20Hobsbawm%20-%20Age%20Of%20Extremes%20-%201914-1991.pdf.

Holland, Joseph. "Linking Social Analysis and Theological Reflection." In *Tracing the Spirit: Communities, Social Action and Theological Reflection*, edited by James E. Hug, S.J., 170–96. New York: Paulist Press, 1983.

— *The Post Modern Cultural Earthquake*. Washington, D.C.: Center of Concern, 1985.

— *The Spiritual Crisis of Modern Culture*. Washington, D.C.: Center of Concern, 1984.

— and Peter Henriot, S.J. *Social Analysis: Linking Faith and Justice*. Washington, D.C. and Maryknoll, N.Y.: Center of Concern/Orbis Books, 1983. Accessed Nov. 17, 2021. https://archive.org/details/socialanalysisli0000holl/page/n3/mode/2up.

Hopkins, Dwight N. *Introducing Black Theology of Liberation*. Maryknoll, N.Y.: Orbis Books, 1999.

— and Edward P. Antonio, eds. *The Cambridge Companion to Black Theology*. Cambridge, U.K.: Cambridge University Press, 2012.

Horvat II, John. *Return to Order: From a Frenzied Economy to an Organic Christian Society*. York, Penn.: York Press, 2013.

Houtart, François. "L'état actuel de la théologie de la libération en Amérique Latine." *RisalInfo*. Sept. 14, 2006. http://risal.collectifs .net/spip.php?article1811.

Houtin, Albert. *L'américanisme*. Paris: Libraire Émile Nourry, 1904. Accessed Feb. 6, 2022. https://archive.org/details /lamricanisme00hout/mode/2up.

— *Un prêtre symboliste: Marcel Hébert*. Paris: F. Rieder et Cie., 1925.

Hudson, Rex A., ed. *Peru: A Country Study*. Washington D.C.: Federal Research Division, Library of Congress, 1992.

Hug, S.J., James E., ed. *Tracing the Spirit: Communities, Social Action, and Theological Reflection*. New York: Paulist Press, 1983.

— and Rose Marie Scherschel. *Social Revelation*. Washington, D.C.: Center of Concern, 1987.

Hugel, Friedrich von. *Essays and Addresses on Philosophy of Religion*. London: J.M. Dent, 1921.

— *Eternal life: Study of Its Implications and Applications*. Edinburgh: T. & T. Clark, 1912.

— *The Mystical Element of Religion as Studied in Saint Catherine of Genoa and Her Friends*. 2 vols. London: J.M. Dent, 1909.

Il Centro Studi "Romolo Murri. *Aspettiamo un'altra generazione di italiani* (da Romolo Murri), dir. Gabriela Eleonori. Gualdo, Italy town square, Sept. 26, 2010. Accessed Apr. 12, 2021. http:// www.romolomurri.org/pdf/giornate/aspettiamo_un'altra _generazione_di_italiani.pdf.

Ingelmo, Hernán. "Entrevista a Diego Irarrázaval." C.E.T.R. May 3, 2008. https://cetr.net/es/entrevista_a_diego_irarrazaval/.

Instituto Ecumenico al Servicio del Desarrollo de los Pueblos. *El mensaje de Paulo Freire: Teoría y práctica de liberación*. Madrid: Editorial Marsiego, 1973.

Inter-religious Task Force for Social Analysis, The, ed. *Must We Choose Sides? Christian Commitment for the 1980s*. Oakland, Calif.: The Inter-religious Task Force for Social Analysis, 1979.

Introvigne, Massimo. *Una battaglia nella notte: Plinio Corrêa de Oliveira e la crisi del secolo XX nella chiesa*. Milan, Sugarco Edizioni, 2008.

Invernizzi, Marco. *Luigi Gedda e il movimento cattolico in Italia*. Milan: Sugarco, 2012.

Irarrázaval, Diego. *Interculturalidad y teología: Interrogantes latinoamericanos*. *Nación Juvenil*, Jan. 5, 2012. Accessed Mar. 29, 2021. http://nacionjuvenil.blogspot.it/2012/01 /interculturalidad-y-teologia.html.

Ireland, John. "Letter to Leo XIII (Feb. 22, 1899). "Ireland to the Pope." *New York Times*, Mar. 22, 1899.

— *The Church and Modern Society: Lectures and Addresses*. New York: D.H. McBride, 1903. Accessed Dec. 24, 2021. https://archive.org /details/TheChurchAndModernSocietyV1/page/n5/mode/2up.

Isasi-Díaz, Ada María. "Mujeristas: A Name of Our Own." In *The Future of Liberation Theology*, edited by Marc H. Ellis and Otto Maduro, 410–19.

Italian Parliament. "Notizie sul convegno di Stella Maris a Chiavari e suoi successivi sviluppi che in Liguria si sono registrati sul fenomeno dell'eversione." In *Commissione parlamentare d'inchiesta sulla strage di via Fani sul sequestro e l'assasinio di Aldo Moro e sul terrorismo in Italia (Legge 23 novembre 1979, n. 597): Allegato alla relazione. Documenti*. Legislatura VIII, Disegni di legge e relazioni, documenti. Vol. 27, Doc. 23, no. 5:99–151. Rome: Parlamento Italiano, 1988. Accessed Apr. 6, 2021. https://www .senato.it/service/PDF/PDFServer/BGT/908256.pdf.

Iturrioz, Jesús. "Nueva teología: Actitud de la iglesia." *Razón y Fé* (Jul.–Dec. 1950): 485–504.

Iung, N. "Révelation." In *D.T.C.*, 13-2e:2580–618. Accessed Nov. 26, 2021. https://archive.org/details/dictionnairedetv13pt2vaca/page/580 /mode/2up.

Jay, Martin. *Marxism and Totality: The Adventures of a Concept from Lukács to Habermas*. Berkeley, Calif.: University of California Press, 1984.

Jiménez, Roberto. "Teología de la liberación: Proyecto histórico y tres de sus conceptos claves." *Paramillo* 5 (1986).

John Paul II. "Address of His Holiness John Paul II, Puebla, Mexico" (Jan. 28, 1979). http://w2.vatican.va/content/john-paul-ii/en /speeches/1979/january/documents/hf_jp-ii_spe_19790128 _messico-puebla-episc-latam.html.

— "Address to the Peruvian Episcopal Conference" (May 15, 1988). Vatican.va. https://www.vatican.va/content/john-paul-ii/es /speeches/1988/may/documents/hf_jp-ii_spe_19880515 _conf-episc-peru.html.

— "Homily at Le Bourget Airport" (June 1, 1980). https://www .vatican.va/content/john-paul-ii/fr/homilies/1980/documents /hf_jp-ii_hom_19800601_parigi-francia.html.

— "Homily at Sixth General Assembly of the Synod of Bishops" (Oct. 29, 1983). Accessed May 1, 2021. http://www.vatican.va/content /john-paul-ii/it/homilies/1983/documents/hf_jp-ii_hom _19831029_chiusura-sinodo.html.

— *Insegnamenti di Giovanni Paolo II*. Vatican: Libreria Editrice Vaticana, 1980.

— "Letter to the Brazilian Bishops Conference" (Apr. 9, 1986). http:// www.vatican.va/holy_father/john_paul_ii/letters/1986/documents /hf_jp-ii_let_19860409_conf-episcopale-brasile_it.html.

— "Speech of His Holiness John Paul II to the Third General Conference of the Latin American Episcopate." Accessed Apr. 9, 2021. http:// www.vatican.va/content/john-paul-ii/es/speeches/1979/january /documents/hf_jp-ii_spe_19790128_messico-puebla -episc-latam.html.

— "Speech to the First National Conference on Popular Missions During the 80s" (Feb. 6, 1981), no. 2. http://www.vatican.va /content/john-paul-ii/it/speeches/1981/february/documents /hf_jp-ii_spe_19810206_missioni.html.

Jolivet, Régis. *Traité de philosophie*. Paris: Emmanuel Vitte, 1949.

— *Vocabulaire de la philosophie*. Paris: Emmanuel Vitte, 1946.

Kaizer de Oliveira, Willian. "Ecoteologia: Perspectivas de novas temáticas da teologia latinoamericana," 668–80. In *Trabajos científicos*. Vol. 1, *La teología de la liberación en prospectiva*. Montevideo: Fundación Amerindia, 2012.

Kantowicz, Edward R. *Corporation Sole: Cardinal Mundelein and Chicago Catholicism*. Notre Dame: University of Notre Dame Press, 1983.

Kellner, Douglas. *Critical Theory: Marxism and Modernity*. Baltimore: The John Hopkins University Press, 1989.

Kellner, Erich, ed. *Christentum und marxismus heute*. Vienna: Europa Verlag, 1966.

Kertzer, David. *Comrades and Christians: Religion and Political Struggle in Communist Italy*. New York: Cambridge University Press, 1980.

— *Prigioniero del Vaticano: Pio IX e lo scontro tra la chiesa e lo stato italiano*. Milan: Rizzoli, 2005.

Kesler, Jean-François. *De la gauche dissidente au nouveau parti socialiste: Les minorités qui ont rénové le P.S.* Toulouse: Editions Privat, 1990.

Killian, David. Introduction to *Basic Christian Communities: The United States Experience*. Edited by National Federation of Priests' Councils, 1–2. Chicago: National Federation of Priests' Councils, 198x.

Kirk, Russell. *The Conservative Mind: From Burke to Eliot.* 6th rev. ed. Chicago: Regnery Gateway, 1978.

Klaiber, Jeffrey L. *Religion and Revolution in Peru: 1824–1976.* Notre Dame, Ind.: University of Notre Dame Press, 1977.

Konstantinov, Fedor Vasilevich. *Fundamentos de la filosofía marxista.* Translated by Adolfo Sánchez Vázquez and Wenceslao Roces. 2nd ed. Mexico: Editorial Grijalbo, 1965. Accessed Dec. 27, 2021. https://www.abertzalekomunista.net/images/Liburu_PDF/Internacionales/Konstantinov/Fundamentos-de-la-filosofia-marxista-K.pdf.

Kristol, Irving. *Reflections of a Neoconservative: Looking Back, Looking Ahead.* New York: Basic Books, 1983.

Kroger, Joseph. "Prophetic-Critical and Practical-Strategic Tasks of Theology: Habermas and Liberation Theology." *Theological Studies* 46 (Mar. 1985): 3–20.

Krupa, Stephen J. "An Introduction to Dorothy Day." *America Magazine,* Aug. 27, 2001.

Küng, Hans. *The Church.* Translated by Burns and Oates, Ltd. Garden City, N.Y.: Image Books, 1976.

— *Truthfulness: The Future of the Church.* Translated by Edward Quinn. New York: Sheed and Ward, 1968. Accessed Jan. 3, 2022. https://archive.org/details/truthfulnessfutu00knrich/page/n1/mode/2up.

Laberthonnière, Lucien. *Essais de philosophie religieuse.* Paris: Éditions du Seuil, 1966.

Labourdette, Michel. "Études critiques: La théologie et ses sources." *Revue Thomiste* (Jan.–Mar. 1946): 353–71.

Lacordaire, Henri. *Conférences de Notre-Dame de Paris,* 4 vols. Paris: Sagnier et Bray, 1844.

— "Discours de réception de Henri Lacordaire." Académie Française. Jan. 24, 1861. https://www.academie-francaise.fr/discours-de-reception-de-henri-lacordaire.

Lalande, André. *Vocabulaire technique et critique de la philosophie.* Paris: Presses Universitaires de France, 1956.

Lamb, Matthew. *Solidarity With the Victims: Toward a Theology of Social Transformation.* New York: Crossroad, 1982.

Lamennais, F. *Paroles d'un croyant: Le livre du peuple.* Paris: Garnier Frères, 1864. Accessed Feb. 5, 2022. https://archive.org/details/bub_gb_YBambHid-WAC/mode/2up.

Lanza, Andrea. *All'abolizione del proletariato: Il discorso socialista fraternitario—Parigi 1839–1847.* Milan: Franco Angeli, 2010.

Latreille, André, J.R. Palanque, E. Delaruelle, and R. Remond. *Histoire du catholicisme en France.* Paris: Spes, 1962.

Laurentin, René, and Michel Corteville. *Découverte du secret de la Salette.* Paris: Fayard, 2002.

Lebreton, Jules. "Modernisme: L'encyclique et la théologie moderniste." In *D.A.F.C.,* 3:665–95. Accessed Nov. 21, 2021. https://archive.org/details/dictionnaireapol03aluoft/page/337/mode/2up.

Lecanuet, L.R.P. *Montalembert, d'après son journal et sa correspondance.* 3 vols. Paris: Poussielgue, 1898–1902.

Leflon, Jean. *La crise révolutionnaire 1789–1846.* Vol. 20, *Histoire de l'église,* edited by A. Fliche and V. Martin. Paris: Bloud et Gay, 1951. Accessed Dec. 15, 2021. https://archive.org/details/lacriservolution0000lefl/mode/2up.

Lenin, Vladimir Ilyich. "On the Road." In *Selected Works: In Three Volumes,* 1:582–587. Moscow: Progress Publishers, 1970.

— "The Tasks of the Youth Leagues," (speech delivered at the Third All-Russia Congress of the the Russian Young Communist League), Oct. 2, 1920. Accessed Nov. 27, 2021. https://www.marxists.org/archive/lenin/works/1920/oct/02.htm.

— *What Is to Be Done?* Accessed Nov. 27, 2021. https://www.marxists.org/archive/lenin/works/1901/witbd/ch02.htm.

Leo XIII. *Actes de Léon XIII.* Paris: Maison de la Bonne Presse, 1925.

— Apostolic Letter *Testem benevolentiae* (Jan. 22, 1899). PapalEncyclicals.net. Accessed Apr. 23, 2021. https://www.papalencyclicals.net/leo13/l13teste.htm.

— Encyclical *Aeterni Patris* (Aug. 4, 1879). https://www.vatican.va/content/leo-xiii/en/encyclicals/documents/hf_l-xiii_enc_04081879_aeterni-patris.html.

— Encyclical *Graves de communi* (Jan. 18, 1901). http://www.vatican.va/content/leo-xiii/en/encyclicals/documents/hf_l-xiii_enc_18011901_graves-de-communi-re.html.

— Encyclical *Immortale Dei* (Nov. 1, 1885). https://www.vatican.va/content/leo-xiii/en/encyclicals/documents/hf_l-xiii_enc_01111885_immortale-dei.html.

— Encyclical *Libertas* (June 20, 1888). http://www.vatican.va/content/leo-xiii/en/encyclicals/documents/hf_l-xiii_enc_20061888_libertas.html.

— Encyclical *Magnae Dei Matris* (Sept. 8, 1892). http://www.vatican.va/content/leo-xiii/en/encyclicals/documents/hf_l-xiii_enc_08091892_magnae-dei-matris.html.

— Encyclical *Rerum novarum* (May 15, 1891). http://www.vatican.va/content/leo-xiii/en/encyclicals/documents/hf_l-xiii_enc_15051891_rerum-novarum.html.

— Encyclical *Satis cognitum* (June 29, 1896). Accessed May 5, 2021. http://www.vatican.va/content/leo-xiii/en/encyclicals/documents/hf_l-xiii_enc_29061896_satis-cognitum.html.

— Lettre à son éminence le Cardinal Richard, archevéque de Paris (Dec. 23, 1900). https://www.vatican.va/content/leo-xiii/fr/letters/documents/hf_l-xiii_let_19001223_au-milieu-des-consolations.html.

Leonhard, Wolfang. *Die dreispaltung des marxismus.* Vienna: Econ Verlag, 1975.

Leoni, Francesco. *Storia dei partiti politici italiani.* Naples: Guida Editori, 1971.

Lepeley, Joaquín. *La teología de la liberación: Un análisis temático cronológico.* Bogotá: C.E.D.I.A.L., 1986.

Le Roy, Édouard. "Comment se pose le problème de Dieu." *Revue de Métaphysique et de Morale* (1907): 129–70; 470–513. Accessed Feb. 6, 2022. https://archive.org/details/revuedemtaphys15pariuoft/mode/1up?view=theater.

— *Dogme et critique.* 6th ed. Paris: Librairie Bloud et Cie., 1907. Accessed Dec. 4, 2021. https://archive.org/details/dogmeetcritique00unkngoog/mode/2up.

— "Sur quelques objections adressées à la nouvelle philosophie." *Revue de Métaphysique et de Morale* (1901): 292–327; 407–432.

Leroy-Beaulieu, Anatole. *Les catholiques libéraux de 1830 à nos jours.* Paris: Plon et Nourrit, 1885.

Lester, S.J., William. *Basic Principles of Saul Alinsky.* San José, Calif.: St. Dismas Publishers, 1970.

Leuwers, Jean-Marie. "Étapes de l'action des laïcs et conceptions successives de l'apostolat du laicat." In *Evangélisation collective: Dossier masses ouvrières,* edited by P. Barrau. Paris: Les Éditions Ouvrières, 1964.

Levy, Jacques. *Cesar Chavez: Autobiography of La Causa.* New York: W.W. Norton & Company, 1975.

Libânio Christo, Carlos Alberto. (See Betto, Frei.)

Lima, Haroldo, and Aldo Arantes. *História da Ação Popular: Da JUC ao PC do B.* São Paulo: Editora Alfa-Omega, 1984.

Lima Vaz, S.J., Henrique Cláudio. Introduction to *Teologia da libertação: Política ou profetismo? Visão panorâmica e crítica da teologia política latino-americana,* by Alfonso García Rubio. São Paulo: Edições Loyola, 1977.

Livi, Antonio. *Vera e falsa teologia: Come distinguere l'autentica "scienza della fede" da un'equivoca "filosofia religiosa."* Rome: Casa Editrice Leonardo da Vinci, 2012.

Llovera, José María. *Tratado elemental de sociología cristiana.* Barcelona: Luis Gili, 1930.

Lois, Julio. "Función crítica de la iglesia en la sociedad." In *Desafíos Cristianos,* edited by Misión Abierta, 170–82. Madrid: Loguez Ediciones, 1988. Accessed Jan. 29, 2022. https://cupdf.com /document/mision-abierta-desafios-cristianos.html.

Loisy, Alfred. *Autour d'un petit livre.* Paris: Alphonse Picard et fils, 1903. Accessed Feb. 5, 2022. https://archive.org/details /autourdunpetitl01loisgoog/mode/2up.

— "L'idée de la révelation," *Revue du Clergé Français* 21 (Jan. 1900): 250ff.

— *Quelques lettres sur des questions actuelles et sur des événements récents.* Ceffonds, près Montier-en-Der, Haute-Marne: self-published, 1908. Accessed Feb. 5, 2022. https://archive.org/details/quelqueslettress00loisuoft /mode/2up.

— *Simples réflexions sur le decret du Saint Office* Lamentabili Sane Exitu, *et sur l'encyclique* Pascendi Dominici gregis. Ceffonds, près Montier-en-Der, Haute-Marne: self-published, 1908. Accessed Feb. 5, 2022. https://archive.org/details/simplesrflexi00lois /page/n1/mode/2up.

— *The Gospel and the Church.* Translated by Christopher Home. New York: Charles Scribner's Sons, 1904. Accessed Jan. 26, 2022. https://archive.org/details/gospelandchurch00homegoog /page/n8/mode/2up.

Lonergan, S.J., Bernard. "Theology in Its New Context." In *Renewal of Religious Thought: Proceedings of the Congress on the Theology of the Renewal of the Church Centenary of Canada, 1867–1967,* edited by L.K. Shook, C.S.B., 34–46. New York: Herder and Herder, 1968.

Lopes, Claudinei Jair. *A relevância teologica da história e a relevância histórica da teologia na teologia da libertação latino-americana.* Doctor's thesis, Pontificia Universidade Católica do Rio de Janeiro, 2009.

López Aranguren, José Luis. "Un modelo profético post-secular." In *Desafíos Cristianos,* edited by Misión Abierta, 331–35. Madrid: Loguez Ediciones, 1988. Accessed Jan. 29, 2022. https://cupdf .com/document/mision-abierta-desafios-cristianos.html.

Loredo de Izcue, Julio. "Allende: il crollo di un mito." *Tradizione Famiglia Proprietà* (May 2007), 23-28, https://issuu.com /tradizionefamigliaproprieta/docs/2018_02_19_16_38_38.

— "Cattolicesimo e comunismo in America Latina." *Tradizione Famiglia Proprietà* (Dec. 2003).

— "Homosexualidad y teología de la liberación." *Covadonga Informa* (May 1990), 8–9. Accessed Nov. 29, 2021. https://issuu.com/nestor87 /docs/covadonga_informa_1986_1990.

— "Il '68 cattolico." *Tradizione Famiglia Proprietà* (June 2008), 19–21. https://issuu.com/tradizionefamigliaproprieta/docs /tfp_maggio_2008.

— "La Waterloo del comunismo." *Tradizione Famiglia Proprietà* (Oct. 2005), 70–76, https://issuu.com/tradizionefamigliaproprieta/docs /plinio_correa_de_oliveira_biografia_illustrata2.

— "Rumbo al socialismo ecológico: Apología de la pobreza en el X Congreso de Teología Juan XXIII." *Covadonga Informa* (Nov. 1990), 7–10. Accessed Nov. 29, 2021. https://issuu.com/nestor87/docs /covadonga_informa_1986_1990.

— "Teología indígena." *Covadonga Informa* 15, no. 162 (Mar. 1992). Accessed Jan. 31, 2022. https://issuu.com/nestor87/docs /covadonga_informa_1991_1992.

— "The 'Catholic Left' on the Border: Adding Fuel to the Fire," *TFP Newsletter* 4, no. 22, 4–6.

Losada, Joaquín. "El posconcilio: El problema de la transformación de la iglesia." In *Desafíos Cristianos,* edited by Misión Abierta, 86–96. Madrid: Loguez Ediciones, 1988. Accessed Jan. 29, 2022. https:// cupdf.comdocument/mision-abierta-desafios-cristianos.html.

Machado Cartagena, Absalón. *Reforma agraria: una ilusión que resultó un fracaso.* Bogotá: Biblioteca Virtual del Banco de la República, 2005.

Madrigal Sanchez, Victor. "Teología india." In *Trabajos científicos,* 131–42. Vol. 1, *La teología de la liberación en prospectiva.* Montevideo: Fundación Amerindia, 2012. Accessed Feb. 4, 2022. http://www.elpuente.org.mx/wp-content/uploads/2013/01 /Libro-I-Congreso-Continental-de-Teolog%C3%ADa -San-Leopoldo-Brasil1.pdf.

Maier, Hans. *Revolution and Church: The Early History of Christian Democracy.* Notre Dame, Ind.: University of Notre Dame Press, 1969.

— *Revolution und kirche: Studien zur fruhgechichte der christlichen demokratie.* Freiburg: Rombach, 1959.

Maier, Pauline. *From Resistance to Revolution: Colonial Radicals and the Development of American Opposition to Britain, 1765–1776.* New York: W. W. Norton & Company, 1991.

Mainwaring, Scott. *The Catholic Church and Politics in Brazil 1916–1985.* Stanford, Calif.: Stanford University Press, 1986.

Malgeri, Francesco. *La sinistra cristiana 1937–1945.* Brescia: Morcelliana, 1982.

Malone, Sylvester L. *Dr. Edward McGlynn.* New York: Dr. McGlynn Monumental Association, 1918. Accessed Apr. 12, 2021. http://www .cooperative-individualism.org/malone-sylvester_edward -mcglynn-1918.pdf.

Malteri, Francesco, ed. *Atti del convegno internazionale di studi promosso dall'Assemblea Regionale Siciliana.* Rome: Edizioni di Storia e Letteratura, 1973.

Marcuse, Herbert. *Eros and Civilization: A Philosophical Inquiry Into Freud.* Boston: Beacon Press, 1966. https://www.marxists.org /reference/archive/marcuse/works/eros-civilisation/ch01.htm.

— *La sociedad carnívora.* Translated by Miguel Grinberg. Buenos Aires: Ediciones Godot, 2011. Accessed Dec. 25, 2021. https://proletarios .org/books/Marcuse-Sociedad_Carnivora.pdf.

— "Talk at Fillmore East Concert Hall, New York, for Twentieth Anniversary of the *Guardian* (Dec. 5, 1968)." In Carl Oglesby Papers, Radical Perspectives, University of Massachussetts at Amherst. Accessed Jan. 24, 2022. https://credo.library.umass.edu/view /full/mums514-b080-i006.

— "Talk at University of California San Diego" (May 23, 1968). In "Herbert Marcuse and the Student Revolts of 1968: An Unpublished Lecture." Jacobinmag.com, Mar. 31, 2021. https://jacobinmag.com/2021/03 /herbert-marcuse-student-revolts-of-1968-ucsd-lecture.

Marechal, Sylvain, et al. *Manifesto of the Equals.* Translated by Mitchell Abidor. 1796. Accessed Dec. 14, 2021. https://www.marxists.org /history/france/revolution/conspiracy-equals/1796/manifesto .htm.

Maret, Henri-Louis-Charles. *Du concile générale et de la paix religieuse.* Paris: Henri Plon, 1869.

Maritain, Jacques. *Humanisme intégrale.* Paris: Aubier, 1936.

— *Integral Humanism: Temporal and Spiritual Problems of a New Christendom.* Translated by Joseph W. Evans. New York: Charles Scribner's Sons, 1968.

— "Letter to the Editor," *Harper's Magazine* (Aug. 1965): 6.

— *The Peasant of the Garonne: An Old Layman Questions Himself About the Present Time.* Translated by Michael Cuddihy and Elizabeth Hughes. New York: Holt, Rinehart and Winston, 1968. Accessed Oct. 10, 2021. https://archive.org/details/peasantofgaronn00mari/page /n7/mode/2up.

Mark, A. Frederick. *Manifest Destiny and Mission in American History.* New York: Alfred A. Knopf, 1963.

Martina, Giacomo. *La chiesa nell'età del assolutismo, del liberalismo, del totalitarismo: Da Lutero ai nostri giorni.* 4 vols. Brescia: Morcelliana, 1970.

Martinez, Richard Edward. *PADRES: A Study of Revolutionary Chicano Priests*. Graduation thesis, University of Michigan, 2002.

Marx, Karl. *A Contribution to the Critique of Political Economy*. Translated by S.W. Ryazanskaya. Accessed Mar. 23, 2021. https://www.marxists.org/archive/marx/works/download/Marx_Contribution_to_the_Critique_of_Political_Economy.pdf.

— *Pre-Capitalist Economic Formations* (1857–1858). Translated by Jack Cohen. Accessed Mar. 23, 2021. https://www.marxists.org/archive/marx/works/1857/precapitalist/ch01.htm.

— "Theses on Feuerbach." Marxists.org. Accessed Nov. 25, 2021. https://www.marxists.org/archive/marx/works/1845/theses/theses.htm.

— and Frederick Engels. *Marx and Engels 1856–58*. Vol. 15, *Collected Works*. London: Lawrence & Wishart 2010. Accessed Mar. 30, 2021. http://www.hekmatist.com/Marx%20Engles/Marx%20&%20Engels%20Collected%20Works%20Volume%2015_%20Ka%20-%20Karl%20Marx.pdf.

Mascitelli, Ernesto, ed. *Dizionario dei termini marxisti*. Milan: Vangelista, 1977.

Mateos, Juan. "La utopía de Jesús." In José Ignacio González Faus, ed., *Utopía y profetismo*.

Mathiesen, Peter. *Sal Si Puedes: Cesar Chavez and the New American Revolution*. New York: Random House, 1969.

Matos Mar, José, and José Manuel Mejía. *La Reforma Agraria en el Perú*. Lima: Instituto de Estudios Peruanos, 1980.

Maumus, Vincent. *Les catholiques et la liberté politique*. Paris: Libraire Victor Lecoffre, 1898.

— *Les modernistes*. Paris: Beauchesne, 1909.

Mayeur, Jean-Marie. *L'abbé Lemire, 1853–1928, un prêtre démocrate*. Paris: Casterman, 1968.

Maynard, Theodore. *The Story of American Catholicism*. New York: The Macmillan Company, 1941.

McAfee Brown, Robert. "After Ten Years." Preface to *The Power of the Poor in History*, by Gustavo Gutiérrez, vi–xvi. Maryknoll, N.Y.: Orbis Books, 1983.

— *Gustavo Gutiérrez: An Introduction to Liberation Theology*. Maryknoll, N.Y.: Orbis Books, 1990.

— *Liberation Theology: An Introductory Guide*. Philadelphia: Westminster Press, 1993.

— Preface and conclusion to *Theology in the Americas*, edited by Sergio Torres and John Eagleson, ix–xxviii. Maryknoll, N.Y.: Orbis Books, 1976.

— *Spirituality and Liberation: Overcoming the Great Fall*. Philadelphia: Westminster Press, 1988.

— *Theology in a New Key: Responding to Liberation Themes*. Philadelphia: Westminster Press, 1978.

— "The 'Preferential Option for the Poor' and the Renewal of Faith." In *Churches in Struggle: Liberation Theology and Social Change in North America*, edited by William K. Tabb, 7–17. New York: Monthly Review Press, 1986.

— *Unexpected News: Reading the Bible With Third World Eyes*. Philadelphia: Westminster Press, 1984.

McAvoy, Thomas. *The Americanist Heresy in Roman Catholicism, 1895–1900*. Notre Dame, Ind.: University of Notre Dame Press, 1963.

McEntee, Georgiana Putnam. *The Social Catholic Movement in Great Britain*. New York: Macmillan, 1927.

McGlynn, Edward. "An Insurgent Priest's Defense of Common Property in Land" (from *The Standard*, Apr. 2, 1887). In *American Catholic Thought on Social Questions: A Search for Social Justice, 1865–1950*, edited by Aaron I. Abell, 161–75. Notre Dame, Ind.: University of Notre Dame Press, 1963.

McNeil, John J. *Scommettere su Dio, teologia della liberazione omosessuale*. Casale Monferrato: Edizioni Sonda, 1994.

McShane, S.J., Joseph M. *"Sufficiently Radical": Catholicism, Progressivism, and the Bishops' Program of 1919*. Washington, D.C.: The Catholic University of America Press, 1986. Accessed Oct. 10, 2021. https://archive.org/details/sufficientlyradi0000mcsh/page/192/mode/2up.

Meller, Patricio. *Un siglo de economía política chilena (1890–1990)*. Santiago: Editorial Bello, 1996.

Ménard, Guy. *De Sodome à l'exode: jalons pour une théologie de la libération gaie*. Montréal: L'Aurore/Univers, 1980.

Menozzi, Daniele. "Cristianità e questione sociale: Da Pio IX a Leone XIII." In Daniele Menozzi. *La chiesa cattolica e la secolarizzazione*. Turin: Einaudi, 1993.

Menvielle, Julio. *De Lamennais a Maritain*. Buenos Aires: Ediciones Theoria, 1967.

Mesa Lago, Carmelo. *Cuba en la era de Raúl Castro: Reformas económico-sociales y sus efectos*. Madrid: Editorial Colibrí, 2011.

Meslier, Jean. *Oeuvres complètes*. Edited by R. Desne, J. Deprun, and A. Soboul. 3 vols. Paris: Editions Anthropos, 1970–1972.

Mettepenningen, Jürgen. "Truth as Issue in a Second Modernist Crisis? The Clash Between Recontextualization and Retrocontextualization in the French-Speaking Polemic of 1946–1947." In *Theology and the Quest for Truth*, edited by M. Lamberigts, L. Boeve, and T. Merrigan, 119–42. Louvain: Leuven University Press, 2006.

Metz, Johannes B. "Carta de apoyo a la iglesia de los pobres que está en Nicaragua." *Tierra Nueva*, 13–14, nos. 52–54 (Jan.–Apr. 1985), 101–4.

— *Theology of the World*. Translated by William Glen-Doepel. New York: Herder and Herder, 1969. Accessed Dec. 5, 2021. https://archive.org/details/theologyofworld0000unse/mode/2up.

Michel, A. "Vérité, véracité." In *D.T.C.*, 15–2e:2675–87. Accessed Nov. 26, 2021. https://archive.org/details/dictionnairedetv15pt2vaca/page/570/mode/2up.

— "Virtuel, virtuellement." In *D.T.C.*, 15-2e:3097–98. Accessed Nov. 27, 2021. https://archive.org/details/dictionnairedetv15pt2vaca/page/780/mode/2up.

Milner, W.M. *The Royal House of Britain: An Enduring Dinasty*. 15th ed., London: Covenant Pub. Co., 1991.

Misión Abierta, ed. *Desafíos Cristianos*. Madrid: Loguez Ediciones, 1988. Accessed Jan. 29, 2022. https://cupdf.com/document/mision-abierta-desafios-cristianos.html.

Moberg, David. "Obama's Third Way." *National Housing Institute*, no. 49 (Spring 2007).

Moncada, Camilo, ed., *Aportes para la liberación: Simposio "Teología de la liberación."* Bogotá: Editorial Presencia, 1970.

Mondin, Battista. *La metafisica di S. Tommaso d'Aquino e i suoi interpreti*. Bologna: Edizioni Studio Domenicano, 2019.

— *Storia della Teologia*. 4 vols. Bologna: Edizioni Studio Domenicano, 2019.

Montalembert, Charles Forbes, count of. *L'église libre dans l'état libre: Discours prononcés au congrès catholique de Malines par le comte de Montalembert*. Paris: Charles Douniol, 1863. Accessed Nov. 28, 2021. https://archive.org/details/BRes112395.

— *Lettre a M. le Comte de Cavour, président du conseil des ministres, a Turin, par le comte de Montalembert*. Paris: Charles Douniol, 1861.

Montes Varas, Juan Antonio. *Desde la teología de la liberación a la teología eco-feminista: Una revolución enquistada en la Iglesia, intenta destruir la civilización y la moral cristiana*. Santiago, Chile: Acción Familia, 2011. Accessed Dec. 25, 2021. https://www.tfp.org/books/Desde_la_Teologia_de_la_Liberacion_a_la_Teologia_Eco-Feminista.pdf.

Morcillo, Casimiro. "Introducción al estudio de la encíclica." In *Comentarios a la encíclica Humani Generis* by Publicaciones del Obispado de Bilbao, 5–36. Bilbao: Ediciones Desclée de Brouwer, 1952.

Morel, Jules. *Les catholiques libéraux.* Paris: E. Giraud, 1864.

Moro, Renato. *Aldo Moro negli anni della FUCI.* Rome: Studium, 2008.

Morrison, Joseph P. "The Liturgical Revival and the Family." In *Family Catholic Action.* Edited by Family Life Bureau. Washington, D.C: National Catholic Welfare Conference, nd.

Mounier, Emmanuel. "Devant Nous," *Esprit* 16, no. 140 (Dec. 1947): 940–42.

— *Qu'est-ce que le personalisme?* Paris: Le Seuil, 1946.

Müller, Gerhard Ludwig. "Liberating Experience: A Stimulus for European Theology." In *On the Side of the Poor: The Theology of Liberation,* by Gustavo Gutiérrez and Gerhard Ludwig Cardinal Müller, 11–31. Translated by Robert A. Krieg and James B. Nickoloff. Maryknoll, N.Y.: Orbis Books, 2015.

— "Liberation Theology in Context," in Gustavo Gutierrez and Gerhard Ludwig Müller, *On the Side of the Poor: The Theology of Liberation,* 54–82. Translated by Robert A. Krieg and James B. Nickoloff. Maryknoll, N.Y.: Orbis Books, 2015.

— "Mis experiencias sobre la teología de la liberación," in *Religión* (Lima), July 3, 2012.

— *Povera per i poveri: La missione della chiesa.* Vatican City: Libreria Editrice Vaticana, 2014.

— "'Vagliate ogni cosa e tenete ciò che è buono.' A 25 anni dall'istruzione *Libertatis Nuntius.*" In *Dalla parte dei poveri: Teologia della liberazione, teologia della chiesa,* by Gustavo Gutierrez and Gerhard Ludwig Mueller. Padua: Edizioni Messaggero-E.M.I., 2013.

Muñoz, Doris. "Experimento entonces mi cuerpo como fuente de plenitud," *Con-spirando* 53, no. 6 (Aug. 2006), 41–43.

Muñoz Iglesias, Salvador, ed. *Doctrina pontificia: Documentos biblicos.* Madrid: B.A.C., 1955.

Murphy, Francis J. *Communists and Catholics in France, 1936–1939: The Politics of the Outstretched Hand.* Gainsville: University of Florida Press, 1989. Accessed Dec. 18, 2021. https://archive.org/details/communistscathol00murp/page/n1/mode/2up.

Murray, S.J., John Courtney. *We Hold These Truths: Catholic Reflections on the American Proposition.* New York: Sheed & Ward, 1960.

Murri, Romolo. *La religione di Alfredo Loisy.* Rome: Libreria Editrice Bilychnis, 1918.

Myers, Minor. *Liberty Without Anarchy.* Charlottesville: The University Press of Virginia, 1983.

National Catholic War Council. "Program of Social Reconstruction." In *Pastoral Letters of the American Hierarchy, 1792–1970,* edited by Hugh J. Nolan, 199–211. Huntington, Ind.: Our Sunday Visitor, 1971. Accessed Oct. 10, 2021, https://archive.org/details/pastorallettersso0000nola/page/210/mode/2up.

National Committee of Black Churchmen. *Black Theology: Statement by the National Committee of Black Churchmen* (Jun. 13, 1969). In *Black Theology: A Documentary History, 1966–1979,* edited by James Cone and Gayraud S. Wilmore, 37–39. 2nd ed. rev. Maryknoll, N.Y.: Orbis Books, 1993.

National Federation of Priests' Councils. *Basic Christian Communities: The United States Experience.* Chicago: National Federation of Priests' Councils, 198x.

Naudet, Paul. *La démocratie et les démocrates chrétiens.* Paris: Librairie Delhomme & Briguet, 1900. Accessed Apr. 12, 2021. https://gallica.bnf.fr/ark:/12148/bpt6k1265217t/f3.item.texteImage.

Negri, Luigi. *Pio IX: Attualità e profezia.* Milan: Ares, 2006.

— Preface to *Omofobia o eterofobia: Perché opporsi a una legge ingiusta e liberticida,* by Gianfranco Amato, 7–9. Verona: Fede & Cultura, 2014.

Neira, Hugo. *Il Perù può diventare una nuova Cuba?* Rome: Samonà e Savelli, 1969.

New York Times News Service. "Poverty Exists for Millions of Soviets, USSR Admits." *Chicago Tribune,* Jan. 30, 1989. https://www.chicagotribune.com/news/ct-xpm-1989-01-30-8903010453-story.html.

Nicolas, M.J., and R.L. Bruckberger. *Dialogue théologique: Pièces du débat entre la Revue Thomiste d'une part, les RRPP de Lubac, Daniélou, Bouillard, Ferrand et von Balthasar d'autre part.* Tolouse: St. Maximin, 1947.

Nicolau, Michaele, and Ioachim Salaverri. *Introductio in theologiam. De revelatione christiana. De ecclesia Christi. De sacra scriptura.* Vol 1, *Sacrae theologiae summa.* Madrid: Biblioteca de Autores Cristianos, 1958.

Nietzsche, Friedrich. *Thus Spoke Zarathustra.* Edited by Bill Chapko. *Feedbooks.* Accessed Mar. 28, 2021. http://nationalvanguard.org/books/Thus-Spoke-Zarathustra-by-F.-Nietzsche.pdf.

Nisbet, Robert. *Twilight of Authority.* New York: Oxford University Press, 1975.

Nitti, Francesco S. *Catholic Socialism.* Translated by Mary MackIntosh. London: Swan Sonnenschein & Co., 1895.

Noland, Richard W. "The Apocalypse of Normal O. Brown." *The American Scholar* (Winter 1968–1969): 59–68.

Novak, Michael. *The Spirit of Democratic Capitalism.* New York: Simon and Schuster, 1982.

O'Brien, David. *American Catholics and Social Reform: The New Deal Years.* New York: Oxford University Press, 1968.

O'Halloran, James. *Living Cells: Developing Small Christian Community.* Dublin: Dominican Publications, 1984.

Oliveros, Roberto. *Liberación y teología: Génesis y crecimiento de una reflexión, 1966–1976.* Lima: C.E.P., 1977.

Omodeo, Adolfo. *Alfredo Loisy, storico delle religioni.* Bari: Laterza, 1936.

O.N.I.S. "Declaración de los sacerdotes peruanos." *Oiga* (Lima), no. 265 (Mar. 22, 1968).

Orleans-Braganza, Bertrand of. "Quo Vadis, Domine? Reverent and Filial Message to His Holiness Pope Francis." TFP.org, Feb. 13, 2014. https://www.tfp.org/quo-vadis-domine-reverent-and-filial-message-to-his-holiness-pope-francis-from-prince-bertrand-of-orleans-braganza/.

Ossicini, Adriano. *Un'isola sul Tevere: Il fascismo al di là del ponte.* Rome: Editori Riuniti, 1999.

Pacika, V.M. "Dialettica dello sviluppo sociale e della lotta ideologica: La teologia della liberazione nella sua versione radicale latino-americana." *Problemi di Filosofia* (Moscow), no. 1 (1985): 92–100.

Pagano, Sergio. *Dalla porpora al chiostro:* "L'inflessibilità di Pio XI verso il cardinale Louis Billot." In *Il papato contemporaneo (secoli xix–xx),* 395–410. Vatican: Archivio Segreto Vaticano, 2009.

Pampaloni, Geno. *Notre-Dame e la Sainte-Chapelle.* Novara: Istituto Geografico de Agostini, 1980.

Papasogli, Giorgio, and Franco Stano, eds. *Antonio Claret, l'uomo che sfidò l'impossibile.* Vatican: Libreria Editrice Vaticana, 1963.

Parada, Hernán. *Crónica de Medellín: Segunda Conferencia General del Episcopado Latinoamericano.* Bogotá: Indo-American Press Service, 1975.

Pattaro, Germano. *Corso di teologia dell'ecumenismo.* Brescia: Queriniana, 1985.

Pellicciari, Angela. *L'altro risorgimento: Una guerra di religione dimenticata.* Casale Monferrato: Piemme, 2000.

— *Risorgimento anticattolico*. Casale Monferrato: Piemme, 2004.

— *Risorgimento da riscrivere: Liberali & massoni contro la Chiesa*. Milan: Àres, 1998.

Perego, Angel. "La teología nueva." *Ciencia y Fe* (Jan.–Mar. 1949): 7–30.

Pérez Tapias, José A. "Balance prospectivo." *Misión Abierta* (Madrid) 77, no. 2 (Apr. 1984): 57–60.

Pesch, S.J., Cristiano. *Fede, dogma e fatti storici: Studio su le dottrine moderniste*. Rome: Libreria Pontificia di F. Pustet, 1909.

Pessen, Edward. *Riches, Class and Power Before the Civil War*. Lexington, Mass.: Heath & Co., 1973.

Peterson, Erik. *Theologische traktate*. Munich: Kösel-Verlag, 1951.

Phelps, Jamie T., ed. *Black and Catholic: The Challenge and Gift of Black Folk; Contributions of African American Experience and Thought to Catholic Theology*. Milwaukee: Marquette University Press, 1997.

Piehl, Mel. *Breaking Bread: The Catholic Worker and the Origins of Catholic Radicalism in America*. Philadelphia: Temple University Press, 1982.

Pierce, Gregory F. *Activism That Makes Sense: Congregations and Community Organizing*. New York: Paulist Press, 1984.

Pietra, Angela. *Storia del movimento cattolico-liberale*. Milan: Vallardi, 1948.

Pike, E. Royton. *Human Documents of the Industrial Revolution in Britain*. London: George Allen & Unwin, 1970.

Pilato, Claudia. "Dall'omosessualità alla pedofilia: Sullo scivolo della rivoluzione sessuale." *Tradizione Famiglia Proprietà* (Oct. 2013).

Pinard, H. s.v. "Création." In *D.T.C.*, 3–2e.:2034–201.

Pius VI. "Allocution de notre très saint-père le pape Pie VI dans le consistoire secret du lundi, 17 juin, 1793 au sujet de l'assassinat de sa majestétrès chrétienne Louis XVI." Rome: l'Imprimerie de la Chambre Apostolique, 1793. Accessed Feb. 2, 2022. https://gallica.bnf.fr/ark:/12148/bpt6k62190727/f5.item#.

— Brief "Quod Aliquantum" (Mar. 10, 1791). Accessed Feb. 2, 2022. https://www.vatican.va/content/pius-vi/it/documents/breve-quod-aliquantum-10-marzo-1791.html.

Pius IX. "Brief Addressed to the President and Young Members of the Circle St. Ambrose of Milan" (Mar. 6, 1873). *La civiltà cattolica* 24, series 8, no. 547, 10:99–100. Accessed Dec. 15, 2021. https://archive.org/details/laciviltcattol10romeuoft/mode/1up.

— Encyclical *Nostis et nobiscum* (Dec. 8, 1849). PapalEncyclicals.net. Accessed Apr. 22, 2021. https://www.papalencyclicals.net/pius09/p9nostis.htm.

Pius X, Saint. Apostolic Letter *Notre charge apostolique* (Aug. 15, 1910). *The American Catholic Quarterly Review* 35, no. 140 (Oct. 1910), 693–711. Accessed Oct. 10, 2021. https://babel.hathitrust.org/cgi/pt?id=chi.74887044&view=1up&seq=707&skin=2021.

— Decree *Lamentabili sane exitu* (July 3, 1907). Accessed Apr. 25, 2021. https://www.papalencyclicals.net/pius10/p10lamen.htm.

— Encyclical *E supremi apostolatus* (Oct. 4, 1903). Accessed Apr. 25, 2021. http://www.vatican.va/content/pius-x/en/encyclicals/documents/hf_p-x_enc_04101903_e-supremi.html.

— Encyclical *Il fermo proposito* (June 11, 1905). Accessed Apr. 13, 2021. http://www.vatican.va/content/pius-x/en/encyclicals/documents/hf_p-x_enc_11061905_il-fermo-proposito.html.

— Encyclical *Pascendi Dominici gregis* (Sept. 8, 1907). Accessed Apr. 23, 2021. http://www.vatican.va/content/pius-x/en/encyclicals/documents/hf_p-x_enc_19070908_pascendi-dominici-gregis.html.

— Encyclical *Pieni l'animo* (July 28, 1906). Accessed Apr. 13, 2021. http://www.vatican.va/content/pius-x/en/encyclicals/documents/hf_p-x_enc_28071906_pieni-l-animo.html.

— Encyclical *Vehementer Nos* (Feb. 11, 1906).

— Motu proprio *Fin dalla prima* (Dec. 18, 1903). Accessed Apr. 13, 2021. http://www.vatican.va/content/pius-x/it/motu_proprio/documents/hf_p-x_motu_proprio_19031218_fin-dalla-prima.html.

— Motu proprio *Praestantia scripturae* (Nov. 18, 1907). Accessed Dec. 5, 2021. https://www.papalencyclicals.net/pius10/p10prasc.htm.

— Motu proprio *Sacrorum antistitum* (Sept. 9, 1910). In Vol. 2, *Acta Apostolicae Sedis* (Annus II). Accessed Dec. 16, 2021. https://www.vatican.va/content/pius-x/la/motu_proprio/documents/hf_p-x_motu_proprio_19100901_sacrorum-antistitum.html. https://www.papalencyclicals.net/pius10/p10moath.htm.

Pius XI. Encyclical *Divini redemptoris* (Mar. 19, 1937). http://www.vatican.va/holy_father/pius_xi/encyclicals/documents/hf_p-xi_enc_19031937_divini-redemptoris_en.html).

— Encyclical *Quadragesimo anno* (May 15, 1931). http://www.vatican.va/holy_father/pius_xi/encyclicals/documents/hf_p-xi_enc_19310515_quadragesimo-anno_en.html).

— Encyclical *Quas primas* (Dec. 11, 1925). http://w2.vatican.va/content/pius-xi/en/encyclicals/documents/hf_p-xi_enc_11121925_quas-primas.html.

— Encyclical *Rappresentanti in terra* (Dec. 31, 1929). Accessed May 5, 2021. https://www.newadvent.org/library/docs_pi11rt.htm.

— Encyclical *Ubi arcano* (Dec. 22, 1922). http://www.vatican.va/content/pius-xi/en/encyclicals/documents/hf_p-xi_enc_19221223_ubi-arcano-dei-consilio.html.

Pius XII. Allocution to the Dominican Friars on the Occasion of Their General Chapter (Sept. 22, 1946). https://www.vatican.va/content/pius-xii/la/speeches/1946/documents/hf_p-xii_spe_19460922_frati-predicatori.html.

— Allocution to the Jesuit Fathers on the Occasion of Their 29th General Congregation (Sept. 17, 1946). https://www.vatican.va/content/pius-xii/la/speeches/1946/documents/hf_p-xii_spe_19460917_compagnia-gesu.html.

— Allocution "La risposta agli auguri della Guarda Nobile Pontificia" (Dec. 26, 1939). In *Discorsi del Summo Pontifice Pio XII*. Modena: Typografia Immacolata Concezione, 1942.

— "Christmas Radio Message" (Dec. 24, 1944). https://www.vatican.va/content/pius-xii/it/speeches/1944/documents/hf_p-xii_spe_19441224_natale.html.

— Encyclical *Humani generis* (Aug. 22, 1950). http://w2.vatican.va/content/pius-xii/en/encyclicals/documents/hf_p-xii_enc_12081950_humani-generis.html.

— Encyclical *Mediator Dei* (Nov. 20, 1947). Accessed May 5, 2021. http://www.vatican.va/content/pius-xii/en/encyclicals/documents/hf_p-xii_enc_20111947_mediator-dei.html.

— Encyclical *Mystici Corporis Christi* (June 29, 1943). http://w2.vatican.va/content/pius-xii/en/encyclicals/documents/hf_p-xii_enc_29061943_mystici-corporis-christi.html.

Pohier, J.M. *Au nom du Père: Recherches théologiques et psychanalitiques*. Paris: Éditions du Cerf, 1972.

Politi, S. *Teología del pueblo: una propuesta argentina a la teología latinoamericana, 1967–1975*. Buenos Aires: Ed. Castañeda—Ed. Guadalupe, 1992.

Ponce, Frank. "Building Comunidades Eclesiales de Base." In *Developing Basic Christian Communites: A Handbook*, 27–36. Chicago: National Federation of Priests' Councils, 1979.

Pontifical Council for Culture. *Via pulchritudinis* (Mar. 28, 2006).

Poperen, Jean. "Y a-t-il encore des idées de gauche?" *Le Débat* 42, 1986/5: 103–7.

Poulat, Émile. *Cardinal Emmanuel Suhard archevêque de Paris (1940–1949): Temps de guerre, temps de paix, passion pour la mission*. Paris: Les Éditions du Cerf, 2011.

— *Histoire, dogme, critique dans la crise moderniste*. Paris: Casterman, 1962.

— *Intégrisme et catholicisme intégrale*. Paris: Casterman, 1969.

— *L'église, c'est un monde*. Paris: Les Éditions du Cerf, 1986.

— *Modernistica: Horizons, physiognomies, débats*. Paris: Nouvelles Éditions Latines, 1982.

Preziosi, Ernesto. *Obbedienti in piedi: La vicenda dell'Azione Cattolica in Italia*. Turin: S.E.I., 1997.

Price, Peter. *The Church as the Kingdom: A New Way of Being the Church*. Basingtoke, U.K.: Marshall Pickering, 1987.

Primavesi, Anne. *From Apocalypse to Genesis: Ecology, Feminism and Christianity*. Minneapolis: Fortress Press, 1991.

Proença Sigaud, Geraldo de, Antonio de Castro Mayer, Plinio Corrêa de Oliveira, and Luiz Mendonça de Freitas. *Reforma agrária, questão de consciência*. São Paulo: Ave Maria, 1960.

Progetto Gionata. "Il teologo Mancuso e le prospettive teologiche sull'amore omosessuale e il suo esercizio mediante l'affettività," in *Progetto Gionata*, Apr. 27, 2012, https://www.gionata.org/el-teologo-vito-mancuso-y-las-qperspectivas-teologicas-sobre-el-amor-homosexual/.

Puyo, Jean. *Une vie pour la verité: Jean Puyo interrogue le Père Congar*. Paris: Le Centurion, 1975.

Quisinsky, Michael. "Congar avec Chenu et Féret au Saulchoir des années 1930." *Transversalités—Revue de l'Institut Catholique de Paris*, no. 98 (Apr.–June 2006): 3–35. Accessed Apr. 25, 2021. https://gallica.bnf.fr/ark:/12148/bpt6k6496960w/f1.item.

Rahner, Karl. *Rélations de la nature et de la grace: Écrits théologiques*. Paris: Desclée de Brouwer, 1963.

— "Richtungen der neuen theologie." *Orientierung* (Switzerland—Dec. 20, 1947).

— "Théologie et anthropologie." In *Théologie d'aujourd'hui et de démain*, edited by Patrick Burke. Paris: Les Éditions du Cerf, 1967.

Ratigan, James. Introduction to *Developing Basic Christian Communities: A Handbook,* edited by National Federation of Priests' Councils, 1–3. Chicago: National Federation of Priests' Councils, 1979.

Ratté, John. *Three Modernists: Alfred Loisy, George Tyrrell, William L. Sullivan*. New York: Sheed and Ward, 1967.

Ratzinger, Joseph. "Intervento del Cardinale Joseph Ratzinger sull'ecclesiologia della costituzione "Lumen Gentium" al convegno internazionale sull'attuazione del Concilio Ecumenico Vaticano II promosso dal comitato del grande giubileo dell'anno 2000" (Feb. 27, 2000). http://www.vatican.va/roman_curia/congregations/cfaith/documents/rc_con_cfaith_doc_20000227_ratzinger-lumen-gentium_it.html.

— Preface to "The Interpretation of the Bible in the Church." Pontifical Biblical Commission (Apr. 23, 1993). http://catholic-resources.org/ChurchDocs/PBC_Interp0.htm. *Origins*, Jan. 6, 1994.

— *Principles of Catholic Theology: Building Stones for a Fundamental Theology*. Translated by Mary Frances McCarthy. San Francisco: Ignatius Press, 1987.

— "Zeichen unter den völkern." In *Wahrheit und zeugnis*, 456–66. Düsseldorf: Patmos Verlag, 1964.

Redzioch, Wlodzimierz, ed. *Accanto a Giovanni Paolo II: Gli amici & i collaboratori raccontano*. Rome: Ares, 2014.

Reher, Margaret Mary. "Americanism and Modernism: Continuity or Discontinuity?" *U.S. Catholic Historian* no. 1 (1981): 87–103.

Reichley, A. James. *Religion in American Public Life*. Washington, D.C.: The Brookings Institution, 1985.

Renan, Ernest. *La vita di Gesù*. Edited by F. Grisi. Rome: Newton Compton, 1994.

Ress, Mary Judith, ed. *Lluvia para florecer: Entrevistas sobre el ecofeminismo en América Latina*. Santiago, Chile: Colectivo Conspirando, 2002.

— Ute Seibert, and Lele Sjorup, eds. *Del cielo a la tierra: Una antología de teología feminista*. Santiago, Chile: Sello Azul, 1997.

Richard, Pablo. *La iglesia latinoamericana entre el temor y la esperanza*. San José, Costa Rica: DEI, 1987.

— ed. *Materiales para una historia de la teología en América Latina*. San José, Costa Rica: DEI, 1981.

— *Morte das cristandades e nascimento da igreja: Análise histórica e interpretação teólogica da igreja na America Latina*. São Paulo: Edições Paulinas, 1984. Accessed Dec. 12, 2021. https://archive.org/details/mortedascristand00rich.

Rivière, Jean. *Le modernisme dans l'église*. Paris: Letouzey et Ané, 1929.

— "Modernisme." In *D.T.C.*, 10–2e.:2009–47. Accessed Nov. 26, 2021. https://archive.org/details/dictionnairedet10vaca/page/352/mode/2up.

Roberts, J. Deotis. *Liberation and Reconciliation: A Black Theology*. New York: Orbis Book, 2004.

Roberts, Nancy L. *Dorothy Day and the Catholic Worker*. Albany, N.Y.: State University of New York Press, 1987.

Rodríguez y Rodríguez, O.P., Victorino. "Godless 'Theology' and Enslaving 'Liberation': A Theological Analysis of 'Liberation Theology.'" *TFP Newsletter* (Nov. 1984), 12–16.

— "Pecado individual y pecado colectivo." *Iglesia Mundo* (Madrid) (Dec. 1, 1984).

— "The Liberating Truth," *TFP Newsletter* (Special Issue, 1985), 11–14.

Rohr, Richard. "An Appetite for Wholeness: Living With Our Sexuality." *Sojourners* (Nov. 1982).

— "Pure Passion: The Holiness of Human Sexuality." *Sojourners* (Oct. 1982).

Roohan, James Edmund. *American Catholicism and the Social Question, 1865–1900*. New York: Arno Press, 1976.

Rops, Daniel. "Il y a cinquante ans, le modernisme." *Ecclesia Lectures Chrétiennes*, no. 77 (Aug. 1955): 11–20.

Rossi, Luigi Guglielmo. "Il modernismo." *Renovatio* (Jul.–Sept. 1990): 377–416.

Rousseau, Jean-Jacques. *Discourse on Inequality: What Is the Origin of Inequality Among Men, and Is It Authorised by Natural Law?* Translated by G.D.H. Cole. Accessed Jan. 15, 2022. https://www.aub.edu.lb/fas/cvsp/Documents/DiscourseonInequality.pdf879500092.pdf.

— *The Social Contract*. Accessed Mar. 23, 2021. http://www.earlymoderntexts.com/assets/pdfs/rousseau1762.pdf.

Rousselot, Pierre. *Les yeux de la foi*. 1910.

— *L'intellectualisme de Saint Thomas*. 1912.

Royo Marín, O.P., Antonio. *Dios y su obra*. Madrid: Biblioteca de Autores Cristianos, 1968.

Rubenstein, Richard L., and John K. Roth, eds. *Liberation Theology: The Challenge to U.S. Public Policy*. Washington, D.C.: The Washington Institute Press, 1988.

Rueda, Enrique T. *The Marxist Character of Liberation Theology*. Washington, D.C.: The Free Congress Research and Educational Foundation, 1986.

Ruether, Rosemary Radford. *Gaia & God: An Ecofeminist Theology of Earth Healing*. New York: HarperCollinsPublishers, 1994.

— "Political Theologies in the Churches: Does God Take Sides in Class Struggle?" In *Churches in Struggle: Liberation Theologies and Social Change in North America*, edited by William K. Tabb, 18–31. New York: Monthly Review Press, 1986.

Ruini, Camillo. *La trascendenza della grazia nella teologia di San Tommaso d'Aquino*. Rome: Università Gregoriana Editrice, 1971.

Ruiz-Gimenez, Joaquín, ed. *Iglesia y derechos humanos: IX Congreso de teología*. Madrid: Evangelio y Liberación, 1989.

Russelli, L. *Teologia femminista*. Brescia: Queriniana, 1977.

Sacred Congregation of the Holy Office. "Warning Regarding the Writings of Fr. Teilhard de Chardin" (June 30, 1962). Accessed Apr. 5, 2021. https://www.ewtn.com/catholicism/library/monitum-on-the-writings-of-fr-teilhard-de-chardin-sj-2144.

Salaverri, Joaquín. "El problema de la 'nueva teología.'" *Sal Terrae* 38 (1950): 143–51.

— "Satisfacción a los padres de Saulchoir." *Estudios Eclesiásticos* 25, no. 96 (Jan.–Mar. 1951): 83–89.

Samuel, Albert. *Le socialisme: Courantes, histoire, pratiques*. Lyon: Chronique Sociale, 1981.

Sánchez, Diego Facundo. *Teología de la liberación: En el derrotero hacia otro modelo de Iglesia*. Final thesis, Escuela Universitaria de Teología, 2009. Accessed Feb. 3, 2022. https://en.calameo.com/read/0000682387ec28db546e2.

Sánchez Egozcue, Jorge Mario, and Juan Triana Cordoví. "Un panorama actual de la economía cubana, las transformaciones en curso y sus retos perspectivos." *Boletín Elcano* (Jun. 2008).

Sanders, Marion K. *The Professional Radical: Conversations with Saul Alinsky*. New York: Harper & Row, 1970.

Sandoval Gonzalez, Raúl A. "La pobreza en Cuba." AucaLatinoAmericano, Mar. 30, 2012, https://aucaencayohueso.wordpress.com/2012/03/30/la-pobreza-en-cuba/.

Santoro, Alessandro. "Il Vaticano deve sparire." *MicroMega*, no. 7 (2012): 117–23. Accessed Mar. 30, 2021. https://www.c3dem.it/wp-content/uploads/2012/10/MicroMega.pdf.

Saragat, Giuseppe. *L'umanesimo marxista*. Milan: Dalai Editore, 1999.

Sardà y Salvany, Félix. *El liberalismo es pecado*. Barcelona: Librería y Tipografía Católica, 1884.

Sarmiento, Nicolás. *Caminos de la teología india*. Cochabamba: Verbo Divino, 2000.

Scaraffia, Lucetta, and Anna Maria Isastia. *Donne ottimiste: L'associazionismo femminile borghese fra otto e novecento*. Bologna: Il Mulino, 2002.

Schillebeeckx, Edward. "I laici nel popolo di Dio." In *La fine della chiesa come società perfetta*, edited by I.D.O.C. Verona, Italy: Arnoldo Mondadori, 1968.

— "Il concetto di verità e i problemi conessi—La toleranza." In Frans Alphons Maria Alting von Geusau, et al. *I Grandi Temi del Concilio*. Rome: Edizione Paoline, 1965.

Schlesinger, Arthur Meier. *New Viewpoints in American History*. New York: Macmillan, 1928.

Schreiter, C.PP.S., Robert J. *Constructing Local Theologies*. Maryknoll, N.Y.: Orbis Books, 1985.

Scoppola, Pietro. *Crisi modernista e rinnovamento cattolico in Italia*. Bologna: Il Mulino, 1961.

Second Vatican Council. Dogmatic Constitution *Lumen gentium*. http://www.vatican.va/archive/hist_councils/ii_vatican_council/documents/vat-ii_const_19641121_lumen-gentium_en.html.

Secretariat for Hispanic Affairs. *Basic Christian Communities: An Experience in the United States*. Washington, D.C.: N.C.C.B., 1982.

Segundo, Juan Luis. *Our Idea of God*. Maryknoll, N.Y.: Orbis Books, 1974.

— "Statement." In *Theology in the Americas*, edited by Sergio Torres and John Eagleson, 280–83. Maryknoll, N.Y.: Orbis Books, 1976.

— *The Liberation of Theology*. Maryknoll, N.Y.: Orbis Books, 1976.

— *The Shift Within Latin American Theology: Lecture Given at Regis College Toronto 22 March 1983*. Toronto: Regis College Press, 1983.

Shook, L.K., ed. *Renewal of Religious Thought: Proceedings of the Congress on the Theology of the Renewal of the Church Centenary of Canada, 1867–1967*. New York: Herder and Herder, 1968. Accessed Nov. 28, 2021. https://archive.org/details/renewalofreligio0001unse/page/38/mode/2up.

Sigmund, Paul E. *Liberation Theology at a Crossroads: Democracy or Revolution*. New York: Oxford University Press, 1990.

Silva Gotay, Samuel. "Origem e desenvolvimento do pensamento cristão revolucionário a partir da radicalização da doutrina social cristã nas décadas de 1960 e 1970." In *História da teologia na América Latina*, 139–164. São Paulo: Edições Paulinas, 1981. Accessed Nov. 29, 2021. https://archive.org/details/histriadateologi0000unse.

Siri, Joseph Cardinal. *Gethsemane: Reflections on the Contemporary Theological Movement*. Chicago: Franciscan Herald Press, 1981.

Sisson, Edward, and William Dembski. "My 'Best Education.'" *World*, Oct. 10, 2008. Accessed Dec. 19, 2021. https://wng.org/sift/my-best-education-1617405732.

Smith, Adam. *An Inquiry Into the Nature and Causes of the Wealth of Nations*. Edited by Edwin Cannan. Vol. 2. London: Methuen & Co. 1904. https://oll.libertyfund.org/title/smith-an-inquiry-into-the-nature-and-causes-of-the-wealth-of-nations-cannan-ed-vol-2.

Sobrino, Jon. Interview. In "O absoluto é Deus, e o coabsoluto são os pobres," by Graziela Wolfart and Luís Carlos Dalla Rosa. Translated by Moisés Sbardelotto. *IHU online* 404 (Oct. 5, 2012): 5–10. Accessed Dec. 5, 2021. http://www.ihuonline.unisinos.br/media/pdf/IHUOnlineEdicao404.pdf.

— "Puebla, serena afirmación de Medellín." *Diakonía* (Managua) no. 9, 27–56. Accessed Apr. 11, 2021. http://repositorio.uca.edu.ni/3438/1/Puebla%20serena%20afirmaci%C3%B3n%20de%20Medell%C3%ADn.pdf.

— *The True Church and the Poor*. Translated by Matthew J. O'Connell.

Maryknoll, N.Y.: Orbis Books, 1984 [1991]. Accessed Dec. 6, 2021. https://archive.org/details/truechurchpoor0000sobr_r1u4/mode/2up.

— and Juan Hernández Pico. *Theology of Christian Solidarity*. Translated by Phillip Berryman. Maryknoll, N.Y.: Orbis Books, 1985.

Socci, Antonio. *La dittatura anticattolica*. Milan: Sugarco, 2004.

Sociedad Uruguaya de Defensa de la Tradición, Familia y Propiedad (Comisión de Estudios). *Izquierdismo en la Iglesia, "compañero de viaje" del comunismo en la larga aventura de los fracasos e de las metamorfosis*. Montevideo: T.F.P., 1976.

Solimeo, Gustavo Antonio, and Luiz Sérgio Solimeo. *As CEBs, das quais muito se fala, pouco se conhece: A TFP as descreve como são; Comentários e documentação totais*. São Paulo: Editora Vera Cruz, 1982.

Spadolini, Giovanni. *L'opposizione cattolica da Porta Pia al '98*. Florence: Vallecchi, 1964.

Spargo, John. "Christian Socialism in America." *The American Journal of Sociology* 15 (Jul. 1, 1909): 16–20. https://zenodo.org/record/1431287#.YWLy7dXMKUk.

Sparrow-Simpson, W.J. *Roman Catholic Opposition to Papal Infallibility*. London: John Murray, 1909.

Spiazzi, Raimondo. *P. Mariano Cordovani dei frati predicatori*. Rome: Belardetti, 1954.

Spini, Giorgio. *Risorgimento e protestanti*. Milan: Il Saggiatore, 1989.

Stark, Rodney. *The Victory of Reason: How Christianity Led to Freedom, Capitalism, and Western Success*. New York: Random House, 2006.

Steiner, Stan. *La Raza: The Mexican Americans*. New York: Harper & Row, 1970.

Stevens Arroyo, Antonio M. *Prophets Denied Honor: An Anthology on the Hispanic Church of the United States*. Maryknoll, N.Y.: Orbis Books, 1980.

St. Matthews Research Committee, ed. *Report on El Paso Inter-Religious Sponsoring Organization (EPISO)*. El Paso, Texas: self-published, 1982.

Stres, Tone. "Il marxismo e la domanda sull'uomo." *CSEO Documentazione*, no. 11 (Nov. 1976): 314–24.

Sturzo, Luigi. *Church and State*. Translated by Barbara Barclay Carter. New York: Longmans, Green and Co., 1939. Accessed Dec. 14, 2021. https://archive.org/details/churchstate0000stur /mode/2up.

Suffert, Georges. *Les catholiques et la gauche*. Paris: F. Maspero, 1960.

Sullivan, William Lawrence. *Letters to His Holiness Pope Pius X, by a Modernist*. Chicago: Open Court Publishing Company, 1910.

— *The Priest: A Tale of Modernism in New England*. Boston: Beacon Press, 1914.

— *Under Orders: The Autobiography of William Lawrence Sullivan*. New York, Richard R. Smith, 1945. Accessed Nov. 28, 2021. https://archive.org/details/underordersautob0000sull.

Susin, Luis Carlos, and Joe Marçal dos Santos. *Nosso planeta, nossa vida: Ecologia e teologia*. São Paulo: Paulinas, 2011.

Tabb, William K., ed. *Churches in Struggle: Liberation Theology and Social Change in North America*. New York: Monthly Review Press, 1986. Accessed Nov. 23, 2021. https://archive.org/details/churches instrugg00tabb.

Tamayo-Acosta, Juan José. "Evolución histórica de los movimientos." *Misión Abierta* (Madrid) 77, no. 2 (Apr. 1984): 61–76.

— "Las comunidades cristianas populares." In *Desafíos Cristianos*, edited by Misión Abierta, 156–69. Madrid: Loguez Ediciones, 1988.

— and Juan Bosch, eds. *Panorama de la teología latinoamericana*. Estella: Verbo Divino, 2001.

— and Raul Fornet, eds. *Interculturalidad, diálogo interreligioso y liberación*. Estella: Verbo Divino, 2005.

Tangheroni, Marco. *Cristianità, modernità, rivoluzione: Appunti di uno storico fra "mestiere" e impegno civico-culturale*. Edited by Oscar Sanguinetti. Milan: Sugarco Edizioni, 2009.

Taparelli D'Azeglio, Luigi. *Esame critico degli ordini rappresentativi nella società moderna*. 2 vols. Rome: 1854.

Taricone, Fiorenza, and Isabella Grassi. *Associazionismo femminile e modernismo*. Milan: Marietti, 2000.

Tarozzi, Fiorenza. "Questione sociale." *Dizionario di storiografia*, edited by A. De Bernardi and S. Guarracino. Milan: Mondadori Bruno, 1998.

Tavares, Emerson Sbardelotti. "Ecoteologia: Do grito dos pobres ao grito da terra na perspectiva da teologia da libertação de Leonardo Boff," 227–35. In *Trabajos científicos*. Vol. 1, *La teología de la liberación en prospectiva*. Montevideo: Fundación Amerindia, 2012.

Taylor, Ronald B. *Chavez and the Farm Workers*. Boston: Beacon Press, 1975.

Teilhard de Chardin, Pierre. *Hymne de l'univers*. Paris: Éditions du Seuil, 1961.

Tenconi, Massimiliano. "I cattolici nella resistenza contro l'anticristo nazifascista." Accessed Mar. 30, 2021. http://xoomer.virgilio.it /parmanelweb/CATTOLICI.htm.

Tesini, Mario. *Gioacchino Ventura: La chiesa nell'età delle rivoluzioni*. Rome: Studium, 1988.

T.F.P. Covadonga. *España anestesiada sin percibirlo, amordazada sin quererlo, extraviada sin saberlo: La obra del PSOE*. Madrid: Editorial Fernando III el Santo, 1986.

— "Teología de la liberación, ¿libertad o pobreza?" *Covadonga Informa*.

Todaro, Margaret Patrice. *Pastors, Prophets and Politicians: A Study of the Brazilian Catholic Church, 1916–1945*. Doctoral thesis, Columbia University, 1971.

Tommasi, Adolfo, ed. *Montalembert*. Turin: Società Editrice Internazionale, 1928.

Topornin, Boris. *The New Constitution of the USSR*. Translated by Murad Saifulin. Moscow: Progress Publishers, 1987. Accessed Dec. 23, 2021. https://archive.org/details/newconstitutionussr /mode/2up.

Tornatore, L., P.A. Ferrisi, and G. Polizzi. *La filosofia attraverso i testi: Profili, temi, autori*. Bologna: Loescher Editore, 1996.

Torres, Sergio. "Goals of the Detroit Conference." In *Theology in the Americas: Detroit 1975*, edited by Sergio Torres and John Eagleson, 255–59. Maryknoll, N.Y.: Orbis Books, 1976.

— "Opening Remarks." In *Theology in the Americas: Detroit II Conference Papers*, edited by West, Guidote, and Coakley, (Maryknoll, N.Y.: Orbis Books, 1982).

— and John Eagleson, eds. *The Challenge of the Basic Christian Communities*. Maryknoll, N.Y.: Orbis Books, 1981.

— *Theology in the Americas: Detroit 1975*. Maryknoll, N.Y.: Orbis Books, 1976. Accessed Nov. 23, 2021. https://archive.org/details /theologyinameric0000unse_e7f9/page/n3/mode/2up.

— , and Moisés Sbardelotto. "'A teologia da libertação pode ajudar a interpretar o mal-estar global de hoje.' Entrevista especial com Sergio Torres." *Instituto Humanitas Unisinos*. Accessed Oct. 22, 2011. http:// www.ihu.unisinos.br/entrevistas/500495-a-teologia-da-libertacao -pode-ajudar-a-interpretar-o-mal-estar-global-de-hoje-entrevista -especial-com-sergio-torres.

Torresi, Tiziano. *L'altra giovinezza: Gli universitari cattolici dal 1935 al 1940*. Assisi: Cittadella Editrice, 2010.

Tradición y Acción por un Perú Mayor. "Teología de la liberación, ¿o marxismo para cristianos?" *Tradición y Acción* (Lima), nos. 6–7 (Dec. 1973).

Trionfini, Paolo. *Carlo Carretto: il cammino di un innamorato di Dio*. Rome: AVE, 2010.

Turi, Tommaso. *L'Azione Cattolica nella chiesa postconciliare*. Bari: La Scala, 1982.

Tuveson, Ernest Lee. *Redeemer Nation: The Idea of America's Millennial Role*. Chicago: University of Chicago Press, 1968.

Tyrrell, George. "A Perverted Devotion." In *Essays on Faith and Immortality*, arranged by M.D. Petre. New York: Longmans, Green and Co., 1914.

— *Christianity at the Cross-Roads*. London: Longmans, 1910.

— *Through Scylla and Charibdis*. London: Longmans, Green, and Co., 1907.

— and M.D. Petre. *Autobiography and Life of George Tyrrell*, 2 vols. London: Edward Arnold, 1912. Accessed Feb. 6, 2022. https://archive .org/details/autobiographyand00tyrruoft/mode/2up.

U.S. Department of State. *The Sandinistas and Middle Eastern Radicals*. Washington D.C.: U.S. Department of State, 1985.

Vacant, Jean Michel Alfred, Eugène Mangenot, and Émile Amann, eds. *Dictionnaire de théologie catholique* [*D.T.C.*]. 30 vols. Paris: Letouzey et Ané, 1902–1950.

Vaillancourt, Yves. "La première rencontre internationale des chrétiens pour le socialisme." *Relations* (June 1975): 174–76.

Valensin, Albert. "Immanence (doctrine de l')." In *D.A.F.C.*, 2:569–79. Accessed Nov. 26, 2021. https://archive.org/details /dictionnaireapol02aluoft/page/288/mode/2up.

Van Vugt, Johannes. "Christian Base Communities." *The Ecumenist* (Ottawa) 24, no. 1 (Nov.–Dec. 1985), 1–8.

— *Democratic Organization for Social Change: Latin American Christian Base Communities and Literacy Campaigns*. New York: Bergin & Garvey, 1991.

Vassallo, Piero. "Da Franco Rodano a Mario Monti." *Riscossa Cristiana* (Sept. 13, 2012). Accessed Mar. 30, 2021. https://anticattocomunismo .wordpress.com/tag/franco-rodano/.

Veckemans, S.J., Roger. "Expansión mundial de la teología de la liberación latinoamericana." In *Socialismo y socialismos en América Latina,* edited by C.E.L.A.M., Bogotá: Secretariado General del C.E.L.A.M., 1977.

Verbist, Henri. *Les grandes controverses de l'église contemporaine: De 1789 à nos jours*. Veviers (France): Éditions Marabout, 1971.

Vercesi, Ernesto. *Il movimento cattolico in Italia (1870–1922)*. Florence: Società Editrice La Voce, 1923.

Verlhac, Jean, and Maurice Caveing. "Monde chrétien et monde moderne." *Esprit* (Aug.–Sept. 1946): 245–49.

Vermeersch, Arthur. "Modernism." *The Catholic Encyclopedia*. New York: Robert Appleton Company, 1911. Vol. 10. Accessed Oct. 2, 2021. http://www.newadvent.org/cathen/10415a.htm.

Vidigal Xavier da Silveira, Fábio. *Frei, o Kerensky chileno*. 2nd ed. São Paulo: Editora Vera Cruz, 1967.

Vidler, A.R. *A Century of Social Catholicism: 1820–1920*. London: S.P.C.K., 1964.

— *Prophecy and Papacy: A Study of Lamennais, the Church and the Revolution*. London: S.C.M. Press, 1954.

— *The Church in an Age of Revolution: 1789 to the Present Day*. Vol. 5, *The Penguin History of the Church*. London: Penguin Books, 1962.

— *The Modernist Movement in the Roman Church: Its Origins & Outcome*. New York: Gordon Press, 1976.

Vigil, José María. "Desafío de la ecología a las religiones." *Revista Vinculum* (Bogotá), no. 238 (2010).

— , Luiza Tomita, and Marcelo Barros, eds. *Per i molti cammini di Dio*. Vol. 3, *Teologia latinoamericana pluralista della liberazione*. Rimini: Pazzini Editore, 2010.

Viglione, Massimo. *La rivoluzione italiana*. Rome: Minotauro, 2001.

— *Libera chiesa in libero stato? Il risorgimento e i cattolici—uno scontro epocale*. Rome: Città Nuova, 2005.

Vinaty, Bernard, et al. *Galileo Galilei: 350 anni di storia (1633–1983): Studi e ricerche*. Edited by Paul Poupard. Rome: Piemme, 1984.

Vivarelli, Roberto. *Storia delle origini del fascismo*. 3 vols. Bologna: Il Mulino, 2012.

Volpe, Angelo. *La questione romana e il clero veneto*. Venice: Tip della Gazzetta, 1862.

Washington, Joseph. *Black Theology: The Negro and Christianity in the United States*. Boston: Beacon Press, 1964.

Weber, Max. *The Protestant Ethic and the Spirit of Capitalism*. Translated by Talcott Parsons. New York: Charles Scribner's Sons, 1930. https://archive.org/details/protestantethics00webe /page/n7/mode/2up.

Weill, M.G. *Histoire du catholicisme libérale en France 1828–1908*. Paris: Alcan, 1909.

Welch, Sharon D. *Communities of Resistance and Solidarity: A Feminist Theology of Liberation*. Maryknoll, N.Y.: Orbis Books, 1985.

West, Cornel, Caridad Guidote, and Margaret Coakley, eds. *Theology in the Americas: Detroit II Conference Papers*. Maryknoll, N.Y.: Orbis Books, 1982.

Whitehead, Evelyn Eaton and James D. Whitehead. *Community of Faith: Models and Strategies for Building Christian Communities*. New York: Seabury Press, 1982.

Whitehead, James D., and Evelyn Eaton Whitehead. *The Emerging Laity: Returning Leadership to the Community of Faith*. New York: Image/Doubleday and Company, 1988. Accessed Dec. 31, 2021. https://archive.org/details/emerginglaityret00whit_0 /mode/2up.

Williams, Raymond. *Marxism and Literature*. Oxford, U.K.: Oxford University Press, 1977.

Winter, Gibson. *Liberating Creation: Foundations of Religious Social Ethics*. New York: Crossroad, 1981.

Wolfhart, Graziela. "O bem viver e uma teologia indígena." Translated by Anete Amorim Pezzini. *IHUonline* 12, no. 404 (Oct. 5, 2012): 32–34. Accessed Dec. 22, 2021. http://www.ihuonline.unisinos.br /media/pdf/IHUOnlineEdicao404.pdf.

— Luis Carlos Dalla Rosa, and Márcia Junges. "O crescimento de correntes teológicas e eclesiológicas." (Interview with Sérgio Coutinho.) *IHU online* 12, no. 404 (Oct. 2012): 26–28. http://www.ihuonline .unisinos.br/media/pdf/IHUOnlineEdicao404.pdf.

Wright, Jeremiah A., Jr. "Transcript. Reverend Wright at the National Press Club." *New York Times*, Apr. 28, 2008. Accessed Dec. 19, 2021. https://www.nytimes.com/2008/04/28/us /politics/28text-wright.html.

Young-Hyun, Jo. *Sacerdotes y transformación social en Perú, 1968–1975*. Mexico City: Universidad Autónoma de México, 2005.

Yrarrázaval, Rafael. "Reforma agraria en Chile." *Ciencia e Investigación Agraria* 6, no. 1 (Jan.–Mar. 1979): 7–9.

Yzermans, Vincent, ed. *All Things in Christ: Encyclicals and Selected Works of Saint Pius X*. Westminster, Md.: The Newman Press, 1954.

Zamoyski, Adam. *16 agosto 1920: La battaglia di Varsavia*. Milan: Corbaccio, 2009.

Zepelena, T. "Problema theologicum." *Gregorianum* 24 (1943): 23–47, 287–326.

— "Problema theologicum." *Gregorianum* 25 (1944): 38–73, 247–82.

Zubova, L., N. Kovalena, and L. Khakhulina. "Poverty in the U.S.S.R: The Population's Point of View." *Problems of Economic Transition* 34, no. 10 (Feb. 1992): 85–98.

Zuccaro, Gian Carlo. *Lui, Mussolini, nel giudizio di mille personaggi internazionali*. Genoa: E.R.G.A., 1983.

Zwierlein, Frederick J. *The Life and Letters of Bishop McQuaid*. 3 vols. Rochester: N.Y.: The Art Print Shop, 1927.

Index